Crossing Over

Crossing Over
Narratives of Palliative Care

David Barnard, Ph.D.
Department of Medicine
Section of Palliative Care
and Medical Ethics
Center for Bioethics and Health Law
University of Pittsburgh
Pittsburgh, Pennsylvania

Patricia Boston, R.N., Ph.D.
Palliative Care McGill
Faculties of Medicine and Education
McGill University
Montreal, Canada

Anna Towers, M.D.
McGill University
Palliative Care Service
Royal Victoria Hospital
Montreal, Canada

Yanna Lambrinidou, M.A.
Center for Folklore and Ethnography
University of Pennsylvania
Philadelphia, Pennsylvania

OXFORD
UNIVERSITY PRESS

OXFORD
UNIVERSITY PRESS

Oxford   New York
Athens   Auckland   Bangkok   Bogotá   Buenos Aires   Calcutta
Cape Town   Chennai   Dar es Salaam   Delhi   Florence   Hong Kong   Istanbul
Karachi   Kuala Lumpur   Madrid   Melbourne   Mexico City   Mumbai
Nairobi   Paris   São Paulo   Singapore   Taipei   Tokyo   Toronto   Warsaw

and associated companies in
Berlin   Ibadan

Copyright © 2000 by Oxford University Press, Inc.

Published by Oxford University Press, Inc.
198 Madison Avenue, New York, New York 10016

Oxford is a registered trademark of Oxford University Press

Library of Congress Cataloging-in-Publication Data
Crossing over : narratives of palliative care /
David Barnard . . . [et al.].
p.   cm.   Includes bibliographical references and index.
ISBN 978-0-19-512343-2
1. Palliative treatment Case studies.
I. Barnard, David, 1948– .
R726.8.C76   1999   362.1′75—dc21   99-29317

Printed in the United States of America
on acid-free paper

Foreword

In a famous 1906 lecture to medical students, entitled "Science and immortality," Sir William Osler referred to his records of 500 death-bed cases. These were studied through the nurses at the Johns Hopkins Hospital, Baltimore, and showed that the actual sensations of dying in the great majority of patients were "like their birth—a sleep and a forgetting." ° The cards on which patient details are recorded are kept in the Osler Library at McGill University and, so far as I know, are the first attempt at such a study. It is moving to see and handle them but it also arouses questions about the illnesses that preceded this peaceful dying.

Nearly a century later, this book describes in perceptive detail the sometimes tortuous journeys toward such final moments. It concentrates on personal and family struggles with inexorable illness rather than on the details of the medical treatments, nursing, and other support that palliative care teams aim to offer.

The authors do not idealize these very real people; rather, like so many patients I recall after fifty years in this field, these people teach us what it means to be human. There are many lessons in living to be learned from the dying, and some of these are described here with quiet objectivity.

Many of us in palliative care spend much of our time helping people face

---

°Osler, W. (1977) *Science and Immortality*. New York: Arno Press, p. 17 (first published 1906).

crises and have to assess and analyze a situation with speed as well as sensitivity. We may have only a small part in a whole continuity of care and family dynamics. It is, however, often from the rarer situation when we can follow a patient alone or with a family through weeks or months that we may learn to meet more urgent needs. One of our patients at St. Christopher's Hospice, London, who had amyotrophic lateral sclerosis was such a person. A lonely musician (a flautist), he challenged all our skills, understanding, and patience. Near the end of his year-long saga with us he dictated the following during a poetry workshop:

Smoke Rings

I can't blow smoke rings any more
My tongue, it will not budge,
But other people's various powers
I never would begrudge.

It's not for me to jealous be
And make a silly fuss.
If everybody were like me
Then who'd look after us?

The more I lose my little skills
The more I see God's plan,
I see what really counts with Him:
The essence of a man.

James Haylock-Eyre°

It is "the essence of a man" that we meet in this book and I believe we will be wiser and more confident in both our service and living because of what we have learned here.

Dame Cicely Saunders, OM., DBE., FRCP.
Chairman, St. Christopher's Hospice, London

°Heylock-Eyre, J. (1992) Smoke rings. In: Saunders, C. (ed). *Beyond the Horizon.* London: Darton, Longman & Todd, p. 11.

Preface

The preface usually gets written last, which seems especially fitting for a book on palliative care. For the preface is as much an opportunity to look back, take stock, and give thanks as it is to alert readers to what lies ahead. In our case, we have much to acknowledge in the way of colleagueship (among the four of us), collaboration (with patients, families, and caregivers), and support (from our sponsors and home institutions).

For the authors, this book grew out of shared interests and experience in care for the dying, and dissatisfaction with currently available stories of what that experience is like. Two of us (Anna Towers and Patricia Boston) are clinicians who are working or have worked directly with the dying. One of us (David Barnard) teaches medical humanities and palliative care to health professionals who care for the dying, and is involved administratively with palliative care programs. And one of us (Yanna Lambrinidou) combines interest in the subject of end-of-life care with a broader interest in the ethnographic study, and faithful rendering, of human experience with illness and health. As we worked together, the four of us came to enjoy a form of collaboration, interdependence, and mutual respect that, we all agree, has been unique in our professional lives.

Almost exactly three decades ago, Paul Ramsey published one of the pioneering works in the young field of medical ethics, *The Patient as Person*. The care of the dying figures very prominently in Ramsey's seminal book. In a chapter entitled "On (Only) Caring for the Dying," Ramsey made an observation that could easily serve to summarize the subject matter of our book:

> Upon ceasing to try to rescue the perishing, one is then free to care for the dying. Acts of caring for the dying are deeds done bodily for them which serve solely to manifest that they are not lost from human attention, that they are not alone, that mankind generally and their loved ones take note of their dying and mean to company with them in accepting this unique instance of the acceptable death of all flesh.°

What is it like, we wanted to know, to "company with" the dying? This book is our effort to answer that question from the points of view of family members, hospice workers, palliative care staff, friends and loved ones, and—to the extent possible—from the point of view of the dying themselves.

To state this goal is to proclaim immediately the enormous debt we owe to the patients and families who accepted us into their living and dying, so that we might tell others of their experiences. In a sense, they are the true authors of this work, and we but the transcribers and editors.

We are also indebted to the staff of the Palliative Care Service at the Royal Victoria Hospital, Montreal, and at the Hospice of Lancaster County, Lancaster, Pennsylvania. These superb and generous clinicians and volunteers were willing to open themselves to our view in the midst of the day-to-day routines and emergencies of end-of-life care, with no time to rehearse—and no protection in the thought that if a case didn't turn out well we would exclude it from the book. We admire these people for their professionalism and for their commitment to improving hospice and palliative care through research and honest self-reflection.

None of these people can receive acknowledgment by name, in keeping with our promise of confidentiality. Several other people, however, can be acknowledged publicly for their crucial contributions to our project.

Eileen Lavery provided essential administrative and clerical support in Montreal. June Watson, Administrative Assistant in the Department of Humanities at The Pennsylvania State University College of Medicine, prepared the final draft of the entire manuscript (as well as several almost-final ones), and supervised all of the complicated administrative aspects of an interinstitutional and binational collaboration. During the writing of this book David Barnard was University Professor and Chair of the Department of Humanities at the Penn State College of Medicine.

Angela Martin, who at the time was a medical student at Penn State, helped lay the foundation for the Lancaster County fieldwork. Gina Tuncil transcribed

---

°Ramsey, P. (1970) *The Patient as Person.* New Haven: Yale University Press, p. 153.

the Lancaster County interviews. Dr. Cathy Jarvis assisted with some of the data collection and medical editing in Montreal. Elizabeth C. Hechtman, at the Philadelphia Center for Social Therapy, provided clinical supervision that was invaluable to Yanna Lambrinidou during the Lancaster County fieldwork. Lauren Enck was our skilled and supportive editor at Oxford University Press.

Finally, we are pleased to acknowledge a major research grant from the Open Society Institute's Project on Death in America. Essential additional support was generously provided by the Greenwall Foundation, the Social Sciences and Humanities Research Council of Canada, the T. R. Meighen Foundation, and the Walter J. Blackburn Foundation.

October 1999   D. B.
                                                                            A. T.
                                                                            P. B.
                                                                            Y. L.

Contents

Part II: Working with the Narratives   395

1

Introduction

The goals of palliative care are easy to state. Realizing them is not so easy. Annette T. Carron, Joanne Lynn, and Patrick Keaney (1999), commenting on the lack of attention to end-of-life care in medical textbooks, assert that "time while dying and near death should be comfortable, supportive of independence and function, enhancing of family relationships, and meaningful." In the course of defining palliative care, J. Andrew Billings (1998) summarizes its primary goals even more briefly, as "alleviating suffering, providing support, and making the best of remaining time." Still more simply, the World Health Organization states that palliative care aims to achieve the best quality of life for patients and families when the patient's disease is not responsive to curative treatment (1990).

When one tries to achieve these goals in the real world, one is brought face to face with institutional limitations, human foibles, problems giving care in teams, and challenges of cultural diversity, among other things. Dying, even with the best possible care, can be messy and difficult. Yet, despite these difficulties, much can be done to make dying more comfortable and more humane, and much is done, every day, by patients, family members, and dedicated hospice and palliative care workers. That is the theme of this book.

A book of stories

This is a book of stories—narratives of giving and receiving palliative care. It is not a textbook that portrays ideal palliative care, or that prescribes specific management techniques. Instead, we present stories of actual patients and families who have experienced terminal illness with the support of hospice or palliative care teams. The names of all patients, family members, and caregivers have been changed, as have many dates, physical features, occupations, and other potentially identifying characteristics.

The cases we narrate were followed prospectively. They were not selected after the fact to illustrate ideal or exemplary care. They are meant to illustrate certain realities of what it is like to die in North America under the palliative care umbrella, in the contexts described. This book helps us compare palliative care ideals with narratives that portray the actual practice of the discipline. Often, the care is exemplary. In other situations many would criticize certain aspects of care. In some cases there are problems, symptoms, or situations that the caregivers could not help. Sometimes, personal, institutional, or social care is, frankly, inadequate, and sometimes it is ennobling and inspiring. The narratives are meant to elicit empathy, understanding, and discussion.

Origins and basic concepts of palliative care

Hospice, or palliative care, has emerged as a specialized field only within the past 30 years. In the United States, Canada, and Great Britain, "hospice care" is often used interchangeably with the term "palliative care," which has been defined by the World Health Organization (1990) as:

> the active total care of patients whose disease is not amenable to curative treatment. Control of pain, of other symptoms, and of psychological, social, and spiritual problems is paramount. The goal of palliative care is achievement of the best possible quality of life for patients and their families.

Increasingly, distinctions in terminology are appearing, with "palliative care" being preferred as the generic term, and "hospice" referring to a particular form or model for providing palliative care (Billings, 1998). It must also be stressed that palliative care is applicable from the beginning of an illness— whenever comfort, support, and quality of life are significant concerns. Despite its origins and growth in close association with cancer, palliative care is not limited to that context. It is also important in any chronic disease where prognosis is limited, e.g., in neurological, renal, and cardiac disease or infection with HIV.

Landmark dates in the modern history of palliative care include the opening in 1967 of St. Christopher's Hospice in London under the leadership of Cicely

Saunders; the opening in 1974 of the first hospice program in the United States in New Haven, Connecticut, under the leadership of Florence Wald; the establishment in 1975 of the first palliative care program in a major academic medical center at the Royal Victoria Hospital in Montreal, under the leadership of Balfour Mount; the recognition in 1987 of palliative medicine as a medical specialty in Great Britain; and the publication in 1993 of the first edition of the *Oxford Textbook of Palliative Medicine*, the definitive scientific textbook in the field.

Four aspects of medicine and society in Britain, Canada, and the United States have contributed to the growth of palliative care in those countries:

1. Medical technology has blurred the line between life and death, leaving many people attached to invasive mechanical life-support, enduring pain, helplessness, and expense throughout their last weeks and days of life, and seeking more comfortable alternatives.
2. Lack of attention to symptom control in medical education and practice has caused caregivers to concentrate narrowly on the pathophysiology and cure of disease rather than the patient's experience of illness, resulting in a great burden of preventable but unnoticed suffering.
3. A loss of extended family ties and community has caused the physical and emotional burdens of caring for a dying person to fall more heavily on the members of isolated nuclear families, and particularly on women, leading people to turn to professionals for necessary support.
4. Strained and evasive relationships, caused by our discomfort around the dying and bereaved, frequently increase loneliness and suffering, making a philosophy of care that emphasizes human contact especially attractive.

The goals of hospice and palliative care are frequently summarized in the slogan "dying with dignity." This phrase has come to mean many different things to different people, including the increasingly popular preference (in the U.S.) for legalizing physician-assisted suicide. David Roy (1988) has provided a definition of dying with dignity that captures many people's goals. "Dying with dignity," he writes, means:

dying without a frantic technical fuss and bother to squeeze out a few more moments or hours of biological life, when the important thing is to live out one's last moments as fully, consciously, and courageously as possible;

dying without that twisting, racking pain that totally ties up one's consciousness and leaves one free for nothing and for no one else;

dying in surroundings that are worthy of a human being who is about to live what should be one's "finest hour." The environment of a dying patient should clearly say: the technical drama of medicine has receded to the background to give way to the central human drama of a unique human being "wrestling with his God";

dying in the presence of people who know how to drop the professional role mask and relate to others simply and richly as a human being.

Palliative care aims to control physical symptoms, not only as an end in itself but also to help the patient attend to his or her relational and spiritual tasks. The unit of care is not only the patient but also the family, or any people whom the patient considers important. Since palliative care aspires to total, or "whole-person" care, including body, mind, and spirit, it is multidisciplinary in nature. The disciplines commonly involved are nursing, medicine, pharmacy, social work, pastoral care, physiotherapy, occupational therapy, music therapy, and art therapy. Nonprofessional volunteers are an integral part of these teams. Leadership styles in palliative care tend to be less hierarchical, and roles more flexible, than in other areas of medicine. Palliative care (as with all care) should be delivered with sensitivity to personal, cultural, and religious values.

Full palliative care programs (of which few examples currently exist) would include the following components: home care, a consultation service for the acute care hospital, adult day care, an inpatient palliative care unit, an outpatient clinic, bereavement support, and staff support. Services and levels of care should be available to patients and families seamlessly, in the setting of their choice. In reality, palliative care is still a neglected area worldwide, and there are millions who suffer needlessly as a result. Economic considerations limit the availability of drugs to control pain and other symptoms. Misguided beliefs abound concerning opioid use and abuse. Morphine is not used or is grossly underused in most countries of the world. There are many areas of the world where professional nursing care for the dying is nonexistent (Stjernswärd and Pampallona, 1998).

We are aware that the style of palliative care depicted in these narratives will not be relevant for most countries in the developing world. This brand of palliative care may be too expensive and sophisticated to serve the needs of the world at large. The developers and leaders of palliative care have a responsibility, we believe, to ensure that research in the immediate future focuses on interventions that are adaptable to areas where costly or high-tech solutions are unavailable, and to advocate for increased access to the full range of care.

"What is in your mind and in your heart"

A hallmark of palliative care since Cicely Saunders founded the modern hospice movement has been the combination of scientific rigor with personal concern. As Cicely Saunders herself has frequently recalled, one of her earliest inspirations was a relationship she had in 1947, as a recently qualified medical social worker and former nurse, with a cancer patient named David Tasma. This 40-year-old Jewish man, who had survived World War II and the Warsaw Ghetto, spoke often with Cicely Saunders about his life, his sufferings, and what he wanted from his caregivers. "I only want what is in your mind and in your heart," he told her one day, in an oft-quoted comment that addresses both the cognitive and interpersonal aspects of palliative care (Saunders, 1993). Accordingly, palliative care and palliative care education have embraced three broad areas: (*1*) the science and techniques of pain management and symptom control; (*2*) knowledge of psychological, social, and spiritual aspects of dying and grieving; and (*3*) self-knowledge on the part of caregivers, especially regarding personal attitudes toward death and loss.

Palliative care is whole-person care not only in the sense that the whole person of the patient (body, mind, spirit) is the object of care, but also in that the whole person of the caregiver is involved. Palliative care is, par excellence, care that is given through the medium of a human relationship. And education for palliative care is not only education in science and clinical techniques, but also in the art of building and sustaining relationships and in using the self as a primary instrument for diagnosis and treatment. This involves a level of psychological risk taking that may be unique in the health field, a process that is demonstrated in several of the narratives in this book. Indeed, one of the aims of this book is to provide students and caregivers with material that will encourage self-reflection and discussion of these emotional issues.

The emergence of palliative care as a clinical discipline (or, perhaps more accurately, as a set of closely related clinical disciplines) has been accompanied by an increasing number of textbooks. The leading example is the *Oxford Textbook of Palliative Medicine,* recently published in an expanded second edition (Doyle et al., 1998). The scientific and clinical aspects of palliative care are now more widely known and documented than ever before. Nonetheless, with all or most of these books, there is a gap. In a recent review of the burgeoning palliative care literature, Timothy Quill and J. Andrew Billings wrote, "Most palliative care textbooks, including the *Oxford Textbook,* do not speak to the heart, nor do they give an adequate sense of the range of psychological, spiritual, social, and existential suffering or the opportunities for personal growth and healing that dying presents" (Quill and Billings, 1998).

Quill and Billings go on to say that the gap is probably filled best by clinical narratives, and they make specific reference to recently published works by Quill, *A Midwife Through the Dying Process* (1996), and by Ira Byock, *Dying Well: The Prospect for Growth at the End of Life* (1997). Another example is *Mortally Wounded: Stories of Soul Pain, Death, and Healing,* by Michael Kearney (1996). These are very important books, but from our point of view each has significant limitations. Quill, Byock, and Kearney are passionate advocates for their own styles of care, which combine meticulous management of physical symptoms with deep understanding of psychological and spiritual distress. It is precisely their passion, as well as their closeness to their patients, that make their books speak to the heart. Yet these very characteristics—advocacy and close personal involvement—limit their books in important respects. As advocates who selected their narratives retrospectively to illustrate the merits of a particular style of end-of-life care, they are apt to minimize some of the inadequacies or ambiguities of their philosophies when applied to particular patients. More important, perhaps, is their narrative point of view. All three books are told from the vantage point of the physicians themselves. As Robert Arnold and Lachlan Forrow (1998) observed in their perceptive review of the books by Quill and Byock, this results in an exaggerated emphasis on the contributions of physicians, as opposed to the non-physicians who in real life provide the vast majority of care; and insufficient attention is paid to the voices, perceptions, and judgments of the patients and families themselves—the very people whose experiences and satisfaction with care matter most.

Our primary goals in this book are twofold. First, we, too, aim to speak to the heart, by portraying as vividly as we can the personal experiences of those who give and receive palliative care. Our narratives portray the application of scientific and technical knowledge, to be sure, but they always situate particular clinical judgments or interventions in the context of a patient's overall experience, including its emotional, existential, and spiritual dimensions. Our objective in each narrative has been to tell the story of the patient's experience of illness and care with particular emphases on the patient's inner life, or subjective experience, and on the caregivers' experience of giving care. Second, we have actively sought out the experiences and perceptions of the widest possible range of participants in each case. Our narratives include the voices and points of view of patients, families, doctors, nurses, social workers, chaplains, volunteers, friends, and neighbors as they interact with each other, and form their often conflicting judgments, over the course of the patient's illness and up to one year after the patient's death.

We thus offer this collection of narratives as a complement to the technically oriented textbooks such as the *Oxford Textbook* or *Palliative Medicine: A Case-Based Manual* (MacDonald, 1998). We recommend that professionally interested readers consult these and other textbooks to deepen their appreciation of the problems of clinical management in *Crossing Over.* At the same time, we believe the narratives in *Crossing Over* will remind students and clinicians of the complex human contexts within which they must apply their knowledge. Illness always occurs in a particular family, social, and cultural context, and always unfolds over time. It is a *biographical* and not merely *biological* process. And the feelings, perspectives, and motivations of the caregivers (both families and professionals) are inevitably part of the story.

Our project: case narratives in palliative care

Extended, richly detailed, multiperspectival case narratives are well suited to portray the physical, psychological, spiritual, and social dimensions of terminal illness, the dynamics of the caring relationship, and how all of these are woven together and interact with each other. Narratives can go beyond conventional case reports in clinical medicine and their narrow concentration on symptoms and treatment to include attention to the processes by which patients, families, and health care providers find personal meaning in illness, and how personal meanings influence the experience and outcome of care. Such narratives can serve as resources that are all too rare in medical education for self-reflection on the part of professionals-in-training.

Vivid and detailed cases are also a valuable contribution to public education on topics related to end-of-life care. In the absence of other forms of empirical data, cases can distort and mislead as well as inform policy makers and the public. Nevertheless, cases convey "truths" of human experience that go beyond the recitation of statistics regarding patients' and families' needs when coping with terminal illness, or data regarding the efficacy of particular medical, psychosocial, or spiritual interventions, thus preventing statistical descriptions from being taken as stereotypes. We believe that this book can be an important part of the current public debate regarding optimum care for the dying, the best allocation of society's resources, and what options ought to be legally available to people at the end of life.

We have constructed our cases by employing a variety of qualitative research methods. We are fully aware of the many methodological, philosophical, and ethical issues that are raised by qualitative and narrative methods in medical and social research. We explore these issues in some depth in a separate chapter on our methodology, which is found in Part II of this book, after the narratives themselves. For the purposes of this introduction, we want to explain just enough of our methodology to help readers understand the context and construction of the narratives. For a fuller treatment of the details, rationale, strengths, and limitations of our approach, readers should consult Part II.

The narratives are derived from a three-year prospective, qualitative, ethnographic study of the experiences of patients, families, and caregivers. We have sought to portray the challenges encountered by patients, families, and health care providers in dealing with terminal illness, and the skills, attitudes, and personal resources required to provide excellent palliative care. We have been especially interested in changes in attitude and orientation accompanying the transition from active treatment to palliative care; the experience of patients, families, and providers over the course of terminal illness and in the bereavement period; the management of symptoms as they occur in the evolving context of the patient's experience of sickness; clinical reasoning and decision making in a complex domain; issues of communication; and cultural and ethical concerns.

We carried out the research in two settings. In the United States, we followed cases in the setting of the Hospice of Lancaster County, Lancaster, Pennsylvania, a large, free-standing, community-based hospice program with an active home care service and a 12-bed inpatient facility for acute symptom management, respite care, and terminal care. In Canada, we followed cases in the setting of the Palliative Care Service at the Royal Victoria Hospital, Montreal, a large, academically based palliative care service at a major teaching hospital, with a 16-bed inpatient unit, consultation service, and—at the time our research was conducted—a fully integrated home care service.

It is crucial to note two major differences between these settings, as they had significant impact on the progress of the cases. The first is the difference in health care financing. Canadian patients were participants in the Canadian Medicare System, which meant that except for private-duty nurses in the home and some medications, patients and families had no out-of-pocket costs for the care they received. Patients in Lancaster County were subject to the confusing and limited coverage for hospice care in the United States. Patients age 65 and over could elect the package of services provided under Medicare Part B, but only after being certified by their doctor to be within six months of death, and by agreeing to receive no further coverage for any active treatment of their disease. Patients younger than 65, unless eligible for Medicaid by virtue of their meager financial means, were subject to the varying limits in coverage for hospice care provided by private insurance. As a result, economic hardship and financial uncertainty play a significant role in the cases from Lancaster County; these concerns were almost entirely absent in the Canadian cases.

The second difference is in the extent of physician involvement. The Palliative Care Service at the Royal Victoria Hospital is staffed with several full-time palliative care specialists, who were actively involved in patient care whether the patient was in an acute care ward of the hospital, in the Palliative Care Unit, or at home. (Since this project was completed, home care has been shifted to local community health agencies, and the role of the Palliative Care Service in the home has decreased.) At the time of our research, Hospice of Lancaster County had no full-time medical staff, but was served by a group of part-time physicians from the community. Especially when at home, patients had very little direct contact with physicians; most physician involvement in symptom management took place via telephone contact from a hospice nurse. As a result, nurses and social workers play a much greater role, proportionally, in the cases from Lancaster County, than in the cases in Montreal, though in each setting the burden of care is distributed across the team. (Since our project was completed, a full-time specialist in palliative care has been appointed medical director of Hospice of Lancaster County.)

We followed our cases from the time a patient was admitted to the hospice or palliative care program (or from the point when a member of the team suggested that a patient or family may be of special interest to our project; this may have been later in the admission). We then followed the case until approximately one year after the death of the patient.

The main criteria for selection of cases were the willingness of the patient and family to participate and their physical and mental capacity to respond to interview questions. Health care providers included all members of the palliative care or hospice team who were involved in the patient's care and who were willing to participate (e.g., physicians, nurses, social workers, aides, psychologists, music and occupational therapists, chaplains, volunteers). Clear explanations of the nature, purposes, and methods of our project were given to all potential participants in order to obtain their cooperation and informed consent to participate in the project. The project was approved by the review boards and ethics committees of both participating institutions.

Four types of data were required for the construction of our narratives: (1) the patient's medical history and significant aspects of the patient's biography, e.g., cultural background, family history, employment, important and meaningful life events, outlook on life, etc.; (2) the clinical course of the patient's illness, through and including the patient's death and the family's bereavement; (3) the patient's and family's perceptions and interpretations of the patient's illness and care; and (4) the caregivers' perceptions and interpretations of the patient's illness and care, as well as significant aspects of the caregivers' own biographies, as these influenced the caregivers' attitudes or behaviors.

We employed the following research methods:

1. *Medical and biographical background:* review of the medical chart and interviews with the patient and family
2. *Clinical course of the illness:* ongoing chart review, direct observation of patient–caregiver interactions, and interviews with the patient and family at regular intervals, attendance at team meetings, and ward rounds
3. *Patient and family perceptions:* interviews with the patient and family at regular intervals, the actual frequency determined by the course of a particular case
4. *Health care providers' perceptions:* providers were asked to keep a journal in order to record their perceptions, reactions, and interpretations of their involvement with the care of the patient; researchers interviewed the providers to amplify journal entries, and also attended staff support meetings.

Tape-recorded interviews of patients, families, and caregivers, chart reviews, and participant-observation were carried out by the authors in both Montreal and Lancaster. While interview questions were not specified in advance, certain broad areas of inquiry were felt to be central to the project, and we were alert for opportunities to pursue them as people told their stories. (For details of our interview guides, see Part II.) A first draft of each case was written by the primary researcher, who is also identified as the narrator of that case (Patricia Boston or Anna Towers in Montreal, or Yanna Lambrinidou in Lancaster

County). The drafts were circulated among the authors for critical comments and questions, and a second draft was written. David Barnard, who formulated the original plan for the project and recruited the other three authors to join him, edited the final draft of each case, which, after the primary researcher's approval, is the version printed in this book. Thus, while the initial selection of data and the narrative stance are the responsibility of the researcher who was personally closest to the events, the final version of each narrative is a collaborative work, growing out of collegial criticism and revisiting the raw data with new or refined ideas about salient themes in the case.

It is important to emphasize that the narrative that results from this process is not *the* story of the patient's experience of dying—as if there could be such a thing. It is *a* story—*our* story—with the limitations of point of view and narrative selectivity that are inherent in our method, as we discuss in more depth in Part II.

A brief stylistic note is in order here. Readers will observe that in the narratives we refer to physicians as "Doctor," while for the most part we refer to nurses and other professionals by their first names. Some readers may feel that this usage conflicts with the ostensibly non-hierarchical nature of hospice and palliative care, and we agree. Yet, even in the well-established programs where we did our research, this hierarchical pattern of address was pervasive and we have reproduced it in our narratives, without meaning to endorse it.

What did we learn?

The narratives in this book are rich in detail, and it would be futile to attempt to summarize them in advance. Nevertheless, we would like to highlight a few of the overarching themes that emerged from our research, in addition to our principal finding of the tension between theoretical formulations of excellent palliative care and the constraints of real life.

1. There is no hard distinction between active treatment and palliative care, and forcing patients to choose between them—either through payment mechanisms or caregivers' ideologies—is hostile to good outcomes.

For patients and families, as well as their caregivers, the norm is a frequent oscillation between hope for cure and acceptance of decline and death. Acceptance and denial rarely appear in pure form. The transition from active treatment (treatment with primarily curative or life-prolonging intent) to palliative treatment (treatment primarily aimed at comfort and support) may happen smoothly and unidirectionally, but more often is a gradual, confusing, ambivalent process for all concerned. Ideologies and systems of care that require dichotomous thinking and black-and-white choices serve patients and families very poorly.

2. High-quality palliative care requires a convergence of personal and institutional effectiveness.

High-quality palliative care depends on the personal qualities of caregivers—warmth, technical competence, and stamina—but can be undermined by system constraints. The extraordinary efforts of individual nurses, chaplains, or physicians to understand and respond to patient or family suffering are frequently documented in these narratives. At the same time, broader system issues, such as financial constraints, bureaucratic structures, the allocation of resources, and interprofessional rivalries, are significant factors in the effectiveness of individual interventions.

3. Variations in socioeconomic status are more likely to affect the quality of palliative care than the patient's diagnosis.

In our research, the vast majority of patients were cancer patients. This reflects the prevailing dominance of cancer in hospice and palliative care worldwide. We maintain, however, that the challenges to patients and caregivers that emerged in our research are quite representative of palliative care as a whole, though as more patients with AIDS enter the system, along with other patients whose disease trajectories are less predictable than those of many cancers, some issues certainly will be different. What we did discover, and what we believe is deserving of further study utilizing quantitative as well as qualitative methodologies, is that socioeconomic status—and, in particular, social or cultural distance between patients and families and their professional caregivers—is a more significant variable than the underlying diagnosis, in terms of the challenges of providing empathetic, patient-centered care.

4. The definition of a "good death" is highly variable.

Among these narratives are stories of patients whose final hours were marked by astounding moments of calm, reconciliation, even humor. There are other patients who died in pain, surrounded by frantic and exhausted relatives. Yet it is impossible on the basis of broad characterizations such as these to declare with finality that one death was "good," another "bad." Few deaths can be simply characterized one way or the other, and the family's judgment may turn out to be quite different from that of the professionals.

5. Patient- or family-centered care can appear more successful to the palliative care team than to the patient or family.

As with judgments of a "good death," patients and families can differ from their professional caregivers as to the genuineness of empathy, or the appropriateness of a particular strategy of care. Invested as they are in their desire to give good care, palliative care workers may not always recognize the situations where the patient experiences not empathy but patronization, not solicitude but the invasion of privacy. Patients and families, moreover, have a great desire to please, and are truly grateful for expert care. This makes occasional lapses or misunderstandings even harder for caregivers to discover.

6. Relationships between patients, families, and caregivers pass through many stages over time.

Rapport, empathy, and trust do not spring full-grown at the outset of a caregiver–patient/family relationship. A major finding of our longitudinal method is that empathy and trust take time to evolve, and that patients and families are frequently selective in identifying a caregiver with whom they feel open enough to share important thoughts.

7. Professional caregivers, as well as patients and families, bring their histories of death and loss into the caring relationship.

Sometimes the histories of loss are immediately evident, as in the case of the patient Klara Bergman, who was a survivor of the Holocaust. Sometimes they are more hidden, as in the case of the nurse who cared for Jasmine Claude and who, having been adopted at the age of two, experienced intense anxiety whenever she cared for a woman whose death left a grieving child.

How to use this book

We have written this book with two types of reader in mind. First, we hope it will interest the general reader who is curious or concerned about how some people have died, with the support of excellent palliative care services. Such a reader will find poignant, provocative, and sometimes inspiring scenes in these narratives. Primarily with this reader in mind we have printed all of the narratives together in Part I, with very little commentary or anything else that would interrupt the narrative flow. It is possible to approach the book simply as a collection of stories of people who are face to face with some of life's most profound challenges.

We have also designed the book for health care professionals and students in the health professions. For them we have included a number of features in Part II intended to make the book useful for teaching and learning about palliative care. We have already mentioned that Part II begins with a more detailed discussion of our research methodology. In addition, Part II contains the following materials:

Commentaries: In order not to interrupt the narrative flow, and also to encourage the most active possible discussion by students, we have avoided explicitly injecting into the narratives in Part I our own opinions and interpretations of many of the salient points in the cases. (As we have already acknowledged, these opinions and interpretations do enter the narratives implicitly, through our editorial selectivity, writing style, and so forth.) In Part II we comment more explicitly on some of these issues, in part to express our own preferences and values for palliative care, and in part to assist student readers in identifying important themes.

Questions for discussion: For each case we have suggested discussion questions to prompt students to reflect on important issues and challenges raised by the case. Depending on the setting in which the book is used, these questions could be the focus of small-group discussion, self-paced learning, or written assignments.

Index of themes: Every narrative raises several themes and challenges related to giving or receiving palliative care. Nonetheless, as a result of the combination of "what happened" and what we selected for inclusion in our narratives, each case brings out some issues more prominently than others. In this section we list the major themes, arranged so that an interested student or teacher can quickly identify which cases best bring out particular themes. Thus, in preparation for a discussion of difficult pain management or requests for assisted death, for example, or the impact of preexisting family conflict on end-of-life care, the teacher can select those cases which most clearly raise that issue.

We do not mean to suggest that the themes we have included in the thematic index are the only ones that are raised in a particular case. Nor do we wish to imply that a given theme only appears in the cases listed under that theme's entry in the index. Nevertheless, the individual narratives raise some issues more prominently than others, either by the nature of a particular case or because of the focus we as authors and narrators brought to it. The index, then, is a rough-and-ready guide to the narratives rather than an exhaustive content analysis.

One entry does deserve comment, however: "Culture, socioeconomic status, and ethnicity." Everyone, of course, lives as a part of a culture, with a particular socioeconomic status and ethnicity. In selecting only a few narratives as especially pertinent illustrations of this fact, we are not trying to limit the reach of these categories to people who are outside the middle-class, European-American mainstream in U.S. and Canadian society. It is precisely because most health care givers and institutions in those societies reflect the mainstream that culture, socioeconomic status, and ethnicity often pose "problems" or "challenges" in caring for patients with different backgrounds. Those are the challenges we have in mind in connection with this theme.

Readers will undoubtedly discover many more themes than we have in the narratives. And they will probably discover, in the selections we have made for the index, more of our biases, as well.

Bibliographies: Although this is not a textbook designed to teach specific techniques of palliative care, we want to guide interested readers to the most useful literature on many of the clinical problems raised by the cases. The background, and in some cases the answers, to many of the discussion questions will be found in this literature. For topics such as the control of various common symptoms, spiritual care, communication, grief, or cultural diversity, we include reading lists that will help students deal with situations described in the cases. As we have said, we hope the book will be read as a narrative companion to these technical and scientific resources.

Some personal words in conclusion

You matter because you are you, and you matter until the end of your life.
                                                        —Cicely Saunders

As we have tried to demonstrate in these narratives, palliative care shows respect for human potential no matter how ill the individual and how limited the prognosis. We were amazed at examples of the therapeutic power of human presence, honesty, compassion, humility, humor, and the affirmation of life. Because these are real cases, we saw examples of communication within families, and with professionals, that were flawed, as well as examples that were good. In an era when patients and families continue to complain about poor communication, we hope that this material will help change attitudes, especially within the medical profession. We also hope that these narratives will help professionals and laypersons alike reflect on the place of death and dying in our society.

The four of us have been profoundly affected by our work and colleagueship in this project. We have certainly been affected by what we have learned from the patients, families, and caregivers who permitted us to accompany them in these significant moments. It is not unusual to hear health caregivers comment that working in palliative care has improved their own quality of life. This has been true to some extent for us as researchers as well. Through our close contact with the people in these narratives, we have learned something about getting back to basics—concern for friends, family, and community. We have learned more about the uncertainty and fragility of life, and we have reaped unexpected joy from this change in attitude and understanding.

There have certainly been personal challenges for us. Ultimately, once we were invited, we had to go into the dying person's world in some small measure to try to understand it. This was risky for us, even if the patients themselves were clearly running the greater risks. But we sincerely believe we have been better able to reflect patients' and family members' first-hand perspectives and those of their caregivers, as a result of trying to share in many of the transient and precious moments of their lives.

The title of this book, *Crossing Over*, is a metaphor for the physical, emotional, and spiritual leaps that we witnessed over the three years of our study. All but one of the patients in the following chapters are now dead. They have crossed over, leaving this world altogether. Prior to their deaths, these patients (and here we include the man who, as this is written, remains alive) took different kinds of journeys. They reached across old barriers to embrace loved ones, to connect to the past, to the future, or to their God. Families crossed over, too. They made efforts to move out of themselves in order truly to understand their dying relatives, to advocate for them, to mend relationships, to stay at their side. In bereavement they had to change again, crossing into a new life without the deceased. Palliative care workers travelled physically—to patients' homes, nursing facilities, or hospice units—only to make yet another leap, an emotional and spiritual one, to try to connect with their patients. As authors, we extended ourselves into the lives of patients, families, and caregivers, trying to understand their different perspectives. Now we hope this book will help readers make their own crossings.

References

Arnold RM, Forrow L. 1998. Caring for the dying, one at a time. *Med Humanities Rev* 12(1):48–59.

Billings JA. 1998. What is palliative care? *J Palliat Med*, 1(1):73–81.

Byock I. 1997. Dying Well: The Prospect for Growth at the End of Life. New York: Riverhead.

Carron AT, Lynn J, Keaney P. 1999. End-of-life care in medical textbooks. *Ann Intern Med* 130(1):82–86.

Doyle D, Hanks G, MacDonald N (eds). 1998. Oxford Textbook of Palliative Medicine, 2nd ed. Oxford: Oxford University Press.

Kearney M. 1996. Mortally Wounded: Stories of Soul Pain, Death, and Healing. New York: Scribner.

MacDonald N (ed). 1998. Palliative Medicine: A Case-Based Manual. Oxford: Oxford University Press.

Quill TE. 1996. A Midwife Through the Dying Process: Stories of Healing and Hard Choices at the End of Life. Baltimore: Johns Hopkins University Press.

Quill TE, Billings JA. 1998. Palliative care textbooks come of age. *Ann Intern Med* 129(7):590–594.

Roy D. 1988. Ethics and aging: Trends and problems in the clinical setting. In: Thornton J, Winkler E. (eds). Ethics and Aging: The Right to Live, the Right to Die. Vancouver: University of British Columbia Press, pp. 31–40.

Saunders C. 1993 Introduction. In: Saunders C, Sykes N. (eds). The Management of Terminal Malignant Disease, 3rd ed. London: Edward Arnold, pp. 1–14.

Stjernswärd J, Pampallona S. 1998. Palliative medicine: A global perspective. In: Doyle D, Hanks G, MacDonald N (eds). Oxford Textbook of Palliative Medicine, 2nd ed. Oxford: Oxford University Press, pp. 1227–1245.

World Health Organization 1990. Cancer Pain Relief and Palliative Care. Technical Report Series No. 804. Geneva: World Health Organization.

I

The Narratives

2

Raymond Hynes
When the Storm of a Lifetime Hits in Mid-Dance

Narrated by ANNA TOWERS

Sometimes a family is fortunate enough to have significant resources to face a world that seems to have fallen apart from one day to the next. This was the case for Raymond Hynes and his family when they learned that he had incurable cancer. The Hyneses had their way of dealing with this disaster, a way that was different from what the palliative care team wanted to see. The different perspectives may have represented cultural differences between the family and the medical professionals. The members of the Hynes family were practical and stoical; when challenged by life events, they typically sought a common-sense, step-by-step solution, and that is how they preferred to deal with the illness. The team, however, kept expecting more expression of feeling. Silence was a powerful force that informed the family's actions. Nevertheless, the family and the team managed to navigate a course that led to a "successful" death at home.

Sickness was not a part of his life

Raymond Hynes loved to dance. In fact, he looked very much like Fred Astaire—tall, slim, and graceful. Even at age 72 he and his wife Margaret went dancing regularly. They were champion ballroom dancers. Mr. Hynes was a fun-loving man, always smiling, always welcoming. He was well known for the parties he organized within the Irish community. He was a baseball fanatic who turned televised games into social occasions. He had many good friends through the church, his work, and his golf group. He was a kidder, and he had a twinkle in his eye. He blamed it on his Irish origins.

If Mr. Hynes had worries, he did not share them with others, for he didn't want to bother people with his woes. He always said that everything was fine. He lived from day to day, was never concerned about his health, and ate and drank what he wanted. He liked to relax and take naps, making it a point to take regular holidays and to play golf twice a week.

Margaret thought Raymond was hard on his body. He had smoked heavily for 60 years, and yet he seemed to have no lung problems. He liked his gin and tonic when he got home. He worked hard and played hard. He had a great sense of humor and made a lot of people laugh. Sometimes, Margaret would say, his positive attitude about everything went beyond reason, but it was pleasant to live with someone who was as lively as Raymond Hynes.

Mr. and Mrs. Hynes lived in a comfortable detached house in an English-speaking suburb of Montreal, and rented a cottage in the country every summer. After retiring as manager of a large furniture company, Mr. Hynes continued to act as a consultant. Everyone said that he was a good manager who was fair and compassionate. Mr. Hynes was a very religious man, serving as a lector and warden at the church. He went to church every Sunday and felt that everyone else should, too. He counted the priests among his friends and worked for Catholic charities. He felt that his religion had helped him through a lot of things in life.

Although not one to express affection in words, Mr. Hynes adored his wife. Sometimes Mrs. Hynes wished that he could be more expressive, but she realized that her husband could, in a few words, express a lifetime of love and appreciation. At his 70th birthday party, for example, he had turned to look at her with deep gratitude in his eyes. All he said was, "Oh, Maggie, Maggie"—and that said it all. Mrs. Hynes was proud of her husband's accomplishments. Although she loved him and enjoyed being with him, she occasionally complained that he did not look after himself, especially because he smoked so much. A tall, graceful woman who was always impeccably groomed, she was good-looking but unadorned, with short, natural gray hair and tasteful spectacles.

The Hyneses had two daughters and one son. They described their family as very close. Mary and Michael lived in Montreal; Jane lived in Florida. Mary was a children's social worker, a lively woman in her mid-forties and tall like her parents. She tended to dress in casual sports clothes and enjoyed exercise and the outdoors. She always seemed to be moving around or saying things to diffuse tension and try to make everyone in the family feel better.

Mary felt very close to her father, describing herself as very much like him.

She told me, "I have a lot of Daddy in me. I'm optimistic, but I do talk about it and work things through." In this last respect, Mary differed from her father, and felt that her father was in denial about a lot of things. When Mary was a child and was upset about something, her father would be dismissive. He wouldn't sit and talk with her, so Mary didn't go to him if she had problems. She preferred to go to her mother. Now Mary seemed to be the linchpin in the family. When Mr. Hynes became ill, he insisted that Mary be present at every medical and nursing visit, and often she was their spokesperson.

Michael had his own business, which was doing well. He was also close to his father, but in a different way. They played golf together, and although they generally did not say much to each other, their feelings toward each other ran deep. Michael had experienced his share of suffering: he and his wife had raised a handicapped son, who, despite all odds, had just started college. They had received great encouragement from Mr. and Mrs. Hynes from the time their son was born. That he had made it to college was a measure of how resourceful this family was. The experience had made the entire family grateful and appreciative. They knew that good health could not be taken for granted.

Mr. Hynes was very involved in the city's Irish Catholic subculture, and he was proud of his origins, as he was of his family. "Nobody is better than the Hyneses," he would say. Mr. and Mrs. Hynes loved their grandchildren—all 10 of them. Because it was important for Mr. Hynes to see his family all together, they all came for his 70th birthday party. On vacations the family would meet at their Vermont chalet and rent two houses near each other so they could all be together.

The family lived within a culture that limited expressiveness. Although they may have been introspective, they were not open concerning their feelings. They were practical and efficient, they knew how to get a job done, and they had financial resources.

Hearing the bad news

When the Hyneses began to recount events to me as part of our research project, Mary began, "This isn't a long story, you know." Mr. Hynes was living and dancing full-tilt when he began to have epigastric symptoms. In September of 1996 he began to feel ill with abdominal pain; he lost his appetite and started to lose weight. In mid-October he went to see his family physician, Dr. Drummond, a former schoolmate, who had been his doctor all his adult life. Mr. Hynes had never been ill before and had never been in a hospital, but 4 weeks after his symptoms started the doctors told him that he had inoperable cancer of the pancreas. An abdominal scan showed a mass in the pancreas with widespread metastases in the liver and within the abdomen.

When all the tests were in, it was the resident on the medical ward who gave Mr. Hynes the diagnosis. It was late morning and Mr. Hynes was alone at the time. Mr. Hynes asked a lot of questions, for he wanted to know exactly what the tests had shown. The resident told Mr. Hynes that his prognosis was two months to two years. When the resident left, Mr. Hynes tried to hold back his tears. He took some time to consider his situation. What should he tell his family? Was there some way he could spare them the pain? He then realized that they had to know everything that was going on. When he was more composed several hours later, he called Margaret and told her the bad news. The family was devastated, and upset that Mr. Hynes had been alone when the physician gave him the news. They would have liked to have been there to support him. Just as Mr. Hynes wanted to spare them, the family wanted to protect him. Everyone in the family wanted to protect the rest of the family, to cushion what could perhaps not be cushioned.

Why had this cancer appeared? Mrs. Hynes privately wondered whether her husband's smoking and drinking might have had something to do with it. Even though the physicians reassured her that the drinking did not, she still felt that lifestyle could have been a cause. Mrs. Hynes was not being critical of her husband; his smoking, drinking and easygoing nature were all of a piece. If anything, she admired his *joie-de-vivre* and felt invigorated by it. But she was looking for a cause. Mr. Hynes felt guilty at having to impose his illness on the family and thought that he might have been able to prevent it if he had lived differently. Now his family was suffering the consequences.

The oncologist offered Mr. Hynes experimental chemotherapy. Mr. Hynes was feeling so shocked and numb that it was hard for him to think. The oncologist told him that the chances that the chemotherapy would prolong his life were not very high, and in fact, the treatment might not help him at all, but it would give the oncologists information that might help others in the future. Mr. Hynes considered this. He did want to make himself as useful as possible. At the same time, he was finding it hard to think clearly. He told the doctors the next morning that he would go ahead with the treatment, not so much because it might prolong his life, but because the oncologists might learn something. His family supported him and respected his decision.

Unfortunately, Mr. Hynes had a pneumothorax (collapsed lung) as a complication of the liver biopsy he was required to undergo as part of the research protocol, and he needed a temporary chest tube to re-expand his lung. This prolonged his hospitalization by several days. According to his wife, he continued to be cheerful and "a very good patient," and didn't complain about the pneumothorax. Margaret, Mary, and Michael were not as forgiving. They insisted that the staff physician consider very carefully whether tests and procedures were really necessary. They did not want Mr. Hynes to go through any unnecessary tests that would lead to additional suffering—a common dilemma for terminally ill patients who are receiving highly experimental treatment.

Consulting palliative care

The ward physicians told Mr. Hynes that they were going to consult the Palliative Care Service to help him with care at home. Mr. Hynes was eligible to receive this service even though he had opted to receive chemotherapy. It is common in Quebec for cancer patients to get hospice-like home care while they are still receiving palliative or experimental chemotherapy. While on the Home Care Program any patient can also opt to be admitted to a regular acute-care hospital ward and be treated aggressively for any medical or surgical complication, if they can find a physician willing to admit them for that. This flexibility contrasts with many hospice programs in the United States, particularly under the Medicare hospice benefit, where the patient and family must choose at the outset the kind of care they want. If they choose the hospice benefit, active treatment for the underlying disease is specifically excluded. In Quebec the transitions can therefore be smoother than in the United States for the patient moving from active treatment to supportive care and eventually to terminal care.

In cases of patients like Mr. Hynes, the request for consultation triggers a visit to the patient and family on the ward. The palliative care team assesses what the patient has been told about the diagnosis and prognosis, evaluates the reaction of patient and family, and proceeds accordingly. At this stage, the palliative care team acts as a support service. They follow the patient at home, assess his symptoms, and provide appropriate symptomatic treatment. They also provide emotional support to the family. As the patient gets sicker, the home care team will mention the resources of the inpatient Palliative Care Unit (PCU). It would be at this point (unless the patient had specifically inquired earlier) that they would talk more about the philosophy of palliative care as it relates to comfort care near the end of life. But the patient and family may choose just to receive the support services and not avail themselves of the PCU—if they opt for aggressive antibiotic intervention for infections, for example. It is only at the point of PCU admission that there is a more formal consent process with discussion of, e.g., do-not-resuscitate orders (DNR), artificial nutrition and hydration, or the use of antibiotics.

When Mr. Hynes met the palliative care consultant, he learned that a nurse from the Palliative Home Care Service would visit him. He was not keen to have a nurse involved. "Why? What is she going to do? Why have someone come to the house?" he asked. He seemed not to want to face the fact that he would get weaker and need help, and may also have felt that this would be a disruption of their family life. Mrs. Hynes and Mary, however, were very happy that they would be getting help. Dr. Roget, a resident physician and palliative medicine trainee, was assigned to follow Mr. Hynes. Dr. Roget was a gentle, soft-spoken man in his early thirties. He had a natural ease in discussing complex issues with patients and families. He came to see Mr. Hynes on the ward, and arranged to see him in the oncology clinic as well as to visit him at home as required.

"Maybe deep down in his heart he was aware"

After Mr. Hynes went home in early November, the home care nurse, Susan, began to make her visits. She had more than 15 years of experience in palliative care, and was cheerful and confident. She loved her work and was well liked by her patients and families. On her first visit, she noted that Mr. Hynes seemed nervous about palliative care. It scared him; he didn't know what to expect. He seemed stunned by his diagnosis and by the whole medical system. Mr. Hynes was very concerned because his symptoms were getting worse. He had now lost his appetite completely. "I can't eat," he would say to Dr. Roget and to Susan. "Why can't you do something about it?" He was trying to force himself to eat and his wife was also trying to push him to eat, as she was very anxious about the appetite loss. Although Mr. Hynes was willing to try to eat more, he resisted pressure when it came from Margaret.

Mr. Hynes insisted that Mary had to be present whenever anyone from the Palliative Care Service visited. Mary arranged her work and her own family's schedule so that she could spend most days at her parents' house. Her husband stayed with their two teenage children after school. It was particularly important to Raymond and Margaret that Mary be there to write down everything that the doctor or nurse said to them. Mary found that she and her mother often had a different understanding of what was said. For example, when Mary heard Susan caution against forcing Mr. Hynes to eat more than he wanted, her mother, who was also listening, said after Susan left, "OK. He can have mashed potatoes and hamburgers."

Mr. Hynes, who had never been ill in his life and was unfamiliar with the health care system, seemed confused. "Who is my doctor, anyway?" he asked Susan. Was it his family physician, his gastroenterologist, his oncologist, the palliative care staff physician, or Dr. Roget? Because Mr. Hynes might opt to be hospitalized for a complication, the palliative care team wanted him to maintain contact with the oncologist.

Mr. Hynes took a ready liking to Susan. On her visits she inquired about his symptoms and general well-being and spoke with the family. She asked Dr. Roget to visit if a physician's input was required. Although Mr. Hynes was very organized in his thinking and expressed his needs clearly, he was not a very talkative man. Instead, he wrote down all his questions, and when Susan visited him, he would go down his list of questions and jot down the answers. Then he would say, "That's fine. You must be tired. You can go now." Mr. Hynes found Susan helpful, but he wanted to stay in control of what she did and of the information that she provided. Mary also liked Susan, for her empathy but especially because of her practical suggestions. Mary told me, "We needed to know: were we reacting as well as possible or not? We're very practical. We want to know how to fix things. She gave us good advice. She said, 'Go with the ball wherever it leads. If he can't eat, don't force him.'"

Mr. Hynes continued to push himself, to get dressed every day, to come downstairs. He wanted life to carry on as before. Although he was too weak to play golf, he tried to see his friends and play cards, or watch baseball on television. But the illness continued, and he had some decisions to make.

He wasn't sure what to do about the chemotherapy. He was beginning to doubt his earlier decision to go through with it. The oncologist had given him time to think about it, and their next appointment was in a few days' time. He contacted Dr. Drummond, who visited him at home. Dr. Drummond, being up to date on all the test results, said, "It's your decision, Raymond, but you have to think about quality of life. Life isn't going to be easy. Why make it more difficult?" Mr. Hynes considered this opinion, but decided to go ahead with the experimental chemotherapy—not for his own sake, but for the sake of others who might benefit. Mary told me that her dad felt it was his Christian duty to do this.

By the time Mr. Hynes returned to the oncology clinic, however, he had continued to lose weight and was too weak to walk more than a block or so. The oncologist believed that he was now too sick to tolerate chemotherapy. She suggested privately to Mrs. Hynes and to Mary that it was time to call out-of-town family and get them to come. She did not think that Mr. Hynes would make it to Christmas. She did not communicate this opinion to Mr. Hynes, however, preferring to leave this to the family or to the palliative care team.

The family decided not to share the oncologist's opinion with Mr. Hynes. No one wanted to say to him, "You have a few weeks at most." Mrs. Hynes did call her daughter in Florida and asked her to come sooner than she had planned, but she did not discuss the reason with her husband. "I had to make up a story about her coming earlier so he wouldn't worry," Mrs. Hynes told me. Then she continued, "Maybe deep down in his heart he was aware." Mrs. Hynes's concerns about her husband's knowledge and emotions also influenced her feelings about participating in our project. The day I telephoned to arrange my first visit she expressed worry that I might discuss something distressing with her husband. I had to promise to tread gently.

On November 24, I visited them in their comfortable, old stone house which was on a quiet, tree-lined street. Mrs. Hynes, dressed neatly in a smart skirt and blouse, greeted me at the door. She was cheerful and welcoming, but she looked anxious. Mary was also there, energetically rearranging seats in the living room. They had just finished making Mr. Hynes comfortable in his reclining chair. I could see that it had been an effort for him to come downstairs. He was very thin and looked tired. He was a tall man, but looked somehow small because of his illness. He, too, was neatly dressed in casual clothes. He jokingly told me how he had taken a lot of trouble to get dressed because I was coming to see him. Cheerfully, he described to me how he was trying to maintain his daily routine: getting dressed on most days, coming downstairs, reading the paper, chatting with his wife over breakfast. He smiled. "You know, we have this chat for about 20 minutes every morning. 'How was your night?' You know, things like that. She makes me hot cereal. She takes very good care of me."

Even though he was getting very tired, he pushed himself to get dressed every day and to be ready for company, because he knew many friends would be dropping in to visit. I asked if it was a problem for him to have to ask all of these visitors to leave once he had gotten too tired. Mary broke in at this point to say, "Oh, no. He's good at that. That's what he did all his life." Mr. Hynes smiled again. "No," he said to me. "I have no trouble asking them to leave."

I could see how easy it was for Mr. Hynes to maintain his sense of control and to be cheerful. It seemed much more difficult for him and his family to communicate about serious concerns. "We joke around a lot," Mary said. "We can't help it. We're Irish." Yet they did have anxieties, especially about Mr. Hynes's disappearing appetite. Their communication with each other became strained over this issue. Susan told me that during one of her visits, Mr. Hynes "blew up at his wife" when, in her frustration and helplessness, Mrs. Hynes coaxed him to eat more. Mr. Hynes acknowledged to me that the stresses and strains were a problem at times. "Sometimes I have a short fuse myself," he said. "That's not like me at all. I want to spare my family. I don't want them to be more stressed than they already are. But I don't know what's happening. I feel lost. I haven't gone through anything like this before."

"How long have I got?"

Mr. Hynes was dying. Everyone in the family knew this, but they did not know how to talk about it. No one wanted to lose control over their feelings, and yet their feelings were sometimes very strong. For example, I had asked Mr. Hynes which persons I could interview for our project, to obtain his consent. He said that his daughter Jane was coming from Florida, but she was very anxious so he preferred that I not talk to her. She was more emotional, and Mr. Hynes was worried that if she talked to me she might get upset and thus upset everyone else. "Mary is OK," he said. "She has feelings, but she can control them." Mrs. Hynes interjected, "We *all* have feelings."

Mr. Hynes simply did not want to express his feelings about his illness within the family. He wanted to live from day to day. Susan continued to advise Mrs. Hynes and Mary: "You have to take the cues from him. He's the boss. However he wants to deal with it, you go with the flow." But Mrs. Hynes would have preferred to talk more.

Instead of talking about Mr. Hynes's illness, they discussed sports. Mr. Hynes continued to watch his baseball games with a passion. They talked about food and, even though Mr. Hynes was no longer eating much, tried to enjoy their meal times together. In other words, they carried on—that's how they had always coped with problems.

Mr. Hynes's appetite seemed to be his personal gauge of his condition. As it continued to dwindle, he became more anxious. He asked everyone he could, "How long have I got?" No matter whom he asked, the answer was always the same: "I have no idea. These things can vary." Susan said to him, "You just have to listen to your body." Dr. Roget told him the same thing; his body would tell him how he was doing. Mr. Hynes found this advice confusing. How could he listen to his body? This was all very strange and new. He didn't know how to listen to his body. He didn't know what was going on, and nobody was giving him a clear answer. He wanted a date! Surely the doctors must know that much. Was everyone avoiding telling him the truth? He wondered if the oncologist might have told Mary something more precise. But Mary said, "They can't tell you, Dad. Everyone has a different body." He always received the same evasive answer.

Mr. Hynes knew that I was a physician who was familiar with the details of his illness, and he wanted to discuss prognosis with me also, even though I was visiting him for our research project and not to provide him with care. This led to some awkward moments for me. "How will I know how I'm doing?" he asked me during one conversation. "Susan said you were going to ask me about pain, but I don't have pain. I don't know what pain is. I feel something here," he said, pointing to his upper abdomen, "and then I burp, but I don't have pain. I know I'll get pain—that's what this friend told me."

"It's not inevitable that you will have pain," I answered. "Many people with this tumor have no pain at all."

"How will I know then?" he asked.

"What do you mean?"

"How do I know when I'm going to die?"

When I paused before answering, he looked angry and impatient.

"You don't know," he said. "Nobody knows."

"Well," I said, "you're weak. But you're eating OK and as long as you're able to eat you'll be OK."

"How much do I need to eat?"

We talked about calories and eating and the futility of pushing oneself to eat. Mr. Hynes lit a cigarette. "Sometimes I get full and my wife nags me about eating," he said. Then he smiled. "But sometimes I can't eat another bite."

I did not want to avoid his direct questions regarding prognosis, but I was not Mr. Hynes's physician. I found it difficult to be both a researcher and a physician at this point. I could have gone into a discussion of "weeks rather than months" in response to his question. But discussions of prognosis are always tricky. We do have patients like him who live on for months, and it does hinge on how good their appetite is. At the same time, force-feeding will not prolong life, as I tried to explain to him. Mr. Hynes had originally been told that his prognosis was two months to two years. One month had now gone by. The practical organizer within him knew that he needed to sort out his affairs and prepare to die, but his feelings had not yet caught up with that.

"We should be saying things and we're not"

At the same time that Mr. Hynes wanted to plan ahead to make things easier on his family, he wanted to spare his family the pain he thought it could cause them to discuss his arrangements. He could not bring himself to make the phone calls to get his affairs in order. Mrs. Hynes had not taken over before, but now she felt that she had to do something to prompt him to look after his affairs. But it was hard for them to talk about dying. They would sit in front of the TV and Mrs. Hynes would say, "We should be saying things and we're not."

Mr. Hynes was more open with his family while I was there, as if I acted as a catalyst. Otherwise his wife and daughter did not ask him any questions—they seemed to be waiting for him to initiate the discussion. But he was not a talkative person. Mary told me later:

> In the hospital he said to Mom, "You'll go off and marry a rich guy." That's as close as he came to saying anything. We're a pretty upbeat family. It's not that we're in denial, but Dad may have been. The rest of us deal with things. There was a lot of talk, a lot of tears, but not in front of Dad.

And Mrs. Hynes said to me:

> He didn't say, "Take care of yourself," to me or anything. He was a man of few words. He would say, "Actions speak louder than words." But we didn't have to talk to each other, because it was *lived*.

But on another occasion she expressed regret that there had been no goodbyes.

Susan continued to visit twice a week and was in telephone contact almost daily. She understood that the Hyneses had to be left to manage things their way. Susan expressed her view in the journal she was keeping as part of her participation in our project:

> They are a stoic Celtic family, and they're not going to show their feelings very much. Big smiles. A lot of appreciation. They say that they have done some good talking together but they're not talking about what they're losing, or anything about death and dying.

Even though Mrs. Hynes often appeared overwhelmed, she did not allow herself to cry in front of her daughter or her husband, and Mary diverted her mother from showing feelings. The family had decided that Susan's role should be to help them with practical rather than psychological or emotional matters. When she spoke with them about how they were coping emotionally, Mary, in particular, would change the subject. It was also difficult for Susan to find the opportunity to counsel the family members individually. Mr. and Mrs. Hynes and Mary were always together when Susan or Dr. Roget visited. No one in the family was signaling that they wanted to have a private discussion with a member of the team.

The family gathers

Although Mr. Hynes's strength was diminishing, he could still walk a few blocks. He was getting thinner, except for his abdomen, which was starting to fill up with fluid. His eyes and complexion were jaundiced. Nevertheless, the Hyneses weren't going around being morbid or sad. Mrs. Hynes was still focusing on getting her husband to eat and drink. What else could she do? Mr. Hynes showed no sign of giving up. He pushed himself to do as much as possible.

Jane had arrived from Florida. She had many questions: what could her father eat, what could be done about the jaundice, how long would this go on. She cried a lot, and the rest of the family seemed uncomfortable with her tears. They were only interested in specific answers to their practical questions. Michael was shy and did not say much. Everyone seemed very scared. Susan wondered: will they panic as Mr. Hynes got sicker?

On December 1, Mrs. Hynes phoned Susan to ask her to come to the house. Mr. Hynes was quite jaundiced. When Susan arrived the next afternoon, Mr. Hynes was still in his pajamas—the first time that he had not gotten dressed for her. He was obviously weaker and much quieter than before. He let his family do most of the talking. Mr. Hynes complained of more discomfort in his abdomen. He seemed very reluctant to consider taking a painkiller, especially when Susan told him that the medication might produce constipation and he would need to take a laxative to go with it. He could not understand why he should take one medication to do one thing and then take another to counteract the effects of the first. When, as usual, he asked Susan how she thought he was doing, she told him that she didn't like seeing him in his pajamas, that it was not a good sign to her. "He seemed to appreciate that," Susan told me later, "because previously I'd always thrown the question back to him. But this time it seemed quite obvious that he had deteriorated."

Mr. Hynes was scheduled for an appointment with his oncologist, who sought to see her patients even when the palliative care team was following them. If the patients were at home, she saw them in the clinic for as long as they were able to come to the hospital. The family wondered if Mr. Hynes would be able to keep the appointment. Although he was too weak to walk, he still wanted to go, and on December 4, Mary pushed him into the clinic in a wheelchair. He saw the oncologist, who gave him another appointment in two weeks, though she told me later, "I don't think he'll be able to make it." This oncologist always gave her patients return appointments.

After the consultation, I observed that Mrs. Hynes looked anxious as she helped maneuver her husband's wheelchair out of the clinic. She looked like she was trying to avoid her own emotions, putting on a formal front. She spoke in a detached way and was very task oriented: "Now we have the medications straight. You have to take those pills." The visit had taken almost all of Mr. Hynes's energy, and he looked terrible. He was thin and jaundiced; he looked to me like he was dying. But he had on his baseball cap and he was going home to watch the game on TV. He reserved his last bit of energy for humor and baseball and for keeping up his family's morale.

Mary had taken a leave of absence from work and was now spending most of every day with her parents. Michael continued to work as usual. Jane stayed for one week, but then went back to Florida because her return airline ticket could not be extended. Her mother and sister had advised her to go back home, even though she wanted to stay, since no one seemed to know how long this would take.

Preparing to die at home

Mr. Hynes was now too weak to go to church, but he had his prayer book on his bedside table. He and Mrs. Hynes discussed calling the priest. They agreed that the priest should come to give Mr. Hynes the Sacrament of the Sick. The priest was one of several who were personal friends of the family. Although Mr. Hynes spent most of his time sleeping, he was awake and alert when the priest came, and he seemed peaceful and accepting after this ritual.

On December 7, Dr. Roget made another home visit. The family asked him to tell Mr. Hynes not to come downstairs anymore, for he was now too weak. The Hyneses had come to trust Dr. Roget, and they were always happy and relieved when he visited them at home. On this day he had to have an important conversation with them: they had to decide now whether they wanted to have Mr. Hynes die at home. Since he did not have any difficult symptoms, both Susan and Dr. Roget felt that it should be possible to keep him at home, which is what Mr. Hynes had already told his wife that he preferred.

Mrs. Hynes tried to be brave, but she was very anxious and found it difficult to make decisions. She wanted so much to respect her husband's desire, but had doubts about whether she could cope. Mrs. Hynes was afraid of her husband's dying at home, but she could not discuss her fears in front of Mary. Mary would say, "Mom, listen. Daddy wants to die at home, and we're going to do all we can. Come on, we've got some things to organize here."

Dr. Roget tried to reassure her: We don't make any hard and fast decisions here. We don't know what's going to happen. We go hour by hour. At one point things could change, and you may say to yourself, this is not working. And then you can call and we can change tack, and sometimes we change tack several times. We might fix the problem in hospital, and he could come home again. So it's a fluid situation, and you should never feel that you're making a hard and fixed decision.

To help Mrs. Hynes cope at night, when she and Mr. Hynes were in the house alone, they hired a night sitter. That first evening, before the sitter arrived, Mrs. Hynes heard a thump while she was in the kitchen. She went upstairs to find that her husband had fallen out of bed. She called her son to come pick him up off the floor, and Michael stayed until 3:00 a.m. The family then decided that they needed 24-hour private nursing to avoid this situation. Mrs. Hynes and Mary organized the nurses for the next day. Since Mr. Hynes had private medical insurance, this was an option for them.

By December 7, the private nurses and sitters were there 24 hours a day. Because they were older nurses and very efficient, Mr. Hynes accepted their presence easily. It was a great relief to the family to have this help. The nurses looked after Mr. Hynes in shifts, cleaning him, giving him medication, and the like, while Mrs. Hynes returned to duties that gave her comfort, such as baking her husband's favorite muffins. Susan told her that her husband could not eat the muffins; they were too dry and he might choke on them. She baked them anyway.

When Dr. Roget next visited Mr. Hynes, he saw him in his bedroom. It did not look like a sick room. There were family photographs on the walls, and a large crucifix. There was a large photograph of Mr. and Mrs. Hynes when they were about 50 years old, photographs of the children and grandchildren, taken on his 70th birthday, a photograph of him receiving a prize at work, and one of him with the bishop and some of his ordained friends. Mr. Hynes looked frail and small in the large double bed. He was now so weak that he could hardly speak, but he continued to smile. In response to Dr. Roget's questions about his general well-being, he raised two fingers and made the signal for peace. He signaled that his morale was "ten on ten." When Dr. Roget asked him how he thought his wife was doing, he gave the same signal and also managed to indicate that she was a strong woman. Dr. Roget thought at the time that by stating this in front of his wife, Mr. Hynes might have been trying to tell her that she was doing a good job, that he was proud of her. Everyone continued to avoid talking about feelings, but they were a bit more open with each other away from the bedroom.

When Susan visited the next afternoon the house was full of activity. There were two nurses there, changing shifts. Michael was walking from room to room, conducting business on his cellular phone, while Mary and his mother dealt with the nurses and the immediate practical affairs. Susan met Mrs. Hynes in the kitchen, and they hugged each other. Mrs. Hynes said, "He is going fast, but he has a strong faith that has helped him through the worst of times, and it is helping him now. I feel comforted by the fact that he seems peaceful and accepting." Mary came into the kitchen and cried in front of Susan for the first time. But she was unable to stay in the room while Susan talked with her mother about what was likely to happen.

Susan explained to Mrs. Hynes how to get in touch with the medical service and what to do if Mr. Hynes should die in the night. Mrs. Hynes called Mary back into the kitchen to hear this information. Susan suggested to Mary that she stay the night. Mary said that she had packed a bag and that she was pre-pared to stay. While Mrs. Hynes listened attentively to Susan's instructions, Mary wrote them all down, trying to control her tears. It was striking to Susan how they really wanted to get things straight. They wanted to know exactly what to do. Reflecting on the scene later, Susan wrote in her journal:

> I felt at that moment how really sad this is, because they were so grateful for that little bit of information. Numbers. That's all I was giving them. Just names and numbers that they will need to know when the time comes. And yet, that was so important to them. It was something that they could hang on to. Something grounding. What they really want is so much more. And I felt humbled by that.

"If it had to happen, that was the way to go"

Mr. Hynes had now become rather agitated and confused. He couldn't seem to get comfortable, partly because of his abdominal swelling. Susan called the palliative care physician and got a prescription for chlorpromazine suppositories, which the nurses or the family could give every six hours as a tranquilizer. Mr. Hynes was in bed almost all the time, sleepy and sometimes forgetting where he was or what was going on, but he still recognized his family and was able to respond to them through signals and facial expressions. He smiled often. Mrs. Hynes kept asking him practical questions: what he wanted to eat or drink, whether he wanted to be in the chair, who had telephoned. She sat by the bed and held his hand. That was the only way she had to express her feelings for him.

The next evening, December 8, Mary and Michael both decided to stay. They were in the bedroom with their parents. Mr. Hynes said he wanted to get out of bed and sit in his easy chair. He was agitated, and after about five minutes he got back into bed, and Mrs. Hynes took hold of his hand. After a few more minutes something seemed to happen with his breathing. Mrs. Hynes asked Michael, "What's happening to your dad?" Mr. Hynes took a last breath and died.

"It was an experience," Mrs. Hynes recalled to me afterward:

> He was conscious of everything up to a few minutes before he died. He was happy in his room and in his bed. He knew that we were there and were helping him. I was happy for him because he had his daughter and son with him. He died peacefully. He didn't appear to be suffering. I'm at peace with the fact that he stayed at home. And I think, for him, absolutely, it was wonderful. He didn't have much pain. He died in his room, with all his pictures.

Mary said to me:

> If it had to happen, that was the way to go. He didn't appear to be suffering that much. He even had a smile on his face. There was nothing that could have been done differently. He didn't even bother us by dying in the middle of the night when he would have awakened us. He did it at such an appropriate time. And it was really, really beautiful. My brother felt that it was a really tremendous experience. He wouldn't have changed it for the world.

The first year: "It's a case of trying to survive"

As was common for the palliative care nurses, Susan attended the funeral that was held three days later. The old church was packed with friends and family, and the service was long because of the many tributes to Mr. Hynes. Mrs. Hynes and Michael came up to Susan and said to her gratefully, "You've been such a good friend." In her journal, Susan reflected:

> It seemed that it was more important to say that than to say "You've been a good nurse," or, "You've done a good job." I think the family were grateful that we were there to discuss practical things like what to do if he died at home, who to call. It was an honor for me to be a part of this team.

I visited Mrs. Hynes and Mary two months after the death. Mrs. Hynes saw her husband's relatively quick deterioration as a blessing. On one of their outings together, Mary and her mother had seen an old man struggling along with a walker. Mary said to her mother, "Dad didn't have to go through that." And Mrs. Hynes had replied, "Yes, I'm grateful for that."

Mary showed me a photograph of her dancing with her father. He was tall, in a graceful pose, smiling. This was the way that she wanted to remember him. We then spoke about how the family communicated among themselves while her father was dying. "We let him do it his way," Mary said. "That's who he was. I don't think it should have been different. But it's not as if we had to make up for lost time. He knew. We knew. Daddy didn't say, 'I'm dying—this is what I have to say to you.' He wasn't that type of guy and Mom took her cues from him. I think it would have upset him. He dealt with it himself, in his own way."

Mrs. Hynes, who was crying quietly during much of my visit, still seemed to be concerned with doing things correctly. Only now, it was not a question of caring properly for her husband but of mourning him. She said:

> I think about him a lot. I feel it. It's the loneliness, coming back to the house at night. It gives me comfort to continue to sleep in our double bed. I need to keep myself occupied. At the same time, I feel it hasn't hit me so much. Maybe it's because it happened so quickly, I don't know whether I've been grieving or not. Years ago, they would go into mourning for six months. My aunts fell apart when their husbands died. It was the thing to do. I'm inclined to want to keep busy. I want to get out of the house during the day. I go to an exercise program twice a week. If I'm in the house all day long, I can't concentrate, I can't read. I get bored or lonely if I have nothing to do, and when I'm busy I feel guilty because I think somehow I should be grieving. Is this how it should be? Is this the way I should be? Active? I just know that I don't feel good if I don't have something to focus on.

Friends phoned, but no one actually came to the house to see her except her daughter. If she wanted to be with people she had to go out. It was especially hard for her to go back to church. "Raymond and I always used to sit in the front of the church," she said. "Now I prefer to stay at the back of the church because my emotions take over. I don't want people to see me crying. I don't want to talk to the people at church, because I feel so emotional. Once I had to leave the church because I could not hold back my tears."

The team originally had some concerns about Michael. He had kept so busy with his work throughout Mr. Hynes's illness, the team wondered how he was going to cope after his father's death. According to his mother, however, "He is emotional. He has a good cry when he needs to." Michael spoke openly of his father's illness and death after the event. He talked about how he missed his dad, especially when he undertook activities, such as golf, that they had previously enjoyed together. Mary said of her brother: "I think that it's made him a gentler guy. I think that it's great that he was there when he died. He couldn't get over how well Daddy died and how he got through his illness." Holiday times were difficult for everyone, especially Christmas and Easter. One of Mrs. Hynes's friends told her, "It's a case of trying to survive."

By summer Mrs. Hynes was describing the typical ups and downs of the bereavement process. It surprised her, how strong the feelings were. "There seems to be a bit more reaction with me now than previously," she told me. "I have days when I'm not as up as I used to be. There's just not enough happening now, with it being summer. There's something that's been taken out of my life that I will never recover from. It comes in waves. The least little thing will set it off." In fact, about six months after her husband died, Mrs. Hynes began to feel more despondent. She considered getting some help from the bereavement service provided through the Palliative Care Service. For many weeks Mrs. Hynes had kept their number by her telephone. Now Mary suggested that she call, but then things seemed to get better and Mrs. Hynes decided not to do so.

That summer, Mrs. Hynes went back to their country home for the first time since her husband's death. It was a place they had been renting for 35 years, so it brought back a lot of memories. She said, "I find it rough when the memories come. It was hard to see the houses again, the views, the people there, now that I am alone." In spite of her painful feelings, she pushed herself. She saw everyone whom she wanted to see, and people greeted her warmly. She thought it would be so difficult to face everyone now, to speak about her husband, but she managed, one step at a time. She spent most of the summer in their country cottage, but organized events so she was not alone.

Even one year after his death, Mrs. Hynes had doubts about whether she was doing things right. "Sometimes I think I should sit back and think a little more," she said. "I think of Raymond a lot, believe me, but sometimes I question whether I shouldn't slow down and give myself time to think about what happened. But I'm a creature of habit. I keep busy." Then, as if to summarize everything she and her family had been through, she said, "We had this illness. There was no way of curing it, and God, mercifully, took him quickly. So it was a blessing that it happened so quickly. I think that all his good works and kindness paid off in the end. That's the only peaceful thought that I can hold on to."

3

Albert Hoffer
Bonds Through Thick and Thin

Narrated by YANNA LAMBRINIDOU

Albert Hoffer was 78 years old when he developed cancer of the throat. An intensely private man, Mr. Hoffer found it painful to endure the invasions of his body and the strong feelings that he experienced in the last months of his life. He was an opinionated, forthright, and mistrustful person, who tested everyone severely before he allowed them to get close. Years of alcohol abuse had cost Mr. Hoffer his career and severely damaged his relationships with his wife and children. The complex, interwoven medical and family issues, in the context of the family's limited financial means, were a tremendous challenge for the Hospice of Lancaster County team.

"I never knew a man who was as sharp as he was"

On the eve of my first meeting with Mr. Hoffer I received a warning from Margaret Gibson, his hospice social worker: if his wife, Julia, disapproved of me, Mr. Hoffer would refuse to participate in our study. Mr. Hoffer's first personal care nurse had been replaced by a second one because she had made Mrs. Hoffer uncomfortable. I found myself wondering what I could do to make a good impression on a woman I had never met. Our first meeting took place on June 26, 1997. When I walked into their home, I found Mrs. Hoffer standing in

the kitchen, staring at the floor and stamping her foot intensely. She was struggling to kill a group of ants. Mr. Hoffer finished the job for her and asked her to
join us in the living room. He and I sat on the sofa. Mrs. Hoffer sat in an arm
chair, put her head down, and started flipping through a magazine.

Looking straight ahead, Mr. Hoffer told me that he didn't know why he was
still alive. His life had no meaning. He was no longer able to work, he was no
longer active, he had no one to talk to about his cancer. His hospice team had
given him the phone number of a support line that would connect him with
other cancer patients, but he had no energy to place the call. Hospice staff
were tactless at times, he said. His nurse cared only about medical symptoms
and ignored the complexity of his existence. His chaplain seemed interesting,
but Mr. Hoffer was not sure if he was the right person for him. Out of all the
people he had met, however, he found him the most likely to rescue him from
his depression. And that's what he wanted. "Pain medications are easier to take
than Prozac," he said, "because they alleviate your pain right away. Prozac takes
time."

Mr. Hoffer, a 78-year-old European American, was a tall and slender man.
One could tell from his physique that in his prime he had been muscular and
strong. His head was covered with thin light hair and his smile revealed two
widely spaced bottom teeth he half-jokingly and half-seriously called his
"fangs." Mr. Hoffer had a strong presence. He was opinionated, fiercely independent, and hard to read. I thought there was a mystique about him that gave
him an air of untouchability. He spoke in riddles. He liked to express himself
indirectly by the use of rhetorical questions, sarcasm, and symbolism. The confusion he brought to his listeners was something he seemed to enjoy. It was his
way of teasing, but it was also his way of testing who really understood him and
who did not.

Mrs. Hoffer was several years younger than her husband and self-effacing.
She was a stout woman with short, white hair whose introversion differed dramatically from the excitability of her husband. Mr. and Mrs. Hoffer had been
married for 48 years. They had three adult sons, Frank, John, and Peter, all of
whom lived in Lancaster County. Mr. Hoffer had one daughter, Eileen, from
his first marriage. He rarely spoke about her. He said that she had moved to
Georgia and was minimally involved in his life.

A retired millwright, Mr. Hoffer had maintained the machinery at a Lancaster County manufacturing company for 33 years. His job had given him
pride. Early in his career, Mr. Hoffer became the director of his company's service department, the company's representative on issues concerning industrial
equipment, and the president of his workers' union. His career came to an
abrupt end at the age of 51 when it became obvious that he was an alcoholic.
He spent the next decade and a half struggling to keep new jobs and to overcome his drinking problem.

Finances were tight. The Hoffers moved into a two-bedroom trailer that stood in a small trailer park, on the edge of a lush hillside. It took Mr. Hoffer 14 years, many Alcoholics Anonymous meetings, and several detoxification programs to give up drinking. Before doing so, he hit rock bottom. According to John, his second son, he drank all day, then "inhaled bottles of aspirin" to treat his hangover and drank again. John remembered him "ruining" things—holidays, relationships, employment opportunities, and his retirement prospects. He recounted a day when his father "clobbered" him with a cane. "There were times when I hated my dad," he told me. It was Mrs. Hoffer who took charge of Frank's, John's, and Peter's upbringing, and she did the best she could to protect them from their father. To the boys she seemed to be an endless source of love and support. Although she kept her feelings to herself, she disapproved of her husband's drinking and despaired at his inability to keep a job.

In 1983, after a close brush with surgery for a bleeding stomach ulcer, Mr. Hoffer decided to stop drinking. This crisis shook him into the realization that his body had suffered from alcohol and that his family had suffered from him. He didn't want to lose either his life or the people he loved.

As a sober man, Mr. Hoffer regained the clarity of mind and the ambition that had pushed him to the top of his manufacturing company years earlier. He started volunteering at a local hospital and enrolled in a university course to become a master gardener. At the same time, he felt the need to make up for the time he had lost with his family. He showed utmost respect for his wife and did everything he could to meet her needs. By the mid-1980s, Frank, John, and Peter had moved out of the trailer and had started families of their own. Mr. Hoffer kept himself abreast of their lives, supported them through hard times, and participated with them in activities they enjoyed. A favorite pastime was fishing. Trips to the water had unified all five of them from the time the children were little, giving them unforgettable moments of happiness that were captured in family photographs. Mr. Hoffer organized more of those trips. In football and basketball season, he placed bets against his sons' favorite teams. When they lost, he teased them.

"My father has always lived life to the fullest," the youngest son, Peter, said to me with love evident in his voice, "even to a fault—to the point he loved to eat, he loved to drink, he loved to party, he just loved all those things about life. He is very much a people-person, my father—he always enjoys talking with people as long as he is the one doing all the talking!"

"I never knew a man who was as sharp as he was," said John. "The alcohol robbed him of a lot of things—it really did. What a metamorphosis as a dad. I really did get close to him [after he stopped drinking]. He was a lot nicer to be around." But despite his love for people, Mr. Hoffer also held his personal cards close to his chest. He was invested in looking strong, intelligent, and independent. He rarely showed a vulnerable side.

"I went into the damndest traumatic shock I ever had in my life"

In June 1996, Mr. Hoffer developed a sore throat. After a month of excruciating pain, he lost his ability to swallow and speak. An ear-nose-and-throat specialist informed him that he had cancer of the nasopharynx. "I went into the damndest traumatic shock I ever had in my life," he said, when he recalled his physician telling him his diagnosis. "Cancer of the throat is the last thing you are afraid of when you are a drinker." Mr. Hoffer consented to a six-week course of outpatient radiation intended to shrink his tumor and bring his cancer into remission. Contrary to his expectations, however, he was not able to eat by mouth again. The radiation stopped the growth of his tumor, but it closed his esophagus. He could not even swallow his own saliva. He had to spit. For nourishment, a tube was inserted directly into his stomach, and through it he fed himself liquid nutritional supplements. Mr. Hoffer's throat became chronically dry. Prolonged talking and sleeping exacerbated his problem and caused him pain.

In January 1997, six months after Mr. Hoffer's radiation treatment, Mrs. Hoffer had a stroke. Suddenly, the pillar of the household was unable to take care of her most basic needs. Mrs. Hoffer's cognitive abilities declined dramatically. As much as she tried, she was unable to keep track of day-to-day activities, including her medication schedule, her personal hygiene, and her nutrition. She began to eat ice-cream—her favorite food—for every meal, which aggravated her diabetes. She became incontinent. It was not unusual for her to soil the furniture or her clothes without even noticing. Home health aides from the hospital visited her several times a week and tested her blood sugar level, gave her baths, and renewed her medications.

After her stroke, Mrs. Hoffer spent hours each day sitting quietly in her armchair or sleeping. Her verbal interactions were minimal. But she didn't like anyone to patronize her. There were times when the nurses who came to see her addressed her husband instead of her or walked into her bedroom without her permission. Some doubted the truth of her statements and turned to Mr. Hoffer for confirmation, and others bathed her with a casualness that humiliated her. Mr. Hoffer became his wife's protector. He took charge of her medications, cooked for her, and cleaned the house as best as he could. Whoever mistreated Mrs. Hoffer was sure to be dismissed.

"A very private man"

In April a computed tomography scan showed a recurrent tumor in Mr. Hoffer's supraglottic deep neck structures, and he was advised to consider hospice. The benefits of further aggressive treatment would not necessarily outweigh the risks. Surgery would require a permanent tracheostomy and a laryngectomy with a voice box. Moreover, it carried a risk of infection. Chemotherapy, on the other hand, was often accompanied by side effects that had the potential to compromise the quality of his life. Yet the possible advantage of either procedure was the prolongation of his life. It was up to him to decide what path he wanted to pursue.

Mr. Hoffer chose everything. He agreed to sign up for hospice, but didn't elect the Medicare hospice benefit. This benefit would pay for all his medications, but it would also require him to rule out aggressive treatments. Mr. Hoffer wasn't ready to do that. Instead, he wanted to pay for his palliative medications out-of-pocket and to explore the possibility of further interventions. He agreed to a second computed tomography scan that would show the full extent of his disease.

He told his hospice team that he suffered from pain, weakness, insomnia, and depression. He was losing weight. Just two days earlier he had fallen. The first time that happened, he lost most of his bottom teeth. He stressed his wife's dependence on him. He wanted the team to understand that he was determined to stay in his home as long as he could. He assured them that his gait would stabilize, for his sons had brought him a walker. Moving to an extended care facility was an option he was willing to consider, but only later. Nursing homes were anathema to him, because both his mother and brother had died in one. In the meantime, he declared, he needed a volunteer to help him with the laundry, dishes, vacuuming, and the rest of his housekeeping duties.

Mr. Hoffer's hospice nurse, Carmen Maloney, collaborated with her patient's attending physician, Dr. Julie McCloud, to design a medication regimen that included long-acting morphine suppositories, concentrated liquid morphine for breakthrough pain, the antidepressant fluoxetine, promethazine for nausea, ranitidine to protect his stomach, digoxin for his heart, and atenolol for his blood pressure. She also assigned Mr. Hoffer a volunteer to help him with housekeeping and a personal care nurse for his hygiene. Margaret, the social worker, took on the responsibility of gathering information for Mr. Hoffer about two subjects he wanted to explore: meal services for his wife and cremation. She also offered him chaplain visits, but he declined. "I don't feel part of hospice yet," he said. He informed Margaret that he would be open to meetings with a spiritual counselor at a later time.

After her first visit to the trailer, Margaret said to me:

> He was testing me—asking me kind of personal questions every once in a while and kind of making little jokes. I think it was to see how I would react to him. I joked back with him a little bit. He was looking for very concrete things—typical man—looking for concrete tasks that I would be doing for him. He had a lot of questions about different things, such as deliverable meals. He was thinking ahead. He just wanted me to gather some information, so he gave me a lot of

homework, and I think it was a test. I came back two weeks later, I had all this information, I explained it to him, and he said, "You are someone who gets things done—I like that." He and I have just hit it off ever since.

On April 30, the day of his computed tomography scan, Mr. Hoffer got his first bath with the assistance of personal care nurse, Jane Pierce. In her nursing notes, Jane stated that Mr. Hoffer was "a very private man." Although he tolerated his bath well, he asked that the person helping him with his personal hygiene remain the same so he wouldn't have to adjust to new faces. He told Carmen, his nurse, that his fears about the future tortured him. The hospital's home health agency that was taking care of Mrs. Hoffer had just informed him that they were considering terminating their services, for Mrs. Hoffer had been satisfactorily stabilized. Who would manage his wife's care if this agency departed? And what about the computed tomography scan he was scheduled to undergo? Would that show a metastasis? Mr. Hoffer feared it would. And if it didn't? Could he afford the aggressive treatments he would want to pursue? He didn't think so.

The scan was negative. His cancer had not metastasized beyond the area of his throat. But before starting him on aggressive treatments, his ear-nose-and-throat physician requested more tests. He wanted Mr. Hoffer to have a physical examination and a throat biopsy. On May 19, two days prior to his physical examination, Mr. Hoffer asked for chaplain visits. His worries had escalated. He feared that the results of his tests would disqualify him from further treatments. The home health agency had decided to terminate their services for Mrs. Hoffer. Mr. Hoffer was also having more drowsiness, weakness, and tenderness in his neck. In collaboration with Dr. McCloud, Carmen increased the dose of his long-acting morphine suppositories and his breakthrough medication. She also started him on lorazepam for anxiety. Mr. Hoffer requested additional housekeeping help from his volunteer. Helen Meyer agreed to visit the Hoffers twice a week instead of once, although this required her to negotiate diplomatically so as not to offend Mrs. Hoffer.

On May 26, Mr. Hoffer requested that his personal care nurse, Jane, be replaced by someone else. I heard three different explanations of Jane's dismissal. The first was that she had made the mistake of talking to Mr. Hoffer about Mrs. Hoffer in Mrs. Hoffer's presence. The second was that she had entered Mrs. Hoffer's bedroom without asking her. And the third was that in a conversation with the Hoffers, she had made the comment that "cancer is a horrible disease." Jane was replaced by Betty Beasly. Betty saw Mr. Hoffer twice a week, and was soon struck by his mercurial moods. "One minute he is very trusting of you," she told me, "the next minute he does not know if he should let you in the door. He is very opinionated about everything. He is very different. You can never get a straight answer out of him. He can joke with you and the next minute be very mad with you. I cannot read him. He did tell me he is an alcoholic. I don't know what to believe: is it true or not?"

"To help people to live until they die"

Mr. Hoffer longed for deep and meaningful interactions with someone he could trust. On his first meeting with the chaplain, Carl Flynn, Mr. Hoffer talked briefly about his love of fishing trips, but switched quickly to pressing matters. He asked questions about Carl's agenda as a spiritual counselor. He also talked about his mistrust toward organized religion. Carl explained that his work was nondenominational and depended on the needs and preferences of each patient. Mr. Hoffer was anxious about the decisions that faced him. All he had to do to prevent his bills from piling up was to stop seeking aggressive treatments, but he was still not ready to give up the possibility of surgery. He explained to Carl that he wanted to do everything he could to stay alive. His wife needed him.

Carl told me later that he sensed how much Mr. Hoffer was probing him, asking, in effect, "Will this work? Is this a fit?" and, "Can this person support me and walk with me?"

"I might have to see if I can be somebody who can support him," Carl went on. "I said to him, 'So when are you going to go fishing again?'—I kind of threw it out there. I said, 'What hospice is about is to help people to live until they die, and I encourage you to do that.'"

Mr. Hoffer was intrigued by Carl, but he wasn't sure he liked him. He found his question about fishing almost offensive. He couldn't understand how a hospice chaplain could have proposed such a trip when Mr. Hoffer had just explained to him that he was drowning in outstanding medical bills. But there was something about Carl's idea that he liked. It was almost too crazy to dismiss. In the meantime, he was anxious to hear from his ear-nose-and-throat doctor if and when he was going to schedule him for his biopsy.

"Something is being built and I have been called to have a hand in that"

Even though the hospital reversed its decision to terminate its home health services to Mrs. Hoffer, Frank, John, and Peter began searching for extended care facilities that would accommodate both their parents. They knew that the day would come when Mr. and Mrs. Hoffer would be unable to live by themselves, and none of them had the room or the finances to take their parents in. Although Mr. Hoffer understood the necessity of such a search, he was devastated by the idea of moving out of the trailer. Giving up even a small part of his independence tortured him. Moreover, he couldn't imagine how he and his wife would be able to afford an extended care facility. He had already spent most of his savings on his medications. In a tender moment with Margaret, the social worker, he confessed that he was used to having "a handle" on every problem that confronted him. This time, however, he felt that his life was beyond his control. He didn't know what to do. He started to cry. Quickly, he turned his face away from Margaret and asked her to leave. On her way out, Margaret encouraged him to call her if he needed to. Warmly, he took hold of her hand and thanked her.

"Even though Albert asked me to leave," said Margaret later, "there was something that happened there, that he trusted me an awful lot, and it was a really neat thing that happened between us. I felt bad for making him cry, but part of me thought he needed to do that, because I think he has really been holding it in. He is a very strong person, and I don't think he cries very easily."

On July 7, Mr. Hoffer told Carl that he was concerned for his wife. He wanted to know what she was thinking about his cancer. He wanted her to share her feelings with him. He asked Carl if he would be willing to help Mrs. Hoffer open up. Carl answered Mr. Hoffer's request with a question: Was it possible that his desire to hear his wife's thoughts reflected his own need more than Mrs. Hoffer's? "I laid it out open-endedly," Carl said when he described this incident to me, "but I think he saw it." When Mrs. Hoffer entered the living room and sat on the sofa next to her husband, Carl asked her warmly, "What do you think about this guy having cancer? I can only imagine that it would be tough, but I don't know how it is for you."

"I don't like it," responded Mrs. Hoffer flatly. She had nothing more to say.

Carl returned to the topic of fishing. He told Mr. Hoffer that if he wanted to organize such a trip, he would be able to help him. In fact, he knew someone who owned a boat and was likely to make it available to him for a weekend. Mr. Hoffer sparked on that idea. He excused himself and a few minutes later he walked back to the living room smiling, with a T-shirt in his hand. On it was an old photograph of him and Peter proudly holding a striped bass.

"I am trying to help this man live until he dies," said Carl afterwards, "and if going fishing is something I can do to support him, that is what I need to do. Something is being built, and I have been called to have a hand in that."

"If I don't get better soon, I'll ask for a transfer of heads"

On July 8, Mr. Hoffer had his throat biopsy. Following the procedure, he spat blood and experienced excruciating pain. July 9 was his birthday. Eileen called her father from Georgia to tell him that she loved him. "Okay," he said, and quickly hung up the phone. I called Mr. Hoffer five days later to see if he would be open to a second visit from me. But he told me that he couldn't talk. The stitches in his throat caused him extreme pain. "If I don't get better soon, I'll ask for a transfer of heads," he said flatly before hanging up the phone.

With Dr. McCloud's approval, Carmen instructed Mr. Hoffer to increase his use of breakthrough medication. A week after his biopsy, Mr. Hoffer reported that his saliva was free of blood. But he also called Carmen to request a new prescription for liquid morphine because he had run out of his old one. Carmen was surprised. She reminded Mr. Hoffer that Dr. McCloud had ordered liquid morphine for him only two days earlier, and asked him if he had picked it up from his pharmacy. Mr. Hoffer confirmed that he had, but explained that sometimes he spilled it or misplaced it. At other times, he said, the morphine "plain evaporated." Carmen found this deeply puzzling. She was struck by a worrisome pattern. Mr. Hoffer had run out of liquid morphine before, even though she always made sure he had enough. Now it crossed her mind that he might have been abusing his medication. (Carmen was correct to be suspicious in Mr. Hoffer's case. However, problems of addiction in cancer care are rare, except in patients with a history of drug abuse. The phenomenon of tolerance—requiring higher dosages of a drug to produce the same analgesic effect—is also not a practical concern in cancer care. If a patient requests more opioids, usually it is because the tumors have grown and are producing more pain.) During Carmen's phone conversation with Mr. Hoffer, Betty, who happened to be visiting her patient for personal care, located an unfinished bottle of liquid morphine in the refrigerator. Carmen was relieved by this discovery, but she also asked Mr. Hoffer to keep a record of the morphine he consumed. As his nurse, she explained to him, she was accountable for the way he used his medications.

On July 17, Mr. Hoffer learned that surgery would require massive tissue removal, because of the residual cancer that was found in his pharynx. Such a procedure would certainly not cure him, but it had the capacity to lengthen his life. At the same time, it would probably debilitate him further.

Early the next morning Mr. Hoffer tripped on a carpet and suffered a two-inch-long laceration over his left eye. In panic, Mrs. Hoffer knocked on the door of their neighbor, Ben Housler. Ben ran to the trailer, saw that Mr. Hoffer was bleeding, and called Peter. Peter called hospice. By the time things calmed down and the family assessed the situation, everyone agreed that Mr. Hoffer required round-the-clock care. In fact, he was a good candidate for symptom management at hospice's inpatient unit. But since Mr. Hoffer was not on the hospice benefit, he would have to cover the costs of that stay himself. The Hoffers were torn. Was it wise to turn down the option of surgery now? Was it time to choose palliation over radical surgery? Was Mr. Hoffer really terminal? After a long discussion with his wife and sons, Mr. Hoffer decided to switch to the hospice benefit. His priority was to receive immediate and intensive palliative treatment. He was admitted to the inpatient unit of hospice on the evening of July 18.

"I am the captain"

When I visited Mr. Hoffer in the inpatient unit, I had to confirm with a nurse that the person I had just seen asleep was indeed Albert. This person looked nothing like the Mr. Hoffer I had known. He seemed older and smaller. He had a large blood blister on his right cheekbone. His skin looked flaccid, his hair more white than I remembered. Since Mr. Hoffer was asleep, the nurse asked me if I would be interested in meeting Eileen, who had flown in from Georgia. At her father's request Mr. Hoffer's oldest daughter was staying at the trailer to look after her stepmother. I told her about our research and asked if she would be willing to take part in it. She was glad to. She and I moved to a private room. Eileen was tearful. She said:

> Yesterday, Dad said, "Don't ask me any questions—I don't want to talk about what I don't want to think about," so he did not want any hugging, or anything like that. In April, when the tumor returned, he called my son and said, "Tell Eileen the tumor is back—I cannot talk to her." That is sort of how he has been treating it with me. He would not even let the doctors talk to me on the phone in Georgia. He completely hid any information from me when his first tumor was diagnosed. A year ago, I just showed up. He was surprised to see me and seemed a little angry, but after that he let me take him to his radiation treatments twice a day. But when I left it was, "Bye, Eileen." So I really think that he does not want to get super close.

Later that day Eileen got the chance to spend time with her father. She then wrote me the following note: "We had a wonderful visit, Dad and I. He was affectionate and loving, and so was I. I was sad I had to leave." After her return to Georgia, Eileen and I spoke on the phone. Eileen reiterated that her father had been open and affectionate, but she added that the reason behind this change was that he thought he was going to die. "Dad asked me when I was coming in again, and I said I don't really know," she said. "I would not come in if his condition got worse. I wanted to be with him when he was alive, so he knew I cared."

The first few days in the inpatient unit, the nurses took complete control of Mr. Hoffer's medications and feedings. He was weak, nauseated, in pain, and discouraged. Whenever he opened his eyes, he stressed one thing: he wanted to return home. Three days later I found him sitting in an armchair. "This pain is an encroachment I find," he whispered as he spit in the cup he was holding.

"It's forever aggressive. Aggressive." It was clear to everyone that Mr. Hoffer was despondent. But he tried to control his frustration as much as he could. A few days later, Carl asked him why he was holding back his tears. Mr. Hoffer explained that he didn't like to cry. "You might need to cry, as there is a lot to cry about," Carl suggested. Mr. Hoffer rolled over in his bed and quietly wept.

Mr. Hoffer was frantic at the thought of leaving his wife alone. He called her every night and, according to a nurse, he lit up "like a Christmas tree" at the sound of her voice. The option of chemotherapy started looking attractive to him again. "I know I will eventually return to the point I am right now," he told a nurse, "but then I'll know I tried it."

Mr. Hoffer was trying to prepare for two scenarios: in one, he would get better; in the other, he would die. During his stay in the inpatient unit he asked Peter, in the presence of one of the nurses, to help him imagine what life would look like with him "in the picture" and with him "out of the picture." Peter told his father that if he were to die, he, Frank, and John would place their mother in a nursing home. Mr. Hoffer's eyes filled with tears. He looked angry. He asked the nurse to leave, saying he wanted to talk with his son in private. Later, Peter seemed distraught. Reflecting on his exchange with his father, he said, "My father is very self-centered, but this is one area where he is not. He is very concerned about what is going to happen to my mom after he is gone, and I can't say I blame him. As a son, that is an awesome responsibility, and I can say, 'Dad, we will do the best we can,' but these are tough decisions we are making right now. These are the toughest decisions I have ever made in my life."

Later the nurse said to me, "I will not forget that exchange. You hope for your patients everything that they want, and it just seems like at the end of your life, you should have everything that you want. But to have to admit that you cannot take care of someone that you love is just very, very hard. You think that you can do everything, or that you should be able to, and when you can't that feels like a failure."

His pain better controlled, Mr. Hoffer got stronger and he fought to regain his independence. He insisted that he feed himself and administer his morphine suppositories without assistance. He despised supervision. During a friendly interaction with nurse Amy Jones, he confessed that he wanted to test hospice's limits. "You know, we are not here to restrict you," responded Amy, "we are here to make you really as free as you can be, but we are really concerned about you." She then touched his shoulder and noticed tears in Mr. Hoffer's eyes. Seeing the tears, Amy told me, helped her "see this gentleman as being kind of rough on the outside, but inside he is just a pretty neat guy, a really caring man." She then recalled an incident when she was kneeling in front of Mr. Hoffer, adjusting his feeding tube while he sat on the sofa. "I am the captain," he said. At that moment Mrs. Hoffer walked in. She asked her husband when he would be coming home. Mr. Hoffer looked first at Amy and then back to his wife. "Well," he said, "considering I have nurses on their knees in front of me, it might be a few more days."

Laughingly, another nurse said:

> For me, Albert is a "bird," a "corker." He loves to dish it out. You can sense he is very much in control, like maybe he wants to shock you a little bit, so if you just give it right back to him he kind of respects you. Albert has his own agenda. The first time I did personal care for him it included a shower, and he kept his back to me, and he let me do his back, and I did the back of his legs. The second time I did him, he was okay. He did turn around and it was like no big deal. I must have passed the dignity test, letting him do what he wanted. The patients who are more vocal, they are more time-consuming, because of their choices. You have to adapt your day to their routine, to uninstitutionalize your thinking.

A family meeting

The Hoffers would need to pull all their resources together to enable Mr. Hoffer to return home. Cassandra Fleming, the inpatient social worker, suggested a family meeting to determine what support Mr. Hoffer would need and who would be able to give it to him. Mr. Hoffer agreed to a meeting. As if he didn't trust the intentions of his sons, however, he asked for an advocate from hospice to represent his interests. He chose Carl.

The meeting took place on July 28. Present were the three sons, the neighbor Ben Housler, Carl, Carmen, an inpatient unit nurse, a hospital nurse and a social worker involved in Mrs. Hoffer's care, Cassandra, and myself. Mrs. Hoffer was invited, but she was unable to attend. Mr. Hoffer said he understood that to return home he needed the help of his sons, hospice, and the hospital that looked after his wife. He therefore wanted everyone to know that he had decided to relinquish some control over his situation. He was willing to accept the care he needed and to cooperate with his caregivers. When he finished, the inpatient unit nurse asserted that hospice had the capacity to make the administration of Mr. Hoffer's liquid morphine easier on him. She would provide him with prefilled syringes for him to inject into his PEG tube. Ben, too, volunteered to help. The same nurse suggested that hospice could also relieve Mr. Hoffer of the burden of morphine suppositories by replacing them with a transdermal fentanyl patch. Carmen offered to purchase a pill-crusher, to turn pills into powder and ease their way through the PEG tube. John volunteered to build a hand-rail in the trailer that would ease his father's movement, and to place bricks under his parents' armchair and sofa. This would make it easier for them to get in and out of their furniture. Mr. Hoffer asked for an elevated toilet seat. He also accepted the suggestion to sign up for meal services for his wife.

By doing so, Mrs. Hoffer would receive one cold and one hot meal every day, and he wouldn't have to cook.

Mrs. Hoffer's care providers reported that Julia's blood sugar level had risen dramatically. They also suggested that Mrs. Hoffer seemed depressed and was possibly in need of antidepressants. Upon hearing that, Peter got angry. He did not want to see his mother go through another round of humiliating psychological tests just to be drugged further. The tests she was forced to undergo after her stroke were traumatic enough for her. As far as Peter was concerned, Mrs. Hoffer had many good reasons to be depressed, and additional pills were not going to solve her problems. Later he told me more about his outburst:

> My mother was the one who really raised us, and that is maybe why I feel so passionate about her and the care she gets as she gets older. My mother feels like she is a burden to us, like, "I really hate to bother you boys." Holy cow, mom! When Dad was working and drinking, who was there? *My mother was there*, and this is the least I can do. She had such an active role in our lives, and after my father stopped drinking, his personality took over and my mother took a back-seat role, and I think she feels kind of bad about this. Is my mother depressed? Probably. That is where I got upset: We will give her some medication so she can be "happy." I don't think that is the appropriate response. I think, as a family, we need to bear her burdens. What better pill can you give your mother than for a son to drop in and say you love her?

Cassandra suggested making a weekly schedule of everyone's duties. After the meeting, Frank, John, and Peter looked exhausted but relieved. Although they vowed to continue their search for an extended care facility, they were happy that their father could return home. On July 30, Peter drove Mr. Hoffer back to the trailer. They were joined by Carmen and Ben to discuss the practical details of Mr. and Mrs. Hoffer's care. When Carmen and Ben walked in, Peter was unpacking his father's belongings. Mr. Hoffer was reading the newspaper and ignored the ensuing discussion. Although he hadn't said so, he disapproved of the plan of care that had been put together for him at hospice. As a result, he decided to take no part in its implementation.

"It was almost a futile effort"

Two days after Mr. Hoffer's return home, Peter called hospice for help. His father had just refused Ben's help in the administration of his medications. Moreover, he complained that he hadn't been consulted about his plan of care. No one had asked him if he wanted Ben's involvement, and Ben was someone he didn't trust. To everyone's surprise, he confessed that his neighbor liked to help himself to his morphine. He further insinuated that it was Ben who had encouraged him to call Carmen for extra refills of breakthrough medication. Ben, he said, had a chemical dependency. He was the last person he wanted to see in charge of his care. Mr. Hoffer withheld further details about Ben's actions and was careful not to incriminate him. He even seemed protective of him. His anger was aimed primarily at his sons who had included Ben in his care without consulting him.

Neither Peter nor Frank believed these accusations. They had heard that Ben had a history of drug abuse, but they still suspected that the missing morphine was the result of their father's accidental overdosing. Even now Peter doubted that Mr. Hoffer followed his medication schedule as he was supposed to. Defying hospice's request to keep a record of the times and doses of his medications, Mr. Hoffer insisted on doing things his own way. Record keeping made him feel watched over. The last thing he wanted in his relationship with his caregivers was to be treated as if he wasn't worth their trust.

"Looking back at that family meeting, it was almost a futile effort," Peter said to me with frustration. "I got so upset with my father, I was ready to just wash my hands of the entire situation and go away. This pattern that Dad showed us at that meeting has been characteristic of a pattern Dad has shown all through his life. He looked at what we did and he said, 'You guys don't really have any clue as to how to do this, do you? Obviously, I need to be in charge of this.'"

Frank patched things up with Ben, apologetically asking him if he would continue to do some household tasks, even if he no longer helped with his father's medications. Ben assured Frank that he would. In Frank's view, Ben was irreplaceable. Neither he nor his brothers had the time to visit their parents as often as someone who lived next door. And his father was still not prepared to move to an extended care facility. He seemed determined, in fact, to break off ties with anyone who even suggested such a solution.

On August 6 Mr. Hoffer cut his ties with Carmen. Alarmed by the reports of stolen morphine, Carmen had told him that she was professionally responsible to notify Dr. McCloud about Ben's unauthorized use of his medications. She had reemphasized the importance of record keeping and had told Mr. Hoffer that if he failed to keep track of his liquid morphine, he would have to consider the possibility of moving to a supervised environment. Mr. Hoffer took offense. Already he felt demeaned by the fact that the nurses pre-poured his liquid medication in syringes. Now Carmen had turned into a menacing power that was going to strip him of his autonomy as well.

Mr. Hoffer immediately turned to Carl. He told him that he no longer trusted his nurse. Carl agreed that Carmen could have related to him differently, but he insisted that the serious problem of the missing medications was not her fault. He suggested that Mr. Hoffer was at least partially responsible for what had happened with Ben. Mr. Hoffer admitted to this, but he also insisted on a different nurse. Hospice complied, and Carmen was replaced by Sharon Brown.

Carl took this incident to heart. "My relationship with him is still intact," he said to me, "and yet I am sure there is a possibility that I could do or say something at some point that he would want to blow me off, too." He went on to reflect on the state of his work with Mr. Hoffer up to that point:

> I think there are some unresolved personal issues relating to intimacy and trust that might need to express themselves at some point, and they also could be an underlying factor in him not being able to say, "I am afraid to die." It has never felt like to me that he has wanted prayer, and I have not offered that, but I think I need to pursue that a little bit just to see where he may or may not be—of course, not being tied to the results. I don't want to go prematurely. Given some of his life history, there is a lot of distrust there, and I think some real rapport building is important. I think we are still running the gauntlet. We are still having to pass his tests in certain ways, and that's okay.

Sharon acknowledged that she was wary about her new assignment, too:

> Knowing that his trust in me could also be destroyed quickly, knowing that in this kind of scenario you are always walking on eggshells, you enter the scene with some anxiety. It presents a challenge for us, as staff, to rebuild trust. This is not just staff having trust in an individual, this is an individual having trust in staff as well. It's a two-way street. So I am responsible for rebuilding trust for him, and I think that is why I may say a prayer before I go there. That is my dilemma: how do I build trust in him, yet also remain non-naive?

When Mr. Hoffer met Sharon, he told her that he didn't need prefilled syringes. He preferred to use his medicine droppers. Sharon decided to respect his wishes. She found it more important to gain her patient's trust than to secure the proper doses of his medications. In fact, she suspected that Mr. Hoffer's diminished dexterity would hamper his ability to use his droppers successfully, but that was an issue she didn't want to raise.

"Now it is just you and palliative"

Mr. Hoffer referred to his cancer as "allegedly terminal." He insisted that his goal was to get stronger. His dilemma about aggressive treatments tortured him. He had decided that if he was to live longer, he was going to invest his savings in a dental plate that would give him a full set of bottom teeth. "You don't lose total thoughts about the esthetics of your face when you look like this," he said. If, on the other hand, he was not eligible for aggressive treatments, he wanted to spend his money on a fishing trip with his family. On August 13, Mr. Hoffer learned from Dr. McCloud that the risks of surgery and chemotherapy far outweighed the benefits. In essence, aggressive therapies were no longer an option for him. Mr. Hoffer dropped his head and started to weep.

A few days later, as Sharon was filling Mr. Hoffer's medication box, she noticed that he was tense. Mr. Hoffer started pacing the kitchen floor and casting furtive glances at his wife. Mrs. Hoffer, who was sitting at the kitchen table, seemed unaware of the tension that surrounded her. Suddenly, Mr. Hoffer looked at her and announced that his disease was terminal. He was going to die. Mrs. Hoffer tensed. Mr. Hoffer's voice cracked. He assured Julia that she would be taken care of no matter what happened to him. After a moment of silence, Mr. Hoffer turned to Sharon and said resignedly, "Now it is just you and palliative."

Leaving no time for anyone to react, he proceeded quickly to his next dilemma: was it wiser for him to invest in dental work or a fishing trip? "It is certainly up to you," said Mrs. Hoffer nervously. Mr. Hoffer decided that it was more important to him to spend his money on the family. He would invite his sons, their wives, and their children to join him and Julia on a weekend trip to the Susquehanna River. All expenses would be paid.

Sharon left the trailer speechless. She had been utterly unprepared to take part in what she saw as an almost sacred interaction. Moreover, she hadn't realized that Mrs. Hoffer had only learned about the untreatability of her husband's condition that day. "It felt like holy ground," she said. "I was not sure why he chose to do it then unless he needed support in the telling. It was an incredible experience. It really did catch me off guard. It even brings tears to my eyes. But it really did seem as though, in some ways, it seemed a relief for him."

"That will be the end of my story"

The next day, I found Mr. Hoffer sitting on the sofa with a pile of old brochures. He was looking for a park that rented cabins by the Susquehanna River. He, his wife, and his sons had agreed to go fishing on the weekend of September 6. "That will be the end of my story," Mr. Hoffer said. "Like all stories, a happy ending. What else would there be to talk about?" At the end of our visit he asked me to "back off" for a few weeks. He reiterated that he had run out of things to say. I wasn't sure how to interpret his request. With Mr. Hoffer I was never sure. Had I done something to upset him or his wife? He assured me that wasn't the case. Moreover, he advised me to make sure to interview his sons and his attending physician, because their stories, he thought, would complete his. He just had nothing more to say. Now that his fight was over, his story was over, too. I never interviewed Mr. Hoffer again.

"I am being pulled in three different directions"

Mrs. Hoffer's home health aides again announced that they were going to discontinue their services. Their last visit to Mrs. Hoffer had been scheduled for

August 27. Mrs. Hoffer's blood sugar level had been stabilized. It was now up to a public agency for the elderly to decide if they had the capacity to accept her as a patient or not. Frank was overwhelmed. As the oldest son and the family representative, he had assumed the responsibility of keeping in touch with hospice, the hospital, and all the people involved in his parents' care. He also organized meetings, coordinated schedules, and hired services. He had committed himself to a 40-minute ride each way, two to four times a week, to see his parents and, when needed, mow their lawn. He asked Cassandra if hospice offered support groups for the family members of the dying, but hospice didn't. When I saw him, he looked despondent. "I wind up feeling I am being pulled in three different directions," he said, "and I don't really feel like I am adequately serving my employer, my own family, my mom and dad. I feel like each one of them is only getting a piece of what I would like to give, so that becomes personally stressful." Yet Frank told me that he had also found unexpected satisfactions. He said:

> There have been some very good times as part of all this. It has brought me closer to my brothers in a number of ways, because we have had to work together as a caregiving team. It has brought me closer to both Mom and Dad. I have felt like this has really allowed me to give back to my parents in a way that otherwise I never would have been able to. Strangely enough, it is a kind of intimate thing to be changing somebody's bandages and to be helping someone administer their medications through one of these feeding tubes. Dad has to trust me at a pretty high level I guess to allow me to change that bandage. In a strange way, those have been kind of tender moments, which was certainly an unexpected thing. Mom is really pretty child-like, so that you know, my relationship with her has become loving in a lot of ways that are unexpected. Would it have been better if her stroke had just killed her? For his cancer to have taken him quickly? You would not have that suffering, but you would not have had all of this closeness that has happened in the midst of it all.

"I still don't know what your definition of God is"

Mr. Hoffer told Carl that he knew he was dying, and he asked him to conduct the funeral service. "I still don't know what your definition of God is," he said to the chaplain. Carl took this as an invitation for a theological exchange. He offered to give Mr. Hoffer an article to read as a basis for some discussion. When Carl visited again a few days later he spoke about the struggle of having to "pass the baton" to others. Mr. Hoffer teared up. "Jesus didn't want to go to Jerusalem either," Carl said after a moment. Mr. Hoffer started to cry. Like Jesus, Carl continued, it was time that Mr. Hoffer allowed his sons to wash his feet. He could use this opportunity to mend fences, grow closer to his loved ones, and not "give up," but "give over" to something that was bigger than him. Just then, Mrs. Hoffer walked into the living room. While wiping his tears, Albert followed his wife to the kitchen and offered her a cup of coffee. Somberly, he proceeded to tell Julia that he wanted Frank, John, and Peter to increase their involvement both in his care and hers.

Carl interrupted. "Can I be 'chaplain' here and help facilitate this conversation a bit?"

"Sure," Mr. Hoffer replied, as if with relief.

Carl addressed Mrs. Hoffer. "Albert knows he is dying, he does not want to die, he is concerned about you, and he knows he is going to miss you, and that is really hard for him. Albert has been the man of the house here and in charge and in control, and he sees he is going to have to pass this baton on, and he does not want to do that, and it is really hard. I bet this guy maybe has not given you as much credit for your ability to care for yourself as you probably can."

"I think I can," Julia said.

"I think he wants to have closure with you and your sons," Carl went on.

"And she got it," Carl said to me later. "And I did a check with Albert, and I said, 'Is this where you want to go? Is this okay?' and he said, 'Yeah.' But a little bit later he left and sat on the living room sofa. It was just so hard, so hard for him, and I knew he wanted to say it, but because of the depth of his emotion and how large it is as well, he just was not able to do that."

Carl marked that day as a breakthrough. It was the first time that he had spoken openly on behalf of Mr. Hoffer with Mr. Hoffer's full support. At the end of that visit, Mr. Hoffer took hold of his chaplain's hand and with teary eyes invited him to the Susquehanna River. If it hadn't been for Carl, he said, he wouldn't have planned the fishing trip at all. Carl was honored by the invitation, but declined it regretfully. He explained to Mr. Hoffer that he saw this trip as an opportunity for him to spend time with his family. If Carl were to join them, he would feel like an intruder. Mr. Hoffer understood. The next time Carl visited, Mr. Hoffer offered him a gift: one of his ties and a $20 bill. "It is my way of thanking the Lord that you came by today," he told him.

A few days later Mrs. Hoffer had a blackout. Mr. Hoffer found her on the floor. Although she wasn't injured, the incident convinced the home health aides from the hospital to extend their involvement with her for another month. In the meantime, Mr. Hoffer was getting physically and mentally weaker. Frank, John, and Peter lost sleep thinking about their parents' safety. They felt burned out. Something had to change. Frank decided to call another family meeting at the trailer to create a new plan of care, four days after the fishing trip. He was going to set the agenda.

"It was a miraculous meeting"

The fishing trip did not turn out as planned. The drive to the cabins was long and the weather was cold and windy. On Saturday morning, Mr. Hoffer woke up with diarrhea that lasted all day. John called hospice and was instructed to discontinue his father's constipation medication. Everyone, except for Mr. Hoffer, went out to breakfast, but when they returned to the cabins, they found Mr. Hoffer crying in bed, pleading to be taken home. Frank drove his father back to the trailer park that evening. The rest of the family stayed at the cabins and returned the next day.

On Monday, Sharon found Mr. Hoffer in bed. He reported feeling queasy. He gave himself a prochlorperazine suppository and reached out for Sharon's hand to express his appreciation for her support. Sharon arranged to increase his personal care visits from three times a week to five. Mr. Hoffer asked to see Carl, and when he arrived Mr. Hoffer—barely able to whisper because of his sore throat—told him that his deceased brother had made an appearance to him. Carl offered to pray with him, but Mr. Hoffer declined.

The second family meeting took place three days later with Albert and Julia, Frank, Peter, Margaret, Sharon, and Carl. Mr. Hoffer seemed alert and oriented, but nervous. He was tearful from the beginning. The discussion opened with Frank's and Peter's gentle comments about their concern for their parents' safety and their worry about themselves. Mr. Hoffer got up and left the living room twice, crying silently. In his absence, the room filled with silence. Carl followed him to the hallway and informed him that the meeting would not continue if he didn't come back. Neither his family nor his hospice team wanted him to fear that decisions would be made without him. Eventually, Mr. Hoffer was able to return to the living room and voice his own frustrations, especially the difficulties he had keeping on top of his wife's needs. He suggested that they hire a private nurse for her, but was told that this was financially unfeasible.

Frank took the opportunity to introduce the option of an extended care facility. He had visited such a facility a few days earlier and thought it would meet the needs of both of his parents. To everyone's surprise, Mr. Hoffer neither cried nor left the room. Instead, he agreed to consider Frank's suggestion. Without wasting time, he stood up, went to the phone, and called the facility himself. He scheduled a family tour for the following day. When he hung up the phone, Mr. Hoffer asked Carl to accompany him for support.

"It was one of the most incredible turnarounds for the good I think I have seen in this job," Margaret exclaimed to me. "That Albert just finally said, 'Okay, I trust you.' That whole trust issue just had been paramount. He was just fighting the boys tooth and nail, and on that day he finally trusted all of us to do this for him. It was just wonderful." Frank had a similar response. In tears, he said, "It was a miraculous, miraculous meeting. I personally feel that the Holy Spirit guided that whole process. I have no other explanation for it."

The visit to the extended care facility went well. In recalling his mother's positive reaction during the tour, Frank said, "I was amazed. Dad was watching all this, and he could see that mom was kind of comfortable, but he said, 'Well, obviously, we do not want to make a decision today, but we will talk about it.'"

On the way back to the car, Carl pulled Frank aside and said, "I think you guys need to understand something here. I don't know what is going to happen, but I have often seen that when the dying person has been struggling with an issue that they need to resolve—whether it is reconciling a broken relationship or making arrangements for a spouse's care once they are gone—that once that issue is resolved, they let go and the end comes fairly quickly."

Three days later, Carl called hospice from the trailer. Mr. Hoffer was nauseous, lethargic, confused, and weak. He couldn't sit up unassisted, and as a result, he had skipped some of his medications. Carl urged Mr. Hoffer's transfer to the inpatient unit. He agreed to go, and Peter took him that day.

"Why should a dysfunctional family suddenly function so well?"

Mr. Hoffer couldn't recognize his surroundings and insisted on driving back home. To prevent an accident, nurses attached him to a personal alarm that was designed to sound when he attempted to get out of bed. Weary and agitated, Mr. Hoffer spoke about his wife. He complained of pain and nausea. The nurses gave him lorazepam for anxiety and short-acting morphine for his pain. They also suctioned his mouth. On September 23, one nurse reported suctioning thick, green mucous. It covered his tongue and, at times, seeped out to his lips.

"It is real clear that we are in the final days now," Frank told me. "Last night he was not even strong enough to spit his phlegm into the little dish they have, so he would just stick his tongue out, and I would have a Kleenex and a little rubber-tipped toothbrush thing that I used to swab it out of his mouth. It sounds kind of disgusting, but to be able to do those little things, they take on a significance that I never would have expected."

Mrs. Hoffer insisted that she be brought to the inpatient unit daily. She told her sons that she wasn't willing to move out of the trailer prior to her husband's death. Frank and Peter picked her up every day before lunch, dropped her off at hospice, and took her back home after dinner. Frank told me how moving it was to watch his parents together:

> You can just see the love between those two people. They just hold hands and look at each other, and she strokes his face. Physical touch is about the only form of communication Dad has left. One time I started to leave without hugging him, and I heard this, "Come back," and I looked around and there he was with his arms out, so I know that's an incredible breakthrough. This whole process has drawn our family closer together in some surprising ways. Given the family history, I do not have any particular answer other than the Holy Spirit. I don't know. Why should a dysfunctional family suddenly function so well?

When I walked into Mr. Hoffer's room on September 24, he was lying in bed, staring quietly at his wife and Peter who were sitting by his side. Suddenly he extended his hand toward them, and whispered, "Get me out of bed." Peter wrapped his arms around his father's torso and slowly pulled him up. "It hurts! It hurts!" cried Mr. Hoffer with every move he made. But his pain did not stop him from sitting up and turning sideways to face his wife. Peter, overwhelmed by the fragility of his father, sat next to him to keep him safe. Shaken as he was, he leaned his head against his father's, and they both started to cry.

"I think Albert is ready, finally," Margaret said to me. "These three boys seem to have all forgiven him, which is incredible, and they have all given so much of their time and effort. So, as many mistakes as Albert must have made, he and Julia must have done something right. I really feel proud about this case. I feel Albert has grown to trust us, and I know that was not easy for him. And it was not easy for Julia, either. And Julia has made tremendous changes. I mean, Julia smiles at me now and talks with me. She never used to do that."

On September 25, Mr. Hoffer stopped speaking. Periodically he opened his eyes and stared at the people sitting by his side. With him were his wife, his three sons, and Eileen, who had flown in to pay her final respects. They took turns holding Mr. Hoffer's hand. Eileen told Carl that she worried about her father's salvation. After the difficult life he had led, was he going to Heaven or Hell? Had he accepted God? Had he been forgiven? Carl told her about the gift Mr. Hoffer had bestowed upon him a month earlier. From that act, Carl said, he had surmised that God was more present in Mr. Hoffer's life than he ever expressed. Eileen seemed reassured.

On September 26, Mr. Hoffer started to moan. He had no longer seemed responsive to verbal or tactile stimulation, but when his wife and children arrived to see him, he opened his eyes, puckered his lips, and indicated that he wanted to kiss them. "I love you," he said faintly to each of them as they bent over to receive their kiss. Eileen had never before been told by her father that she was loved. Carl encouraged Mr. Hoffer to lift his fears, doubts, and concerns to God since he wasn't able to verbalize them. He blessed his journey and encouraged him to let go when he felt ready. Mr. Hoffer's hands were cool and dusky, his knees mottled. The next day his breathing changed. Nurses noted periods of apnea and gave him morphine to ease his respirations. Julia kissed him goodbye, and a few minutes later he died. His family held hands around him and prayed.

"Amazing Grace"

John wasn't sure what he wanted to say about his father at the funeral. Their relationship had been complicated by alcohol. The night before the service he was going through his father's belongings at the trailer when he found an old diary in which Mr. Hoffer confessed his guilt about his alcoholism and his abusiveness toward his family. In that diary, Mr. Hoffer took full responsibility for his actions, including the clobbering of John many years earlier. Neither John nor his brothers had ever before heard their father acknowledge the role he had played in shaping his own life. Now John knew what he wanted to say. He spoke about the two people he had known in his father: the one who was an alcoholic and detached, and the other who was sober, caring, and involved in everyone's affairs. He proudly declared that he had learned a big lesson from his father: to take responsibility for his own behavior.

The service was attended by approximately 75 people. Carl officiated. As a sign of Mr. Hoffer's closeness to God, Carl wore the tie Mr. Hoffer had given him. After the eulogies, and with the accompaniment of guitars, Frank, John, and Eileen's son sang "Amazing Grace," Mr. Hoffer's favorite hymn. In tears, the audience joined in. But people laughed as intensely as they cried. In the background stood Mr. Hoffer's urn (he had been cremated), surrounded by photographs and memorabilia. Looming large was an old T-shirt that reflected humorously Mr. Hoffer's cantankerous nature. It read: "Pieces of Fatherly Advice: No. Absolutely Not. Never." After the service, Mr. Hoffer's older sister stomped her cane and declared that she was tired of reuniting with her family only when someone died. She invited everyone to join her two weeks later in celebration of her 90th birthday.

When I spoke with Carl a few days later, he said:

> I had a little time of closure after the funeral service. I stood underneath a tree and just kind of spoke to Albert from my heart and said goodbye. For Albert to have really given himself over to the process, to have mended fences with his family, and to be reconciled and have healing occur—I counted this as a good death. I think I tend to have more sadness with those who are not open to living until they die. I am planning to go deep sea fishing in October, and there is no doubt in my mind that Albert Hoffer is going to come to my awareness. I know I will have a few words with him, and maybe it will be praying to St. Albert to help me catch a good fish.

"If you don't grow close to someone when you're a child, their dying is a good time to do it"

Prior to her move to the assisted-living facility, Mrs. Hoffer stayed with Frank. Together with her three sons, she decided to go through all of her and her husband's belongings to throw out what she didn't need, keep what she did, and auction off the rest. The four of them needed the money to pay 13 outstanding bills, including taxes, funeral home expenses, and hospitalizations. In memory of his life with his parents, Frank kept two reference books from his father's gardening classes that were filled with hand-written notes. John kept a pitcher that he remembered his mother using for lemonade and iced tea. And Peter kept a set of china and a book about the Civil War that he used to browse over and over again as a child. It reminded him, he said, of his father's passion for history.

Mrs. Hoffer moved to the extended care facility in the beginning of October. Her sons saw a positive change in her. At their aunt's 90th birthday party, they were surprised to see her be social and solicitous. But Julia still kept her feelings to herself. The only time she revealed a hint of her feelings about her new life was when Peter referred to her extended care facility as her "home." "It is not my home," Mrs. Hoffer asserted. "It is just the place where I live."

None of the Hoffers felt the need for follow-up bereavement services from hospice. Mrs. Hoffer turned down the option of visits from a volunteer. Frank, John, and Peter all stated that they had already lived through the hardest part of their grief. The times when they needed the most support were the times when their father was suffering. "Even with all the support that I had through hospice," Frank said, "there were times when it was just very lonely."

None of the Hoffer brothers attended the auction in May 1998. Among the objects left behind was a New Testament given to Albert by his Sunday school teacher in the 1920s. Frank, who had never seen this book before, was thrilled that it wasn't sold. He saw it as tangible evidence that his father had a relationship with God. "This little Testament," he said, "I am really saving for Eileen. She was so concerned with whether Dad was going to go to Heaven, and I am hoping that it might be comforting for her."

Six months after Mr. Hoffer's death, his sons still worried about their mother. Although they saw her often, she felt lonely, for she couldn't remember their visits. As usual, her short-term memory failed her. Frank decided to take photographs of family gatherings to remind her that she wasn't abandoned. He looked back at his father's dying as a time of healing. He was thankful to have reunited with Eileen and vowed to keep in touch with her. And he was thankful to have grown closer to his father. Peter felt the same way. Remembering the time when he cried with his father in the inpatient unit of hospice, he concluded, "If you don't grow close to someone when you're a child, their dying is a good time to do it."

A year after Mr. Hoffer's death, I was informed that the Hospice of Lancaster County had created a support group for the caregivers of terminally ill patients. The catalyst of this initiative was Frank Hoffer, who wanted such a group when his father was alive, but had to do without it.

4

Klara Bergman
Burdens from the Past

Narrated by PATRICIA BOSTON

When Klara Bergman's doctors told her that she had an incurable lung cancer, she did not question the diagnosis. But she felt it was a terrible injustice. She felt that she had been cheated and was being punished for no good reason. Mrs. Bergman, who was 80 years old, had suffered in Nazi concentration camps during World War II and lost most of her loved ones. She had cared for her sick father for many years after they were freed from the camp. Since then she had strived to repair and alleviate the suffering of victims of concentration camps, never thinking of herself or of her own needs.

Why had God inflicted such a terrible injustice on her? A good and loving God would not do such a thing. Perhaps there was no God. All her life she had been deeply religious and committed to her Jewish faith. But if God existed, He was not there for her now.

Hurts in the past

Mrs. Bergman was a Polish Jew who married and had her first child at age 22, just prior to World War II. After one year of marriage she was taken along with her husband and child to a German concentration camp; her mother and father were taken to a different camp. Klara survived. When she returned from the

59

camps she was 24, having lost her 14-month-old son, her husband, and her mother. Still, she felt lucky because her father had survived. Although he was very sick, he was alive and she could now care for him.

Not only was she well and her father alive, she also managed to find work. A friend in the Polish government helped her find a job, which was to establish an office of the World Jewish Congress in Warsaw. Klara's mission was to bring together Jewish families who had been separated by the war or incarcerated in concentration camps. It was a difficult undertaking because communication systems were very poor and there was no mail service. But through many contacts and "sheer determination" she managed to bring people together.

Hundreds of Jewish families were reunited as a result of her efforts. But then Poland became occupied by the Soviet Union and she and her father had to flee. With the help of people from the World Jewish Congress, she went first to Paris, then to London where Klara met the man who became her second husband. They had a daughter, Ellen, and when her husband was offered a position in Montreal, the family decided to move to Canada. Klara was able to find a job right away with a Jewish organization and continued her work of reuniting separated families. She also went to law school, enabling her to help people settle legal problems incurred during the war.

All in all, it was a wonderful life in Montreal. The Bergmans settled into a comfortable suburban neighborhood where they raised Ellen. She was a bright, intelligent girl who excelled at school and later went on to study law at the local university. Klara and Ellen had an especially close relationship, and when Ellen left home to study abroad in Paris, Klara found it hard to be without her. Ellen had excelled beyond all of her parents' expectations, winning a scholarship to study at the Sorbonne.

In Ellen's final year at the Sorbonne, her father became ill with cancer, his illness progressing rapidly. Klara took time away from her law practice to nurse him. After her husband died, it was hard to be alone, without him. But time passed and she gradually took up her law practice again. She enjoyed the company of her friends and traveled to Europe to see Ellen. Life began to have meaning again.

Three years after her husband's death, Klara noticed that she was beginning to have some trouble with breathing. At first she wondered if it was her imagination or if it was simply due to asthma. She had smoked cigarettes for 50 years, but now she stopped. She saw her family doctor, Dr. Gupta, who scheduled her for a chest X-ray, thinking that perhaps the difficulty was due to a chest infection. The X-rays showed a much more serious problem.

Dr. Gupta referred Mrs. Bergman to an oncologist, Dr. Lieberman, who told her that her symptoms were due to lung cancer. Dr. Lieberman was optimistic about her recovery, however, and scheduled her for surgery to perform a right upper lobectomy and biopsy of her lymph nodes. Following the surgery she had four weeks of radiotherapy treatments to decrease the chance of local recurrence.

"Why now?"

When she heard after the surgery that there was no immediate evidence of metastases, Klara Bergman was not only relieved but felt confirmed in her strong belief in God and the Jewish faith. Though she had spent two years in a concentration camp and had lost all of her loved ones except for her father, she had always believed in God's goodness and purpose in all that happened in people's lives. Two months after the radiotherapy, however, she began to have increasing shortness of breath and trouble swallowing liquids. Six months later, Dr. Lieberman told her that a bone scan and X-rays showed that she had multiple bone metastases. He offered external beam radiotherapy to help control her pain.

Mrs. Bergman found it hard to understand why this terrible thing had to happen now, just when she was enjoying the fruits of her labor. For her, dying was the end of everything. When I met her and began talking with her about the onset of her illness, she told me that she couldn't sleep at night for trying, as she put it, "to put together the puzzle." She said:

> Why now, when I could relax and enjoy old age? Because I have really enjoyed old age. Old age was never something I have worried about and been frightened of and all those things people think about getting older. I thought this would be great. I would be old and live to a good age as my father had done. I didn't even look forward to retiring. I didn't feel that my mental powers were in any way diminished, and I liked what I was doing.

When Mrs. Bergman realized that there was no cure for her cancer, it became difficult to continue seeing her clients—not only physically but because of her increasing feelings of resentment. Her clients' problems and grievances became irritating and seemed trivial compared to her own. They were pursuing claims for compensation for losses that resulted from the war; she felt they did not appreciate the life and the wonderful resources they already had. She explained:

> They came to me with measly little complaints. Everybody I saw wanted more money and I couldn't understand it. I knew all of their past histories and that they had more now than ever before. There was no logic to asking for more money. Maybe a friend had told them they had an increase in their pension and that person would want an increase in their pension. People always came to me saying, "Everybody's getting more than me."

Mrs. Bergman could no longer sympathize with these problems. Here she was, "wracked with pain and a dying woman," and "all they wanted was a few dollars!" It was even more frustrating that her clients really did not sympathize with her. They saw themselves as victims of purposely inflicted injustices, but to them Mrs. Bergman's situation was different because no one had inflicted her illness upon her. It was no one's fault.

But Mrs. Bergman felt that her illness was a punishment, and the injustice of it made her more and more angry and confused. She examined her past life. Was she being punished for something? Had she done some terrible wrong? Certainly, she had been luckier than many; she had come home from the camps. But Mrs. Bergman's memories of the camp were of an intense struggle to keep her strength and health and to survive. Perhaps she had been too lucky. "There were others," she recalled, "many others who were much more damaged by the persecution. People who suffered in three, four different camps—much more difficult camps—who were physically mistreated and who, in spite of that, bore up quite well." She was fortunate by comparison. She had not suffered the same brutality as some.

Yet she had experienced terrible losses. There was a pain in her heart that had remained for the rest of her life. She said:

> You see my husband and I had a young son when I was taken to the camp. And when we were told we had to go there, there was a chance to leave my son with some friends who were not Jewish and who would have cared for him. I could have left him behind. There was, for that moment, that opportunity. I knew he would be safe. But I was reluctant to part with my child. He was, after all, 14 months old and I thought he needed to be with his mother. So I took him with me to the camp. He didn't survive. He became ill with pneumonia. There was no treatment available for him, and I lost him.

Klara had never stopped thinking about her son. It was never possible to come to terms with that kind of loss. Now, as she contemplated her own suffering and death, the memories of her son and the question of whether she should have left him in safe custody plagued her. There were, of course, women who had lost two or three children in the camps and had suffered greatly. To this Klara responded, "I don't think that the loss of two children amounts to more than the loss of one child. Because the pain is always there. And your life is never the same again, especially if you think you could have avoided the loss."

As I listened to her story, I wondered how I as a mother or as another human being, could ever understand this woman's pain. I had raised two children of my own who were healthy and always full of life and energy. It was hard to relate to her loss. Although my own parents were now dead and I still felt their loss, they had both lived full lives and I had good memories.

Pain: A punishment from God

In the fall of 1995, a few months after Dr. Lieberman told her the news that she had bone metastases, Klara Bergman began to have gnawing pain in her legs. It was controlled to some extent by acetaminophen, and she could have increased doses if needed. But the thought of increasing her pain medication only increased her anguish. She feared becoming confused and losing control of her mind.

As her pain persisted the whole ordeal felt increasingly like a "punishment from God." It was unfair, and could only mean that God was unjust. Perhaps God did not even exist! During the war, she had always held on to her Jewish faith. Since being released from the camp, she had tried to lead a good life. Although her faith was tested at times, in the end she had always been able to feel that God was there for her. But now it was impossible to make peace with God when she had been given a terrible punishment for a crime she had not committed. She prayed for God's help. Sometimes she joked that she was preparing a speech "for when I get up there and what I will tell Him." But she doubted whether God was even listening.

Why did she have this terrible cancer? Perhaps it was the result of smoking for so many years. But why wouldn't a loving God protect her after all she had suffered in her life? She could find no answers to these questions. Meanwhile, the pain in her chest increased. The radiological reports showed lesions consistent with metastatic bone disease. Over the next few months, a widespread invasion with pain in her left femur and chest wall developed. She lost weight, and didn't feel like eating. Her situation seemed to get more and more hopeless.

I met Mrs. Bergman during this period of her illness, first visiting her home in November 1996. She lived alone in a cottage-style house in a middle-class neighborhood of Montreal, a comfortable home with many personal mementos scattered throughout the rooms. There were old photographs, some of which might have been taken 60 years before, and souvenirs, which varied from a tiny Portuguese doll in traditional costume to an Irish tea towel that hung on the wall in the tiny kitchen. Most of these souvenirs came from all the countries she had visited over the years, and the rest were the result of Ellen's travels.

Klara Bergman looked much younger than her 81 years, and it was hard to believe she was as ill as she was. Her face was unwrinkled, with porcelain-like, clearly defined features. Her long, white-blond hair was elegantly rolled into a chignon, giving her a majestic, regal air. She had a pink shawl draped over her shoulders and sat up in bed, propped up by five or six large pillows and floral cushions. Although the bed seemed very large for her tiny, delicate frame, it seemed well suited to the ambiance of grace surrounding her. Two large, soft, stuffed rabbits sat on the bed beside her. "I love stuffed animals, rabbits and teddy bears, all animals," she said. "Ellen gives them to me and I have names for all of them. That one is Clarence," she said, pointing to a large brown bear.

Because of the way she held herself and looked at me through clear blue eyes, she impressed me as a woman of profound dignity, as well as elegance and beauty. Much later, she told me that many young men had admired her and declared their love for her, which was not hard to believe. She had a way of regarding one intensely with admiration and interest in what one had to say, no matter what it was. She was well schooled in drawing out information, and I liked talking to her. There were times when I would catch myself enthusiastically chatting about my own life, only to remember that I was the interviewer. I thought she must have been a superbly competent lawyer.

Changing relationships and roles

Mrs. Bergman knew she was going to die. Her question was whether she would be able to handle her illness with her accustomed dignity. She found it hard to adapt to the role of a person who was dying. She wasn't able to talk about it to the people who visited, even though many were old friends. It was not that she was ashamed of her illness, but she didn't "want to make a well person feel embarrassed or anything." "I don't want to make a well person feel that I'm envious or that I feel that he or she should have it and not me," she said.

One December day when I visited, Mrs. Bergman was with an old friend, Sophie, who was also born in Poland. The two women had been close friends for 35 years. Sophie was about to leave for her yearly winter sojourn in Florida. Sophie and Klara knew that this was probably the last time they would see one another, as Mrs. Bergman recounted:

> We sort of said good-bye to each other. And she was the one who was crying. And I felt so bad about it. Because I know her. And I know what she thinks and feels. And I felt really bad about having to say good-bye to her because it made her feel she was privileged, you know? I felt that she would feel that I am envious of her position. And I almost said, "so help me God, I'm not." I'm glad that she is in this position. Thank God she has a good life, a good daughter and grandson. She worked hard all her life. She was an immigrant, just like me!

Mrs. Bergman found herself in a very strange situation: she wanted to be frank and honest about her feelings and illness, and she wanted to be intelligent about it. But she feared that she might be hurting the other person's feelings. From some innocent remark, people might consider that she thought they were "lucky." She didn't want to awaken such feelings, and she didn't want people to feel that she expected their pity. "I want my friends to be just as they have always been," she said.

Mrs. Bergman had no biological family to speak of, except for a brother in England, whom she seldom saw. Ellen was all the family she had, and Ellen made her life in Israel, where she had an excellent job with the government record office. After leaving for Israel in 1992, Ellen returned to Montreal only to observe religious holidays, such as the Jewish New Year. For the most part, the friends Klara Bergman had made over the last few years were her family. Now they were coming through.

Many of her surrogate "family" were even older than she was. It was amazing to her to see how people with crippling arthritis, asthma, or even heart congestion would struggle through the snow and ice in the cold, Montreal winter, just to come and help her. Mrs. Bergman wasn't sure if she herself could have done it. "Frankly," she said, "if I were going to visit somebody who is sick and as old as I was, or even older, I would probably feel a bit put out. I might think to myself, 'in this weather, why do I, an old woman, have to go out?'" Once her friend Naomi found Mrs. Bergman vomiting on the bedroom floor. It was "demoralizing," throwing up on the floor and then watching her friend, with whom she had only shared philosophical debates and intellectual discussion, mop up the remains of breakfast and lunch. As Mrs. Bergman recalled: "She stood with me, over the sink, holding my head while I was throwing up. She is 83 years old. And I said to myself, I am really fortunate, you know? She was talking to me like one talks to a child, holding my head and stroking my back with the other hand. It's a wonderful feeling."

If there were doubts in Mrs. Bergman's mind about the presence of a loving and beneficent God in the face of this terrible event that had befallen her in the "peaceful autumn" of her life, there were no doubts regarding the goodness and compassion of humankind. People complain these days, she said, "about how selfish and self-serving the world had become." But the care and love she now received from friends, some of them old and crippled themselves, convinced her that there was indeed hope for the world.

Medical care

Dr. Gupta had cared for Mrs. Bergman for the past 15 years, and was more than a family physician to the Bergman family. Dr. Gupta and Mrs. Bergman's husband had been friends and colleagues for a number of years before she became his patient. He wanted to continue to care for Klara, but when he saw how ill she was, he felt that the palliative care team should be involved. Dr. Fitzgerald, one of the physicians with the Palliative Care Service, visited Mrs. Bergman at her home to see how he could help, and to discern whether she wanted him to take care of her.

It was not a difficult decision for Klara to make. She had heard of Dr.

Fitzgerald from a good friend and knew that he was kind and compassionate. She needed to be able to talk to someone about the thought of dying; it was impossible for her to talk about it to her friends who were well.

Dr. Fitzgerald visited Klara Bergman regularly. He enjoyed his visits. They would often talk about her life experiences, though she didn't want to talk much about her time in the concentration camps. Dr. Fitzgerald had cared for other patients who had suffered greatly in their past, and sometimes this had a profound impact on the way they reacted to a diagnosis of terminal cancer. If Mrs. Bergman had made a connection between her present suffering and the past, however, she struck Dr. Fitzgerald as a woman who would decide for herself how to respond. He recalled:

> She was a firm woman. She was a woman who I felt I could let take the lead on how she was going to handle her situation, maybe more than some other people who had experienced similar events in their lifetime. I thought she was in charge of the things she needed to discuss and would raise quite comfortably whatever needed to be raised. I didn't think it was necessary to push her and to elicit material that either she wasn't ready or had decided not to talk about.

Mrs. Bergman was fully aware that she was going to die within a relatively short period—several weeks or perhaps a few months. She told Dr. Fitzgerald that she wanted to die in the best way that she could, free from pain, if that was possible. What she asked of him, and what was most important, was that her mind remain clear until the end. Mrs. Bergman worried that pain medications "would cloud her intellect" and that she would lose control of her mind. Dr. Fitzgerald prescribed oxycodone, which would help alleviate her pain and yet might have less risk of producing confusion, compared with other opioids. He felt that oxycodone might be a drug with fewer side effects for someone of Mrs. Bergman's age.

Alone in a separate world

The oxycodone did not make her drowsy or confused. She was able to read and enjoy her friends. Still, Mrs. Bergman felt alone. The differences in roles and the way people related to her now magnified her sense of aloneness. People had busy lives; they had careers and families, they traveled the world. They had lives to look forward to and memories to make. Ellen was young and perhaps would marry. But even if she did, Mrs. Bergman would never know the person.

Whom could she talk to who could really understand? She felt she could not share her grief or her fear of death with even her closest friends, thus making everything seem more isolating and extreme. She certainly couldn't talk about these things with Ellen. If she made a remark about dying, Ellen would cut her off, saying, "Oh, stop it." It reminded Klara of when her own father had wanted to talk about his fears and feelings about death, and she had said the same thing Ellen was saying to her now: "Oh, don't talk like that!"

Ellen

Ellen Bergman took an extended leave from her job in Tel Aviv so she could care for her mother. Klara felt secure and safe when Ellen was around. Although Mrs. Bergman had many helpful friends, good doctors, and the support of home care nurses if needed, Ellen was the person to whom she had delegated most of the responsibility. As her parents' only child, Ellen felt alone with this responsibility. She worried continuously, describing herself to me as the "worrying type."

Ellen took up her caretaker role in the midst of another loss: months before Mrs. Bergman was diagnosed with lung cancer, Ellen had hoped to marry a man she had known in Israel for some time, but the relationship fell through. Ellen didn't want to talk much about her broken relationship. She rarely showed extreme emotion. She did say to me once that she would like to marry, but now probably would not. She had good friends and an interesting job. "Life could be worse," she said. I could never tell whether she was resolved to the idea of being unmarried or whether it was because she still felt pain from the breakup of her relationship.

Ellen was attractive, soft spoken, slight in build, and looked much younger than 38 years old. Her dark brown, curly hair framed her fine features. I thought she had beautiful eyes that somehow stayed sad when she smiled and even giggled as she told me her story. Mrs. Bergman worried about Ellen not being married. She still felt angry toward the man who had "broken his obligation." "I'd like to see Ellen happy and cheerful," she once said. "She's cheerful enough but I think that it is just a dress-up, for me. I know she is sad and would like to be married with children."

When her father died of cancer Ellen was left with a lot of regrets. He had died while she was studying in Paris. She had been engrossed in her studies and had little time for anything until after her final exams. So Klara took care of her husband until he died a few weeks after the diagnosis. Ellen felt upset about her own lack of involvement, reasoning that she had not been more involved because she had not been told the full truth about the seriousness of her father's cancer. At the same time, student life at the Sorbonne was full and demanding, and she now wondered if perhaps she hadn't pursued the truth as much as she should have. She had not called home as often as she should have. On her father's birthday, when she had called to speak to him and there was no answer, she had not followed up with further calls. "The next day," she recalled,

"I got a message that my father was seriously ill in the hospital. I flew back to Montreal the next day, but three days later he died. There is a lot of guilt in me, and unfinished business which I can never repair."

Now it was vitally important to her to be in Montreal and to be a "good" caretaker. It felt good to have a chance to make up for her neglect of her father by being in charge of her mother's care. She took over the household affairs, paying bills, cleaning, cooking, monitoring medications, and coordinating the doctor's and nurse's visits.

Ellen found it very difficult to take any time off from these duties. Once she went for an overnight trip to Ottawa, one of the first full days she was away from the house since her return from Israel several weeks earlier. She worried the entire day she was out and was not able to relax. She knew her mother was anxious and fearful the entire time that she was in Ottawa, and she had felt a kind of "catastrophic feeling." Although her friends in Ottawa had planned a day of sightseeing, with a lot of distractions to help her relax, Ellen spent the whole day worrying that something could happen if she didn't get back to her mother's bedside. The experience made her feel physically ill. She said to me:

> I'm not going to do any traveling anywhere anymore, because what if something happens to me? I was sitting there with my friends, thinking and sensing my mother worry. And I realized I had a sort of soreness here [she pointed to her chest] and I worried that if I get sick and I can't look after her. . . . My mother needs me here now.

In the past, Ellen had always felt like a little child in relation to her mother. In spite of her 38 years, her studies at the Sorbonne, her travels to Europe, and the fact that she had an independent life in Israel, she had always felt like the child who was being looked after. Klara Bergman had been strong, always there for her, watching over her. Now the roles were reversed.

"If you cannot control my symptoms, you know what you can do"

Ellen felt that she had to try to keep her mother home at all costs. For a while, things went well. Klara received oxycodone for chest pain, metoclopramide to prevent nausea, and lactulose, bisacodyl suppositories, and docusate to prevent constipation. But as the days went by, her breathing became more difficult, and she barely managed to eat the kosher food that Ellen prepared. Dr. Fitzgerald began to feel that his patient needed greater access to the palliative care home services. He asked Dr. Thompson, another palliative care physician more closely connected with the home care service, to take over Mrs. Bergman's care. Dr. Thompson began to visit Mrs. Bergman at home regularly.

One day the home care nurse was so worried about Mrs. Bergman's breathing that she called Dr. Thompson and asked her to visit immediately. When Dr. Thompson arrived, Mrs. Bergman was visibly more short of breath and was wheezing. "I am dying," was the first thing she said. Dr. Thompson's assessment was that Mrs. Bergman had a parenchymal spread of tumor. She ordered oxygen, salbutane, and dexamethasone. She considered that her patient might be anemic, which would also account for her shortness of breath. She thought that if Mrs. Bergman did have anemia a blood transfusion might help. But it would involve a short stay at the hospital.

Mrs. Bergman appeared despondent. "I am dying," she said to Dr. Thompson. "Why do you want to transfuse me?" Dr. Thompson recalled that she hesitated for a moment before answering Mrs. Bergman, and Mrs. Bergman said to her, "Don't look at me like that—you know it's true." When Dr. Thompson explained that her intentions were to make Mrs. Bergman more comfortable, not to prolong her life, Mrs. Bergman agreed to the plan, but added, "I want to go soon. I don't want this to drag on."

Above all, Mrs. Bergman did not want to suffer. She said to Dr. Thompson, "If you cannot control my symptoms, you know what you can do." It was clear to Dr. Thompson, at least at this moment, that her patient was alluding to euthanasia. Dr. Thompson responded that she would discuss various treatment options that were available in palliative care, including how to keep her comfortable without prolonging her life. Mrs. Bergman said she would like that, although their conversation did not continue at that time.

Home or the Palliative Care Unit?

A few days following Dr. Thompson's home visit, Dr. Gupta called at the house. Mrs. Bergman told him that she now had intense pain over her left hip and could no longer put weight on the left leg. When Dr. Thompson heard this, she thought it best to admit Mrs. Bergman to the hospital. She could obtain radiological confirmation of metastases and assess her overall physical condition. Dr. Thompson worried that Mrs. Bergman might have a fracture of her left hip due to her advancing disease. It was also necessary to achieve better control of her pain.

Ellen worried that she was not nursing her mother competently enough. As her mother's pain increased, Ellen felt inadequate. Then, one of the visiting nurses noticed that Klara was beginning to get bedsores from lying in one place in her bed. This confirmed Ellen's fears:

> When the nurse mentioned bedsores, I remembered there was some material for bedsores that someone had recommended a week or so back. And I thought I

could have got it. I hadn't got round to ordering it. So I felt really anxious and blamed myself. Because it really was my fault. I should have ordered it right away.

Mrs. Bergman's pain was keeping her awake at night, despite the medication she was taking to prevent it. Ellen worried that if she didn't stay by her mother's bedside all the time, her mother might fall out of bed. She thought of hiring a private nurse "who could be paid to stay up and keep an eye on her." She tried putting a baby monitor in her mother's room so she would hear if Klara called out in the night, but it didn't work properly.

The situation was all too much to handle. Even her mother felt it was time to go to the Palliative Care Unit for control of her pain and some relief for the shortness of breath.

The Palliative Care Unit

Klara Bergman was admitted to the Palliative Care Unit in December 1996. Barbara, the nurse who took care of her on the unit, settled her into a sunny, spacious room. Mrs. Bergman liked the colorful, homespun bedcovers on her bed, for they reminded her of the shawls her mother had crocheted many years before. The bed was comfortable and the bathroom was close by. Being at home in her own bed was nice, but it had meant a difficult walk to the bathroom. Ellen also settled into the room. Though she didn't plan to stay overnight, she spent most of the daytime with her mother and wanted to be fully involved in her care.

Klara Bergman impressed the palliative care team with her charm and graciousness. Dr. Crevier, one of the palliative care doctors who also took care of Mrs. Bergman, recalled:

> In my first meeting with her, I had a hard time believing she was very ill. Her face was almost like that of a young woman. Her eyes were bright and clear. She was alert, poised, and inquisitive about all of us. Her hair was beautifully coifed. She wore a white crocheted shawl elegantly draped across her shoulders. To me she looked like she should be sitting on a veranda somewhere sipping tea.

Dr. Crevier thought she was dignified and cultured. "She wasn't going to let her illness compromise her sense of grace and dignity," she recalled.

"A special caregiver challenge"

Ellen also impressed the team with her industriousness and dedication. She helped give her mother her morning bath, carried the meals, and set up the tray at the bedside. Frequently, Mrs. Bergman went for a stroll, walking slowly up and down the hallway, leaning heavily on Ellen's arm. Sometimes they would walk to the palliative care lounge, where they could sit and look out onto heavily wooded areas or, at night, see the twinkling lights of the city. Sometimes there was a concert or some other activity going on. More often than not, Mrs. Bergman wanted to chat with people. She wanted to know their story and how they were coping.

To me, Ellen still appeared tired and even overwhelmed by her mother's needs, even though she now had direct access to the palliative care team. Mrs. Bergman preferred that Ellen be her caregiver. Once when I was visiting, I noticed Mrs. Bergman seemed a little short of breath. I asked if I might go and ask a nurse to help attach the oxygen mask. "No!" she replied. "It is not necessary, I don't need it just now." But as soon as Ellen came into the room, her mother asked her to fix the mask. Ellen was visibly irritated. "Why didn't you ask someone else?" she said. "Why must it always be me?"

Some of the nurses saw taking care of Mrs. Bergman as "a special caregiver challenge," in part because Ellen also needed a lot of attention. She was so fearful, so anxious to meet her mother's needs. Lena, another nurse, told me:

> Sometimes Ellen will come to us and say, "My mother needs a laxative. I think you should give her a lower dosage than you did last time." Or she'll say, "My mother needs something for pain. But don't give her as much oxycodone this time. You gave her 5 milligrams too much last time." Or Ellen will ask you to try another type of medication that perhaps she heard about from another patient. So you are constantly trying to balance Mrs. Bergman's needs with Ellen's needs and what you are able to do in the nursing role.

Ellen did not want to usurp the nurses. She wanted the team to care for her mother, and to provide her with respite from demanding and wearisome tasks. Yet it was important for her to feel that she had explored every option to improve her mother's care. As she explained:

> I will never forgive myself if my mother doesn't get exactly the care she needs. Already I feel I should have been a much better daughter—more competent. My mother has always wanted perfection. And I should be prepared to give her perfection in the way she is cared for.

Managing pain and other symptoms

At times, Mrs. Bergman's pain was excruciating. The pain seemed especially acute in her left hip, though it seemed to be spreading to all her limbs. Radiological studies showed extensive bone metastases. "How much worse will it become?" she asked Dr. Thompson. "I am afraid. I am afraid of pain. I am afraid of this dragging on, of losing my dignity. What will happen to me?"

Dr. Thompson told Mrs. Bergman that there were a lot of options for controlling her pain. She began by discussing the option of increasing the dose of opioid medication. Mrs. Bergman often chose to live with her pain because she still did not want to be confused or drowsy. As it became absolutely necessary to increase the dosage, Dr. Thompson tried to increase it so gradually that it would not cause drowsiness or result in Mrs. Bergman feeling out of control. She also arranged for radiotherapy to the painful area, and prescribed lorazepam to calm some of Mrs. Bergman's fears and reduce the anxiety that accompanied the pain.

After a few days, the pain seemed better. Dr. Thompson urged Mrs. Bergman to let the nurses know when it seemed that the medication was insufficient. But the cancer in her bones was not the only source of Mrs. Bergman's pain. She also had two small bedsores at the base of her spine. Ellen was still worried that they were due to her own previous care of her mother at home. Barbara reassured her that bedsores happen easily with patients who are bedridden for lengthy periods. The nurses cleaned the bedsores with Hibitane and applied regular heat lamp treatments to them. They provided oxygen if Mrs. Bergman needed it to alleviate the distress of feeling short of breath, and she could have the drug dexamethasone to help relieve her breathing difficulties. Klara was impressed. She told me:

> I feel good, now that I am here. Of course it is not like home. Home is always nicer. But now everything is readily available for me. If I have pain, there is something for it. If I need other things, the nurses are already here.

For a while, Mrs. Bergman experienced some relief from physical discomfort. When it became difficult to breathe she took salbutamol and oxygen, and these measures helped. She felt in control, and chatted with people who stopped by to visit. She always seemed to downplay her own discomforts and concerns when I visited her, focusing instead on other people's worries and misfortunes. One afternoon, after her friend Helga visited, Klara worried that her friend might not go home to a hot meal that evening. Helga's stove had broken and couldn't be fixed until the following day.

"Please don't leave me alone"

After two months passed, it seemed less and less likely that Mrs. Bergman would go home, even for a short stay. Her pain was now controlled, but she was becoming much weaker. She didn't feel like getting up at all. "I am tired and my body is weary," she said.

Ellen also seemed weary. She would almost snap at her mother when her mother asked for something. She found more reasons to leave the unit "to do errands," especially while her mother was asleep. Just as Ellen finally allowed herself to get away, however, Klara seemed to want her daughter's presence even more. Ellen needed to be with her mother, but she was exhausted. "How long do you think this will go on?" she would ask Mrs. Bergman's various care-givers. No one could say for sure.

The nurses saw how much Ellen needed time away from the unit. They also saw that when Ellen was gone, Mrs. Bergman wanted one of them in the room with her all the time. Often, Barbara would go to Mrs. Bergman's room to turn her onto her side or to reposition her pillows. Mrs. Bergman would ask her to linger, then ask for something else, such as changing the water in the flower vases, folding the clothes and towels, or tidying up papers—anything, as long as it involved staying in the room; there was fear in her eyes. But Barbara had four or five other patients in her care who were very ill and dying, and she needed to be there for them as well. This emotional challenge was even more complex than the physical management of Mrs. Bergman's symptoms.

Barbara asked one of the volunteers, Linda, if she would sit with Mrs. Bergman. But Mrs. Bergman didn't feel secure with just anyone in the room; she wanted the presence of Ellen, or if not Ellen, then Barbara or Lena.

"I want to die with dignity"

One day, Mrs. Bergman told Dr. Crevier that what she most needed and wanted was "freedom from fear." "How can I get rid of that constant sense of fear inside me?" she asked. To me she said:

> I hate it, I hate it! This sense of being a child again—not in a good sense, for some-one like me, but in the sense that I must now depend on others to be sure that I eat without making a mess and that my body functions without making a mess. All the time I think of this and I am afraid of it. For some perhaps, it is not so impor-tant, but for me it is impossible to bear.

She continued, "I've always been one for keeping beautiful and elegant. Loss of dignity . . . there is something ugly about it. I want to keep as beautiful as possible in these circumstances." Yet now she was losing control of her bladder. On occasion she had to ask Ellen, Barbara, or Lena to change the bed clothes. It was not so bad if Ellen or Barbara were around; they knew her situation. But what if it were one of her friends? One day, when several friends were visiting, her incontinence was especially bothersome. The team thought that she might benefit from a urinary catheter. Mrs. Bergman was pleased with that idea. Any-thing was better than "wetting the bed and invading my dignity," she said.

There was also the advantage that the constant leakage of urine would no longer chafe her skin or irritate the bedsores, which had now begun to heal.

"I am afraid God is not there"

As she lay in her bed, Klara again wondered whether she could trust the religion of her childhood. She struggled with questions such as "Does God exist?", "Who is God?", "What exists after I die?", "Is there a benevolent God?", and "If there is, then why am I suffering?" Sometimes we would be chatting about topics such as a recent visit from a friend, or the lunch menu, and she would suddenly interrupt with thoughts about her faith. Once she asked me, "Do you believe in God?" I said I did. She replied:

> You see, I don't know if there is a God. So many bad things have happened. What is His logic? It doesn't make sense! How is it He permits so much to happen to people? Why would such a God, if He exists, allow these bad things to happen? I have spent most of my life dedicated to helping others in need. There is no justice in this.

Sometimes she could alleviate her fears by talking to her rabbi or to staff members who had impressed her with their own faith. Kyle, one of the nurses on the unit, had great faith in the existence of God. She felt a little easier after his visits. Kyle believed that whatever happened after death was surely something good. A believer himself, he felt he could comfort people spiritually. Although Kyle practiced a different religion, his "sheer faith" gave her momentary hope. Although Kyle saw that Mrs. Bergman felt a little less anxious after his visits, he still felt her restlessness and deep underlying fear. "She listens and we have good interactions," Kyle said to me, but he felt she was struggling.

After one of the rabbi's visits, she told me, "His faith in God does not waver. He believes in the goodness of mankind. He told me to focus on the good times I have had, and I have had many." Indeed, she could see the dedication and goodness of so many people on the Palliative Care Unit, she said. Certainly what the rabbi had said was true for the people she saw working here. She continued:

> I struggle with my fears: fears of losing all of my faith, fears that God does not exist. But my sense of logic—you see, I work on logic —tells me that there is goodness and compassion in others. These people—the nurses and doctors here—have no reason to be here. They don't have to choose this work, to be with dying people day after day. Such love and such dedication! And it is sincere.

Mrs. Bergman also marveled at the devotion of some family members toward their loved ones on the unit, especially the devotion of adult children toward their parents. She had noticed a young man in his early thirties caring for his mother. He had cared for her unselfishly for four years, she explained to me. Then she said, "I am so impressed by the devotion of that young man. He stays here with his mother all night and then leaves to work and then comes back here. You can't imagine it. He is young with so much life ahead of him, and yet he has made such a great sacrifice." At these times she could relate to her rabbi's argument about the goodness of human beings. Still, she said, if God does exist "it follows that I must be angry with Him for making me afraid and for allowing my and others' suffering."

Looking to the past

No one on the team knew quite how much pain Klara Bergman had endured in the concentration camp. We all knew that she had suffered and that she had fought to survive. But no one could tell exactly what she had endured. Although she talked freely about the events of her life following her release from the camps, we knew little about her life inside. All she would say was, "My life was difficult in the camp and I suffered. But everyone suffered and the most fortunate thing for me was that I came home. Many others did not."

She did mention some of her dreams. "Sometimes they are not just ordinary dreams," she said. "They are troubling dreams where I can't seem to control the events." She dreamt she was falling down a steep slope. She couldn't remember the details, but when she awoke she felt a sense of helplessness. When I asked if she wanted to talk about her dreams to someone on the team who might be able to help, she responded:

> I am not interested in speaking with anyone who will try to rationalize my situation. My situation will not improve if I talk about my dreams. I am going to die. I am dying. I hate it, and when I say I hate it, I hate it. Of course if someone is going to tell me that I am *not* going to die—well then, it would be quite another story.

Some members of the team did try to broach the subject of Mrs. Bergman's past experiences. The music therapist, Sue, asked if she wanted to tell the story of her past. Mrs. Bergman responded abruptly, "I like to talk, but you shouldn't talk to me about my Holocaust experiences." She told Sue that she did not like people who were "Holocaust professionals."

Dr. Thompson thought there was no real evidence of clinical depression in Mrs. Bergman's case. Mrs. Bergman was eating as well as she could. She was talkative (if not about past events), she enjoyed the company of many friends and visitors. When she felt up to it, Mrs. Bergman would read, look at television, or attend the musical concerts that were available in the palliative care lounge. She readily acknowledged to Dr. Thompson that she was sad about what had been happening to her for the past two years, but she also felt proud of her many achievements. Besides, even if she were clinically depressed, Klara Bergman had little interest in seeing a mental health professional. She "didn't believe much in the benefit of such help," Dr. Thompson noted.

As the days passed she said she felt she was losing her grip on "this inevitable and pervasive progress towards my final end." Over and over again, she would ask, "Where is God and why is He doing this?" She did take the lorazepam that Dr. Thompson had prescribed to alleviate anxiety, but her fears seemed to penetrate the effects of the medication.

"I'll be here with you"

Most of all, Mrs. Bergman feared dying alone. "There will always be someone here for you," Barbara told her. "Even if I can't be there on one of the days, Lena is here." Ellen now began to stay with her mother at night as well as during the day. She slept in a cot beside her mother's bed, listening for any sound her mother made. Ellen didn't sleep much herself. "It is as though my mother knows whether I'm here or not," she told me. "Even if she's sleeping, as soon as I go out into the hallway, even for a short walk, she wakes up. I hear her call out my name. I know that she is really scared."

Sue, the music therapist, tried to work with musical images that would provide comfort and relief for Mrs. Bergman. To a small extent it worked. As Sue explained:

> I suggested she try putting on some quiet music and really to try to imagine with all her senses that she was back within the beauty of the images she was experiencing. She thought about the good memories she had had. We created an image of her sitting at home on her favorite chair with her beloved cat on her belly, where the pain was. And I looked at her as she was describing the cat and how much fun she had with this cat and how the cat meowed and how she loved it and the special communication she had with this animal—and for a while, her face looked very relaxed. She enjoyed it and she said she had, at least for those moments, forgotten her pain and her fearfulness.

When Sue returned the next day to try a similar experience, Mrs. Bergman told her, "This form of imagining with music" wasn't for her. After Sue had left the previous day she had felt "frightened," "isolated," "with a terrible feeling of abandonment." "All my nightmares came flooding back again," she said. Sue offered to make a cassette that Mrs. Bergman could listen to with headphones. Sue made the cassette in which she guided the images, and Mrs. Bergman tried to use it sometimes.

"I wish they could give me something to just end it all"

One day she said to Dr. Crevier, "I don't want this to just drag on and on. I don't want to suffer endlessly. If I am to die, then let it happen soon and quickly." Then she asked, "Maybe I could go to sleep and simply stay asleep?" Klara Bergman wanted to die. She was asking to be freed from her struggles. Her pain was well controlled by hydromorphone, and chloral hydrate, a sedative, also offered some relief. "But I am afraid," she said. "I thought I was above being afraid like this, but I am afraid, all the time, and there it is!"

Even if euthanasia were legal and available, however, which it was not, Ellen made it very clear that *she* was not willing to accept such an option. She was not willing to let her mother go. "I hate it when she talks that way," she said to me. "I told her she needs to try and be strong for my sake, if nothing else." To her mother she said, "We'll manage. I won't leave you alone."

Ellen helped with her mother's morning bath and coaxed her to eat the yolk of an egg and a little juice, no matter how long it took. Every day she brought home her mother's night clothes and special towels to launder and would return within an hour with fresh, clean, scented clothes for her mother to put on. She brought in religious books, magazines, and newspapers, even though I could see that Mrs. Bergman was less and less interested in anything. Ellen's eyes looked bloodshot and they had dark shadows under them. Sometimes I saw her sitting facing the side of her mother's bed with her head resting in her hands. One nurse wrote in her notes:

> We should try to encourage Mrs. Bergman's daughter to take some time off. She is afraid to leave. But she is extremely exhausted. I have gently approached her to see if she will allow one of us to replace her.

When one of the nurses tried to coax Ellen at least to sit in the family kitchen and perhaps make herself a cup of coffee, Ellen became irritated. "I am not tired!" she insisted. "I am not in the least bit tired."

Fears of persecution

In the beginning of February, seven weeks after Klara Bergman was admitted to the Palliative Care Unit, she began to show signs of confusion and suspiciousness. She would hear the sound of footsteps in the corridor and wonder if someone was coming or waiting to give her some order. On one occasion she heard the voices of two of the volunteers chatting as they wheeled the library book cart down the hallway outside her room. "Who is there?" she called out.

"Are we under surveillance?" On another occasion she asked me if we should try and get alternative accommodations. "Perhaps," she said, "we won't be able to stay here for too long." If you looked directly at her, she might ask, "what are you looking for?" Even when familiar nurses entered her room to fix her bed or give her a back rub, she would awaken abruptly and ask what they wanted from her. She wanted to know who was waiting outside, what people's names were, why they were there. More often than not, she would refuse to eat the food that was offered.

Dr. Crevier noted:

> She is starting to talk about wanting to see the police record of the nurses. She believes that someone wants to come and get her back to the concentration camps. She sees men in her room behind us. Her daughter found her this morning with two coils of oxygen tubing around her neck. She was restless in the bed, moving about and never finding a comfortable spot.

The last days

In consultation with the psychiatric consult team, Dr. Thompson and Dr. Crevier worked to ascertain dosages of haloperidol and lorazepam that would alleviate Mrs. Bergman's fearfulness. The drugs worked. Once her mind was clearer, she began again to reiterate that what bothered her most was not knowing what to expect. For her, dying was the end of everything. If her life had to end, then surely it should end quickly. Her list of fears was now enormous.

Despite her previous insistence that she had to remain alert and awake at all times, Mrs. Bergman said she was now ready to sleep. To be able to have a peaceful sleep, free of anxiety, was more important than anything. She was ready to let go. The physicians adjusted the medication so that she slept more and more. Ellen, struggling to come to terms with the reality of her mother's imminent death, stayed constantly beside her mother's bed. Over the next couple of days she looked more calm and prepared.

Early on a mid-February morning Mrs. Bergman died. Ellen held her hand during the last hours. It was good, she said, that her mother died with people close beside her. Most of all, she had wanted Ellen to be there with her. Dying on this particular day was, in her own way, "doing a favor to me," Ellen said. According to Jewish custom, the time of Mrs. Bergman's death did make things a little easier for Ellen, for her mother died just before the Sabbath. Had she died on the Sabbath, Ellen would have needed to ask the Palliative Care Service not to allow anyone in the room for 24 hours.

5

Frances Legendre
The Price of a Death of One's Own

Narrated by ANNA TOWERS

Frances Legendre was accustomed to being in control. When she came to the Palliative Care Unit suffering from advanced ovarian cancer, she was prepared to die. She exuded acceptance and calm, and she drew her family and the palliative care staff into her plans and images of eternity. But Mrs. Legendre did not die then, and a few weeks later, convinced that it was not yet her time, she launched into a relentless effort to find a cure. She insisted that her oncologists enroll her—against their own judgment—in high-risk experimental treatments, and the palliative care team found itself advocating more aggressive care for their patient. When all the treatments failed, Mrs. Legendre came back to the Palliative Care Unit to die again. This time she and her family wanted the end to come quickly, peacefully, *now*.

Beginnings

Frances Legendre was 51 years old when she learned she had cancer. At that time, she was a businesswoman and housewife, married to Jacques Legendre. Like Frances, Jacques was French Canadian, 57 years old, and a wealthy and successful businessman for 30 years. The Legendres had traveled widely. They had four daughters who lived in Montreal, Paris, and the Bahamas. Mr. and

Mrs. Legendre usually spent winters in the Bahamas, the rest of the year enjoying their home a few miles outside Montreal. Mr. Legendre had built the house for their retirement, as a gift to his wife. The tall, majestic, Mediterranean-style villa stood overlooking the fields and hills of the Quebec countryside, flower-filled gardens, and a manmade lake. Mr. Legendre had also built a fountain in the garden calling it their wishing well. The home reminded them of Italy, where they had lived for a few years—the best time of her life, Mrs. Legendre recalled.

When she first visited her doctor, complaining of lower abdominal pain, he told her that she had "a little cyst on the ovary." While she was initially reassured, the pains persisted. Her doctor reexamined her and again found nothing of great concern. Nonetheless, Mrs. Legendre couldn't understand why the pain was there all the time, and eventually her doctor ordered more extensive tests. By the time these tests revealed the ovarian cancer, two years had passed since her initial diagnosis of a benign cyst. The news was a terrible shock, but Mrs. Legendre had already known that the pain she was having meant that something must be seriously wrong.

The cancer was already quite advanced, and experimental therapy was all that was available. The couple decided to pursue any treatment that might give her even the slightest chance of remission. It didn't matter how expensive the treatment was or how difficult it might be to find it. The Legendres had resolved to try all possibilities and to pursue all odds. "I wanted to fight," Mrs. Legendre said. "I am still a young woman. My life is wonderful. I have a good husband, wonderful children. They all did well and there is so much love in our family. I have a young grandson, everything to live for. I felt cheated. I wanted to keep my good life."

"Something might work!"

Although the experimental drug paclitaxel resulted in a slight remission, this lasted only two months, and Mrs. Legendre's tumor progressed. At that point, Mrs. Legendre said, she felt "cheated and mad that my life was being taken from me." She and her husband pressed on with their determined search for a cure, only now they felt that they were alone in their mission, for her doctors were offering no more treatments. Mrs. Legendre interpreted this as a loss of interest in her and a withdrawal of support. "We had to take matters into our own hands and think up answers on our own," Mr. Legendre said. They did their own research, pored over New Age–type journals, and sent away for literature described in the advertisements. They sought out unpublished information by word of mouth. At times during their quest they felt they were being taken advantage of, Mr. Legendre said, by people who were "probably making a lot of money by giving out 'recipes' to cure cancer." But they were prepared to pay anything, and besides, Mrs. Legendre asked, "what choice did we have?"

They tried organic foods, nutritional formulas, home remedies, vitamin therapy, herbal remedies. But trying to find a successful alternative cure proved frustrating, expensive, and painful. One Chinese herbal remedy, a blend of 170 herbs, proposed, as Mrs. Legendre recalled, that "it could make the tumor melt." It didn't work and it was costly—$300 "under the table." But whenever there was even a chance, the Legendres would find the money. After all, they said, "something might work!"

After several weeks and many thousands of dollars, Mrs. Legendre began to feel sick again and she was in intense pain. All the treatments, of whatever type and from whatever source, had ultimately failed to stop her cancer. It appeared that there were no other options. When Dr. Singer, her oncologist, examined her, he found that the tumor had grown and had spread into her liver. "I'm sorry," he told her, "but your sickness is now at a very advanced stage." "I'm not ready to die," she answered, "what do you have to offer me?" But he had no other suggestions for stopping the growth of the tumor. Moreover, the side effects of the experimental drugs had made her feel sicker than she could ever remember. At that point, Mrs. Legendre gave up trying. "I knew I had to stop," she recalled later. "I wanted to live, but I just couldn't take feeling sick."

"That's the beginning of the end, you know"

In the fall of 1995 the Legendres returned to their home in the Bahamas. Over the next few weeks Mrs. Legendre's abdominal pain intensified. Dr. Singer had prepared her for the symptoms that were to come: "you are now in the terminal phase, first the bowel, then your stomach gets hard like a rock, you have nausea and your stomach is not able to process food anymore." He prescribed morphine for her pain, but Mrs. Legendre was reluctant to take it. She was like many patients with advanced cancer who resist taking pain medication as a way to stave off the reality that their disease has progressed. To take the medication was to admit that the pain was getting worse. To admit that the pain was getting worse was to admit that the cancer was getting worse. And to admit the cancer was getting worse was to begin to look into the face of death. Mr. Legendre, relieved that at least something could be done for his wife's pain, argued with her. "Why suffer?" he would ask. "It's there for you." Mrs. Legendre took the morphine but thought to herself, "Well, that's the beginning of the end, you know."

The morphine Dr. Singer had prescribed was not enough to control her pain. He suggested to the Legendres that they return to Canada where services to manage her pain and other distressing symptoms would be more readily available. At the end of December, Mrs. Legendre flew back to Montreal, accompanied by her daughter Lily. She arrived at the hospital's emergency department late on a Saturday afternoon, certain that the end was near.

When Dr. Raymond, a physician from the Palliative Care Service, met Mrs. Legendre for the first time, she was lying on a stretcher in the emergency department, with Lily sitting beside her. Dr. Raymond could see immediately that Mrs. Legendre was in pain and that she had a look of panic in her eyes. He had already spoken with Dr. Singer and the resident in the emergency department, who had told him that Mrs. Legendre had small bowel obstruction. The disease was too far advanced for her to safely have surgery to relieve the obstruction. Dr. Raymond knew that there was a 50% chance that the obstruction might resolve on its own or with the help of steroid medication, only to recur again within a couple of months. In the worst-case scenario, if things did not improve now, she would not be able to nourish herself, and she would probably die within a few weeks.

Though he was a young man, Dr. Raymond was an experienced palliative care physician. He had seen many patients die under these circumstances, and it was hard for him, even though he knew he could control his patients' pain. He thought it was probably easier caring for soldiers at the front in wartime than caring for a patient who was alert and aware, knowing she was starving to death, because at least he would not have come to know the soldiers as intimately as his patients on the Palliative Care Unit (PCU). No matter how much experience you had with dying persons, Dr. Raymond had once said, and no matter how much could be done to relieve their distress, "When people are dying, for those last days and hours and minutes, you must be close to them in a human and very compassionate way. And sometimes there can be three or four deaths in the space of one or two days. You get to be with the families, you are closely involved in the lives of those families, and there is a relationship that is highly significant for them and for you."

At that moment, however, Dr. Raymond's responsibility was to reassure Mrs. Legendre. What could he offer her? Seeing how panicked she was, Dr. Raymond guessed that Mrs. Legendre expected to die within a few days. In fact, the actual time of her death was almost impossible to predict. "You know," he said to her, "I don't work for any psychic alliance, but in my experience I've learned one thing: I cannot make predictions. I've also learned that for people who are quite sure when they will die, very often life will do something else." At the moment, he continued, there was much he could do to make her more comfortable. Dr. Raymond arranged immediately for Mrs. Legendre to be admitted to the Palliative Care Unit and ordered adequate morphine for her pain and intravenous dexamethasone and metoclopramide to try to get her intestines working again.

"I am going to a beautiful place"

People seemed kind and friendly on the PCU. Her nurse, Ena, settled Mrs. Legendre into a bright, sunny room. The 16 rooms on the unit are especially designed to be cheerful and bright with pastel-colored furnishings, homespun-style bedcovers and blankets, and brightly colored curtains. Mrs. Legendre's room was situated at one end of a carpeted hallway. At the other end was a small kitchen and dining area where families and friends could cook and visit if they liked. Near the kitchen was a spacious carpeted lounge with colorful easy chairs, floral-covered sofas, coffee tables, and a large grand piano that occupied a central space. The lounge looked out onto a large woodland area and provided an impressive aerial view of the city. Mrs. Legendre felt good here. It wasn't like the hospital wards she had experienced before. In fact, "it wasn't really like a hospital at all," she said. "People had time."

It was at this point, in early January 1996 and just a few days after her admission, that I met Mrs. Legendre. Dr. Raymond had explained our project to her, and she was very open to participating in it. The Legendres told me about their earlier experiences with Mrs. Legendre's illness and the events that had led to her present admission to the PCU.

When I first saw her, she was sitting up in bed, propped up by colorful pillows and dressed in a floral pink nightgown. I thought there was a radiance about her. Her pain was now under control. She seemed vivacious and happy. She looked like a strong, well-built woman, and her tanned and ruddy complexion made her appear younger and much healthier than she actually was. She laughed often, and even when she was serious, her eyes twinkled as though she were ready to break out into laughter.

Mr. Legendre was sitting on the bed holding Mrs. Legendre's hand. He was a rather short, strong-looking man. His sunburnt, weather-beaten complexion led one to think that he worked outdoors a lot. He was a quiet man who didn't smile or laugh as much as his wife. Whereas Mrs. Legendre chatted animatedly and easily, Mr. Legendre looked at the floor when he spoke or just simply stared ahead. He often seemed thoughtful, sometimes hesitating before answering a question. His slightly drawn face often showed sadness and concern when the conversation revolved around his wife's illness. When Mrs. Legendre seemed to be in pain, he would rub her back or massage the back of her neck and shoulders. They often sat together just holding hands.

The day I first met the Legendres the atmosphere in the room felt warm and serene. Mrs. Legendre's family had brought in pillows, bedcovers, pictures, and mementos from home, as all families on the Palliative Care Unit were encouraged to do. The Legendres, however, had gone further than most families; they filled the walls with family photographs, scenic posters, religious pictures, and

Catholic icons, such as a small statue of the Virgin Mary and a Crucifix that they hung over the bed. They brought fresh flowers and pictures of the sacred heart of Jesus. A large photograph of the Legendres' grandson, André, stood on the night table.

André was the eight-year-old son of the Legendres' daughter Josée, who spent much of her time in Europe. Despite the long distance between them, André occupied a very special place in his grandmother's life. This may have been because the Legendres had lost a son in infancy, and when André was born it was as if their loss had been made good. Mrs. Legendre saw herself as one of André's teachers, a source of special wisdom and experience for him. Both of them were always excited to see each other.

Pinned onto the back of Mrs. Legendre's door was a large, poster-sized map of the Milky Way with several red stickers on it in the shape of stars. Periodically a new red sticker would appear on the map, and after awhile I saw that the map was quite full of stickers, each with someone's name written on it. For her the map "had a very special purpose," which was clearly connected to her death. The map showed the constellations of the stars, and the red stickers being added represented all the people who were surrounding her. "Those people will always be close, we will always be running in the same constellation . . . so we cannot say death is the end, but the beginning of something," she explained. After my third visit, Mrs. Legendre asked me to take a red sticker from her night table, put my name on it, and place it on the map.

Mrs. Legendre told me that she was ready to die. Why did she look so bright and happy? "Because I am going to a beautiful place," she explained. "There is a place I am close to in Italy called Monte Stelle—'Monte' for the mountain and 'Stelle' for the star—and between the two peaks of the mountain, there is a bright, bright star." She believed that her soul "would go and get installed on that bright star" and that every time people thought of her she would be glistening there. That is how she would remain close to her loved ones.

Mrs. Legendre never talked about having any formal religious beliefs, though she did talk about prayer and how it comforted her. The beliefs she expressed were an eclectic mix of traditional Catholicism, in keeping with the religious adornments in her room, and personal and idiosyncratic ideas, such as when she spoke about becoming a shining star in the galaxy. She spoke with assurance, firmly believing that what she had worked out in her mind was true for both herself and all people. For the Legendre family her beliefs also rang true. The family had asked their mother "to give a code or something" so they could be in touch when she had gone. "That's where my mother came out with this most extraordinary plan," Lily said, referring to the map of the galaxy and to all the named stickers surrounding her star. "My mother is going to come back and watch over us, so you see she will always be with us. I feel very comfortable with the idea of my mother visiting all of us after she dies, and I don't doubt it."

André told the Palliative Care Unit psychologist that he would be able to keep a spiritual contact with his grandmother by means of a star (as well as through a pendant she had given to him, which he would keep forever as a symbol of their close bond). Lily added, "It would give continuity. You know that saying—'in the world, something is created, nothing is destroyed . . . matter can be transformed but never destroyed.'"

Acceptance or denial?

Mrs. Legendre's doctors, nurses, and other caregivers did not know how to interpret her beliefs and her way of preparing for death. They were grappling with a challenge in caring for Mrs. Legendre that was, as in the care of many palliative care patients, more confusing and complicated than the management of her physical symptoms. How should they respond to Mrs. Legendre's serene and calm acceptance of imminent death? Her attitude was particularly puzzling to some of the staff because it abruptly followed the Legendres' ferocious pursuit of a cure. Were the staff witnessing a profound transformation in Mrs. Legendre's attitudes and outlook, or was her serenity a façade? Should they attempt to probe beneath the surface in case Mrs. Legendre was denying her true situation?

Whatever their private suspicions, outwardly the team fully supported Mrs. Legendre's needs and wishes. More and more stickers appeared on her galaxy map, most being placed there by caregivers. A nurse or volunteer might give Mrs. Legendre a special bit of help on a particular day, and as that person was leaving Mrs. Legendre would ask, "Have you put your star there yet?" To my knowledge, no person declined. Some caregivers went even further, adding their own creative contributions to Mrs. Legendre's beliefs—one of the volunteers found a poem about the constellation of the stars; the music therapist found a song called "There is a Star for You." Ena was quite convinced of the reality of her patient's plan. "She has a remarkably strong faith," Ena said. Without exception friends, family members, and all the other caregivers added their own personal stars to the map.

While Dr. Raymond also wanted to support Mrs. Legendre, his past experience as a palliative care physician made him cautious. Her dying was almost too easy. Everything was planned out, and he saw no sign of any sadness or regret that her illness was now truly terminal. Why the sudden change to full acceptance of dying? He thought it was important to "really listen attentively to what was happening" and asked the psychologist to have a talk with Mrs. Legendre.

The psychologist described the patient as "healthy with a good outlook" on her coming death. Her notes from this visit read:

> She has a very special spiritual way of seeing her death. We rarely hear and witness this particular kind of rapport with death. There is a mixture of strength, peace, joy, poetry, realistic, and idealistic views. This kind of view is difficult to share as some people automatically expect to experience suffering in the process of saying good-bye.

Nonetheless, Dr. Raymond was concerned, for there was something that didn't quite fit for him. It was hard to accept Mrs. Legendre's sudden readiness to die, when only a few days ago, with her pain under control, it had seemed so important to her to enjoy life.

To the Legendre family, the relief of Mrs. Legendre's pain and the security of being on the Palliative Care Unit had given Mrs. Legendre a special opportunity to organize her death. Indeed, Mrs. Legendre said that she felt "secure and safe now." She envisioned the afterlife as another dimension to the life she was leading now, but first she had to prepare for her death properly. "I'm the one who has to control and organize my death before going to the other dimensions of my life," she explained. The pastoral counselor who visited with Mrs. Legendre heard her express these thoughts, and he, too, wondered if Mrs. Legendre was not *too* organized." He would have expected more uncertainty, more grappling with the unknown, or at least some signs of sadness at the prospect of saying final good-byes. On the other hand, he said, "She was a manager in her own life and she was managing death as though she were managing her own business."

This was the palliative care team's first encounter with Mrs. Legendre's intense need for control. It would not be their last.

Going home again

A month passed and Mrs. Legendre did not die. It was now the first week of February 1996. She had begun to drink and then eat more, and her intestinal obstruction slowly resolved. Although she sometimes complained of pain, this was usually alleviated by morphine in varying dosages. She was comfortable enough to receive many visits from friends and family, and when she was alone she was usually chatting, often laughing, on the telephone. During a one-hour visit I made, the phone rang at least five times. While everyone seemed to like her company and it was easy to be with her, we felt as though we were all waiting with her for death to happen.

Occasionally Mrs. Legendre would cry, and she told the psychologist that she sometimes felt depressed. The psychologist's notes continue:

We explored the fact that one can face death with trust, or healthy curiosity, and at the same time be in touch with sadness and fear. She is now in a slow process of negotiating contradictions within herself in facing the final phase. She is afraid to go back home, which in her mind represents going back to life, and again, in her mind, being here means preparation for dying, as if she would practice the act of dying ahead of time.

Ordinarily, however, Mrs. Legendre almost never talked about dying. She seemed relatively well in comparison to other patients on the unit. The volunteer who visited her said, "It's not her time yet." Mr. Legendre said, "She wants it to happen now, just now, but maybe it's up to God." Her daughters Yvonne and Lily began to feel the strain of waiting for their mother's death while also enjoying the time they still had with her. "It's hard," Lily told me at this time. "We are waiting in one way, but we don't want her to leave. We want to know she's happy and we're happy for her." She paused. "But we're feeling it, you know?"

One day, toward the middle of the month, Dr. Raymond went to see his patient to tell her he would be going away from the unit for a week. "I won't be here when you get back," Mrs. Legendre responded. Dr. Raymond interpreted his patient's absolute prediction of the time of her death as a defense on her part against the excruciating uncertainty of her situation. He tried to convince her that, in truth, she was not dying that fast. "Loss of control is terrible," he reflected later. "You need to be able to make plans even if it is to die. It's very difficult to abandon that." Dr. Raymond thought that Mrs. Legendre's map and all the names on the red stars were an effort to guarantee a sense of organization and control. He did not press this interpretation on her, however, and left shortly after for a week's break.

When I talked with Mrs. Legendre during the week that Dr. Raymond was away, she didn't seem quite as radiant and spontaneous as before. She still smiled, but it seemed to be an effort. Mrs. Legendre missed Dr. Raymond's presence on the unit, even it if was only for a week. She remembered his talk with her before he left and she seemed to be thinking about it. "Dr. Raymond understands me," she said. Moreover, she trusted him. He was "human and kind" with a "good philosophy;" he was "a very extraordinary man."

A naturally open and sociable woman, she had started to get to know some of the other patients and their families. "I feel sorry for them," she said, "to see them suffer, and you feel bad for the families." The unit was busier than usual; there had been 21 deaths on the unit in the past 17 days. Gentle crying, sometimes sobbing could be heard in the hallway not too far from Mrs. Legendre's room.

When Dr. Raymond returned, Mrs. Legendre informed him that she had thought her situation over. "It is not time to die yet," she said. She wanted to go home. Even though everyone on the unit was wonderful and kind, it had been a very hard few days seeing so many families lose a loved one. "Maybe it isn't my time yet," she repeated. "Maybe He is not ready for me yet."

On February 20, Mrs. Legendre returned to her home in the Bahamas. I spoke to her on the telephone from time to time over the next several weeks, and she sounded active and happy, "busy driving my car and enjoying the ocean." Dr. Raymond kept in close touch with the Legendres and observed, "She doesn't see herself as sick anymore. The last time I talked to her she was giggling, laughing, busy in her house, doing her household chores."

Mrs. Legendre began to talk again about treatment to arrest her cancer. The Palliative Care Unit was far from her thoughts now, though she still relied heavily on Dr. Raymond's support. In her mind she had moved into a new and different place and it was as if I, and our project, had become part of an old memory. Her talks with me were still enthusiastic but they were now totally centered on pursuing the means to live "by any way possible." She laughed a lot during our conversations. "My tummy is full of tumor," she said. "I look nine months pregnant and my feet are swollen." But she felt good. "The morphine is working!"

"Dying a third time"

While Mrs. Legendre was in the Bahamas, she and her husband learned from a television documentary program that a new "vaccine" for arresting tumor spread had been discovered. While the vaccine was still in its experimental stages, the Legendres heard that it could be available within six months. Mrs. Legendre wanted that vaccine. She was going to fight for her life.

In May, Mrs. Legendre came back to her home in Quebec and immediately contacted Dr. Singer to get information about the vaccine. He offered to find out what he could. At the same time, he contacted Dr. Raymond, who was still managing Mrs. Legendre's symptoms. Mrs. Legendre was experiencing more abdominal pain and swelling in her legs. Dr. Raymond suggested a readmission to the Palliative Care Unit. Mrs. Legendre agreed to go back to the unit to try to relieve her symptoms, but she still wanted to pursue information regarding the new treatment. At least she might get one more winter in the Bahamas and she could spend most of it with her young grandson, André.

Mrs. Legendre returned to the unit on May 18, and Dr. Singer and Dr. Raymond began to work as a team. Dr. Singer was experimenting with a new cytotoxic chemotherapy agent and he arranged for Mrs. Legendre to receive the drug. Dr. Raymond continued to try to manage her symptoms, using large experimental doses of diuretics to try to relieve her massive leg and abdominal swelling. Although the swelling was reduced, her pain got worse. It was unclear whether this was a side effect of the chemotherapy or whether it was from growth of her tumor. Whatever the reason, her symptoms became very difficult to manage at this point. She vomited and suffered intense abdominal pain that her nurse Ena described as "horrible to watch." Ena would go into her room to find her screaming, crying, holding onto her stomach. All Ena could do was to sit with her, rub her abdomen or back, or apply a heating pad. She felt helpless. Mrs. Legendre would look up appreciatively through her pain, thankful that Ena was there. Later she would smile and even laugh in spite of her pain, saying, "I don't care what it takes. Something is still being done."

Jean, the volunteer who had worked with Mrs. Legendre, also noticed an air of defiance, even joy, despite Mrs. Legendre's symptoms. For example, when Jean saw that the room was no longer elaborately decorated with the posters and the map of the galaxy, and asked Mrs. Legendre where the decorations were, Mrs. Legendre replied, "Well, I'm not going to die, so I know I'll go back home and so I don't need to decorate."

Dr. Raymond not only cooperated with Dr. Singer in managing Mrs. Legendre's symptoms, he also often took Mrs. Legendre's side in urging Dr. Singer to continue an aggressive treatment plan, sensing how much it meant to her to feel she was actively fighting her disease.

Dr. Raymond's willingness to work closely with Dr. Singer while Mrs. Legendre fought fiercely against her cancer highlights an important distinction between supportive, or palliative, care and hospice care. Although these terms are commonly used interchangeably, for many people, *hospice care* is care that is directed solely toward relieving symptoms at the very end of life. It is incompatible with the fierce struggle to prolong life with the sort of aggressive treatments Mrs. Legendre was receiving. Many hospice programs are resistant to patients' efforts to fight their disease, both for philosophical reasons (e.g., it is better to "accept" death) and for economic ones (in the United States, for example, reimbursement for hospice care typically requires patients to forego treatments intended to be curative). The model of *supportive care* that Dr. Raymond was following did not make such a rigid distinction, which in the real world is rarely as clear-cut as some hospice policies and philosophies would suppose. He was prepared to apply his expertise at symptom control and psychological and spiritual support according to where his patient was in her own struggle in coming to terms with her disease.

This approach permitted Mrs. Legendre to benefit from palliative and active treatment simultaneously. But everyone paid a price for this tactic. Mrs. Legendre paid in the form of her intense suffering, though at this point it was a price she was willing to pay. Dr. Raymond and the others on the palliative care team had to witness Mrs. Legendre's suffering, which they believed would prove futile in the long run, while trying to support and encourage her in every way possible. Furthermore, they had to do this without eliminating the tension between the goals and effects of active treatment and palliative care. Instead of firmly choosing one course over the other, they had to remain on the boundary between the two, experiencing the intense ambivalence inherent to Mrs. Legendre's situation.

Mrs. Legendre saw what was happening to those around her. "I know Ena doesn't want me to suffer and I know my family doesn't want to see it and I know it hurts my husband," she told me, "but I want to take this drug as long as they will give it. I want to take up all possibilities [of experimentation] and the doctors do have them."

Ena felt a special closeness to her patient. She felt she understood her and wanted to protect her. Yet it often took a special effort for Ena not to react personally to Mrs. Legendre's anger, especially when, in the last few weeks of her life, Mrs. Legendre became very demanding and short-tempered. One day, as Mrs. Legendre asked Ena to help her into the bathroom, Mrs. Legendre looked up at her and asked, "Are all your patients like me?" "What do you mean?" Ena replied. "Oh," Mrs. Legendre said, "demanding." Ena answered, "You're not demanding. You're going through a rough time. And everyone is different." As far as Ena was concerned her own reactions were beside the point, even though she was fully aware of just how angry and demanding Mrs. Legendre had become. "I never let her feel that I felt that," Ena recalled. "Because I don't know how I would feel to be dying a third time."

Sometimes Mrs. Legendre expressed anger and frustration toward her doctors, feeling that they had been too hesitant to prescribe or search out more experimental therapies. When further treatments were not immediately forthcoming, she sometimes expressed a feeling of injustice. She "felt abandoned," she claimed, and "not listened to." One day she complained bitterly to me, "I feel like they [doctors] don't give a damn for me. I'm here to die and that's it and so let's pass to the next one."

One day Mrs. Legendre asked Dr. Singer why he had not responded to her request for treatment earlier. "Why do you turn your back on me?" she said. When he tried to explain to Mrs. Legendre how risky any further treatments were in light of her very advanced disease, she replied, "I know I'm a bad risk . . . but I'm just 54 years old . . . You see, I have the energy inside. I have to stop those tumors." Then she told Dr. Singer, "You know what? My ashes will turn around on you if I die and the day after they discover something good for tumors!"

Mr. Legendre also paid a price for his wife's determination to fight. One day early in June I saw him crying openly in the hallway as he walked toward the elevators. He stopped for a moment to say, "You shouldn't go into her room right now. My wife is very bad, to watch her suffer like that, to look in her face, it is too difficult." Watching his wife scream out in pain was unbearable; he couldn't stay in the room. He would come back later.

The physicians did not know whether the increased pain was related to the chemotherapy. However, the patient, family, and the other staff believed that there was a link.

Later that same day Mr. Legendre reflected more on his wife's condition. Her choice to put herself through the anguish and pain she was suffering puzzled him. "I don't know why she has to go on suffering, she's been through so much already," he said. "You just go on watching her suffer, but she doesn't want to give up." He went on, "She's a strong woman, and always very determined. But I don't know why she wants to go through all this . . . too much suffering . . . it's not human."

Ena suggested that Mr. Legendre stay home during the day, and be with his wife at night. Mrs. Legendre was often afraid at night, and was comforted by her husband's presence. At the same time she also slept more then and so Mr. Legendre would not have to witness as much of her agony.

Meanwhile, Dr. Raymond was observing his patient closely and trying to manage her pain the best he could. He felt that her pain was more than physical, that she had "total anguish" as she now truly faced the reality of dying. In addition, Mrs. Legendre had always been a woman to whom physical appearance was important. It was very difficult for her to accept the swelling and the other physical changes that were occurring. Mrs. Legendre had been able to share some of her feelings with Dr. Raymond: "She was feeling more and more disfigured," Dr. Raymond recalled, "and that was very difficult for her." At the same time, she continued to have hopes of remission. But the treatments did not work.

Trying to control the end

On June 14 Mrs. Legendre went home for a short period, but she had to come back to the Palliative Care Unit two weeks later because of her steadily worsening abdominal pain and the swelling in her legs. When I went to see her on the unit this time, a sign on her door confronted me: "No Visitors Please. Please Ask the Primary Nurse." I requested to see Mrs. Legendre when I saw Linda, her nurse for that day. Linda knew Mrs. Legendre well, often taking care of her when Ena was away. Linda said that Mrs. Legendre was not doing well. Her breathing was more difficult now, and she needed oxygen most of the time.

"She seems to have given up this time around," Linda added. "She's different—not so feisty, and it's like she feels there's no hope anymore. She's not fighting." Mr. Legendre was finding it hard also, Linda said. "He feels there is very little hope, and that waiting there, just waiting, is long and painful." Linda mentioned that Mr. Legendre was talking about selling their house in the Bahamas and tidying up their affairs—an indication to me that Mr. Legendre, who had not spoken of these matters before, had also given up the fight.

I knocked gently on Mrs. Legendre's door and entered the room. The walls were nearly bare, so different from the richly adorned walls I had seen seven months ago. There were no decorations from home: no pictures or photographs, no map or stars—nothing except some pictures the unit provided. The room was large, bright, and spacious, but at that moment it seemed clinical and lifeless. There was something forlorn and lonely about the woman who lay flat on the bed with her eyes closed, breathing quietly with oxygen prongs in her nose. After a few moments Mrs. Legendre opened her eyes and looked at me. "It's no good," she said. "I'm not going to make it this time. This is it. They couldn't do it. They couldn't get me the drugs. There's nothing left for me . . . no hope." She pointed to her stomach. "I can feel the tumor here. I can feel it pressing. It's pressing on my chest and I'm having trouble breathing. I just don't think I can go on like this anymore."

Mrs. Legendre was very weak now, and almost completely bedbound. The woman who took such pride in her clothing and elegant bedwear was now in a standard hospital gown for ease of nursing care. Though her physicians were able to control her pain, she began to have periods when she would lose complete control of her bowel functions. According to her husband, this had happened "not once but four times and it was totally unacceptable to her, an absolute affront to her dignity." She continued to have swelling in her legs and abdomen and her breathing was difficult despite the oxygen.

Mrs. Legendre began to talk openly about wanting her doctors to help her die. On July 8, she asked Dr. Clermont, a fellow in training on the Palliative Care Unit, to give her something to end her life. Dr. Clermont explained that he was unable to do that. Euthanasia was illegal, and beyond that, Mrs. Legendre was so weak at this point that it was not possible to have an extended conversation with her. Even if euthanasia were legal it would be wrong to accede to her request with so little opportunity to explore its meanings and ramifications with her. What Dr. Clermont could offer, however, was to help her sleep comfortably, so she would not suffer.

This was not good enough for Mrs. Legendre. She had made another decision. She told Linda, "I'm as good as dead. I want them to give me something so I can go now." Just as she had decided to fight for her life despite all the odds, and before that, to take her leave and settle among the stars, now she had decided the fight was over and it was time to die—now.

Sedation or euthanasia?

For the next 10 days Mrs. Legendre fluctuated between demands for immediate action to help her die and equally fervent hopes that chemotherapy would extend her life. In the last week of July, Dr. Raymond had to be absent from the unit, and Dr. Thompson, another palliative care physician, took over Mrs. Legendre's care. It was not unusual for the palliative care physicians to take care of patients in each other's absence, as they took care to be informed and familiar with each other's patients. Dr. Thompson was an experienced palliative care physician who had cared for people with terminal illnesses for many years. Patients and families liked her and expressed confidence in her. She was easy for the Legendres to talk to—"caring, a good listener, kind. You felt secure with her," Mr. Legendre later recalled.

Dr. Thompson got to know the Legendres over a period of a few days. During this time Mrs. Legendre's breathing had become worse. Dr. Thompson believed that this was probably due to pulmonary emboli. She formed the opinion that Mrs. Legendre would probably not live more than another week or two. Dr. Thompson also felt that when Mrs. Legendre said, "This is it, I can't take it anymore," she was expressing her frustration, the affront to her dignity caused by the loss of control of her bowels, and the anxiety of her increasing shortness of breath. Mrs. Legendre had not asked Dr. Thompson directly for help to die, though she had readily agreed to Dr. Thompson's suggestion that she be made to sleep so she would not experience respiratory distress or anxiety. Dr. Thompson's offer was to provide Mrs. Legendre with "terminal sedation," which was not the same as complying with her earlier request to Dr. Clermont to just "end it." Dr. Thompson could give Mrs. Legendre the drug midazolam and maintain her in a state of sleep from which she could be aroused, if necessary, to permit further interaction with her family, though only if she could tolerate being awake without an increase in suffering from her symptoms.

Dr. Thompson discussed her plan with Mr. Legendre and the Legendres' daughters, Lily and Yvonne, on August 2. Dr. Thompson confronted directly their fears that their mother was suffering intolerably and their belief that Mrs. Legendre now wanted to die immediately. Dr. Thompson explained that she herself had not received a specific request from Mrs. Legendre to do anything beyond helping her sleep. She related to the family that Dr. Clermont had received such a request, and explained why Dr. Clermont believed he could not agree to it. Dr. Thompson also observed that, while there certainly appeared to have been some days when Mrs. Legendre was so frustrated by her struggle that she just wanted to give up and have it all come to an end, there were other times when she still hoped to gain a little more time to live.

Mr. Legendre said he found it very hard to witness his wife's discomfort. There were some very difficult times, he believed, when euthanasia was the best possible course of action. He remembered, in relation to other family members, when it would have been best for them if they hadn't been forced to stay alive. (In Mr. Legendre's mind, refusing to grant his wife's request for euthanasia seemed to be the same as "forcing her to stay alive.") Both he and Mrs. Legendre had watched her mother and father being kept alive by artificial tubes even though there was no hope for recovery. "That was totally unnecessary suffering," he said; "it was not human."

Dr. Thompson explained that the medicines they would give Mrs. Legendre would keep her comfortably sedated so that she would not suffer from either respiratory distress or general anguish. Yet the sedatives would allow for her to wake up at any time so she would be able to communicate with her loved ones. She wouldn't be unconscious or so heavily sedated that she could not awaken. It might still be possible in a good, comfortable moment to have a brief conversation with one of her loved ones, perhaps to speak some last thoughts. It allowed for any of her family to say things they needed to say to her.

Mr. Legendre and his daughters agreed to the sedation, though they were adamant that Mrs. Legendre not suffer. Mr. Legendre was especially concerned about the possibility of his wife's choking when her last hours came. Even if it were only for two seconds, he said, that was really her worst worry. Dr. Raymond had assured Mr. Legendre that they could almost certainly prevent that from happening, and Dr. Thompson repeated this reassurance now. She said she would go ahead and give Mrs. Legendre the midazolam. It would guarantee a comfortable sleep, although if needed, Mrs. Legendre could be awakened.

The last hours of life

Mrs. Legendre's physical condition rapidly deteriorated over the next two days. She became more short of breath, so Dr. Thompson increased the frequency of the midazolam from every six hours to every four hours. Her daughters, Yvonne, Lily, and Marie traveled from their respective homes to be at their mother's bedside. Mr. Legendre was there all the time. They sat together in Mrs. Legendre's room for hours. They brought food and warmed it in the kitchen. They tried to relax in the lounge, where they met other people going through a similar experience. As Marie recalled to me later, it sometimes just helped to talk to someone who was "going through the same kind of sorrow." Mr. Legendre telephoned their fourth daughter, Josée, at her home in Paris and told her of the gravity of her mother's condition. Josée arranged to travel to Montreal as soon as she could.

On August 4, Dr. Thompson came to Mrs. Legendre's bedside and found her sleeping peacefully. Her breathing had been made easier with the drug hyoscine, which helped to reduce the secretions in her upper respiratory tract. Lily was at the foot of the bed and seemed relaxed. Mrs. Legendre's brother came to say goodbye. Now all the family were there except for Josée, who was delayed on the last part of her journey from Paris. Josée had telephoned and said she would make it to the hospital within the next two hours. Mrs. Legendre had asked for Josée several times in the last days. Mr. Legendre moved closer to his wife and said, "Try and wait. Hang in. Stick with it. Josée is on her way. She just called me." But his wife couldn't wait any more. She shook her head. "I can't wait," she said, and died a few minutes later.

The family stayed in the room with Mrs. Legendre's body for about three hours after she died. Josée arrived during this time. "It was not painful to see her dead," Mr. Legendre recalled. "She had a smile on her face. She always had that same smile on her face, even after she had gone."

Looking back

I spoke with members of Mrs. Legendre's family several times in the months following her death. Despite their uncertainties about Mrs. Legendre's wishes for euthanasia, and the periods of great suffering she endured during her last fight against her disease, the family expressed genuine satisfaction and gratitude for the way Mrs. Legendre had died. To Mr. Legendre, his wife had died in a way that was ideal. "She died the way I'd like to go," he said to me: dying in the company of all one's loved ones and surrounded by kind and caring people as his wife had been "would be a good way to go." He felt that at the end his wife had not suffered as her father had, which had been one of their greatest fears. "The way they were doing things [on the Palliative Care Unit], that was good for her and good, 100%, for us. You know people are going to die anyway when they are there. They are ready for it. I knew my wife was going to die . . . even about eight days before. But to take such good care, right up to the last moment of death like that, it was marvelous."

In another conversation months later, when Josée was also present, Mr. Legendre returned to the same theme. Having the palliative care support "was a big thing for us," he said. There was a difference, he thought, between dying in a hospital and dying on the unit. "Because on the Palliative Care Unit," he explained, "you know what happens and the moment, almost the moment, that it happens. You don't panic because you know what will happen ahead of time from the people who are specially trained to do the job. It is an enormous help. Maybe as a family, yes, you are suffering [because you are losing somebody], but with that support, you are sure everything will go well."

Mr. Legendre also reminded me of Mrs. Legendre's wishes and plans for life after death. She had made her last plans calmly and without fear, he said. Mrs. Legendre had wanted to be cremated. She wanted to have her ashes in Italy, close to Monte Stelle, the mountain she had often spoken about when she first came to the Palliative Care Unit. "That's what I did," Mr. Legendre said. "I took her ashes to Italy and I put them there. Everything was orchestrated to be like that."

She knew exactly what would happen, he continued, and it was clear that at the very end she had no fear. "She gave that big smile, a beautiful smile, and that's how it stayed," he concluded. "She died the way I'd like to go when I die. Because I'll die with all my people around me, the way she did. And I'll be looking at them and saying goodbye."

6

Shamira Cook
"Who Am I?"

Narrated by YANNA LAMBRINIDOU

Most hospice patients in the United States are white members of the middle class, even in communities with ethnically and socioeconomically diverse populations. To some extent, this results from Medicare's requirement that at least 80% of hospice days be spent at home, with a primary care provider available. People of poorer economic means are less likely to have the flexibility to meet this requirement when a patient is critically ill, or even to have the stable housing arrangements hospice programs prefer. Many African-American patients, in particular, may be mistrustful of the hospice approach if it appears that beneficial, life-prolonging treatment might be withheld.

Shamira Cook was a 34-year-old African-American woman who was not only terminally ill but also a single mother with a history of heroin addiction. Her social situation, attitudes toward her cancer, and life history posed great challenges to her hospice team. Her desire to fight her disease at all costs provoked tension within the team and aggravated long-standing conflicts with her daughter. Yet, Ms. Cook felt that she was on an urgent mission, which made it impossible for her to give in to her cancer despite its physical and mental toll.

"I got clean to die"

Shamira Cook had been a heroin addict from the time she was 13. By the age of 33, her dilapidated group home in western Pennsylvania had turned into a crack house. She had been incarcerated several times. Her 12-year-old daughter, Rowena, would hide every time she heard the police. Finally, Ms. Cook had had enough. She moved to Lancaster County, placed Rowena in foster care, and entered a drug rehabilitation program. In February 1996, she walked out clean. She got a job at a convenience store, rented a small apartment in a subsidized housing complex, and regained custody of Rowena.

Ms. Cook relished every moment of her new life. Lancaster County came to symbolize her rebirth. She saw her transformation as a divine gift, and treated it as her second chance to show herself, Rowena, and the rest of the world that she was worthy of a good life. More importantly she treated it as her second chance to be a good mother. But the day before Christmas 1996, severe respiratory distress brought her to the emergency room. She was eventually diagnosed with non–small-cell lung cancer with metastases in her lymph nodes, kidney, and abdomen.

A week after her diagnosis, Ms. Cook made arrangements with her next-door neighbor to look after Rowena and began chemotherapy and radiation treatments. The radiation impeded her ability to swallow, requiring her to be fed by a percutaneous endoscopic gastrostomy (PEG) tube. The chemotherapy gave her nausea and made her lose her hair. She came home bald, weak, pale, and exhausted. Rowena was so frightened at the sight of her that she extended her stay with the neighbor for another week.

Ms. Cook began to receive visits from fellow members of her Narcotics Anonymous group, co-workers from the convenience store, nurses from a home care agency, and the hospital's chaplain-in-training, Yolanda Dixon. Mrs. Dixon, a friendly and energetic European-American woman in her forties, had met Ms. Cook at the hospital and had bonded with her instantly. In the hospital, she had noticed that Ms. Cook rarely slept—she either cried through the night or held her eyes open for fear of dying in her sleep. Mrs. Dixon promised Ms. Cook that she was going to stand by her side no matter how her illness evolved. "I worry about Shamira every day, every minute," she said to me. "When she started relaying her life to me, I realized I cannot let this woman die alone. I don't want this woman to go out of this world and people not to know the goodness of her, regardless of the badness that was there." From her second day in the hospital, Ms. Cook adopted Mrs. Dixon as her advocate. She refused to make decisions without her and requested her presence every time she felt depressed.

Confronted with her mortality, Ms. Cook concluded that her life was filled with lessons. She had advice for drug abusers, thoughts for cancer patients, and motherly stories for Rowena. She wanted to help others before she died. She wanted to explore the meaning of her existence. She bought a small cassette player and a box of blank tapes, and when she had the physical strength she spoke into the recorder about her life.

For better control of her symptoms, hospital staff offered to refer her to the Hospice of Lancaster County, and on February 5, 1997, Ms. Cook, Mrs. Dixon, and a hospice admission nurse met in Ms. Cook's apartment. "I got clean to die," said Ms. Cook solemnly. She proceeded to talk about her family history. Her mother had passed away seven years earlier, her brother was killed two weeks after her mother's funeral, her father was absent from her life—she didn't know if he was alive or dead—and her 18 half-siblings were scattered throughout different parts of the country. One of her sisters, Keisha, lived in neighboring Dauphin County. Because Keisha was a hard worker and a good disciplinarian, Ms. Cook had called her to discuss the possibility of passing on to her Rowena's guardianship.

For the present, however, Ms. Cook was determined to continue with chemotherapy. She vowed to try any treatments that would arrest the growth of her tumors, to both improve and prolong her life. The admission nurse informed her that hospice required all patients to have a "primary care provider." This person would be responsible for making decisions for her if and when she lost her mental clarity. Ms. Cook asked Mrs. Dixon if she would become not only her primary care provider but also the attorney-in-fact in a durable power-of-attorney agreement. Mrs. Dixon accepted both roles.

Ms. Cook left a lasting impression on the hospice admission nurse. After that meeting the nurse said, "I was overwhelmed with Shamira's courage and bravery and her awareness of what was happening to her. At some point she took me back to her bedroom. She wanted to show me her PEG tube; then she broke down. She started to cry and apologized then for crying. I just remember saying to her that I thought she was so brave and so open. I just think she is a courageous person."

Following the recommendations of Ms. Cook's attending physician, hospice nurse Elly White provided medications for pain, anxiety and depression, nausea, and diarrhea, as well as injections of filgrastim to increase her white blood cell count. At the request of Ms. Cook, Elly locked all medications—except for the breakthrough morphine—in a lockbox. This way, Ms. Cook was assured that her drug-addicted friends would stay away from her supply of prescription drugs. The hospice social worker, Barry Prout, connected Ms. Cook to a hospice volunteer and asked her if she wanted to participate in our project. Ms. Cook expressed enthusiasm for the opportunity to tell her story. The idea of educating others through her life experiences gave her both pride and purpose. If her story could be distributed to a wider readership, she thought, then she had a better chance of making a difference in this world. She was eager to start our interviews.

I met Ms. Cook on a joint visit with Barry a week after her admission to the home care program of hospice. She greeted us warmly at the top of a long flight of stairs. She was a tall, thin woman with prominent cheekbones and big, expressive eyes. A blue bandanna covered her head. Her apartment was small and unadorned, but it appeared clean and tidy. Without wasting any time, Ms. Cook led us to her living room, sat down on the couch, and started talking to us about her life. She wanted to spend the time she had left away from drugs, so that she would be able to smell the flowers, feel the sun on her skin, and develop a new relationship with her daughter. "Rowena and I don't know each other," she said; "I've always been high." Rowena was acting out, skipping school, and asking her mother for large amounts of money. Ms. Cook knew no other way to show her daughter that she loved her except to give her everything she wanted. Her preference, however, was to spend "quality time" with her. It was time, she said, to put her own pain aside and work on creating better relationships. She wanted to show the people who had hurt her, blamed her, rejected her, and lacked faith in her that she loved them. "I want people to know who I am," she said.

As I was listening to Ms. Cook, I found myself both moved and perplexed by her openness. She was speaking to Barry and me as if we were old friends. She was sharing with us painful and personal information without any indication of discomfort. Did her activity mean that she trusted us? Did it signify that she was bonding with us? Or did it lack a relational quality? Our discussion was interrupted by the arrival of Chloe Maxwell, Ms. Cook's personal care nurse. Barry and I offered to leave, but Ms. Cook insisted that we stay. She wanted to play her tapes for us. In those tapes, she spoke about her desire to show the world that she was a good person.

In retrospect, I think that Barry, myself, and everyone else who walked into Ms. Cook's life at this time presented her with another opportunity to start with a clean slate—to shed the parts of herself she didn't like and to present herself anew as the person she wanted to be. In this context, our relationships were probably not only meaningful to her but also instrumental in her preparation for death. With her permission, I quote a composite of excerpts from her own recordings:

> Hi. My name is Shamira Cook. I came to Lancaster County because I wanted to get my life together. I am not using today, and I am very proud of myself. Since I have learned that I have cancer, I have not given up the fight. It is very hard. The hospitals and all of the needles and all of the tests—just so much for me to handle in such a short time. I have a lot of wonderful, caring people in my life today, such as Yolanda Dixon, who is just one of my dearest, dearest friends. Then there is the hospice team that works with me. I just feel like I am so loved and that is something that I always wanted, but I did not think that I would get it this way—being sick. But love is love, and I guess it does not matter when you get it.
>
> I am just thinking back when I was a child how I always just wanted someone to love me. I just got beat every day, and I got beat so much that I thought it was normal. I thought it was love. I thought, "Well, if my mom is beating me, she must love me." My life was centered on drugs, sex, alcohol, lying, cheating, deceiving

and whatever other slimy thing that I could do because I was an addict. And that is thanks to my father. My parents were both addicted to alcohol and drugs. I loved my father very much. I wanted to be with him all the time. That turned out to be a bad idea, because [when I was] seven he molested me and turned me onto drugs, and that went on for seven years.

They say when you are an addict you only have three things to look forward to, and that is jail, institutions, and death. For the last few days, I have not been able to pray, and I have not been able to thank God for the days of living and the days that I have not used. I don't want to go astray again. And that is so easy for me, being a recovering addict. When things get tough, I usually run, and I'm not going to do that. I want to live each day to the fullest without the use of drugs.

I remember how large my family was at one time, but mostly everybody is dead now. And if they are not dead, they are sick or they are too good for me to be a part of their lives, which I think is so sad. I don't want no enemies. I don't want to die knowing that no one likes me. With or without hair, I am still a beautiful person. I did not give up on using when I was out there, I am not going to give up on living now that I am sick. So I, myself, I choose life over death, although I know, when my Heavenly Father calls me home, I am going.

Rowena

Although she showed love for Ms. Cook, Rowena didn't seem overly attached to her. For the biggest part of her life, her mother had meant more trouble to her than good. I saw Rowena only a few times. She was a tall and radiant young woman with high cheek bones and a very sweet smile. When I visited her mother at home, she was usually in school. I heard that she was a troublemaker, that she got into fights with her classmates, and that she was expelled from school on a regular basis. But every time I saw her, she either disappeared into her bedroom or sat quietly in the living room with her mother and me. Several people suspected that she harbored intense anger toward Ms. Cook, which I do not doubt. What I remember of Rowena, however, is her warmth. She was quick to smile with every affectionate comment that was made and quick to laugh at every joke. Ms. Cook filled with joy when she saw her daughter's face light up. I lost count of the times she told me about the day she brought Rowena to her knees with laughter by taking off her bandanna, putting a shiny earring on one ear, and proceeding to clean her entire apartment while singing the song of Mr. Clean.

Whether as a disciplinarian, protector, entertainer, or teacher, Ms. Cook was determined to leave some positive mark on her daughter's life before she died. In the middle of February, she decided that she owed it to Rowena to host a belated Christmas dinner. Never before had she had the wherewithal to do that. "My addiction was so bad," she recalled, "at one time, I used to sell my baby's Christmas toys." This time, Shamira was going to buy a Christmas tree, Christmas ornaments and presents, and she was going to make ham, sweet potatoes, and beans for Rowena, Mrs. Dixon, and a few other friends. She scheduled the dinner for February 21, three days before her next chemotherapy.

"I wish I could fly"

I never heard the details about the Christmas dinner because on February 21, Ms. Cook became so nauseous that she wasn't able to enjoy it. Three days later, she was taken to the hospital with excruciating pain. Her oncologist, Dr. Mark Jenks, canceled her chemotherapy and scheduled her for a computed tomography scan to determine the cause of her symptoms. The scan revealed metastases in her retroperitoneum. The tumors in her lungs and mediastinum, however, had shrunk.

When I saw Ms. Cook on February 25, her morphine had been doubled over a span of four days, and she was lying in her hospital bed, half-conscious. Her eyes were three quarters closed and she was mumbling. "I am taking 21 pills a day, and that is way too much," she said. "I am tired of this. I am really tired of this. I wish I could fly." Given her condition at the time, I didn't know if she was talking to me, or if she cared for a response. But her demeanor changed instantly when Rowena entered the room. Rowena had been expelled from school once again and had decided to join her next-door neighbor on her visit to Ms. Cook. At the sound of Rowena's girlish voice, Ms. Cook opened her eyes and broke into a big smile. Rowena sat at the foot of her mother's bed. Mother and daughter teased each other and laughed. "C'mon, man!" exclaimed Rowena in response to one of Ms. Cook's jokes. "How come you're calling me 'man'?" asked Ms. Cook strictly. "Do I have a beard on my face?" Rowena laughed. "Do I have a moustache?" Rowena laughed again. Still, when it was time to leave, she hopped off the bed and walked toward the door without saying goodbye. "Where do you think you're going?" asked Ms. Cook with affection. "Come over here and give me a kiss!" Playfully, Rowena approached her mother, gave her a big kiss on the cheek and left.

When Ms. Cook returned home, her hospice team was worried about her. Her needs had increased, yet she spent significant portions of the day alone. In addition to weakness, loss of appetite, and nausea, she reported feeling overwhelmed and discouraged. The discovery of the new tumors devastated her. Barry thought that the hospice inpatient unit would be a better environment for Ms. Cook, but Ms. Cook was not eligible. Hospice did not perform cardiopulmonary resuscitation, and that was an intervention that Ms. Cook insisted on having available to her.

On March 10, Ms. Cook learned from Dr. Jenks that most of the areas in which her cancer had settled were inoperable. During our interview two days later she said, "Two years ago, if I would have found I had cancer, I would have been dead. I would have overdosed myself. I would have went and got me a bag of dope, shot it up—all the liquor and beer I could get. See, that is the first thing we do as addicts when we cannot handle something or something is not going right in our life: we go get high." As we were talking, the phone rang. When Ms. Cook answered she heard the screams of an angry mother who informed her that Rowena had just hit her child with a bag of ice. The caller announced that she planned to beat up not only Rowena but also Ms. Cook. Shamira put down the phone in dismay. In her tape that day, she said:

> I need to say that I have been having a hard time with my child and her acting out in different ways, because she does not understand, really, what I'm going through. That reminds me of when I was a child, when my mom was busy drinking and drugging and not having time for me. I feel as though, since I have been sick, it is like I have been paying myself a lot more attention than I have her, even though I'm not using. It seems like we don't really have a relationship going on, and that is something that I really want, because like I said, only God knows how much time I have left here. I just feel helpless and one thing I have learned by doing the First Step before is that I am really powerless right now, and I need to keep my health together, if not for me, for Rowena.

Several hospice nurses wondered why Ms. Cook insisted on chemotherapy treatments when these treatments compromised the quality of her life. A few nurses suspected that she was in denial. Why else would she put her body through so much pain? Others, however, expressed a more nuanced view. "She knows that she has a terminal disease," said one nurse who had gotten to know Ms. Cook, "but I don't know if she has a real hard and fast awareness that she is going to die. There is probably some denial there, and I have to say that maybe the system is almost feeding into it somewhat. I asked the attending physician when I first met Shamira what his thoughts were as far as prognosis, and he said, 'Probably about three months, but I would not tell the patient that.'"

Chloe, Ms. Cook's personal care nurse, spent hours watching television with her, discussing topics that concerned her, and lifting her spirits with good humor and jokes. On the topic of Shamira's "denial," Chloe said to me:

> The first time I met Shamira she said, "You can come in, but I don't want you to talk to me about dying because every time the other nurses [from a previous home care agency] came here they never, ever gave me hope. It was always, 'You are dying, you are dying, you are dying.' If I want to talk about it, fine. You can be open with me. But I don't always want to hear I am dying because I still need hope."
> I cannot imagine being full of cancer and [having to call] a taxi to go to the doctor's. But then the part of me who is 38 and who is a mom understands why she is fighting and why she is not ready to give up. Getting her chemotherapy for her hope, even that little bit of hope, might be doing her a lot of good. It is hard to say.

The nurses were particularly concerned about how Ms. Cook would cope when her needs increased. Mrs. Dixon proposed gathering a team of volunteers from her church who would stay with her friend during the night. Church members had already donated funds to cover Ms. Cook's rent, and they seemed willing to help her in other areas as well. Mrs. Dixon then made another offer: to take Ms. Cook into her own home. Although she hadn't secured her family's permission to do that, she was confident that her proposal was feasible. Barry was impressed by Mrs. Dixon's commitment, but he also worried that her offer might be an indication of an unhealthy "enmeshment" with Shamira. Did Yolanda realize what she was getting herself into?

Rowena moves out

On March 21 Ms. Cook and Rowena had a serious fight, and in the heat of their argument, Rowena left the apartment; Ms. Cook did not know where she went. Panicked, she decided that she didn't have the strength to raise Rowena the way she wanted and that it was time to let her go. She called Keisha and asked her to pick up Rowena two days later and take her into her home. That evening, Ms. Cook vomited uncontrollably and developed severe abdominal pain and dysuria. In the morning, when Rowena returned home, Ms. Cook was suffering from excruciating pain. Yolanda was out of town, so Ms. Cook asked a friend to drive her to the emergency room. The emergency room physician stated that either she had a urinary tract infection or her cancer had spread further. He performed a urine test and gave her medications for pain. Since Mrs. Dixon was not available, Ms. Cook's Baptist pastor, The Reverend Anthony Johnson, came to the emergency room and took her home. An African-American community leader in his fifties, Reverend Johnson had never spent time with Ms. Cook before, but he knew about her and had held prayer for her at church.

On March 23, Keisha came for Rowena and took her to her apartment in Dauphin County, about 40 miles away. The next day, Ms. Cook was rehospitalized at the recommendation of her oncologist. Dr. Jenks wanted a new scan of her abdomen, pelvis, and bones to evaluate the effectiveness of her chemotherapy. The scan revealed that Ms. Cook's retroperitoneal metastases had increased greatly. It was clear to Dr. Jenks that the chemotherapy had not worked. When she heard this, Ms. Cook appeared calm and accepting. But she announced that she wanted to continue with chemotherapy. More than ever, she desired any interventions that had the potential to help her. Surprised by her equanimity, a resident asked the hospital psychologist to see her for an evaluation, suspecting that she was in denial. But the hospital social worker had a different view. "[Shamira] had to be a survivor to get where she was," she said, "so she did not lay in bed and ask for pity. She knew she was sick and would recognize it, but then not focus on it. I don't know how you can be in denial when people keep telling you what is wrong. I mean, she was alert enough to hear it—how she chose to interpret it, I think, would be more of a coping way, not a denial way."

With prompts from Barry and Elly, Ms. Cook contemplated leaving her apartment. If indeed she was in need of round-the-clock care, where would she prefer to go? Barry and Elly encouraged her to consider moving to a nursing home. The inpatient unit of hospice was still not available to her because she continued to desire chemotherapy and resuscitation.

When I saw Ms. Cook later that day, she told me that if she were to rely solely on hospice, she would die. An extended care facility, on the other hand, would allow her to seek aggressive treatments. But she was torn. The idea of moving to a nursing home at the age of 34 shocked her. She missed Yolanda. She remembered telling her that she didn't want her to leave Lancaster, even for a few days. She knew that something bad was going to happen during her absence. Now her fears had come true. Hesitantly, she asked Barry to help her fill out an application form for the nearest nursing home.

"Do I look like I need 24-hour care to you?"

"Shamira feels as if decisions are being made behind her back," Mrs. Dixon said to me when she returned to Lancaster. "She does not want to die in an institution. She has made that very clear. I hate nursing homes. I would personally like to see her stay in [her] apartment if that is where she wants to be. If we have to set a 24-hour vigil with all the people that I know, we will do that." Mrs. Dixon had informed Barry that she wasn't able to take Ms. Cook in her own home, because her husband had recently lost a young relative and wasn't ready to relive another death.

On the eve of her hospital discharge, Ms. Cook asked Elly if she would be allowed back home once her pain was under control. Like all members of Ms. Cook's hospice team, Elly regarded the transfer to the nursing home as a permanent solution. She realized, however, that her patient wasn't ready to hear her view, so she responded indirectly: it was important, she said, to take one day at a time. Ms. Cook exploded in anger. "You never say what I want to hear!" she exclaimed. Later, Elly said to me:

> I truly empathize with her. She says she wants to deal with reality, but she does not really want to. It is sort of like a no-win situation, and I know that anger is part of the grieving process. I mean, she has to go through this anger before she can reach acceptance. I try not to be negative, but I also would not play into what she wanted to hear, and that just made her furious. I don't think that we could any longer fol-

low her if she stays in her apartment, because it would be an unsafe situation. I am not sure her physician would follow her. We try to follow what a patient wants, but in this case, because of the circumstances of her life, it may not be possible.

On April 1, Ms. Cook was discharged from the hospital, but because the nursing home had still not reached a financial agreement with her program of medical assistance, she returned to her own home. Ms. Cook was delighted to be back in the apartment. She assured Barry that she did understand the severity of her condition, but she emphasized that she wanted to live positively. She couldn't tolerate "negative" messages from her caregivers. She was 34 years old, and she was determined to spend her remaining time as happily as her disease allowed. Again and again she declared that she wasn't ready to move to a nursing home. Sandy Glass, her hospice volunteer, took this statement to mean that Ms. Cook didn't realize she was dying. "I let her have her fantasy," Sandy said. "I figure that she is entitled to that. She is 34 years old, and this is a hard enough thing to be dealing with. One day I did say that death is something we must all face, and then I dropped it. I did not want to depress her."

By the next day Ms. Cook's pain was under control, and she felt so well that she decided to go shopping. But first she called Elly and apologized for her angry behavior. I saw her the day after that. She was in a hurry to go to Dauphin County to see Rowena. Excitedly, she led me to her bedroom and showed me her new outfit, a pair of green athletic pants with a matching jacket and white sneakers. She couldn't wait to leave. Without notifying her friends, her neighbor, Mrs. Dixon, or hospice, she arranged for a taxi to take her to the bus station. I was struck by the quickness with which she erased her caretakers from her mind; although she appreciated their help, it was as if she wished that they, like her cancer, were part of a bad dream she could leave behind. When I asked her about her last pain crisis, she started to cry. She said:

> I thought I was going to die. That is the scariest feeling, because when you have a disease like I have that cannot be cured and it is spreading, it is very scary. They kept throwing hospice at me, like that is where they wanted me to go, but see, when you go to hospice you have to be getting ready to die, and when you go there, they stop all your treatment, and all they do is pain management until you die. One of the nurses from hospice kept pushing the nursing home on me, because she felt like I needed more care—24-hour care. Do I look like I need 24-hour care to you? I don't think so! This nurse has gotten overprotective of me. Every time I am feeling good and I tell her how wonderful I feel, she is like, "Well, you know that you can get sicker. . . ." I know that! I have a serious disease of cancer. I know it is serious! That is why I'm doing everything in my power right now to keep my health up!

Ms. Cook's attitude elicited strong reactions from hospice staff. Some nurses stated that if she was indeed averse to the idea of receiving only palliative care, hospice had no role in her life. If all that Ms. Cook wanted was someone to fill her pill box, another nurse agreed, then a home health agency would serve her better. Other staff believed that Ms. Cook was both hospice-appropriate and realistic. They argued that she had a right to die in the way that she saw fit, even if that involved avoidable hospitalizations and preventable pain crises. They felt that some of her caregivers were trying to push Ms. Cook to decisions more in keeping with an ideology of "the good death" than with her own beliefs and values. One of these nurses said:

> I just think not all cases go smoothly. I mean, I know there is probably going to be a crisis again, but that is Shamira's choice, and I think we just have to deal with that. She wants to be able to focus on what living she has left. She knows she is going to die. She does not need someone coming into her room and telling her, "You are going to a nursing home, and you are not going to come out." I certainly do not feel that we should pull out [of her care]. She is terminally ill. I think we need to realize that when we walk into families there are problems that have been there a long, long time, and we are not going to be able to fix that. Not all cases are going to be your white, middle-class, *Leave It to Beaver* or *Ozzie and Harriet* family. So part of me is really frustrated when they say she is not hospice-appropriate just because she does not do exactly what we tell her to do.

In the midst of this tension, I asked Dr. Jenks to explain how he viewed Ms. Cook's treatment. He commented that in cancer care the distinction between palliative and curative is not always meaningful. In Ms. Cook's case, for example, her cancer was incurable. It would definitely not go away with treatments. But this didn't mean that it was untreatable. He told me that her chances for complete remission were less than 5% and for partial remission, between 25% and 30%. Therefore, the prolongation of Ms. Cook's life was a possibility, albeit a slim one. I never learned if Dr. Jenks had shared these numbers with his patient, but I could see why Ms. Cook seemed to like him. In his words I heard a sense of hope, which Shamira craved.

When Ms. Cook told Felicia Johnson, her pastor's wife, that Elly squelched her optimism, Mrs. Johnson immediately called hospice. She argued that Ms. Cook was not in denial. Shamira knew she was dying, Mrs. Johnson said, but she was not yet ready to stop fighting for her life. In a conversation I had with her, Mrs. Johnson said, "We know Shamira is terminal; Shamira knows she is terminal; but Shamira is not *being* terminal; she is not dying right at this moment. I think when hospice goes into a home [they should] assess it: assess the needs, assess where the people are, assess where the families are, and don't come in with their preconceived ideas of how it ought to be."

"Don't ever, *ever* come to me with negative shit no more"

Ms. Cook returned from her visit to Dauphin County on April 7. She was exhausted and lethargic. Upon her arrival, Chloe informed her that she had been removed from her case. Since she was now able to take care of her basic needs by herself, hospice didn't deem it necessary to offer her personal care. Chloe assured her, however, that she would resume her visits if Ms. Cook's needs increased. Shamira liked her personal care nurse and would miss her. "So I have to act like I'm dying to get you back?" she asked Chloe in frustration.

Ms. Cook told Elly that all had gone well with her trip to Dauphin County. Though she had felt ill, being in Keisha's home gave her a peacefulness that one feels only among loved ones. Seeing Rowena with Keisha assured her that her daughter was in good hands. Her visit reminded her that she had come a long way from who she was only a few years earlier. The last time she visited Keisha, she was financially broke and high on drugs. This time, she had brought gifts for Keisha's family and money for Rowena.

When I visited her a few days later, Ms. Cook rummaged through her drawers to find an enlarged photograph of her with her daughter. It had been taken two years earlier at her drug rehabilitation center. Shamira had a full head of hair and wore a lovely colorful outfit. The picture symbolized total victory: her triumph over her addiction and her reunification with Rowena.

Now, Ms. Cook said, the mere thought of hospice brought a "black cloud" over her head. She continued:

> I know God is not going to take me away yet, because I do not think I was put here to live the life that I lived. I think He had better plans for me. That is another reason why I hate to be around the negative hospice nurses. I had agreed to go into the nursing home until Elly said I might not come out. I don't need that negative crap, even if I won't be put in remission! Let me live the rest of my life, whatever it might be, in peace!
>
> Elly thinks that I think I'm going to get better and better. I know better than that! I know that cancer is a very serious disease! Especially since I have it in my lungs, I got it in my kidney, now something is going on in my stomach and my back. What makes her think that I am that naive or that damn stupid that I am not thinking about the death part either? How does she know how I feel when I am here by myself at night? How many nights I have cried myself to sleep? How many times I have asked God to have mercy on me because I am not ready to die? I told her, "Don't ever, *ever* come to me with negative shit no more." So, *shoot!* They better leave me alone!

A tense team meeting at hospice

Over the next week Ms. Cook's weakness and exhaustion increased. She reported severe pain in her back. Every day she appeared more lethargic. She ate little and lost weight. Her apartment was in disarray, dirty dishes piled up in the kitchen sink and her medications scattered throughout the living room. Elly felt that Ms. Cook's death was imminent. Although Ms. Cook's insurance provided no coverage for continuous home care services from hospice, Elly offered to ask her supervisor if Shamira could spend the last few days of her life in the inpatient unit. Her rationale was that if Shamira declined further, she was likely to refuse chemotherapy and give up on her desire for resuscitation.

In the weekly meeting of hospice providers, a nurse supervisor informed Ms. Cook's team that her health plan did not cover hospice inpatient unit stays, nor would it pay for any further inpatient chemotherapy treatments. Ms. Cook's next chemotherapy, which was scheduled for the following day, was planned on an outpatient basis. The supervisor expressed frustration, again stating that she didn't understand why Ms. Cook was a hospice patient. She viewed her as someone who was so eager to fight her disease that she sought treatments uncritically. "Any time she has a crisis, it becomes our problem," she said to the team.

Elly argued that Dr. Jenks kept giving Ms. Cook false hopes and making it hospice's responsibility to deliver bad news to her. Barry, the social worker, giving a new spin to the conversation, had heard some of Shamira's tapes, and asserted that she was fully aware of her condition; he did not think she was in denial. When someone mentioned Yolanda's promise to keep Ms. Cook out of a nursing home, tension flared around the table. One nurse said, "If Yolanda made this promise, then *Yolanda* has to deal with Shamira." Another person exclaimed, "This is not our problem anymore!" And a third person said, "We are not responsible for the promises Yolanda is making."

The meeting closed uneasily. Barry seemed perplexed. He told me that his own impression of Ms. Cook differed significantly from the way she was presented in meetings. He didn't see Ms. Cook as unrealistic, he just thought that her way of dying was different from other people's, and he wanted to find a way to respect that. He had even come to admire Yolanda for the support she offered to her friend: "At first, I thought, 'Yolanda, you are so enmeshed,'" he said. "So what? This is what the world needs sometimes—for people to reach out and do a little more. So I scolded myself."

"They don't bother me and I don't bother them"

When I visited Ms. Cook two days later, on April 22, I asked her how things were going with hospice. "They don't bother me and I don't bother them," she said. She stated that her relationship with Elly had improved—Elly was no longer as "negative" as she used to be.

Three days later, Ms. Cook reported to Dr. Jenks's office for a follow-up examination, appearing weak and pale. During the visit, she coughed up blood and was immediately admitted to the hospital. She reported increasing back pain, dyspnea, weakness, unsteadiness, and a tender abdomen. Her chest X-ray revealed radiation pneumonitis—an inflammation of her lungs that was caused by the radiation she had received three months earlier.

In the hospital, Ms.Cook's pain reached an unprecedented level. She rolled in bed, screaming. Everyone thought that she was going to die. Her attending physician placed her on an intravenous morphine drip. Dr. Jenks informed her that her white blood count had dropped dramatically, and under these circumstances, he could not possibly keep her on chemotherapy; there was nothing more he could do for her. He then told Elly that it was time to transfer Ms. Cook to the inpatient unit of hospice, for he didn't think Ms. Cook had much time left. In fact, he wasn't certain if she was going to leave the hospital alive. Still in pain, Ms. Cook agreed to the transfer.

"We thought we were on a roll with it," Yolanda recalled. "Shamira agreed to go and the doctor even went in with me and said, 'You know what this means: that there will be no attempt made to resuscitate you, it would just be medication to keep you comfortable.' I think the pain was so great that she would just do anything to make it stop. A little while later hospice called back and said, 'No.' They know she changes her mind so much, they were not going to take her until she signed a consent form."

Ms. Cook was in so much pain that she wasn't in a position to read medical documents and evaluate her options. Hospice turned to Mrs. Dixon, who, as Ms. Cook's power-of-attorney, had the legal right to make decisions for her. Yolanda felt overwhelmed by this responsibility. "What if the pain gets under control and she gets back to normal?" she wondered. "Then she is going to want out of there. Was she at the point of saying, 'I'm done'? Was she going to come back? I didn't know."

Mrs. Dixon was freed from her dilemma the next day. When she walked into Ms. Cook's room on April 27, she found her friend surrounded by her family from Dauphin County. Mrs. Dixon had informed Keisha about Ms. Cook's condition and was pleased to see that Keisha had traveled to Lancaster County to see her sister. Ms. Cook was jovial, but when she saw Yolanda her mood changed. She appeared indignant. "I am leaving for Dauphin County," she announced. "I am going with my family. I want to be out of here today! Get it moving!" Mrs. Dixon walked into the hall and cried.

The hospital social worker informed Mrs. Dixon that the doctors had not yet discharged Ms. Cook, so she wouldn't be able to travel to Dauphin County as quickly as she wanted to. Hesitantly, Yolanda returned to Shamira to give her the news. By that time, Keisha and her family had left, and Shamira was lying in bed, alone. Before Yolanda had the chance to say anything, Shamira apologized for her outburst, explaining that her relatives had brought the "street" out in her. She told Yolanda that she depended on her friendship, and she didn't want to lose her. She was scared. Gently, she took hold of Yolanda's hand, and they both started to cry. With tears rolling down her cheeks, Ms. Cook leaned back and fell asleep. "When she held my hand so tight and fell asleep," recalled Mrs. Dixon later, "I felt a sense of safeness, that she felt safe with me. I have developed a real closeness with her."

I saw Ms. Cook two days later. She was lying in her hospital bed next to her teddy bear, looking frazzled. With her address book in her hand, she was making arrangements for her departure. She was excited to move in with Keisha, but she was also upset. "I imagine that it is going to be kind of strange," she said. "You know, being in a house and your sister is telling your daughter what to do. But I have been there. I am not going to take over. I had my chance for that, you know. I had my chance to be a mom twice. The first time, Rowena got put in the foster home, the second time, I am sick. Yolanda and me been crying all morning. She don't want me to leave here."

As I listened, I realized that there was a possibility that I would never see Shamira again—Dr. Jenks had said that her death was imminent. But even if she were to live longer, I wasn't sure if my schedule and the goals of our project would permit me to visit her in Dauphin County. Still, I asked her if she would be interested in having me and my tape recorder visit her in her new home. She said that she would: "Because I want to give," she continued. "I want to give all that I can after everything that has been given to me."

I was struck by her answer, sensing that in the turmoil of her life, her generosity was often overlooked. In the few months that I had known Ms. Cook, she was seen more as someone who drained the system than as an asset of any sort. We agreed that I would try my best to proceed with our work, even if that entailed only periodic phone interviews. Not knowing if that was a feasible plan, however, I asked her if there was anything she wanted me to include in the story I would write about her. "What is important to you to tell?" I asked.

She paused for a while, and said: "That I was not the bad person that even my family tried to make me out to be. That I was really a loving and caring person—it was just that I was always directing my love in the wrong way to the wrong people. And that if you do have kids, make them your number one priority."

To Dauphin County

On May 1, Ms. Cook's care was officially transferred to a hospice in Dauphin County. When I arrived for my last visit to her apartment I found her in the living room watching a horror film on TV. She looked drowsy, but she insisted that I watch the most gruesome scene. She told me that her new medication regimen gave her the same high that she experienced when she abused drugs. Her eyes narrowed and her eyeballs rolled back. One moment she was looking at me and participating in our conversation, and the next, she was gone. I didn't stay long with her that day. By that time, I already knew that I would be able to visit her in Dauphin County, so we agreed to see each other in her new home.

Keisha arrived in the early afternoon. She found Elly, Barry, and Yolanda all waiting to carry her sister's suitcases to her car. Ms. Cook was on the phone, crying. Keisha appeared to be overwhelmed. Privately, she told Elly that she hadn't realized how sick her sister was. The news that Shamira was dying had shocked her. She was a single mother herself and worked all day, so she didn't know if the few evening hours she would be able to devote to Ms. Cook would suffice. Clearly upset, she walked into the bathroom and sobbed. After loading Keisha's car, Elly and Barry said their good-byes. Ms. Cook promised to write to them. The last one to leave was Yolanda. The hospital chaplain assured her friend that she would visit her soon. The two women embraced, and Yolanda left. That evening Ms. Cook crossed the border of Lancaster County for the last time.

To come to terms with her friend's departure, Yolanda told herself that no matter how attached she felt to Shamira, Shamira still saw her as a stranger. She had fled from Lancaster County as if she were besieged. "I think when Shamira gets bad, they will take her to a hospital," Mrs. Dixon said with disappointment. "I think Shamira will die in a hospital in Dauphin County. I feel maybe a little bit jealous, because I wish I would be able to be there with her. I would like to be with her when she dies, I would like to be sitting with her. I think that when she gets closer to her death, she is going to be a lot more scared. It would not surprise me if she calls and asks me to come. I hope she does."

"Patient denies the cancer"

Ms. Cook declined personal care visits from her new hospice program, insisting that she could maintain her hygiene without assistance. However, she accepted a bedside commode, a walker, and a shower bench. She reported weakness, unsteadiness when she walked, a distended abdomen, and increased shortness of breath on exertion. An oxygen cannula became a permanent part of her attire. To gain strength, she began filling her diet with wholesome foods and supplementing it with vitamins. Upon hearing that, Marilyn Beck, the hospice social worker, started to worry. She didn't want Ms. Cook to nourish false hopes of a recovery. She explained to her that her weakness resulted from the progression of her disease and was not likely to dissipate with improved nutrition. Ms. Cook was outraged. Later, Keisha's daughter called hospice to say that hospice workers were not allowed to talk to her aunt about the seriousness of her condition.

"Patient denies the cancer. Does not want to talk about the 'D-word,'" a hospice nurse wrote in Ms. Cook's chart. Dr. Robert Bridges, her new attending physician, was left with the same impression. "She is in big denial with her terminal illness," he said. Ms. Cook's request for aggressive treatments surprised him. In his opinion, her condition was untreatable. She also complained of pain in her back and neck, reporting that a lymph node in her clavicle had enlarged so much that it bothered her. Aware that she was receiving an unusually high dose of morphine, Dr. Bridges consulted a pain specialist. Never before had he worked with a patient who had such a high tolerance for narcotics. The pain specialist, Dr. Robert Neff, switched Ms. Cook from long-acting morphine to 50 mg of liquid hydromorphone every 4-6 hours. But in Ms. Cook's eyes, pain management wasn't enough, and she requested a visit with oncologist Allison Hopkins to explore the possibility of surgery. She wanted her lymph node removed.

Meanwhile, life in Keisha's home struck the new hospice team as chaotic. Ms. Cook lived in a small row house with Rowena, Keisha, Keisha's three adult children, and her four grandchildren. "They have Rowena babysitting all of the little kids," said Marilyn Beck, "and every time any of our staff goes in, they are all in there running around naked and screaming, and it has been pretty wild. There are casts of thousands in there most of the time." Mrs. Dixon, who visited Ms. Cook soon after her move to Dauphin County, wasn't at all pleased with the new arrangements. Ms. Cook's hospital bed stood in the dining room, next to a television set. When Yolanda saw Shamira smoking in bed while feeling so drowsy that she could barely keep her eyes open, she was horrified. She found Keisha's home entirely inappropriate for a terminally ill patient. The only advantage she saw to Keisha's family was that they were African American. "I think she [felt] close to that black family," Yolanda said to me. "I think the blackness of that environment [felt] good to her. They understood her, whereas we were just caregivers to her."

When I saw Ms. Cook on June 3, I found her alone in her new home. She was lying in her hospital bed, watching television. The enlarged photograph of her and Rowena was the only decoration on the living room walls. I noticed that she had lost weight. Her eyes seemed more prominent than I remembered. And she was scared. "It's rough," she said as she cried. "I don't know if people realize how serious my cancer is." Later, speaking into her tape-recorder, she continued, "If it wasn't for my sister Keisha, I would probably be dead right now, because I was not going to go to no [nursing] home, no way. I was not going to go in a [nursing] home because if I went to a [nursing] home that is where I was going to die at—and I probably would have killed myself anyway." The following day, she told me, she was scheduled to see her new oncologist. Aside from her breathing problems, she suffered from thrush, which impeded her ability to swallow, a vaginal infection, and urinary incontinence.

She had started wearing diapers. She missed Yolanda. "This has just been one hell of an experience," she said.

On June 18, two weeks after her first meeting with the oncologist, she asked Dr. Hopkins if she would be willing to radiate her retroperitoneal tumor. The doctor said that there was nothing she could do now to contain the cancer. But to control Ms. Cook's neuropathic pain, she doubled the dose of her gabapentin from 300 to 600 mg three times daily. "I don't want to die!" exclaimed Ms. Cook in agony when she saw her nurse Faye the next day, "I'm so scared!" Faye wrapped her in her arms. Warmly, she assured Shamira that she wouldn't be left alone. Her family, friends, and hospice team were all there to support her in the days ahead.

"We don't have time no more to be playing—I am dying!"

On June 24, Dr. Hopkins increased Ms. Cook's liquid hydromorphone to 125 mg every 6 hours. The next day Shamira met with Dr. Neff to ask if he knew of ways to arrest her cancer. She could barely walk, appearing lethargic and confused. She asserted that her disease was God's way of telling her to "clean up" her life. Now she wondered why Dr. Neff had referred her to Dr. Hopkins when Dr. Hopkins could do nothing to control her cancer. Gently, Dr. Neff told Ms. Cook that her disease was untreatable. Like Dr. Hopkins, he didn't know of any treatments that would help her. Ms. Cook looked shocked. She burst into tears, stood up, and walked out of Dr. Neff's office as fast as she could. "I don't think I was the first one to tell her," reflected Dr. Neff later, "but it was the first time it really stuck. That was hard on me."

When I telephoned Ms. Cook on the hot summer day of June 26, she sounded alarmed. She hadn't heard from me in three weeks, and she had forgotten that I had told her I would be away. "We don't have time no more to be playing—I am dying!" she exclaimed. She continued:

> There is nothing else they can do for me. They can't stop my cancer no more. My sister already knew. Everybody else already knew but me. I told them it was best not to tell me yet, because I was not ready. What they should know is that you never get ready to hear that you're going to die. It is at the point now, we were discussing the dress that I am going to be buried in. Since I have been told, it seems like I just became sick. It could be mind over matter, you know. I was feeling so healthy again, until [Dr. Neff] told me, 'Well, you know, you are dying, there is nothing else we can do for you, period, besides keep you comfortable.' I don't know how to feel, Yanna! I just don't know what to think, what to do. I feel like a piece of glass. I feel like if I move the wrong way that I am going to go to pieces.

There was a pause and I heard a rustling sound. Then Ms. Cook resumed speaking:

Excuse me, I am sweating and I'm trying to wipe the phone off. I don't feel like I'm ready to go nowhere yet, so death better go ahead on and find somebody else, because I ain't ready. Because I don't think God brought me this far to drop me on my head. Because I think there is something He wants me to do before I leave here. I just don't know what the plan is, and I ain't going to worry about it, because when it comes to God, you ain't got to worry about nothing.

I found the agony in Ms. Cook's voice jarring. Until then, I had been fooled. Her feistiness, good humor, and youth had convinced me, to a certain degree, that she was going to make it—that somehow she was stronger than her disease. Now I felt sad and close to her. I knew that I would miss her. I told her that I wanted to see her soon. We agreed to meet on July 3.

When I arrived that day, I was struck by the change in her appearance. Her face was swollen from her steroids, her eyes were bulging, and a thin layer of facial hair covered both of her cheeks. She told me that her legs had become too heavy for her body. She suffered from stomach pain, especially around her navel. The wig she had chosen to wear in her coffin was on display at the foot of her bed. It was a set of long, straight black hair with bangs. She looked tired and upset. She was struggling, especially with the fact that Rowena continued to avoid her. "I can't get no sleep," she said. "I try to be everybody's everything, and I can't do it. I am only one person, and I don't even know who I am. For real, I don't even know who Shamira is. I know my name is Shamira, I know I am not a dumb woman, I know I have a beautiful child, I know I am dying, I know I have taken care of all the responsibilities as a mother for when I die. I want to go back to Lancaster County, because I don't think my daughter wants me here. It's like I spoiled something for her when I came."

By July 7, Ms. Cook reported pressure from her distended abdomen, back pain, swelling of her left foot, increased weakness, tightness in her chest, confusion, and forgetfulness. Dr. Hopkins doubled the dose of her breakthrough morphine from 100 mg to 200 mg every two hours as needed. Keisha was worried. She told Faye that her sister had started to hallucinate. Three times she had heard her talking to her deceased mother. Ms. Cook recalled those moments vividly. Her mother had appeared to her so suddenly that it had scared her. With her was a small child who was playing peek-a-boo behind the living room chair. Shamira's mother looked proud. She didn't speak to Shamira, but through her thoughts she gave her courage. "She was looking at me," Ms. Cook recalled, "like she was saying, 'Well, you look like you doing pretty good, like you are handling it,' and, 'Just keep on doing what you're doing.' That is how I took it, and that is how I feel—I am doing the best I can."

But on July 9, Keisha called hospice in a panic. Ms. Cook had heard threatening voices and, thinking that people were trying to attack her, she placed a knife under her pillow for protection. Keisha feared for the safety of Rowena and her own grandchildren. She didn't know how violent Ms. Cook was capable of becoming. Hospice called Dr. Hopkins for help. The oncologist was baffled. "What the hell am I supposed to do about that?" she thought to herself. She quickly suggested that Ms. Cook be hospitalized for a psychiatric evaluation. Hoping that the scary voices would quiet down, Ms. Cook agreed to go.

After a few days, she returned home with a diagnosis of "psychotic depression." She was taking an increased dosage of antidepressant medication, an antipsychotic, and a new antibiotic. Keisha wasn't happy about her sister's return. Shamira's mental deterioration scared her. Fearing for the safety of her grandchildren, Keisha worried every time she left for work.

On July 21, Ms. Cook agreed to go back to the hospital for a reevaluation of her condition and an adjustment of her medications. Dr. Hopkins instructed her attending physician to decrease her pain medications until he felt confident that he had struck a balance between pain control and mental clarity. Four days after her admission, Shamira seemed stable. Though depressed, she was alert, oriented, and reported no pain. She was scheduled to return home once more on July 26. On the eve of her departure, she spoke on the phone with Yolanda and told her that she loved her. The two women laughed about some photographs they had taken together during Ms. Cook's previous hospitalization and agreed to meet at Keisha's home the next day.

The following morning a hospice nurse found Ms. Cook "wildly anxious." Ms. Cook was refusing to be discharged from the hospital, crying out that she was afraid to die. When Keisha arrived to pick her up, she found her sister rolling feverishly in her bed. She had lost control of her urine, and defecated involuntarily. Frightened and agitated, Ms. Cook asked Keisha to hold her hand. She looked like she was struggling to breathe. "Can't you make this stop?" she asked Keisha in panic. Keisha took hold of her sister's hand and tried to calm her. Gently, she encouraged her to close her eyes and rest. As Keisha started rubbing her leg, Shamira stopped moving. A few minutes later, Keisha realized that she was dead.

"They brought her out of the morgue, put her in a box, and that was it"

"Shamira had a good heart, she really did," said Faye when she heard about Ms. Cook's death. "She just did not have a fair chance." Dr. Hopkins called Keisha at home to apologize for her poor judgment in authorizing her sister's discharge. She explained that she hadn't expected Shamira to die so quickly, and she wasn't even certain what the immediate cause of death was. When Yolanda arrived at Keisha's house, she, too, was shocked to hear the news.

During her visit, Yolanda sensed that Keisha was frazzled. When she asked her what was the matter, she received another shock. Keisha informed her that she wasn't Shamira's real sister. She was a woman whom Shamira had met and grown to admire while still in her addiction. In fact, Ms. Cook's only blood relative was Rowena, and someone needed to take responsibility for organizing the funeral. Keisha could not afford it, and the hospital was pressuring her to remove Ms. Cook's body from the morgue. Yolanda offered to arrange the funeral herself. "I just never gave it a second thought," she said to me later. "I just thought that the Lord would provide it, I really did. I am going to have to put it in God's hands, and He will have to provide the money, because I don't have it."

The next day, Mrs. Dixon raised $800 at her church. This amount covered the expenses for a grave site. Other funeral expenses amounted to another $1,500, which Mrs. Dixon paid out of her own savings and additional donations she received in the mail. When Keisha called the funeral home to ask who would be able to dress Ms. Cook in her new dress and wig, she was told that no one was available. Since Ms. Cook wasn't going to be embalmed, the funeral home refused to touch her body. "So what they did," Yolanda told me, "is they brought her out of the morgue, put her in a box, and that was it. They really didn't do anything."

Ms. Cook's burial took place in Dauphin County on July 30. Under a small, maroon tent, Rowena, Keisha, Keisha's children and grandchildren, and a few friends from Lancaster County gathered. The two rows of chairs set up by the funeral home faced Ms. Cook's light blue casket, which was decorated with a bouquet of white flowers. Against the casket leaned the photograph of her and Rowena. In the picture she was beautiful, free of drugs and full of hope. Now Rowena sat in front of her mother's casket, crying on Keisha's shoulder. At the service, Yolanda recounted her first meeting with Ms. Cook at the hospital. Reverend Johnson spoke about the time when he and his wife encouraged Ms. Cook to fight for her life until the end. He admired Shamira for having done just that. The Reverend then announced that he and Yolanda welcomed everyone to a memorial service for Ms. Cook in Lancaster County.

About one hundred people attended that service two weeks later: Ms. Cook's extended family, former co-workers, friends from her drug rehabilitation center, her Narcotics Anonymous group, members of the church, and members of Yolanda's religious community. Looking around me, I couldn't help but notice the diversity of people Ms. Cook had touched. Young and old, rich and poor, black and white had all gathered under one roof to honor a person they had grown to love as a relative, or recovering drug addict, or conscientious employee, or cancer patient. Toward the end of the service, one of Ms. Cook's co-workers came forward with a large envelope. He said that one time when Ms. Cook was confined to her couch because she was too sick to move, she asked him for help to write a letter. She then dictated a message for Rowena. This message was now in the envelope he was holding. He gave it to Rowena and sat back down. I never learned what Ms. Cook's letter said, but the mere fact that she had prepared it reminded me of something she had told me on several occasions: that she wanted to leave Rowena with at least one thing she would remember.

Yolanda Dixon

After her mother's death, Rowena visited Lancaster County often. She saw her friends during the day and spent the nights with Mrs. Dixon. She told Yolanda that life with her mother had been difficult, and, in many ways, she didn't miss it. Yolanda was convinced that Rowena needed counseling, but doubted if Keisha would offer it to her. She contemplated raising Rowena herself, but she questioned the cultural appropriateness of such an arrangement. She invited Rowena to spend holidays with her family and volunteered to buy her clothes. On one of her visits, Rowena gave Yolanda a copy of the photograph with her and Ms. Cook. Yolanda displayed it prominently in her office.

As time passed, Mrs. Dixon saw less and less of Rowena. But she spoke about her with an intensity that never wavered. She spoke about Ms. Cook as well. She told me that she thought about her every day. No matter how much she tried, she could not accept her friend's death as a good one. If only the doctors had explained to her that her disease was incurable, Yolanda reflected, Shamira would have been able to enjoy the last few months of her life, not suffer through them. In Yolanda's opinion, Shamira would then have refused chemotherapy, lived longer in her apartment, enjoyed Rowena, made plans for her funeral, and accepted the hospice inpatient unit as a good place to die.

The Reverend and Mrs. Johnson

"Our attitude affects our physical condition," Reverend Johnson commented when I spoke with him after Ms. Cook's death. In his experience as a pastor he had seen patients outlive their prognosis—and even defeat their disease—because they fought to live. The Reverend made a distinction between accepting one's diagnosis and resigning to it. He believed that Ms. Cook had accepted the seriousness of her condition, without giving in to the inevitability of her death. Reverend Johnson's wife, Felicia, observed that the last few months of Ms. Cook's life gave her the opportunity to grow spiritually. In the end, she left this world with an improved relationship with God, a renewed relationship with Rowena, and a newfound relationship with her loved ones in Dauphin County. Reflecting on people's tendency to assume Shamira was in denial, Mrs.

Johnson said, "I was intimidated by Shamira [at first] because I had to change my whole mind-set. I had to change my whole thinking about this girl. I had to just shut up, and look at her, and try to go where she was. I think about her because she was such an influence to me, because now when I look at death and dying, I think of it differently. And I will tell people, 'It is not over until it's over.'"

"She was an inspiration," Mrs. Johnson continued, "and that word is not strong enough to really describe the impact that she had on people. Her determination was overwhelming. Shamira has really made me realize that just as there is a quality in living, there is a quality in dying. She did it. She did it with elegance, you know. She was an extraordinary woman."

Then Mrs. Johnson recalled warmly a time in April when Ms. Cook had mustered the strength to attend a Sunday service. The Reverend saw her sitting in the balcony and asked her to rise and greet the congregation. Slowly, Ms. Cook stood up and smiled. Everyone turned toward her and applauded loudly.

7

Rose Picard
"I'm Allowed to Be Happy Even Though I'm Dying"

Narrated by ANNA TOWERS

Rose Picard had led a full and happy life. When at the age of 72, the gynecologist told her that she had ovarian cancer, she adapted quickly to the news. When chemotherapy failed and she transferred to the Palliative Care Unit, she did so with equanimity. Her husband and children had more difficulty. Mrs. Picard had an unshakable faith and *joie de vivre* that impressed her health care givers. She prepared for her death; when she was ready, however, death did not come quickly.

A life of joy and gratitude

Mrs. Picard was a tiny woman with straight, natural gray hair, a prominent beaked nose, and lively, large brown eyes. She seemed always to be smiling, joking, and inquiring after the welfare of those around her. She and her husband Philip had been married for 52 years, since they were both 21. They had two daughters, Mary and Linda, a son, Mark, and six grandchildren. The family got together almost every Sunday. In between, the men played golf together and the women went out for lunch or shopping for clothes.

Mr. Picard had been manager of a plastics factory. He and his wife often gave

120

parties for the employees at their home. Mrs. Picard kept track of everyone's birthday and made certain that they were all remembered. Her husband was a well-built man with a gray moustache and was soft-spoken. Although talking about feelings did not come easily to him, he was an affectionate man, and I often witnessed him holding his wife's hand and doing little favors for her comfort. He was a sentimental man who valued family and religious rituals and special occasions. Anniversaries were important to him.

On balance, Mrs. Picard felt that their relationship had been a good one. "What I lived with my children and my husband is exceptional, exceptional," she told me one day, after she became ill and had agreed to participate in our project. "It's beautiful! I will never forget this. I hope they, too, will remember after I'm gone." The love that she had experienced in this life she also linked with the afterlife. She was Roman Catholic, and her faith was "very, very important" to her. Philip and the children were also practicing Catholics. "God helps us a lot," she would say. "We might leave this life but we go to another one. I will go to another life. I don't know when. He above knows, and I accept it."

Of her marriage and her faith, Mrs. Picard said, "I always tried to be a good spouse, but it doesn't mean that I always was. We have ups and downs in life. There are good days and bad days." In fact, Mrs. Picard would have said that her daughter Mary was her best friend and confidante. Mary told me that her parents supported each other in practical ways but they never really talked. Mr. Picard was not one to talk through problems or share feelings easily. So Mrs. Picard would confide in Mary instead. As Mrs. Picard became sicker, this became an issue.

Mrs. Picard came from an Irish-French family of 14 children. She was the youngest daughter, and looked after her four younger brothers. She started working at age 12. Though her family went through a difficult time during the Depression, Mrs. Picard was never bitter, and learned to be grateful.

Mrs. Picard had a deep respect for the individuality of others. She would say that each of her children was very different and she had allowed them to be who they were. This came back to her later, in that the children respected her in the same way. For example, Mrs. Picard explained, "When my children were growing up, I never pushed them to eat. It's normal for children to be hungry one day and not hungry the next. That's how I brought them up. So they don't push me to eat when I don't feel like it. They just say, 'Mom is ill and not hungry right now.'"

She was a natural mother. Throughout her life she was open to others and attentive to their needs. She was an affectionate person, with a great sense of humor. She enjoyed gatherings, parties, and traveling on business with her husband. Whenever people got together, she wanted to speak with everyone there, showing genuine interest and enthusiasm. At any gathering, Mrs. Picard could be heard above the crowd when she laughed, which she did often. Her husband said to me, "I don't know what it is about her, but everyone wants to be around her." Mrs. Picard said, "I tried to be affable with people. You can't show yourself to be higher or better than them. I wouldn't leave people alone at a gathering. Like, at a convention, someone would arrive and the others wouldn't know how to welcome them. I would say, 'Look, this is what you do. You don't leave a lady like that all alone.' I was like that."

"She was famous for that," her husband chimed in. "Even in our apartment block, when she went to the laundry room, it was time for a big party."

Illness comes

Mrs. Picard had been well all her life. Then, at age 72, she began to have abdominal discomfort and in February 1995 was found to have cancer of the ovary. The tumor was advanced at the time of diagnosis. The gynecologist told her after surgery that 50% of the tumor was still there. He said to Mr. Picard, "We'll try to prolong her life. I don't know how long she has—two months, four months, six months, a year—I don't know." Mr. Picard said of the gynecologist, "He was frank. And I respect that, when the doctor is honest enough to tell us the truth. He couldn't do more. He did what was possible."

The oncologist did not encourage Mrs. Picard to have systemic chemotherapy, and she and the family accepted this. They understood that the aim was to keep Mrs. Picard as comfortable as possible in the time that remained. However, the oncologist did give her intraperitoneal mitoxantrone. By September, she was requiring paracentesis every two weeks to remove fluid from her abdominal cavity. She and the family found it hard to come to the hospital for this. They lived far away. The clinics were busy and they had to wait two or three hours. Mrs. Picard was also referred to the Palliative Care Service at this time for pain control. She lived in a rural area where palliative home care was not available, so Dr. Morin, the palliative care physician, followed her via telephone, along with the family physician who visited her at home. Her abdominal pain was soon controlled.

By December, however, the ascites had become a very significant problem. Mrs. Picard's abdomen was heavy and uncomfortable. She still needed peritoneal taps every two weeks. She decided that she did not want the intraperitoneal chemotherapy anymore, since it didn't seem to be working. However, she did agree to try oral cyclophosphamide, another chemotherapy agent. In mid-January 1996, Mrs. Picard was admitted to the gynecology ward with vomiting due to a small bowel obstruction. She was treated conservatively with a nasogastric tube and IV rehydration. She very quickly became the "darling" of the ward. She was considerate of the nurses and would make them laugh.

Within a few days, Mrs. Picard's symptoms settled, but she was not well enough to go home. The gynecology staff and Dr. Morin, the palliative care physician, discussed with Mrs. Picard and her family the possibility of a transfer to the Palliative Care Unit. Perhaps there she would get stronger and be able to go home again. In the meantime, the palliative care staff would try to control her symptoms. Dr. Morin explained to the family that bowel obstruction was a serious complication but occasionally the symptoms resolved and the person could go home again. Mr. and Mrs. Picard and their daughter Mary were visibly upset, but then seemed to accept the situation. Linda, on the other hand, was constantly in tears when she came to see her mother. She would stay for a few minutes but then had to leave because she was so upset.

Mary and Linda

Mary, who was 50 years old, was Mrs. Picard's oldest daughter. She was a remarkably good-looking woman, with long blond hair kept tidily coifed. She was warm and open about her feelings and also concerned about the welfare of others. She seemed to me to be a "natural carer," like her mother. Mrs. Picard was very close to her. I often saw the two of them chatting quietly, holding hands on the hospital ward. They had spoken openly about the cancer from the time of diagnosis. Mary felt prepared. She said to me, "We have known for a year now that she is dying, and I went through it with her. You know, the asking 'Why me?' and feeling angry. And then she would feel like crying and I would say, 'It's OK to cry.' So we would cry together. And then she would feel better."

Linda, however, who was a year younger, was more withdrawn and had great difficulty accepting the diagnosis. She would not talk about it and would not come with her mother to the oncology clinic for treatments. Later, when her mother was sicker, I would see her rushing into the hospital to see her mother. She walked very fast, looking very anxious and upset, and never stayed very long. Linda was somewhat overweight, had long black hair, and always seemed a bit disheveled compared to her sister. She never looked me straight in the eye and could never chat easily, as Mary could. Linda had always been closer to her father, and she found it difficult now to speak with her mother.

Mr. Picard and Mark did not say much either, though they supported Mrs. Picard in a practical way. It was clear that Mrs. Picard was able to share her feelings with Mary in a way that she could with no one else. Mary had an explanation for this. "I've been through suffering in my life," she told me, "so it's easier for me to accept this than it is for my sister or my father perhaps. When I was 33, I developed a colon infection that led to perforation of the bowel. I almost died. I was in intensive care for a couple of weeks. I went part way into the other world. It took me months to recover. I had two young children at that time. So I came face to face with death then. It made me unafraid. I'm no longer afraid of the dying process."

"It changed my life," Mary continued. "I learned to live 24 hours at a time, and to appreciate what is beautiful in the world. When I love someone, I tell them. I'm a grandmother now, and when I'm with my granddaughter, we talk about the lovely flowers and how nice they smell, and the sounds of the birds. We have a great time together, just appreciating what's around us. So my mother and I spoke about that. My mother said, 'I'm afraid of dying.' 'So?' I said. 'That's normal.' Then she said, 'What was it like when you were sick?' And I explained to her that it felt very peaceful, and was a beautiful experience. So she had a dream, and she said she dreamt that she was dying and she saw stars. And it was so beautiful, she said. She said, 'I'm not afraid anymore.'"

Mrs. Picard had related this dream to the occupational therapist some days before I heard Mary's version of it: "I was in my coffin and I saw how things were. I saw stars coming from the sky to pick me up. I saw blue. I saw some beautiful things." She said she was reassured by this dream.

"I'd like to call you Rose"

On January 20, Mrs. Picard was transferred to the Palliative Care Unit, in a separate wing of the same hospital, and settled into a private room overlooking a wooded park. Within a few days her windowsill was full of cards and her grandchildren's drawings adorned the walls. The nurses from the gynecology service came to visit Mrs. Picard often. They had become fond of her and would come during their lunch break or after their shift.

Most patients find a nasogastric tube uncomfortable, and as soon as Mrs. Picard arrived on the Palliative Care Unit Dr. Morin ordered it removed. She tried to relieve the symptoms of bowel obstruction with medication, including antiemetics, somatostatin or anticholinergics, and steroids. These medications prevent nausea and minimize gastrointestinal secretions, thus reducing vomiting.

Mrs. Picard never demanded anything and tended not to complain so the nurses quickly learned that they had to ask her if she had pain. She tried to be as active as possible, walking in the hallways aided by her husband or one of her children. She enjoyed sitting in the solarium or in the family kitchen, chatting with other patients, family members, and staff.

At one point, Mrs. Picard became disoriented, and she was afraid; she woke up and thought she was dead. She preferred to always have company with her. As always in her life, she did not like to be alone. Mostly, she was serene in her outlook, exhibiting remarkable openness in discussing her terminal illness. She spoke calmly to the priest of her decision to refuse treatment. "Life is a pilgrimage," she said to him. "When the time comes to finish, it comes." But she wanted to enjoy a good quality of life for as long as possible. For her, this meant being able to enjoy her family and feeling supported by them.

Mrs. Picard was worried that her husband was not accepting of the fact that she was dying. Mr. Picard often appeared anxious; but Linda seemed to be having the most difficult time. Though she came to the unit to see her mother almost every day, she still did not stay long. She was usually pacing the hallway whenever I saw her, and often her face was puffy and her eyes red from crying. She didn't share her feelings, and usually left without speaking with staff.

Mrs. Picard developed a very warm and friendly relationship with Father Francis, the pastoral worker who was assigned to the ward. Despite a 30-year age difference between them, Father Francis, who was normally quite formal, was moved to ask her, "May I call you by your first name—Rose? It's a beautiful name. I'd like to call you Rose." She said, "Of course," and started to call him by his first name also. Father Francis came to see her regularly. She appreciated his visits and received Communion almost every day. She commented that Father Francis had been to Haiti and that "he has seen a lot of suffering." She was obviously fond of him.

As January drew to an end, Mrs. Picard began vomiting again, evidence that she might be developing bowel obstruction once more. Mrs. Picard asked the oncologist directly what her prognosis was and was told that it was approximately four weeks. She took the news with equanimity, continuing to say that she was not afraid of death.

Preparations

Over the next few days, Mrs. Picard grew weaker. Although the symptoms of her bowel obstruction were controlled with metoclopramide (which prevents nausea and aids gastric emptying) and prochlorperazine (a second antiemetic), she was unable to eat much. She asked to go home to spend a final day there. "I want to see my things," she said.

Her family organized themselves to bring her home by car. Mark had to carry her up the front stairs. She immediately went to lie down on the cot in her conservatory, in the sun, among her favorite plants. She lay there happily and fell asleep. A few hours later, her family brought her back to hospital. They would have liked to have kept her at home, but she still had intermittent vomiting, and was so weak that she needed total care. Mr. Picard felt more secure with her being in hospital, as he was physically unable to provide his wife with the care she required and his children all worked. Although Mary was willing to take time off, she did not feel that she would have enough support in looking after her mother. Linda was too upset and anxious to give practical help.

Nonetheless, Mr. Picard wanted to try to bring his wife home on day passes as often as possible. Mrs. Picard accepted that her family did not have the resources to care for her at home and did not put any pressure on them to keep her there.

On February 8, Father Francis asked Mrs. Picard if she wanted to receive the Sacrament of the Sick. Formal Catholic rituals were important to the Picards. Mrs. Picard agreed, and she wanted all her children to be there. However, Mark said that he could not take time off work, and Linda didn't come because she was too anxious, saying she couldn't bear to be there. But Mr. Picard and Mary were present, along with two volunteers from pastoral services. Father Francis later told me that it was one of the most beautiful ceremonies that he had ever experienced—Mrs. Picard participated fully in spite of her suffering and weakness, and she embraced and kissed everyone at the end.

The music therapist visited, and Mrs. Picard requested that she play Schubert's "Ave Maria." Mrs. Picard was very moved by this, and said that she wanted this played at her funeral. She was clearly preparing herself for her death.

In early February, Mrs. Picard expressed an interest in having a video made of herself speaking to her family. The staff found a video filmmaker who volunteered to do this for her, and they organized themselves in the solarium for the filming. Mrs. Picard had a brief prepared text in which she thanked her caregivers and addressed her family. "The time has arrived for me to leave you," she read into the camera, "without regret, but with a lot of serenity. For you, Philip, good-bye and I hope to see you soon. And similarly, for Mary, my daughter and confidante, and Linda, who has learned to adapt to the situation even though you are going through a lot of grief. We have all had a lot of grief. And Mark, you were a joy in my life." Mrs. Picard quickly came to the end of her prepared text and then wasn't quite sure what to say. The music therapist asked her, "What makes it possible for you to be so accepting of what is happening? I find it remarkable." Mrs. Picard smiled and replied:

> I am not afraid of dying. I am facing it with serenity. I want it to be beautiful. I want it to be me. Then, in the church, I don't want any fanfare. All I want is for the ones I love to be there. I have accepted this, but it hasn't been easy. I don't want to flinch too much, but it hurts. Like, for my children—Linda in particular—she can't be there when I talk about dying. And my son, too. It's hard for them to be with me.

Mrs. Picard was pleased to have made the video and wanted all her family to look at it with her right away. She would ask caregivers who came into the room, "Have you seen my video?"

By this time she needed multiple medications to prevent vomiting, as she had total bowel obstruction. She received a cocktail of subcutaneous medication consisting of 20 mg famotidine, 40 mg metoclopramide, 20 mg morphine, 300 µg somatostatin, 100 mg dimenhydrinate, and 2 mg haloperidol via a syringe driver. Another syringe driver contained 16 mg dexamethasone. In addition, she took laxatives by mouth. With the aid of this medication she was relatively comfortable. She was still able to walk slowly, with help, wearing the two syringe drivers in small fitted pouches strapped to her shoulder. Despite all this, she still managed to look cheerful. One day, as she was returning from the whirlpool bath, I saw her wearing a big smile.

Decreasing the life-prolonging medication

By mid-February, Mrs. Picard was too weak to walk. At this point she said to Dr. Morin, "I'm tired and fed up. I have done everything I need to do and I want it to be over." Dr. Morin considered the situation, realizing that her patient was now dying. The bowel obstruction had not resolved, and Mrs. Picard had a lot of tumor in her abdomen. Dr. Morin explained to Mrs. Picard the medication she was on, and what the dexamethasone was doing. Perhaps it was prolonging her life by keeping her bowels open. Mrs. Picard told Dr. Morin that she wanted the dexamethasone decreased, thinking that this might bring death sooner. Dr. Morin began to taper the dexamethasone in accordance with her wishes, and would increase the medication for pain control and nausea if required.

Now it was even more important for Mrs. Picard to have her family with her. "I like to have people around, otherwise I panic," she said to me. Her family organized their time so there would be someone there most of the day and in the evening. Mrs. Picard felt slightly somnolent, but her mentation was otherwise clear. She had practically no appetite, and was especially grateful to her family for not pushing her to eat.

On February 22, Mary visited her mother in the afternoon as usual. The two of them were alone, which made it easier for Mary to speak with her mother about dying. Mrs. Picard felt very comfortable having this discussion. "Don't think about us," Mary said to her. "We will be all right."

Mark started talking to me about his mother's death. He said that he hoped to take a trip with his dad after this was all over. Linda still seemed more fragile. She was often tearful and would say to me, "This is so difficult."

When I saw Mrs. Picard around this time, she was amazingly cheerful. She said, "I have some Irish blood in me so I'm allowed to be happy even though I'm dying. It's like *pfft!*" She made a sound like a fire going out, then laughed out loud.

A couple of days later it was quiet on the ward. Mrs. Picard looked the most tired that I had seen her. She was having some periods of confusion, and some frightening dreams. She had some visual hallucinations, seeing mice and ducks in her room, but she seemed not to be too bothered. (Dr. Morin believed that this could be from the morphine, so she adjusted the medication.) Mrs. Picard said to me, "It's like I wish it were all over. Because I'm so tired. It's long, always waiting, waiting, waiting. And I'm always afraid that I might choke. I've never choked, but I'm afraid! I'm afraid because I had a friend, and she choked to death. As soon as she drank water, she would choke."

Mr. Picard was there, too, anxious to help in whatever way he could. He said to his wife, "I gave you a bit of ice just now, and you were able to suck on it. That helped, didn't it?" He turned to me. "And I helped her clean her teeth and her mouth, and that helped."

"Uh-huh," she agreed. Then her thoughts drifted to her home, which she might never see again. "It's so quiet," she said. "Many patients have left for the weekend, eh? But it's not easy for the families, it's hard for them to get organized. But maybe I can spend a little time at home tomorrow."

"If you're strong enough," Mr. Picard said. "We did it last week because you were a little bit stronger than this week."

Mrs. Picard seemed to drift off a few times during our conversation. Then she would perk up for a few minutes. She spoke about her video. She had viewed it once, and wanted to see it again. Several other patients and families on the ward had seen it, and she was very happy about that. Each of the children had their own copy.

We sat silently for a few moments. Mr. Picard was holding his wife's hand and looking at her. Then he turned to me and said slowly and deliberately:

> When you've been married almost 53 years, and you see that your wife is in the hospital, it does something to you. To see her suffer, it does something. I can't help her, but she says my being here helps, so every day I come to see her. We spoke this week, and she told me that she's tired of living, because of all the physical symptoms. So she made me promise not to hold on to her. Then she said that when she's up there, she's going to speak with me every day. So that's what helps me. And the children support me, too. I hope that God comes to take her as fast as possible, because she tells me she's tired of suffering.

Mrs. Picard, who had been listening to this, added, "It looks that way."

It impressed me how this couple, who had been together for so long, could speak so openly about letting go of their earthly relationship. I could sense their deep faith in a relationship that could continue in the afterlife. Mr. Picard continued, "We said everything that we had to say to each other. And our children were there, too. So, this week she received the Last Rites, and we were here. So she's ready to go in peace. That's what we wish with all our hearts. And as far as we're concerned, it's understood that we'll talk to her every day and she'll monitor us, eh, Ma?" Mr. Picard said, turning to address his wife.

Mrs. Picard replied, with no hesitation, "There'll be nothing to monitor."

"You'll keep an eye on us, anyway."

Mrs. Picard said, with a twinkle, "You're old enough to do your own monitoring." This made Mr. Picard laugh.

"Don't worry, I'm here beside you"

Father Francis commented to me that Mrs. Picard seemed to bear her physical decline with an unwavering faith. "It's surprising to me," he said, "because the more she declines physically, the stronger her faith. But it is a balanced faith, not an exuberant faith. It isn't, 'I believe in God no matter what, everything rests with Him, and you'll see—He will save me.' It isn't the kind of faith that's like a lifesaver."

Mrs. Picard was not expecting a miracle. When she saw her children and her husband now, she made them promise that they would let her go, that they would not try to hold on. Linda continued to have difficulty with this, and was very tearful whenever she saw her mother. Mary, on the other hand, was able to be more realistic and cool about the situation. The next day, February 25th, Mary asked whether the dexamethasone might be decreased further. She felt that the dexamethasone might be prolonging suffering now, rather than prolonging useful life. "She wants to die and is exhausted," Mary said. "It's so hard to see her this way."

Mrs. Picard was too weak for me to interview her. She acknowledged my presence, but was very sleepy. She seemed calm, relaxed. Mary was concerned but seemed relatively relaxed compared to Linda, who averted my gaze and never smiled. Dr. Morin continued to taper the dexamethasone. There seemed to be no conflict in Dr. Morin's mind: her patient was dying and her goal was to keep her comfortable, not to try to get her to eat or drink again.

Mrs. Picard found it difficult to be alone at night now. She had had nightmares the day before that were possibly related to her medication. Mr. Picard was afraid that she would have them again, so he said that he would stay with her and keep an eye on her. He could help Dr. Morin, by observing his wife and reporting back what happened during the night. The nurses prepared a cot so he could sleep beside his wife, but he did not sleep much that night, having never slept in a hospital before. He would get up every hour or so to check on his wife. "Don't worry, I'm here beside you," he would say if he saw that she, too, was awake.

Periodically, Mr. Picard would listen to her breathing. "And when I couldn't hear her breathe," he explained to me, "I would get up to have a look. Then suddenly, she would start breathing again. So, I would say to myself, 'she's still alive.'" Mr. Picard found it impossible to rest. Mrs. Picard woke up many times, too. Mr. Picard would say, "Don't worry, I'm next to you. I'm sleeping." Finally, at 7 a.m., having hardy slept, he went home. He slept for a few hours and then came back because he knew that his wife needed him to be there.

Linda was too anxious to spend nights with her mother, and Mary had been admitted to the hospital with pain from kidney stones. The family decided not to tell Mrs. Picard about this. Mr. Picard did not dare ask his son to stay the night because Mark had his work and his own family, and he had not offered to stay. The ward staff tried to ensure that there was a volunteer to sit with Mrs. Picard late into the evening.

Sometimes Mrs. Picard was confused. "I want to go home," she said one evening, in her confused state.

Mr. Picard said, "You can't go home."

"Why?"

"Because it's Dr. Morin who gives permission to go, and now it's too late, you can't go."

"Oh," Mrs. Picard retorted, "she's the boss then."

Mr. Picard tried to explain. "You know, the three or four other times that you came home, she gave her permission and I didn't refuse to bring you home. But now I can't bring you."

"OK, but try tomorrow, and tell me what she says."

Mr. Picard tried to avoid the subject the next day, so as not to upset her. He was hoping that the end would come soon. "She's so tired," he said to me. "I don't know what keeps her going. She wanted to see Peter, one of our grand-children, and she was so happy to see him. She was holding on for that. And then, it's her birthday in five days. I think she's waiting for her birthday to come. Is she waiting for her birthday, to die on her birthday? I don't know. Only God knows. But I hope that she goes soon, because to see her suffer— she hasn't eaten, she feels sick to her stomach. If only I could be the one to suffer, to spare her, but she's the one that has to suffer." He sobbed. Then he continued:

> I can't say that the nurses and doctors aren't doing their job. It's extraordinary what they do. But it's difficult anyway, to see her day after day and to see that she's still alive but that her color's changed and she's lost so much weight. She weighed 126 when she came in hospital and now she can't weigh more than 100 pounds. In the summer, she weighed 170 pounds. Yesterday we stopped by the Oratory and we prayed God to take her because it's difficult for us to see her suffer. The doctors can't do more than what they're doing. No, I can't ask more of them. They're doing their best, but she's the one who's suffering.

Mr. Picard had trouble containing his tears. The family looked exhausted. They had many questions about what would happen now. How was she going to die? Mrs. Picard had been weaker and confused for a few days but occasionally she seemed to perk up and be able to sit up in bed. Mary said, "She is such a lively person, always smiling. Even now, we were in the solarium and she wanted to talk with everyone, to touch everyone. She enjoys touching people. So do I. There was a Spanish-speaking woman there and she tried to talk to her in Spanish! She was so lively."

Whenever the music therapist came now, Mrs. Picard only wanted to hear the "Ave Maria." She looked sadder now, though she smiled occasionally. Death did not come.

Tired of waiting

It was early March and Mrs. Picard again expressed frustration—she was tired of the whole situation. She started to feel anxious that the dying process was taking so long and she was afraid that she might have more pain. When she asked Dr. Morin to give her a sedative so that she could sleep more during the day, Dr. Morin decided to increase the midazolam. Mrs. Picard now needed small amounts of medication (15 mg each of morphine and midazolam subcutaneously over 24 hours) to keep her asleep; the dexamethasone had been stopped.

Over the next two or three days, Mrs. Picard mostly slept. She ate very little. She complained of thirst at one point, but this was alleviated by increasing her mouth care. By March 4, she was confused and was obviously dying. I tried to talk with her but could not get a response. Mr. Picard, Linda, and her husband were at the bedside. Linda was visibly upset and was not able to talk to me. She was trying her best to control her strong feelings and spend more time at her mother's bedside, especially since Mary was still in another hospital with her kidney stone problem. Mrs. Picard was so somnolent and confused that she seemed not to notice that Mary was absent. Still, Mr. Picard wanted his wife to receive even more sedation. "Mary and I spoke with Dr. Morin about it," he told me. "To give her an injection to relieve her—not euthanasia, but to relieve her. My wife also spoke to Dr. Morin about it. She is thinking about me, saying, 'You'd be better off at home.' I am staying with her all the time and she didn't want to bother anyone. She always thinks of others before thinking of herself."

Linda either paced in the hallway, her eyes red from crying, or she sat by her mother's bedside, holding her hand. Her mother was barely responsive now, and when she was more wakeful, she was agitated and confused. Linda wondered whether it was the medication that was making her mother behave in this way. "She is trying to take her bedclothes off," she said to me, distressed by this behavior that was so unlike her mother and seemed so undignified. Speaking as a doctor, I explained to her that it was not the morphine that was making her mother confused but her general debility and state of imbalance. We often see this in the last days of life, and it is usually controlled easily with tranquilizers. I explained that if the family's presence by the bedside was not enough to calm her mother, the medical team could sedate her more. "Her throat seems sore," Linda said, a moment later. I explained about mouth dryness and that the family could use sponges to keep her mouth moist and make her more comfortable. Linda seemed reassured by my explanations and went back to holding her mother's hand.

In one of her rare wakeful moments, Mrs. Picard said again, "I'm tired. I'm fed up, let me go." By this time she was not eating anything. Linda and her father wanted the nurse to give Mrs. Picard more tranquilizer, as their tolerance for any sign that she might be in discomfort or confused was low. They wanted her completely asleep. Although the nurse was very busy she understood their anxiety and gave Mrs. Picard another injection, even though to the nurse the degree of agitation was minor. Mrs. Picard was now receiving 5 mg midazolam every 4 hours, as required, to keep her asleep.

Mr. Picard was the most anxious that I had seen him. He said that Mrs. Picard seemed uncomfortable in the bed and he kept ringing the bell for the nurse to come. He got impatient when the nurse was not immediately available to help reposition his wife, whose legs were rubbing against the bed rails. He was trying to be polite, but his anxiety came through. He paced in the room. If he got upset, he would pace in the hallway. He said to me: "It is her 75th birthday today. She will have lived through it, but not experienced it. I have brought her flowers, but she is not aware of this. I am praying the Lord to take her today. I have been speaking with Linda over the weekend. I've told her, 'You have to accept that your mother is dying. You have to let her go.'"

"Don't ask me—Mary is the mother now"

The next day, March 5, Mrs. Picard continued in her comatose state. She did not require any extra tranquilizer. Mary was now out of the hospital after a four-day stay, and had come to be with her mother again. The family accepted live flute music at the bedside, particularly Mrs. Picard's favorite pieces, "Ave Maria" and Pachelbel's "Canon." Mary sang along. Mrs. Picard seemed calmer after the music. The family also used cassettes to play her favorite classical music. They all looked exhausted, waiting for God to take her. Mary looked tired, too, but at the same time, calm and accepting.

As I got up to leave she followed me outside, wanting to have a chat with me. We sat in the family kitchen. Mary said:

> It's hard for my father. He is having a hard time over the last few days, since it has become apparent that Mom is dying. He can't bear not to be able to communicate

with her now. It's easier for me than for my sister, and maybe also easier for me than for my father.

Today is the first day that I have not seen her smile, because she can't smile. She always had a smile on her face. Everyone said, "Oh, your mother, she's the one who is always smiling." That's how they knew who she was. She likes to touch people and to be touched, so we touch her. We hold her and caress her. She likes that.

Linda is having a hard time. She is afraid of death. I told her, "Linda, you have to get some help." She is so anxious. The other day, Linda asked my mother something, asked for her advice. And my mother said, "Don't ask me—Mary is the mother now." I have to be the strong one now. But my mother is there for me. Last night I felt her actual presence there beside me, so she will always be a presence for me.

I met Mr. Picard in the hallway. He was agitated. "It upset me today when I walked in and saw all those catheters," he said. The nurses had put in a urinary catheter because Mrs. Picard was too weak even to use the bedpan. There was only one catheter, but the tube and bags seemed to multiply in Mr. Picard's mind. "I don't know," he went on. "I didn't look closely, but I didn't like to see that. She is so much weaker, but she's holding on. She's gone through her birthday now." Tearfully, he went into the elevator.

The family and staff made sure that Mrs. Picard's favorite music tapes were played continually. Even though she was comatose, the music played all night. She died early the next morning. The family was not present, but they arrived soon after. Her death was described by the staff as peaceful.

"Evenings are the worst"

At first, Mr. Picard called Mary 20 to 40 times a day. He was crying all the time. He insisted that his children clear Mrs. Picard's things out of the house the day after the funeral—her clothes and jewelry, the mementos. Mary told me that she found this difficult, but they respected their father's wishes.

When I spoke to Mr. Picard five months after his wife's death he still seemed to be deep in his grief, though by this time he was calling Mary only five or six times per day, usually about "little things." He carried his wife's photograph with him as he wandered around the house. He put it on the dining table while he ate. "I try to avoid the house," he said, "because all the furniture and decorating was done by my wife." He was considering moving the next year, to get away from "the memories in this place." He played golf during the day, and this was a good distraction, but he found it difficult when he got back in the evenings. "Evenings are the worst," he told me. "I get so lonely." He went on:

After 53 years I was wondering if I could continue. But I spoke with her and it helped. She told me in the hospital, "I will be there for you." I go to the cemetery on the 6th of every month [the anniversary of the death], but my daughter Linda says, "Don't go so often." I don't listen to her. I listen to my heart. If I feel like talking to my wife, I talk to her. I talk to her all the time. Mary understands this, but Linda is having a hard time. When Linda comes over, she just wants to go through and look at her mother's things. She is suffering a lot.

Mr. Picard obtained a lot of comfort from being with his grandson. "I play golf with him and we talk about his grandmother and I feel better," he said. He also spoke with another grandson, who was a nurse. "His grandmother was his idol," said Mr. Picard. "I need to speak about these things. I know that some people must get bored or annoyed with me."

On what would have been their 53rd wedding anniversary, Mr. Picard went to the cemetery with his daughters and one granddaughter. He found the ritual helpful. However, he found the day of the six-month anniversary difficult, even though his daughters were there.

When I phoned him shortly after this, he sounded relaxed, calm, confident, steady, and in control. "I'm doing better," he said. He was thinking about his wife almost constantly. "She said to me before she died, 'I hope you'll continue to live.' But I can't go out with just anybody. I like to go out with my daughters. I see friends and play cards on Wednesday nights. I don't feel the need for a woman friend right now, although my friends are pushing me in that direction."

Mary, Linda, and Mark

Mary expressed disappointment in her relationship with her father at this time. She told me, "My sister and I are trying to help my father, but we are also suffering, and he doesn't see that. Linda talks to him about how sad he feels and they cry together. Linda has a different way of talking with my father. She will ring Daddy up and say, 'Are you crying? Are you lonely? Poor Daddy, you're all alone.' Whereas I will say, 'How is your day going?' I ask him that way, but I guess we're all different."

"My father," Mary continued, "according to him, he's the only one who has the right to mourn. He never asks how I'm doing emotionally, only physically. My son and daughter, and Linda, I can speak to. Linda asks me a lot, how I'm doing. And I need to talk. My mother and father never really talked. She always talked with me. Maybe he feels guilty about not having communicated better with her. But I try to tell him not to feel guilty, that Mom forgave everything before she died, that she died in peace. But I think that he feels guilty about things that he didn't do in their relationship."

Mary had begun to volunteer in a palliative care program three months after her mother's death. "Even if it's just to hold someone's hand," she said, "I feel that I'm contributing something. I'm a listening ear. I love that work." She then spoke of the joy and comfort that her granddaughters brought to her in her grief:

> My granddaughter Kim is extraordinary. She is three years old. A few days ago we were walking by a pond with ducks. She said, "The ducks will die. Will Grandma feed them after they die?" She speaks incessantly of Grandma Rose. I have another granddaughter who was born on May 6—my mother died the 6th of March. I felt her presence there in the delivery room. This is a baby who is always smiling. Jade is her name. We associate her a lot with my mother. My mother used to say, "I won't see this baby born, but speak to this child about me." Kim said, "Doesn't Jade smile like Grandma?" I hope my grandchildren continue to grow like this. They're extraordinary.

Mr. Picard had also spoken to me about Jade. "This last grandchild," he told me, "born three months after her death, on the 6th—it's as if my wife sent her. She's here to guide us, this grandchild." The sixth of the month had became an important, difficult day.

Linda was doing better now than when she first learned of her mother's cancer diagnosis. She was very anxious, however, about her father's welfare, not wanting him to go far, and was worried about him dying, too. Linda was very close to her father, continuing to call him every day, as she had done even before her mother died. Mark seemed to be coping in a different way; he never spoke about his mother. Mary was never able to speak with him alone, without the children there, to see how he was feeling, and he didn't seem to encourage such discussions.

Getting on

Mr. Picard was experiencing the change of seasons differently now. As autumn came, he said to me, "I didn't want to go out. My children had to come see me here. Between the sixth and the ninth of this month, it was difficult. I felt the winter coming. Then the leaves fell, there were no leaves. The trees looked different. I was glad to have my family around."

The first Thanksgiving was difficult. They were not looking forward to Christmas. "I have to buy Christmas cards," Mr. Picard said. "My wife used to do that. So I'm trying to do that in the same way my wife did it. We're trying to carry on living, even though she's not here. Last week, I cooked dinner for the whole family. The year before she died she taught me how to cook, do the laundry, clean the house. She used to do everything. If she hadn't taught me, I would have had a hard time right now. She was understanding and practical. I could not have had the same life without her. She was wise. She was always right when she said things."

Mr. Picard found it difficult to plan vacation trips, since he had always traveled with his wife. But now he was planning to visit his grandson in Texas. When Christmas came the family coped by celebrating in new ways. They rented a house in Vermont and had pot-luck dinners. Mr. Picard found it helpful to have done something different.

When I spoke to Mr. Picard one year after his wife's death, he was still very conscious of her presence. This was both reassuring and distressing to him. "In July, I will move to another apartment," he said. "Because she's here with me all the time. We speak often. Is this normal?" I reassured him that it was. "She tells me, 'Rest, you've had enough,' or, 'Continue with your life.' When I play with my granddaughter, I see my wife's brown eyes and that helps me."

"I'm lucky that my children are so helpful," he went on. "Like when I told them I would move, they told me not to worry. They would help. Here I see her everywhere. I know I won't forget her, but by changing surroundings, maybe it will help me get on with my life."

8

Victor Sloski:
"I Want to Die at Home"

Narrated by PATRICIA BOSTON

Victor Sloski learned that he had lung cancer when he was 57. The news was hard to take. He had lived happily with Shirley, his live-in companion, for 20 years. Still, when experimental treatments failed, he was prepared to die, hoping the end would come soon. It didn't. His cancer metastasized from his lungs to his stomach, spleen, colon, and finally, to his brain, causing him to go blind. The palliative care team offered to arrange an admission to the inpatient unit, but Mr. Sloski insisted that he wanted home care. He wanted to die at home regardless of how ill he became.

Victor Sloski did die at home. Afterward, Shirley said, "Caring for a dying husband was the biggest challenge of my life. But if I had to do it all over again, I would do it." Getting to that point had been very hard. At times Shirley felt that she was too exhausted, emotionally and physically, to go on.

Life before: a new beginning

Victor Sloski had never been afraid of hard labor. He was 18 years old when he first arrived in Canada to look for work. Born in Poland just before World War II, he was raised with a brother and two sisters on a farm some 30 miles from the city of Warsaw. Most of what he knew about reading and writing came from four or five years of elementary school in Poland before he went to work on the family farm. When times got difficult in Poland, he emigrated to Canada, where his experience in farming stood him well. He found a job on a small French-Canadian farm 20 miles north of Montreal.

This job lasted only a few months, but the farmer helped him find work at the local farmers' market, loading and unloading fruit and vegetables from the trucks that brought produce to the markets every day. When that job folded, he found work at a larger city market, unloading fruit and vegetables from rail cars and from the ships at the city's dock. He held that job for the next 20 years. He might have been able to get other work if he'd had an education, but this had not really worried him; it was more important to go to work than go to school, and anyway, Victor said, work never hurt anybody. Sometimes he worked 18–20 hours a day. The pay was not much, but it was honest and put bread on his table. He was able to send money back to Warsaw, to his now widowed mother and his sisters. Most years he'd been able to send $300–$400 a year.

In the kind of work he did there was little chance to meet women. When he was almost 40 years old, he met Shirley, an accounts clerk at one of the central market offices. Shirley came from a farming family in Manitoba, about 1000 miles from Montreal. Victor wasn't one for marriage; he couldn't guarantee enough security. But he liked Shirley a lot. She was "kind" and "a good looker." She liked Victor. He was "the strong, silent type." Victor and Shirley lived together for the next 20 years, in a small, one-bedroom apartment over a grocery store in the small working class suburb of Ste. Marie, four or five miles from downtown Montreal. They had no children as they couldn't afford to raise a child. "You never knew whether or not you'd be out of work and have to go on welfare," Victor said.

The guys who worked with Victor were good buddies, who, "if you were short of a dollar," would help you out without asking why. After a day's unloading at the dock, they'd had many a good night at the tavern with a few beers and a smoke. Victor had been a smoker all of his life, smoking two to three packs of cigarettes a day, sometimes lighting one cigarette with the last. He never thought about it much, for everybody had smoked. Some of the guys never had a cigarette out of their hand, Victor said to me. Besides, he added, when you were the worrying kind, a good cigarette helped you relax.

Something's wrong

In 1993 Victor began to notice a nagging cough. He had always had a smoker's cough, but this cough was more persistent. It kept him up at night and made him feel tired on the job. He began getting short of breath, and even small tasks became hard to cope with. Some days, instead of stopping off for a beer at the tavern or fixing gadgets around the house after work, he needed to go straight to bed.

In October, Mr. Sloski saw Dr. Gregory, his local general practitioner, and asked him for some cough syrup. After listening to Victor's chest, Dr. Gregory ordered chest X-rays and a computed tomography (CT) scan. The X-ray showed a large mass, and the CT scan showed a hilar mass and a small lesion in the right lung. Following a transthoracic needle aspiration to obtain a small biopsy of lung tissue, the pathology report indicated a large-cell undifferentiated carcinoma. Further tests revealed metastases to the liver and spleen.

A few months later a surgeon at the city hospital performed a splenectomy in an attempt to arrest the spread of the cancer, but it was immediately clear that further surgical intervention would not be effective. At this point, Mr. Sloski was referred to Dr. Limberg in medical oncology. From March to August of 1994, Mr. Sloski received six courses of experimental chemotherapy. After the protocol was complete, a follow-up CT scan showed there was no change in the tumor. Chest X-rays revealed further progression of the disease. Over the next year the oncologists tried two more experimental drugs, but Mr. Sloski's cancer responded to neither. In December 1995, Dr. Limberg consulted with Dr. Webster of the Palliative Care Service. Mr. Sloski was experiencing pain in his chest and abdomen and had frequent headaches. Dr. Limberg expected that Mr. Sloski's pain would intensify and hoped the Palliative Care Service could control it.

Around the time of this consultation, Mr. Sloski began to complain of difficulty with his vision. Things started to look blurred and unclear, and the blurring seemed to be getting worse. He also began to feel unsteady on his feet. He would be walking along and then suddenly keel over to his right side. In January 1996, Dr. Limberg ordered another CT scan, which showed that the cancer was in Mr. Sloski's brain.

"I knew the real story"

The best option that Dr. Webster and the palliative care team could suggest was to refer Mr. Sloski for a palliative course of external beam radiotherapy to the brain. Radiotherapy is sometimes used therapeutically in palliative care to alleviate a tumor's pressure by reducing its size. However, while radiotherapy might alleviate some of the pain Mr. Sloski felt in his head, it could sometimes produce acute and uncomfortable side effects, such as nausea and vomiting. Nevertheless, hoping it would help in the long term, Victor agreed to undergo five radiation treatments. Fortunately, he did not suffer any side effects and the medical report noted that he tolerated the radiation therapy well.

Mr. Sloski knew that the radiation treatments would not make his cancer go away. In that sense, he said, he knew "the real story." He had never been one for avoiding things that needed to be faced. Still, he recalled to me later, "they said the radiation would stay with you at least for a month. So I thought it would do some good. Maybe stop the pain in my head." While it may have helped reduce his headaches, it seemed that his sight was still worsening. As the days and weeks passed, he couldn't read the paper even with his glasses.

Despite these setbacks, his appetite was good—at least for the moment. Shirley prepared tasty meals of his favorite foods, even if it was an expensive piece of steak, just to get him to eat a few mouthfuls. But eating was small comfort when so many other things were going wrong in his body. He was beginning to have seizures, or "fits," as he would call them. At times everything would go black for a few seconds. Dr. Webster prescribed phenytoin, which seemed to work, and after a few days Mr. Sloski reported fewer seizures. By March, however, he was having more abdominal pain. Dr. Webster prescribed omeprazole, which helped to alleviate the discomfort.

Mr. Sloski was in emotional turmoil. What would happen next to his body? He couldn't sleep through the night and he had panic attacks almost every day. He also experienced periods of intense depression. Dr. Webster prescribed nortriptyline, which helped to lift Victor's spirits, and clonazepam and rivotril to calm him and control the acute panic attacks.

By this time, Grania MacDonald, the palliative home care nurse, was following Mr. Sloski. When she visited their home in Ste. Marie, Grania found that Mr. Sloski and Shirley were very comfortable talking about the progression of his illness. Mr. Sloski talked easily of his experiences with his symptoms and what it was like "to be living like a sick person when you had worked all your life." Moreover, they both thought it important that doctors and nurses be aware of what these experiences could be like. When Grania mentioned our research project to them, they said they would be very willing to participate. I visited their home for the first time in early March.

"I want to die at home!"

Ste. Marie is a community that visitors might pass through on their way to other places. It is a world of commerce and small-housing tenements that sprawls untidily along the northern end of Montreal, the main road leading to the ski slopes in the mountains some 30 or 40 miles to the north. The stretch between Montreal and Ste. Marie includes factories and some fine 19th-century stone buildings and churches, blackened by age, and French-Canadian homes built at the turn of the century that open directly onto the sidewalk. Mainly immigrant families live in these homes now, families of Italian, Polish, Greek, Ukrainian, Russian, or Czechoslovakian descent, many of whom arrived at the turn of the century or immediately following the world wars.

Some of these buildings are three or four stories high, with heavy lace curtains veiling windows so that passers-by cannot easily look inside. In late summer and fall, painted window boxes are full of hardy perennials. In the spring, tulips, daffodils, and hyacinths are in bloom, the bulbs having been carefully stored in dark basements over the winter. Other stretches of the road to Ste. Marie are less well kept. Buildings with dull, uncleaned windows or frames filled in with cardboard or plywood, stand on grounds littered with old beer bottles, cans, and cigarette butts. Some former apartment buildings are used to store materials for nearby factories. Many stores and shops line the route, with several *depanneurs* (corner convenience stores), and local bakeries producing delicious smells of breads and other goods, where one can buy a dozen fresh bagels—baked on hot coals while you watch—croissants, or a fresh baguette. In the packed shopping areas, buses travel bumper to bumper among cars, delivery vans, and in summer, bicycles. Fast food cafes and restaurant chains are everywhere; at lunch time workers line up for inexpensive hot dogs, souvlaki, pizza, or french fries and gravy (a popular local snack known as *poutine*).

Victor Sloski could not imagine living anywhere else; he and Shirley had made their home here for 20 years. Although their apartment over the grocery store had three rooms, to me it looked no larger than two regular-sized rooms. The main room doubled as a sitting room and a bedroom. A large television took up one corner. The rest of the room was dominated by a king-size bed with red, braided bedcovers and bright red and pink satin cushions. There was one other small bedroom. Most of their socializing took place at a tiny kitchen table, at the back of the apartment, where they ate, talked, and entertained, whether their guest was a friend, neighbor, nurse, doctor, or priest. Most of our conversations were at that table, too.

On my first visit, Victor Sloski appeared as a tall, lean, broad-boned man who must have looked more muscular before he got sick. He was almost bald, which, Shirley explained, was due to the radiation. Most of the time, Mr. Sloski didn't look directly at me when he spoke; he stared straight ahead, as if he were recalling some event. On this occasion, he spoke freely and easily, in carefully chosen words, about his life and the progression of his illness.

It was hard to understand, he said, how he could have become so sick, with so many things going wrong all at once. He had no illusions—he knew for sure that he was going to die. People were kind and helpful, but there was too much wrong with his body. The worst part was just having to sit and wait, with all this time on his hands, worrying that more pain would come. All his life he had worked hard and had kept busy. Here at home he still had a lot of work to do— fixing the place, painting, caring for the tomatoes and flowers on his balcony. But he could do nothing. "If I lay down, I can't breathe," he told me. "It's like something choking me. I cannot stand up and walk. It's too much. I know that I'm getting blind, too. Every day I see less and less. I eat a little bit at a time. But even my appetite is going. I got pain in my stomach and chest. I'm scared of all this." He motioned toward Shirley. "It's scary for me and scary for her."

At this point, Mr. Sloski was receiving hydromorphone 10 mg by mouth every four hours for pain, phenytoin 100 mg orally three times a day for control of his seizures, and clonazepam 0.5 mg twice a day for anxiety. Because constipation and heartburn were also problems for him and contributed to his stomach discomfort, Dr. Webster had also prescribed colace 100 mg taken orally twice a day and a liquid antacid whenever he needed it after eating. Victor wondered if taking so many pills contributed to his blindness. How could you know?, he thought, it could be anything.

On this particular day, Shirley said, things weren't too bad. She had been able to persuade Victor to eat two soft-boiled eggs. The previous day he had eaten some Cream of Wheat and a little boiled beef with mashed-up potato, carrot, and turnip. He had liked that and it had stayed down. He had managed to take a shower without any help and watch his favorite science fiction programs on TV.

Shirley said that the best thing for Victor right now was when his family called from Poland. In all these years, he had not been one to have much contact with his mother or his brothers and sisters. He hadn't even wanted to mention his illness. But after a lot of discussion and persuasion from Shirley, he finally called his older sister Melinka and told her about it, and that he would not get better. Victor still wasn't convinced that his family needed to know so much. As he put it to me, "How you gonna call it? Boring! It's not pleasant for them. Now they're all crying about me. What can they do back there?" When Shirley and Dr. Webster wondered if some of his family might come over now to see him, Victor objected that it was just not worth it, it was too far to travel, his mother was too old at age 84, and so on.

Anxious and depressed as he was, and even though he feared more pain, Mr. Sloski did not want to die before his time and he didn't want anyone to help him do it, either. Although as an adult he had not gone to mass every Sunday, he had been raised Catholic in Poland, attending mass regularly with his mother and sisters as a child, and saying prayers together nightly. In many ways, his childhood faith had remained with him. Although it wavered sometimes, he still believed in God and he was sure there was a life after this one. What was happening to him was God's will; his life was in His hand.

Speaking of the possibility of suicide, he told me, "I've thought about that. But I don't believe you have the right to take your own life and no one else has the right to do it for you. When your time is come, He will decide for you, and if you have to suffer, you have to suffer." Victor believed that if one suffered, it was probably for all the wrongs one had done in this life. One had to pay for them—if not here then in the next place—and it was better to pay for them now. Even if he were to suffer more, he said, the most important thing was to die at home, in his own bed, with Shirley at his side.

"Why don't you two get married?"

Over the next several weeks, Mr. Sloski weakened rapidly, and he seemed to withdraw more into himself. "I'm just a burden to everybody," he would say. "Why bother with me? I'm finished already!" At times, both Victor and Shirley were openly angry. "He worked so hard all his life and now this!" Shirley shouted during one of my visits. "Why him? Why not some of those miserable people who never did anyone any good?"

Grania MacDonald spent most of her visits counseling and consoling the couple and trying to alleviate their fears of what was going to happen next. It was hard. She later recalled to me:

> Everything had gone so fast. It seemed like they got hit by one blow after another. They would have liked the stomach problems to be ulcers, fixable with Maalox or another antacid. But the stomach problems were not ulcers, they were cancerous tumors. There was no radiotherapy for that because it could do more harm than good. Then a lump he felt under his arm was radiated, but it didn't get smaller, it just got hotter. And it went on and on. It seemed that from one week to the next, there was another affront to this poor man's body. They really seemed to be in a boat with no oars.

Grania really liked Victor and Shirley. She felt tremendous empathy for them, yet she felt helpless in shielding them from the ceaseless rain of problems.

At this point, Grania was visiting them twice a week. She tried to focus on the things she could do that would make a positive difference to Victor and Shirley. There didn't seem to be much. Victor worried what would happen to Shirley when he passed on. There wasn't much money—a few government retirement bonds and a small pension. While they lived in a common-law marriage, they were not legally married, and he wasn't sure whether she could legally benefit from the small estate he would leave.

Grania saw an opportunity. "Why don't you two get married?" she asked during a home visit in March. "It could easily be arranged and perhaps legalize things so that you could put some of your affairs in order." Victor and Shirley liked this idea, though things would have to happen quickly. Victor's mind was still clear now, but there was the distinct possibility that as the metastatic disease in his brain increased he would become more confused and disoriented. By the time a civil service could be arranged at city hall in Montreal it might be too late. Grania knew another nurse who was also a minister, and called her, explaining the situation. Later that month the minister came to the house, married Victor and Shirley with some neighbors as witnesses, laid out the refreshments on the kitchen table, and took the photographs.

Afterward, Victor told Grania he wished they had thought of this earlier, so Shirley could have had a nicer wedding. He took satisfaction from the assurance that Shirley would be provided for more securely, but he still worried about her. It seemed to him that Shirley was denying things. She should realize that he was a dying man, he said. "She shouldn't go down to the stores and tell the neighbors and the store people that I'm not too bad. She's lying to herself and to the other people. She lets them think I'm getting better." Actually, Shirley did know her husband was dying. "But," she said, "I try to put it to the back of my mind, and look on the bright side." This did not suit Victor. As he put it, "I'm sick and I'm dying and that's it."

Grania shared some of Mr. Sloski's concerns about Shirley. Whereas Victor talked about what he felt, Shirley seemed more fragile, more isolated. She had a sister and brother in Winnipeg, but that was 1000 miles away. Victor's family were in Poland and he didn't want to see them. Here in Ste. Marie, Shirley had few friends. There had been some good friends over the years, but many had left to find work elsewhere. Her neighbors worked 12-hour shifts in the factories, they had their own troubles. How could she ask them to come in and look after Victor for even an hour?

Financial problems and other worries

The Sloskis' lack of financial means was a more immediate problem. In Quebec, the government allows certain financial benefits to defray the cost of medication and treatment measures, but not all of these are covered by the government allowance. The most convenient option for opioid delivery for Mr. Sloski would have been a fentanyl dermal patch (changed every three days) to replace the oral hydromorphone he was receiving every four hours. At the time, that preparation was not available on the government formulary. When Dr. Webster called the local pharmacy, she discovered that the patches would cost $250 for two weeks, which the Sloskis could not afford. The next most convenient option was long-acting morphine rectal suppositories, given every 12 hours. This cost $200 for two weeks—again, too expensive. Grania suggested that the cheapest option of all would be oxycodone suppositories, which she could obtain free from the hospital. The problem was that Mr. Sloski might need two or three suppositories every four hours to equal the hydromorphone he was receiving now. Dr. Webster finally decided simply to increase the dosage of oral hydrodmorphone, which seemed to offer Mr. Sloski some relief, at least for as long as he could swallow. Grania brought the medicine from the hospital pharmacy to save Shirley the trips.

Another problem was that Mr. Sloski would get a rare burst of energy that allowed him to climb out of bed—even though he was in a hospital bed with rails—and wander around the apartment in the middle of the night. He was confused during most of these escapades and was likely to hurt himself. Dr. Webster suggested haloperidol 2 mg at night, and possibly during the day, and made a note to ask Grania to titrate that dose upwards as required. This would have to be switched to chlorpromazine suppositories when Mr. Sloski was no longer able to swallow. Dr. Webster also felt that eventually Mr. Sloski might need midazolam subcutaneously to prevent seizures, once he was no longer able to take his oral antiseizure medication.

Dr. Webster knew that as Mr. Sloski deteriorated there would be a risk of aspiration pneumonia if Mrs. Sloski continued feeding him as she was. At this point, Dr. Webster chose not to dwell on this with her, as she was just getting used to the idea that her husband was dying. Still, Dr. Webster did mention to her that there was a possibility that her husband could develop pneumonia, so that she could be prepared for that eventuality.

"If I could pull God down from heaven I'd beat Him up!"

Victor had metastatic disease throughout his pelvis by now, and it had made it difficult for him to urinate, among other symptoms. "It's no good. Just leave me alone!" he would sometimes snap at his wife. "Why doesn't everyone just leave me?" he said to me during one of my visits in the spring. "Can't they see there's nothing to be done? Everything has been tried. Nobody should bother." He would sometimes stop in the middle of a sentence, as if it hardly mattered to him whether he finished it or not. "Forget it!" he would say at last after a long pause.

Shirley, who had always felt a strong faith in God, had stopped praying. She was Catholic, went to church regularly, and received the sacraments of the church. But now she was angry. "This morning I cried all morning," she told me one day. "I just couldn't stop. I called out to God, 'Why are you doing this to us? To me?' After I had cried for what must have been a good two hours, I felt more peaceful inside. Maybe God *was* there?" If He was, she told Grania, she had some business with Him. "If I could pull God down from heaven, I'd beat Him up!" she said.

Victor, who seemed more resigned that he was dying, was not sure that God was necessarily at fault. He had always believed in miracles, even if he was not a practicing Catholic. But perhaps the miracles were not meant for him. Some people, if they prayed hard enough, would get their prayers answered, he said, but he was resigned to the idea that maybe God was punishing him for some wrongdoing. After all, the couple had lived together unmarried for 20 years. They were married now, of course, but they had not been married in a Catholic church, and in the eyes of the church, that was a sin. No doubt, there were also other sins for which he was now being punished. Grania suggested a visit by the local priest, which seemed to bring some comfort. He heard Victor's confession and spoke to Shirley at length. She was relieved that Victor had been able to receive the Sacrament of the Sick. "If he has sins on his mind, now they will be forgiven before he leaves this world," she said.

The priest had helped Victor, but Shirley was still worried about how she was going to cope, especially at the end. On one of Grania's next visits she flung question after question at her: "What shall I do? How will I know when he's gone? What have I not done that I am supposed to do? Should I find the funeral home now? Do I have to give his papers [Social Security card and ID cards] to the funeral home? How will I know what to do when the time comes? Victor just wants to be left to die, but what about *me*? What will *I* do?"

Grania actually believed that Mr. Sloski ought to be admitted to the Palliative Care Unit for the last days of his life. Even as she tried to reassure him that his wife was a strong woman who would come through for him in whatever ways she needed to, privately she wondered whether Mrs. Sloski might break down in a crisis. At the same time she was also aware of Mr. Sloski's unshakable determination to die at home. For the moment, therefore, she focused on each of Mrs. Sloski's concrete concerns, and tried to give her as much information and reassurance as she could.

She explained that all Shirley would need to do when the time came would be to make a telephone call to the city emergency health services. Everything would then be arranged from there. The city emergency service ambulance and a physician would come. The Palliative Care Service would have already appraised them of Mr. Sloski's situation, so everything would happen smoothly. It was possible that when Mr. Sloski died, Shirley might have to wait for an hour or so—sometimes that could happen. But the emergency services would come, she could be assured of that. Grania described how things usually worked with respect to funeral organization and planning, the papers she would need to have handy, and what would be expected of her. Later, Grania told me:

> I tried very hard to stay with what she needs to know. At some level she doesn't want to deal with the hard cold facts of funeral homes. Ideally, I think she'd like to feel he'll improve. But she knows he won't, and I reiterated that, because I think it helps her deal with what she has to know. I hope I was gentle with the information. I know I must be careful to say things gently, kindly. But lies would be no better.

Nursing Victor at home

In addition to Grania's twice-per-week visits, nurses from the local community health center came to the apartment to help Mr. Sloski with bathing and dressing, and to administer medications. They were not available on a full-time basis but could supplement other forms of care. More often than not, it was Shirley who needed the most support, as there were times when she felt despair. Yet she had to go on: "A couple of cigarettes and a good cry and I just carry on," she said. It didn't matter what kind of care was needed. If Victor needed a bedpan, a back rub, or help with his bath, she would do it. Shirley still seemed to have the feeling that if she pushed Victor to eat more, he would get stronger and perhaps the end could be delayed. "He's so thin and undernourished," she said. "Perhaps a little soup or some ice cream. I keep thinking and thinking, 'I could help him to get a bit stronger.' Maybe I'm not being very realistic, but I can't stand the thought of him dying, of having to see his life end. Surely there are things I can do."

She wanted guarantees that Victor would not have any more pain. "What can I do to prevent his pain?" she asked Grania. "Can the doctors predict ahead of time what pain he will have and prepare for it?" Grania did her best to explain the effectiveness of the medications and to explain the potency of hydromorphone and its equivalency in morphine. Shirley seemed to understand that Victor's pain medication was already at a very high dosage, and that his pain was well controlled. On the other hand, he became more bedbound, and he had become very thin. His thigh bones and coccyx were barely covered by skin and his body had little protection against getting bedsores. Thin as he was, however, he was a well-built man. Even with two people it was hard to lift him in the bed or to maintain balance when getting him out of the bed into a chair. Grania and Dr. Webster marveled that Mrs. Sloski could keep on doing so much by herself.

On one visit in June, I witnessed firsthand how much Mrs. Sloski had learned about nursing care, despite her fear, anxiety, and fatigue. We went together into Mr. Sloski's room. He seemed much less responsive, although he occasionally opened his eyes and made eye contact as if to acknowledge us. Mrs. Sloski knelt beside the bed and brought her face very close to his. He said something to her that I could not hear, and then she straightened up and deftly rearranged the pillows. Gently she moved her husband's head and in no time she had placed three or four pillows in comfortable positions beneath his head and arms. I offered to help, and Mrs. Sloski promptly gave me instructions, undoubtedly unaware that I am a nurse myself. Under her direction we arranged ourselves on opposite sides of the bed, took hold of the sheet, and—on her count of three—scooted Victor up toward the head of the bed. Then she gave him his medications, holding his head forward and supporting it carefully while he drank from the cup and swallowed the pills. When all was done, Mr. Sloski opened his eyes and looked wide-eyed into his wife's face.

A family visit

Beyond an occasional phone call to see how her husband was doing, people didn't come around much, so Shirley Sloski often cried alone. She tried not to cry in front of her husband. She could cry with Grania there, and sometimes she cried on my visits. The team worried that there were not enough support services for not only her but for all of the family caregivers who wanted to care for their loved ones at home. Grania contacted the community social service agency so they would visit, and she asked the priest if he could make regular visits. Shirley was willing to talk to the priest and the social worker, but for the most part, she was taken up with caring for her husband. In such a tiny apartment it was hard to talk about things that were on her mind with any real privacy or without constantly feeling that Victor needed her.

Grania and Dr. Webster still wondered whether it might be helpful to both Shirley and Victor if his family could visit from Poland. Dr. Webster was aware of the many arguments the Sloskis had had over this and whether the family should even have been told about Mr. Sloski's illness. On one of Dr. Webster's home visits she sparked one of these discussions when she asked Mr. Sloski how his family was reacting to his situation. "They are upset and they feel helpless," he replied. "They are upset because I am young to have this. But I don't think they should come over. It's too late for them to come over. I could die tomorrow."

Mrs. Sloski jumped in, "They *could* come over."

"Where would they stay?" Mr. Sloski asked her.

"They could stay here."

"What would they do?"

Mrs. Sloski thought for a moment. "Well," she said, "I think it would be good for you to see them." She turned to Dr. Webster. "Don't you think it would be good for him if he saw his family again?"

Dr. Webster tried to be diplomatic. "It's not up to me to say," she replied.

"Well," Mrs. Sloski went on, "I tried to organize for them to phone again on Sunday—"

Mr. Sloski interrupted. "I'm having problems with my speech."

"Your speech isn't that bad today," his wife countered, with another glance at Dr. Webster for confirmation, "is it, Doctor?" She turned back to her husband. "It's just on and off that your speech is a problem."

"Well, it's too late for them to come," Mr. Sloski said, as if to put an end to the matter. "And they are not well themselves."

Despite her husband's doubts and protests, Shirley made a point of keeping regular contact with Melinka. Meanwhile, Mr. Sloski was sleeping more and more, and at last Shirley took it upon herself to call Melinka and invite her to visit. Regardless of Victor's preferences, she wanted Melinka to come.

In late June, Melinka arrived from Warsaw with her 20-year-old daughter, Miriam. Though Victor was now too ill to have much meaningful interaction, Melinka wanted to see him before he died. She had not seen her brother in 30 years. Melinka and Miriam stayed for one week, during which time Grania made one of her visits. She told me that Melinka seemed horrified at her brother's appearance, even though she knew he was dying, and that Miriam looked frightened when she was with her uncle, whom she had never met before. Yet Grania also thought Mr. Sloski was able to recognize them, and seemed to appreciate the fact that they had come because he was dying. As the three women nursed him together, he seemed more at peace.

A week after Melinka and Miriam returned to Poland, Mr. Sloski's breathing became more labored. Grania suggested to Mrs. Sloski that he might go soon, and once again offered the option of transferring Mr. Sloski to the Palliative Care Unit. "I don't want you to take him to the hospital," Mrs. Sloski cried. "I want to have him here at home. If I can't manage then I'll just have to tell someone and I'll just call." Grania reminded her that all she needed to do was pick up the telephone and a Palliative Care Unit admission would quickly be arranged. The next day, Mr. Sloski seemed more congested in his chest and his breathing became more labored. Shirley went to the phone and called the hospital. When she returned to the bedroom, Victor was dead.

Bereavement

Mrs. Sloski remembered everything that she needed to do. She had written a note to herself that contained all of Grania's instructions. She called the city emergency health services, and the physician and ambulance arrived within minutes of her call. Even though she knew her husband was gone, she told me later, when the ambulance came and the attendants were taking the body from the apartment she asked them, "Are you sure he is dead?" and they said, "Yes, madam, he is." She had felt bad when they had taken off Victor's watch and his cross and chain. They had also taken off his wedding ring and put it on the kitchen table. Mrs. Sloski said to them, "I didn't want you to do that." They told her, "We have to do this, but you can ask the funeral parlor to put them back on." Later she took the wedding ring and cross and chain to the funeral parlor, and a woman there helped her put them back on.

Shirley organized a big party for the funeral. Everyone whom Victor and she had ever known was invited to come back to the house after the funeral service. She ordered food from a local catering company, and because they had personally known Victor they gave her a special discount. Only about a dozen people came back, but Mrs. Sloski said it didn't matter. Victor would be looking down from heaven and he would know she had made the party for him anyway.

During the next few months, I visited Mrs. Sloski on several occasions. What had bothered her most of all was having to watch Victor suffer, she told me. There was very little she felt she could do. Sure, she could nurse him and do the necessary things. But as time had gone by and he got sicker and sicker, she felt more and more helpless. "I felt I did not do enough," she said. "Or maybe there was something else I could have done, even the day he died. Maybe I shouldn't have left him for that minute to make the phone call. Sometimes I think I did things wrong out of sheer desperation. Like trying to feed him and forcing him to eat, which I'm sure didn't help him."

It was odd, she said. She knew Victor would die. The odds were against a miracle happening. But she was often able to put this on the back burner and deny it to herself. Being so busy with all the nursing care, she didn't need to think about it if she didn't want to. It had been difficult when she went to the funeral home to choose the casket. She told me that she couldn't even enter the showroom at first. The man at the showroom had been very patient, and she had gone outside for a cigarette. When she came back in, she picked out a casket that seemed all right. The man began to suggest some additional items, she recalled, smiling at this memory. "Now," he had said, "would you like—" "No! I wouldn't!" Mrs. Sloski told him. "I would like to get out of here!" She was laughing now. "And I left."

When I visited her three months after her husband's death, Shirley said she was often having "fits of crying." The nights were long and lonely. Twenty years was a long time to live with someone; being in the house alone still required some getting used to. She had always felt safe having a man in the house. Before he got sick, Victor was a strong man who could tackle anything. There wasn't much chance of a break-in with Victor around. She usually stayed in at night now. If she did go out and it was dark when she returned, she was very careful. "I don't just walk in and turn the lights on," she said. "I creep up the stairs. I turn the light on." She laughed again. "I check all the cupboards, and under the beds."

The bereavement team from the Palliative Care Unit had been very kind, Mrs. Sloski said. A social worker from the local community agency had visited regularly and she had been able to talk about some of her fears. Dr. Webster had called to see how she was coping. And Grania still visited regularly. Reflecting on the help she had received, Mrs. Sloski said, "I could not have expected any more and I don't think my husband expected any more. He knew at the end there was nothing to be done, no cure. Things weren't ideal, but he knew we were all caring for him in the best way we knew how." Then she said, "Caring for my husband, knowing he was going to die any day and not knowing what would happen, was never easy. I would say it was probably the biggest challenge of my life, if you can call it that. But if I had to do it all over again, I would do it."

Now she planned to attend a bereavement group at the hospital, made up of other family members who had lost a loved one to cancer. "I want to try it. The neighbors have been very kind, but they have husbands who come home to them at night and someone to have supper with." The bereavement group would be good for her, Mrs. Sloski said. These were people who had gone through the same thing, "who knew what it was like to sit home alone and watch TV and feel empty."

9

Leonard Patterson
Jagged Edges

Narrated by YANNA LAMBRINIDOU

Leonard Patterson was a 62-year-old European American with colon cancer. His poverty, tumultuous relationships with his family, and unmanageable pain produced a cluster of unresolved problems in the final months of his life. Despite the painstaking efforts of hospice to offer Mr. Patterson a peaceful death and his family a smooth transition to a life without him, this case left many of its participants unsettled. One of the many questions it raises is whether the best of palliative care can ease shattered lives in cases that are not only complex but also depart from an economic, social, and cultural mainstream.

"His heart was as big as a bushel basket"

My first attempt to meet Mr. Patterson was unsuccessful. Unknowingly, I drove to the wrong house and knocked on the wrong door. No one answered. I called Mr. Patterson from the nearest pay phone, but no one picked up the phone. I left surprised and disappointed because I had spoken to him only 20 minutes earlier, and he had sounded happy to meet me. I remembered him playfully pretending to calculate if my 20-minute ride to his place would give him enough time to put on his pants. I worried. Did Mr. Patterson not want me to visit him after all? Was he too shy to tell me on the phone? When I returned to hospice, I mentioned the incident to Chaplain Steve Holbek. Steve knew Mr. Patterson and often had good insights about the patients with whom he worked. He informed me that Mr. Patterson was "somewhat of a simple man," at the very low end of the socioeconomic ladder, who might have been intimidated by the language I used to introduce our work. The term "research project" itself might have scared him.

Steve's hypothesis was certainly not the full explanation of my failed meeting with Mr. Patterson—I quickly discovered that I had the wrong address for him and replaced it with the right one. Steve's thoughts had nonetheless captured an important essence in this case. Mr. Patterson had had a difficult life. He was 62 years old and very poor. He had a wife and a daughter who depended on him. For years he had made a living driving a truck, delivering bread to neighborhood grocery stores. When I met him he had already left that job, but I could see that something about it fit him perfectly: the hard-working hours behind the wheel, the silence that must have accompanied his work, the delivery of bread. Mr. Patterson was a quiet man and a self-effacing provider. Not only did he pay the rent and put food on the table for his family, he also served his community. In an indirect way he spent years bringing bread to people's homes. More directly, he worked as a handyman for neighbors—cleaning, painting, gardening, building, and repairing were all tasks within Mr. Patterson's expertise and everyone knew it. His physical appearance revealed both his kindness and strength. He was a thin man, but muscular and strong. Moreover, his round brown eyes communicated a sweetness that many people in his community recognized and cherished. His best customers were elderly women. Mrs. Hillary Milford, a 77-year-old native of Lancaster County, had relied on him for 12 years. She recalled:

> Mr. Patterson would do anything under the sun that you asked him to do. He would wash and wax my kitchen floor. He washed and waxed my car. He did the yard work and raked leaves. He clipped the bushes. He planted a whole row of arborvitae trees down in my back yard. His heart was as big as a bushel basket—nothing was too much. When my dog got sick one time—she got somehow into a bag of chocolate—I called Len. He said, "Hillary, just put kitty litter on it and come and get me." Now, not everybody would do that.

As a young man Mr. Patterson left his home in Kentucky to start a new life with several "guys," as he called them. He spent much of his time on the road moving from town to town and making a living out of household projects. His skills gave him pride. But that same period in his life brought him shame as well; he saw it as the beginning of his troubles. While on the road, Mr. Patterson developed an addiction to alcohol. "I drank my way up to Pennsylvania," he once told me. When he reached Lancaster County he decided to end his trip. He met his wife, Ruth, and got married. But alcohol continued to rule his life.

Ten years later, Mr. and Mrs. Patterson gave birth to their daughter Sarah. The three of them lived together in a first-floor apartment.

Mr. Patterson assumed all the responsibilities of running the household. He cooked, cleaned, looked after Sarah and his wife. He was the glue that held his family together. Mrs. Patterson required protection. Since her pregnancy with Sarah 21 years ago, she had been unable to work and was on welfare. Her husband explained her condition as "pinch nerve"; their daughter thought it was "laziness." Regardless of its etiology, Mrs. Patterson presented her inability to work as a permanent and indisputable condition. She appeared unkempt, with her hair as well as her clothes often looking unwashed. Several of her teeth had fallen out, and the ones that hadn't seemed to be in bad shape. Chewing was a challenge for her, so she limited her diet almost exclusively to liquids. Mentally, she seemed slow.

Whenever Mrs. Patterson talked about her marriage she focused on what she called "the rumors" that Mr. Patterson's friends spread about her. These rumors said that Mrs. Patterson wasn't a good wife. She didn't satisfy her husband sexually, she didn't want children, and she didn't know how to care for Mr. Patterson. Rumors also had it that Mr. Patterson had had affairs with other women. A decade ago, a 28-year-old woman called to say that she was Mr. Patterson's daughter. Later the Pattersons were told that a neighbor considered Mr. Patterson to be the father of her new baby. And in 1991 someone sent a letter to the Department of Children and Youth claiming that Mr. Patterson had molested Sarah. Frustrated, Mrs. Patterson asked:

> Who would be spreading around these rumors and why? What kind of sick people are they? And my mom said that Len can't have no kids. Len was fixed. How am I supposed to know if he was or wasn't? Sarah still believes that he did get somebody pregnant, and she still believes that girl who called is his daughter, and I said "no!"

Mrs. Patterson never confirmed if her husband was unfaithful to her. Yet she always wondered. Astoundingly, the one time she went out to look for him in the middle of the night she was raped. "It seems like somebody's pickin' on me, you know?" she'd often say to me. She realized that her image of Mr. Patterson was different from that of neighbors. "Some people didn't see him as a heavy alcoholic," she said. "They saw him, the opposite side of him, you know, religious, stuff like that." And although the rumors blamed Mrs. Patterson for her troubles, she blamed her husband's drinking. She believed that if it weren't for Mr. Patterson's addiction, they would have a better life. As it was, she was not only poor and unhealthy, she was also lonely. Her most dependable companions were Squeaky, her cat, and Flour, her dog. Without them she would have had no close relationships at all.

Sarah, the third member of the Patterson household, had a tumultuous relationship with both her parents. She was 21 and a single mother of three boys.

Chris, the father of her oldest son, had fled to Nevada, and Jason, the father of her other two children, was in jail. For Sarah it was extremely hard to make ends meet. Although she was a full-time employee at a local restaurant, she depended on her father for a roof over her head and on her mother for babysitting her oldest boy. Her two other babies stayed with Jason's mother. Sarah had deep appreciation for her father. In one of our conversations she said, "If it would not have been for my father letting me live here, I would never have been able to get my life back in gear." A few years earlier, Sarah had quit high school to move in with Chris' family and give birth to her first child. This arrangement failed, and Mr. Patterson invited both Sarah and Chris to move into his home. When Chris refused to work, however, Mr. Patterson kicked him out. He left for Nevada, and Sarah fell in love with Jason. Jason, a crack-cocaine user, got in trouble with the law on a regular basis. Mr. Patterson urged his daughter to get rid of him as well, but Sarah fought back. Although she loved her father, she also resented him for the marred childhood he had given her. She said:

> He is my father, I love him. There was just a lot of stuff that my father did to me when I was younger that I can just never get rid of. That is always going to be in me, that is always going to be inside me. I mean, you know, all my life he was physically abusive. He used to beat me with a belt, and he would call me names. Before, I used to weigh 200 pounds, and he would call me "porky" and make fun of me, and that hurt me. When I got older he would also be abusive with my mother, and I wouldn't allow that. I would step in and say, "You are going to hit her, you are going to deal with me." And we would get into fights—we would get into fistfights and everything. There is a lot of that. There is a lot of that hatred. I do love my father, but there is just that hatred, it stays inside of me because he has put me through a lot of stuff.

Sarah's relationship with Mrs. Patterson was equally complicated. Although she tried to get close to her, she always felt rejected. Sarah was convinced that her mother didn't like her. The fact that she had joined gangs, that she was a single mother of three children, and that the fathers of her children were professionally unaccomplished went contrary to her mother's expectations. Mrs. Patterson, according to Sarah, wanted her daughter to comply with conventional social rules. "My mother wanted her girl to be Miss Little Goody Two-Shoes," she once told me. But Sarah never fit that role, and this brought perpetual tension between them. Through the years, Mrs. Patterson called Sarah a "slut," a "whore," and an "unfit mother," among other things. Sarah's theory was that her mother's anger stemmed from her own two miscarriages and two stillborn births years earlier. The Pattersons had tried to have several children, but didn't succeed. As a result, according to Sarah, her mother placed all her hopes and dreams on the one child she did have. But she was disappointed. More importantly, Sarah claimed, Mrs. Patterson was jealous. She had always wanted the two things Sarah took for granted: fertility and Mr. Patterson's attention.

"It was a shock to Len"

In October 1996, Mr. Patterson noticed a dramatic decline in his health. Severe abdominal pain and a lack of stamina started to disrupt his daily existence. He resorted to Maalox and soft foods, but neither helped. He felt increasingly unable to work. On October 31, he was hit with the most unbearable pain he had ever experienced. He also noticed rectal bleeding. Reluctantly, Mr. Patterson went to the doctor. After several tests, he was told that he had cancer of the rectum with liver metastases. Mr. Patterson heard the news in disbelief: "Are you sure you're talking about *me*?" he asked. Mrs. Patterson explained that her husband's diagnosis shattered them all:

> It was a shock to Len. And even though I went through rough times with him, with his drinking and stuff, I love him. Some people say, "How can you, when you went through rough times with him?" Sarah, too, you know? It bothered her.

Mr. Patterson underwent a colostomy. He also started chemotherapy. But he didn't stop working, or helping out his neighbors. Mrs. Milford recalled that he helped her until the last day his body allowed him to. He continued taking the bus to her house, although the work exhausted him at a much faster rate than usual. At 62, with a recent colostomy and the side effects of chemotherapy, all he asked from her was a ride back home.

Four months of nausea, vomiting, diarrhea, and dehydration had passed when Mr. Patterson was told that his chemotherapy had not worked. The side effects alone had taken a toll on his body. In February 1997, his medical report described him as "a disheveled, poorly kept white male with terrible hygiene" suffering from a small bowel obstruction. His chemotherapy was terminated. One month later, upon the suggestion of a friend at the Welfare Office, Mr. Patterson called the Hospice of Lancaster County. He sought help to control his symptoms so that he would be able to continue his life as normally as he could. Nausea, vomiting, occasional loss of appetite, diarrhea, and pain on the left side of his abdomen were his main symptoms. To control them, he was given prochlorperazine, megestrol, loperamide, long-acting morphine tablets, and oxycodone for breakthrough pain. Otherwise, he was functional. He also asked for chaplain visits. Although he was not a member of a faith community, he believed in God and wanted spiritual support.

After his first visit to the Pattersons', George Tiles, the hospice social worker, reported: "The patient cleans the home and does all the cooking. He continues to ride his bike to the grocery store, but he fell yesterday and scraped his head."

The same report indicated that Mr. Patterson's goal was to remain as active as he possibly could. Karen Blackwell, the hospice nurse, learned to plan her weekly visits around Mr. Patterson's busy schedule. Mr. Patterson liked to go to McDonald's for breakfast with other regulars and visit his neighbors during the day. Even on quiet days when he stayed home, he liked to sit on the porch and watch the traffic. Something about his pastime always seemed to indicate a desire to connect with others; Mr. Patterson had a need to be in touch. Steve, the chaplain, saw him as the heart of his neighborhood, adding, "He kind of has his fingers out in the community."

"He is going to the Hospice House, he is very sick"

Mr. Patterson's hospice team was happy that their patient was able to maintain the busy life he wished for. But in the middle of April, a few weeks after his admission to the home care program of hospice, they also noticed that his disease had progressed. Mr. Patterson was markedly weaker and more somnolent than before. He had lost weight, and having been a thin man to begin with, he now looked bony and pale. The unpleasant chills that started racing through his body led him to decrease the frequency of his baths; just the idea of undressing became intolerable to him. Of course, along with his own decline came a decline in the condition of his house. Squeaky started peeing on the rugs, possibly because her litter box had been taken over by cockroaches. The house reeked of urine. Fleas hopped freely between the walls, the pets and the furniture. Someone from hospice warned me not to bring my bag into the Pattersons' unless I intended to transport "critters" back home with me. And yet, Mr. Patterson made every effort to keep his house clean. Karen, his nurse, once found him scrubbing the bathtub. But like his cancer, the dirt in his house spread faster than he could control it.

On May 27, 1997, two months after his admission to hospice, Mr. Patterson collapsed in his neighborhood grocery store. Unresponsive, he was taken to the hospital. Because he regained consciousness with naloxone, an opioid antagonist, it was presumed that he had overdosed on narcotic analgesics. Yet the possibility that he had taken "too many pills," as he put it, disturbed Mr. Patterson greatly. It confronted him with the threatening reality that he was no longer able to take full charge of his life. Steve saw this hospitalization as a critical turning point in Mr. Patterson's life, for it raised the specter of his mortality. Even more than his own death, however, Mr. Patterson seemed to fear for his family. As Steve said: "He's imagining: how is it going to be for them with him being laid up in the hospital? And then the real distressing piece for him is coming to a deeper relationship with what that might mean, you know, when he dies: how are they going to manage?"

Mr. Patterson was not a man of many words. But from his first meetings with Steve he expressed a need and appreciation for prayer. He liked to be reassured that things would be all right "in God's hands." He benefited from an affirmation of faith—a reason to trust and hope. In the hospital, Steve lifted his fears up to God, and that seemed to relax him.

As a family, the Pattersons never recovered from the grocery store incident. When Mr. Patterson returned home things had changed forever. Mrs. Patterson and Sarah both knew that the head of their household, the person on whom they had depended for years, now needed their help to survive. Frightened by the events of the previous days, they asked a hospice nurse to explain to them which medications might have caused the overdose, and how to prevent this incident from recurring. The on-call nurse labeled all bottles clearly, set up a pill-tender for easy tracking, and reviewed the times that each medication was to be administered. She also encouraged Mrs. Patterson to keep the morphine in her possession. This way, she thought, the amount of narcotic taken by Mr. Patterson would be monitored. Two days later, Sarah called hospice to announce that her parents were overwhelmed. Mr. Patterson refused to take his medication, and Mrs. Patterson spent a sleepless night trying to look after both her husband and Sarah's crying boy. Hospice offered their 12-bed inpatient unit as a temporary respite option. There, Mr. Patterson would receive 24-hour care, while his wife and daughter would get the chance to regroup and plan their next step. Sarah and Mrs. Patterson agreed. Mr. Patterson turned down the offer without further consideration. As the head of his household he was unprepared to abandon his family. Moreover, he harbored a great fear of life in health care institutions. As he once said: "When you get diagnosed with a terminal illness people put you in a home, and they don't care about you anymore."

Word went out that the Pattersons were in crisis. A chain of telephone calls reached a friend, Mr. Paul Hankin, who also happened to be a long-time volunteer at the Hospice of Lancaster County. Mr. Hankin called Mr. Patterson to find out how he could help. Mr. Patterson didn't have an answer. He admitted that he had spent the day alone in bed, for his wife had been at the park with Sarah's son. But when Mr. Hankin suggested that he may need a little more care than what he was receiving and that the Hospice of Lancaster County would be a good place for him, Mr. Patterson asserted: "I am not going to the hospital." Mr. Hankin explained that hospice was not a hospital, and Mr. Patterson replied that he wouldn't know how to get there. Mr. Hankin assured him that he could give him a ride. This conversation came to a close, however, when Mr. Patterson declared that he was not ready to leave his home.

His position changed the next morning. After some thought, and possibly pressure from his family, Mr. Patterson agreed to transfer to the hospice inpatient unit for five days of respite care. Mr. Hankin recalled:

Ruth called me and said Len is ready to go, and he would like it if you could come to the house. So I immediately left and went to the house, and it was a picture, you know, driving up in front of an apartment building and seeing Len's wife for the first time, on the front porch holding this little three-year-old fella and Len sitting on the front porch step, looking very sick, carrying a little plastic bag with a pair of soiled long pants, waiting for me to take him to the Hospice Center. . . . We stood and talked, and I introduced myself to his wife, and a neighbor lady came by and said, "Len, are you going away?" And Ruth responded with, "He is going to the Hospice House, he is very sick, and he may not come back home." So I got Len in the car and we had a nice talk from his house to the Hospice Center, and I refreshed his mind with what this was all about—this was *not* a nursing home, and it was *not* a hospital, and that it was brand new—and he kept saying, "Oh, thank you, oh, thank you, but I want to go back home. I want to go back home."

"Would you look at these fine pajamas?"

I met Mr. and Mrs. Patterson three days later in the inpatient unit of the Hospice of Lancaster County. Mrs. Patterson and Kevin, Sarah's three-year-old son, were sitting in the unit's living room, surrounded by comfortable furniture, color-coordinated wallpaper, a brand new fireplace, a cozy alcove with a variety of toys for children, and a view of hospice's flower garden. They had walked from the bus stop, about half a mile away, and looked fatigued. They were waiting for Mr. Patterson to wake up. Mrs. Patterson looked disheveled with her stained clothes, untied sneakers, and no socks. She was visibly distraught. I noticed that she kept twirling her hair around her finger with intensity. In tears, she told the social worker, George, that she wanted her neighbors to stop spreading rumors about her. Word had it that she was to blame for Mr. Patterson's transfer to the inpatient unit. The accusation seemed to be that if she were a capable and caring wife, Mr. Patterson would have been able to stay at home. George attempted to divert her attention to her family and her relationship with Mr. Patterson, but to no avail. The neighbors and their insistence on bad-mouthing her took primary importance in Mrs. Patterson's mind. Overwhelmed by the rumors, her husband's condition, and her fear about her own future, Mrs. Patterson cried, "If Len dies, I want to go, too." George asked if she intended to kill herself, but got no answer. He left suspecting that Mrs. Patterson was suffering from paranoia. He also called the county mental health office to see if Mrs. Patterson had a case worker. She didn't.

Mrs. Patterson's visit with her husband was brief. I later learned that that was normal. She often came in, asked him for money, and left. When I walked into Mr. Patterson's room he was lying in bed quietly, his eyes half closed. No one was around him. It felt peaceful. Although I hadn't seen the Pattersons' home at the time, I had a feeling that Mr. Patterson was not used to the ambiance of the inpatient unit. This man who occupied the lower end of the socioeconomic ladder was now lying in a private room with wall-to-wall carpeting, brand new, hand-crafted maple furniture, a leather couch with pillows that matched the carpet, an entertainment center, a large private bath with all amenities, and two French doors leading to the hospice gardens. The trees and bushes had only recently been planted so they weren't big enough to block the view to the highway running by the hospice. I saw this as a drawback, a distraction from the serenity of the inpatient unit, but Mr. Patterson thought otherwise. "I like looking at the highway," he said, "I've always loved watching trucks and vans and big vehicles." Humbly, Mr. Patterson expressed gratitude for hospice, but in the next breath he looked up at me and said, "If I had the choice, I'd want to be at home any time." The first few days in the inpatient unit he felt alone and isolated. He questioned whether his family and friends still cared for him. But it seemed that they did, for next to him, on his bedside table, stood several cards sent by friends. Mrs. Patterson visited as often as she could. She gave him a brand new, cellophane-wrapped *Playboy* calendar as a gift, now prominently positioned against his reading lamp.

The combination of his fear of hospice and his gratitude for every service offered to him touched many of the nurses in the inpatient unit. Descriptions of Mr. Patterson as a "sweet man," "a sorry little soul," and someone you would want to "take under your wing" were offered freely at every mention of his name. Mr. Patterson was transformed in the inpatient unit. As difficult as it was for him, he began to accept the care of others. He had walked in as the head of his household who needed no one's help. Yet he was too sick and humble to turn down support. In the inpatient unit, Mr. Patterson accepted all medications and reached a level of physical comfort he had missed for several weeks. Moreover, the day he entered the unit, he received a used pair of pajamas from a nurse and new underwear, socks, sweatpants, a pair of slippers, and a matching robe from Mr. Hankin. One nurse recalled: "I'd go in his room and he'd say, 'Would you look at these fine pajamas?' You know, they were just typical, everyday pajamas. And his slippers, he's like, 'Look at those slippers!' And he'd show them to me, he'd show me the bottom and the soles, and these are just the greatest things that he ever saw. And I thought, this is so neat. You know, I've never looked at a pair of pajamas and thought, 'This is the greatest thing.' And that's how he was."

The most tangible sign of Mr. Patterson's transformation was his relationship to whirlpool baths, which he came to refer to as "miracles." Originally adamant about staying unwashed, for fear of taking his clothes off and freezing, Mr. Patterson resisted the whirlpool with a passion. But soon he was convinced to give it a try. The heat was turned up for an hour prior to his arrival, so when it came time for him to undress he was able to do so without discomfort. He loved the water, loved the warmth. "It was so great to see him enjoy that bath," said one of his nurses. "He needed a bath because he had not been taking them at home because they gave him chills. He really did need one." Another nurse recalled that "you could scrape off a layer of old skin, dirt, that kind of thing. He actually had little black specks in the bed when he was laying in there before we got him in the tub. He was unshaven. Mouth was pretty disgusting. He smelled like urine. His colostomy, I'm sure, hadn't been changed for quite some time. So he was just in a real bad state." For Mr. Patterson, the whirlpool became a ritual of cleansing—both physically and emotionally. Wrapped by warm water, hot steam, and the nurturing of his nurses, he found his baths conducive to intimate discussions about his life and imminent death. He was relentless at expressing worry for his family, for he couldn't imagine how they would fare without him. Steve worked intensely on these fears with him. He often reminded him, "you've done a lot for others and maybe, speaking theologically, this is a time when Jesus wants to wash *your* feet—that you need to be cared for and loved in certain ways, and it can happen through the hospice and through others."

During his 10 days at the hospice inpatient unit, Mr. Patterson left a lasting mark on the staff. Again and again, nurses told me that he was one of those patients they would never forget. As reserved as he was, he managed to develop friendships with not only staff but also other patients. There was one elderly woman in particular with whom he liked spending much of his time. "Neither of them had a lot of visitors, and they connected," said Debbie, an inpatient unit nurse. They shared meals together and he loved to make her laugh. The friendship between Mr. Patterson and Mrs. Myers was mentioned to me by several of the nurses. I could tell that there was something powerful about the fact that two dying people were able to create joy together. Despite his own weakness, he often liked to go on walks with Mrs. Myers by pushing her wheelchair by himself. Nurses remembered one warm day when the two of them decided to go for a stroll in the gardens. Both were in wheelchairs that time, pushed by two nurses. At some point during their outing, Mrs. Myers' wheelchair got stuck in the ground. Without hesitation, Mr. Patterson got out of his seat and started lifting his friend's chair. He held up the front of the wheelchair while the nurses pushed from the back. This was one of those moments when utter exhaustion must have been worth it to him. What he missed most was his ability to help others.

Evelyn, an inpatient unit nurse, stressed that Mr. Patterson helped her as much as she helped him. She said:

> I am only 25, and when I think of older people and having such a drastic illness as this, I relate them with my grandparents. They are so conservative and so private, and they don't talk about anything, and they certainly don't talk about their private life. Len was just different. He would talk with you and he would relate things, and it was like, "Wow, not everybody is so hush, hush." He was one of the first patients I really talked with, and he treated me like an equal, not like a little child. When I

came here, I knew I liked hospice, I knew I liked the concept and what it meant, and I liked everything behind it, yet I did not know if I was going to be good at it. Len showed me that I *could* be and that I could give anything I wanted, and I could give my heart, and it would be all right. I don't know how else to put it.

Despite the fact that he warmed up to staying at hospice, Mr. Patterson had to leave when his condition stabilized. The inpatient unit at the Hospice of Lancaster County accepts patients only for symptom management, temporary respite care, and palliative care in the last days of a patient's life. Once his symptoms were controlled, Mr. Patterson fit none of these categories. Moreover, his medical assistance did not cover private-duty nursing at home. George, Mr. Patterson's social worker, and Karen, his home care nurse, thought that Mr. Patterson's only reasonable option was to transfer to a nursing home. They saw Mrs. Patterson as paranoid, retarded, and incapable of taking care of her husband, and Sarah as an overwhelmed young woman who could barely manage her own life, let alone the death of her father. They also ascertained that there were no relatives or neighbors who would take responsibility for Mr. Patterson's care. George made arrangements to have Mr. Patterson transferred to a nursing home that accepted patients on medical assistance. At the same time, he tried to locate support systems for Mrs. Patterson. Mr. Patterson's deep concern for his wife had made it clear to hospice staff that Mrs. Patterson had to be looked after with equal seriousness. Her well-being was going to be a fundamental requirement for Mr. Patterson's peaceful death.

In the beginning, Mrs. Patterson rejected all of George's efforts to help her. George suspected that she had the ability to take care of her basic needs without the help of Mr. Patterson, but that the parent–child relationship she had developed with her husband had deprived her of the opportunity to exercise her independence. Eventually, and with Mrs. Patterson's reluctant permission, George connected her to the Mental Health/Mental Retardation Office for a psychological evaluation. George's rationale was that if Mrs. Patterson was diagnosed with a mental or physical disability, she would be able to apply for Supplemental Social Security Income (SSI). Without the support of welfare, George worried that Mrs. Patterson would be unable to survive. The limited income she had lived on until then came primarily from Mr. Patterson's meager earnings, which would now be absorbed by the nursing home.

I visited Mr. Patterson in the inpatient unit on the day of his transfer to the nursing home. Again, he was lying in bed with his eyes half closed. He seemed quiet and withdrawn. The day before, he had had a conversation with the hospice's medical director that had revealed how hard this transfer was going to be for him. According to one of the nurses who witnessed the exchange, the doctor saw him and said, "Tomorrow is the big day!" "Yes," replied Mr. Patterson, and either out of confusion, denial, or misunderstanding he stated, "I'm going home." Surprised by his response, the doctor asked rhetorically, "Now, where are you going tomorrow?" But he got the same answer: "I'm going home." To clear up the confusion the nurse gently intervened by asking Mr. Patterson again, "Don't you remember where we were talking about Len?" to which Mr. Patterson finally responded, "Oh, yeah, I'm gonna go over to the nursing home for a little bit." Later, the nurse commented: "A lot of times you have to be careful how you say things. Everybody else says, 'Just be honest,' which we do, but sometimes that's too hard. If you would have just said, 'You're going there and you're gonna die there,' that would have been too much."

Although George and Karen seemed relieved to have found a place that would offer Mr. Patterson 24-hour care, some nurses in the inpatient unit felt ambivalent about this transfer. Emily, for example, wondered how much Mr. Patterson's caregivers had taken over for him. She asked, "Who are we to go in and say 'this house is too dirty and your wife doesn't take good care of you, therefore, you know, you've served the community well all of your life, so we want to do something "nice" for you'"?

"It's an awful thing when you tell yourself you're gonna die"

The next time I saw Mr. Patterson, he was lying alone in a four-bed ward in a local nursing home. His slow-release morphine had been increased from 30 mg twice a day to 100 mg twice a day. He looked comfortable. Next to him were more cards from friends and the still unopened *Playboy* calendar. Clearly, he was lonely. "It isn't like the Hospice Center," he had told Mr. Hankin. The first thing he mentioned to me was that he wanted a television. His roommate spat, cursed, and hollered obscenities at all hours of the day. Not only did he not make a good friend, he disturbed Mr. Patterson's sleep. Mr. Patterson explained that his cancer exhausted him. Frequently he experienced excruciating pain. Emotionally, he had to make great efforts to adjust to his new and unstimulating life. His daily activities had been reduced to looking out the window, taking pills, cleaning his colostomy, drinking the liquid supplement he could digest, and sleeping. This was not an easy adjustment for him to make. Moreover, he blamed himself for his condition. He was convinced that it was his alcoholism that gave him cancer. "The doctor told me *that* was what ended my life. . . ," he said, "that's what ended my life, drinking and drinking. Drinking this wine and whiskey—too strong. I thought I'd have a little more time with my family, a little more living. . . , but I don't think so. But it's an awful thing when you tell yourself you're gonna die." Soon, our conversation shifted to Mrs. Patterson. Mr. Patterson was extremely worried about her: "I don't have nobody to watch my wife. Nobody at all to watch my wife. She's a very nice woman though. Me and her have been married 20 some years. And she's always been right there by me. She's always been right there."

For Mr. Patterson, life in the nursing home was yet another reminder of his decline. At each stage, his deterioration was even more dramatic. In the nursing home, Mr. Patterson became weaker and thinner. Physical activities exhausted him quickly. He also experienced more pain. Pain management in the nursing home was sometimes a problem. Three days after his admission, he was accidentally overmedicated. In the morning he was given his 100 mg slow-release morphine. A few hours later, however, he experienced pain. Helen, a substitute nurse from hospice who was visiting him at the time, asked one of the attending nurses to give him a short-acting medication for breakthrough pain. Accidentally, the nurse gave him the 100 mg tablet that was to be taken 10 hours later. Helen recalled the nurse shouting, "Oh my God! Gross med error! Oh my God, oh my God, I made a terrible medication error!" Terrified by her mistake, the nurse called the nursing home's medical director who instructed her to observe Mr. Patterson closely. Extreme sedation or respiratory depression would be signs for worry. As it turned out, Mr. Patterson slept his medication off .

When he wasn't in pain, Mr. Patterson displayed a perpetual state of lethargy. He slept a lot, and when he had visitors he had a hard time keeping his eyes open. I remember him trying to keep up with conversations while his eyeballs rolled back into his head. But his withdrawal was not complete. As much as his condition allowed him to, Mr. Patterson still expressed worry about his family.

Sarah hadn't seen her father since the day he entered hospice. In our conversations, she sounded ambivalent toward him. She presented Mr. Patterson as both her enemy and her strongest ally. Mr. Patterson had abused her in the past, but in her adult years he insisted on protecting her from relationships that seemed destructive. Sarah resented his advice, but she recognized—then and now—that her father cared for her deeply. His admonitions haunted her. She was unhappy with Jason who insisted on getting her pregnant against her will and failed to support their growing family. "My father was right," she would often say to me, "My father was right." Mr. Patterson's voice seemed to be with her all the time. But its tone had changed; it was no longer authoritarian and it didn't threaten her. She could hear love in it now, and she trusted it. It was a voice she would miss. She said:

> When my father dies, it is going to hurt, and I know that day is going to come soon. Right now I pray every night that he lives, I pray that they find a cure. That is mostly what I pray for. I had told one lady at hospice, "If anybody hurts my dad out in the nursing home, I am going to beat their butt," you know, being protective. I mean, that is my father and if anyone hurts him then they deal with me, that is the way I am. But, of course, my father has hurt me, which don't make sense, but I still feel like that.

There was hardly anyone on whom Sarah could rely during her father's illness. Mr. Patterson was sick, Jason was in jail, and her mother, Ruth, seemed unable to cope with the hard realities that faced them. Sarah was worried for her. She expressed concern that Mrs. Patterson had not admitted to herself the seriousness of her husband's condition: "She always claims, 'He's coming home, he's coming home,' and he is *not* coming home. You know, she claims that he told her he was coming home, and from what the lady at hospice said, he wasn't coming home. He is staying in there."

Now that her husband was in the nursing home, Mrs. Patterson's only consolation was her pets. Flour, the dog, was with her everywhere she went. Seeing them together, it was hard to discern if she was taking care of him or he of her. Squeaky, the cat, was a source of stability inside their house. Apart from the fact that Mrs. Patterson spent much of her time with her pets, she also talked about them as members of her family. She was as worried about their well-being after Mr. Patterson's death as she was about her own. She didn't want to lose them. And this was one of the reasons she rejected George's proposal to seek low-income housing. In the high-rises, she said, "you're not allowed pets."

"I wanna see them happy before I go anywhere"

When I visited Mr. Patterson on July 11, three weeks after his admission to the nursing home, he was eager to relate to me an interaction he had with his wife a few days before. This interaction had eased some of his worries about Mrs. Patterson, for something about her demeanor had told him that his wife was being cared for. She looked calmer than usual, and he was able to reach out to her in a way he had never done before. He said:

> People are trying to help her out, and evidently, they must be doing pretty good. All they got to do is talk to her. When she left here, she was in a great mood. We was watching my roommate's television. And I said, "Ruth, I wanna tell you . . . Sit down there now." I said, "Sit down there and take it easy. I just wanna tell you: if I have *any* time, *any* time whatsoever that I could spend it with *anybody* in this world, it would be with you." Well, she gets up and she goes back in the kitchen. You could tell she was crying a little. And about an hour after that she started to laugh and shakin' my hand and kissin' me. That's what I've gotta keep on doing—being nice to her. Got to. I wanna see them happy before I go anywhere.

From the day he entered the nursing home, Mr. Patterson kept asking when he'd be able to go home. "I want to sit around the house, watch television, go to the store, get a soft drink, drink it. Just like normal people. We're not different than normal people. I'm normal," he said one day to Steve and me. Steve affirmed his goal, but also asked him what he was going to do if getting well and going home wasn't in the cards. Mr. Patterson paused. "That's a superduper big question," he said. He declared that he was willing to accept his fate, but that he still wanted a week with his family.

With Steve's help, Mr. Patterson acknowledged that his wife had grown. She was not as helpless as he thought. She displayed a level of competence that was higher than he expected. Steve was moved by this discussion. He saw it as a stepping stone toward self awareness, for it enabled Mr. Patterson to see his blindness to his wife's potential. Without the assurance that his family would survive without him, Steve worried that Mr. Patterson wouldn't be able to let go. At the end of our visit, Steve asked Mr. Patterson if he wanted prayer. Mr. Patterson always did. Steve knelt down while stroking Mr. Patterson's right hand. Mr. Patterson turned his head toward me and gave me his left hand. I held his hand with both of mine. Together, we tuned out the noises on the floor and prayed. Steve asked God to hear Mr. Patterson's wishes—to receive his desire to go home. He said that we know things might not end up the way Mr. Patterson wants them, but asked God to help Mr. Patterson receive and grow from whatever was given to him. He closed with a plea for God's blessing. Mr. Patterson said he felt better. He definitely looked better. His skin and eyes seemed energized. He had perked up. "God bless you," he said to both of us as we left.

The hospice staff had mixed feelings about Mr. Patterson's desire to go home. An employee who was familiar with the case but not directly involved in it told me that she couldn't understand why a patient who was receiving 24-hour care in a nursing home would want to return to an unhealthy environment and risk his safety. Karen, Mr. Patterson's nurse, and George, his social worker, feared that Mr. Patterson's pain would escalate at home. Keeping his pain under control required close supervision and a strict medication schedule, neither of which were possible in Mr. Patterson's house. Moreover, the Pattersons could not afford private-duty nursing. Steve, on the other hand, thought his hospice colleagues were overprotective. Mr. Patterson had promised that if he went home, he wouldn't do any work. And even if he did, Steve argued, hospice could not assume the responsibility of controlling the choices of its patients. Steve found it extremely important that the prospect of going back home had given new meaning to Mr. Patterson's life. It gave him reason to wake up in the morning, it gave him hope, and it strengthened his determination to stay alive. Knowing he would need strength for his return home, Mr. Patterson had made a point of fortifying his diet. He forced drinks down his throat to make sure he gained weight. "You feel ready to go home?" I asked Mr. Patterson a few days later. "Sure do!" he replied, "I think I feel ready now. I feel a little better. It's not up to me though." "Whom is it up to?" I asked. "I don't know," he said, "some big wheel in here. I don't know who that is. I don't know. They decide whether you're ready to go home for a week, whether you're ready to go home for a month, or whether you're ready to go home for good." The decision in Mr. Patterson's case was made jointly by hospice and nursing home staff. Mr. Patterson was given permission to go home for four hours.

"Our boy is going home today"

"Our boy is going home today," announced Karen when she first saw me one morning. Her big smile revealed pride. She, George, and Steve had worked hard to find a safe way to realize Mr. Patterson's wish. They arranged for a hospice volunteer to drive Mr. Patterson to his house at 1:00 p.m. and return him to the nursing home at 5:00 p.m. During those four hours, Karen scheduled a nursing visit as well. This way she'd be able to check on her patient and make sure that his return home was smooth. The volunteer, Robert Gardner, dropped Mr. Patterson off as scheduled. But he was surprised to see that neither Ruth nor Sarah were at home. Mr. Patterson ambled into his house without keys. The door was unlocked. He assured Robert he was going to be okay and encouraged him to leave.

A couple of hours later, Karen arrived. I went, too. We expected to see father, mother, daughter, and grandchildren gathered together, but we were confronted with an entirely different scene. Sarah, apparently, was at work. She had not been informed about her father's visit home. Ruth and little Kevin were outdoors, playing on the sidewalk. They had left Mr. Patterson alone to sleep. Mr. Patterson was inside, lying on his bed with his eyes half closed. Karen and I tiptoed into his bedroom and sat on two kitchen chairs next to him. His room was small and dark. It was hot, and the smell of the cat's urine was overwhelming. But Mr. Patterson seemed blissful. Turning his head slowly, he looked around at his room and said to us, "This is my life." He paused for a second and continued: "I'm proud of it." Two hours later he was taken back to the nursing home.

"I would be ready to go if it is the time"

When Mr. Patterson returned to the nursing home everyone noticed a decline. Karen, his hospice nurse, reported that he was weaker, slept more, had increasing difficulty cleaning his colostomy, and was unable to keep up with conversations. Periodically, he would lift his arms up in the air while opening and closing his fists as if he were trying to reach something—a relatively frequent sign of drug toxicity or metabolic complications. Several of his caregivers got the impression that he had entered the liminal space between the world of the living and that of the dead.

The week of Mr. Patterson's visit home, Mrs. Patterson called George for the first time since hospice had been involved with her, to seek his help. Apparently, her welfare had come up for review, and she had been denied the minimal support she was receiving. Both cash assistance and food stamps were going to stop because a doctor wrote on her chart that she was capable of working. George explained to her that in order to apply for SSI she needed a psychological evaluation. Although SSI is designed for persons with an extremely low income, one still needs a physical or emotional diagnosis in order to qualify for it. George scheduled a meeting for her with the Mental Health/Mental Retardation Office and accompanied her there the day of her appointment.

Karen was perplexed by the Pattersons' difficulties:

> I kind of marvel sometimes at how basic human life can be and how so many things that I expect as normal or beneficial are just not even in their reality. With her limited mental function, plus probably some psychological/psychiatric pathology, plus the social/financial situation, you kind of wonder what makes Ruth feel good—what makes Ruth feel like it is worthwhile getting out of bed this morning.

Mrs. Patterson's welfare was extended for a month. In that interval a doctor was going to reconsider her capacity to work. Although a month's extension was nothing reassuring, it offered Mrs. Patterson a temporary cushion. I expected that she would announce the good news to her husband and daughter, but she did not. It was George who updated Mr. Patterson on the fortunate developments. Money was a private matter among the Pattersons. There wasn't much of it, and everyone protected what they had. Mr. Patterson was afraid Ruth would coopt his limited savings, so he hid the $160 that he had. Sarah spent her salary extremely carefully and demanded that her mother babysit Kevin to compensate for not bringing money into the home. Mrs. Patterson feared that if Sarah knew that she had any money at all, she would take it all from her to pay the rent.

Meanwhile, after six weeks in the nursing home, Mr. Patterson was lonely and depressed. He couldn't sleep at night. He couldn't understand why friends and relatives didn't come to visit. "I do not mean that much to them," he said softly. "It's hard to tell who might show up. So all you can do in a situation like that is just wait."

"Waiting" meant sleeping, staring out the window, or looking at the bare walls surrounding him. Mr. Patterson still didn't have a television. I could see him withering away. His complexion had acquired a yellowish tone, and he looked even thinner than before—"emaciated" might be a better word. I could see his skull; his skin was tight around his bones and his eyes looked sunken in. His voice had lost its power and his words had started to run into each other. I struggled to understand him. Our conversations were slow and tiresome. I repeated almost everything he said to check if I had heard him right. He corrected me, again and again, until I understood him. Staff from hospice offered Mr. Patterson a second trip home. Initially, he responded positively, but soon his pain started to overwhelm him. His abdomen had become distended and hard with tumor.

On August 4, I visited Mr. Patterson with Karen. He was lying in bed as usual. He told us that his pain had become worse, running from the left to the right side of his abdomen. It was unbearable. Karen left the room to ask the ward nurse for a short-acting painkiller. The nurse looked harried, and although she agreed to administer the medication, she quickly disappeared into someone else's room. Forty minutes later she still hadn't given Mr. Patterson his pill. It was clear that Mr. Patterson was in severe pain. He was quiet but pale and tense. In the few sentences he was able to utter, he expressed worry for his dog. He didn't think Mrs. Patterson and Sarah would be able to care for Flour without him. Then came his lunch, but he couldn't touch it; he was in too much pain.

Karen was distressed. Although she was confident that there were medications that would alleviate her patient's pain, her hands were tied. As a hospice nurse, she had almost no authority in the nursing home setting, and, even worse, she posed a threat to the ward's overworked and underpaid staff. In contrast to nursing home staff, Karen worked for an agency known in Lancaster County for its luxury and comfort. She didn't have to wear a uniform, she had only a comparative handful of patients to look after, and she worked on a flexible schedule. More importantly, she was an expert in palliative care. By giving directions to Mr. Patterson's caregivers, she risked more than her welcome in the nursing home. Karen explained to me that the slightest criticism of nursing home staff could turn them against her. Such a scenario would be anathema to any hospice nurse, for it would render her opinions irrelevant and deprive her of the chance to improve the care offered to her patient.

Frustrated and unwilling to make further appeals to the nursing home staff, Karen sat by Mr. Patterson's side and advised him to become his own advocate. She told him that he had to place demands on his nurses by asking for painkillers when he needed them. Mr. Patterson nodded. "I've got to say something," he said. He told us that he wanted more help cleaning his colostomy as well. Several times it had filled up and no one was there to empty it out. That humiliated him. It was clear that if Mr. Patterson were to start speaking up for himself, his care would improve. As it was, he just lay in bed waiting to be noticed. And to complicate matters further, when he felt pain, he often didn't look uncomfortable. "On those times when he said he was painful, he wasn't acting painful," Karen said. The frequent discrepancy between Mr. Patterson's subjective experience of pain and his physical appearance required that he be asked about his pain on a regular basis. This, however, was something that nursing home staff had neither the time nor energy to do. Would someone as self-effacing as Mr. Patterson learn to voice his own discomfort? Or was he doomed to stay silent and receive insufficient care?

After much thought, Karen decided to try and make a change in Mr. Patterson's medication. As it was, Mr. Patterson was scheduled to take 100 mg of slow-release morphine twice a day and an additional 30 mg of short-acting morphine syrup at regular intervals. The frequent administration of the liquid morphine, however, posed an overwhelming burden to the pressured schedule of nursing home staff and was sometimes overlooked. Karen's idea was to eliminate the liquid morphine by increasing the dose of the slow-release pills. This way, Mr. Patterson would enjoy constant pain relief, without having to be tended to on a regular basis. Moreover, he might be less drowsy.

Karen's plan was not received well by the nursing home staff. She recalled:

> When I suggested the change, I kind of think that the nursing home's medical director interpreted that I was trying to increase the morphine, when in fact I was trying to move the major portion of the morphine dose from the rapid-acting to the time-release—which would be a better delivery for the patient and the staff also, but I don't think they ever listened to me. I don't think they really understood, and the doctor's response was, "Well, what we are doing is working, so there is no reason to change it." Once he said that, the staff really became defensive and did not want to hear any more about it.

Steve was also worried about Mr. Patterson's care. On August 6, he and I made a joint visit to the nursing home. Mr. Patterson looked more bony than ever. Steve stroked his hand the entire time. Mr. Patterson said he couldn't sleep at night because of the pain from his abdominal and rectal tumors. Steve asked him what he wanted God to do for him and Mr. Patterson replied faintly, "To take away the pain." One could hardly hear his voice anymore; he was devoid of strength. At the same time, he wondered if God was really with him. The previous day, he had prayed to not be given a bath, but he got one anyway. He suffered because it was too cold for him. He confessed that although he did feel God by his side, he felt Him only "a little," adding, "I would be ready to go if it is the time." Together with George, Steve began exploring the possibility of transferring Mr. Patterson back to the hospice inpatient unit.

The next day a nurse substituting for Karen was sent to check Mr. Patterson's condition. She was asked to determine whether it would be a good idea to transfer Mr. Patterson back to the inpatient unit, but she saw no indication of pain in him. She said:

> From what I see, pain is an emotional pain for him. I think that's a big factor for him. The nurses are telling me they give medication every two hours. I did not have the nerve to check the med sheet. They may skip one dose in one shift, they said. We need to make sure the next time that they are doing exactly what they say they are doing. I don't like to do that. I don't like to question somebody's authority

on their grounds. That is *their* game over there. Two or three visits ago, I asked a nurse what they were doing for breakthrough pain, and she said they would give it to him when he asked for it. I said, "Well, he is complaining of pain now, so he should probably have it now." She said, "It is interesting that he only complains about pain when you guys from hospice are here."

"I wish Len would come back home"

At the Pattersons', the nauseating smell of Squeaky's urine had started to creep out of the apartment and up to the second floor. Angry neighbors called the landlord demanding an immediate solution. The landlord responded with an ultimatum: Sarah and Mrs. Patterson had until September 1 to get rid of Squeaky and Flour. If they failed to do so, they would all be kicked out of the house. Mrs. Patterson panicked. She declared that she would rather live on the street than part with her pets. Sarah tried to convince the landlord that only Squeaky caused the problem. She pleaded for permission to keep Flour, but to no avail. The landlord was adamant: both pets had to go.

Not only did Mrs. Patterson not have enough money to move, she was also told that she would be taken off welfare. Apparently, a doctor confirmed the previous assessment that she was fit to work. In a brief phone conversation I had with her, she sounded despondent. "I wish Len was here," she cried. "The doctor said I can work, but I can't. I'm tired and weak, my ankle and foot hurt from arthritis, I get bad headaches from my teeth, my neck and back hurt. People are not going to hire you if you don't have good shoes and nice clothes. I wish Len would come back home."

"Let's hope this will not be it"

It was the end of August, and it was hot. Mr. Patterson's illness was progressing. His medications were unsuccessful in alleviating the pressure and pain caused by his rectal tumor. For the first time in her work with him, Ann Marie, a personal care nurse from hospice, noted that Mr. Patterson refused to close his eyes. He told her he was afraid that if he were to fall asleep he would die. Ann Marie asked if he wanted to pray with her. He said yes. She later recalled:

> I just prayed that God would provide someone to help take care of his grandson, and that God would help open the door for his wife to get maybe a part-time job, and that God would make a way for her financial needs to be met, and that God would help him with his fear and comfort, and he just seemed to feel really good about that, thinking of it that way.

When I arrived in Mr. Patterson's room on the morning of August 29, Ann Marie was giving him a sponge bath. Although she had drawn a curtain around them and I couldn't see Mr. Patterson's expressions, I could tell he enjoyed the personal care. Long silences and a few faint words of appreciation revealed contentment. Moreover, when the bath was over he declared that it had been the "best thing in the world." But he also had the feeling that he would never receive another bath. The curtains opened, and Mr. Patterson turned to greet me. Two red, unblinking eyeballs stared right into my eyes. Mr. Patterson was worried not only about his family but also about himself. He was alarmed by the fact that he seemed unable to tolerate solid foods. His diet had been reduced to a few cans of liquid supplements a day. Ann Marie assured him that drinking these liquids was like eating an entire meal. "Your body doesn't know the difference," she asserted. "Just like I told you with Jesus. It might not feel like He's here, but He is, and everything will be all right." On her way out, Ann Marie called Steve, George, and Karen to let them know that Mr. Patterson was declining. "I would not be shocked if he died tonight," she said before she left.

Steve arrived minutes later. "You're sick and tired of being sick and tired, aren't you?" he asked softly, to which Mr. Patterson nodded. He also reassured him that he was in God's hands. Mr. Patterson expressed a desire to see Sarah. There was a sense of urgency about him that convinced us all he was ready to let go. Steve left to pick Sarah up from work. I sat next to Mr. Patterson and waited. I remember not knowing what to say. Soon I found myself repeating the comforting words of Ann Marie: "Everything will be okay, and Sarah will be okay, too." To my surprise, Mr. Patterson refuted me: "No she won't. I know she won't be okay. Everyone says she will, but I am her father, and I know."

Sarah arrived, looking composed but afraid. Nervously, she sat in a chair by her father's bedside. Mr. Patterson slowly turned his head toward her and asked her questions. Was she still working? Was she making enough money? Did Jason have a job? Sarah assured him that everything was okay. The last thing he asked her was to promise that she would take care of her mother. Sarah did. "I have flashes that I'm going to die in a day or two," Mr. Patterson asserted. His eyes remained wide open, but his conversation with his daughter seemed to have given him a sense of comfort. He sunk his head back into his pillow and seemed to withdraw into himself as if in a state of meditation. There was an awkward silence in the room.

Mrs. Patterson came through the door. Someone from hospice had called her to notify her of her husband's condition. As usual, she had walked from the bus stop, so she looked sweaty and disheveled. Her arrival broke our silence. Steve walked over to her, and the two started talking. Mrs. Patterson stopped at the foot of her husband's bed, staring at him from a distance. Mr. Patterson seemed disconnected from his surroundings. With a glazed look in his eyes, he was staring at the ceiling. It wasn't clear if he knew that his wife had arrived. He showed no sign of following the conversation that had started. I assumed he wasn't listening at all until Mrs. Patterson made reference to a bill. "What bill?"

he suddenly exclaimed. Mrs. Patterson would have proceeded to answer his question if Steve hadn't cut the conversation short. Both hospice staff and nursing home staff feared that Mr. Patterson would suffer a torturous death if he didn't stop worrying about his family. He was seen as defying nature by holding onto life in a body that was almost dead. Everyone felt that his spirit needed soothing, otherwise he wouldn't be able to leave this world in peace. With Steve's redirection, Mrs. Patterson walked closer to her husband, looked him in the eyes, and said, "I love you." "I love you, too," responded Mr. Patterson, eyes still fixed at the ceiling. But quickly, their tones changed. "What do you want me to do with your clothes?" "What do you want me to do with your tools?" "What do you want me to do with all your things?" cried Mrs. Patterson in desperation.

Mr. Patterson gave no response. He looked exhausted. His wife and Sarah left. Steve sat by his side, quietly. "Having Ruth and Sarah over was the best thing," said Mr. Patterson after a brief period of silence. "It would be a lie not to say I love them." He then asked for a pill that would put him to sleep. I could sense a heaviness in the air, feeling that everything around me had slowed down. The interaction between Steve and Mr. Patterson seemed to unfold in slow motion. There was silence and a set of burning, unblinking eyes crying out for help. The man who could not ask for painkillers when he needed them was now firmly requesting pills to help him die. Steve was at a loss for words. Finally he told Mr. Patterson that he wouldn't want to give him such a pill because doing so would prevent him from experiencing the good things that can happen during one's death. I later asked Steve what was going on in his mind at the time. He replied:

> Inside myself I am thinking, "Holy shit! We are not going down that road." It is not appropriate and, of course, [I]remember[ed] that he was afraid to close his eyes because he did not want to go to sleep and not wake up, and [him] thinking about being put away now, and [I] recogniz[ed] that he was in that tension. What I have seen is that there are still miracles and blessings that can occur with people of faith in their understanding of who God wants to be for them, experiencing God in some very powerful ways that are awesomely reassuring and, of course, sharing their struggle with their family members. So I think euthanasia would be inappropriate because he was not clear at that point. He was still struggling and trying to negotiate that and come to some kind of resolution.

When I said good-bye to Mr. Patterson later that day, he said, "Let's hope this will not be it."

"Nothing is going right"

On August 31 Squeaky and Flour were still in the apartment. Mrs. Patterson had one more day to decide what she was going to do with them. "I am going out on the streets tomorrow," she cried to me on the phone, "because we have to get rid of our dog and cat. It is just so hard for me, and I really don't want to babysit Kevin, and they claim I can work." "Nothing is going right," she continued, "and I just don't like moving." I could hear agony in her voice. Mrs. Patterson had spent several days calling friends and neighbors to see if they would be willing to take her and her pets in with them. One night, Sarah deliberately locked her and Flour outside in the rain.

On September 1 the tension between Sarah and Mrs. Patterson climaxed. Fearing eviction, Sarah insisted that the animals leave the house. Mrs. Patterson refused to give them up. A screaming fight ensued. Mrs. Patterson's parents were called in, and they invited their daughter to move into their house. But Mrs. Patterson refused, for they wouldn't accept her pets. Then the police came. Apparently, they were notified by neighbors. When the fighting broke up, Mrs. Patterson and the animals disappeared. They were gone all night.

In an effort to resolve the situation, George offered to take Squeaky and Flour to an animal shelter. Sarah accepted the offer, but Mrs. Patterson, who was back home the next day, refused it. Sarah kicked Squeaky out of the house and made arrangements behind her mother's back for George to take Flour to the Humane League. George transferred Flour on September 5. Hoping to prevent his death, however, he continued looking for a family that would adopt him. At the same time he dreaded seeing Mrs. Patterson. He was afraid that Sarah would tell her mother the truth about what happened and that she, in turn, would fill up with hatred toward him. To his surprise, when Mrs. Patterson saw him at the nursing home, she expressed joy. I don't know if she knew what role he had played in Flour's disappearance and neither did George.

By this time Mr. Patterson had lost almost all the energy it took to speak. Most of his conversation was limited to faint nods and shakes of his head. He indicated to Steve that he was no longer worried about his wife, but he did want to see his sister from Kentucky because he wanted her forgiveness. Apparently, his sister had been extremely critical of Mr. Patterson's alcoholism, and her disapproval haunted him. Practically, however, Mr. Patterson's wish was unachievable. No one knew how to get in touch with his sister, and even if she were to telephone, Mr. Patterson was unable to speak. Steve had been unaware that this part of Mr. Patterson's history disturbed him. He recalled asking Mr. Patterson, "Do you know that God has forgiven you for that and the mistakes you made as a result of your drinking?" Mr. Patterson said, "No." Steve continued, "So that opened a whole new territory to explore. I reassured him that God is with him and is compassionate, merciful, and will take care of him, and that God is also forgiving."

By the end of this visit with Steve, Mr. Patterson declared that he was ready to let go. Karen put in a request for round-the-clock hospice care. She had a strong feeling that Mr. Patterson would die within the next three days. She noticed mottling on his feet and back. But unlike Steve, she had difficulty reassuring her patient that his family would be okay after his death. In a worried tone she said to me, "You see most of our families through this difficult time and you know they are going to be all right eventually, once they allow themselves time to grieve. You know they are going to do fine. This family, there is just no way I can make myself believe that they are going to be fine, and that is frustrating."

"Every day he looks ten times worse than he did the day before"

A week later, Mr. Patterson's medical records indicated significant periods of unresponsiveness, sleep with intermittent apnea, and no urine output. His pulse was too weak to be felt at the wrist, so the attending nurse measured it with a stethoscope. After a long week of intensified visits, Steve had a strong feeling Mr. Patterson's last day had come. He decided to go to the nursing home, and I accompanied him. Mr. Patterson was lying in bed with his eyes three quarters of the way closed. Steve talked to him about the love of God. He also told him what a good person he thought Mr. Patterson was, how much he loved him, and how thankful he felt for having gotten to know him and walk with him on his journey. Mr. Patterson remained unresponsive. The only answer he gave that day was a nod to the question: was he going to go with the Lord if the Lord reached out to him? Several hours later, after Steve had left, Mr. Patterson sat up suddenly and raised his hand as if he was reaching out to someone at the foot of his bed.

Sarah, too, visited her father that day. She recalled:

> I thought, "Oh my God, he is dying." I was there and I touched him and I told him I was there, I said, "I love you, I am here," but it was like touching nothing. I know he is going to go, but it hurts me. I had a lot of anger and a lot of hurt. My anger and my hurt are towards my dad, but I mean now that he's on his death bed, I mean you really can't have that towards him because he is dying. And then I feel guilty for having that towards him.

By September 10, Mr. Patterson was unresponsive to almost all verbal and tactile stimuli, markedly jaundiced, with no urine output and no bowel sounds. His breathing was labored, his mottling had spread to his elbows, knees, and hands, and he showed signs of pain when anyone tried to move him. "Every day he looks ten times worse than he did the day before," remarked Karen. Both hospice and nursing home staff were convinced that Mr. Patterson was holding onto life out of concern for his family. To ease his fears, George asked Mrs. Patterson to reassure her husband that everything was going to be okay, but within Mr. Patterson's hearing, Ruth said, "Well, he knows I won't be okay!" For the first time, Mr. Patterson's caregivers started seeing Mrs. Patterson as a liability.

They instructed each other to try to control Mrs. Patterson's interactions with her husband because her need for his support prolonged his suffering.

Mr. Patterson's swallowing ability had diminished so he was unable to take his pills. To circumvent this problem, nursing home staff began crushing his slow-release morphine and inserting it into his stoma, even though the slow-release feature of long-acting morphine is dependent on an intact tablet coating. Crushing the coating eliminates the time-release. Thus, the nursing home staff were essentially administering a 12-hour dose all at once. Problems also accompanied the administration of Mr. Patterson's short-acting, breakthrough medication. Because the nursing home physician did not want to increase Mr. Patterson's slow-release dose, Mr. Patterson required increasing doses of his breakthrough medication hourly. The nursing home nurses were reluctant to give this medication, fearing they were going to hasten their patient's death.

"In God's hands all is well"

On the morning of September 11, Steve went back to the nursing home. He was astounded to hear that Mr. Patterson was still alive. To his amazement, he found Mrs. Patterson worrying aloud to her husband about her future. Knowing how hard it was for Mr. Patterson to hear his wife's concerns, Steve said to him, "If Jesus comes for you to take you home, it is okay to go with Him." He then reassured Mr. Patterson that "in God's hands all is well—even when it does not look, seem, or feel that way." "At that point," Steve recalled, "came a tear at the corner of Mr. Patterson's eye that welled up enough that it trickled down his cheek. I was rubbing Mr. Patterson's arm, making contact with him and trying to be comforting, and Ruth on the other side started doing the same thing. You know, kind of modeling a little bit as it turned out, and she even eventually said, 'I love you.' I said, 'Len, did you hear that? Ruth said she loves you and she really cares about you.' That was short lived. But it did happen!"

On September 12, with prompting from a hospice nurse, Mrs. Patterson told her husband that it was okay to let go. That night Mr. Patterson died.

"If you see George, tell him thanks for all his help"

Since her husband's death, Mrs. Patterson has moved in with her parents. Sarah and Jason have had a fourth child against Sarah's wish to limit their family to three. Thanks to George, Flour has been adopted by a new family in Lancaster County, but Mrs. Patterson has not been informed of his whereabouts. Squeaky was killed by a car. Although hospice expected Ruth to require intensive support from its bereavement counselors, she did not. After seeing her at Mr. Patterson's memorial service, both George and Steve confirmed that she was not as unskilled as she had seemed. Mrs. Patterson had appeared with a new haircut, clean clothes, and the determination to introduce her family members to each and every hospice employee who had come to pay their final respects. I remember her confidently taking me by the hand to her sister to whom she explained articulately the reason behind my presence there and the purpose of our research.

A few months later, in December, I got the chance to talk with Mrs. Patterson again. Excitedly she announced to me that her Supplemental Social Security Income (SSI) had been approved. In only a few more weeks she was going to be back on welfare. "If you see George," she said, "tell him thanks for all his help and tell him that I'm getting SSI for sure." And she quickly added, "I just don't want Sarah to know about it."

10

Miriam Lambert
Total Pain and the Despair of an Unlived Life

Narrated by ANNA TOWERS

It happens rarely in palliative care that a person's pain remains uncontrolled despite the best efforts of the team. Miriam Lambert was referred to our study because of the difficulty of her case. She had not had an easy life, and emotional issues compounded her situation. The palliative care team tried to control her pain with a full spectrum of medications as well as anesthetic blocks (see medication record at the end of the chapter). They tried supportive nonmedical and psychological interventions, such as art therapy, music therapy, and massage, to reach her in any way they could. Nonetheless, the pain persisted.

"I'm not a very open person, you know"

Mrs. Lambert was 68 years old when I met her in the Palliative Care Unit on October 1, 1996. Pale, with blond, neatly combed, shoulder-length hair, she sat rather stiffly in her hospital bed. She looked proud and dignified, and was soft-spoken. She had just recently been diagnosed with melanoma, which had started in her foot, and had now spread to her pelvis and spine. She had been in almost constant pain for three months. Her affect seemed flat, even as she spoke of her discomfort, and she avoided my gaze as we spoke, her face mask-like. I wondered: was this demeanor a result of the pain? Although she did not

177

look like she was in pain, when asked directly, she would say the pain was unbearable. It was always there, especially in her back and her left leg, and it was
excruciating when she moved.

In her room I noticed tasteful art posters on the walls, with books about
music on her bedside table. Judging from the books and the way she spoke, I
thought that she must be well educated. I was surprised to learn that she had
done odd jobs all her life; most recently she had been a supermarket cashier.
There was something that didn't fit. Over several visits, I tried to engage her in
conversation about herself. "I'm not a very open person, you know," she said.
Slowly, through my conversations with her, but mostly through conversations
with her brothers, nieces, and the caregivers on the Palliative Care Unit, a por-
trait of her life emerged.

She was of working-class, French-Canadian origin, born and raised in a small
town, the tenth of 12 children. Two siblings had died in infancy. According to her
older brother Peter, Miriam was the "glue" for the family. Her brothers felt that
Miriam had not realized her potential, as she was very bright and was always top
of her class at school, but then she settled for menial jobs. Peter said of her:

> As a person she is closed, isolated, and does not speak of emotions. She is a pleas-
> ant person in company, but she isn't open. She is very reserved. She doesn't speak
> much. She never had a life with a rhythm of her own. She is very generous and did
> a lot for her husband. He demanded all of her time. She couldn't live a full life.
> She went from one small job to another. She tried to look after other people's
> problems, but not her own. What a waste of potential! She did very well in school,
> but she didn't socialize well. She had always been alone before she got married.
> Maybe it's because of the relationship with my parents.

She had a few friends but no intimate friends. When she spoke of her
mother, she said that she didn't feel loved; she felt left aside when she was
growing up. She saw a psychiatrist for depression when she was an adolescent
and periodically later in life. She felt as if she had done something wrong,
though she didn't know what it was, and that she had not been forgiven. As an
adult, she continued to live with her parents. When her father died, she looked
after her mother through a long illness. Her mother died when Mrs. Lambert
was 37 years old.

Mrs. Lambert had never been involved with men until she met Roger, a man
who was 30 years older and about to get divorced. Miriam Lambert was not the
reason for the divorce—she was clear that her values would not have allowed
that. She and Roger started to live together, but after six months Mrs. Lambert
realized that she did not love him. Nonetheless, they had stayed together 30
years in a common-law relationship, out of convenience.

They were able to enjoy life for a few years, but after that one hardship after
another occured. Mrs. Lambert had to spend a lot of time looking after her ill
sister, who died within a couple of years. Roger, who had been a young-spirited,

active person when she met him, developed heart and lung disease, making him more dependent on her. Now he was 98 years old and had been in a nursing home for six months, ever since Mrs. Lambert had become ill with cancer. Mrs. Lambert felt guilty about this. Although she did not readily share her feelings, she spoke frequently about Roger and her concerns regarding his comfort. According to her brother, she was not emotionally close to Roger, rather, she felt a great sense of duty toward him, making her feel very tied to him.

Before Roger got ill, she had gone through a series of temporary jobs. She did not feel fulfilled in these jobs, and she expressed a lack of personal realization: "I have always been in the service of others," she said to me. "I don't know who I am." Her only objective had been to look after her mother, her sister, and then Roger. They had no children of their own. Roger had children from his first marriage, but they were not close to him and were not involved in his care.

Her one relaxation was listening to classical music. She had played the violin briefly as a child and would have liked very much to have studied more, but she had had no opportunity to do so. She hadn't gone out much for the last four or five years, as Roger demanded all of her time. When she did go out, it was mainly to take Roger to the doctor. She panicked now, thinking Roger would die, for it was as if she didn't exist without him.

Among Mrs. Lambert's family was an 84-year-old sister who was too frail to come see her and two of her brothers who lived in town and visited her regularly. Mrs. Lambert's nieces were the most significant people in her life. She looked after her husband out of a sense of duty, but she loved her nieces, particularly her niece Carole, who was in her mid-40s. Another niece, Sandra, was a successful lawyer, and Mrs. Lambert was very proud of her. A third niece had been murdered by her boyfriend. Mrs. Lambert occasionally spoke about this, but without emotion. Although Mrs. Lambert was close to her nieces, they did not confide in each other.

Mrs. Lambert came from a religious Roman Catholic family, but she had lost her faith early in adult life. She had felt betrayed and deceived by the church: there was so much ritual and dogma, but where was the truth? She read a lot and contemplated questions about religion and philosophy. She was looking for answers within herself, but she had not reached a state of peace. As Carole put it, "She does not love herself, she is extremely hard on herself, and she is hard on others. I have the impression that life was difficult for her. She got lost somewhere along the way."

Beginning of the illness

In October 1995, Mrs. Lambert developed swelling and pain in her big toe. At the time she was busy looking after her husband. He was needing more and more care and Mrs. Lambert was getting tired. When she finally took the time to see her doctor he told her that she had an infection or an ingrown toenail and gave her antibiotics. It seemed to get better for a few weeks, but then the swelling returned and Mrs. Lambert could hardly walk because of the pain in her foot. After Christmas she went back to the doctor for a biopsy, which confirmed that she had melanoma. The tumor did not seem to have spread, but the surgeon told her that she needed to have the toe amputated.

Mrs. Lambert had mixed feelings about this. She had been having so much difficulty coping with her husband, who was chair-bound because of his illness and had started to become forgetful and demanding. His vision was also very bad. Mrs. Lambert had to look after him and every aspect of the household. She had promised him that she would never place him in a nursing home, but now she needed to go into the hospital. So she was almost happy to have the amputation and to get Roger into a nursing home.

In the hospital she at last had time to consider her own situation. She had not had to deal with doctors before, except for psychiatrists. Could the doctors not have diagnosed the melanoma sooner? She was angry and felt that she could not trust physicians, losing faith in them just as she had lost faith in the church.

Following the surgery, she convalesced at her brother Peter's house for three weeks. While she was there, she spoke non-stop about her life and people she had known, but said little about her feelings, except for remarks like, "I've always been in the service of others. I feel like a servant." Although she spoke a lot about Roger and the constant care he had needed for the past three years, during the three weeks she was in Peter's home, not once did she call her husband. Later Peter said to me, "It's as if she felt totally liberated."

In May 1996, a few months after her surgery, she went to see the surgeon again. He had bad news: the melanoma had spread to her groin. She was devastated, but she wanted to fight for her life. She agreed to have surgery to remove the lymph nodes in her groin. The oncologist offered her experimental chemotherapy. Though the chance that it would help was not great, Mrs. Lambert wanted to go through with it.

"How can my life be ending? It hasn't started yet"

In July, Mrs. Lambert began to have pain in her left leg. During July and August she spent up to 10 hours each day in the bathtub, trying to get some relief. One day she spent 20 hours there. By August she had developed tumor in her pelvis and severe pain in her left lower abdomen; the pain in her leg got worse. A scan showed tumor in her lumbar spine with nerve root entrapment. The chemotherapy had failed.

Things were happening so fast that Mrs. Lambert didn't know what to do. When the surgeon offered her radiotherapy, she refused. She wanted to go home and think about it. So far everything had failed, so why have more treatments? But when the pain got worse in late August she was admitted to a general surgical ward for pain control. She now accepted a course of radiotherapy to try to reduce her pain and started taking small doses of the opioid analgesic hydromorphone.

At this time, her attending surgeon told her that she had a prognosis of a few weeks. Mrs. Lambert became despondent, saying to her brother Peter, "How can my life be ending? It hasn't started yet."

Her pain was out of control. The surgeon consulted Dr. Bonin of the Palliative Care Service. Mrs. Lambert rated her pain 10 on a scale of 0 to 10—the worst pain possible. When pain is due to tumor invasion of nerves, opioids alone are often not sufficient to control it. Dr. Bonin suggested an increase in hydromorphone and the addition of carbamazepine (an anti-epileptic agent) and amitriptyline (an antidepressant) as co-analgesics.

The oncologist also considered offering her palliative chemotherapy to try to control the pain. However, within two or three days, Mrs. Lambert was feeling better. She was walking around and in better spirits. The oncologist, seeing that she was more comfortable, said that he would not favor more chemotherapy, unless the pain could not be controlled by other means. The medical team felt that she might be able to go home.

A few days later, however, burning pain was back in her left leg and groin. She rated its intensity as *fifteen* out of 10. Any movement made the pain much worse. Dr. Bonin transferred her to the Palliative Care Unit on an urgent basis. Mrs. Lambert hoped that with the more specialized care on the Palliative Care Unit, her pain would soon be controlled and she would be able to go home.

On August 30, 1996, she was admitted to the unit, receiving a room with a private bath so she could have hot baths as often as she wanted to ease her pain. One of the nurses described her as "stoical, friendly, open and afraid to bother others for help." Her nieces brought her gifts and things she needed. They related to each other in practical ways, Mrs. Lambert not discussing her more serious concerns with them.

Within a few days, her pain medications seemed to be working, as the pain was less and she was able to walk. The staff began planning her discharge home, and she began to look forward to resuming her normal life. But the relief was short-lived. Mrs. Lambert began to have hallucinations, which Dr. Bonin believed were from the high doses of hydromorphone. She switched medication and asked the anesthetist for help. Perhaps an epidural or a nerve block would reduce the need for medication. On September 11, Mrs. Lambert tried the epidural analgesia, but it did not help. She was unable to move her legs when she received the epidural medication, and the pain was still there.

It is rare that epidurals do not work in this context. Mrs. Lambert was so discouraged that she cried. Dr. Bonin was surprised and disappointed. Once or twice a year they had a patient like Mrs. Lambert on the unit—a patient whose pain persisted despite their best efforts. Dr. Bonin continued to try different kinds of medication but she was rapidly running out of options. The oncologist was not enthusiastic about giving Mrs. Lambert palliative chemotherapy because the predicted response rate was so low.

In mid-September, Mrs. Lambert's older sister died, also of cancer. Mrs. Lambert said of her, "She was like my mother—sensitive to pain." Mrs. Lambert wanted to go to the funeral but was physically unable to do so. Her family tried to include her at a distance, sharing their plans for the rituals and prayers. She was touched by this, but her sister's death, along with her worry over her own tumors growing, provoked feelings of despair. She asked the psychologist, "Why live when death seems to be the way out for all of us?"

In the nursing home, Roger would occasionally remark to his niece or nephew, "It's not going well for Miriam, is it?" Once in a while he telephoned Mrs. Lambert. Commenting to me about these calls, she said, "I feel so helpless. He calls and says things like 'I need help. No one is here to get me to the toilet.' What can I do? This is what happens when you don't have children." In fact, her husband did have children from a previous marriage, but they did not visit him.

Trying to get closer

The nurses found it difficult to communicate with Mrs. Lambert at a deeper level. Linda, her primary nurse, told me, "Her conversation is superficial—difficult to pierce. She will barely skim the depths. I couldn't get down in there, like I can with other patients. She is bright, and loves to play with words, but somehow it is difficult to get close to her." Though she had very little to work with, Linda tried to interpret Mrs. Lambert's reserve. "She could not use her potential," she speculated to me. "She did not have a career. She has a sense of failure about this. She feels a great sense of responsibility toward her husband. I think that her emotional pain is linked to the fact that she can no longer look after her husband."

Closeness of patients in palliative care to staff is quite individualized. Patients are selective in the caregivers with whom they will share their feelings, if they choose to open up at all. In Mrs. Lambert's case, it was Gloria, the art therapist. She told Gloria that she saw her life as a failure. In an art therapy session Mrs. Lambert made a painting of a swirling bluish cloud, bordered by a blue square, and wrote the word "fiasco" underneath, in large blue letters. "I don't do anything well," she explained. "My life is a fiasco." Of the painting she said, "This is bad. It doesn't look good. It's horrible, but that's how I feel." She wanted to put the painting on the wall of her room, along with others that were more cheerful and comforting to her. Despite these moments of self-disclosure, Gloria felt that Mrs. Lambert was "hiding."

When her pain was tolerable, Mrs. Lambert listened to music or watched TV. On her birthday, September 27, many visitors came. The staff encourage families to celebrate birthdays, if possible. Mrs. Lambert had two birthday cakes and a birthday supper with 12 people.

A few days after this, Mrs. Lambert developed a new burning pain, this time in her right leg. Crying with pain, she stayed in bed and did not move. X-rays confirmed that the tumor had spread. She was scheduled for more radio-therapy, but sometimes she was in so much pain and was so tired that she did not go down for the treatments. Dr. Bonin continued to increase the opioid and coanalgesic medications, adding new ones to replace those that seemed ineffective.

During this time, Mrs. Lambert met with the psychologist; she kept away from serious subjects, expressing the desire to talk only about light things. After about half an hour she told the psychologist that what she really needed to talk about would make her break into tears and, she said, "If I cry I will feel more physical pain." The serious talk would have to wait.

Mrs. Lambert also received music therapy. During a relaxation session in her room, Mrs. Lambert reported no pain when she listened to the sound of ocean waves. In early October, she began to attend a creative arts group. She collabo-rated with another patient on certain images of a house. At the next session she asked Gloria to make some drawings for her. Gloria recalled this session to me: "She spoke a great deal about 'feeling sad or angry inside but smiling on the outside.' She created an image of a woman smiling, but holding a more somber woman inside of herself. She reacted favorably [to it] but did not want to place it in her room." Gloria wondered aloud, "Perhaps it's a little close to home?"

Mrs. Lambert's conversation was becoming more superficial, even with Glo-ria. Gloria wanted to see if she could explore Mrs. Lambert's world more deeply by using visualization techniques. "I brought her a peaceful picture," Gloria said, "seeing if she could imagine herself in it. She always blocked me when I tried to image with her. She is playing 'hostess with the mostest,' want-ing to please me by *trying* to image." Subsequently, however, Mrs. Lambert be-came more involved with these techniques. One day, Gloria reported, Mrs. Lambert and one of her nieces visualized together that they were entering into one of the drawings that Gloria had made for her—a peaceful, happy city scene. Mrs. Lambert imagined a rooftop restaurant in the scene, and she and her niece went in to have a meal there together. Another day Gloria brought a number of magazine photos, and Mrs. Lambert chose one that showed two small children kissing.

The team was trying everything they could think of to make contact with Mrs. Lambert. They wanted to help her to have some life before she died, to rescue her in a small way. Perhaps she could experience just a little bit of life that she could call her own. They hoped that she could be as open as possible to life now, despite her extraordinary physical, emotional, and spiritual handicaps and limitations. Of course, there was also an important temporal limitation—she was dying.

Total pain

On October 10, Mrs. Lambert had another pain crisis. Dr. Bonin realized that her regular medications for neuropathic pain were not working. Believing that this was a case of "total pain," in which physical, psychological, and spiritual elements are combined, she had already asked the psychologist to help. Now she also consulted the anesthetist and the psychiatrist. Mrs. Lambert did not react well to the latter referral, saying to her brother, "The doctors don't believe that I have all this pain. They even got me to see a psychiatrist." In fact, Dr. Bonin knew very well that Mrs. Lambert was experiencing intense physical suffering. But because of the interrelation of physical, emotional, mental, and spiritual elements in Mrs. Lambert's suffering, the team was trying to adopt a holistic approach, an approach that Mrs. Lambert either did not understand or did not want to accept. She did appreciate massage therapy, however, the nurse, occupational therapist, or volunteer taking turns at massaging her legs and back. She also continued to use music and imagery techniques, even though she worried that she was taking up too much of the therapists' time.

By this time, I was visiting Mrs. Lambert regularly as part of our project. During my visits, Mrs. Lambert would usually stare straight ahead, looking vague and distant. When she spoke of her pain, her affect stayed flat, even when she used expressions such as "It's like my bones will break." She accepted my silent presence but wouldn't allow me into her world, even after many visits. Yet she did say, "The only thing that helps my pain is if someone sits with me." One morning, when she was having a particularly bad pain crisis, she could not keep from crying out loud: "It's not humane. It hurts when I cry. I can't even cry!"

When the pain was this bad, she preferred to be alone. She said to Linda afterwards, "When the pain is really bad, nothing helps. It's better if you leave me alone then. I hope I'm not offending you. I don't want you or anyone else to take it personally. I need to be angry or cry without having to explain myself each time." Linda reassured her that it was all right to do that.

Mrs. Lambert began to feel frustrated and even angry with Dr. Bonin. Her brother reassured her, "Dr. Bonin is doing her best." She replied, "I know that she's doing her best, but even if she controls the pain I'm going to die anyway." Mrs. Lambert was totally desperate. She had feared pain all her life, and now here it was, with no relief in sight. Although she had some spiritual beliefs, she could find no meaning in her suffering. She did not think that God had inflicted this pain on her; she had no concept of God.

To the staff there seemed so much more that she could not express, and they felt shut out. Linda commented that Mrs. Lambert was "not accessible." Gloria was trying to use the art sessions to help Mrs. Lambert become more open about her feelings, but she did not have much success. She told me:

> There is something that blocks her from investing in other people. She must have been very hurt. Any art work that is more probing, more personal, she shuts away. Or maybe there was something basically missing in the mother–child relationship. But it's really sad.

Toward the end of October, Mrs. Lambert was completely bedbound because of her pain. She had periods of confusion and seemed to be giving up. "I am dying," she told Dr. Bonin. "I am losing everything. It's not that I'm accepting of it." She phoned her lawyer and arranged for him to come to the hospital to help her get her affairs in order.

Dr. Bonin wanted the advice of the other physicians and members of the team on how to treat Mrs. Lambert, so she presented Mrs. Lambert's case at the weekly multidisciplinary ward rounds. At the meeting she offered her opinion that "the pain is not only physical—she has a total pain syndrome." She mentioned that Mrs. Lambert had told her, "I need a mother." Another physician commented that Mrs. Lambert was a classic example of what Michael Kearney (a palliative care specialist in Ireland) called "soul pain," a deep-set anguish due to unexpressed unconscious conflicts. But the various methods that Dr. Kearney used in such cases, often with some success—visualization, guided imagery, deep relaxation—had all failed for Mrs. Lambert.

What was the team to do? The anesthetist, having reassessed her that day and found that she continued to have back pain, believed that an intrathecal block would be possible, but Mrs. Lambert was not keen on that option. Dr. Bonin was considering using more sedative medication so Mrs. Lambert could sleep through these periods; however, this was not an easy decision to make. She knew that when sedation was used for pain it could shorten the person's life because the person would be asleep and not able to eat. However, Mrs. Lambert had already eaten hardly anything for weeks and had been losing weight steadily. Parenteral nutrition was not an option for her because it does not significantly prolong life in cancer patients who are losing weight because of the effect of the cancer on their metabolism. The other physicians on the team agreed that sedation was the only option left.

When Dr. Bonin mentioned this to Mrs. Lambert as a possibility, she was receptive, but she hesitated because the lawyer was coming to help her sort out her affairs. She met the lawyer on two occasions, and Dr. Bonin tried to ensure that she was as lucid as possible during those times, waiting until Mrs. Lambert had signed all her papers. Then, with Mrs. Lambert's consent, Dr. Bonin ordered more sedative medication—ketamine and midazolam.

Ketamine is an anesthetic agent that, in lower doses, produces a dissociative reaction, whereby a person may still have pain but will experience it as if it were happening to someone else. The person may therefore feel less distressed. Because ketamine has side effects, however, it is usually administered with a sedative drug such as midazolam to try to minimize the frightening hallucinations or other so-called emergence phenomena that can occur with this drug.

"When the pain gets better is when I feel worse"

Within two days of starting the ketamine, Mrs. Lambert was pain-free. She was not confused or hallucinating. As Dr. Bonin expected, Mrs. Lambert entered a dissociative state. She said to Dr. Bonin, "I feel drunk, but I don't care!" Later, she said, "I feel like I'm not myself. I don't know what to do without the pain. The pain was so present before, and now I feel lost."

She was able to enjoy visits, and was particularly pleased to see her youngest brother who had come from out of town. She was beaming when I entered the room, and introduced me to a strapping, fit-looking blond man. She said, "This is my baby brother. Isn't he handsome?" She found his visit stimulating and entertaining as they joked around, keeping the conversation light. I wondered if she was actually connecting with anyone.

At this point, I began to understand how difficult she was to reach. I had seen her at least 15 times by now, and although these were relatively brief visits, I still felt that it was taking so long for us to connect! During my previous visit was the first time I felt any human connection at all. She had cried and cried, like a small, abandoned child, but she did not respond to me as a person. She needed a warm body at her side; it could have been any warm body. When she spoke of her pain (now usually in her right leg), she looked straight ahead of her, eyes unfocused, as if in a trance. Her voice was almost expressionless, even before the ketamine was started. I wondered whether she would be labeled a borderline personality disorder on a formal psychiatric evaluation. Such patients have difficult, long-standing character problems and are considered challenging to manage.

I reflected on what I knew of her family constellation. She came from a very large family, the first three children being girls, then four boys, then Miriam, then two more boys. "I was sandwiched between brothers," she once said with a vague smile on her face. Was this a sexual reference? I wondered if there was a history of incest or abuse.

Mrs. Lambert said something at this time that sounded paradoxical: "When the pain gets better is when I feel worse." I wondered what terrible inner anguish emerged when she no longer needed to focus on her physical pain.

By October 23, she was sleeping most of the time because of the ketamine and midazolam. The staff felt that she was suffering less now and agreed that it was better to keep her sedated. The ketamine dose was reduced, however, because Mrs. Lambert began to have bizarre and vivid dreams of fire or boiling water rushing into her room. Such distressing visions are a possible side effect of ketamine.

During one of the periods when she was more wakeful, I visited her. As I walked into the room, she was drinking water from a glass, trying to get her pills down. For the first time, she looked angry to me. Though I was visiting her in the context of our research, I tried to listen as actively and as therapeutically as I could. She motioned with her glass of water and medication cup. "I could throw this at someone," she said.

I responded, "You're angry."

She continued, "Last night I would have killed myself if I could, because of the pain in my legs and in my abdomen." She started to cry. "Nothing they try works and the syringe driver hurts my arm, or wherever they put it. Wherever they put the needle, it hurts. They have to change it every day. Before, I wanted to be alone, but now I always want someone with me—over the last couple of weeks." She was still crying. "Before, I was too proud."

"Are you afraid?" I asked.

"No, I'm not afraid. I'm only afraid of having pain. I have pain, that's all. If only this could be all over." She was silent for a while. "Everyone brings me biscuits or candy. But I'm not hungry. If I listened to them I would have a roomful of biscuits and candy. It's not that I'm not grateful for their good will."

"Nothing helps."

"No. I always like to have someone with me. I don't know why. I have less pain somehow. I feel less alone." She started to cry again.

"That's it," I offered. "You feel alone."

"One has pain, pain, pain," she replied, "and there's nothing that can be done about it." She cried. "[The psychiatrist] came. He said to me, 'There is nothing I can do here.' I don't think he is coming back."

"What about our psychologist?"

Mrs. Lambert paused. "She came a few times. I don't know if she'll come back. I guess it depends on me."

In fact, the psychologist did try to see her on several occasions in the weeks that followed. Usually Mrs. Lambert was asleep, or tired, or in too much pain to have lengthy discussions with her.

Glimmers of trust

After this conversation, I felt that there were so many things that she did not know how to talk about. But she was able to open up in art therapy, where she did not need to be verbal. The next day, at the art therapy session, the pain was better. She was in a recliner in the solarium, joking and talking. She did not want to paint or draw herself, but she wanted Gloria to draw and paint in her presence. She found this a safe way to express herself—to respond to the drawings Gloria made. Her response to a picture of a tree was, "It looks like a peaceful place." Her response to a painting of flowers was, "That's beautiful. You keep it somewhere for me." It was as though she did not feel ready or able to own the beautiful object, to keep it in her room. Yet, in a previous session, she had found a particular picture beautiful—one of children playing in a natural setting—and had asked Gloria's permission to keep it in her room. Now she said to Gloria, referring to that picture, "I had to throw it in the garbage." Then, "If I didn't like you, I wouldn't have told you. I like you and I know you will understand."

Was she afraid of experiencing beauty for herself, and of the closeness to Gloria that this represented? Was she in some strange way angry at what Gloria represented—the possibility of intimacy—as she felt herself getting closer to her? As she became more open with Gloria she spoke of a brother and a sister who had died when they were young and of mothers loving small children. "We're always related to somebody," she said. "And we're always somebody's baby." She thought a lot about her mother and occasionally spoke of her husband with fondness and sadness. Mostly, though, she thought about the distant past.

Linda asked Peter what Mrs. Lambert had been like when she was young. Peter said that she was always hit on the head as a child, but he did not directly state that there was further abuse, referring to it obliquely. He said, "She was an unhappy child. You shouldn't go deeper in discussing it. It might hurt her." The staff understood that they had to tread softly. While they did not want to abandon her, given her troubled past, their goals in Mrs. Lambert's case had to be very limited. They would try to control her symptoms and help her achieve some quality of life in the short time left to her, but they could not resolve her deep-seated psychological problems.

Over the next few days, Mrs. Lambert was more sedated from the ketamine and midazolam and she slept most of the time. When she was awakened by the pain, the nurse, occupational therapist, or a volunteer would be there, giving her a massage that she found helpful.

Slowly, the kindness of the staff began to touch her. One morning, when she was more wakeful, I visited her as Linda was finishing putting Mrs. Lambert's hair in rollers. Mrs. Lambert looked happier than I had ever seen her. She said,

"People are so kind here. They don't have to do this," referring to Linda, who was doing her hair. I admired the art work on her walls. "Gloria leaves me this art work and she says to me, 'It warms my heart to give them to you,' Mrs. Lambert said. Her eyes opened wide, as if she were marveling at love freely given.

"The angels are telling me to die peacefully"

On November 7, Dr. Bonin presented Mrs. Lambert's case at ward rounds again. Mrs. Lambert had developed more tumors in her pelvis. None of the medical solutions they had tried so far had relieved the pain for any length of time, and the pain was increasing again. Dr. Bonin and the nursing staff found it difficult to tolerate her dissociated state. She was not herself and seemed detached and distant as she spoke, but she said that she still had pain. She expressed guilt about not being able to be with Roger, but said she did not want him to visit—he'd been exhausted after the one time they had tried it.

Only a few times a year did the staff have patients as challenging as Mrs. Lambert. These patients always made everyone distraught, for palliative care staff like to feel that they can relieve suffering in all cases. They had known other patients who, like Mrs. Lambert, had symptoms that were difficult to control. Sometimes they saw the patient undergo a shift of perception: the pain would still be there, but it would be experienced differently, and the suffering reduced. The patient would reach a deeper level of understanding, almost as if the suffering had been given new meaning. Unfortunately, this transformation had not occurred in Mrs. Lambert's case, and Dr. Bonin was running out of ideas.

Just before ward rounds, the anesthetist had tried to perform a spinal block at the L2–L3 level but the attempt was unsuccessful. Dr. Bonin decided to try another coanalgesic drug, gabapentin. The other physicians considered the case carefully but could not come up with any other ideas. Mrs. Lambert said that she did not mind being more completely sedated—she was preparing to die.

On November 18, Dr. Bonin reported:

> She feels that she is getting weaker, especially over the past week. She is very sad about this. She was hoping to make it to Christmas. She was so glad when people put up the holiday decorations in her room. She especially likes the little white angels, but now she says, "The angels are telling me to die peacefully." She asked me questions about how and when she would die.

The next time Gloria saw her, Mrs. Lambert was too sick to do art therapy. When Gloria said to her, "I'll see you Wednesday" (in two days' time), Mrs.

Lambert replied, "Yes, if I'm here." This was the first time she had spoken to Gloria about dying.

But she did not die, she continued to suffer. She developed dizziness that she attributed to the gabapentin, so she asked that the drug be discontinued. She stopped eating and drank very little. Her brother reported that she was more closed in on herself now, not speaking to family members when they visited. She slept most of the time now, and when Gloria came back two days later, Mrs. Lambert was barely responsive. Gloria sat with her, holding her hand. When Mrs. Lambert opened her eyes, she seemed to recognize Gloria, then closed her eyes again.

Inducing sleep

On November 25, the pain became unbearable; the ketamine was no longer having an effect. Dr. Bonin came to see her and found her lying in bed, "asking for something to be done." Dr. Bonin interpreted this as a possible request for euthanasia. Since euthanasia was morally unacceptable to Dr. Bonin and was not a legal option in any event, she offered Mrs. Lambert deep sedation, to which Mrs. Lambert agreed. She was already much weaker and was barely responding. Dr. Bonin stopped the ketamine and started methotrimeprazine, a medication that is both analgesic and sedative. It would give Mrs. Lambert some respite, and the sleep induced by this medication could be reversed at any time.

Around this time, Linda sought me out. She wanted to speak with me because Mrs. Lambert had aroused strong feelings in her. Linda saw that Mrs. Lambert was deteriorating and thought that she might die soon. She told me how patients often affected her as a nurse, how she tried to empathize, and the repercussions of this:

> I'd like to speak now, because after they die, I forget. That's how I protect myself, I guess. I'm remembering everything that she said now, but when they die, I forget. I have to forget so that I can carry on with the next patient.
>
> In the beginning, her pain was uncontrollable. One day she had severe electric shock–like pains that made her scream. She knew that her screaming wouldn't upset me and that knowledge reassured her. She appreciated getting consistent nursing care. She leaned on her two primary nurses quite heavily.
>
> I entered her pain at one point. I was in pain, too. We had tried absolutely everything and nothing was working. On that day, my neck went into spasm from stress and I had to go home early because of the pain. I had had neck pain in the past, but when I feel that people need me all at once, my neck pain comes back. I knew then that I had overstepped my boundary and that I couldn't get so involved. She greeted me crying, saying she'd never get out of bed again because of the pain, and she never did. She told me that her emotional pain is more than her physical pain.

> She has learned to express her needs, which she had difficulty doing before. She is able to ask the volunteers for help. She makes volunteers feel special. However, she realized that some people may come for their own comfort and not hers. Sometimes we need to feel that we are doing something, but it doesn't help.

Mrs. Lambert's family and friends organized a visiting schedule to ensure that there would be someone with her most of the time. Mrs. Lambert slept quietly over the next few days. She did not eat or drink. By December 3, she was clearly close to death. Dr. Bonin felt that she had probably developed septicemia, a bacterial infection in the bloodstream. She decided under the circumstances not to investigate this further, nor to treat it with antibiotics. Although Mrs. Lambert could no longer speak with the members of her family, she was able to have important, albeit brief, exchanges with Dr. Bonin about the sedation. She was still in pain. She said, "The physical pain is now worse than the mental pain. I can't bear this any more." Dr. Bonin asked her if she wanted the sedative increased. She said yes.

The next day, Mrs. Lambert slept continuously. She was not responding when people spoke with her. The music therapist continued to see her every day and to play for her even though she seemed to be in a coma. On the evening of December 5, Mrs. Lambert was sleeping peacefully in her room, her niece Carole beside her. The light was subdued—only the Christmas lights were on—and soft, relaxing music played. Carole lit some incense, and read silently from a Catholic prayer book. Mrs. Lambert died later that evening, with two of her nieces present.

Roger

Roger had not planned that his wife would die before him. At the funeral, he cried as he touched his wife's body. But he never spoke of her after that. One of Mrs. Lambert's nieces and her husband, who were now the closest people to Roger, told me that he never showed any emotion if someone mentioned his wife by name. If someone reminded him that she had died, he would say calmly, "Oh, yes."

It seemed that Roger had reached a certain tranquility. He died in July 1998, 18 months after his wife's death and four months after his 100th birthday, a milestone he had hoped to reach.

Conclusion

Although the palliative care staff had tried their best to help Mrs. Lambert, they were frustrated by the inadequate pain control and by their inability to get in touch with her inner world. Over a period of almost three months, they tried everything they could in their approach to Mrs. Lambert's total pain. On the biomedical side, they tried every drug and anesthetic intervention that was appropriate. On the psychosocial side, they tried to get her to open up to others, to learn the meaning of trust and love, even this late in life. Yet the great tragedy of her life became evident—the tragedy of a life unlived because she was unable to trust herself or others.

At various points during her time on the unit, Mrs. Lambert showed signs of beginning to share her inner life. Once during the final period of her sedation she awoke when the music therapist came, and asked her to play some music on her flute. She cried, which was a big step for her. She started to come alive in her contacts with some of the staff, especially with Gloria and Linda. She could not fully express herself to them, however; the journey had just begun. Perhaps she understood that she was to get no further in this lifetime. Would the outcome have been different had the staff had more time to work with her? On this we can only speculate.

Medication and pain control record

August 23	Admitted to surgical ward for pain control. CT scan showed destruction of right side of sacrum. Tumor extended into the S1–S2 neural foramina and possibly into the spinal canals. She received radiotherapy to this area. Hydromorphone 4 mg SC q4h was started. (She did not tolerate a nonsteroidal anti-inflammatory drug, which gave her epigastric burning even with a gastroprotective agent.)
August 25	Pain intensity 10/10. PCU consulted. Palliative care physician ordered syringe driver medication: hydromorphone 36 and haloperidol 3 mg to prevent nausea, to be administered over 24 h.
August 27	Seen by oncologist considered offering her palliative chemotherapy. Patient walking around and in better spirits. Pain 5/10.
August 28	Hydromorphone 12–16 mg PO q4h; increased to 16 mg PO q4h. Syringe driver discontinued to prepare her to go home. Naproxen 250 mg twice daily, lorazepam at bedtime, carbamazepine 150 mg twice daily.
August 29	Patient says that most helpful pill is the lorazepam. Pain 10/10. Amitriptyline 25 mg at bedtime started, with plan to titrate upwards.
August 30	Mrs. Lambert was transferred to PCU on an urgent basis be-

cause of left leg and groin pain that she described as 15 on a scale of 1 to 10. Hydromorphone 16 mg PO q4h. Carbamazepine 150 mg then 200 mg PO bid. Naproxen 250 mg PO bid. Amitriptyline 50 mg PO at bedtime.

September 3   Changed to room with a tub, since hot baths help pain.

September 5   The pain was better—she was walking. The staff considered starting to plan her discharge home.

September 9   Mrs. Lambert began to have hallucinations and myoclonus, which Dr. Bonin believed was from the hydromorphone. Started fentanyl patch 125 mcg/h. Regular hydromorphone was discontinued. Increased carbamazepine 200 mg three times daily. Increased amitriptyline 75 mg at bedtime. Naproxen discontinued. Dexamethasone 80 mg IV over 1 h, tapering over 5 days. She was totally pain-free for 4 days.

September 11   Epidural for 48 h (bupivacaine and hydromorphone)—paralyzed legs but no effect on the pain. Pain in groin 7/10 after epidural. Anesthesia: Epidural catheter well placed. Decreased strength in right leg and decreased sensation. As she was also getting weaker and was bedbound, oncology decided not to offer her any chemotherapy. Dr. Bonin: "Long discussion about where we are at in terms of pain control, disease progression, past history. Understands disease is progressing with tumor along S1–S2 nerve roots."

September 14   Mexiletene added

September 16   Epidural not helping. Not moving at all because of the pain, 10/10 on movement, 8/10 at rest. Discontinued epidural.

September 22   Mexiletene 100 mg PO three times daily × 3 days then increased to 200 mg PO three times daily. Increased amitriptyline 100 mg PO at bedtime. Started choline magnesium trisalicylate 500 mg PO q12h

September 24   Trial of transcutaneous electrical nerve stimulation prior to mobilization.

September 27   No relief with repeated trial of TENS, up to 50 min.

September 30   New burning pain R leg X-rays: osteolytic metastases bilaterally on sacrum. Treated with radiotherapy. Increased fentanyl transdermal patch to 150 mcg/h q3 days. Increased mexiletene 300 mg PO twice daily. Continuing to have incident-type pain.

October 4   Increased pain. Increased fentanyl 200 mcg/h q3 days. Lorazepam 1 mg twice daily. Increased mexiletene 300 mg q AM 400 mg at bedtime.

October 9   Music therapy. Patient reported no pain during relaxation session.

October 10   Pain crisis. Pamidronate 90 mg IV. Fentanyl patch 250 mcg/h. Hydromorphone breakthrough. Carbamazepine 600 mg PO daily. Amitriptyline 100 mg PO at bedtime. Mexiletene 700 mg PO daily.

October 12   Amitriptyline discontinued (ineffective). Clonazepam 0.5 mg PO bid and 0.5 mg PO at bedtime. She continued to complain of back pain. Anesthetist was consulted. Ketamine 240 mg and midazolam 24 mg q24h were started via subcutaneous infusion. Patient was dissociated, but she said that she still had pain. Anesthetist: An intrathecal block would be possible, but the patient was not keen on this option.

October 15   Discontinued carbamazepine (ineffective). Temazepam 15 mg PO at bedtime. Lorazepam discontinued. Increased clonazepam 1 mg PO bid. Discontinued choline magnesium trisalicylate (ineffective).

October 19   Pain-free but blurred vision and slowed language. Not confused or hallucinating. "Feels drunk, but does not care!" Dr. Bonin: Plan: gradually decrease medication other than ketamine.

October 20   Decrease clonazepam 0.5 mg bid. Decrease mexiletene 300 mg bid. Decrease fentanyl patch to 200 mcg/h q3 days. Pain 3/10 at baseline, 9/10 with movement.

October 21   Less pain. Some nausea and vomiting.

October 23   Severe pains in legs and abdomen. Despairing. Expresses suicidal thoughts.

October 25   Pain better. Enjoyed solarium and art therapy session.

October 28   Sedated from the ketamine and midazolam combination. Sleeping most of the time. Ketamine dose was reduced because she began to have vivid dreams. She started to have myoclonus, so fentanyl had to be reduced. Consult with psychiatrist, psychologist, and anesthetist. Psychiatrist reports: "There is nothing I can do here."

October 30   Discontinued mexiletene. Gabapentin 100 mg three times daily started, increasing doses. Hydromorphone 6–12 mg PO q3h prn.

November 5   Mrs. Lambert said that keeping the radio on all night helped keep her mind off the pain. Spinal block failed at L2–L3 level—no CSF obtained. Anesthetist feels there is tumor there.

November 7   Presented at ward rounds. Team has tried massage but this is no help over last 48 h. She has been having more pain. Anesthesia: Will try caudal block this week. When she had epidural

	a few weeks ago she got weakness of legs but pain was not affected.
November 13	Continues ketamine 200 mg and midazolam 24 mg SC over 24 h. Gabapentin 400 mg PO three times daily.
November 13	Variable pain; variable mood.
November 15	Bad pain. "I'm suffering. I'm suffering."
November 18	Was on gabapentin up to 400 mg three times daily. She developed general muscle weakness with this so she could not open her eyes ?etiology. Although it was not felt to be secondary to the gabapentin, the patient wanted to reduce the dosage. Pain 10/10. On amitriptyline 125 mg PO daily. Still on ketamine. Gabapentin decreased to 300 mg PO daily.
November 22	Ketamine 240 mg SC over 24 h.
November 25	Gabapentin stopped. Fentanyl increased to 300 mcg/h.
November 26	Ketamine was discontinued, and methotrimeprazine was started at 30 mg SC over 24 h. Methotrimeprazine helped her pain, but she was sedated.
December 3	Mrs. Lambert still had "a bit" of pain. Sedation was increased after discussion with her. Methotrimeprazine 50 mg SC over 24 h. Case presented to visiting professor. Her commentary: "This was a case of mixed neuropathic and somatic pain—conus (medullaris) syndrome, which started with L2 radiculopathy. She probably also had vertebral body involvement and spinal instability. Although melanoma is not a very radiosensitive tumor, radiotherapy is indicated for pain control in these cases. The patient had chronic neuropathic pain with thalamic neuronal involvement and its concomitant brain neurophysiological changes. This is the reason why the epidural analgesia did not work. The team could have tried a neurolytic epidural block earlier in the course of this patient's pain. Methadone might have helped but sedation is a possible side effect."
December 4	Mrs. Lambert is comatose, unresponsive to verbal commands.
December 5	Comatose. Still seemed in pain when she was moved. She died later that evening.

11

Sadie Fineman
A Question of Denial?

Narrated by PATRICIA BOSTON

Sadie Fineman was 80 years old when her doctors discovered that she had a large cancerous mass in her pancreas. Despite a course of experimental therapy the tumor continued to grow, and the best option that Mrs. Fineman's doctors could offer was palliative care. Mrs. Fineman and her family made it clear to the palliative care team that she wanted to be cared for at home, even though there were many times when the nursing care she required exceeded the knowledge and skills of her family. This was not her caregivers' only challenge; the Fineman family insisted that the word "cancer" be avoided in all dealings with the patient to keep the truth from her at all costs. It was not until the last days of her life that Mrs. Fineman actually began to believe she was dying.

A family meeting without the patient

Sadie Fineman lived in a middle-class, immigrant, suburban Montreal neighborhood with her 54-year-old daughter, Rachel. Widowed 40 years ago, she had raised two children, without much money. Rachel was now an executive business secretary and Henry was a 57-year-old lawyer. Rachel never married and had always lived with her mother. She had received many opportunities to marry but, as she told me when I met her, she "enjoyed her freedom" and felt most comfortable with her mother in the home where she had been born and raised. Rachel shared the housework, cooking, and financial expenses. When her mother became ill, she became the main family caregiver.

Mrs. Fineman's son, Henry, lived with his wife, Julia, in a neighborhood about two miles from his mother's home. Although they did not live with Mrs. Fineman, Henry was always available, "on call 24 hours a day" as he put it to me. Both Rachel and Henry loved their mother and felt close to her. Rachel in particular said she felt "very bound and connected emotionally." It was impossible for her to imagine what life would be like without her mother in the world.

At the time Mrs. Fineman was diagnosed with pancreatic cancer in the spring of 1991, the tumor could be only partially resected. By August 1995, the tumor in the body of her pancreas had enlarged. Mrs. Fineman was now beginning to complain of mid-back pain and pain in her shoulder. The tumor had spread and there were both a local recurrence and the possibility of bone metastases. Although no further surgical treatment was available, a number of courses of action, such as experimental chemotherapy, palliative chemotherapy, or supportive care, were possible. Mrs. Fineman's oncologist, Dr. Levitan, suggested a family meeting to discuss these options.

Mrs. Fineman did not attend, as she did not care much for these kinds of meetings; they involved a lot of medical talk. Dr. Levitan was not surprised. In his previous conversations with Mrs. Fineman, it had become clear to him that she was not ready to talk about her illness. Her major worry, and all that she was willing to deal with, was her back pain and the nagging pain in her shoulder. As she explained to Dr. Levitan, "the main problem is my arthritis." If that could be looked after everything would be okay. She was a busy woman and needed to get on with things.

Dr. Levitan conducted the family meeting with Henry, Julia, and Rachel. Mrs. Fineman was especially comfortable having Henry involved. He had a "good mind," as she put it to me, and she was used to relying on him when decisions needed to be made. At the meeting, Dr. Levitan assured the Fineman family that pain control would not be a problem. But how should they proceed with treatment? It was difficult to know, Henry said. Yes, there was the possibility of offering his mother experimental treatment, but why do it when it would make her very sick and prolong suffering? On the other hand, his mother still enjoyed her life, even loved life, so why not provide her with whatever could be made available?

Dr. Levitan felt that his patient had the right to decide for herself what to do. But to make this kind of decision she needed to know the seriousness of her condition. He told Henry that in his opinion it was always best to tell the patient the truth. Dr. Levitan preferred to tell people the gravity of their condition so that they could take care of their affairs, complete unfinished business, and perhaps even do some of the things in life that they hadn't done up to now. While no one could say for sure, it was possible that Mrs. Fineman might only live for a few more weeks. Surely she needed to be prepared for that possibility.

Henry and Rachel implored Dr. Levitan not to tell their mother how ill she was. Henry argued that his mother was already 80 years old, had taken care of her affairs, and she had already done all that she wanted to in life. She was happy and content with her life at home with Rachel. "Besides," Henry said, as far as he and Rachel were concerned, "what if her affairs are left in a mess?" When the time came to deal with their mother's affairs, they would do it. Why rush? For the most part, Henry said, he "preferred to avoid those kinds of realities." As he explained to me later, "My attitude is, everything one has to know about death, one will find out when the time comes." At that point he preferred to focus his energies on how his mother was living, not how she was dying. After all, the only thing that was of any real concern to her just then was her "arthritis."

They agreed to try to tell their mother of the seriousness of her disease. But at the same time, they needed to offer her some hope. Dr. Levitan agreed to give her the option of the experimental therapy. Henry and Rachel told Dr. Levitan that they would explain to their mother that there were drugs available to help her condition, but that the drugs might not work.

The ability to hear what she wanted to hear

With Rachel's agreement, Henry explained to his mother that Dr. Levitan had told him that her illness was serious—she had a recurrence of her tumor—but that some experimental drugs were available for her to take. Henry decided not to use the word "cancer" in any of his discussions with his mother because it was too frightening a word. When people hear that word, he believed, they think of it as a death sentence.

Mrs. Fineman readily agreed to the experimental therapy. Henry and Julia accompanied her to the oncology department, and sat with her while she underwent the treatments. Henry told me that it was hard to see all those people down there in the chemotherapy clinic, suffering with cancer. They looked so ill, and yet some of them seemed braver than the people accompanying them.

Mrs. Fineman's therapy did not work. Dr. Levitan said her cancer was rapidly metastasizing. He continued to worry after his talks with his patient because she seemed not to realize how very ill she was. Again he emphasized to the family that Mrs. Fineman really ought to know the full extent of her condition. Dr. Levitan feared that she might survive only two more weeks. Henry agreed to talk again with his mother. Together with Julia, he explained to Mrs.

Fineman that the treatments had not worked, but quickly added that the doctors would be trying to do all that they could for her. Henry realized that he was not being as blatant about his mother's situation as he could be. But that was how he preferred to handle things. "Besides," he told me, "even when you told my mother what the reality was, it wouldn't necessarily be a reality for her." He continued, "My mother is a tough, courageous woman. There was never a problem in telling her about her illness. But she also had the ability to hear what she wanted to hear."

Henry and Rachel both rationalized that their approach in giving information to their mother was driven by their belief that "hope should not be taken away." As Rachel asked aloud to me, what if there were family events planned for the next year or the year after that? Their mother loved a good family wedding and all the gossip and planning that went with it. Why should she miss out on that hope? "Why," Henry chimed in, "should I say, 'No, you are not going to live to make that wedding'? Why would I be so stupid, so blunt? Even if there was not much time, better to let my mother think, at least, that she had some future to look forward to."

"The realm of miracles"

Mrs. Fineman's tumor progressed. She began to lose weight and looked ill and pale. But she did not die. Dr. Levitan was amazed. Five months had passed since the experimental treatments. He said to Henry, "You know, we're not dealing in the realm of medicine now, we are dealing in the realm of miracles. I have no medical explanation for why she is still alive."

Mrs. Fineman was continuing to live as fully as she knew how. She boasted to me of winning at cards, going for car rides with her friends, and "talking too much on the phone." Henry and Julia felt confirmed that it was a very good thing that Mrs. Fineman had not known or realized "the truth." Henry later recalled to me:

> She lived better, as things turned out, than if we had overrealistically told her. She knew the tumor was growing. She saw the symptoms progressing. Her legs were swollen and her stomach was protruding. Still, she enjoyed her life in the fullest sense of the word.

Dr. Levitan requested a consultation from Dr. Webster of the Palliative Care Service. When Dr. Webster visited Mrs. Fineman, she noted that Mrs. Fineman had lost 35 pounds during the preceding six months. Mrs. Fineman was still complaining of pain in the middle of her back, and in her left shoulder. The back pain, she explained to Dr. Webster, was "from gas," and the shoulder pain was "from arthritis."

Palliative care

It was at this point, in February of 1996, that Sadie Fineman entered our study. My first meeting with her was at the small apartment she shared with Rachel. Dr. Webster had explained our project to her and she was very open to participating in it. Dr. Webster described Mrs. Fineman to me as a "strong, stoic lady" who was very able to express her own views on her illness. Dr. Webster also observed that Mrs. Fineman asked few questions about her prognosis. She had inquired neither whether her illness was serious nor whether it was life-threatening. As Doctor Webster noted at the time, "I am not really sure what she knows. No one in the family is actually discussing it. When the subject [of her illness] is broached, she offers her own explanations."

When I met Sadie Fineman she certainly didn't strike me as a woman who was concerned that she might be dying. She was tiny and frail, and slightly stooped, yet she stood up as straight as she was able. She had a tremendous aura of authority, her voice clear, loud, and purposeful. I had the feeling she was a tremendously strong lady in spirit. She wore a green and yellow floral housecoat and comfortable, fluffy, yellow slippers. Yet her greeting to us (I made my first visit with Dr. Webster) was almost formal. As she shook our hands in welcome, I noticed how pale she looked. There was a hint of jaundice around her eyes, which were otherwise dark, clear, and sharp.

We sat around the dining table, which was situated at one corner of her large living room. The table was covered with a dark brown wool cloth protected by yellow, colorful plastic place mats. Old newspapers and magazines were piled at one end of the table and a portable telephone sat at the other end. The room felt cozy, containing a few pieces of well-worn furniture, the sofa decorated with large, plumped-up, green pillows, some covered with tapestry. The crocheted floral blanket draped across the sofa was clean and well cared for. The walls were painted a shiny cream and were decorated with family photographs, some of which were faded and taken perhaps some 30 years earlier. Many marked special family events: a large photograph showed a young man in graduation attire and another showed a young woman holding what might have been a graduation certificate or a diploma. There were also photographs of family weddings, couples, and children. At one end of the room, several small coffee tables were piled up with papers, envelopes, and magazines.

Mrs. Fineman didn't look directly at us when she spoke. Sometimes I wondered if she was paying attention. But I quickly realized that not only did she hear everything that was being discussed, she was also quick to correct us on the date or time of an event. She could recall not only those events leading up to her illness in recent years but also life events that had occurred 40 years before. Sometimes as she spoke I thought, "How ill she looks!" But it was also easy to forget her cancer and its prognosis, for she spoke with energy and vitality about her life, and about the future as if there could be no doubt about its coming.

During our visit Dr. Webster observed to me that Mrs. Fineman's abdominal tumors were easily palpable—it was difficult not to be aware of her large, protruding abdomen. Yet Mrs. Fineman did not seem concerned and she didn't ask Dr. Webster any questions about it. Instead, she chatted easily and amiably about how she felt inconvenienced by diarrhea because it interfered with her lifestyle and her outings. She liked to go to the senior citizens' organization across the street to play cards. She confirmed that she was being visited frequently by the palliative care nurses from the home care service, but all that was really needed, she said, was "something to stop the diarrhea" and some ointment to stop her skin from itching. It was annoying, she said, to have to keep scratching her hands and arms.

"She's not going to die from an overdose of ice cream"

A few days after my visit, I heard from the home care nurse that Mrs. Fineman had been admitted to the hospital because of biliary obstruction. Dr. Brant, her surgeon, inserted a biliary tube to help relieve the obstruction caused by her growing tumors. Although she now had a tube draining through her abdominal wall, Mrs. Fineman didn't seem at all concerned about this procedure. One of the palliative care physicians, Dr. Thompson, recalled that Mrs. Fineman's major concern at this time was being able to get her hair washed. "It has been three days and they haven't washed my hair," she told the nurse and Dr. Thompson. Later, the nurses washed her hair.

Once the tube was inserted, Mrs. Fineman went back home again. When Anita, the home care nurse, came to see her, Mrs. Fineman's major concerns were "to get something for my diarrhea" and "to get some foods that I'll feel like eating so I can put some weight on." She also wanted Anita to see if she could obtain some more comfortable undergarments to take care of her itchiness and skin rash. Anita suggested some special underwear from a medical and nursing supplies store, and arranged for these to be delivered directly to Mrs. Fineman's home. Dr. Webster also continued to make home visits. She would always allow time for Mrs. Fineman to talk at length about how she was feeling and any concerns she might have. She also tried to broach the subject of Mrs. Fineman's advancing cancer. But Mrs. Fineman wanted only to discuss practical nursing issues, such as making sure her biliary tube was draining properly, getting medicine for the pain, and making sure the wound around the tube was cleaned properly.

Rachel worried a lot about whether her mother was eating enough or whether she was taking enough vitamins. She worried about the quality of the food her mother ate. "She doesn't get enough protein in her diet and she shouldn't really be eating so much dairy foods," Rachel said to me. "I shouldn't really eat so much ice cream," Mrs. Fineman said on one occasion when I visited. "Rachel says it's not very good for my digestion. It never was. I always loved ice cream but it didn't love me!"

Sometimes Rachel would call Henry to share her worries about their mother's dietary habits. This irritated him. These were such small things! If their mother liked ice cream, and wanted to take a chance and try to eat some, why shouldn't she? He explained to me:

> Sometimes [Rachel] will call me with the smallest things and she'll worry about some food that Mother is having—maybe too much sugar. So what? Let her do whatever makes her happy. I say, "Why are you worrying about things? She's not going to die from an overdose of ice cream. Let her do what she wants."

The tube

Biliary tubes are shaped something like a letter T. One end of the cross of the T passes into the liver and the other end passes into the patient's duodenum. Routinely, it is necessary to clamp the external part of the tube, the long stem of the T that protrudes out onto the patient's abdomen. Clamping the tube ensures that the internal part of the tube is draining. Health professionals with surgical training have detailed knowledge of the various ways a biliary tube drains and have little difficulty with its management, which is a common practice for them. But for people who are not specially trained in surgical techniques, management of a biliary tube can be daunting. Mrs. Fineman's biliary tube needed care daily, perhaps even hourly. It would have been easy to manage her care if she were in the hospital or on the Palliative Care Unit. But admission to the Palliative Care Unit was not an option; Mrs. Fineman and her family felt that staying at home was best. Sadie Fineman did not seem to know, or want to know that she had advanced cancer or that she was dying.

The community agency nurses visited Mrs. Fineman twice a week, and Anita, the palliative care nurse, visited once a week, sometimes once every two weeks. But management of the drainage tube nonetheless posed a real challenge for both nurses and the family. As Anita put it, the tube drainage could be a "messy business" when the biliary fluid leaked out onto Mrs. Fineman's abdomen. Not everyone felt comfortable handling a tube that seemed simply to protrude from a gap in the patient's stomach. Often the biliary fluid would drain copiously and soak the dressings around the drainage tube, and sometimes Mrs. Fineman felt pain at the site of the tube insertion. The tube would appear to be loosening and seem to slip. Rachel would get worried and often wondered if she was doing something wrong when she changed the dressings around the tube. Henry would then telephone Dr. Brant or Anita and ask if something could be done to reposition the tube. On one of these occasions, Mrs. Fineman was readmitted to the surgical unit for reinsertion of the tube by Dr. Brant.

As often happens, the procedure was effective for only a brief period, in this case, for two weeks. Once Mrs. Fineman was back at home the tube drained effectively into a large plastic bag taped to her abdomen, but the stitches at the site of the tube insertion gave way. The copious amounts of biliary drainage may have weakened the suturing. Dr. Brant re-sutured the area and for a while, the tube seemed to work satisfactorily again. The team embarked on a schedule of increasing the daily amount of time that the tube was clamped by one hour every day. Eventually, Dr. Brant hoped, the tube could be left open at night time only, and after this Mrs. Fineman might not need to wear the drainage bag. But this plan did not work. Two hours after the tube was clamped by Dr. Brant, the dressing around it was saturated and had to be changed. After leaving the tube unclamped, the dressing was again saturated and had to be changed by the community agency nurse who was on evening call that day. Despite the best efforts of Dr. Brant and his surgical team, the drainage tube worked only sporadically. The spread of the tumor was the principal cause of the problem.

These events were frustrating and somewhat of an ordeal for the nurses, doctors, and the Fineman family. Mrs. Fineman began to complain of pain in the area where the tube had been inserted, and in her back. Dr. Brant had prescribed oxycodone and acetaminophen, but it didn't seem to work. Rachel didn't know what to do, for the pain medications were not working and heating pads didn't help at all. Mrs. Fineman was frightened and called Henry. She was sure he would be able to do something.

Henry tried to leave most of the day-to-day caregiving to Rachel, since she was the one who was at home with their mother. Rachel oversaw the medication regime, the tube drainage, the meals, and the general duties of the household. But if things didn't go smoothly, Rachel became upset and nervous and wanted Henry to intervene. Now was such a time. Henry decided to take his mother directly to the hospital's emergency department.

At the emergency department, Mrs. Fineman was examined by Dr. Boileau, the on-call palliative care physician. He prescribed morphine, which was immediately effective, and gave Mrs. Fineman a prescription for morphine to be taken every four hours. Following their return home, Dr. Webster telephoned the Fineman family and explained some of the services that were available from the palliative care staff. For example, there was a 24-hour emergency telephone service available. If there were a next time when pain relief was needed, the palliative care physician on call would be able to provide more immediate assistance.

"I'm looking forward to going to the casino"

During my visits to her home, Mrs. Fineman rarely alluded to the seriousness of her condition. One morning she greeted me at the top of the three flights of stairs to her apartment. It was a long climb. She called out laughingly, "I came up those stairs myself the other day. You have to take them slowly!"

It was extraordinary to me that although Mrs. Fineman looked ill and frail, most of our conversation was completely unrelated to any of her symptoms or her illness. On this particular day she was busy sewing extra straps onto a pair of pants so that they would be easier to manage when she had to use the toilet. She wanted to wear the pants when she went out to play cards and Mah Jong at the seniors' center, which she was planning to do the following week. It was hard to visualize such a tiny, frail, underweight woman going out to play card games. She looked to me as though she were dying. Six months earlier her doctors had suggested that she might have only a few weeks to live. But clearly, dying was not in her vocabulary.

"Do you know where I can buy something that is waterproof other than plastic underpants?" she asked me. She was having some problems with diarrhea. "I know that the nurses can get me some plastic underpants, but I need to go to a store where I can find another kind." When I suggested that she speak with Anita, she responded, "Oh, well, if I can just find out the store where they sell them, I can go on the bus, or, if not, my son will take me."

When I asked Mrs. Fineman about her illness directly she would talk about it, but only when prompted. She told me she knew she had had a tumor four years before and that the tumor had been removed. "I felt fine after that," she explained. "Now I have another small tumor." This didn't really bother her, Mrs. Fineman said. It was a real nuisance that she had to put up with the diarrhea, especially when she went out to see people.

It was not only games at the senior center that interested Mrs. Fineman. "I'm looking forward to going to the casino," she told me. "I'm going this summer with my son Henry." She also loved horse racing. "I don't have much money," she said, "but I like to put a bit of money on the horses, and when you win you've had a bit of fun." Sometimes it was frustrating for her to have to wait for Henry or Rachel. "They don't want me to go out alone," Mrs. Fineman said, "but I like to be independent."

Rachel and Anita

There was no question in my mind that even if Sadie Fineman was aware of the seriousness of her growing tumor, the implications of her pain and bowel incontinence, or the reasons for the biliary drainage, she was not thinking about dying and had no plans to die. It was also clear to me that both Henry and Rachel were enjoying life with their mother, ill as she was. Rachel described herself to me as a "nervous person" even in "normal times." It had been difficult after her mother was first diagnosed to get used to the idea that she was so ill. All her life she had lived with her mother. She had never left home and they were very close. She couldn't imagine life alone. She did have a man friend at one point, but she had ended the relationship because it had meant traveling 60 miles or so out of town to his home. She just didn't see how she could keep it up after her mother became ill. In any case, the relationship hadn't been that important. Rachel explained, "I know I'm 54 years old. But I like living at home with my mother. I've never wanted to marry and be on my own. We're a good team. She has her opinions about things and I have mine. But we get along just great."

Rachel continued with her full-time secretarial job even after her mother became seriously ill. The job was demanding. Sometimes her supervisor would ask her to do extra paperwork, which meant staying late at the office until six or seven o'clock. She would then come home to doing meals and housework. There was no doubt that Rachel got tired and "worn out." But having her mother at home and living for a bit longer was worth it, Rachel said. She continued:

> I really want to stress that I feel privileged to have this extra time with my mother. It's a gift. She carries on and I feel we've been given a reprieve so many times. My brother and myself, we're amazed that she carries on. We've thought so many times over the months and now years that she was going to die. I want to take advantage of the fact that we have the extra time.

Rachel said she could manage her mother at home as long as she could have some nursing help, such as with the biliary tube. Sometimes, though, things didn't go as smoothly as everyone would have liked. Rachel felt especially nervous about the tube, not feeling comfortable handling it. The procedure of clamping the tube for periods of time according to the community nurse's instructions made her feel very nervous. Henry would call or send a fax to Anita and ask if there couldn't be more intense and frequent home nursing care. But full-time nursing care at home was expensive and difficult to find. Of course, there was always the option of being admitted to the Palliative Care Unit. But Henry and Rachel felt that Mrs. Fineman was far from ready to go to a place for dying people, no matter how kind the people were. Henry wanted more skilled nursing help to support the care that Rachel was giving.

Anita felt pressured on these occasions. Whereas Anita made home visits once weekly, the community agency nurses visited twice weekly, sometimes more often if needed. Since Mrs. Fineman was still functioning well at home, the front-line caregivers were the community agency nurses. (As Mrs. Fineman's illness progressed and the role of palliative care increased, Anita became more involved in the case.) In many ways, the biliary tube constituted an active form of treatment. To care for the tube was really the job of the community agency nurses. "It's difficult," Anita said to me, "because Mr. Fineman [Henry] will ask for a faster intervention when things don't go well. He will send a fax or telephone anyone and everyone—myself, Dr. Brant, Dr. Webster—and ask for faster service. I don't really blame him—he's wanting to get the best care for his mother—but we are constantly working between an active role and a palliative care role."

Mrs. Fineman might be terminally ill, Anita continued, but at the moment she was being cared for as if she were not. Anita was accustomed to nursing people at home who were dying and who, along with their family, were trying to come to terms with the process of dying. Sometimes, Anita said, she felt guilty about making these distinctions. She explained:

> I realize that this is a very sick patient and I shouldn't feel this way, because she is an old lady who is going to die. She's got a huge tumor. She's got this big bag hanging down strapped to her abdomen and all these horrible symptoms—pain, diarrhea. . . . My life is great compared to hers. But when I go there, somehow it is not for palliative care. Somehow I am second in line to the community agency nurse, and that's how the family sees me.

It was hard to nurse someone who was so ill and who would ultimately die from their illness, and not be able to deal with them on that level, Anita said. Perhaps when Mrs. Fineman came to a stage of her illness when she would need to be admitted to the Palliative Care Unit it would be possible to talk openly about some of these issues.

But the Fineman family did not plan to encourage Mrs. Fineman to be admitted to the hospital unless it became absolutely necessary. It wasn't a question of not accepting the concept of palliative care; Henry didn't see a problem in admitting his mother to the Palliative Care Unit, if and when the time came. From what he had seen of the unit, "it was immensely impressive." People were decent there, creating a "culture of caring" that was perhaps greater than at any other hospital he had ever seen. Certainly, he would encourage his mother to go, if and when the time came. In the meantime, he would have time to try and cope with her illness in his own mind. He said, "I guess for the next little while, my sense is that I have to try and cope with this myself, to face reality."

For her part, Rachel hoped that she would be able to care for her mother at home and that she would never have to go to the Palliative Care Unit. Rachel encouraged her mother to embrace life and to do as much as she could. Sadie Fineman was a strong-minded, determined woman, she said. This was the way she wanted to manage things. She wasn't thinking about dying. She was busy with her life, and ill as she was, she still did her share of the household chores. "She's thin and ill, yes," Rachel continued, "and maybe she's even dying. And she just keeps walking around, regardless of that. Just yesterday, she cleaned out the fridge—cleaned it all out—and I had told her I would do that. But when I came home from work, there she was, stooping down like the little skeleton that she is, and she'd cleaned it out. She has pain, she has diarrhea and this tube, which must be terrible. But she's never let anything beat her."

"Cancer was cancer"

Never did Mrs. Fineman or her family speak about dying. By July Mrs. Fineman's abdomen seemed much more extended and Anita noted that her ankles were becoming more swollen. It was clear to Anita that her patient was developing ascites. When Dr. Webster made a home visit Mrs. Fineman told Dr. Webster that she and Rachel were managing quite nicely. Her pain was reduced by the morphine, and her diarrhea was being controlled. Although the biliary tube could be "troublesome sometimes," Mrs. Fineman didn't see the need for any specific medical intervention. She did worry, however, about the expansion of her abdomen. "But, well, what could you do?" she said; that was the way it was.

Dr. Webster wondered: Was Mrs. Fineman not pursuing questions about her enlarged abdomen because of what she might hear? Was there a part of her that knew she had cancer? It was hard to tell whether Mrs. Fineman was anxious not to know how ill she really was, or if she was simply too busy getting on with her life to worry about it.

Anita was also concerned about what she described to me as the family's "general avoidance," especially their absolute refusal to utter the word "cancer." She worried that perhaps the Fineman family was in some kind of denial, and that when the truth did come, it would be hard to take. And it would come, Anita said, no matter how determined Mrs. Fineman was to carry on. After all, she said, "cancer was cancer."

Yet Rachel kept reminding the team that her mother had always been aware of her "growing tumor." Maybe the family had not used the word "cancer," but she knows how ill she is, Rachel said. It had just never been her mother's way to talk about defeat. Even if she was going to die, Rachel went on, "she'll keep doing for herself until she drops. She knows she's sick, but if she can do it, she will. She gets up, makes her food, takes her medications, and as long as she can walk and move her hands, she'll do it."

One day in early October, Dr. Webster made another home visit. Mrs. Fineman mentioned that she still liked to go out once or twice a week. "Every day I try to just get out of the door for a breath of fresh air," she said. Then she commented, "I'm losing more and more weight. I've stopped weighing myself now." She paused briefly. "There's no point." Dr. Webster listened very attentively now. Was Mrs. Fineman ready to speak more openly? She had lost 60 pounds by this time, and she began to ask more questions about pain. What would it be like to get more and more pain? She was feeling sharp shooting pains in the upper part of her neck. Dr. Webster thought the pain might be related to the cancer or be due to degenerative disc disease. She decided not to mention the possibility of a neck tumor, since there was no firm medical evidence to support this. However, it now seemed possible to talk more openly about Mrs. Fineman's advancing tumors. She reassured Mrs. Fineman that many people, even those with her kind of tumor, manage to avoid increasing pain, and that in any event the team would be able to control it.

Before Dr. Webster left that day Mrs. Fineman told her, "My telephone never stops ringing. My friends call me a lot with their stories." She loved a good bit of gossip, she said. She had plans to go to the casino and the horse races "when the weather gets better." And there was a family wedding coming up next year. "I might go to that," she said.

A blood transfusion

One Saturday evening in mid-December, Rachel telephoned Dr. Stevens, the palliative care physician on call, to say that her mother had fallen down. The day before, Mrs. Fineman had gone out for pancakes with a friend, but then she had started to feel dizzy and now she had fallen and injured her eye, and may have broken her left arm. Dr. Stevens suggested that Mrs. Fineman come to the Palliative Care Unit for a reassessment of her status as well as for immediate care for her present condition. When Mrs. Fineman arrived she said the room was comfortable enough, but she would not be staying long. "No use getting more things from home," she said. "My son and daughter would only have to carry everything back home when I go."

Dr. Stevens, in consultation with Dr. Boileau, another palliative care physician, ordered blood tests, which revealed that Mrs. Fineman had a hemoglobin of 48. This explained why she had felt dizzy and fell over. She had probably suffered from an internal gastrointestinal bleed, and it was very possible that she was still bleeding. In consultation with Dr. Stevens and the palliative care team, Dr. Webster decided to offer Mrs. Fineman a blood transfusion, which is not a routine practice in palliative care. On this particular palliative care service, patients receive a blood transfusion only if it will help them be strong enough to get out of bed and walk around. In Sadie Fineman's case, the palliative care physicians believed that a transfusion would allow her to go home again, if only for a short while. It would raise her hemoglobin, at least temporarily, which would give her a little more energy, and enhance her overall sense of well-being. Mrs. Fineman certainly expected to be allowed to go home. She was still busy living life!

Giving the transfusion was not easy, for it was hard to find a good vein that would sustain a few hours of intravenous therapy. Dr. Boileau tried to insert a small butterfly needle into the larger vein of her left arm, but this did not work. The nurses began to wrap Mrs. Fineman's arms in warm towels for several minutes at a time. Mrs. Fineman did not mind. The doctors could "poke" her all they wanted. What was important was to "get some blood inside her" so she could get back home. The fall had been "such a nuisance."

The hot towels worked, and Mrs. Fineman received her transfusion. I visited her just a few hours afterward. The room seemed less cozy and inviting now, the atmosphere feeling clinical, sterile, somber. The easy chairs that normally surround the patient's bed on the unit were pushed aside to allow the nurses easier access to their patient. As I stood near, the nurses came in, looking efficient in their white uniforms, purposefully checking the flow of the intravenous tube and the small pieces of equipment—extra tubing and butterfly needles—which are there in case they are needed. Mrs. Fineman looked tiny in the bed, her pale, frail form propped up by pillows in the semi-darkness. The lights in the room had been dimmed so that there was just enough to see her face and to see a wristwatch to check her pulse. She gave me a big smile and leaned forward to squeeze my hand with her "good arm," as she put it. I stared at her in amazement as she called out laughingly, "You see! I've pulled through again. I'll be home by the weekend!"

But Sadie Fineman did not go home again. As the days passed, she got visibly weaker, despite the blood transfusions and despite the intravenous fluids that she received for better hydration. She was not getting better, and for the first time, it seemed, she began to realize this herself.

"I'm not up to it anymore"

"Don't send me home for good behavior," she laughingly told one of the staff physicians. Even though she was feeling better, she said, "I'm weak and I can't take care of myself. Besides, I like it here." This was a change. Despite the continuing flashes of humor, Mrs. Fineman was showing many signs that she was aware of how sick she was. She began to talk openly about things that were on her mind in relation to her life and unfinished business. Her children had been good to her, she told me. She felt very proud of both of them. Rachel was wonderful. She told Rachel that no daughter could have been better to her.

She was worried about Rachel. "She doesn't realize I'm so sick," she told me. She had to try to prepare Rachel for the worst. She wouldn't be able to live forever. Rachel would have to take care of things from now on. Before, during all these months, she had recovered very well. She had been busy with her life. But now, "I'm suffering from things I didn't have before," she said. Rachel would have to manage on her own. "I'm not up to it anymore," she said. But how would Rachel manage? Mrs. Fineman explained her worries:

> You see, I'm all she's got. She never married, she always relied on me. My daughter has a job, but she's not a young woman. She's at an age now where she's too old to get a job and too young to get a pension. If I'd be a wealthy woman . . . she would have no worries.

Mrs. Fineman's expressions of concern for Rachel seemed to illustrate the subtle, delicate ways people have of moving in and out of awareness of their impending death. For months the team and I had wondered whether Mrs. Fineman had been in denial. Had she been? Could it be so simple or black and white—then she was in denial, now she is not?

The nurses shared some of Mrs. Fineman's concerns about her daughter. Anita, for example, recalled how difficult it had been to approach the subject of her mother's dying with Rachel, even though Rachel and Henry had always spoken as if it were their mother who was afraid of the topic. "When I tried to discuss her mother's possible death," Anita said, "you could see the tears and the anxiety come into her eyes. And it was like she was asking me, 'Please don't say that. Please don't talk.' So I did little at the time. Because if you confront it too much, or if you say or do too much, ironically, you may lose the relationship and the trust that you have built."

As the time of her death approached, it was Sadie Fineman who confronted this reality with her daughter. She began to talk about the household business that needed attention. There were bills to be paid. Rachel would need to fill in certain forms to cancel her pension money. "I don't want you to go to pieces over this," she told Rachel. "But you must take care of things. Don't pay the gas bill," she said. "There is a credit coming!"

To me, Mrs. Fineman said that she was prepared. "I know when I am so sick that I won't make it," she said. "I won't recover now. I know it. Who lives forever, anyway?" She continued, "The time has come. And I'm ready for it. I've lived my life span. I'm 80 years old. And that's a long time. There'll never be a time when I'll go and my children don't need me. But I'm not leaving babies."

Now, four weeks after she had been admitted to the Palliative Care Unit, Sadie Fineman began to talk less and sleep a lot more. She had more pain, experiencing it "like something I never had before," she said. She began to have difficulty breathing, so the nurses gave her oxygen. She received morphine, which seemed to relieve her pain. I could no longer have a conversation with her. "She sleeps most of the time now," her nurse, Ena, said, and added, "she is dying." On one of these times, I visited to find Mrs. Fineman sleeping. She looked gray and listless, yet peaceful. Rachel now visited more often. She would sit for long hours beside her mother's bed. She looked calm and I thought that she and her mother must have been able to talk about at least some of the things they had wanted to talk about. The nurses went in and out of the room to bathe Mrs. Fineman and turn her gently, talking in soft whispers.

One day in early January, Sadie Fineman stopped breathing. Ena and Barbara, another nurse, were with her. She looked happy and peaceful, Ena said. Henry arrived 15 minutes later. "I would like to have been with her," he said to me. "But she had been preparing us for the inevitable." Then he said, "My mother was in control right up to the end. She was with it. She was open and she knew what was happening. She wanted us to know it, too. And when she felt convinced that we were prepared for it, she gave in."

12

Stanley Gray
"Like Lazarus, He Came Back from the Dead"

Narrated by YANNA LAMBRINIDOU

When Stanley Gray was admitted to the home care program of hospice, he appeared to be dying from congestive heart failure (CHF) and end-stage chronic obstructive pulmonary disease (COPD). Then, to everyone's surprise, his condition improved. Although dependent on oxygen, morphine, and eight bronchodilator treatments a day, Mr. Gray started to lead a relatively independent and deeply religious life. A year and a half after his admission to hospice, Mr. Gray's social worker believed he was no longer "terminal." His nurse, on the other hand, argued that although Mr. Gray was functional, he could die at any time.

Mr. Gray is the only patient in our study who is still alive as we complete the writing of this book. His case demonstrates the unpredictability of diseases like COPD and CHF, and the challenge they present to the current system of hospice care in the United States. The case unfolds on the borderland between palliative and long-term care, even as it illustrates the immense personal and relational transformations that can take place near the end of life. It also raises important questions of religious faith. Mr. Gray's totally consuming relationship with God made some members of his hospice team uncomfortable. The nurse and chaplain even suspected that it compromised his health. And yet Mr. Gray was convinced that it was God who had caused him to outlive his original prognosis.

"He is dying, he has no lungs left, nothing!"

Even for South Carolina, the first week of May 1996, was unusually muggy. Stanley Gray, a 57-year-old European American with CHF and COPD, confined himself to his small Charleston apartment—he couldn't imagine surviving outdoors, without his rickety air-conditioner. The cooler and dryer air at home was a necessity, just like his oxygen tank and his regular bronchodilator treatments. But two days into the heat wave, Mr. Gray's air-conditioner broke down. Having neither the strength to repair the unit himself nor the money to hire a professional, he sat quietly in his bedroom and concentrated on his breathing. He could feel the heat creeping into his apartment like a noxious gas. He could also feel the stiff resistance of his lungs. Two days later he was gasping for breath. His skin was tinged blue. Without wasting time, he drove to the hospital for what turned out to be his third admission in five months.

When he arrived at the emergency room, Mr. Gray was immediately admitted to the intensive care unit. There he was placed on intravenous steroids, a bronchodilator, and two antibiotics. After a few days he was deemed stable enough to transfer to a regular hospital room, but he continued to deteriorate. His oxygen saturation level dropped, and he was confused and combative. He didn't want to die. The thought that God had not forgiven him tormented him. His physician gave him an antianxiety medication that made him deeply somnolent. In reaction to his decline, the hospital called his only sibling, Mrs. Florence Laxton, to tell her that Mr. Gray was dying. Mrs. Laxton, a 53-year-old packaging company worker, lived in Lancaster County, Pennsylvania. She took the next plane to Charleston.

At the hospital, Mrs. Laxton found her brother unresponsive. She noted that he was not receiving any nutritional support. Didn't Stanley need food to survive? she asked. The physician responded impatiently that her brother was in no position to eat. "He is dying, he has no lungs left, nothing!" he exclaimed. Upset but undeterred, Mrs. Laxton began giving her brother small amounts of juice, then spoonfuls of ice-cream and pudding. Mr. Gray seemed to respond well to all, but he remained somnolent. After a week, Mrs. Laxton began to lose hope. Although she wasn't pious, she remembered vividly leaving her brother's room to pray. She told God that she knew she didn't have the power to cure her brother, she recalled to me later. She realized that his health was in God's hands. If He wanted to take Mr. Gray, she was ready to let him go. But she hoped that He would cure him instead.

The next morning, Mr. Gray opened his eyes. Although extremely weak, he recognized his sister for the first time since her arrival. His physician explained to him that he had two choices: he could die in the hospital or receive hospice services at home. Mrs. Laxton wanted to take her brother back to Lancaster County. The physician argued that a long trip in Mr. Gray's condition was entirely inappropriate. Mrs. Laxton retorted that if her brother had only a short time to live he would be happier spending it with family in Pennsylvania than alone in South Carolina. Though he could only utter a few words, Mr. Gray seemed to agree. He accepted the idea of hospice, gave Mrs. Laxton the responsibility of signing a do-not-resuscitate order on his behalf, and said he was prepared to risk the flight to Pennsylvania by air ambulance. The hospital made arrangements with the Hospice of Lancaster County to equip Mrs. Laxton's house with oxygen tanks and a hospital bed.

In Lancaster, an ambulance met the two siblings at the airport and took them to Mrs. Laxton's house. Mr. Gray was unconscious. Hospice informed Mrs. Laxton that her brother was actively dying and sent a continuous home care team to help him through his final moments.

"Bless the Lord"

I met Mr. Gray at his sister's farm house 15 months later. It was a warm August day in 1997, and he was sitting in shorts and an unbuttoned shirt in the living room. Mr. Gray was a strapping man with expressive blue eyes, a full set of graying brown hair, and bushy eyebrows. His arm bore a tattoo that said "Born to Lose." An oxygen cannula was blowing air into his nose. His walker, together with the two portable oxygen tanks that hung on its sides, was standing directly in front of him. Mrs. Laxton, a rotund woman with big blue eyes and rosy cheeks, smiled sweetly as she asked me what I wanted to drink. Tiffany Hadley, Mr. Gray's vivacious hospice nurse, had arrived only a few minutes before me and was already sitting comfortably on the living room couch enjoying a cup of coffee. I asked for iced tea. On her way back from the kitchen, Mrs. Laxton instructed her three barking Irish setters to quiet down and sat in an armchair across from her brother.

Mr. Gray looked drowsy. He told Tiffany that he was having a bad day—he felt sluggish. With embarrassment, he confessed that the previous night he had smoked two packs of cigarettes. He saw smoking as a careless act that destroyed the human body and insulted God, and the thought that he had consciously compromised his health when God had given him a second chance to live had tortured him all night. Still, he was eager to talk. Tiffany encouraged him to give me a short version of the story about his reunification with Mrs. Laxton. It was a story he loved to tell.

Mr. Gray recounted that he was born and raised in Lancaster County. From the age of 9 until 12 he had been confined to bed with rheumatic fever, with only a small, battery-operated radio for stimulation, and his daydreams, he emphasized. He created a fantasy world of his own in which he and Superman were the strongest people on earth. But when he finally recovered and was able to return to school, Mr. Gray realized that he wasn't strong at all. Because he had missed three years of school, he was set back to third grade. Older and taller than his classmates, he was teased ruthlessly. He quit school and when he turned 17, he joined the Army.

In 1969, after the death of his father, the end of his third marriage, and a jail sentence, Mr. Gray decided to move to Georgia. For 16 years he had no contact with his relatives. Then, homesick, he made an appearance at his sister's farm in 1985. Mrs. Laxton, her husband, and their two children were very happy to see him. But Mrs. Laxton had to inform him that their mother had passed away a few years earlier. Mr. Gray was shocked by the news. When he left, he told no one where he was going. He was planning to move out of Georgia, but he didn't yet know where he would find a new home.

Ten years later, in December 1995, his housemate in Charleston tried to convince him to send Mrs. Laxton a Christmas card, but Mr. Gray resisted. "I have been a black sheep in this family," he told his friend. "I have been kind of dragging the name through the dirt pretty bad." Since Mr. Gray assumed that his relatives wouldn't want to hear from him, it had been 10 years since his last visit with his sister, and 27 years since he had seen his own daughter, Cynthia. Arithmetic told him that his little Cynthia was 35 years old already, but because her mother kept her away from his side of the family, his relatives couldn't tell him anything about her. "So this is how I got separated from my family," Mr. Gray said, "through embarrassment." Still, his housemate insisted that he at least send his sister a card, and so he did.

Around 6:00 in the evening on New Year's Day 1996, Mr. Gray was lying in his bed at home. By this time he had been diagnosed with emphysema. "I had a phone in my room," he recounted, "and I was lying down sleeping, and the telephone rings. I picked up the phone, and this woman's voice says, 'I am not sure if I've got the right number, but I am looking for Stanley Gray.' I am laying there and thinking that I've got a few bills down there; I figured it was just the bill collector. I said, 'Well, you've got him. This is Stanley Gray.' And right away she said—I can't remember her exact words—but I think she said, 'Oh my Lord! This is Flo!'"

"I am going to cry," Mrs. Laxton interjected as she listened to Mr. Gray tell the story.

"Yeah, right," Mr. Gray said, "I got a knot in my throat, too." Then he continued, "When she said that, my whole world just lit right up. What a New Year's! I knew then that God was with us."

Mrs. Laxton had traced her brother's telephone number from the return address on the Christmas card. By that time, her husband had passed away in the care of hospice, and her two adult children had moved into their own homes. Though she had the Irish setters to keep her company, she was extremely lonely and had a strong desire to see her brother and her cousins.

Though they all lived far away, they happily agreed to come for a family reunion.

Mr. Gray paused. He had run out of breath. He closed his eyes and expanded his lungs slowly—once, twice, three times until he had inhaled enough air to go on. He then recounted that the family reunion didn't go as planned. Exhausted from the flight, he was carried off the plane unconscious, and immediately transferred to the hospital. By the time of his discharge, four days later, his cousins had left. His sister wanted him to extend his stay in Lancaster County, but not wanting to burden her, Mr. Gray insisted that he return to Charleston. To spare him the hazards of another flight, Mrs. Laxton drove him back herself. Nine days after her return home she received the call from the hospital informing her that her brother was dying.

To everyone's surprise, Mr. Gray survived. His explanation for his turn-around was God. "Bless the Lord," he said again and again as he spoke about his recovery. He asserted that God had healed him to give him the opportunity to repair the wrongs he had committed. "I get sick just thinking about my life," he said, as he explained that he had spent most of his adult years in disgrace.

Despite his drowsiness, Mr. Gray talked for half an hour that day. Toward the end of his story, he struggled to catch his breath. He pursed his lips and leaned forward, resting his elbows on his knees, clearly struggling to inhale. He clasped his oxygen mask to his face, but this didn't seem to help much. His sister offered him a glass of water to prevent his mouth from drying out. Tiffany encouraged him to make use of his short-acting morphine to ease his breathing and to take a nap. I thanked him for his story and made arrangements to visit him again soon.

"I just wish all the patients of hospice could feel as good as I feel"

The next time I saw Mr. Gray, he was sitting alone at the kitchen table reading the Bible. He told me that Mrs. Laxton had gone to the doctor. A few months earlier, she had injured her back at work and was placed on temporary disability. At the time, I didn't realize how unusual Mrs. Laxton's absence was. Because of her own health problems and the protectiveness she felt toward her brother, she spent most of her time at home. With the exception of that day, interviews with Mr. Gray were three-way conversations. When Mr. Gray ran out of breath, Mrs. Laxton spoke for him. And when he regained his strength, he elaborated on her statements. Mrs. Laxton, he explained to me, had done everything for him. Although she struggled financially herself, she had not hesitated to pay the $3,500 fee for the air ambulance to bring him back to Lancaster County. And for over a year, she had devoted her entire life to his well-being. He wanted not only Mrs. Laxton but also their friends and caretakers to know how much he appreciated her. "I feel like Flo is my wife, not my sister," he said tearfully, as he told me that he loved her. Then he chuckled, recalling the day when a waitress at a restaurant assumed that he and Mrs. Laxton were husband and wife. "We need to start going out separately," he said. "Flo ruins the possibility of me ever getting a date!"

Mr. Gray looked strong on this visit. With the cannula blowing air into his nose, he spoke rather effortlessly. "I just wish all the patients of hospice could feel as good as I feel," he said, and thanked the Lord. He quickly added that although he had only recently accepted God into his life, God had always been there for him. That was a point he wanted to make sure I understood and a message he wanted to communicate loud and clear to the readers of his story. Remembering his childhood, he described a farm accident when he had been run over by a tractor at the age of five or six:

> I was in just such a position that the tractor ran over my body, the wheel ran across my body and ran across my belly—it did not run over my chest now. The wheel of the tractor ran across me and the two wheels on the trailer ran across me with a loaded trailer and the ground was just soft enough, I guess, the imprint of my body was being pushed down into the ground just enough that the full weight of the tractor never—

Mr. Gray stopped to catch his breath. He closed his eyes, pursed his lips, and concentrated on his breathing. A few minutes later he was able to continue.

> Praise God. Now this is God again. This is the Lord, which at that time I did not even realize. But with God and His angels—and I say this with a lump in my throat now—but the Lord sure got me out of that because the tractor and trailer ran over me.

God had saved him many times, Mr. Gray asserted. The rheumatic fever that had caused him three heart attacks before the age of 12 had left him with only a mild heart murmur. And now, 44 years later, God had given him hospice. Mr. Gray couldn't imagine what he would have done without the physical, emotional, and spiritual support he received from this agency. And he certainly appreciated that Medicare covered the high costs of his medications. The only complaint he had he directed at himself. "I know that I still do things that are not of the righteous man," he said. "I have not given myself fully to the Lord. I want to. I tell myself I want to, and yet I realize by my actions that I have not totally made that commitment to Him. I am still smoking cigarettes from time to time, even when I don't terribly have a bad craving, and I know I can do better."

Hellfire and brimstone

Mr. Gray's medication regimen consisted of steroids, a bronchodilator, a tranquilizer, and short-acting morphine. He received regular hospice visits from his nurse, personal care nurse, chaplain, and social worker. The hospice social worker, Thelma Barron, referred to Mr. Gray's recovery as a miracle. "Like Lazarus," she said laughingly, "he came back from the dead." Thelma had come to see Mr. Gray's illness as more of a chronic than a terminal condition. Any kind of specific prognosis, she said, would probably be grossly inaccurate.

"Stanley was supposed to have died a couple of times now, and he has just bounced back," Tiffany, the nurse, observed to me. Mr. Gray's lungs were severely damaged. Through the stethoscope, Tiffany could hear air exchange only after his breathing treatments. She believed that Mr. Gray's religious beliefs had a direct impact on his health. She explained that because Mr. Gray feared eternal punishment, he was anxious. As a result, his two main symptoms fed each other—his anxiety exacerbated his respiratory distress, which in turn increased his anxiety.

Hospice chaplain Carl Flynn agreed. A friendly and unassuming man in his forties, he told me that Mr. Gray operated out of a conservative, evangelical paradigm. His religiosity, according to Carl, was rooted more in fear than in love for God. "I am sure he came out of a hellfire-and-brimstone kind of upbringing," Carl said. He found Mr. Gray to be extraordinarily self-critical and attributed this not only to his background but also to the teachings of Pastor Lowel, a Southern, evangelical minister Mr. Gray had recently started to watch on television. In Carl's opinion, this show had given Mr. Gray the impression that there was only one way to understand God, and that was through the Bible. Carl, a practitioner of a theological movement that views reality as a process of growth and change with infinite possibilities, found himself offering Mr. Gray counterpoints to the absolutist statements of the television preacher.

Carl remembered his initial visits with Mr. Gray as being unsettling. "There was something that was always missing. Always missing. Always missing," he said. "Here is a person with chronic obstructive pulmonary disease who cannot get his breath, but on a spiritual level it speaks to a kind of lack of openness to being inspired by the movement of God's spirit." As a chaplain, Carl wanted to loosen up the tightness he perceived in Mr. Gray's religious life and tried to show Mr. Gray that there were ways to enrich Bible study by breathing life into his relationship with God. He came to believe that Mr. Gray would benefit from a personal and nurturing connection with the divine that transcended Scripture.

When, one day late in August, Mr. Gray accused himself of having sinned because he smoked a cigarette, Carl devised a spiritual exercise. He sought Mr. Gray's permission "to invite Jesus into his home." Mr. Gray agreed, reluctantly.

Carl, acting as if he could see Jesus, asked Him to sit at the head of the kitchen table. Then he instructed Mr. Gray to share his worries with his guest. Mr. Gray started talking, but he faced Carl instead of the empty seat. Carl redirected him to Jesus. Nervously, Mr. Gray turned his gaze sideways. When he finished talking, Carl invited him to a few minutes of silence. It was time, he said, to see if God had a response. Mr. Gray sat quietly, but didn't get a sense of a divine message. Carl did, however. "I got that Jesus loves you very much," he told Mr. Gray, "that you are His own child and in fact your name is written in the palms of His hands." Extending his own palms toward Mr. Gray, Carl asked him to place his worries in them. Carl, in turn, would offer them to Jesus. "Jesus," said Mr. Gray as he positioned his hands over Carl's, "I am placing my struggles, my concern about smoking, in your hands and I know that when I am tempted or when I am bothered by this, I will know it is in your hands, and I don't have to worry about it anymore." As if he were holding Mr. Gray's concerns, Carl turned in his chair and made as if to give them gently to Jesus. More silence. Then Carl chuckled. He had a mental image of Jesus holding a lit cigarette and laughing. "And I shared that with Stanley," he told me later. "I said, 'I don't know what it means, but I have a sense that Jesus is saying, 'I can hold this for you. It is no big deal.'"

Carl was happy with the exercise. He felt confident that he had helped Mr. Gray relinquish some control over his struggles and allow a force greater than himself to guide him to the righteous life that he desired. Mr. Gray told me later that he felt less comfortable with the enactment. On the one hand, he was relieved by the opportunity to unburden his worries, and on the other, he saw his interaction with Jesus as a convenient but immoral way of detaching himself from his responsibilities. He argued that God expected His followers to take charge of their own lives. Nevertheless, he stopped smoking.

"Everything I do in my life is either illegal or immoral"

A month had passed since my first meeting with Mr. Gray, and I still didn't know what he meant when he referred to the sinful life he had led in the South. I also didn't understand what had prompted him to leave that life behind and turn to God. Although he spoke frequently about his transformation, Mr. Gray routinely circumvented his troubled past. When he made yet another reference to his sins, I asked him if he could tell me what he meant. For a moment he hedged, then he said that he had been an alcoholic and had allowed prostitutes and drug dealers in his house. Sometimes he made money for the safe haven he provided them, but more often he loaned it back to them and lost it. For years, Mr. Gray felt bad about his profligate lifestyle. But one day, he decided to change. "I suddenly got to a place where I did not like who I was or what I was," he said. He told his friends that they were no longer allowed to carry out illicit activities under his roof. Most of them never visited him again.

"What led you to that change, do you think?" I asked him.

"Although I was not thinking of it at the time that way," he replied, "I know it was the Lord. I knew that He had a purpose for me, and I truly believe that the Lord was actually touching me and trying to nudge me: 'This is not what I want for you, and you know this is not what you want.' And deep down inside, I believe it was my knowledge of the Lord and what was right and wrong."

He continued, "I have done everything in my life, short of kidnap or murder. I have stolen things that I knew were not mine, I have forged signatures on checks. I have been guilty of lying and cheating. I have been guilty of adultery. I suppose I have broken a lot of God's commandments." He glanced at Mrs. Laxton and suddenly he paused. "While we are being taped," he said as he tried to take a few deep breaths, "I might as well tell my sister something, because I looked at her, and I don't know if she is thinking about this or not." He then asked Mrs. Laxton if she remembered his engagement to a young woman 39 years earlier. At the time, he was stationed in a military base in the Southwest. Mrs. Laxton nodded, recalling that her brother had mailed her a photograph of his fiancee. "That was in my imagination," Mr. Gray said apologetically, and he explained that he had never gotten engaged. To elevate his status in the Army, he had lied about his life both to his family and to his military commander. The woman in the photograph was a waitress he hardly knew. Eventually he was caught and court-martialled.

"I used to say, 'Everything I do in my life is either illegal or immoral,'" he stated, "and most of the time it was both."

"I don't know how to bring it out—that it is okay for him to cry"

I had visited Mr. Gray several times before asking him about his daughter. Although an enlarged photograph of her hung prominently on Mrs. Laxton's living room wall, Mr. Gray didn't talk about her often. His first marriage ended just about the time Cynthia was born and his wife had insisted that he never see Cynthia again. He recalled that when Cynthia was in grade school, he missed her so much that he waited on streets she frequented to catch glimpses of her from a distance. One time, he even sat in the house of her next-door neighbor hoping to see her return from school.

I met Cynthia, who was now 37, in September 1997. She and her husband lived in an apartment complex in Lancaster County with a daughter from her previous marriage. As a social worker in a nursing home, she worked long hours and looked exhausted. "It is kind of strange that I did not know my dad until a year and a half ago," she told me. "I knew who he was, I was given a name, and I was told he was my father. At one point—in fact I think twice—I had been told that he was already dead." Cynthia had spent her entire childhood wondering why her father had left her. "I wanted to know what was wrong with me," she said.

In June 1996, Cynthia received a call from Mrs. Laxton's daughter, whom she had never met. Would Cynthia be open to meeting her father? the cousin asked. Cynthia was shocked. She felt defensive. "Dad can never get those 36 years back no matter what he does. They are gone," she thought to herself. "But," she told me, "there was no sense in holding a grudge and denying myself the chance to get to know the man who helped my being come into existence. So I said that I would talk to him, but he would have to call me." Mr. Gray called his daughter a week later. He told her that he was terminally ill, that he was staying with her aunt Flo, and that he was receiving the services of hospice. He also asked to see her before he died. "So I came to him with an open mind," she said, "and very honestly told him that there was no way he was going to make up for the last 36 years, so do not bother trying and let's start from here."

For a year and a half, Cynthia had visited her father weekly. Mr. Gray avoided talking about his life, and Cynthia had come to accept that she would never learn the details of her father's past. "Sometimes we seem like polite strangers," she said. "I get the feeling that he does not trust himself or he is afraid that I am going to walk out if I learn too much." At the same time, her fear that her father didn't love her was slowly dissipating. Only a few weeks before I met her, she had found a letter that Mr. Gray had written to her mother. In this letter, her father admitted that he was not fit for parenthood, confessed that he was in trouble with the law, expressed his love for baby Cynthia, and promised to stay away from her until he became a better person. "That is an act of love," asserted Cynthia.

Cynthia had grown to love her father and admired him for his transformation. But she also felt sorry for him. She found him too isolated and alone. "Sometimes I think he hides his fear," she said. "He is so upbeat and he watches what he says, and he tries to be so positive, and yet there are times I know he is having problems breathing. And he is taking morphine, and he is cramping, and his fingers are contracting, and it is like he will still put on that happy face, and he is like, 'It is fine.' And I don't know how to bring it out—that it is okay for him to cry." Cynthia worried for Mrs. Laxton as well. In the previous months, she said, her aunt had given up the things that gave her happiness: knitting and taking care of her two horses. "[Flo] lives for her daughter and her son, and she lives for my dad," she said. "She is a very good woman, but she stopped taking care of what she needs for herself. She stopped saying, 'Okay, I need time away.' There are times when she will not sleep right. And yet I cannot get her to let me in."

Cynthia continued with a tone of disappointment, "Sometimes I feel like I am still on the outside, that they are protecting me. If I am going to be there for the good, I need to be there for the bad, and Dad is going to die. I am not afraid of death. But I am afraid of not being able to give to him."

"I want to get deeper into the true word of Christ"

As I continued my visits I began to see what Carl meant when he told me that Mr. Gray's religiosity was rooted in fear. Mr. Gray came across as a perfectionist, who feared that his wrongs had the capacity to bring him eternal damnation. "I want to learn God's word as it is meant to be," he asserted, "and I want to follow those who are more learned about it, such as a minister, who wants to teach it as it is supposed to be taught—as God wants it taught—verse by verse, book by book. Not trying to change it to suit man as he would like to have it."

As much as he loved talking about religion, Mr. Gray seemed uncomfortable doing so. He almost invariably stopped himself and interjected a series of disclaimers—that he didn't want to speak for God, that he didn't know if his understanding of the Bible was correct, that he didn't want to lead anyone astray. "God's word says that whoever says something and misleads somebody then your soul is in jeopardy," he once told me. One day he decided to share a dream with me. He had had it in Charleston a few years earlier, but until now he wasn't sure he could relate it without somehow distorting its divine message:

> I had a dream where I saw a vision of fire falling from the sky—just balls of fire coming out of the sky. The sky was all red, all around. People were running and screaming, fire falling on them, more or less like Armageddon, and out of all this fire a figure came through the fire or came out that was Christ or Christ Jesus. At least that is the way it looked to me. I immediately fell down and began to worship and say how much of a sinner I was, which was really the truth, begging for forgiveness.

Mr. Gray's initial interpretation was that Jesus had given him the opportunity to confess his sins and had finally granted him eternal life. But with the help of Pastor Lowel, he realized that the figure in his dream was not Christ at all. Christ, he learned, would have automatically turned him into a spirit. The fact that this figure didn't transform him, but watched him beg for forgiveness, meant that he was the Antichrist. It was thanks to God, Mr. Gray went on, that he had come across Pastor Lowel, and it was thanks to Pastor Lowel that he had learned that one needs to know the Bible in order to be saved. "God was telling me," he said, 'Hey, you need to pay a little closer attention to my word.' I would have been truly lost. My salvation would have been just thrown right out the window, but knowing the difference now, I want to get deeper into the true word of Christ."

Mr. Gray's voice started to shake. "It is so important that people who are where I was at know that no matter how lost they think they are out there, whatever they have done, there is nothing that God won't forgive." Then he started to cry:

> What I am saying is, I feel like I was so far out, I was so lost that I was just getting in deeper, and God left a flock of sheep that is already saved when He heard my cry in the wilderness, and like a true shepherd, He came and found me, and He brought me back into His flock where I have my salvation now, a true salvation. And He can do it for anybody.

Proudly, Mr. Gray announced that he had not smoked for three weeks. Tiffany was impressed with his improvement, he said with a smile. He had been able to cut down on his morphine, and only a few days earlier, he had managed to accompany Mrs. Laxton to the mall. "I used to pray for healing, yes," he said. "I thought how nice it would be to be completely healed. But under the circumstances I don't pray that way anymore. Each year that I have got this disease I am supposed to be getting less and less. Instead of that, I am doing more and more and more. So you tell me, what is it? Well, in a sense as far as I am concerned, I am healed. So why keep praying for healing? I am alive, so as far as I am concerned, I am as good as cured."

Given his improvement, I wondered if Mr. Gray's condition was still serious enough to justify his remaining under the care of hospice. He had been a hospice patient for 16 months. When I asked Tiffany if she had thought about discharging him, she answered, "He is still really a sick guy. I hear air now, but it is still not that great, and he still cannot walk from the bedroom to the kitchen without having to stop and take a rest period. It is just that he is not needing to use the mask and rely so much on morphine. We have been discussing him in our team meeting, and he is still really symptomatic, and he still has a lot of the criteria that justify us staying involved." Tiffany added that Mr. Gray benefited greatly from hospice's emotional and spiritual support. "I believe that Stanley is terminal just based on the [way that] his disease progressed in the beginning and, like he said, he's got some purpose right now for this happening, and when his purpose is up, he is ready."

Tiffany's opinion was shared by Dr. Katherine Marsh, the pulmonary specialist overseeing Mr. Gray. Dr. Marsh acknowledged her patient's physical improvement, but she also asserted that from a medical perspective, Mr. Gray's level of functioning remained low. Flipping through the chart, Dr. Marsh informed me that she had spoken with Mr. Gray about a living will. The only reason he was able to maintain a relatively high quality of life, she explained, was because he received the services of hospice. Good palliative care and the occa-

sional checkups she gave him guarded Mr. Gray against recurrent deterioration. Prevention, she observed, was what kept her patient alive. "Even the
smallest infection or a change in fluid status, if his heart did not function well,
could tip him over into a bad situation where he could not recover even with
medications," she said. "His prognosis for three years survival is probably zero.
His prognosis for a one-year survival is probably 15% to 20% as best I can give
you. We don't have good statistics in pulmonary medicine, because there is so
much variability in chronic lung disease. We see people who, if they don't get
an infection, may remain stable for a year or two. But his disease is very severe,
and I am actually surprised that he has done well this long."

Pastor Lowel

In early October, a family emergency forced Carl Flynn to leave hospice.
Tiffany offered Mr. Gray a new spiritual counselor, but he declined. "If I find
myself needing any real strong spiritual help, so to speak, I can pretty much
just take it straight to Christ himself," he said. Mr. Gray's main worry was that
he had not had time lately to watch Pastor Lowel's television show. Visitors
from hospice and outings with his sister had filled his days with social activities,
and he had started to miss his Bible study. One day, aware that he made recordings of the religious program, I suggested canceling our interview and spending
our time together watching one of his tapes. Mr. Gray seemed surprised and
excited by my proposal. He stated that he would never pass up the opportunity
to spread God's word. We moved to the living room and sat around the television set. I was eager to see Pastor Lowel. But when Mrs. Laxton inserted the
videotape in the VCR, I felt catapulted into sacred territory. Suddenly, I felt
nervous. I realized that the situation I had put myself into was extremely sensitive. The show I was about to watch embodied Mr. Gray's and Mrs. Laxton's
deepest values. What if I made a facial expression, or a move, or a comment
that offended them? What if I inadvertently came across as disrespectful? But
now it was too late to do anything except sit quietly and watch.

The focus of the show was the Book of Daniel. One verse after another appeared on the screen while Pastor Lowel discussed its meaning and significance. Suddenly, Mrs. Laxton disappeared into another room to fetch her
Bible. For the sake of accuracy, she said, she liked to compare the verses on the
screen with the printed version in front of her. The pastor, a scholarly man who
sat next to a statue of an eagle and before a big American flag, spoke at great
length about the dream of the King of Babylon. He compared the competing
empires of the past with Russia and the West today. The tape lasted longer than
I expected, and after 45 minutes I had to go. I apologized to Mr. Gray and Mrs.
Laxton for interrupting, explained that I had another meeting to attend, and

thanked them for allowing me to watch the show. On my way out, Mrs. Laxton told me that she found Pastor Lowel's teachings invaluable. Because of him, she said, she had finally understood how there can be many human races when all of humanity started from one. All the non-Jewish races, she said, came into existence on the sixth day of creation. Adam and Eve, however, were created on the eighth. And Jesus was their descendant.

"Needed reassurance"

On October 8, Mr. Gray's personal care nurse, Naomi Barnes, found Mr. Gray sick in bed. He was wearing his oxygen mask and struggled to speak. Having spent the previous day picking tomatoes in his sister's yard, he had strained his muscles. He reported that the sharp, grabbing pain in his chest, back, shoulders, and scapula was so severe that he couldn't breathe. Two doses of short-acting morphine had not helped. Naomi applied warm, moist heat on the affected areas of his torso. When Tiffany arrived she could hear no air entry at the bases of Mr. Gray's lungs. Breath sounds in his upper lobes had decreased as well. It took Mr. Gray a few days to start walking again, but Tiffany suspected that he was sicker than he showed.

"When he knows you are coming at 11," she remarked, "he will be sure to be out in the kitchen, have the coffee ready, and he will be there, and you see him sitting there completely comfortable." To see how Mr. Gray fared during the walk from his bedroom to the kitchen and how long it took him to regain his breath, Tiffany started appearing early for her visits. This way, Mr. Gray was still in his bedroom and had no choice but to walk in front of her. She noted that, even with his oxygen mask on, his shortness of breath came sooner and seemed more persistent. After he sat down at the table it took two minutes before he could speak.

In late October, Tiffany congratulated Mr. Gray for surviving his second smoke-free month. He looked embarrassed. He said that he didn't deserve congratulations, because the previous day he had smoked again. Tiffany tried to discourage him from punishing himself and explained that backslides were normal. But Mr. Gray didn't seem convinced.

"Needed reassurance," wrote Tiffany in her nursing notes that day. She left Mr. Gray, wishing that Carl was still available to help him. She had already referred him to hospice's new chaplain, Jane Madder, and hoped that she would be able to give him the support he needed. She worried, however, that Jane and Mr. Gray wouldn't get along. Jane was more formal than Carl. "She is not as laid back and as easy-going," she remarked, "which I know Stanley really liked about Carl. Carl would sit there and tell you a dirty joke, you know. And Stanley liked that. Because, you know, Stanley is rough around the edges."

Jane Madder

Jane Madder left her first meeting with Mr. Gray and Mrs. Laxton puzzled. What they had told her about Pastor Lowel disturbed her. She disagreed with the philosophy that there is only one truth in the world and that the Bible has an explanation for everything. But she sat quietly and listened. Later she learned that Mr. Gray and Mrs. Laxton felt bad about monopolizing the conversation.

The next time Jane visited, she invited Mr. Gray and Mrs. Laxton to talk more about their lives. Again, Mr. Gray focused the conversation on the Bible. Jane asked him if he found any Scriptures especially meaningful. Mr. Gray couldn't come up with anything. Jane then proceeded to talk about a prayer she had given at a hospice meeting in which she asked for gratefulness "for new things that happen and a kind of acknowledgment that while we celebrate what we have received in the past, we also look forward to new gifts from God and from the spirit." "So I was just reporting this to them," she told me later, "to kind of challenge them in a little bit of a way—the tendency of [Pastor Lowel] to nail everything down, that this is the way it is, and their tendency to buy into that—and so I was just saying, 'Some new things may happen for us.' Well, I think they got the message." In a slow and subtle way, Jane hoped to help Mr. Gray move beyond what she called the "closed system" that Pastor Lowel promoted. Such systems, she argued, made people disinterested in new ideas, gave them a false sense of security, and prevented growth.

Thelma and Tiffany

By November, Thelma, Mr. Gray's social worker, was also trying to redirect discussions with Mr. Gray away from his faith, but to no avail. "He is more consumed with the spiritual aspect than he is with the illness," she remarked. Although she had grown tired of Mr. Gray's preoccupation, Thelma conceded that his religious life, and his ability to share it, gave him happiness. She even reluctantly agreed to borrow two of Mr. Gray's religious videotapes. "I think it is really helping him," she said. "I think it is a real source of strength for him, and I think it is as important as his medications."

Tiffany felt more comfortable with Mr. Gray's religiosity because, unlike the other members of the team, she found him open to differing perspectives, and she agreed with some of his convictions. She also believed that God had given him his illness for a reason: because of his COPD, Mr. Gray had made amends with his family, reestablished a connection with his daughter, and brought Mrs. Laxton closer to God.

"Every day I thank God for bringing you back into my life"

On December 7, Mr. Gray celebrated his 58th birthday. Cynthia's gift to him was a framed photograph of him sitting at the kitchen table with her standing behind him, her arms wrapped around him and both of them smiling. On the border of the frame Cynthia had written, "Every day I thank God for bringing you back into my life. Love, Cynthia."

Naomi Barnes

By the middle of December 1997, Mr. Gray was smoking regularly again. Due to increased weakness, he spent many hours in bed. On December 17, Tiffany watched him stop three times on his way to the kitchen. Even though he was wearing his oxygen mask and holding onto his walker, he needed to rest. When he reached the kitchen, he leaned against the doorway. Once he caught his breath, he walked to his chair and leaned over that. Finally, when he sat down, he dropped his head, closed his eyes, and tried to take even breaths. Three to four minutes later, he turned to Tiffany and said, "I am doing really good, all things considered."

Tiffany was worried. She offered to ask Mr. Gray's primary care physician to increase the frequency of his sustained-release morphine from twice to three times a day. She also encouraged him to consider using pills or patches to stop smoking. Mr. Gray resisted. He stated clearly that he didn't want any help fighting his addiction. "Right now this is between me and God," he said. Tiffany was perplexed. "He is feeling like he needs to punish himself," she told me later. "Some of him is starting to get a little weird, I think."

I saw Mr. Gray the next day. He was sitting at the kitchen table as usual. Mrs. Laxton had made a fresh batch of coffee, which was steaming in the middle of the room. Right away, Mr. Gray told me that the sustained-release morphine had eased his breathing. The fact that he was still functional made him happy. Being end-stage, he said, he knew that he couldn't take his independence for granted. "You have been 'end-stage' for 20 months now," commented Mrs. Laxton. She had just offered me a cup of tea when Naomi, the personal care nurse, arrived. It was three o'clock. "He is my last one!" Naomi exclaimed. "I told you I save the best for last!" Naomi was an outgoing and good-humored woman, and she had grown very close to Mr. Gray. She claimed that she liked to "save" Mr. Gray for the end of her work day so as to have the freedom to extend her visits beyond the time it required to take care of his hygiene. She had gained Mr. Gray's trust, helping him take showers, massaging his back and neck to relax his muscles, emptying his bedside commode, and conversing with him about her life and his.

I had the sense that Mr. Gray felt less inhibited with Naomi than with any-one else. "With Naomi there is always this joke," said Mr. Gray, "and I can do most things, but one problem I do have is emptying the portable toilet." Mrs. Laxton interjected, "There are times when he doesn't get it done, and when Naomi comes, he says, 'I have a little present back [in my bedroom] for you,' and it is kind of like a joke." Naomi came from a family that was socioeconomi-cally similar to Mr. Gray's. She was also a devout Christian. Drawn to people in need, she had served many patients in her life. When she told Mr. Gray that she had worked in a prison, his guard dropped. Gradually, he began sharing with her experiences from his past. Every now and then, he even told her dirty jokes. He would cry with Naomi and laugh. "He is the type of guy that you have to let your hair down with and not be offended at anything he says," said Naomi. "He is a sweetheart." Mr. Gray excused himself and went to the bath-room to start his shower. Naomi was going to help him if he called. Mrs. Laxton offered to continue with our interview. "[Stanley] is still concerned about smoking," she said quietly. "He has days when he smokes more than others, and he wants to quit, and yet I think part of it is that he is bored." Mrs. Laxton expressed guilt for smoking herself. She knew that if she didn't buy cigarettes, her brother wouldn't be able to continue his unhealthy habit. But Naomi held a different view. She said:

> I am a nurse, and I am not saying that he should smoke, but by the same token I have been around him and when I do his back and massages and all, I can feel the tension when he has this internal struggle with the smoking. And then when he does smoke, it is a release for him. It's a physical release for him. I mean I can feel it in his neck. I guess maybe I am just as much to blame. I did not say [to him], "Go ahead and smoke," but I just said, "You have to choose the lesser of two evils here." And I said, "Of any time, if the good Lord is going to be understanding, it is going to be now."

"I don't want to go back again and have 10 more tapes waiting for me"

By the end of December, Thelma felt worn out by Mr. Gray's religious fervor. Without realizing it, she had accepted eight videotapes of Pastor Lowel, but had neither the time nor the desire to watch them all. Uncomfortable with the intense religious focus of her meetings with Mr. Gray, she found herself post-poning her next visit. "Maybe we are going to have to set some limits," she said with a perplexed look on her face. "I don't want to go back again and have 10 more tapes waiting for me."

"She just could not believe how well I am doing"

In January 1998, Mr. Gray had a respiratory crisis that he managed to survive with antibiotics and a new prescription for 100 mg capsules of sustained-release morphine. Naomi increased her personal care visits from two to three times a week. Mr. Gray requested bedbaths. He told her he was not ready to die. Naomi sat next to him on the bed and cried.

On February 15, Mr. Gray and Mrs. Laxton both quit smoking. When I visited around that time, Mr. Gray asserted that his condition had improved. The combination of his new morphine capsules and the absence of cigarettes had reduced his need for short-acting morphine from eight times a day to three times a week. "[Dr. Marsh] was tickled to death when she saw me," he said as he started to describe a recent appointment with his physician. "She just could not believe how well I am doing."

I asked Mr. Gray if Dr. Marsh had an explanation for his progress. "Let's face it," he responded, "the doctors are not going to just come right out and say, 'Yeah, it is God doing it. It is not us.' But in a manner of speaking, they are also saying that they have done everything that they can, and they don't understand how I am doing as well as I am doing. But they are glad that whatever it is, it's working, you know?"

"Sometimes I think I get strength from him"

"I think his faith is 80 percent of it," said Naomi when I asked her how she explained Mr. Gray's surprising stability. Naomi was sitting sideways in her living room couch with her leg propped up with pillows. A few weeks earlier, in the beginning of March, she had broken her ankle. She had taken a temporary leave from work, so she invited me to interview her at home. With enthusiasm she told me that Mr. Gray and Mrs. Laxton had paid her a surprise visit the previous week. She recalled that she was having lunch with a friend when she heard Mr. Gray shouting, "Hey! Hey!" She looked out the window and saw Mrs. Laxton imploring her brother to quiet down. Naomi couldn't believe her eyes. Excitedly, she opened the door and welcomed them in. Mr. Gray, wearing his cannula and mask, made it into her house with the help of his walker. When he caught his breath, he told Naomi that he wanted to see how she was doing. He then joked that a little "present" was waiting for her in the car.

Naomi laughed as she recounted this. "He just seems so much better," she said. "I even said to my husband, 'If I lose Stanley right now, that is going to be it.' That is going to tear me apart, because I just think the world of him. For him to come in here—he is terminal, God bless him—he trucks into my house because I cannot come see him! Nobody could have done anything that would have made me feel better. That was really neat. He is a such a neat man. In fact, sometimes I think I get strength from him." Although impressed with her patient's perseverance, Naomi affirmed that Mr. Gray was still very sick. She suspected that he, himself, didn't realize that. Drawing from his faith in God, he put on a happy front that seemed to dissipate at times of crisis. When he couldn't breathe, he became angry for losing control over his condition. Naomi believed that Mr. Gray would require a lot of emotional support when he started to die. She missed him. She couldn't wait to start working with him again.

A nurse supervisor corroborated Naomi's view that, although Mr. Gray gave the impression that he was chronically, rather than terminally, ill, he definitely belonged in hospice care. The dose of his medications increased steadily. When he skipped a dose, his symptoms worsened. But apart from the inherent ambiguity of defining Mr. Gray as "terminally ill," the nurses and administrators at hospice were united in recognizing the many benefits they were giving Mr. Gray and Mrs. Laxton in terms of support, nursing care, close monitoring of symptoms, and availability in moments of crisis. If they were uncomfortable with the length of time Mr. Gray was enrolled in their program, it was not because they doubted the value of these services to him but because the bureaucratic regulation of hospice care in the United States creates an artificial dichotomy between chronic care and hospice care.

"To me, he is a clear-cut case," asserted the supervisor. "I do not think, if we would ever get questioned on this case, which may happen, I think we have enough documentation of what is going on. We are continually doing things for him. It is not as if we are not doing anything, socializing when we go in. We are readjusting the medications. So this is a very comfortable case for me."

"I know we may seem like fanatics"

In May 1998, Mr. Gray announced that he wanted to explore other people's religious beliefs. He asked Tiffany if he could meet another one of her patients who, Tiffany had told him, was a retired minister. The next time Tiffany saw this patient, Peter Stone, she mentioned Mr. Gray's interest to visit with him. Mr. Stone agreed to call Mr. Gray.

Tiffany was delighted, but she worried that the two men wouldn't connect. Although both pious, she told me, they were very different. She characterized Mr. Stone, an end-stage cardiac patient in his seventies, as a "three-piece-suit guy" who distrusted medicine. He was a vegetarian who relied primarily on alternative forms of healing and held strong views. Tiffany feared that Mr. Stone had the capacity to shatter Mr. Gray's beliefs. "I do not want Peter to make

Stanley feel like everything he thinks is wrong," she told me. "I said to Stanley, 'You know, some of the things you guys believe might be different,' and Stanley acknowledged that. But he is just kind of interested in getting another point of view. We will see."

Peter Stone visited Mr. Gray three times. Tiffany was pleased to see that they enjoyed each other's company. But in the beginning of August, their relationship broke off. Mr. Stone borrowed a videotape of Pastor Lowel and instead of returning it himself, as he had promised, he mailed it back with a note. He wrote that he disagreed with some of Pastor Lowel's statements, and that for a while he was going to be too busy to continue his visits with Mr. Gray. Mr. Gray seemed hurt. Protectively, Mrs. Laxton reminded him that Mr. Stone was a busy man, but Stanley wasn't convinced. He suspected that it was differences in their religious views that had pushed Mr. Stone away. Mrs. Laxton turned to me and said apologetically, "I know we may seem like fanatics to an extent. But it is excitement, and I do feel that we have learned the right path."

Meanwhile, the hospice team was concerned about Mrs. Laxton's health. Having brought Stanley into her home expecting him to die at any moment, Mrs. Laxton had spent the last two years doing little except monitoring her brother's every breath. Thelma thought it would be important to help Mrs. Laxton switch her mindset from short-term, intensive care to chronic, long-term care, even though the team resisted that very distinction when faced with the need to justify retaining Mr. Gray in their program. So far, however, Mrs. Laxton had shown little interest in following Thelma's suggestion.

"I do not have to be ashamed to say I am a Gray"

When I saw Mr. Gray in July he was sitting at the kitchen table with Florence and Cynthia. He had been smoke-free for six months, but he looked pale and exhausted. For two weeks he had had difficulty urinating. His body was bloated, his feet, ankles, and toes visibly swollen. His skin felt so tight that he thought it was going to break. He struggled to breathe. A few days earlier, his primary care physician had increased his diuretic from 60 to 80 mg a day, and that made him feel better. "I am quite sure that [the diuretic] is going to be the key to this whole thing," Mr. Gray said with a smile, "and, praise the Lord, in a day or two from now maybe I will be feeling quite a bit better and ready to get out there and dance again."

"That's right!" Cynthia interjected. "We have got a baby to get ready for, so you have got to get yourself feeling better." Cynthia turned to me and explained that she was three months pregnant. She had told her father a few weeks earlier, and they were all thrilled. They saw the baby as an opportunity to live precious moments that they had missed. Mr. Gray had not held Cynthia as a baby, and for 16 years, he didn't even know that Cynthia had given birth to her daughter. "I will be there this time the best I can," he said as he reached out and held his daughter's hand.

Speaking privately to me later, Cynthia told me that she believed that the most healing time of her father's life was yet to come—that he would experience the most growth in his final days. That period in his life was bound to rob him of his strong facade and force him to reach out in ways that would permit his loved ones to give back. Only then, Cynthia believed, would he be able to let go. In her opinion, two and a half years after his admission to hospice, Mr. Gray continued to keep most of his struggles to himself. She was amazed to see that even when he found himself in a crisis, he apologized for burdening his caretakers. Cynthia vowed that she was going to "bully" her way into her father's world when he started to die. In the brief time she had known him, she said, she had changed. She felt more complete and confident, and more loving toward her father. "The man I know now I can be proud of," she said. "It is not like I have this terrible black cloud on that side of the family. I do not have to be ashamed to say I am a Gray. Before, I was not quite sure."

In September, Cynthia learned that her baby, another girl, had died in her womb. Mr. Gray accompanied his daughter to the hospital for emergency induction of labor. Once born, the lifeless baby was handed to Cynthia. She, in turn, passed her to Mr. Gray. Mr. Gray sat down and placed the baby on his lap. He stared at her quietly. Tears rolled down his cheeks.

13

Martin Roy
Trying to Live and Die Well

Narrated by ANNA TOWERS

Martin Roy was only 37 years old when he learned that his cancer was far advanced. By his own account he had already had a full and fulfilling life, and he spent his final months preparing his family for his death. Although controlling Martin's symptoms was not easy for the palliative care team, with a combination of inpatient and home care, they succeeded in finding a style of care that kept him comfortable and suited the family. Something other than symptom control proved challenging to the staff, however: Martin seemed almost too accepting of his situation. What accounted for his exceptional ability to adapt to dying at an early age? Was he simply a "good coper" or was he "euphoric" and in denial? What was really going on with him?

A life of travel and social justice

Martin Roy was a well-traveled French-Canadian who loved life. The center of attention at any social gathering, he loved parties and dancing. He made and kept friends for a lifetime. He was gracious, soft-spoken, with a charming smile, and looked straight into one's eyes when he spoke. He was a slight man, and very thin as a result of his illness, but he had been a well-built athlete before cancer began to ravage him. After receiving an M.S. in sociology, Martin had worked for the Peace Corps, then managed a travel agency and a solar energy firm, and had been a scuba-diving instructor in the South Pacific. Martin and his wife Alexandra had lived in Nepal for eight years and their two children, Justin, 8, and Caroline, 6, were born there.

Martin, the eldest of five children, now lived in Montreal, as did his brothers and sisters. His wife and his sister Diane provided his main emotional support, being the only people with whom he felt totally comfortable. Martin also had many friends from various walks of life, including some whom he had known since his childhood.

I met Martin at the beginning of our research project, approximately three years after he had been diagnosed with stomach cancer. He and his family were still in Nepal when he first developed digestive symptoms. Martin related the onset of the cancer to a boating accident in which he had been involved six months prior to this. He was alone, sailing a small craft in a busy harbor, when he was hit by a larger boat. He explained:

> When I had my accident, I saw the first moments of death as Dr. Raymond Moody describes in *Life After Life*. It's true what they say. I saw the image of my son Justin appear, when I stopped a 23-foot-long boat with my head and my shoulder, at 55 km/hr. A ton! That's when everything started, I think. Something blew inside. I was in a state of burnout for about six months, and the cancer appeared after that, and I think it was because of that trauma. All that centrifugal force that I had to summon up to stop [the boat] just made something burn out inside me.

Although his travel agency was doing well, Martin and his family moved back to Montreal, mainly so the children could go to school there. Returning to Canada was a big change, and not just because it was on his return that Martin received the definitive diagnosis of stomach cancer, and underwent an esophagogastrectomy. He explained to me:

> It wasn't easy to come back, I have to be honest. There we lived without money, no kidding. At our house it was always a great food party. Some people stopped at our house; they thought it was a restaurant. Other people thought it was a bar. So we said, "Come in, have a drink."
>
> Traveling, when you change country, money, food, history, clothes, expression— everything changes. So I've never been afraid of change. I spent 10 years of my life in Nepal, Bhutan, Indochina. I've lived in many countries, and I've been through a lot. I've experienced discomfort, places where they had had drought for three years, illnesses, epidemics, the heat. But we lived 24 hour days, intensely. We lived off love. We loved what we did, we did it with people who loved. You see that the people are poor, but they're beautiful, they're gentle. They were kind and they never, never let me down.
>
> So then I come back here and there's violence, murder, pollution. So I would go traveling again. I would do different things, go to the Pacific, go swimming with dolphins. I lived with iguanas, herons, turtles . . . Scuba-diving in the Pacific Is-

lands, I saw things under the sea . . . You know, there are beautiful things on this planet!

Elaborating on his philosophy of life, Martin continued:

> I'll take the best from all these places and I'll make something new, something good. For me it's Martin Luther King, Gandhi, or it could be Jesus Christ, or Mother Teresa. Or it could be a little boy that I meet in a poor village. If we want to lessen pain, suffering, evil, then we have to realize that we have the means and put ourselves to work. I read everything that Gandhi and Martin Luther King wrote. I got inspiration from them because in the Catholic religion I didn't feel very much at home.

But now his illness had interrupted everything. As Martin explained to me during our first long conversation:

> It was working, except this wrench came into the works . . . a large wrench. . . . I'll tell you honestly, a large wrench. It's hard for me to talk about it. When I talk about it for the first time with someone . . . (sobbing) excuse me . . . I was saying, a large wrench, but not necessarily. Because death is a subject I've read about over the last 20 years. And with life, I think, there's quantity and there's quality. . . . In the sum of a life, be it 30 years, 40 years, or 100 years, there's an equilibrium. It's normal that I'm used up at age 37. I've done what some do in 100 years. It's like an automobile, the motor is finished, I've gone over 300,000 km. "Sorry, Mom, Dad. I've run for too long. I need a new motor, and they can't install one."

Martin and Alexandra had been together for 17 years. She was the same age as Martin, a small, rotund woman with a calm demeanor. Barbara, the home care nurse from the hospital-based Palliative Care Service, described her as a "saint" because of her patience and warmth. She always had a hint of a smile on her face, none of the staff ever saw her upset. It seemed as though she could cope with anything. Alexandra described her husband as a joyful and charismatic person, a comic and a clown, who always spoke the truth.

After surgery . . . more surgery

Following the surgery, Martin had a long convalescence. He felt "cut up, amputated . . . a whole train had passed over me." Because Alexandra worked full-time as a dental assistant and could not look after him, Martin went to live with his parents for five months in their modest, one-story dwelling about 10 miles away. Alexandra and the children visited every two or three days. Martin's mother helped nurse him, in addition to looking after her handicapped brother Robert, who had suffered from severe neurological dysfunction since contracting meningitis as a child. Mrs. Roy had been looking after her brother for eight years, since their mother died. Robert was bedbound and tube fed and had a tracheotomy that needed frequent care. He lived in a hospital bed that Mr. and Mrs. Roy had set up in what was once their dining room. When Martin and his brothers and sisters were growing up, their uncle Robert was a key person in their lives. They called him "Bo-Bo," and would play together, considering him like a brother. Martin and Diane spoke of Robert with great affection. Now Mrs. Roy cheerfully looked after him, even though it meant that she could not go out.

A year after his first surgery, Martin developed headaches and was found to have a brain metastasis. This came as a surprise to everyone, including his physicians. He had a craniotomy with excision of the tumor, followed by radiotherapy and chemotherapy. Since he seemed not to have any tumor elsewhere, the oncologists offered to treat him as aggressively as possible, even though they did not expect a cure. Following the brain surgery Martin was left with double vision. He had to give up reading, one of his greatest passions, and driving. During this second convalescence he had plenty of time to think and reflect. He described some experiences that he had at this time that were fascinating to him, and that made him aware that he could use mental techniques to control pain:

> After my brain surgery it took me four, five days to come back. And I remember that I was very happy. I wasn't tired, I was totally comfortable. And I noticed my surroundings differently, because I wasn't in my conscious mind, I was in my subconscious. I was feeling so good that I didn't want to sleep, and I didn't sleep for five days. Then I realized that my subconscious doesn't know what fatigue is. It doesn't know what pain is. My subconscious is total comfort. It's when we're in our physical body that we can suffer, but when we're in our subconscious, it's universal, it's grand, it's peace, it's infinity. It's eternal life. It's in that state that we feel the most loving, collegial, relaxed, devoted.
>
> I only speak about this with my wife and my sister, because I know that not everyone can understand this. It's incredible! I didn't want to come back into my conscious mind. I was feeling so good in my subconscious! I was in paradise, I had no pain. And I wasn't taking any medication, not even Tylenol.
>
> The day after my stomach surgery, when I started to feel pain for the first time, morphine didn't help at all. And the pain was so strong that I couldn't breathe or move. So I got a hold of myself, and the pain disappeared within five minutes. Forever. They had opened my ribs and I had this sword-like pain that came in front of my chest here and came out my back. So I got a hold of myself and reminded myself that I have certain powers, which I had discovered in my travels, like when I was in that boating accident. I learned that I had a physical and mental power whereby I could, by necessity or instinct, summon all the energy I needed in a thousandth of a second. There could be consequences afterwards . . . but I found that I had great powers.
>
> The subconscious doesn't go to bed and doesn't sleep. It's there all the time. If I have pain, I know that I can seek refuge there.

Six months later, in January 1996, Martin was found to have multiple lung and liver metastases. He wanted no further chemotherapy and was referred to the Palliative Care Service. Dr. Frank, a consultant in the oncology clinic, saw him and referred him to the Home Care Service. On his own initiative Martin started to take shark cartilage, an alternative treatment. He was hopeful that this might prolong his life, or at least reduce his symptoms.

Barbara, the home care nurse, visited weekly. She was an experienced, efficient, no-nonsense nurse who had a good sense of humor. She monitored Martin's symptoms and reported back to Dr. Lawrence, who became his regular palliative care physician. Barbara was the first to comment on Martin's demeanor in the face of his devastating disease:

> In January, I found he was too euphoric, inappropriate, too good to be true . . .
> When you're that young . . . I wondered if he had a problem from his brain
> metastasis. I think that he might have been denying things. He was a non-stop
> talker. I think that when he was stressed, he became very intense. It was very
> draining for me because of the energy he had. It made me think of Rasputin—he
> had that intense look in his eyes.

I met Martin in early April 1996, when he came to the hospital to see his palliative care physician. He looked tired after his one-hour journey. He wanted to tell me about his two children, and how he had explained to them that their father was very sick. He told them that "I would become an angel soon. You won't be able to see me, but I will be able to see you." He felt that the children were not coping too badly with this.

Because Martin's current regimen of acetaminophen and codeine was not controlling his lumbar and epigastric pain, Dr. Lawrence suggested switching to morphine. Martin was reluctant to do so, thinking he would try harder to control the pain with other means. The pain had to be bad before he would resort to medication. Barbara continued to visit him weekly and to monitor his symptoms.

Reflecting on death

In mid-April, I interviewed Martin in his home, a two-bedroom apartment in a working-class neighborhood. As he opened the door to welcome me, he looked thin and tired but had a big smile for me. Their dwelling was very simply furnished. It reminded me of a student's apartment; all the furniture looked second-hand. There were framed photographs of mountains, scenes from India and Nepal with family, and friends. In family photographs from three years ago Martin appeared fit and muscular, very different from the frail man in the reclining chair next to me now.

Martin was at home alone during the day, except for two days per week when his daughter Caroline was home. Toward the end of the interview, his children came in from school. They greeted their father and me warmly, and then went to play quietly in an adjacent room. Martin spoke with me for three hours on this occasion, eager to discuss his travels and his illness. He was still refusing morphine, preferring to take hot baths and deal with the pain mentally.

Martin had many feelings and ideas about death and dying that he was eager to share with me. Words flowed out of him.

It's not serious being sick. I have been meditating on death since I was 15 years old. And I saw a lot of death, in the revolutions, the social upheavals. All my life has been a series of adventures into the unknown. I never retreated, I went forward because I wanted to get to know the unknown. There is nothing worse than dying ignorant! Not to know that there are beautiful things at our doorstep, and not touching them, examining them, observing them, or at least tasting them! But I led a good life. Maybe I abused my body because I lived too intensely. But I saw that we were about to contaminate our planet, and I wanted to see things before they got polluted. I had the chance to see that. So I can't complain.

I don't have 100% proof that there is a life after this one, but I've had several experiences, like that in the hospital with my pain, and after the brain surgery, where I spent five days in my subconscious. That was the ultimate! But I can't discuss this with people because it's not something that is valued in our society. And it's a shame, because that's where we find the joy in living, the realization of one's self. And it's hard to grasp. As we approach it, it moves away a bit. But we get a taste and that makes us accept death. And I've accepted death for a long time, because otherwise I wouldn't have gone to those countries where I saw all sorts of things and risked my life.

We have to teach and learn about death in our society, not from a negative point of view, but constructively, because to see death negatively is to strip it of all its value. There are countries where death is nothing serious. When we watch a funeral in Bhutan, or we see the infant mortality in some parts of India—they see death every day. They're not afraid of it. But here, as soon as we talk about death, well, no, death doesn't exist. "Come on! Is my car still in the parking lot? Good, OK." *That's* important. But death, that's *not* important. And what makes me feel sorry for [people here] is that they allow death to take them by surprise. If they were ready to face death, they would assume the task of dying without destroying the life of others. Because there are those who destroy others in their dying, with their agony, their perceptions, their views and by what they say.

Because death is beautiful also. I had a taste of it at the time of the boating accident. . . . I'm not afraid of death. I don't run after it, but I am blooming, flowering, I have realized myself. And I know one thing: you also have to trust in death. I know it's going to come. What's difficult, though, is when we suffer, before. Dying, apart from the emotional problem of leaving others and seeing them suffer, is nothing. It's the suffering of others that concerns me more than my own—my wife, children, brother, sisters. I worry about my children's future and what kind of world they will live in.

Coping with physical symptoms

Two weeks later I saw Martin again at his home. He seemed peaceful, accepting, as before. Alexandra was at work. She had a lot to deal with: she had to work full-time, wanted to find an apartment in a more convenient location, and had to deal with all the usual family concerns in addition to Martin's illness. When I arrived, Martin was making arrangements with her over the phone about putting supper on.

He spoke more about his physical symptoms and how he coped with his illness on a daily basis. We discussed his pain, which he said had become more severe over the past two weeks. He had tried every means he could to control it, but the pain in his chest and flank was getting worse. He had finally agreed to take long-acting morphine, and was now on 45 mg taken twice daily. He said it helped a lot, and explained how he had been in pain for two years since his surgery. In the past week, since he had started to take morphine, he was pain-free for the first time.

Martin did not like to complain, and he didn't like it when other people complained. He had not talked to me about the pain he was having when I saw him the first time. But now he was getting to know me a bit better and he was more open about his symptoms. In this interview, Martin did not mention using mental techniques to control his pain. I suspected that his morphine requirements might have been a lot higher if he had not adopted such techniques.

In spite of his improved appetite, he only felt like having milk, milkshakes, and cookies. Since his stomach surgery he tolerated snacks better than meals, and he had a significant problem with reflux. He had to take frequent naps, even though he was sleeping 12 hours per night. He tried to make himself useful with the little energy that he had. After he got the children off to school he would watch TV, listen to music, or meditate. He was unable to read more than a page at a time because of the double vision. Otherwise he seemed to adapt well to his vision impairment and he didn't complain about it. He wondered if the shark cartilage had started working. "The man said it would take three or four months to work," he said. "Or perhaps I feel better because of the morphine."

Martin spoke with friends on the telephone, but he was becoming more selective about his company: "I find that I can't tolerate foolishness, if someone says something stupid, illogical. . . . If I meet someone who's really zero, zero, zero across the board—well then, I'd rather not be there! I used to have a lot of time for that, but now I don't." Martin wanted to spend time either alone, with his family, or with people "of substance," which to him meant people who shared his humanistic concerns.

Preparing the family

Martin focused a lot of his mental energy and attention on preparing his family for his death. As he put it to me:

> Inside, I'm at peace. Alexandra is also doing well with this. We have informed everyone. So that's a lot that's already done. It feels like a hurricane has just gone by. Because to make the whole family aware and not to hurt them, and to comfort them in all this—it takes time. No one has died in my immediate family. So, for them, it's something new. We have to consider that. I've tried to help them, with all the precious advice I've been given [by palliative care], and all the information I've been able to pick up, here and there, to try to make them see the positive side of things.

Only Alexandra, and perhaps Diane, knew how the illness was affecting him: his pain, his lack of appetite, his lack of energy, his sadness. Alexandra reported:

> We have been in another phase since January. Before that we thought there was some hope. I tried always to show my hopeful side, to hide my tears from Martin. But after January it became clear that he was in the terminal phase. We decided to share our feelings, to cry together. So after that, I didn't hold back the tears.

In May, Martin started to spend weekends at his parents' house. Although Mrs. Roy, being in her early seventies, was fit for her age and wanted to find the time and energy to look after Martin's needs, she felt physically and emotionally overwhelmed. She was upset with how fast Martin's illness was progressing. She was also concerned about her husband's reactions and how her other children would deal with the situation. Martin was concerned about her:

> [Being here] gives me a chance to prepare my mother. She is having trouble. She has to realize that this is reality and that we have to accept what destiny presents. My mother is a good person but she's not very spiritual. She doesn't accept human limitations. She is trying to fight this. My mother has already lost her parents, brothers, and sister. Nevertheless, she is suffering with this. Perhaps it's more difficult because I'm her son. She has had six children, so you'd think it would make it easier, but perhaps it doesn't.

Coming into the Palliative Care Unit

By early June, Martin was feeling so weak that he stayed in bed all day. He started to have more vomiting and abdominal pain. Alexandra could not look after him anymore because she still needed to work. Martin therefore moved into his parents' house full-time, but after a few days his parents realized that they could not cope with the situation either. Therefore, in spite of Martin's desire to die at home, he came into the Palliative Care Unit on June 9. Alexandra felt guilty about this, but they had no choice.

Alexandra came to the hospital to visit every evening after work while Martin's brother and sister-in-law looked after the children. Justin and Caroline came to see their father every other day. Diane visited several times per week and would stay for several hours. She would take her brother out into the hospital gardens to enjoy the summer sun, where they would sit, chatting together, for long periods of time.

Alexandra shared Martin's view that one had to enjoy the present. "How does it help to be sad?," she would say. "Why be dead before you're dead? We want to live in the present, to make the present pleasant. We're not sad now. In January perhaps, we went through a phase where we would cry together. But we don't cry now. Martin and I have seen the world together. It has been a spiritual experience for us. We share the same spiritual views. That has helped us deal with this. Even when he is very ill I tell him, 'I find you beautiful.'"

Mrs. Roy, on the other hand, found it difficult to accept that her son had entered the final stage of his illness. She said to me, "The first time I went to the hospital to see him, he said, 'Now I'm all organized.' He had his funeral organized. He wanted his brother Simon to sign his advance directives. He was very clear about what he wanted for the funeral, all the details. We didn't expect this—we had to leave the room—we couldn't take it."

"That man is euphoric"

Within a few days Martin's pain and vomiting were controlled by moderately increasing the dose of oral morphine and anti-emetics. He continued to show good spirits. The head nurse, who observed Martin when he was admitted to the unit and the first interactions he had with the staff, said to me, "There's something not right about that man. He's too light. That man is euphoric." Dr. Lawrence's reaction was, "That's OK. I think it's better to be a bit euphoric."

Both the head nurse and Dr. Lawrence were very experienced in palliative care, so I had to take their assessment seriously. But the possibility that Martin may have been euphoric was not something that had crossed my mind in the many meetings that I had had with him over the previous three months. I had formed the impression that he was a man who felt things deeply. I found the ward staff's label of "euphoria" surprising, and was taken aback. Had I missed something? Was I too close to the situation to see that Martin's reactions were unusual, and perhaps abnormal? My doubts grew when I read some of the other staff's notations in the chart. The occupational therapist, for example, wrote: "The patient is euphoric, extremely positive (over-positive). Seems to push himself too much and does not respect his limits." Nurses' notes read: "Lots of hopes and wishes. . . . Smiling and engaging everyone in conversation. . . . Very nice man. Smiling, joking and socializing with staff. Spirit very good and +++ high."

I observed myself as researcher slipping into the institutional mode, and taking the opinions of fellow caregivers more seriously than the data that Martin was presenting to me. I subsequently alternated between the two points of view—seeing Martin as a remarkable man, or looking for pathology in him— and was never able to integrate the two viewpoints in my mind.

I was not alone in alternating between admiration and doubt. Dr. Lawrence recalled that the main question Alexandra had for him was, "Should the children come after the death to see the body?" "It's amazing," he continued. "You meet them together or alone, and there is that serenity, that feeling of completion. And at first I had trouble assessing whether this was a pathological reaction. But now I've come to the conclusion that, although I don't understand it totally and we're not used to that, I see both of them coping the same way— very nicely, very peacefully. . . . It's a spiritual process, not religious, but a spiritual process. It's almost a rebirth. . . . It's a question of surrendering. She has that sense of completion as well, in her life with him. Not that she's tired of it, but when I asked her, she said, 'He was given to me and now he's needed elsewhere.'"

Alexandra explained her sense of completion to me by saying that she and Martin had asked a lot of questions at the time of the diagnosis. "But now we don't need to know anything, so we're not asking many questions. Martin and I are talking to each other." Alexandra found Dr. Lawrence's advice (about having the children view the body) very helpful. "Dr. Lawrence said that we shouldn't leave a doubt in their minds about the reality of the death. I found this logical and sensible."

The staff and I (in my researcher role) were deeply impressed by this couple's attitudes. And yet, Dr. Lawrence spoke for all of us when he commented:

> I'm careful, because you know, you don't have so much light without shadow. With Mr. Roy there is not much shadow presently. Then, you're always saying, well maybe if it's totally repressed, what will happen when he stops being able to repress? Because at one point, and that is my experience, there's a period when the filter between your unconscious and conscious becomes more and more porous. And then the shadow becomes more evident and then sometimes it can be quite ugly. I've seen that in "saintly" individuals. They were the best mothers and the best fathers and then they become quite difficult during the last few days. And, for those who remain, it's very difficult. So I feel much better when I see both sides.

I also had this feeling about Martin. I was looking for evidence of fear or doubt in him that would make him seem "whole" in my eyes.

A video for the children

The unit provided video equipment for patients to use, so in mid-June, Martin made a video for his children, to leave for them after his death. He set up the camera in his hospital room, enabling him to address the children privately. When I went to see him one afternoon, he was reviewing his video, so we watched it together. In the video, Martin is lying in his hospital bed, speaking directly into the camera and addressing his children, unscripted:

> The body is the prison of the soul. What will happen is that Daddy will become an angel. But stay strong. I hope that you will accept my departure with a bit of wisdom. Look after each other, and your mother, too. You know that Alexandra, your mother, is eternal love. She loves you as Daddy does.
>
> Daddy is proud of the two of you (crying). I could say that you saved my life. Eight years ago, there wasn't much in Daddy's life, and then big Justin came along. I remember your first steps, and Caroline, who jumped in the swimming pool.
>
> You will create your happiness by doing the things that impassion you. The important thing is to have pleasure in the realization of your being. What you do, do it well, for the good. In the final count, one must love continuously. In life, it's important to be able to get close to others. The friendships that we create, outside of blood ties, are important. We need to love and help our friends unconditionally. We shouldn't attach ourselves to material things; suffering comes from possession.
>
> Don't be afraid to take risks, calculated risks. We are in a difficult era in the world, socially, economically. You'll need to read a lot, find out, equip yourselves. Carry a book with you and read whenever you can. Don't waste your time in life. Protect life on the planet.
>
> Death isn't something frightening, in itself. I have taken many risks in my life, I had many adventures, some of which made me afraid. I've had close brushes with death. God is generous and gives us a lot of chances. I should have been dead a long time ago, but God let me live a bit longer so that I could prepare you. Eternal life exists. Daddy still exists in the message of love on this video.
>
> I will wait for you in God's kingdom, and I imagine that it will be restful, peaceful. I'm sure that it will be beautiful in paradise. Not that it's not beautiful on earth—the blue sky, the clouds that we see when we fly—they enrich our soul and bring us closer to God, and eliminate our fear. Justin, Caroline, your dad will surely be sad to leave you (cries) but while we were together, you gave me pleasure and happiness. You are like two jewels. You have creative beings within you. Let your imaginations loose and create, no matter how small or large. I am confident that you will succeed in life.

Toward the end of June, Martin began to have more epigastric pain and gastric reflux, and he developed a cough. The pills left a bad taste in his mouth because of the reflux, which he found unbearable. Feeling that he was at the end of his rope, he told the nurses that he was uncomfortable and he wished it were all over. "You have to do something," he said. In an attempt to achieve better symptom control, the physician stopped the oral medication and ordered subcutaneous medication through a special pump (syringe driver). Martin received morphine 70 mg and metoclopramide 30 mg subcutaneously over 24 hours. The chest X-ray showed increasing metastatic lung disease, but no pneumonia. He was put on an oral antibiotic for bronchitis and on famotidine to reduce stomach acid secretion and help his epigastric pain.

Over the next couple of days all his symptoms improved, and Martin's morphine requirements remained stable throughout the rest of his admission. The staff noted, however, that he appeared increasingly tired, thinner, and sadder. He expressed the need for more privacy. He was quiet and more withdrawn. He rested with eyes closed most of the time. He expressed some anxiety over his wife and children moving to a different apartment on July 1. He hoped that they would be able to manage on their own.

After their move, Martin began to go home for four days every week, maintaining his medication schedule with the syringe driver. He wanted to be with his children as much as possible, and Justin and Caroline seemed more settled now that they saw more of their father. At the end of every visit he would hold the children and cry.

On the ward, he looked happier. He expressed no concerns to the nurses and continued to be pleasant and agreeable. I visited Martin when he returned from his first weekend at home. He was lying in bed, and seemed his usual cheerful self again. He offered me some of his Swiss chocolates. "You can't just have one," he said. "You have to make it a total experience. Have several."

Alexandra continued to visit every evening during the week, and his children visited every other day, even though the hospital was one hour away from their home. Martin insisted on Alexandra's company every day, which was not easy for her. She commented to me:

> It's almost selfish of him. I have to keep the family together and work and look after the children, to keep everything together and he just thinks of his own needs. When I arrive at the hospital through the traffic I have to take a big breath to calm myself before I can talk to him. He lives in a different relaxed space and he doesn't need to think of my troubles. I have to make the transition in order to see him and relate to him, from my busy practical world to his world. But once I move into his world it's like being in a sanctuary. I forget everything, all the stresses.

When is death going to come?

By the end of July Martin looked weaker but he was still cheerful, calm, uncomplaining, and outgoing. He would joke about his illness, "I'm not fat, am I?," and seemed to want to enjoy every moment. "Until you die, you must appreciate life. You can't just think about death," he would say. The syringe driver had improved his symptoms considerably. He had no pain or nausea. Whenever he could, he would slowly wheel himself out to the hospital gardens where he enjoyed the trees, flowers, and birds. Often, his sister Diane would be there with him. They had a deep connection with each other that they could share in the silence. His other brothers and sisters felt less comfortable visiting. They would ask Diane, "What do the two of you find to talk about?" They couldn't understand it. Martin confided in Diane as much as he did with Alexandra. He was always thrilled to see either of them, and he never wanted them to leave. Martin's mother, on the other hand, could not bring herself to visit him in the hospital. She found it too upsetting.

Dying was taking a long time. Martin had thought he would die within a few weeks of coming to the Palliative Care Unit, and was fed up with waiting. "Let it come," he would say. "Let's get it over with." He was now experiencing a combination of fear, boredom, and despondency. He felt guilty because he was taking up a bed that someone else might need.

By early August, he showed signs of increasing anxiety. He started to take up smoking again, which he had quit following his stomach surgery two years previously. Over the next few weeks this turned into chain smoking. The staff expressed concern that, since he was weak, he might set fire to himself and his nylon jacket when he went outside in his wheelchair to smoke. He sometimes smoked while alone in his room, which was against the rules. Occasionally, Dr. Lawrence smelled marijuana in Martin's room and on his breath.

"My time is approaching," Martin said. He had suffered with his stomach for over two years, and he saw death as a liberation. He felt he had no unfinished business. Previously, he had been satisfied with his visits home. Now he complained that there had been too many visitors, too much noise, too much commotion. Also, the trip itself was beginning to drain him. Martin was ready to die.

On September 16, he developed a cough. The chest X-ray was suggestive of mild bilateral pneumonia. In his discussion with Dr. Lawrence, Martin expressed the wish for death to come, and requested comfort care only. He didn't want to get weaker and become a burden to anyone. They agreed not to start antibiotics unless Dr. Lawrence felt that this would help control his symptoms by decreasing lung secretions.

When I saw Martin the next day, he looked extremely weak and spoke very slowly. I wrote in my notes: "He looks like his battery is winding down." He continued to speak, however, of his philosophy of love and friendship. I became desperate to establish deeper contact with him. "Do you ever have any doubts, any fears?" I asked him.

He replied, calmly, "No. Once you see how things are . . . you see how things are. You see that life and death are the same thing. How can we be afraid then?" He was somnolent as he said this. It was frightening to me. He spoke as if he were reciting to himself, as if he were in a trance. I was upset, disappointed. What was I expecting of him? He sounded like he was preaching and that's not what I was looking for! I was looking for more meaningful communication with him. At the very least, I wanted to be able to say to him that our own contacts had been important to me. I wanted to tell him that I thought that he was a remarkable person. But perhaps he was now too ill for us to have that kind of closure.

Death comes

Martin went home as usual for his weekend pass two days later. His brother had to carry him up the three flights of stairs to the apartment, and then went off to pick up a tank of oxygen, which Martin now needed very often. He was out of breath, his cough was getting worse, and he was getting weaker. Alexandra felt that she would not be able to cope with him for the whole weekend, but she knew that he was dying and wanted to remain as calm as possible, for his sake. Neither of them slept. They talked all through the night. Martin needed reassurance that his family would be there when he died, that he would not be abandoned. Alexandra said to him, "Even if you can't do anything physically, we can still talk, we can still relate. You can express your needs. It means a lot to me, to be able to relate." Martin replied, "Me too."

The next morning Dr. Lawrence gave Alexandra instructions over the phone to give Martin some extra morphine, but after 30 minutes he was still very short of breath. Alexandra and Diane realized that they could not keep him comfortable at home, so they convinced Martin that they should call an ambulance and take him back to hospital. Once he made the decision, he seemed at peace with it. Before the ambulance arrived, he asked to see the children. He squeezed their hands and opened his eyes to say good-bye to them. Alexandra went with Martin in the ambulance, and Diane stayed behind with the children. Diane knew that this would be the last time the children would see their father alive. Judging from the look on Martin's face as he looked at his children, he knew it, too.

"I am going to die," Martin announced to me when he arrived on the ward on a stretcher, pushed along by two ambulance men, with Alexandra in tow. He was in great respiratory distress. He was rushed into his room where he improved slightly with oxygen. Alexandra said to him, "Stay calm. We prepared for this. Stay calm and think of yourself, don't think about us."

Dr. Lawrence and the nurse adjusted the oxygen to make Martin as comfortable as possible. Alexandra stood at the bedside, holding Martin's hand and trying to comfort him. I also stood beside him. The whole scene was so peaceful. I had practiced obstetrics for many years, and it felt to me as if Martin and Alexandra had rehearsed for this moment as one rehearses for a birthing. Martin reached out to grasp my fingers and looked at me with acknowledgment and gently shook my fingers in gratitude and farewell. It was such a peaceful look, even though he was cyanosed, congested, and breathing rapidly at a rate of 60 breaths per minute. I was impressed with the generosity that he demonstrated in that last hour. When Dr. Lawrence finished adjusting the oxygen, he told Martin that they would give him an injection to make him more comfortable. He then put his hand on Martin's shoulder and held it there for a few moments.

Martin's parents and brother arrived, and they took turns being in the room with Martin while the palliative care team worked. Dr. Lawrence ordered a small dose of midazolam to try to reduce Martin's awareness of respiratory distress. Alexandra stepped briefly out of the room. She looked tired and dazed. She said, "We were expecting this to happen, but when it does happen, it's still a shock."

Martin died with Alexandra, his parents, his brother, and his nurse John present. He had remained as calm as a person could under the circumstances. Given that normally this can be a most distressing way to die, his was the most peaceful respiratory death out of dozens that I have witnessed. The family contacted Diane, and she arrived a half hour later with the children. Justin and Caroline, guided by Alexandra, spent some moments saying goodbye to their father. The team then organized a brief ritual at Martin's bedside, where everyone congregated and recited a Universal Prayer.

The first year: carrying on with living

At the funeral service, Justin was very protective of his father's body. He said, in an aggressive tone, "No one will bury my father. I will bury him. He's my father. I will take the shovel and bury him." He wanted to help carry their father's coffin after the service, and was allowed to do so. Justin was upset with his mother, because he would have liked to have been there when his father died. Alexandra said afterwards, "I think it might have traumatized him, and it would have been difficult for Martin if Justin had been there. I think it was OK the way it happened." Justin couldn't quite understand what had happened to his father's body after it was cremated. Alexandra decided to keep the ashes in a wardrobe at home until the children were older. Then they could decide what they wanted to do with them.

Two weeks after Martin's death, it was Alexandra and Justin's birthdays. They knew that Martin would have wanted them to celebrate, so they did. In the months that followed, the family did their best to resume a normal life, for Martin's sake. Two months after the death the family seemed to be adapting well. Alexandra commented:

> The fact that the family was there when he died—his mother, father, and brother—that helped a lot. That helped his mother accept. Martin would have been happy with how things went. There was no significant loss of autonomy. Bowel or bladder incontinence would have been unacceptable to him.
>
> During the illness I did not have much time to think. Now I revisit the memories. I'm trying to let go. But I'm functioning OK. Martin and I talked a lot, so we were somewhat prepared. He said, "Be ready. Be ready." But now there's a void. We communicated so well, sometimes without words.

Justin showed some aggressive behavior at school during the first three weeks, but this subsided. His teacher expressed surprise at his maturity. Both children did well in their school work. They spoke about their father often, saying how they missed him. They also felt his presence. Alexandra said, "Last week I was crying and Caroline came up to me and said, 'Mom, why are you crying? Daddy is among us!' Justin often identified with his father. "I want to be a comic, like my father," he would say. And he tried to make people laugh.

Three months after Martin's death, Alexandra and the children took a trip to Nepal "to try to make closure," revisiting their old house and meeting old friends. Alexandra said, "It was a big shock for me, because we had spent most of our married life there. All the memories came back. The children used the time to fill in holes in their memory."

Alexandra considered the first six months to be the worst. She cried often. Then she noticed a shift. Things started to improve as the warm weather came. She went out as often as possible with the children; they would enjoy the outdoors, for Martin's sake. Alexandra also began to feel Martin's presence more. She continued to have this sense of Martin's presence well into her second year of bereavement.

"First there was a void," she told me. "A part of me was gone. We were together 17 years—that's half of my life. I felt like something was torn inside me. Then I started to sense Martin talking to me. Now we have conversations. Whatever I am doing, I hear him making comments. We knew each other so well. I know what he would say. It's as if he's with me all the time now, and I feel less sad. I hear him talking. Maybe it's my imagination, but does it matter? The void is gone." She smiled. "And I feel him alive within me. Whenever I see something beautiful—the sky, the clouds—I think of him. Because we experienced a lot of beauty together."

It was not until one year after the death that Alexandra could bring herself to view the video that Martin had left for the children. She decided to wait until the children were older before showing it to them, so they would understand better what their father was saying to them.

Six months after Martin's death I visited his parents in their home. They had plenty of time for me and spoke very freely about their son, so that I had trouble getting away even after two and a half hours. They told me how Martin's death had brought his brothers and sisters closer. Mrs. Roy's brother Robert had also died in the meantime, three months after Martin's death. Mr. and Mrs. Roy experienced Robert's death as a release, whereas the loss of Martin was exquisitely painful. Mr. Roy said, "It was worse when we found out the diagnosis. The end was not too bad—he was well looked after."

Mrs. Roy said, "It made it easier that he didn't suffer. Suffering is the most difficult thing, seeing a loved one suffer." Nevertheless, their pain was now profound. Of all the family members, Mrs. Roy seemed to be the most affected by Martin's death. She explained:

> When you lose a child, you feel like you're missing something, a part of your body. I hope that time makes it better. But it's getting better. At first, when he was dying, I was thinking of him the whole time. Now in my mind, I often see the image of him being ill. I dreamed about him for the first time last week. He was ill and then he died. I was so glad to have that dream. I cried.

She began to cry. Mr. Roy said softly, "My wife cries a lot."

"Martin wouldn't have liked that," Mrs. Roy said, drying her tears.

Mr. Roy agreed. "He hid his emotions. You know that."

"But he cried when he spoke of his children," Mrs. Roy remembered.

Mr. Roy had tears in his eyes. "It's not easy to lose a child. I hadn't planned this—that he would leave before me."

14

Richard Johnson
"Do Not Go Gentle Into That Good Night"

Narrated by ANNA TOWERS

Many people, especially those who are relatively young, opt to fight their cancer to the end. At first, Richard Johnson refused chemotherapy. But when his disease became far advanced, he asked for aggressive treatments. Although Mr. Johnson understood that his chemotherapy was a purely experimental treatment, he nonetheless hoped that his life would be prolonged. It made him feel safe to be on a medical ward where he thought that he might get aggressive biomedical interventions for as long as possible.

Both Mr. Johnson and his wife wanted to be totally involved with the decision making concerning his illness, down to the last detail. Yet Mr. Johnson did not involve his wife in some of the crucial choices he made. Mrs. Johnson disagreed with his aggressive approach at the end when she saw him get sicker and realized that he was dying. Mr. Johnson died a conflicted death, and the course of his wife's and son's bereavement reflected this.

Refusing chemotherapy, at first

Mr. Johnson was a 51-year-old engineer who had advanced carcinoma of the prostate when we met him as part of our project. Even when ill, he was a handsome man, who looked younger than he was. He was a gracious man who communicated in an intense way, making good eye contact, articulating his words carefully. However, there seemed to be two sides to Mr. Johnson. On the one hand, he seemed wise, spiritual, and accepting of his situation, and was able to surrender to life events and learn from them. He could be warm and relate cordially with others. "I feel supported and loved by the people around me," he said to me soon after I met him. "I'm very lucky. That's what's important. Family and friends. I have a good little family. I see people who are collecting toys [instead of focusing on true values]. I have a brother-in-law like that. He's a doctor in the States. He wants a Porsche. I used to be like that. But now, even though I don't have my health, I feel that I have everything I need. I'm a rich man."

On the other hand, he had the determination to control and fight, needing things to be perfect. He did not like to take medication, especially tranquilizers and analgesics, because he was afraid of losing control. Dr. Allan, his palliative care physician, described to me how both Mr. Johnson and his wife Linda kept note pads on which they wrote down everything he said—every observation, every prediction, and every dose of medication that Mr. Johnson received.

Mrs. Johnson described her husband as a nervous man. He had a history of manic-depressive illness, experiencing his first episode at age 36. He had required lithium and a tricyclic antidepressant for many years. In his words, the depression arose "from a series of very difficult events." When he was 31, his mother died of cancer on the palliative care ward of the same hospital in which he was now a cancer patient. Mr. Johnson seemed to have unresolved feelings about that event. His tendency toward depression and his generalized anxiety were documented regularly in the hospital chart, which dated back 15 years.

Mr. Johnson had never really found a direction in his professional life. He didn't care much about his engineering work, which he found very stressful, nor did he enjoy working for others. He had tried to change careers and started a full-time business of his own that did not work out. Nevertheless, Mrs. Johnson seemed proud of her husband's achievements. One advantage of the five-year period when he worked from home was that he became very close to his son Simon, who was now 12 years old.

Mr. Johnson was raised a Roman Catholic and went to church every Sunday with Simon. Although his wife was Anglican she went to church with them occasionally. Mr. Johnson had a deeply spiritual view of the world, and claimed that his faith helped him throughout his illness.

Mrs. Johnson, a bright, beautiful 38-year-old woman of English origin who worked as an assistant manager in a bank, was a capable individual who liked to be well informed. She had been married to Mr. Johnson for 16 years. Simon, a well-spoken, handsome boy, went to a private high school and was a good student. He was quiet, a loner, and, according to his mother, had always been that way.

Mr. Johnson was diagnosed with adenocarcinoma of the prostate in the summer of 1994. He had consulted his doctors, complaining of genital pain, and was diagnosed within a month. Two weeks later, scared and angry, he was recovering from a radical prostatectomy. After the surgery, Mr. Johnson's father, who lived in the same city, came to see him, even though they had a history of rarely seeing each other. They had not been close, and they could not talk now; the distance between them increased as Mr. Johnson's illness progressed. Mr. Johnson was not close to his three brothers or sister, either. During Mr. Johnson's terminal illness, his wife was the only family member who was there to support him.

At the time of the surgery the tumor had spread to the lymphatic system. Although the urologist suggested chemotherapy, Mr. Johnson chose to undergo hormonal treatment. He had witnessed his mother dying of chemotherapy-related toxicity on the Palliative Care Unit 20 years ago. He made this decision himself, without involving his wife, who thought the tumor had been removed completely at the time of surgery and that her husband was cured. This discrepancy exemplified an issue that persisted throughout Mr. Johnson's illness: his wife felt left out. In his mind, Mr. Johnson was trying to protect her. He was often confused, however, as to what he should do, and then didn't know how to speak with his wife.

In January 1996, Mr. Johnson developed pneumonia and was readmitted to the hospital. He was found to have liver metastases and recurrent tumor in the pelvis. The oncologist offered him experimental chemotherapy. Again, Mr. Johnson refused, and again, neither he nor his physicians involved Mrs. Johnson in the decision.

She was trying to get information on her own. She would be on the Internet for hours looking at cancer research, searching for alternative treatments. "But by January," she told me, "it was too late." She resented the fact that she had been kept out of the decision-making process. The doctors had asked her to leave her husband's bedside when they had discussions with him. "Sometimes doctors seem to treat people like they're stupid," she commented. "But doctors have to realize that people have access to treatment information. They read up about it. And doctors should talk to family members because patients will only hear what they want to hear and sometimes the messages don't get through."

The oncologist, Dr. Logan, was a sensitive and mild-mannered man who was ordinarily regarded as having excellent communication with his patients. But he found Mr. Johnson to be a challenge. Mr. Johnson had strong feelings about how he should be treated, and sometimes these feelings seemed to prevent him from hearing the information that was being presented to him. Two days after Dr. Logan had presented the option of experimental chemotherapy, he went back to see Mr. Johnson in his hospital room. Mrs. Johnson was not present. What Dr. Logan had intended to be an exchange of information and a therapeutic encounter turned into a tirade by Mr. Johnson about how oncologists were "just out to poison people." After this meeting Dr. Logan put a note in the chart that expressed (for him) unusual frustration with his patient:

> I have spent more than 30 minutes with Mr. Johnson. He swore at me and accused me of entertaining an "infantile approach" with him. Mr. Johnson is very upset because he thinks that I plan to use chemo. My reply to him was that this was a misunderstanding. There will be no chemo. He can read my consult [to this effect] in his file ad libitum.

From my observations, Mr. Johnson, who had trained as an engineer and could be a logical, reasonable man, had moments when his feelings would overtake him. He had trouble understanding his feelings, which was part of the reason he did not talk to his wife about them, though he did occasionally express his feelings to the nurses. During this admission, for example, he was in a four-bed room. One of his roommates was dying. "The family are keeping a death watch," Mr. Johnson said to the nurse, "I don't like it."

Mr. Johnson opted to receive more hormonal treatments. In the meantime, his tumors were growing rapidly. He started to experience abdominal and leg pains due to sciatic nerve involvement from a new tumor mass in the pelvic wall. He was given carbamazepine, which helped relieve the pain, though the nurse noted that Mr. Johnson often refused analgesia even if he was in pain. He was afraid to take morphine, especially if it was given by injection. He needed to have all medication and dosage changes discussed with him first.

Toward the end of January, Mr. Johnson went home for a weekend pass. He spoke to Simon about his cancer, for the first time. On his return to hospital, he asked for psychological support for himself and his family. The nurse gave him the name of the cancer support volunteer agency, which he phoned to obtain a referral for therapy that involved visualization techniques. A psychologist at a sister institution taught him this method, which Mr. Johnson subsequently used to try and control his pain.

About turn

In May 1996, Mr. Johnson was found to have widespread bone metastases and his liver tumors were growing. He complained of fatigue, increasing pain in his right upper abdomen, and right shoulder. All of this was because of his huge liver, most of which was now involved with tumor.

Mrs. Johnson pleaded with him to get another opinion regarding possible treatments. Mr. Johnson was not keen to have treatment, but he did go along with her to see a specialist in a cancer institute in another province. The specialist told him about some experimental treatments that were available. On hearing this, Mr. Johnson decided that he was not ready to die. He had been against "poisons" of all sorts and preferred vitamins and meditation. He had thought for sure that the hormonal treatment would work. Now he saw that he was in trouble and he changed his mind, asking for the experimental chemotherapy. He wondered whether he should have had chemotherapy sooner. Linda wondered if she should have pushed her husband to have the chemotherapy before this.

Upon returning to Montreal, the Johnsons found another oncologist, Dr. Peters, who agreed to give him the experimental treatments. Mr. Johnson had many concerns about the treatments, especially whether they would severely compromise the quality of his remaining life. "Don't take a good day of my life and turn it into a bad day with your treatment," he admonished Dr. Peters. "If I would live one month and your drug makes me live two months but the second month is poor quality, then don't do it."

"No, the odds are better than that," Dr. Peters replied.

Mr. Johnson was admitted to the oncology ward to receive the experimental chemotherapy. For pain from his enlarged liver and neuropathic-type pain in his right leg he received the following medication: 4 mg hydromorphone orally every six hours, 400 mg carbamazepine orally three times daily, and 25 mg amitriptyline at bedtime. But the pain was not well controlled. Mr. Johnson preferred to put up with pain rather than take an opioid dose that would produce mental clouding and make him feel he was losing control.

Meanwhile, Palliative Care was consulted for pain control. When Dr. Allan came to see Mr. Johnson on the oncology ward he noted that Mr. Johnson was very drowsy from the hydromorphone. He switched him to morphine elixir to "facilitate fine-tuning." Mr. Johnson was also receiving steroids, 30 mg prednisone by mouth daily, which was not only part of the chemotherapy protocol but was also to alleviate his liver pain.

Mrs. Johnson took a leave of absence from her work and spent a large part of every day at her husband's side. She dutifully recorded the medication orders and every drug dose that he received in her notebook, which came to serve as a diary of her husband's condition. Some of Mr. Johnson's physicians had difficulty with this. "At first," Mrs. Johnson recalled to me, "the doctors asked me to leave the room while they did their rounds. And then they realized that I have a few brains so they started to give me information and asked me what I thought. The junior doctor especially didn't understand why I had so many questions about the blood tests and everything that was happening to my Richard."

After two weeks, Mr. Johnson was discharged home. By the end of June, he began to feel worse. He took to his bed and could not eat solid food. He became more somnolent and had tremors and mild confusion. The physicians felt that this was due to his deteriorating liver function. He was started on 30 ml lactulose by mouth three times daily. Within 2 days he seemed more alert, and the oncologist resumed the experimental chemotherapy.

By July 4, however, Mr. Johnson had not eaten anything in three days because of nausea and vomiting and was readmitted to the medical ward. He had lost 14 pounds in one month, was confused, and showed signs of hepatic encephalopathy. He complained of increasing back pain, abdominal distension, and pain in his right leg, both of which were swollen. The physicians thought that he might have an infection, so they started intravenous antibiotics. Dr. Peters noted in the record:

> He is obviously very ill and he knows it. He feels that all his systems are shutting down. I agree that he should be a "no code." However, if he was to improve a bit, I would like to restart his experimental drug, perhaps by the weekend. This admission, and the deterioration, are due to his cancer, not the [experimental] drug. I would ask Palliative Care to see him with a goal of putting him on as little medication as possible.

The medical goal at this time was to try to improve Mr. Johnson's functional state by readjusting any medication that might be making him somnolent, with a view to continuing the experimental treatment. Dr. Peters also wanted Palliative Care to get to know him and the family to facilitate transfer to the Palliative Care Unit when the time was appropriate.

Mr. Johnson still experienced mild pain in his abdomen. He was on small doses of morphine for this (3 mg subcutaneously every 4 hr), and he continued on carbamazepine for his leg pain. He refused to take breakthrough doses of morphine. Dr. Allan suggested boosting the steroids, then tapering, as this would help minimize the amount of morphine required. Dr. Allan noted that Mr. Johnson did not want to be sedated.

Do-not-resuscitate (DNR) orders, which were discussed with Mr. Johnson but not with his wife, were written. When Mrs. Johnson saw the "no code" in the chart she asked her husband about it. He replied, "Yes, I told them and don't you change it because I'll never forgive you," admonishing her like this several times.

"How long do we carry on with this?"

The oncologist resumed the experimental treatment on July 6. Now, however, Mrs. Johnson wanted it to be stopped. She would follow Dr. Allan into the corridor after many of his visits to her husband. Wiping away tears, she would ask, "How long do we carry on with this?" She looked exhausted, and Dr. Allan appreciated how hard it was for her to watch her husband, who he knew was dying. Still, he would usually answer her by saying something like "we have to meet him where he is. As long as he wants drugs, I'm not going to tell him to quit. Not because I believe that drugs are going to help, but because I believe

that's what he wants." Mr. Johnson was not unique in his attitude. In our ter-
tiary care institution, we often encounter patients with advanced cancer who
desperately cling to experimental therapies that offer little chance of producing
remission of the disease.

Mr. Johnson's physical condition seemed to fluctuate dramatically from one
day to the next. But over the next few days, Mr. Johnson felt better—his appetite improved and he became more alert. He began to organize his affairs,
preparing his will and discussing plans and finances with his wife. But then his
appetite got worse again. When Dr. Allan went to see him this time, he was
lying in his bed, his head in the pillow, crying silently. Dr. Allan sat with him.

"I feel so discouraged," Mr. Johnson said, "and so useless. My appetite is
gone. When I tell my wife about it, she's upset that I'm not eating more. What
am I supposed to do?" Then after a while he said, "What if the pain in my leg
gets worse?"

Dr. Allan tried to reassure him. "You know I will continue to do my very
best to make sure that you get the right medications that will keep you
comfortable."

"I'm sorry," Mr. Johnson said, holding back his tears. "I think I just haven't
had enough sleep."

Dr. Allan recognized Mr. Johnson's despair, and continued to sit quietly with
him. He knew that Mr. Johnson had fears about dying and that he was concerned about his son.

"How's Simon doing?" he asked.

"Oh, he's OK"—the reply that Dr. Allan always heard when he asked after
Mr. Johnson's son.

Simon was waiting for the day when his dad would return home. Although
aware of his father's illness, he did not seem to realize its extent or seriousness.
Simon found the change in his routine to be difficult. Mrs. Johnson's parents
looked after him, but Simon missed his own parents. The social worker
arranged a counseling session with Simon and continued to see Mr. and Mrs.
Johnson regularly. Other members of the family visited Mr. Johnson infre-
quently, and his brothers and sisters didn't visit him at all. Mrs. Johnson said
that they were afraid of hospitals after what had happened to their mother.

When Dr. Allan saw Mrs. Johnson later that day, she pleaded with him again:
"Do you think that we should stop the chemotherapy treatment? Richard is
dying." The staff often saw Mrs. Johnson in the family lounge, by herself, crying. But she tried to control herself in the presence of her husband and her
son.

By this time I was seeing Mr. Johnson regularly as part of our project. I visited him in his room on the medical ward. He lay in his bed, dressed in the
standard blue hospital gown, too weak to sit up. He was friendly and alert, but
his cheeks were sunken. He seemed to be relating well to the other patients in

the room; as I walked in, he was trying to support and encourage the man in the bed opposite him.

He spoke with me openly and at length about his life and his values. Even though this was only our second encounter, he spoke about very intimate things:

> Maybe the chemotherapy is working because I feel better this week. I have a great oncologist. He and Dr. Allan—they are doing everything possible. Last week I thought I was dying. But I'm ready to die. I have a lot of faith. I keep saying, "God, if you want to take me, I'm ready." I didn't used to be this way. Five years ago I was ready to leave my wife. You know, you get married, you go through the honeymoon that could last a few weeks to a couple of years, then children come and it gets hard. It's not so much fun any more. I wanted things to be perfect and they weren't perfect, so I wanted to leave. Not that there was another woman. But then something happened to me. I decided to stay. I committed myself, and I began to see things in a different light. I matured. It was a gradual thing, but I realized that my priorities had changed. I know men who get involved in serial marriages, and they don't have solid relationships. There's nothing solid there.

Mr. Johnson spontaneously discussed with me the effect of the treatment on his sexuality. "This room is quite noisy so I wouldn't mind moving into a single room," he said. "The men around me are very ill, but you know they dream at night, and they have very hot dreams. I know because I can hear them talking in their sleep. You know, I had a chemical castration in March and since then I haven't had such feelings."

"That must have been difficult for you," I said.

"You know, I don't miss it," he replied. "It's good not to be a slave of those feelings."

Although this view surprised me, I noted that he did not seem sad or upset.

More physical problems

The experimental chemotherapy continued. By mid-July, Mr. Johnson had developed clinical signs of ascites and increased leg swelling, which was thought to be related to his low albumin. He also continued to have abdominal pain. Although there were days when he felt a bit better, the residents felt that this might be the time to ask for a transfer to the Palliative Care Unit. Mr. Johnson was now so weak that he spent all his time in bed. Nonetheless, he continued to ask that the chemotherapy be continued.

I went to see him again and found him asleep. He now spent a lot of his time sleeping. Linda was seated at his bedside, reading. We went to find a quiet room, and she was tearful as she spoke to me. "I'm all right as long as I don't talk about it," she said. "It's hard for our son. He and his father have been so close. For a large part of when he was growing up his dad was working from home, so they saw a lot of each other. Yesterday Simon said, 'Is Daddy coming home soon?' I couldn't let him know how sick he is. He is used to his dad being in and out of hospital, so I don't think that he realizes that his father is near the end."

Linda paused and then continued, "Richard wants to have this experimental treatment. That's how he is. He wants to keep on pushing. And I don't know what to say to him. I don't know if Richard wants me around as much as I am. Yesterday I left the hospital early so he would have a break from me."

"He told me that he really appreciates your being here," I said to her. Instead of relief at this remark, however, Linda looked distressed, anxious, and confused. It seemed that for all their closeness, she and Richard had trouble sharing negative feelings with each other, particularly being sad together.

Over the next few days, Mr. Johnson appeared to be doing better again, his abdominal pain now well controlled. He got out of bed, moving about his room with his walker. He asked that the morphine dosing time be adjusted to decrease sleepiness during meal times—perhaps he would then feel like eating more. He became anxious about developing bedsores, wanting everything done to prevent him from getting bedsores. According to the nurse, there had never been any signs of bedsores appearing.

A few days later, Mr. Johnson developed shortness of breath, a symptom that is particularly frightening for patients. The resident told Mr. Johnson that his shortness of breath could be from his lung metastases or he could have "water on the lung." The scan for pulmonary emboli was negative, so the resident offered to treat him with diuretics. That evening Mr. Johnson was anxious and frightened that a tumor could be starting to compress his lungs. But the shortness of breath responded to diuresis, so the physicians concluded that he had developed pulmonary edema. Throughout these episodes Linda continued to ask the doctors many questions. Why was the albumin in his blood low? Why had he developed pulmonary edema? As she explained to me, "This keeps my sanity and it's for the control part. It makes me feel like I have some control. It's just to keep it together. It's my way of coping."

Mr. Johnson's breathing was now better, but he was feeling weaker and weaker. Dr. Peters monitored the prostate-specific antigen (PSA) every week to see if the chemotherapy was working. Every week, Mr. Johnson and his wife would wait anxiously for the result. So far, the PSA had been stable, but the oncologist suspected that it was now rising. Mr. Johnson knew that this would mean that the chemotherapy was not working. After a discussion with Dr. Peters, Mr. Johnson agreed that he would transfer to the Palliative Care Unit if the PSA were in fact rising. Dr. Peters also offered him another option. If he was responding to the chemotherapy, Mr. Johnson could still go to the Palliative Care Unit and continue to receive the oral chemotherapeutic agent there.

Perhaps he would be more comfortable with the specialized nursing care on the Palliative Care Unit, and Dr. Allan could supervise his care more closely.

I went in to see Mr. Johnson that evening. His wife had left for the night. He looked very weak and ill, out of breath despite the oxygen mask, and hardly able to speak. He was pondering his options. He was beginning to talk about how sad he was to leave his son, who only came to visit him in the hospital two or three times a week, for a half hour at a time. He said, "I would like to go to PCU, no matter what. The only thing is my mother died there 20 years ago. I remember it was a nice sunny place, but she died there and I still have feelings about that." He paused. "One of the things that bothers me about palliative care is that there is no life there. The nurses are there when you need them but they come in less often because they are single rooms. Here there are four in a room so there is more action, more life." He paused again, then said, "I know I could die tonight or I could die three months from now."

Mr. Johnson was feeling particularly ill the next evening, so Mrs. Johnson decided she would spend the night with him. Because of general bed shortages in the Canadian hospital system, there is often a wait for beds on the Palliative Care Unit, and this was the case now. The nurses brought her a cot so she could sleep beside him. This was the first night that she had spent with him since he was admitted to hospital. She was glad that she stayed, for she could note when he had pain and note his reactions to the morphine. She didn't get much sleep, but she didn't care. The next day, his pain seemed better and Mrs. Johnson went home to sleep. Simon was not very happy to see her. He wouldn't talk to her or let his mother kiss him.

"What's wrong?" she asked him.

"You didn't come home last night."

Mrs. Johnson explained to him that his father was sicker. She did not tell him that he was dying. Simon did not say anything more that night. The next morning at breakfast, he seemed his old self again. "I understand that Daddy needs you now more than I need you," he said.

The life review

Something now changed with Mr. Johnson. On July 25, Mrs. Johnson said, "He had a need to bare his soul, to get everything out of himself." Mr. Johnson had come to trust Dr. Allan and began to speak to him about his life. He spoke for about 40 minutes, longer than he had ever talked before. He talked about everything. "I've done my work," he said at one point. "I never liked engineering. My father pushed me into it and I did it anyway." He talked about guns, planes, and pain. It seemed to Dr. Allan that he just needed to say who he was. Mrs. Johnson had to leave the room because she was crying so much.

He spoke of the things he had liked, armaments and planes, saying at one point, "When you come to think about it, I would get depressed that all these wonderful inventions do one thing, kill human beings." He was philosophical, asking, "Who am I? Who are we as individuals? We're all nobodies. Nobody's big. If you die, you die, and the world goes on." And then, Dr. Allan recalled, Mr. Johnson related to him that when his mother was dying, somebody called him on the phone and told him he should come right away if he wanted to see his mother alive. "I just could not bring myself to her side," Mr. Johnson recalled. "I went over, but I waited outside and drank coffee or whatever, and then she died. I've sort of felt guilty about that all my life." But then he dropped the subject and started to talk about something else. It seemed that this experience was too painful for him to explore any further.

Up until this point, Mr. Johnson had wanted to continue the chemotherapy, but now he did not want it anymore, even though he was afraid he might offend Dr. Peters by telling him that. He respected Dr. Peters and had developed a close bond with him. He said to Dr. Allan, "I don't know if he'll be upset if I don't want the chemotherapy. And he will want me to come to PCU. He will want his bed freed up for another patient."

Dr. Allan replied, "Dr. Peters hasn't put any pressure on me at all to bring you to PCU, and if you come to PCU he will willingly say yes. He will remain your friend, he will come to see you practically every day. There is no obligation in any of this."

Mr. Johnson thought about this for a while. Then he smiled and his voice took on an odd, almost sarcastic, tone. (Dr. Allan described it as "snarky.") "I guess if I live, Dr. Peters will always pull another drug out of his back pocket," he said.

Later that day Mr. Johnson said to his wife, "If I go to PCU, it means I'm going to die sooner." It was as if a door opened for the first time. In the meantime, Dr. Allan suggested to them that Mrs. Johnson might want to visit the Palliative Care Unit to get an idea of what it was like.

"It seemed gloomy"

Simon saw that arrangements were being made. His aunt had now come to stay with them, and his mother was spending more and more time at the hospital. Mrs. Johnson told me that he had come into her bedroom that evening, and was more open with her than ever before. He said, "I know that Daddy is dying. He's going to be with his mother, and he'll be able to look down on us. He'll see everything that we do." Mrs. Johnson hugged him and they cried together. She said to me, "He is 12 years old and he's telling me all this. I hadn't mentioned anything about his father dying."

On the morning of July 27, Mr. Johnson was asleep when I went by the ward.

His wife was there, and she followed me out of the room. She said, "He's sleepy because of the morphine. He was having more pain so they had to increase the morphine from 3 to 4 mg every four hours, by injection. Dr. Allan mentioned something [methylphenidate] that might wake him up a bit. I will ask him about it."

Mr. Johnson was very sensitive to morphine and required very small doses. He also developed side effects very readily. Dr. Allan was trying to fine-tune the medication in a very delicate situation, in the interest of keeping Mr. Johnson as awake and aware as possible, which is what Mr. Johnson wanted. Dr. Allan was considering starting a syringe driver which might better control Mr. Johnson's pain while minimizing somnolence.

Mrs. Johnson said to me, "I went to have a look at the Palliative Care Unit yesterday afternoon. I didn't like it. It was dark. It seemed gloomy. I didn't say that to my husband. I said that it was quiet, there were carpets so you didn't hear the nurses walking down the hallways, but I didn't like it." However, she did like the idea of her husband being in a single room.

When I went back that afternoon, Mr. Johnson had just awakened. He was up in the chair trying to shave himself, lathering his face in spite of his weakness, desperately trying to keep up his routine. He had agreed to try the syringe driver, though he told one of the nurses that for the most part his physical pain was controlled. It was the psychological pain, he said, that was worse.

The next morning, Mrs. Johnson left a message for me at the Palliative Care Unit. She knew I was on call and covering for Dr. Allan. She said that her husband had had a bad night. Could I go and check on him? I said I would. For the next two days I added to my researcher role the role of Mr. Johnson's treating physician.

There were no PCU beds available so Mr. Johnson was still on the medical ward. I went and checked Mr. Johnson's medication record and noted that he had required morphine injections every two hours. Mr. Johnson was now on 40 mg of morphine per day subcutaneously, a relatively small amount, but he was receiving it by frequent injections. The syringe driver was not started until later that day. Mr. Johnson had also been more short of breath during the night. The resident had assessed him and had ordered heparin in case he had pulmonary emboli. She ordered a chest X-ray to ensure that Mr. Johnson had not developed a pleural effusion, which could have been drained to relieve his breathlessness.

When I went into the room, Mr. Johnson was asleep. He had had his 4 mg morphine just one hour before; he was so sensitive to these injections he became sleepy even with small doses. He wore an oxygen mask, and he looked ill and frail. Mrs. Johnson looked anxious and perturbed, and her face was pale and puffy. I spoke with her outside the room. She had spent the last two nights with her husband. There was never anyone with her to help her take shifts.

"You look very tired," I began.

"He had a bad night with the pain."

"He might be more comfortable on PCU where the nurses are more used to managing pain medication," I suggested. I could see the hesitation on her face.

"I think he's dying," I whispered to her.

"I know he's dying," she said, somewhat impatiently. "I know that. Dr. Allan said it would be a couple of days. I know that that's just a probability. It could be three weeks. Last night he said, 'I want to go home. I want to go home.'"

"He was confused?" I suggested.

"No, he wasn't confused. I don't know if he meant that he wanted it to be over. But he wasn't confused."

I wasn't so certain. I believed that this was a sign that Mr. Johnson was entering his final days.

The Palliative Care Unit

Mr. and Mrs. Johnson agreed to transfer to the Palliative Care Unit when a bed became available. Mrs. Johnson hoped that the symptom control would be better on the PCU. She asked again about the medical management policies there and was reassured to hear that apart from the fact that we did not usually use continuous IV drips, the medical care would be no less aggressive. I told her that because her husband was so weak, we were at the point where no further diagnostic tests would be done, whether he stayed on the medical ward or came to the PCU.

Mr. Johnson was transferred on July 29, arriving on the unit with Linda and Simon. Simon stood calmly at his mother's side. I noticed that he looked big for being 12 years old. His blond hair was neatly combed and he was tastefully dressed. He smiled shyly when I spoke with him. Simon was having difficulty adjusting to the reality of his father's illness and was getting some counseling through his school. The PCU pastoral worker noted, "Simon looks 'too well.' People expect him to behave older than his 12 years because he looks older."

As Mr. Johnson was being settled into his room, Simon said to his mother, "I'm glad Daddy's here. It means he'll get better."

"Daddy's very sick," his mother replied.

Later that day, he said it again: "Daddy's going to get better."

After consulting with Mrs. Johnson, we decided not to change the medication very much. I reasoned that it would help the transfer process if we kept the medication about the same, but tried to monitor it carefully to see if he would need extra morphine. The PCU resident physician noted Mr. Johnson's strong desire to remain alert and to be advised about any proposed changes in medication. Indeed, the Johnsons' need for meticulous control had been clear to the Palliative Care Service from the beginning. A few days before, Dr. Allan had been visiting on the medical ward when Mr. Johnson needed to use the bedpan. "The angle of the bed had to be just so," Dr. Allan told me. "He asked his wife to adjust the angle, and a few degrees seemed to make a big difference to him."

When I saw Mr. Johnson that afternoon, he was alone in his large single room. There was a comfortable chair beside the bed and plenty of room for a cot if anyone wanted to stay overnight. The room had a pleasant view over the city but was otherwise bleak, as Linda had not had the opportunity to bring anything from home. Mr. Johnson did not seem to be in pain but was somnolent and confused, and he looked very ill.

He said to me, "I feel the whole thing is out of control. I don't know what's going on."

I replied, "Your wife is telling us what to do—the medication, everything. It's in her control now. Is that OK?"

"Not one hundred percent," he said.

He said he was thirsty so I gave him something to drink, even though it was hard for him to manage to drink now. Then he fell asleep. He was still sleepy despite efforts to minimize the morphine dosage. Dr. Allan had increased his steroids (dexamethasone) in an attempt to keep the morphine dose as low as possible and still control the pain in Mr. Johnson's liver.

The next day, Dr. Allan considered reducing the morphine. He was torn, however, because Mr. Johnson had had his first comfortable, pain-free night in several days. The challenge from the opioid point of view was that there was such a narrow margin for error in Mr. Johnson's case. When Mr. Johnson was at home, he would get 6 mg of morphine by mouth and he would be fine. Raising the dose to 8 mg would make him somnolent.

"Control is so important to him," Dr. Allan said to me. "I think that he must feel terrible being confused. The big question is to decide with Mrs. Johnson when to stop attempting to give him a clear mind. She is always asking, 'Is he getting a little too much morphine?' He was willing to bear pain for the sake of mental clarity. He has been totally clear-minded until today. I discussed methylphenidate with her [an amphetamine to make him more awake], but she refused. Both he and she did not like the idea of any more pills."

"I don't know whether I did the right thing"

Mrs. Johnson began to express guilt about the course of the last couple of months. She was getting tired and was full of doubts. She looked flustered when I spoke with her outside her husband's room. "I worry that I'm making the wrong decisions," she said. "I want to know what's going on but then I worry about having to decide. In March, we could not accept that he was dying.

We went to see Dr. Peters and asked if he had any treatment at all. I don't know now whether I did the right thing to have encouraged him to do that. Maybe he would have lived longer if he had not followed the treatment?"

She burst into tears. "It's hard seeing someone so young die. And I'm afraid that I won't know what to do after he dies. I've been so involved in looking after him."

She had some questions about how aggressive we were going to be on the Palliative Care Unit. "Would you give him [furosemide] if he developed water on the lung again?" she asked.

"We would do whatever was necessary to keep him breathing as comfortably as possible," I explained. "Sometimes this does involve giving a diuretic."

She asked, doubtfully, "How do I know when it's time to restart the morphine again?"

The syringe driver had been temporarily turned off since her husband was so somnolent. Dr. Allan had hoped that he would wake up a bit, but eight hours later, he had still not awakened. This signaled to me that Mr. Johnson was dying.

"You decide, when you think he's getting uncomfortable again," I suggested, knowing that until now she had wanted to maintain control of the dosage interval.

"I decide? I think a doctor should decide," she replied anxiously.

This was the first time I had seen her wanting to give up control.

Later that day something happened that I heard about in two different versions. According to one of the nurses, as the nurse was repositioning Mr. Johnson in the bed, Mrs. Johnson suddenly grabbed her by the wrist and angrily told her, "You're hurting him!" The nurse objected to Mrs. Johnson's tone. When I saw Mrs. Johnson later that afternoon, she was in the room with her husband, who was semi-comatose. She was sobbing. "That nurse is a real bitch!" she cried. "She was trying to move him and I said, 'Be careful! He's got metastases there.' And she said, 'Don't talk to me like that. I'm the nurse here and I deserve more respect than that.' No nurse has ever spoken to me like that ever since we've been in hospital."

I was disappointed and dismayed by this incident, since we had tried so hard to be supportive to Mrs. Johnson. There had been a change of nursing shift and the nurse was perhaps not aware of the tensions that were there.

On August 1, the nurse reported that Mr. Johnson himself was agitated and irritable. He was confused and restless, and sometimes would lash out. At one point the nurse said to him, "I'm your nurse," and Mr. Johnson responded, "Nurses don't—nurses don't deal with cemeteries." He began calling out, "Mommy, help me! Help me!"

The resident physician was notified of Mr. Johnson's distress, and he ordered an immediate subcutaneous dose of 2.5 mg midazolam. He also added 5 mg midazolam to the syringe driver, which contained 35 mg morphine and 1 mg haloperidol, to be administered over 24 hours.

The next day, Mr. Johnson was restless when he was turned, but was otherwise unresponsive. He could barely be coaxed to drink small quantities of juice or to suck water from a mouth sponge. Mrs. Johnson was alone with him when I went to visit. Simon had come earlier, with his aunt, but had left. Mrs. Johnson seemed sad, but relatively calm and accepting. She said to me, "He was agitated before and they gave him the tranquilizer and he's more peaceful now. He's bad, isn't he? But I'm talking to him. I'm sure that he can hear me. I think I'll stay with him tonight."

I replied that it might be a good idea if she did. Her father and Mr. Johnson's father also came. Mr. Johnson died at 7:00 that evening, with the three of them present.

"I'm too young to go through this"

The next week at the PCU rounds, the team signaled Simon as a bereavement risk, noting that even up to the day that his father died, Simon had been hopeful that he would get better. Simon was keeping to himself. Counseling was available through his school but he refused it. "I don't want anyone to mess with my head," he said.

One month after her husband's death, Mrs. Johnson felt a lump in her breast and underwent a biopsy. Her mother had just been diagnosed with breast cancer. Mrs. Johnson looked extremely anxious and overwhelmed when I saw her. Her biopsy result revealed carcinoma in situ. She was relieved that all she needed was careful follow-up.

Two months later, she reported to me that her mother had started her second round of chemotherapy. "She is not too sick. She is doing well. What she shows us is the outside. Emotionally, she seems O.K." It struck me that Linda was like this, trying her best not to show her emotions. "My biopsy was relatively benign," she said to me, "but I still think about it." She had another mammogram booked in a month's time.

Mrs. Johnson went back to work after three months but required regular counseling sessions with a social worker. Five months into her bereavement, she seemed to have more problems than average, with poor concentration and insomnia. "We tried to get a routine," she told me when I spoke with her at this time. "It was a shock to go back to work. I notice that my memory is not as good as it used to be. I used to have a great memory for details. I can't handle the same volume that I used to, especially when it comes to multitasking. I guess that's normal. I'm taking something to help me sleep that [my family doctor] gave me in October. That's the last time I saw him. Even then I'm usually up at 5:00 a.m."

She continued, "Sometimes I can't understand why Richard's cancer couldn't be controlled. Prostate cancer is supposed to be one of the easiest cancers to control. The surgery went well, but then I don't know what happened. I have a copy of the whole medical file but I can't bear to look at it." She became tearful. "I think about it a lot—everything that happened. I'm not at peace with everything yet. I think about whether he could have had different care, a different kind of treatment, whether he should have had more aggressive treatment earlier on. Sometimes I think that it's something that I have to live with. I can't let it kill me inside. Sometimes I feel that I'm to blame."

Mrs. Johnson spoke with the social worker at the hospital four or five times, but then the social worker went on maternity leave. Mrs. Johnson didn't want to go for group bereavement counseling, even though this was an option. The social worker said that she would look for one-on-one alternatives for her. The volunteer counselor from the Palliative Care Service also contacted Mrs. Johnson and they spoke on the telephone a few times. But this did not help. "I still think that bereavement is for older people," Linda said. "I'm too young to go through this."

Mrs. Johnson told me that Simon, too, had some problems paying attention in school, although he managed to get good grades. He would sometimes disrupt class, which his mother believed was an attempt to get attention. He was more socially withdrawn than usual and had given up his sports activities. He went to the library every day. He didn't talk to anyone except his one good friend. "He doesn't talk about his father much," Linda said. "He keeps it inside. I bring it up but he never brings it up. I give him the opportunity as often as I can. I talk about his father. He was very close to his father. I'm sure that he thinks about him." She began to cry again. "He says that he thinks about his father every day."

At six months, Mrs. Johnson canceled an interview that I had arranged with her. She sounded tense, like she was trying to keep the lid on things. "I've been up and down and I'm up right now," she explained. "I'm afraid that if I talk to you, it will bring things up and I'll be down again."

She decided to see the Palliative Care Service psychologist, and received counseling for three months. Then they somehow lost touch, and Mrs. Johnson decided she would try to handle things on her own. She started to take a benzodiazepine daily, commenting to me, "I don't think it's a good thing to take in the long term, but it's a security for me."

One year after her husband's death, Mrs. Johnson was still having difficulties. Even with the tranquilizer, she slept only two or three hours every night. She had tried everything to sleep and nothing worked. The volunteer bereavement counselor continued to telephone her, asking her if she wanted more intensive counseling, which Mrs. Johnson considered. Simon, meanwhile, was back to his old self—the quiet loner.

15

Jenny Doyle
"Do I Really Belong in a Hospice Program Yet?"

Narrated by YANNA LAMBRINIDOU

Jenny Doyle was a hospice patient for eight and one-half months, much longer than is typical for a U.S. hospice program. Her time with hospice was tumultuous, however, marked by periods of anger and resentment amid other periods of gratitude and affection. Mrs. Doyle was 47 years old when she was diagnosed with inflammatory breast cancer, an aggressive form of the disease that she fought bitterly to the very end. Her struggle led her to a series of doctors and created serious tensions for the hospice team. Throughout this time the legacy of early years of strife with her children created additional stresses and strains, which persisted throughout the bereavement period. "At least let the moment of her death be peaceful," the family prayed. But even that was not to be.

A rebel with a cause

Jenny Doyle was a stout, European-American woman with wavy brown hair, a pronounced chin, rosy cheeks, and a smile that emphasized her bright eyes. Her high-pitched voice, fast speech, and excited tone revealed an enthusiasm that many of her loved ones saw and appreciated. Mrs. Doyle was a passionate woman. Since 1983, she had worked as an administrative assistant for a manufacturing company. Her office was on the first floor of a dilapidated old building with leaky pipes, damp walls, and a steady flow of insects. The mold on the walls and the monthly spray of insecticides that had seeped into the carpet brought out allergies in many employees. Some filed complaints with the company's management, but could offer no proof to connect their poor health to the air in the office. But when, in a short period of time, two of her co-workers developed cancer, Mrs. Doyle was convinced that there was something wrong. In May 1995, after a series of doctors' appointments and medical tests, she was diagnosed with occupational asthma. Her physician gave her a letter stating that her work environment was detrimental to her health. She was immediately transferred to a branch office. But Mrs. Doyle also wanted financial compensation for the work days she had missed and filed a workers' compensation lawsuit against her company.

Two months into the trial, she was diagnosed with inflammatory breast cancer, an uncommon form of the disease that involves the lymph vessels under the skin, often making its first appearance as a dermatological irritation. She was 47 years old. She had two adult children, and only nine months had passed since her second marriage. Her dreams for a new, untroubled life with a man she loved were shattered. At the same time, she couldn't stop thinking that she was the third person in her office to develop cancer—a nightmare come true. Her desire for compensation now turned into a desire for revenge. Although her lawsuit addressed her asthma and not her cancer, she was determined to win it.

In September 1995, she started four courses of chemotherapy. The treatment was hard on her, but she continued to work. Her co-workers admired her for her courage, good nature, and ability to laugh, and they respected her for being the only one who had taken a stand against the company. Affectionately, they named her "the rebel with a cause." Mrs. Doyle was flattered by this title. "If the cause is my life, you bet I'm going to be a rebel!" she laughed as she described this phase of her life to me. She bought a T-shirt and printed a message on it: "I am not calling in sick. I am calling in dead." She planned to give it to her supervisor when she won her case.

In November 1995, Mrs. Doyle lost her job when she disputed the company's finding that the air in the office was healthy, and she declared that she was unwilling to return to a decayed building. A few days later, another of her co-workers was diagnosed with cancer. For the next six months Mrs. Doyle had no income of her own. To live, she was forced to rely on the limited income of her husband who worked at a small advertising agency, as well as the charity and good will of relatives, childhood friends, and co-workers.

"There is virtually no reading material on my cancer," she said to me. "Dr. Susan Love's book that deals with breast cancer has a half page, and she says that is why there is no more in this book—because it is so rare." Even if inflammatory breast cancer were uncommon, however, Mrs. Doyle believed that it wasn't likely to stay that way. She had heard that it afflicted migrant workers, which convinced her that it was linked to pesticides. Aware of the wide use of such agents, she concluded that her type of cancer was bound to become more prevalent.

To educate herself about her disease, Mrs. Doyle joined a support group. Her group consisted of five members and met twice a month. She liked the meetings because they gave her the opportunity to learn and help at the same time. She exchanged support, advice, and information. She cried and laughed. In the third meeting she attended, one of the women in her group announced that her cancer had metastasized to her liver. Six weeks later, she died. Mrs. Doyle was shocked. For the first time, she had come face to face with the deadliness of her disease. She wanted access to new treatments.

After informing her oncologist that she would be willing to receive experimental therapy, Mrs. Doyle was invited into a study testing the effect of bone marrow transplant in the early stages of inflammatory breast cancer. Since her tumors had not spread beyond her breast and local lymph nodes, she was admitted to a hospital for three weeks for a bone marrow transplant. Though the procedure is usually grueling, Mrs. Doyle told me little about it. What she did say was that she left the hospital with renewed hope. She had finally entered the front line of the battle against inflammatory breast cancer. But she didn't stop there. She also underwent a preventive double mastectomy and agreed to a five-week course of radiation to her chest wall and lymph nodes. By September 1996, 13 months after her initial diagnosis, she had done everything she could to contain her cancer. That thought in itself reassured her.

In January of the following year, after a bout of intense pain between her shoulder blades, her oncologist, Dr. Silverman, detected metastases throughout her spine. Mrs. Doyle remembered him saying that she had one year to live. To control her pain, Dr. Silverman prescribed slow-release morphine. He also suggested that she receive radiation, chemotherapy, or radioactive strontium. Mrs. Doyle chose to start with radiation. It acted fast, she said, and had the potential to shrink her tumors at the same time.

The radiologist, Dr. Stein, explained that in contrast to her first radiation treatment, this one would be strictly palliative. "A lot of what we try to do [at this stage]," Dr. Stein told me, "is keep people as functional as possible during their care. Jenny makes it easy because she is very positive, and she always gets better. One of these times she won't, and that will be sad, but [up until now] all of our interactions with Jenny have been good because she gets better, so that makes it a lot easier on everybody—myself, the therapist who gives her the treatment, and Jenny."

Mrs. Doyle remained optimistic. She cherished informational materials from the bone marrow study and waited anxiously for them every day. But suddenly, these materials stopped coming. She discovered that she had been removed from the study because her disease had progressed. She said to me:

> You are no longer part of the study, so they don't share any information with you then. You lose your information rights, so to speak. You think, "What? Is it only for women who they think have been cured by the bone marrow transplant?" You get the feeling that you are detrimental to their program or their funding. Like if they cannot show a certain amount of success rate they would lose their funding. And I think that's what it's all about.

Calling hospice

Now that her breast cancer had spread to her spine, Mrs. Doyle feared that she could die as quickly as the woman in her support group. "Since the girl ahead of me with this disease died so very quickly," she said, "I thought it was probably to my advantage to have hospice. It took her about six weeks to pass away. She went very quickly." Though she was not yet finished with her spinal radiation, Mrs. Doyle called the Hospice of Lancaster County for admission. Dr. Silverman confirmed the terminal nature of her disease and Mrs. Doyle was admitted to the home care program of the Hospice of Lancaster County on February 6, 1997.

The next day she met Lucy Stephens, her hospice nurse. Soon after, the hospice social worker, Sandra Dunn, arrived for a visit. Sandra used her first visit with Mrs. Doyle to learn about her life. Mrs. Doyle had been born and raised in Lancaster County, where both of her parents still lived. She had married her first husband in 1966 and had Kim, who was 28, and Peter, who was 25. That marriage had dissolved. In 1992, she met Andrew Doyle, who became her second husband two years later. But there was something inauspicious about this marriage. Nine months into it, Jenny was diagnosed with inflammatory breast cancer and a year later her husband had a heart attack. Between the two of them, Mr. and Mrs. Doyle had already been through chemotherapy, a bone marrow transplant, two mastectomies, radiation, and bypass surgery.

Sandra noticed that the style of Mrs. Doyle's delivery didn't match the gravity of her words. Mrs. Doyle's tone was upbeat, positive, and energetic. She spoke fast. She came across as self-assured, fearless, and good-humored. She expressed concern about the coping abilities of her family, but said little about herself. She expressed worry for her daughter, Kim, and her husband. Mr. Doyle had lost many members of his family to cancer and now feared both his own death and that of his wife. He had no support system of his own and seemed to cope with his wife's illness by pretending it didn't affect him. That disturbed Mrs. Doyle. She wanted her husband to get help.

Mrs. Doyle assured Sandra that she, herself, was all right. She was working with a wonderful counselor who offered her services for free. She had a strong faith in God and a supportive spiritual community. The only help she wanted involved her landlord. She was already having difficulty climbing the stairs to the second floor. She and Andrew had found a first-floor apartment that they liked, but without their landlord's permission to break their lease, they were not able to afford it. Sandra called the Doyles' landlord immediately and got his permission to end their lease. On March 1, the Doyles moved into their new apartment. Mr. Doyle took it upon himself to carry and unpack the heaviest of the boxes despite his heart condition. He was a stodgy man who tired easily, but he injected humor anywhere he could. Mrs. Doyle tried to lift light items, but she was stopped by a dull pain in her shoulder.

The only thing that bothered her about the new apartment were the long and lonely hours she spent in it. Mr. Doyle often worked overtime, and she missed her job. She would have liked to have a part-time position, but wasn't interested in returning to the environment that had made her sick in the first place. Instead, she spent her days watching television and visiting with friends. On the weekends, she often took day trips to the seashore or went to dance clubs with Mr. Doyle. Traveling and dancing were her favorite activities. At the same time, she also prepared for her decline. Her support group had brought her close to a woman who was deteriorating rapidly. Mrs. Doyle was both frightened and encouraged by this experience. On the one hand, it showed her the devastating effects of her disease, but on the other, it gave her an example of how to cope with her own deterioration. Although she was still ambulatory, she followed Dr. Silverman's recommendation to acquire a wheelchair. With prompts from Lucy and Sandra, she also named the people who would be able to help her when she needed more intensive care. Andrew was one, her father and daughter would also be available, so would her mother, but Jenny didn't feel comfortable around her; she found her to be too negative, critical, and unsympathetic. Her son Peter lived in New York and wouldn't be able to stay with her for long periods of time.

In the beginning of April, the second woman in the support group died. Mrs. Doyle was devastated. Five days after the funeral, she awoke with excruciating pain in her left shoulder. Her experience was similar, though more severe, to the one she had had a month earlier. It took her a double dose of oxycodone to get back to sleep. But she continued to experience low-grade discomfort. This frightened her. Tests showed that her cancer had metastasized again; she had two small tumors in her shoulder socket and one on her collar bone.

Jenny started a third course of radiation. After her first treatment, she told Lucy that her arms felt sore, she coughed frequently, had lost her appetite, and was tired. "Otherwise I am well," she asserted, moving on to a happier subject. Her daughter Kim had become engaged. She and her fiancé, Patrick, had just announced that in October they were going to get married in Europe. Upon their return, on the first weekend of November, they planned a wedding reception in Lancaster County. Mrs. Doyle was delighted. November seemed far away since it was only April at the time, but she felt confident she would stay well enough to make an appearance at Kim's reception.

In some ways, Lucy identified with Mrs. Doyle. She, too, was young. She had children of her own. She also had a family history of breast cancer and expected to develop it as well. But Lucy didn't think she would have as much courage as Mrs. Doyle. She was relatively new at hospice and had never met a dying patient with the feistiness of Mrs. Doyle. She told me:

> She is so upbeat and accepting of everything, much more so than me. I am just wondering if it's all show for everybody, and if underneath she is really scared to death, or if this is really just Jenny. But everyone says this is how she has been with everything all along. I actually admire her for being able to handle it like that, because I know I could not. I am an upbeat person for the most part, but if it came to something like that I know I could not be as upbeat as she is. I know when her time comes it is going to be difficult for me. I am feeling somewhat attached to her. I try not to be, but you cannot help but be sometimes with her. It is just that she pulls you in. I actually miss the weeks when I don't get to go out and see her.

Sandra had a different reaction to Mrs. Doyle's cheerfulness. "I find it almost a difficult thing about Jenny," she observed to me, "that you talk about hard things, and she always uses this very bright tone of voice. The affect and the content just don't go together. Maybe she is dealing with things internally or with her counselor. I don't know. Sometimes you are not sure exactly where she's at." Mrs. Doyle's independence, self-sufficiency, and close relationship with her counselor made Sandra feel like "a fifth wheel" in her care, she said, though she still found it important to build a good relationship with her patient. She wanted to be prepared for the day when Mrs. Doyle would be unable to visit her counselor and would turn to hospice for emotional support.

"I know I have done things wrong"

At the end of April, Mrs. Doyle invited Kim and Peter to one of her counseling sessions. She had something to tell them and needed her counselor's support. At the counselor's office, Mrs. Doyle admitted she had not been a perfect mother. "I know I have done things wrong," she said. She didn't delve into details, but her implication of repentance made both Kim and Peter cry. In tears, they promised their mother that they would stay by her side until she died. That was a groundbreaking commitment. Prior to her cancer diagnosis, Peter did not speak to Mrs. Doyle for a year and Kim maintained a cordial, but distant relationship with her. The rift between Mrs. Doyle and her children went back 15 years when her first husband, Peter and Kim's father, abused Kim. Mrs. Doyle sent Kim away temporarily with the promise that she was going to make things safe before bringing her back. That promise was never realized. Instead, she decided to continue living with her husband and invited Kim to return. Kim refused. Feeling betrayed, she moved in with her grandparents and kept minimal contact with her parents. Her father had abused her in a way she never spelled out to me, and her mother, she said, had chosen to stay with him at her expense. What hurt Kim even more was the preferential treatment she saw them give Peter.

Kim remembered telling her mother, "Mom, it looks like you screwed up so bad with your first kid that you just brushed that one under the rug, and you did everything you could to make the second one work out okay. I mean, you didn't send him to live with someone else, you sent him to college, you supported him, you were at his high school graduation. You didn't do any of those things for me, and I didn't just vanish. I am still here, and I am still hurt, and I am still wondering why." As if in reply, Mrs. Doyle stopped paying for Peter's college education and asked him to move out of her house. In 1994, Peter relocated to New York. He developed a drinking problem. "I felt responsible for that," Kim said to me. Since that time, Kim recalled that she and her parents vacillated between periods of closeness and distance. Peter hadn't made any effort to stay in touch with his mother. When he learned about her terminal diagnosis he said, "Well, it's not like I know what it is like to have a mom right now anyway."

"They tell you in the video: 'This is not a cure'"

In the first week of May, Mrs. Doyle began using her wheelchair. The palliative radiation to her spine had caused her blood count to drop, which made her weak. She had lost her appetite and experienced increased constipation and shoulder pain. Her hips ached. At the suggestion of her radiologist, she decided to start radioactive strontium treatments. Just one shot of this substance, Dr. Stein told her, had the capacity to bring her long-term comfort. It could alleviate her pain for a period of three to six months, free her of her need for narcotic analgesics, give her flexibility, and possibly prevent further metastases. Mrs. Doyle was thrilled to hear about these benefits. She finalized her decision to accept the strontium when she saw a promotional videotape about it and confirmed that her health insurance would cover its high cost. She spoke excitedly about the new treatment, but always added, "They tell you in the video: This is not a cure."

Because strontium is radioactive, Mrs. Doyle was told that she would have to take special precautions for a week after receiving it to protect others from exposure to her bodily flu·ʿls. Moreover, if she were to die within six months of the shot, her body would be considered hazardous and ineligible for cremation. Lucy seemed apprehensive. "Jenny is really almost hoping for a miracle," she said. "Not as far as a cure, but as far as being able to go off almost all her medications and increasing her level of functioning. But my understanding is that strontium either works—and when it works it is fantastic—or it doesn't work. There is no in-between."

Mrs. Doyle received the injection on May 23, and my first meeting with her took place five days later. When I arrived at her apartment, she opened the door, greeted me with a big smile, and walked back to the couch with ease. She was wearing a pair of cotton sweat pants and a white T-shirt. She looked comfortable. Her speech was fast and excited. She told me that the reason she agreed to participate in our study was because she wanted to educate others about inflammatory breast cancer and remind the medical establishment that it was a disease deserving further investigation. "I am thinking, well, sometime maybe if I talk to somebody it will hit a nerve and maybe there will be research money somewhere to help those who are going to come on with this," she said.

The strontium had already helped. Mrs. Doyle was almost pain-free and limber. She had been able to cut her nightly dose of oxycodone in half and hoped that soon she could eliminate it completely. She had also been able to dance. If these effects were to last for six months, she calculated, she would be eligible for another strontium shot and would live well for a whole year. "I am a little radioactive," she giggled, explaining that she had to wash her clothes separately from her husband's, flush the toilet twice, bring her own utensils to restaurants, and wash her dishes with special care. "We circled on the calendar when I do not have to do this anymore," she said.

The downside of Mrs. Doyle's improvement was that it led many of her friends to assume that either she had been cured or that her prognosis had been extended. Such assumptions made Mrs. Doyle feel alone and unsupported. What frustrated her even more was that many people were hesitant to learn from her the hard realities of inflammatory breast cancer. She suspected that they were in denial. When she tried to tell a friend from church that the strontium was not a cure, she failed. "That woman had a hard time with it," she said. "It is like a mind thing. She doesn't see a person who is crippled and bent over and everything like this. She thinks, well, they cured the disease. But people seem to be on their guard a little bit with you. They don't want to come right out and ask you what is going on. I like when a person asks me if they have a question. I don't like this guessing stuff."

Mrs. Doyle noticed her daughter looking at her curiously. She sensed that Kim was surprised by her limberness and afraid of her radioactivity. At the same time, Kim expressed an optimism about her prognosis that bothered her. In preparation for her wedding reception in November, Kim asked her mother to buy herself a new dress. But when Mrs. Doyle told her that she preferred to wait until she was sure she would be able to attend, Kim exclaimed: "That's a defeatist attitude!"

Strontium's magic didn't last. Within three weeks Mrs. Doyle returned to her original medication doses. Her blood count remained low. She felt extremely weak, and pain returned to her right hip and left shoulder. But she didn't lose hope, because Dr. Stein said that it was normal for her condition to worsen before it got better.

In anticipation, the Doyles bought a four-day vacation to Las Vegas. They scheduled their trip around the 4th of July holiday to celebrate the warm summer day on which they had met four years earlier. They had always wanted to visit Las Vegas. "I will put $10 in the slot machine, and then that will be it," Jenny laughed. More than anything, they wanted to attend variety shows, go dancing, enjoy the sun, and relax together. Until then, they intended to spend a quiet month at home.

"We have to be the voice of reality"

In the middle of June the spasms of pain in Mrs. Doyle's right hip worsened. Oxycodone and the local application of heat reduced but didn't eliminate her pain. She couldn't sleep. To walk, she needed a walker. The pain persisted even after the oxycodone dose was doubled. In a matter of days, she lost nine pounds. An X-ray revealed that her cancer had metastasized to both her hips and pelvis. Dr. Silverman instructed Mrs. Doyle to replace the oxycodone with 100 mg of slow-release morphine twice a day. He also advised her to take her Las Vegas vacation immediately. The way her cancer was spreading, he couldn't see her having the strength for a long trip in July. Mrs. Doyle was disturbed by her doctor's recommendation. It struck her as alarmist. She wanted more information.

In the weekly nursing meeting at hospice, several of Lucy's colleagues were startled to hear that Mrs. Doyle had questioned Dr. Silverman. They believed now that her disease was progressing much faster than she expected and that, in all likelihood, her prognosis had been reduced to weeks. They suspected that Mrs. Doyle was in denial. A supervising nurse commented that Mrs. Doyle needed to start preparing for her death. She instructed Lucy and Sandra to pay their patient an informational visit and explain to her the gravity of her condition.

Nervously, Lucy called Mrs. Doyle and made an appointment to see her the following day. "I dreaded that visit," Lucy told me later. "It is like when you have an exam, and even though you studied, you just have this sinking feeling in the pit of your stomach you don't want to take it, even though you know the answers. I just had that sinking feeling in the pit of my stomach all day long, because I felt like I was dropping a bomb."

Mrs. Doyle caught the nervousness in Lucy's voice. Panicked, she immediately called her husband to ask him to attend the meeting with her. She also called her attorney, told him she was dying, and urged him to put pressure on the judge to make a decision about her case. Two years had passed since she had filed her lawsuit. She wanted to see it settled soon. Finally, she called her travel agent. She told her that she and her husband had decided to cancel their vacation.

The next day, Lucy, Sandra, Mr. and Mrs. Doyle met in the Doyles' living room. Lucy looked Mrs. Doyle in the eyes and slowly explained that hospice was concerned about her. The strontium shot had failed both in alleviating her pain and in preventing a new metastasis. Radiation was not a solution, either; it worked only temporarily. Moreover, many of the spots on Mrs. Doyle's body had already received the maximum amount. Her disease was progressing rapidly. Her prognosis was now a matter of weeks instead of months. If she still wanted to go to Las Vegas, she had better leave immediately. And if she wanted to make her will or tie up loose ends with loved ones, this was the time to do it.

Everyone cried. Mr. Doyle hugged his wife and assured her that he would take family medical leave to stay at her side. Mrs. Doyle assured Lucy and Sandra that the trip to Las Vegas was off. She talked about the anger she harbored for her supervisor at work. She felt it was time to send him the T-shirt, but her attorney had advised her against that. For the first time, Mrs. Doyle gave Sandra permission to contact her parents and children for emotional support. At the end of the meeting, a tearful Andrew escorted Lucy and Sandra to their cars. Softly, he asked them if cremation was going to be an option for his wife. Lucy explained that it wouldn't be, because only a month had gone by since the administration of the strontium. The crematorium would not accept her body before November.

A few days later Mrs. Doyle bought baby gifts for the grandchildren she would never see. She also got into the habit of checking her mailbox every day for the judge's decision. And she returned to Dr. Stein to receive radiation for pain in her sacrum and ilium.

To her surprise, Dr. Stein gave her a very different picture of her condition. Having seen not only her X-ray but also her most recent blood tests, he concluded that her death was not imminent at all. Yes, her cancer had spread to her hips and pelvis, which meant that the strontium shot had probably not worked, but there was no reason to believe that her prognosis had changed. Her major organs—that is, her lungs, liver, and kidneys—still seemed healthy. All of a sudden, Mrs. Doyle saw the meeting with Lucy and Sandra in a different light. She was furious that on the basis of the single X-ray report Lucy and Sandra had taken it as their duty to convince her that she had only a few weeks to live.

"How could they do this?" Mrs. Doyle asked angrily as she told me about the news from Dr. Stein. "Lucy had the need to show me that her way was right—almost maybe to scare me into seeing what she thought was the truth, and that caused a lot of pain, a lot of pain. I guess it kind of opened my eyes. This is one of the complaints that I understand there is with hospice. They sometimes tell the patient the way they perceive things, and that is not always correct."

Lucy abandoned hospice's alarmist position as soon as she heard Dr. Stein's view. "I don't think she is going to go downhill as quickly as I was thinking before our meeting," she said to me. "My nursing supervisor really thought that she would not be here come the 4th of July. I don't know. Jenny is a fighter. Now here we are, June 18, and I cannot see her not being here in three weeks." Sandra, too, was disturbed by the fact that she had sounded a false alarm. At the same time, she saw a positive side to the meeting. At least, she argued, it prompted Mrs. Doyle to think seriously about her death. Then she elaborated on her philosophy.

> Because of what we do, we maybe tend to lean more on the negative—forecasting the worst—and then sometimes it does not happen that way. I guess I feel like it is still better to err that way and have things turn out better than to be looking on the bright side and not be prepared. We may tend to lean more on the negative, because we know that out there in the world people don't know about death, don't understand about death, don't expect death, and therefore are working hard to believe that it is not coming. We kind of feel as if we have to be the voice of reality.
>
> I don't think that talking to somebody about dying really hurts that much. For us to do that with Jenny did not make it happen any sooner, it did not really do anything to hurt, it probably was good. The vision of Jenny going out to Las Vegas and dying there was pretty upsetting, and that was enough to make you get in there and really say something.

Sandra expressed confidence to me that Mrs. Doyle understood hospice's perspective. In their last, lengthy conversation, she had detected no anger or tension in Mrs. Doyle's voice. Their exchange had been friendly, she said. Sandra had no reason to believe that Mrs. Doyle was upset. Sometimes, however, she wondered if her patient was honest. Did Mrs. Doyle feel resentment toward hospice after that meeting? Did she hold a grudge against her and Lucy? Had she lost her trust in them, but was unable to say so?

In fact, Mrs. Doyle decided to quit hospice. At first she thought of complaining about Lucy and asking for a new nurse. But she liked Lucy, and Lucy had shared many aspects of her life with her. Among other things, she had told her that she was a single mother. She had also shown her photographs of her youngest child who was chronically ill. Mrs. Doyle actually felt protective of her. She didn't want her to lose her job. She thought it would be better to leave hospice all together. She saw herself as stronger and healthier than the patients hospice was designed to serve. "Maybe I shouldn't be in this program yet," she said to me.

Mrs. Doyle wasn't ready to die. She had just finished her 52nd radiation treatment and planned to start driving again as soon as her hips allowed. The day I saw her, however, she was pale and cold, and had a catch in her breathing. Sitting with an electric blanket on a heating pad, she attributed her chills to the radiation. But she was thankful for all the treatments she had received. Even the strontium had been worth it to her and she planned to receive it again as soon as she could. In contrast to Lucy and Dr. Stein, she thought it had worked. It had eased her shoulder pain and, in her opinion, couldn't have possibly prevented her metastasis. The pain in her hip had developed before the strontium shot. To her, this meant that the metastasis had come before her treatment. She was disappointed that Dr. Stein had a different opinion. Moreover, she was hurt by the fact that he didn't kiss her on the last day of her treatment. Dr. Stein always kissed Mrs. Doyle goodbye. She worried that his recent lack of affection signaled his discouragement.

A sister in the struggle

By July Mrs. Doyle had still not received a decision about her lawsuit. The occasional catch in her breathing had become a more regular symptom and her morphine had been increased to 130 mg twice a day. The rest of her medications included the hormonal treatments anastrozole and megestrol, a diuretic, an antiemetic, and prednisone. Every day that passed without trying a new intervention seemed like a waste. Then she found Dr. Richards, the oncologist of one of her friends, who had a different opinion about her prognosis. Dr. Richards told Mrs. Doyle that she wasn't hospice-appropriate. Mrs. Doyle's voice filled with fervor when she recounted the oncologist's words: "When I see someone functioning as well as you are—walking, talking, breathing, telling me that they are caring for their apartment, telling me that they are looking to get back to driving and things like this—this does not spell 'hospice patient' to me," she exclaimed.

Dr. Richards was an investigator who conducted experimental studies. She told Mrs. Doyle that if her major organs were cancer-free she would be eligible for new treatments. Mrs. Doyle was filled with hope. But when she informed Dr. Silverman about her new options, he sounded disapproving. He doubted that experimental studies would benefit her. His pessimism disturbed Mrs. Doyle, but it didn't stop her from traveling a long distance to be treated by Dr. Richards.

Dr. Richards scheduled Mrs. Doyle for tests that would determine the extent of her disease. She also offered her a monthly infusion of the bone-resorption inhibitor, pamidronate. This drug's primary purpose was to strengthen Mrs. Doyle's bones. At the same time, she believed it might prevent further bone metastases. Pamidronate, explained Dr. Richards, was a perfect treatment for Mrs. Doyle, for it strengthened her bones without compromising her blood count. Already, Mrs. Doyle's platelets were so low that she was covered with bruises.

Mrs. Doyle described her new physician as an extraordinary person who was determined to fight breast cancer with all her might. Dr. Richards had lost her mother to breast cancer, and she herself was a breast cancer survivor. "It is a relief to know that we have a sister in the struggle," Mrs. Doyle said to me. "She understands all those things that I don't see how it is possible for someone who has never been there to understand completely, and she was so nice."

Mrs. Doyle decided to tell Lucy that if her cancer had not metastasized to her major organs, she would leave hospice. "I'm going to tell Lucy that I choose to fight for my life," Jenny told me. "At this point in time, I am very excited about Dr. Richards's program. I am going to tell [Lucy] too that I see no reason why I should not go for everything that is available, and that is what Dr. Richards is all about. I said, 'at 48 years old I have a lot of kick left yet.' It is so nice to know that you have not been given up on."

Dr. Silverman no longer had a place in her care, either, as she was going to replace him with Dr. Richards. More than anything, she wanted to attend Kim's wedding reception in November and, if she could, see her first grandchild. When she spoke to Lucy she explained that she was switching physicians but actually did not mention leaving hospice. Lucy was happy for her. "Be it beneficial or not physically," she said to me at this time, "this is something Jenny needs to do, and if she needs to do that, I have to stand behind her. I think emotionally it is helping her a lot." Lucy felt reassured that her patient didn't see Dr. Richards's interventions as a cure. She also called Dr. Richards to confirm that her work with Mrs. Doyle was strictly palliative. Dr. Richards assured her that her goal was to give Mrs. Doyle comfort and, in the best of circumstances, buy her more time. "That pretty much falls right in line with hospice's philosophy," said Lucy after hanging up the phone.

Mrs. Doyle received her first infusion of pamidronate on July 10. She noticed that her appetite and overall energy improved. Her spirits soared. Now that she had gained some strength, she started dreaming of a weekend visit to the Atlantic coast.

"It has been a long, long time since I have felt this terrible"

On the third weekend of July, the Doyles took a trip to the Atlantic coast. They returned home rejuvenated. Mrs. Doyle's blood count had started to rise and her bruises had faded. On July 23, Dr. Richards informed her that, according to her test results, her major organs were healthy. Once her platelets reached a normal level, she would be able to receive chemotherapy. Mrs. Doyle was ecstatic. "We made it over that hurdle!" she exclaimed with relief. But six days later, she woke up with the most excruciating pain. She assumed she had broken a rib. At 6:00 a.m., she took breakthrough morphine and two hours later, her slow-release dose. Soon after her husband left for work, she started to vomit. She couldn't keep any of her medications down, not even her antiemetic. She experienced cold sweats. Kim happened to call her just as she was getting sick. Realizing that her mother was in trouble, she left work to see her. Between her episodes of vomiting, Mrs. Doyle managed to hit the speed-dial button on the phone and tell Mr. Doyle to hurry home. She also contacted Lucy. When Lucy examined Mrs. Doyle she called hospice and made arrangements to have 24-hour nursing care placed in her patient's home. She also contacted Dr. Richards. Surprised by this turn of events, Dr. Richards instructed her to give Mrs. Doyle her medications rectally. But she wanted to see her patient as soon as possible to verify whether Mrs. Doyle's pain was caused by a fracture due to metastatic cancer in her bone.

Everyone was alarmed. "It has been a long, long time since I've felt this terrible," Mrs. Doyle said. Her pain subsided with an increased dose of slow-release morphine, but it didn't disappear. Vomiting made it even worse. "I cannot win right now," she said. "But we will make it through. We just have to keep the faith."

When Dr. Richards examined Mrs. Doyle three days later, she determined that she hadn't fractured a rib. However, her blood count had dropped even further. Dr. Richards proceeded to give her a second infusion of pamidronate. A few days later, Lucy told me that I would not believe the changes in Mrs. Doyle. She had regained her energy. Although her appetite remained poor, she experienced no pain. Once again, she was able to walk by herself to the mailbox at the bottom of the driveway to check for the judge's decision on her case. Another hospice nurse was standing nearby listening to Lucy's report. "Stay tuned for Jenny," she exclaimed laughingly. "She's always a surprise!"

"Before I opened the letter I said a little prayer"

On August 22, when Lucy arrived at the house for a scheduled visit, she found a note on the door on which Mrs. Doyle said that she had to leave. She had won the lawsuit! She had been awarded worker's compensation from the day her company's branch office had closed until the last day of her life. I saw her a few days later. She beamed with happiness. She said:

Everybody is really happy for me over this. Before I opened the letter I said a little prayer. I said, "Please, God, please!" At first I just read the back part for myself that I had won. I was so happy that day. I just feel vindicated. I feel that justice did prevail, and it makes you believe in the system again.

Our discussion turned to Kim's wedding reception, which was to take place in a luxury hotel. Two hundred people were invited to a sit-down dinner and ballroom dancing. Mrs. Doyle planned not only to attend the reception but also to organize a bachelorette party for Kim, scheduled for September. She giggled. Kim had requested a male stripper, and it was Mrs. Doyle's job to find one.

Things looked good. She and her husband had decided to use some of the money she would receive to rebook their vacation to Las Vegas. This time, however, it would be a 10-day trip that would include not only Nevada but also New Mexico and Arizona. The trip was tentatively planned for the beginning of September. When I asked Lucy what she thought about Mrs. Doyle's travel plans, she said:

Thrilled for her and baffled for me. She is like a Timex. She takes a licking and keeps on ticking. No matter what setback she has, she seems to come out of them with flying colors, so you are not quite certain if the next setback is going to be the final one, or if she is going to bounce back again. I am really stunned that she's doing so well, but have a feeling when she really, truly does start to go back, it is going to be a quickie, because she has so much metastasis in there. I know she wants to make it to her daughter's wedding, which is in November I guess, and boy, at the rate she's going, there is a chance she might.

Dr. Richards appreciated the "free rein" given to her by hospice. She was confident that the pamidronate infusions helped Mrs. Doyle with her pain and spared her from further radiation. But she saw a fine and unclear line between mere symptom management and aggressive treatment. On the one hand, she asserted that the treatments she was giving her patient were palliative. On the other hand, she explained that the category "palliative" was contestable. "I think everything I do is palliative," she said, "but there is palliative and palliative. I mean, there is palliative like giving morphine, and there is palliative like giving intravenous hydration, blood products, the pamidronate. . . . That is kind of pushing it." (In fact, many palliative care services would find it entirely appropriate to administer such treatments to patients with advanced cancer. Palliative care represents a spectrum, and there is no clear demarcation between comfort care and care that involves certain types of life-prolonging treatments.)

All Mrs. Doyle could think about now was her trip to the Southwest, set to begin on September 12. Mr. Doyle was equally excited. He saw the vacation as an opportunity to "regroup" with his wife and create intimacy in an environment that wasn't dominated by her illness. He explained that for him and his wife cancer had become greater than a mere disease. It was a way of life. The undivided attention that Mrs. Doyle's physical condition demanded of them had led them to neglect other parts of their lives. "We have lost a lot of the physical contact," Mr. Doyle said. "Not that I want the moon, the sun, and the world, but it's time to get away and try to get back to a little bit of normalcy along with relaxing and doing things couples do."

"You worry sometimes that she is in denial, but I don't really think that is true," commented Sandra, who continued to be amazed by Mrs. Doyle's perseverance and who seemed to me to have modified her interpretation of it since June. "That is just her way of handling it and having as good a life as she possibly can with what she has got. Because when you scratch a little bit, she cries. She talks about it and acknowledges what is going on. Jenny has hopes, goals, dreams, the daughter's wedding, all this stuff and just how devastating it is going to be for everybody when—and if—she does not make it to the next goal. Because she is so young and so neat."

"I made it through with flying colors"

"I made it through with flying colors! I did not have any problems!" Mrs. Doyle exclaimed when she got back from her trip. She found no checks in the mailbox, however. The manufacturing company's attorney had appealed the judge's decision and, although his case was dismissed, payments to her had been put on hold. Her attorney was at work to solve that problem.

Mrs. Doyle felt hopeful and strong despite the fact that she was tired, puffy from her corticosteroid, and low on platelets. But she was dismayed to learn that while she and her husband were away Lucy had decided to leave hospice. Certain conflicts at work had drained her. Mrs. Doyle's case had been transferred to another nurse, Roberta Smalley.

Lucy knocked on Mrs. Doyle's door the next day. She confirmed that she had left hospice. She also told her that she considered her a friend and hoped to continue supporting her in any way she could. She gave Mrs. Doyle her home phone number and encouraged her to use it. Mrs. Doyle was upset. She had grown close to Lucy despite the events of June. She trusted her as a nurse. Her sadness was deepened when she shared the news with Dr. Richards. Dr. Richards found Lucy to be a capable and committed hospice worker. She worked well with her. And she liked the fact that Lucy had shown a real interest in keeping Mrs. Doyle out of pain. She was sorry that Lucy had left. Like Mrs. Doyle, she would miss her.

"My mom is a very big part of my life"

The male stripper brought laughs and blushes to everyone at Kim's bache-lorette party. Kim was pleased, and so was Mrs. Doyle. The wedding was now around the corner. Kim was scheduled to leave for Europe on October 11. She would be gone for three weeks. She worried about leaving her mother. The possibility that Mrs. Doyle wouldn't be alive when she returned frightened her. She instructed Peter to inform her of every emergency. She explained to her fi-ancé that if her mother were to decline, she would need to return home. Mrs. Doyle, however, seemed well. For the first time, she even talked about the dress she planned to wear at Kim's wedding reception. She expected to be alive for at least a few more months. She even hoped that her platelets would allow her to start chemotherapy.

Kim was less optimistic. She had learned not to take anything for granted. The roller-coaster effect had trained her to worry when things were going well. In tears, she said to me:

> I think things are good, and that is when I get scared. Am I missing something? I was with Mom last night, and I was paying attention to her, and I did not see any-thing. She looks great, she is acting fine, she is energetic to the point that she can really talk about her trip. My mom is a very big part of my life. She is this vital per-son, this source of energy and enthusiasm, and she is a friend. She is someone I want to embrace and hold on to. I am going to lose so much. My criticisms of her are just kind of part of the background now. I can see her, appreciate her, and love her just because she is who she is.

For the first time in her life, Kim said, she felt proud of being Jenny Doyle's daughter.

Another crisis

While Mrs. Doyle was making dinner on the evening of October 1, she felt a sharp pain in the right side of her abdomen. She dropped the plate she was holding and doubled over. A few minutes after regaining her composure, she was stricken again. Breathless, she leaned over the dining room table and in-structed her husband to call hospice. Her pain resembled the pain she had ex-perienced in July, when she thought she had fractured a rib. This time, how-ever, she didn't vomit. With the help of a hospice nurse, the Doyles managed to control Mrs. Doyle's pain, but they didn't eliminate it. In the morning, Mrs. Doyle called Dr. Richards for her advice. Dr. Richards recommended comput-erized tomography (CT) scan of her abdomen. Mrs. Doyle had the scan the following evening. When I saw her on October 6, she told me that if her cancer had metastasized to her liver, Dr. Richards would be unable to offer her more treatments. She would have to give up her fight.

Mrs. Doyle was weak and lethargic, and her voice was noticeably more raspy. She yawned with every sentence and seemed to be short of breath. But she was hopeful. The scan did suggest changes in her liver, but, according to Mrs. Doyle, it was inconclusive. She complained that hospice had neglected her. Since her husband's phone call on the evening of October 1, no one had contacted her to see how she was doing. "Roberta has not done diddley," she said. "So far, I did not contact her about this crisis, because I'm doing it with Dr. Richards. Now she was supposed to call me today to arrange for a visit sometime later on this week, but I have not heard anything yet."

On October 11, Mrs. Doyle saw Kim and Patrick off to Europe. She gave them her blessing and insisted that they stop worrying about her. "I wished they could take me with them," she said. Upon her return home, she found her first worker's compensation check waiting for her in the mailbox. Three days later, she started to vomit uncontrollably. She also experienced severe pain and shortness of breath. Not trusting Roberta, she didn't call hospice. Dr. Richards instructed her to get a blood test immediately. Mr. Doyle took her to the nearest hospital. There, her platelets proved so low that she was instructed to stay for inpatient treatment. She had multiple bruises on her arm, abdomen, and back. Her face, neck, and arms were puffy. She received a blood transfusion immediately.

Sandra was shocked to hear about Mrs. Doyle's hospitalization. She was unaware that her patient was in crisis. What disturbed her even more was that, contrary to the impression I had received from Mrs. Doyle, she had been trying to contact her for three weeks. She said:

> I think what she is doing is wanting to protect herself rather than wanting to actually get rid of us. She understands what we are about, and she knows that is a reality for her. If I got her alone, I would probably just comment on the no-return phone calls. I am sure I would say, "Listen, I don't want to put you on the spot, so please don't feel defensive if I ask you: do you feel as if you would rather not have me visit, or really rather not think about hospice right now?"

When Sandra did see Mrs. Doyle in the hospital room, Mrs. Doyle spoke non-stop, leaving no room for dialogue. To Sandra it was a facade. Behind Mrs. Doyle's confident appearance, she saw fear and anxiety. On her way out, she looked at Mrs. Doyle's chart. In it, she saw a letter written a few months earlier by Dr. Richards, stating that Mrs. Doyle was too active to be hospice-appropriate. "Well, you know," Sandra said to me, "if Dr. Richards communicated that to Jenny, that certainly puts a distance between Jenny and us."

"I think I am dying"

I saw Mrs. Doyle in the hospital on October 17, three days after her admission. She was lying in bed with an oxygen mask, her nose bleeding. Her head and extremities looked hard and swollen and her eyes were yellow. She struggled to stay alert. She kept her words to a minimum, but she did manage to tell me that she was "hanging in there." Mr. Doyle was sitting by her side. The rhythmic sound of machines underlay the heavy silence.

Suddenly the phone rang. A friend of Mrs. Doyle's wanted to talk to her. Upon hearing her voice, Mrs. Doyle started to cry. "I think I'm dying," she said with a frightened tone, as tears rolled down her cheeks. Her friend told her she would be there right away. Mrs. Doyle turned to us and said she was confused. She had a look of horror on her face. She sobbed. She insisted on being informed about her condition, wanting to know what was happening to her. Looking her in the eyes, her husband leaned over the bed railing and softly said, "Your platelets are low." He then started to cry. His voice shook. "Probably they won't be able to raise them, Jenny," he said. Had any doctor said she was . . .? She couldn't say the word. Mr. Doyle shook his head. The tension on Mrs. Doyle's face eased. If she were dying, she said, she wanted the opportunity to speak to her parents, her cousins, and Peter. Mr. Doyle reminded her that her parents had visited her that morning and lived close enough to come again. Her cousins were available, too, he said, and Peter was on his way from New York.

Mr. Doyle invited me to join him in the lounge. He looked distraught. He had not slept in days. He cried. He told me that he didn't know what to do. He knew his wife was dying, but he didn't know how to tell her that, or when. Peter was scheduled to arrive the next day. Kim had just gotten married in Europe, but because Mrs. Doyle did not want to ruin her trip, he wasn't going to notify her about her mother's condition. Lucy was the only person he would have felt comfortable calling for help, but she no longer worked for hospice. When I mentioned Sandra, he had difficulty remembering who she was. He cried some more, then he laughed, then he cried. He was tired, he said, somehow he needed to take care of himself as well. Before I left, a nurse walked into Mrs. Doyle's room. As the nurse was giving her a blood transfusion, Mrs. Doyle pointed upward to show us a bird flying in the room. We all looked up, but saw nothing there.

"Jenny is gone in spirit, but her body is still here"

Two days later, Mrs. Doyle learned that her cancer had metastasized to her liver. She asked now to be kept comfortable and to be spared from further blood transfusions. She was no longer able to get out of bed. She required a urinary catheter. Her respirations were shallow and labored. She was given an antianxiety medication for a panic attack. She asked for a pill that would help her die. Peter was by her side. Seeing his mother in an unresponsive state, he left a message on his sister's answering machine, asking her to call the hospital. Mr. Doyle declined Sandra's offer to transfer his wife to the hospice inpatient unit. He felt that Mrs. Doyle was comfortable in the hospital and wouldn't want to be subjected to an unnecessary transfer. He asked, however, for a visit from Lucy.

Later in the day, Mrs. Doyle opened her eyes and asked to see her husband, parents, two of her cousins, and Peter all at once. She seemed alert. When everyone gathered around her, she told them she was dying. Looking at each one, she spoke about the things she appreciated about them. She said she loved them. She instructed her parents to take the baby gifts she had bought for Kim's and Peter's unborn children and give them to them after their birth. Finally, she led a prayer. When she finished, she closed her eyes.

The next day, Mr. Doyle encouraged his wife to let go. Mrs. Doyle moaned with every breath. She was covered with bruises under the surface of her yellow skin. On her right arm she had a large, fluid-filled blister. Mr. Doyle applied water to her lips to keep them moist. He spoke to her affectionately without knowing if she could hear. He assured her that he loved her. Suddenly, Mrs. Doyle opened her eyes, gave him a kiss, and said, "I love you, too." Her gesture made him laugh and cry. A friend called on the phone. "Jenny is gone in spirit, but her body is still here," said Mr. Doyle softly. He had already made calls to inquire about funeral arrangements. To his relief, he was assured that since five months had gone by since Mrs. Doyle's strontium injection, she was eligible for cremation.

Kim called from Europe and, together with her husband, she took the first flight back home. Softly, Mr. Doyle told his wife that her daughter was expected soon. Mrs. Doyle was declining further. Her mother, anxious and distraught, had to take sedatives to calm herself.

Mrs. Doyle's breathing started slowing down. At times it stopped completely. Every three or four breaths, someone would shake her and she would start up again. Her body was very hot. Mr. Doyle and one of their friends wrapped ice cubes in rags and placed them at pulse points, and worked that way for a couple of hours. Then, at five o'clock in the afternoon, Kim walked in with her new husband. They took the oxygen mask off, and Kim hugged her mother, crying and crying.

The next day, at the recommendation of a hospice nurse, Mrs. Doyle's intravenous hydration was terminated. Now neither Peter nor Kim left their mother's side. The following morning, Mrs. Doyle's respirations were labored and noisy. Once again her family gathered in her room and watched. Mr. Doyle brushed her hair and sprayed perfume on her body. Mrs. Doyle was swollen and covered with black, blue, and yellow patches. All her family hoped for was that she would leave this world in peace. But to everyone's horror, her last gasp came with vomit. "She threw up all this brown, pus-looking, oatmeal stuff," Mr. Doyle recalled. "It must have been bile backing up from her liver. We had to carry her mother out of the room."

"For me, Jenny's death was sort of a mess"

Half an hour after Mrs. Doyle's death, a hospice nurse walked into her room to support the family. When she asked how she could help them, Mr. Doyle said, "Could you give me another 30 years with my wife?" Kim answered first. "That will be in heaven," she said.

Two hundred and fifty people paid their final respects at the viewing. The next day, Mrs. Doyle was cremated. Mr. Doyle was having trouble sleeping. His wife's death had fallen upon him quickly and unexpectedly. Kim was depressed. She couldn't understand how her mother could have declined so rapidly. Her wedding reception was scheduled to take place in six days, but she canceled it. Dr. Richards was disappointed that she failed to raise Mrs. Doyle's platelets. "We had tried to get her on an experimental drug," she said, "and the red tape was a real stumbling block. But I am not so sure even if we had been able to actually get it into her system, it would have made a difference. But I guess Jenny took the approach that she wanted for a period of time. She did not beat the cancer, but she gave it a run for a while."

Sandra was disturbed by Mrs. Doyle's death. "For me, Jenny's death was sort of a mess and not the way I would have liked to see it go for her," she said. "She was treating herself as if she was not a hospice patient, when really, underneath, all this stuff was going bad and then just caused her to totally crash. I could not escape the feeling that she was not dying comfortably." Sandra suspected that if Mrs. Doyle hadn't sought aggressive treatment all the way to the end, she and her family would have been better prepared for her death. She didn't think they denied reality. She thought they ignored it. At the same time, she acknowledged that her own preference for a more gradual ending in the in-patient unit of hospice might not have been Mrs. Doyle's priority.

Not everyone at hospice shared Sandra's feelings, however. "Jenny was a very powerful person," Roberta said to me. "I wrote in the chart that we need more people like Jenny Doyle in this world. Just her strength, her vision, her drive to stay alive, looking out for her family even though she knew she was dying, not talking about dying. If I were her, I would be the same way. I wouldn't want to give up at her age. Hospice people think you need to talk about your dying. No. These people are so sick, they know. Deep inside, they know. Why do I have to badger her with that? She knew she was dying. She was just visionary. Just a perfect hospice kind of patient."

Five weeks after his wife's death, Mr. Doyle had melted their wedding bands into a cross that he placed over her urn. He felt guilty about his wife's final moments. Why did she vomit? Could he have prevented that? The hospice support groups he attended brought him in touch with other widowers, but they consisted of people much older than him, which he found depressing. "It is a transition period, and I don't particularly care for it," he said. "I still choke up five or six times a day. Like, last week I hated love songs. But I moved stuff around a little bit, and I know after a while I will have to put a picture away or something along those lines, but there is no rush right now." One thing he didn't want to repeat, however, was spraying his wife's perfume in the house. The memories that brought him were overpowering.

"I am angry at her, and I'm hurt"

When I saw Kim two months after her mother's death, she told me she had been reluctant to take part in another interview. She felt uncomfortable talking because her feelings toward her mother were not all positive. At the same time, she didn't want to squelch them. On the one hand, she explained, she missed her mother, but on the other, she resented her. "I am angry at her, and I'm hurt," she said. After her death, Kim learned that her mother had left her and Peter only a minor fraction of her assets. The rest of her fortune went to Mr. Doyle. Kim emphasized that her hurt had nothing to do with dollars. That was a point she wanted to make sure I understood. Once again, in Kim's opinion, Mrs. Doyle took no responsibility for the well-being of her children. In essence, she let them fend for themselves, which is exactly what she had done years earlier. "I remember my mom saying to me she was going to make sure I was taken care of with her death benefit," she said. "That was how she was going to make it up to me."

"Now I'm wondering if all the healing that went on in our relationship was just strictly for her benefit," Kim continued. She felt like a fool for having forgiven her mother. At the same time, she questioned if holding a grudge against someone who was gone would help. "I can either let this hurt me for the rest of my life or accept it," she said. "I think it will just take some time." The memory she thought would ease her anger was that of her mother regaining consciousness when she came back from Europe. She knew that Mrs. Doyle had been unresponsive prior to her arrival. She said, "Once I got to the room she started breathing really strong, and her heart was good for almost two days. She could not talk any more, but she gave me a kiss. So she stuck it out. I really appreciate that she stuck it out." Kim didn't want to go through her mother's clothing. She didn't want her jewelry. All she would have liked was photographs from her childhood, but she knew her mother had thrown those out.

Even a year after Mrs. Doyle's death Kim was unable to make use of hospice's bereavement services. She told me that hospice, as an agency, reminded her too much of her mother. Then she said, "There were many years that I did not have contact with my mom, and in a sense, it just feels like that period again. I am 15 again and don't know if I will ever see my mom again. So I tell myself, my mom is dead. I remind myself, 'It is not that your mom is not coming, your mom is dead. Your mom is dead. *Gone.* She is not living any more.' I don't miss her. That I don't like. But I don't think it is the result of anything I have done."

Mr. Doyle told his hospice support group that he was in the "second half" of his grieving period. To the support group leader, he gave the impression that he was moving on with his life. In fact, Mr. Doyle was contemplating moving out of Lancaster County all together. He was lonely. He felt rejected by Mrs. Doyle's family. He had been accused of greediness, selfishness, and an over-zealous determination to get rid of his wife's belongings. He said, "The second six months is more difficult because I have to find out who I am as an independent person, and what I want to do, because at my age in life that gets a little worrisome. I have to build up a whole different network that I don't have. It still gets lonely and quiet around here at night, but I am sleeping a little bit better. You can't run through this period. You just have to walk through it. I think I would just like to find ways to walk through it quicker."

16

Jasmine Claude
A Study in Faith

Narrated by ANNA TOWERS

Initially, when Jasmine Claude's lymphoma was first treated with chemotherapy, the cancer was stopped. But then the tumors started to grow again, and her oncologist tried three different regimes to get her into remission. In her fourth year of treatment, she began to develop abdominal pain. The oncologist consulted the Palliative Care Service to help control her symptoms, and the service followed her as an outpatient. She continued to receive palliative chemotherapy for many months after this. When the oncologist told her that the abdominal tumor was growing in spite of the chemotherapy and that he would have to stop the treatment, Mrs. Claude began to receive palliative home care. She was feeling tired and less able to go out, but was otherwise not feeling too bad. She carried on with her daily routine as much as she could, and seemed surprisingly cheerful and serene.

Over the years, Mrs. Claude had developed an unshakable faith in God. It was unusual for the palliative care staff to witness such serenity, and their reactions ranged from curiosity, fascination, and inspiration, to skepticism. This narrative describes not only an experience of palliative care but also an exploration of the experience of faith, as seen within a palliative care context.

The birth of faith through adversity

Jasmine Claude had not had an easy life in her native Haiti. In her early twenties she experienced terror at the hands of the Tonton-Macoutes military police that destroyed her young family. Her husband died while a political prisoner, leaving her to raise their son, then only three years old. Fifteen years later, Mrs. Claude developed lymphoma. She was working as a secretary at the time, and had managed to save some money. She moved to Montreal, where there is a large French-speaking Haitian community, to have further medical investigations and to receive treatment. Mrs. Claude knew some friends with whom she could stay until she was settled. She had been a devout Jehovah's Witness in Haiti and was able to fit into a new "family" in Montreal, which helped her through an otherwise difficult transition to a new society. She also kept in touch with old friends in Haiti, and others who were spread out across North America. She continued to be concerned about the unstable political situation at home. The democratically elected leader Aristide had been ousted by the Haitian military and an economic embargo was in force. Mrs. Claude, like most Haitians, had invested great hope in Aristide, and she corresponded with friends who were hoping for restoration of democratic rule.

I first met Mrs. Claude in December 1995, one month after the oncologist had stopped her chemotherapy. She lived near a densely built working-class section of Montreal, in an area consisting of apartment buildings and the occasional street of smaller units where two or three families might live. All the streets were lined with trees, but there were no parks or green spaces. Mrs. Claude shared a modest two-bedroom apartment, which was in a 10-unit building near a major highway, with her 20-year-old son Paul, who was a full-time student.

When Mrs. Claude, a tall and slim woman, answered the door, I was struck by her gracious, aristocratic bearing and warm, engaging eyes. As we settled around her kitchen table, I noticed her markedly protuberant abdomen. Only by frequently shifting her position did she manage to remain seated throughout the interview. The apartment was spotless, and I surmised that she must be spending all of her physical energy cleaning. She said that Paul helped with the household chores.

She looked very sad as she spoke of her husband's death in prison, but she brightened as she spoke about her faith. "I was very depressed after my husband died," she said, "even suicidal at times. Then something happened to me about six years ago. Things changed. I started to have faith. I felt strong again. So now, no matter what happens, I know that God is there for me. I often wonder why this had to happen to me, of all people. I don't know what it all means. But I can look death squarely in the eye. Don't get me wrong: I do feel angry and frustrated about all this, but I won't allow it to get me down."

She went on to talk about her hopes for Paul. "He's in college and he's doing great," she told me. "I brought him up alone, but I did my best to bring him up well. I want him to grow up in a way that would have made his father proud. And he's a good boy. He gets on well with people and he adapts well to change. I don't think he'll go back to Haiti after I die, because of the political situation there. But with his skills he could go anywhere in North America. So that's what's important for me—to make sure that my son will be OK and settled."

Mrs. Claude continued her pattern of trying to support others. She counseled needy members of her church community on the telephone and wrote letters to her friends. She kept busy with chores in the apartment, as much as she was able to. Her abdomen was so bulky that she felt like she was nine months pregnant, and she found it difficult to breathe.

"One thing I do enjoy is writing letters to my friends," she said. "I write to them about all sorts of things. I try to encourage them. So many of them ask me for advice about their problems."

"Do you write to them about your illness?" I asked.

She answered without hesitation. "No, I never do. I never write about my illness."

"Whom *do* you talk to about your illness?"

"Oh, my son is good. Whenever I get upset or depressed, he has a way of sitting me down at the kitchen table and having a chat with me. We talk and he doesn't give up until I feel better."

Mrs. Claude still had close ties with her family in Haiti. She was trying to arrange for her mother to come to Canada to help look after her during the terminal phase of her illness. That was her wish, to stay at home under her mother's care. She also had two brothers in Haiti and a sister who was a nurse in Switzerland, with whom she spoke regularly on the phone. She had several close and supportive friends in her church community who helped her both practically and emotionally. Her church friends regularly took her shopping for her groceries so she didn't have to go by bus. She organized the schedule herself.

I was deeply impressed after meeting Mrs. Claude. She made me feel good, and hopeful for the future of humanity. She was a warm and competent person, of strong faith, facing death and lovingly raising her son. Her physical state was not good, her prognosis was grim, and yet she seemed to be at peace.

By the time I met Mrs. Claude, Susan, the home care nurse, had been visiting Mrs. Claude weekly for quite some time. She assessed how Mrs. Claude was managing, checked on symptoms, and communicated with the palliative care physician regarding medication. Susan was very experienced with symptom control and terminal care. Cheerful, outgoing, and able to see the humor in situations, Susan cared deeply for her patients and went out of her way to help them. Her observations in the journal she kept as part of our project indicated that others from the Palliative Care Service shared my reaction to Mrs. Claude. Around the same time as my visit, Susan noted:

> There's been a remarkable change in this lady in the past year. She is much more optimistic; very, very peaceful. She has made all her arrangements. She is going to have her last will and testament done on Monday. She's quite a remarkable lady, I think. Every day I've gone, for about the last month or six weeks, she's had a radiance on her face, even though she'd been very uncomfortable with ascites and edema in both legs. She knows she's very sick, she knows she has a short time to live, but she takes every day as it comes and tries to live it the best she can. There's just something very wonderful after being with her. It's a feeling of being wrapped in soft, soft cotton, a feeling of peace that I have when I leave her. She knows there are hard times ahead, and yet I come away feeling that I've been touched by something blessed. She's not looking for consolation or comfort or anything—that seems to be within her. And I take this serenity with me when I leave her.

"A calm heart is the life of this body of flesh"

Around Christmas, Susan noted that Mrs. Claude was becoming more subdued as she began to have more physical symptoms. Her abdomen was getting bigger and more cumbersome, so she could hardly walk. She was losing her appetite and getting weaker. She was now bedbound. Her sister visited from Switzerland, and one of her brothers came up from Haiti. Mrs. Claude expressed to Susan the feeling that there was lot of power inside herself to change the course of the illness, possibly leading to a miraculous improvement. At the same time, she was exhausted from too much company over the holidays. There was a sign on the inside door of her apartment, requesting that visitors not stay for more than 30 minutes.

By early January, Mrs. Claude's sister and brother had left, and Mrs. Claude insisted that she wanted to be alone. She refused additional help at home through the community health services, saying that she was capable of looking after herself with some help from Paul. We observed, however, that Paul never seemed to get involved in direct nursing care for his mother. Mrs. Claude just wanted her family around her, her religious magazines, and her Bible. She wanted to be alone to reflect and meditate, without having to be sociable. An inspirational quotation was mounted on the wall above her bed: "A calm heart is the life of this body of flesh."

Mrs. Claude was still waiting for her mother's visa to come through, and was looking forward to her mother coming in about three months. She seemed to be unaware that her prognosis was shorter than that. When the oncologist had stopped the chemotherapy two months earlier, he had told Mrs. Claude that she might live another year. Mrs. Claude's health had markedly deteriorated since then, but no one else had discussed her prognosis with her, and it seemed that she was unaware that her disease was progressing faster than her oncologist had estimated.

Bursts of anger as energies dwindle

In late January, Susan's weekly home visit with Mrs. Claude had to be delayed because of another more urgent visit. She telephoned Mrs. Claude to let her know, offering to come one hour later than her scheduled appointment of 2:30 p.m. She added that she would be accompanied by a physician who had been visiting the Palliative Care Service. Mrs. Claude replied in a curt tone that Susan had not heard from her before, "You will either come before 3:00 or not at all."

"But, Mrs. Claude, that's not possible," Susan replied, perplexed by Mrs. Claude's tone of voice. "And I really want the doctor to see you because he'll be leaving us this week and it's the last chance for him to see you."

"A doctor isn't necessary because I have the Lord who will look after me," Mrs. Claude replied. She sounded angry now.

This did not sound like the Mrs. Claude that Susan knew. "But you really need to be seen," she persisted, "and we can't come sooner because we have another patient whom we urgently have to see right now."

"Well, I'm sorry, but I need my rest."

Susan paused for a few moments. "Well, I guess I'll have to come next week then."

"I think that would be better. Because if you come later today it will interrupt my rest."

Susan was upset by this encounter. Mrs. Claude's manner was a real surprise, and Susan's other patient really did have an emergency: he was dying, and in fact, died shortly after Susan got off the phone. A week later, when Susan arrived, she was greeted by an angry Mrs. Claude. Susan started cheerfully, "So, Mrs. Claude, how has it been having your brother and sister here? You had lots of other visitors, too. That was a lot of company."

Mrs. Claude said, irritably, "It's really tired me out. It was good to see my family, but some other visitors are really inconsiderate when they come to see you and they have all kinds of advice to give that you don't need."

"I'm sorry I couldn't make it last week at the time we'd agreed," Susan said. "I had a patient who was in a crisis situation."

"Some people will say anything to get attention and they'll call any little thing a crisis," Mrs. Claude responded bitterly.

"No, Mrs. Claude. My other patient was really sick. The crisis was that my other patient was dying."

Mrs. Claude sighed and softened her tone. "I'm sorry," she said. She then resumed in an angry tone. "But I'm having problems here. My mother can't get a visa from the Canadian consulate in Haiti. She ought to be here now to help me, but we need the papers."

"You asked the doctor to give you a letter last week," Susan said. "And she faxed the letter to Haiti. Didn't that help?"

"The visa is still delayed. I'll need a stronger letter." Mrs. Claude puffed up her face and clenched her teeth in anger. "They treat people from poor black countries like we are all criminals!" she said.

Once more, Susan felt hurt and unfairly treated. At the same time, she tried to rationalize her experience with Mrs. Claude, to depersonalize it by reframing it in terms of Mrs. Claude's advancing disease. "I felt she was turning inward," Susan commented afterward in her journal, "and that was normal as she got sicker. It did not change my admiration for her as much as I filed away the thought in my mind, 'Now she is really sick!' And she was."

I had had a similar encounter with Mrs. Claude around this time, when she was curt and angry. I reacted differently from Susan, however, possibly because as a researcher rather than as Mrs. Claude's physician I was not actually responsible for her care. Mrs. Claude's expression of anger actually made me respect her more, for I now knew that she could express her needs directly and that she could be angry when she felt she had to be. Rather than putting distance between us, it strengthened the bond that I had with her. To me, the fact that she could get angry made her serenity all the more authentic.

On February 14, 1996, Mrs. Claude called Susan to say that she was experiencing abdominal pain and it was hard for her to breathe. Susan discussed this with Dr. Morin, the palliative care physician, and they suggested to Mrs. Claude that she come to the hospital. They thought that a paracentesis (to remove fluid from the abdomen) might relieve her abdominal distension and improve her breathing. She could then go back home. However, an ultrasound test revealed a solid tumor. There was no ascites liquid to be extracted. It was the tumor that was making her abdomen protrude to the size of a massive twin term pregnancy. Susan felt that she should be admitted to the Palliative Care Unit, and Mrs. Claude reluctantly agreed. She assumed that her stay would be short. Paul was taking exams at this time and Mrs. Claude did not want him to quit his studies to look after her. But she expected her mother to obtain her visa any day, so that she could go home under her mother's care.

"Now I want a rest"

On admission to the Palliative Care Unit, Dr. Morin started Mrs. Claude on diuretics and steroids. The music therapist found classical music that helped relieve her abdominal pain. Paul came to see his mother every evening, and Mrs.

Claude's church friends also continued to be a practical support to her. They were busily organizing medical aides and generally trying to prepare for her eventual return home. Two friends, Jacques and Brother Demers, a church leader, visited almost every day. She was clearly aware that her condition was terminal. At the same time she was hoping that she could just have a few tests and go home again. She switched back and forth between thinking she would go home and being afraid that she would die on the unit.

When I went to see Mrs. Claude in her room, she was still too uncomfortable to lie down and so was propped up on several pillows in a reclining chair. She had some difficulty breathing because of the pressure from her abdomen and had to stop in mid-sentence to take a breath. But she was generous in cheerfully taking the time to chat with me. We got talking about her relationships. "I was always the organizer in the family," she explained. "When I'm not there, the people around me don't know what to do—they stand there with their arms by their sides. So, I'm trying to organize my mother to come. But it's not easy because I have to get Paul to phone, and he's young and not so able to organize things."

"Why don't you get a phone in your room?" I suggested.

"If I get a telephone then too many friends call me and they want to talk for a long time and get advice about their problems."

"They want *you* to help *them* even though you're sick?"

Mrs. Claude replied calmly, "I'm always the one who has helped other people with their problems and now I want a rest. I don't want to see any visitors except my son and two men friends from my church." She had a hint of a smile as she paused. "I prefer male visitors—they don't talk as much as the women."

"That's true, isn't it?" I replied. We both laughed.

Along with Mrs. Claude's sense of humor, the staff appreciated and found fascinating her ability to get her needs met without making them feel manipulated; instead, they felt worthwhile and successful. I discussed this with Rosemary, her ward nurse, who had worked on the unit for many years. She had formed a close bond with Mrs. Claude.

"Rosemary," I began, "what I find interesting is that she has absolute control over her world, but it's something positive as far as the staff are concerned. I mean, there are patients who take charge—"

Rosemary finished my sentence, "And they abuse. On thinking about it, it's that she doesn't control me. She controls her affairs but without controlling those around her. She uses me, but it's OK for her to use me; it's part of my role. But I know that she isn't going to abuse my services or abuse my goodwill. I can be myself. I'm not risking my skin in helping her. She is realistic in her demands. She expresses real needs."

Rosemary, who was a calm and patient nurse, was expressing how difficult it can be to look after palliative care patients who become demanding, angry, or moody as they get sicker. Nurses have to constantly monitor themselves and not react emotionally in return. But where does a nurse set limits? Rosemary was relieved that Mrs. Claude didn't put this sort of pressure on her, that she freed her from the constant self-monitoring that is part of the daily work of a nurse.

On February 16, within two days of her admission, Mrs. Claude's breathing and leg swelling started to improve, presumably in response to the diuretics and steroids. She still got short of breath when she talked but she was now able to walk down the hallway. She liked to stay up at night writing letters, and she seemed to have a voluminous correspondence. Since she didn't nap during the day either, I wondered whether her insomnia might be a sign of fear or anxiety, but Paul told me later that his mother had never slept much.

Mrs. Claude was trying to process the fact that nothing could be done to markedly reduce her abdomen, that there was no fluid to remove. The implications of this were just starting to sink in, and she expressed the desire for space and time to think. She limited her visitors even further to those whom she truly wanted to see. During the second week of her admission she was looking thinner, and she was too weak to leave her room. She developed new symptoms: nausea and increasing abdominal cramps. The pain was quickly relieved by oxycodone, a strong opioid, but Mrs. Claude was reluctant to take the medication regularly. She was under the common but mistaken impression that if she took regular analgesia now, medication wouldn't work if and when the pain got worse. Even after we explained to her that this was not the case, she continued to be stoic about her pain.

When I visited her on February 24, she was lying on her side, her face slightly contorted. She was holding her abdomen.

"Mrs. Claude, do you want me to tell the nurse to bring you a painkiller?"

"No, I think I'll wait. A little rest might ease the pain. Anyway, my spirits are good. I have a spirit of steel. It's been four years that I have lived with this, and my spirits have always been good. They say that if one can keep one's spirits up, it's 90% of the battle. But I am eating less, and I'm feeling weaker." She paused. "I'm not afraid of dying. I consider it a deep sleep. I think my son is also more prepared now, about my going."

I asked Dr. Morin later about her relationship with Mrs. Claude and the issue of Mrs. Claude's faith in particular. She said, "At first, I was a little skeptical. But after two or three discussions with her, I realized it's clearly all right for her to be like that. The deeper you go into her history, the more you realize that she needs her religion. I don't make it a habit to confront people, because religion is something personal. I said to myself, 'This woman—if we push her, if we challenge her too much about her personal beliefs—it would be to her detriment.' So it wasn't something that I tried to challenge, but it's something that I tried to listen to. One day I asked her, 'What about your son? Is he a believer?' Her answer was very interesting. She said, 'He can't really understand this. He is too young.' So, for her it was clearly a long spiritual journey that she had undertaken."

Dr. Morin did not have such a powerful, unquestioning faith. But alongside her skepticism was a real fascination with Mrs. Claude's faith, and she often found herself drawn back to the subject in her interactions with Mrs. Claude. "I often brought it up," she told me. "It was clear that one couldn't play around too much in there, to question too much. I didn't try to do that, but I certainly used the patient, in the sense that I made her talk about how she got to believe what she believed. People with these strong fixed beliefs have always intrigued me. What's going on in their heads? How can they believe something so totally? It penetrates to their very marrow."

I also interviewed a ward volunteer who had looked after Mrs. Claude and who had been with the Palliative Care Service for 21 years. She described Mrs. Claude's faith as "radiant."

"You have a tremendous faith," the volunteer had said to her.

"Yes," Mrs. Claude had answered, "with so many evil forces around the world. The wild dogs are out there, I don't know what my son will do. I despair about my country. I worry about the political situation, about Aristide. It never gets better. My country is torn to pieces, and there are so many negative forces in the world. But we have to keep our faith in the Lord."

The volunteer was very moved. "I couldn't get over it," she said to me as she recounted her time with Mrs. Claude. "She had been through so much in life, and still she could look so calm and radiant. She was not in despair for herself, she was not afraid of anything. I haven't seen a patient like her in all these years. When I sat with her, she communicated so much. Her eyes, her body language just spoke 'peace' so clearly!"

The last days

Meanwhile, Mrs. Claude's increasing abdominal cramps heralded trouble. On February 26 she vomited and had other symptoms and signs of small bowel obstruction. Because of the extent of the tumor, she was not a candidate for surgical treatment to relieve the obstruction. Dr. Morin explained all this to Mrs. Claude, who remained fully alert, and continued to ask for as much control as possible over her medical and nursing care. She did begin to accept opioid medication on a regular basis for pain relief.

She looked weak and dehydrated when I went in to see her that day. "I'm having more pain," she told me, "but my breathing is better." She smiled and said, "I had a great whirlpool bath yesterday! So pleasant. I even told my sister in Geneva when I spoke with her on the phone yesterday. I said, 'You have money in Switzerland, but here we have whirlpool baths!'"

Mrs. Claude was not the first patient I had heard give the whirlpool a rave review. Many of the ward patients were comforted by it, which was a large gift from the grateful relative of a patient who had died on the unit a few years ago. This is one example of a detail of care that can give comfort even in the very last days.

Mrs. Claude told me she was thinking that she would go home again. She said that she was looking forward to seeing her brother, who was planning to come from Haiti in two months' time. Again she didn't seem to be aware that her prognosis was shorter than two months, and the staff decided to leave it at that for the time being.

Sometimes when patients develop signs of bowel obstruction, they spontaneously get better within a day or two. Perhaps the bowel gets kinked around the tumor and then this resolves. But the next day it was clear that Mrs. Claude was seriously obstructed. Even if she took nothing at all by mouth, she was vomiting bile. Medication controlled the nausea and reduced the vomiting, but she could not eat or drink. I spoke with her again, with Rosemary present at the foot of the bed.

"Mrs. Claude, you know your bowels are blocked," I said gravely.

"Yes. I was so afraid this would happen." She looked calm and dignified.

"There's a 50% chance that this will get better either by itself or with the help of medication. But that would be only a temporary improvement, I'm afraid."

"Well, I've told my brother to come sooner. I've also organized everything: my funeral, money for my son. I even wrote my own obituary notice to be printed in the newspaper in Haiti after I die."

"Your own obituary notice! Amazing!" I cried. "You're a great organizer. I think I'll hire you!"

Mrs. Claude smiled. "To work with you in the next life?"

"Yes," I said softly. "In the next life."

I reached out and held Mrs. Claude's hand and she started to cry. This was the first time I had seen her cry. I continued to hold her hand for a minute or two, and then she spoke again.

"I can't cry in front of my son. I must be strong for him."

"So who is there that you can speak with?"

"There is my friend from the church."

I sat silently with her for a couple of minutes more. When she was more composed, I left and Rosemary continued to chat with her. I remember feeling at the time that this exchange had deepened the bond I had with her. It was the type of meaningful encounter that happens occasionally in palliative care, and so often at unexpected moments.

The next day, February 28, Mrs. Claude was switched to continuous syringe driver medication, which led to better control of the vomiting. She still couldn't eat or drink, but she seemed in good spirits, saying that she wanted to be positive. Susan returned that day from a vacation and went immediately to see Mrs. Claude. When she got to the room a volunteer was sitting next to the bed, gently rubbing Mrs. Claude's stomach. Susan had heard about the bowel obstruction, and for a few moments they discussed the serious implications. But Mrs. Claude soon changed the subject. "She asked about my vacation," Susan recounted to me, "and wanted to know if I had any photographs. I promised I would bring them. She then said, 'You look good!' and flashed that amazing smile of hers. I was so touched. I found myself crying as I walked down the hall."

That evening, Mrs. Claude called her two church friends, Brother Demers and Jacques, and said, "I'm not feeling well. Come see me." When they arrived she discussed her life with them, the funeral arrangements, and she was able to cry with them. Brother Demers was too emotional to speak with her and had to leave, but she and Jacques spoke at great length. "We will see each other in another world," she reassured him. She reviewed her life, every phase of her illness. It was the only time that Brother Demers and Jacques had seen her cry. She cried with Paul that night, too, the only time that she cried in front of her son. She told him, "I'm satisfied with my life. I am going in peace." They discussed what would happen to him. Would he be able to live in the apartment alone, "with all the memories?" But mostly they discussed practical things together and finalized some financial details.

Paul phoned his mother early the next morning, as he did every morning. For the first time, he found that his mother was confused. He was concerned and came immediately to check on her. I met him on the ward, and he looked worried. I told him that his mother's condition had changed. He visited her briefly and looked even more worried as he came out of the room. But he couldn't stay. He had to go to school to write some exams. He was already late, he said, and quickly disappeared into the elevator.

Around 2:00 p.m., Rosemary left Mrs. Claude's bedside to attend to another patient. She returned to find that Mrs. Claude had suddenly died. No one had expected her to die suddenly that day. Usually, patients who develop bowel obstruction live on for days, sometimes weeks. Dr. Morin guessed that Mrs. Claude had probably had an internal hemorrhage. Although Rosemary is an experienced palliative care nurse, she was shocked and distressed, and could not carry on working. She went to sit in the nurse's lounge for the remaining hour of her shift.

I went into Mrs. Claude's room, to spend time there alone. Her body was still warm. I touched her and thought of how much I respected this woman. I thought of our last conversation, where I had jokingly said to her that she should work for me in the next life since she was so well organized. And I was moved by a sense of continuity, even though I am not a formal believer. I had a sense that everything was happening as it should, that life was all right, and that death was all right, and that they were part of one process. It was not a feeling of resignation, rather, for a moment at least, I had a taste of something beyond acceptance.

But what I could not accept was that the death had been so sudden. We knew that she was dying, but it wasn't supposed to be today! She didn't fade away. She went, just like that. It was a shock for me as well.

In the meantime, Dr. Morin and several other staff were milling around the nursing station. Dr. Morin had tried to reach Paul at school to tell him of his mother's death; however, the exam was over and Paul had already left. Repeated phone calls to his home failed to reach him. Everyone was afraid that Paul would arrive without having been forewarned that his mother had died.

Finally, at around 4:00 p.m., Paul arrived on the ward. The nurses were in their change-of-shift meeting, taking report from each other, and the only staff around was a volunteer who had just started her shift and who was not yet aware herself that Mrs. Claude had died. Paul went to his mother's room, which she had shared with another patient, and found that his mother's bed was no longer there. If a patient dies in a two-bed room, the practice on the ward is to give the grieving family more privacy by moving the body into another, quieter room at the end of the corridor. The volunteer saw Paul come back out to the hallway looking worried and puzzled, and immediately realized the situation. She took him to the meditation room where his mother's body had been taken. He looked completely bewildered. It was dark outside, but he did not want the light on. He just wanted to sit in the dark room with his mother. When Rosemary heard that Paul had arrived, she went immediately to the meditation room to see him and she put her arms around him. She had stayed well beyond her shift to wait for him.

When Paul got his bearings he said he had to make some phone calls. The volunteer offered to help him get through to his aunt in Switzerland. When he had finished his business he ate some food the volunteer had found for him, and then sat in the darkened nurses' lounge for half an hour. He went back to be with his mother's body, and then returned to the lounge. After another half hour, he went to pick up his mother's belongings. The volunteer watched him collect everything in sight, even the half-dead flowers. A friend from the church had arrived by then, who was very calm and seemed very supportive.

The psychologist who was there that evening spoke briefly with Paul and with Brother Demers, who had also arrived. She reassured herself that Paul had some good support immediately available. Over the next few days, it was Brother Demers who helped Paul look after all the affairs. Mrs. Claude's mother did not get her visa papers until after her daughter's funeral and she finally arrived from Haiti three weeks after Mrs. Claude died.

Reactions to the sudden death

The next day, I spoke with Rosemary. She described her reaction to Mrs. Claude's sudden death:

> She went fast. I left her room to give another patient some medication. It took five or ten minutes. I came back and she had died during this time. I was so surprised because—you know, we expect people to die here—but it was so sudden, she was already gone! Everyone expected that there would have been time for the family to come from Haiti. So I cried. It's bizarre, isn't it? I've been working here for 12 years, and thought that I had built a shell around me, but it had been a while since I had cared continuously for a patient many days in a row. She always told me she was happy when I was there. That same morning, the day she died, she told me, "You're a marvelous nurse."

Rosemary interrupted herself to look at me and say, "She was kind, wasn't she?" Then she reflected further on her emotional reactions:

> It's me, and it's a very personal reaction. When I'm with a mother and a child—when it's the mother that dies, but not when it's the child—there's a kind of unconscious identification, that I can't control. I couldn't control myself when she died yesterday. And I couldn't leave without having made the bridge between the mother and the son. He arrived, and I was there. I was waiting for him to come. I was waiting for something. I don't know what. I had to make the connection. I was there when she died and I had to make the bridge between her and her son. And I felt responsible! I've noticed that on several occasions, it happens when it's a sudden death. It's like an abandonment. She left, without giving us a chance to prepare, not like the others.

Rosemary paused. "Mind you," she continued, "I was adopted at the age of 20 months, so I have these crises of abandonment."

I also talked with Dr. Taylor, the resident physician, about the suddenness of Mrs. Claude's death. She said, "My feeling, when I walked into the room yesterday and she had just died, was that I just didn't do enough. I wasn't there enough for her or for her son. Something else could have been done. There was a sense of unfinished business. My expectation was to walk in and see her a couple of more times and be able to interact with her."

When I spoke with Paul afterwards he, too, commented on what it had been like for his mother to die so unexpectedly that day. "I spoke with Rosemary and Dr. Morin," he said, "and they told me it was OK for me to go to my exam. I looked at the chart and Rosemary had written that my mother was confused, that she was speaking Creole. Rosemary couldn't understand what she was saying, but I could have, had I been there." Paul wondered aloud to me, "Did she have a final message for me in Creole before she died? I feel that I should have stayed with her."

The year after

Dr. Morin and I both felt that Paul was at high risk for bereavement complications. He was relatively young and was now orphaned. He might still have unresolved feelings about having lost his father. He was a recent immigrant and seemed socially isolated. Although his mother had been critically ill, the actual moment of death had been unexpected—there might be unfinished business. Dr. Morin thought he was at risk for developing prolonged grief reactions or a depression that would interfere with his daily functioning. She planned to speak with the bereavement coordinator to try to get extra help for Paul, over and above the usual follow-up offered to families.

As it turned out, the members of Mrs. Claude's church community looked after Paul, even though he was not an actual member of the church. The church friends came by, called him up, and generally treated him like a member of the family. Paul failed the exams that he was writing at the time of his mother's death. He rewrote them the next month, however, and passed them all.

Within two months of his mother's death, Paul told me that things were getting better. He had spoken with many of his friends and found it easier to talk about his mother. Whenever I spoke with Paul after his mother's death, he seemed calm, confident, well organized, and in control. He was also more open and talkative with me, very different from the way he had been when I saw him with his mother, when he seemed shy and more of a little boy.

By four months, Paul had gotten himself a temporary job and he hoped to study electronics at the university the next year. When I spoke with him around the time of the first anniversary of his mother's death, things were continuing well, although he described some common signs of grief. "Every day is a battle," he said. "I'm anxious. Every time the phone rings, I'm afraid that someone is phoning to give me bad news, that someone has died. I'm also more sensitive to the grief of others. I talk more. I'm more open. There have been many changes in me over the past year."

He continued to sound confident. He was coping with his job, had retained his hope for the future, and was planning to further his studies. There seemed to be no cause for concern about the course of his bereavement.

The meaning of faith

After Mrs. Claude's death I continued to explore the theme of faith, which had emerged as such a major thread in this narrative. Paul shared the palliative care team's admiration for his mother's spirituality. When we spoke several months after her death he said:

Everyone who met her said what a remarkable person she was. Looking back on it, I see that religious people believe, but this was different—the way her faith played a role in every decision that she made, everything she faced. I am not sure that I could have done it. She witnessed in a special way. In the funeral speech the theme was the faith that she had, even in the end. It prevented her from being afraid. She didn't worry. She knew that it wouldn't be the end, that there was a future.

The physicians expressed intellectual and scientific curiosity, but also skepticism, regarding Mrs. Claude's spirituality, and were ambivalent about the issue of faith. On the one hand they assumed, tacitly, that religion isn't adequate. They took a psychodynamic view that is often taught in medical school and saw faith as a maladaptation, even as pathological. At the same time, however, they could not deny, and even admired, the enormous power of what they had witnessed, a power that called into question the narrowness of their skeptical psychological interpretations.

Dr. Taylor's comments were typical:

Unquestioning faith has always been difficult for me, because that is not my approach. It is not my experience. I have always admired people who can just be that convinced. And yet I wonder what else could be going on. And I think that maybe I am not getting at the underlying fear, or the underlying questions, because I don't know how many people are really fearless. Maybe I was being presumptuous or parental or something, but I just would get the feeling with her that things were much more fragile than she made them out to be, and I wanted to help and yet didn't, or couldn't.

The physicians did not openly negate or disaffirm Mrs. Claude's faith. It was hers, and they respected it. But they were torn between admiration and suspicion. Dr. Morin expressed the ambivalence of several of her colleagues when she said to me, "It always creates a difficulty for me, a faith like that, because I have a hard time adhering to something that dictates everything in advance for me. But it was clear to me that it helped her to get through everything she had to face."

I could easily relate to the team's fascination with Mrs. Claude's faith, on the basis of my own work as a palliative care physician. We are all struggling with our own questions of spirituality and transcendence. We learn on different levels and we plateau at different levels, as caregivers and as persons. In palliative care we are actively relating to the mystery of living and dying as a vital entity. We learn to relate to the mystery through the care of our patients.

17

Katie Melnick
Living and Dying with God

Narrated by YANNA LAMBRINIDOU

God was omnipresent in Katie Melnick's life. She saw signs of Him everywhere she went. Even during the last stages of lung cancer, after the disease had spread to her brain, Mrs. Melnick felt a deep sense of peace. Her caregivers from hospice were amazed at the depths and consistency of Mrs. Melnick's faith. At the same time, painful secrets in the Melnick family caused pain, confusion, and guilt, especially for Mrs. Melnick's daughter, Lena. During the time of Mrs. Melnick's dying, which took much longer than she had been prepared by her doctors to expect, the family relived old hurts, but also found unexpected possibilities for love and reconciliation.

"I am with you"

"I am very busy for a dying woman!" Katie Melnick jokingly exclaimed the first time I spoke with her on the phone. Mrs. Melnick was a 52-year-old, third-generation Polish Catholic who, at the time I spoke to her, had a 14-month history of lung cancer. After her initial diagnosis in August 1995, she underwent a lobectomy of her left lung. Now the cancer had metastasized to her brain. To explain why she didn't have time to meet with me that week she referred to the doctors' appointments that filled up her calendar. First she had to see her radiation oncologist in Lancaster, and then she was to travel to New York City for an appointment with a brain tumor expert. Her lungs were too weak to survive brain surgery, but she was suffering from seizures, forgetfulness, difficulty seeing, and tingling in her right arm. Mrs. Melnick had been offered stereotactic radiosurgery, an alternative method to conventional brain surgery that uses highly focused radiation beams to treat brain tumors. She was told that this procedure had the capacity to not only improve, but also lengthen her life.

Mrs. Melnick felt ambivalent about this new option. The last thing she wanted was to undergo a procedure that would compromise the quality of her remaining life. She knew she was going to die from her disease, and had already contacted Hospice of Lancaster County herself. Hospice staff had been visiting her for several weeks by the time I met her. In the end, she succumbed to pressures from her children who asked her to get a second opinion before turning down a potentially beneficial offer. She scheduled an appointment with a New York oncologist, and she and I agreed to meet a few days after her return.

On November 21, 1996, I visited Mrs. Melnick in her second-floor apartment in a small town in Lancaster County, Pennsylvania. She was a tall, thin, and attractive woman. She had a soft voice and elegant features—youthful skin, high cheekbones, a delicate nose, and light brown eyes. Her hair had only recently fallen out from her radiation. Despite the deforming effects of her illness, Mrs. Melnick prided herself on both physical and emotional strength. "I am like the matriarch of the family," she said to me the first time we met. She was sitting in an overstuffed chair at the corner of an unadorned living room, alone. Her husband John and her daughter Lena were at their family-owned dry-cleaning store. By her side was a coffee table with her essentials: medications, cigarettes, ashtray, and her beloved Bible. She smoked nervously, joked and laughed, and asked me questions about our study. She expressed eagerness to start our interviews, for she had a story she wanted to tell. At her suggestion, we moved to her bedroom for fear that the squawks of Anabel, her African gray parrot, would distract us. Already, Anabel had made a point of announcing her presence in the living room. "Anabel bird!" she shouted in between a polyphony of undecipherable sounds, "Melnick bird!"

In the bedroom Mrs. Melnick began her story by telling me about the neatly folded, hand-knit wool blanket that I sat next to at the foot of her bed. It was an ivory-colored throw with a pink cross in its center. Mrs. Melnick began:

> After my lung surgery, I still was not feeling that good, but I had still worked six days a week at our dry cleaner's. I was pretty depressed. This lady came in one time to drop off some clothes. We had no conversation. She did not know me. She does not know whether I am Jewish, Christian, anything. She had no idea that I had the lung cancer. When she left, God put it on her heart to pray for me, and she makes these prayer blankets; at each stitch she prays for the person that she is

making it for. She gets home and God kept telling her, "Pray for that lady," and she was, like, arguing with God, "I don't know her!" "Make a blanket for her!" So, she says, she was in the process of making one for somebody else, but God kept putting it on her heart. It took three weeks. She argued with God and said even when she would go to bed He would say, "Pray for that lady." Really! A total stranger! Anyway, she did. So in she comes with this blanket. She put it on my counter, and I figured she wanted to have it cleaned. I said, "Oh, isn't that pretty," and she goes, "It's for you." Well, I'm telling you, from a total stranger! That is why I have such a strong faith in God, that He could send a total stranger. It is just unbelievable! See the cross at the center? A total stranger! So to me that is confirmation of God telling me, "I am with you."

Mrs. Melnick practiced Catholicism until 1988. Then she switched to Protestantism and now attended a local Pentecostal church. The Scriptures gave her courage and inspiration. Now that she had difficulty reading for long periods of time, she explained to me, she limited her study to her favorite verses, those that exhorted contentment with one's fate and confirmed the love of God for all His people. "I know I should be experiencing anger, denial, and all these different things, but I am not," she told me. "I just pray. I say a little prayer to God, and I'm fine. I am just at peace. I am probably going to be like this right up until the end because He is with me—unless I tear my eyes away from Him and stop praying."

Mrs. Melnick was not fatalistic. She considered every form of palliative treatment available to her. She also attended healing services—Catholic, Protestant, and Pentecostal—in the hope of getting cured. She believed both in the power of medicine to extend her life and in the power of God to eliminate her tumor. Her appointment in New York gave her courage. She was told that she was a good candidate for stereotactic radiosurgery if her cancer hadn't metastasized to new organs and if her brain tumor hadn't enlarged. The procedure would give her six months to a year of life. Without it, the New York physician estimated that she had two months at the most.

Back in Lancaster County, Mrs. Melnick's radiation onocologist informed her that the mass in her brain had doubled. The 14-course radiation treatment he had given her only weeks before had not helped at all. In his meeting with Mrs. Melnick, the physician seemed detached, his voice, cold. Mrs. Melnick was startled to see a doctor lose all emotion as he handed her what amounted to a death sentence. She felt more sorry for him than she did for herself. She recalled, "I hugged him, and I said, 'I'm fine. I feel so bad that you have to tell people this.' My heart went out to him, and he just, like, got a tear in his eye and hugged me. So doctors are compassionate, but I guess they have to say these things over and over to people, and it is not easy. I have been really praying for the doctors because it is a tough, tough thing."

Since radiosurgery was no longer an option, a surgeon offered Mrs. Melnick brain surgery—the very procedure that two months earlier she had been told she wouldn't survive. After a period of prayer and talking things over with Lena, she decided against the surgery. "I don't want to spend my last days fighting cancer," she explained to me. "So now I feel that the growth of my tumor is a blessing because I don't want to linger and watch my family suffer. So I believe God answered my prayers because my tumor is growing. I am going to live shorter now. It is going to be a quicker death, and I would rather [it be that way]."

Her children supported her decision. Mr. Melnick, on the other hand, wanted his wife to try every procedure available to her. He didn't want her to give up, but wasn't able to convince her that brain surgery was worth the try. Mrs. Melnick had made up her mind. When she spoke with the brain surgeon, however, she was shocked to hear how short her prognosis actually was. Without brain surgery, the surgeon told her on December 2, 1996, she would live no longer than two more weeks. That was, she remembered, "the first time I have prayed for my life. All I was thinking was, 'God, help me make it to Christmas. Let me be around for Christmas, so I don't ruin the holiday for everybody for the rest of their lives.'"

A family secret

John and Katie Melnick had been married for 36 years, and together with their three children they had spent almost all of their lives in a small town in Maryland. Mr. Melnick worked at a fabric store while Mrs. Melnick raised the children. Although they loved each other, Mrs. Melnick told me, she and her husband weren't close. She liked openness and affection whereas he kept mostly to himself. Mrs. Melnick said:

> My husband is not a very warm person. I think he has hugged me twice since I got sick. He was never a huggy person. You'd think living with me all these years he would have changed a little bit, but he didn't. He is just not a warm person. He is not like me and my kids. I love him. He is a good man. But he just is not warm at all. He is just very cold, very cold. He was always like that. Because I am dying now, I would like him to be a little more warm, but he is not. I would like him to be a little more comforting or just say, "We'll get through this together," but he doesn't. But he does not have the same peace in the Lord as I do, either.

Mrs. Melnick poured all her love out to her children. Paul, 31, Carl, 29, and Lena, 22, were the essence of her life. Motherhood was the most important part of her existence, the only aspect of herself she cried about losing. "The happiest time of my life was raising my kids," she would say when reminiscing about her past. Mrs. Melnick described herself as a playful mother who took part in water fights, snowball fights, camping trips, dancing, and many other activities that brought happiness to her children's lives. In contrast to other parents, she said, she relished summers because her youngsters were out of school.

In December 1993, the fabric store that had employed Mr. Melnick for 27 years closed down, and both he and his wife started looking for new jobs. When they heard that a profitable dry-cleaning store in Lancaster County was for sale, they bought it and moved north. Neither of them were happy to leave Maryland, however. And neither of them wanted to leave their children behind. Their only consolation was that now Paul, Carl, and Lena were grownups. Paul was married, had one child of his own, and was in the middle of a training program to become a cook. Carl flew commuter planes and was himself engaged. And Lena worked happily at a hair salon in her neighborhood. Lancaster County was a 4-hour drive from the Melnicks' hometown, but daily phone calls between mother and children kept their bonds intact.

The dry-cleaner's was an exhausting business. Mr. Melnick was unhappy in his new job. The hours tired him. The responsibilities of running his own business overwhelmed him. And the fact that he was an introvert—quiet and uncomfortable with strangers—made his interactions with his customers an unrelenting challenge. Mrs. Melnick fared much better. She loved to work. The long hours at the store didn't bother her. It could be said that they energized her. Without a second thought, she took charge. She orchestrated the store's remodeling, she bought new equipment, and she paid the bills and taxes. Moreover, she enjoyed meeting customers and made a point of establishing personal relationships with the regulars.

Eight months into their new business, Mrs. Melnick was diagnosed with lung cancer. She was devastated. Her lung surgery took such a toll on her that, according to Paul, she lost her will to live. She stayed in the hospital for a month. After her discharge, she stopped eating. Mr. Melnick started blaming her for chain-smoking and for needlessly bringing a tragedy not only upon herself but also upon her family. He put the dry-cleaning store up for sale. He felt that without the help of his wife the business would destroy him both emotionally and financially. However he received no offers for it.

Eventually, Mrs. Melnick stopped smoking, resumed her work, and life went back to normal. But in October 1996, she started feeling weak and unable to control her right hand. She knew something was wrong. Mr. Melnick, on the other hand, believed that his wife was only overworked. Mrs. Melnick didn't look nearly as sick to him as she claimed. He was sure she would outlive him. She was surprised by her husband's reaction. She suspected that he was in denial and resentful that she could no longer remain strong for him.

Tests showed that Mrs. Melnick's cancer had metastasized to her brain. She immediately called Lena in Maryland. "It's a brain tumor," she said. "Can you come out right now? Can you quit your job and come out right now?" Four days later, Lena relocated to her parents' home in Lancaster County. Yet her decision to support her mother was difficult. Only a year before she had gone through the death of her maternal grandmother, a woman she loved deeply and had cared for at home until the end. In the meantime, she had ended a long relationship with her boyfriend and had had her dog put to sleep. Furthermore, her relationship with Mrs. Melnick was, as she put it to me, "not a very good one." "I know it sounds sick," she told me, as she explained that her move to Pennsylvania was motivated more by love for her father than for Mrs. Melnick. "I have a lot of respect for him," she said, "and I know what he has been living with for the past how many years, and I know how rough it is. He has become dependent on my mother, and I wanted to help him."

Lena got up and shut her bedroom door so that Mrs. Melnick, who was sitting in the living room, wouldn't be able to hear her. She then told me how, during her teenage years, her mother had abused both alcohol and her children. Physical fights, injuries, obscenities, and unpredictable outbursts of anger were not uncommon in the Melnick household. "There have been a lot of things that have happened over the course of my relationship with my mom that I thought were just irreparable," Lena said. "It was awful, and my dad has no recollection of that whatsoever. He is in denial, although he would sit up with her for nights, many nights. I remember one time I came in and he was choking her and another time she was choking him, and—oh my God! It was awful." Lena went on: She and her brothers had become suicidal. Paul developed a drinking problem of his own. But Lena said she suffered the most. She became the target of her mother's violent eruptions, although she never understood why. She suspected that Mrs. Melnick was jealous of her because she had many friends, she did not suppress her feelings, and she enjoyed a close relationship with her father.

To protect herself from her mother's violence, Lena said, she "disconnected" from her family. For a while she moved in with her grandmother. Later, she rented her own apartment and visited her parents only occasionally. Even then, however, she continued to feel discomfort around her mother. At times she "could not stand to be in the same room" with her. Now, however, she had come to Lancaster County "with an open heart" and a renewed belief in God. She had forgiven her mother for the pain she had caused her, and she had forgiven herself for the ways in which she might have contributed to her mother's rage. Her hope was that she and Mrs. Melnick would finally bond.

"I'm going to Heaven"

The Hospice of Lancaster County had been involved with Mrs. Melnick for a month and a half before she refused the brain surgery. Because she was younger than 65, she did not qualify for the hospice benefit payable under Medicare. When she discovered that the benefits from her private insurance company were very limited she was shocked. She was covered only for "skilled nursing visits"; equipment such as an electric hospital bed, a wheelchair, and a walker would have to be paid out of her own pocket. She also learned that during the final days of her life, the insurance would not pay for hospice to provide her with continuous home care. Neither she nor her husband had the money to pay for the support she would need to live comfortably through the last weeks of her life.

Fortunately, through interventions that Mrs. Melnick interpreted as further evidence of God's providence, the local Cancer Society provided her with a walker right away and promised an electric hospital bed and a wheelchair if and when she needed them. For hospice purposes, Lena was named Mrs. Melnick's "primary care provider." Mr. Melnick, who would have been the most likely candidate for this position, did not want to get too involved in his wife's care. He did not cope well with crises, and the responsibilities of the business were more than he could handle.

Sue Elwood, the hospice nurse, tried her best to address Mrs. Melnick's symptoms with acetaminophen and codeine (for headaches), lorazepam and temazepam (for anxiety and insomnia), amitriptyline (for neuropathic pain in her arm), and prochlorperazine (for nausea). Mrs. Melnick's seizures, the symptom that upset her the most, were controlled with phenytoin. When free of pain, Mrs. Melnick was relatively comfortable. But her unsteady gait and shaking hand prevented her from carrying out day-to-day activities. "A lot of times she will try to feed herself and the spoon will go to her chin instead of her mouth," Sue observed.

In a hospice staff meeting, Mrs. Melnick was compared to a time bomb. The fact that she was functional one day did not mean that she couldn't decline dramatically, fall, or have a seizure the next. To prevent her from hurting herself, Sue recommended that Mrs. Melnick not be left alone. Immediately, Lena hired an assistant for the dry-cleaning store so she could stay at home all day. Nadia Lantz, a personal care nurse from hospice, saw Mrs. Melnick five days a week. This assured Mrs. Melnick's safety and gave Lena the opportunity to take breaks. Nadia's primary purpose was to assist Mrs. Melnick with her personal hygiene. Mostly, however, she found herself sitting in the living room, socializing with her patient.

Mrs. Melnick was exceedingly modest. She didn't want anyone to see her naked—not even her husband. She told me that she belonged to a generation in which "women kept their private parts private." Also, despite Nadia's reassurances that she was still a beautiful woman, she had started to feel shame about her body because she had lost weight. Mrs. Melnick insisted on washing herself alone. She always shut the bathroom door behind her and had Nadia wait outside in case of an accident. The only help she accepted was an elevated toilet seat with handles and a bathtub chair for taking showers.

On the basis of the surgeon's prognosis, Mrs. Melnick expected to die about a week before Christmas. She became remarkably pragmatic. Whether she would make it to Christmas or not, she wanted to take care of business. She gave Lena durable power of attorney. She also passed on to her the ownership of the dry-cleaning store and the responsibility for managing the family's finances. She instructed Nadia to keep her comfortable on the last days of her life and to remember to moisten her mouth and straighten her sheets when she was no longer able to speak. She asked her family to gather around her bed and pray when she died. She pleaded with her children to stay together after her death and make sure to take care of their father. Convinced that Mr. Melnick was incapable of carrying out such a task, she made her own funeral arrangements.

Time and again, she talked to me about the adjustments she was having to make to manage a physical self that changed daily. New medications, new equipment, and new assaults on her dignity were becoming ordinary aspects of her life. Mrs. Melnick despised the cliché about cancer patients' "courageous battle" against their disease, for she didn't see herself as a fighter. "You don't have a battle, you are stuck!" she often said in exasperation. "I got this disease, and there is no 'courageous battle.' It is a battle with your God and your peace, but not with the cancer. There is nothing courageous about it."

Mrs. Melnick told me that she dreaded everything that would come prior to her death. She didn't fear being dead; she feared getting there. How much longer would she live? How much longer would she be able to maintain even a bit of independence? How much longer would she be conscious enough to comprehend what was happening to her? Would she lose her mind so fully that she would start lashing out? Would she be forced to give up her modesty just to stay physically clean? More than anything, she feared being bedridden. To her, the inability to stand up in the morning and sit upright for the rest of the day seemed the most violent assault of all.

Despite her family's discomfort with "morbid conversations," Mrs. Melnick had no difficulty discussing her death. Proudly she remarked, "I talk about my death like I would talk about going to work." Through her openness, she said, she ripped some of the mystique away from death and prepared her children better for her imminent demise. She showed everyone around her that she was neither distraught nor devastated. "I just have this inner peace," she said. "I feel God is with me. Dying is not scary to me at all. I could die tomorrow and I will be at peace because I know where I'm going. I'm going to Heaven. I am going to be with Jesus, so I am not afraid of that. God promised me that, and I live on His promise. I just believe in His word."

Mrs. Melnick returned to smoking. Cigarettes gave her a sense of satisfaction and something to do during the long and lonely hours she spent in her chair. "Now that I'm dying, I am doing a lot of reminiscing," she said. Flipping through the pages of her life, one by one, she concluded that she had wasted time. "I think of mistakes I have made," she said. "Boy, if I could turn back time and change the things that I may have said to somebody to hurt their feelings." She wished she had gotten closer to people. Mrs. Melnick knew she couldn't go back, but she hoped that through her illness she would get the chance to reach out to her children more than she had done before.

Her main concern was Lena. During one of our meetings in her bedroom, still trying to isolate ourselves from her parrot Anabel, Mrs. Melnick explained to me that she and Lena had not been as close as she wanted because, as a teenager, Lena had cut her out of her life. She had avoided spending time with her, and resented her motherly advice. "She is our only girl, so we spoiled her and, oh! those teenage years were horrible," she said. I wondered if she was going to bring up the subject of her alcohol abuse, but she did not. "Lena was stubborn, she was going to do what she wanted to do. She even left home for a while and stayed with my mother. We had a couple of shaky years, and it is possible she is feeling a little bit guilty about that." In Mrs. Melnick's view, Lena went through a normal, adolescent, rebellious phase. Now, she suspected, Lena had come back to repair the damage she had caused and free herself from the guilt that burdened her. It was evident that Mrs. Melnick was uneasy around Lena. "Lena is real hyper," she said. "A lot of times she snaps at me for no reason, and she keeps telling me she is praying for patience."

One of the flashpoints between them was Nadia, the personal care nurse from hospice, who, Lena complained, was cutting into the time she had with her mother. "My Nadia," as Mrs. Melnick had started to refer to her, was a young and vibrant woman. On a daily basis, she applied lotion to Mrs. Melnick's scalp to moisten the skin that had dried out from the radiation. Standing behind her, she rubbed her head with slow and rhythmic movements, giving her a few moments of human touch that Mrs. Melnick both missed and cherished. Hesitantly, Mrs. Melnick started to call her into the bathroom as well. One time she needed help scrubbing her back, another time, getting out of the bathtub, a third, drying her legs. To respect her patient's privacy, Nadia would walk in, assist with the task at hand, and leave the bathroom as soon as she was finished. It took time for Mrs. Melnick to get used to Nadia's help. But she also came to like her for her professionalism, warmth, gentleness, intelligence, humor, sensitivity, and—most importantly—her Christian faith. It was very important to Mrs. Melnick to be surrounded by Christians. She was delighted to discover that the other hospice staff she had met belonged to Christian churches as well. "Christian people are caregivers. Like nurses in the hospital, hospice nurses could not do it if they weren't. They couldn't do it." Nadia would say, "Praise the Lord" at the end of every sentence that expressed a good thought. Anabel learned to say it, too. "Praise the Lord!" she would shout during my visits, "Praise the Lord!"

Old hurts boil over

"I feel as though I am going to make it for Christmas," said Mrs. Melnick on December 16. "After that, every day is going to be a blessing—what God gives me, you know." The approach of the holidays excited her, but it also filled her with a "bittersweet" feeling. As she explained, "The hardest part for me is the loss. That is something you feel because of little remarks people will say: 'I am going to do this this summer,' 'I am going to do this a month from now or two months from now,' and I know that I may not be here and that will go through my mind right away. The sweetness is that I'm going to be with my Lord, my God. I am not going to suffer. I am not going to be bedridden as long. That is a blessing to me."

Mrs. Melnick pulled the family Christmas tree out of storage and asked Lena to set it up and decorate it. It looked like mother and daughter would be able to plan an unforgettable holiday together. Paul was due in four days with his wife and son. But the newly hired assistant at the dry cleaner's got sick, and Lena was forced to resume her normal working hours at the store. Days went by and Lena did not find the time to decorate the tree. Mr. Melnick returned home overworked, irritable, and unable to devote his attention to anything other than the television. Lena was equally exhausted not only from the long hours at the store but also from worrying about her mother. To decompress, she went out with her friends and stayed up late. The household was filling up with tension. Mrs. Melnick's hopes for a joyous holiday started to crumble. When Paul and his family arrived, everyone cheered up. But the Christmas tree was still leaning against the wall, long and thin, waiting to be unbound and decorated. Mrs. Melnick was getting increasingly uncomfortable looking at it.

On Christmas Eve she decided, "This is my last Christmas, and I am not going to get aggravated over a tree!" She mustered all her energy to pick up the tree, drag it to Lena's bedroom, and drop it in the corner. "Lena," she said, "if you don't feel like putting the tree up, we won't have it then, but I don't want to see it sitting in the living room. It's making me nervous!" Shocked and enraged, Lena grabbed the tree, ran back to the living room, and set it up. "Everything has been falling on my shoulders," Lena told me in an exasperated, exhausted tone as she recalled the scene to me. "I have got to take care of the business, I have got to take care of both parents, everything is my fault, I have got to take care of everything. Paul could have gotten the Christmas decorations out easily, but they wanted *me* to do it for some reason." She hunted for the decorations but couldn't find them. Paul came in. He had been drinking and was upset at all the commotion. Lena finally located the box with the decorations, threw them on the couch, and on her way out the door, swore and pushed her brother. He hit Lena in the face. "I still have a scar right here on my head," Lena told me. "He was choking me, he was trying to kill me. I have never felt so betrayed and so upset in my life." Mrs. Melnick took Paul's side. "Lena," she said, "that is your brother and you don't expect your brother to stand there and get manhandled."

"I don't have any respect for my mom after the Christmas tree incident," Lena told me. The incident brought to the surface her old hurts and convinced her that Mrs. Melnick did not deserve to be forgiven. She now knew that she would never get close to her mother. It's not that she didn't love her mother; she did, she grieved for her. She was convinced her mother was unhappy and saw her confinement to her chair as the most brutal form of torture against her strong-willed and active spirit. But at the same time, she wondered if this person who was now at the brink of death had grown from her experiences, had recognized her mistakes, and had changed inside in any way that made her a better person. Lena doubted it. She was angry and confused. Was she a bad person to feel resentment toward a woman who would soon be dead?

The victory tree

"The patient had an enjoyable Christmas with her family," wrote Sue in her chart on January 2, 1997. After the holidays Lena was back at home on a full-time basis. The assistant at the dry cleaner's had returned to work, too. Anabel had mastered the phrase "Merry Christmas," which she repeated ceaselessly. The fact that Mrs. Melnick had lived to see the holidays meant a lot to her. "To me, it's a victory," she said. "A victory in Jesus." She saw her survival as proof of God's power and the Christmas tree as a symbol of His presence in her life. She named it her "victory tree" and vowed to leave it up until the day she died.

The undertaker stopped by to discuss her wishes for the funeral. When he left, she felt relief, but Lena was in shock. She had been unaware of Mrs. Melnick's funeral preparations and couldn't believe how coldly and calmly her mother had discussed the technicalities of her own interment. In tears, she called her father to tell him what had happened, and he, too, sounded surprised. When he returned home that day from work, Mr. Melnick looked at his wife and said, "Aren't you jumping the gun a little?" Mrs. Melnick didn't expect such a reaction. "I have been tying up loose ends by myself," she said to me, "but that is what I have always done. All my life. It has worked. It is working still. I would have liked my husband to have helped me, but I know he would have never [done it]." She did not want her family to fear reality—even worse, to maintain false hopes—for she knew that she was protected by God. She said, "I tell my family, 'I am going to be up in Heaven. I'm going to be having a good old time, and you're going to be down here working!'"

When I visited Mrs. Melnick in the beginning of February, I couldn't help but notice her decline. For the first time she seemed small in her chair. Her world had shrunk to a small circle around her. She was surrounded by her walker, a newly arrived bedside commode, several feet of cable that brought the telephone to her lap, and, as always, her coffee table, which was filled with medications. From that day on, we stopped conducting our interviews in her bedroom, for moving from one room to the next had become too risky. Anabel greeted me with a few hellos and goodbyes and Praise-the-Lords, but overall, she remained quiet. Mrs. Melnick smoked with slow and careful movements of her left hand. She was eager to talk. She wasn't sure how many more interviews we'd be able to conduct.

"I am progressing," she said as she started to cry. Her legs and abdomen had swollen even further. Her right arm and leg had become increasingly harder to control. Nadia had to help her take showers. At night she couldn't lift her leg to get into bed. Moreover, she had started to lose control of her bowels. "My stools just shot out, and I was mortified, and Lena cleaned the whole bathroom down," she said. She would watch a movie and an hour later, forget all about it. Only a week earlier she was able to fold clothes, but the day I saw her that seemed like an unmanageable task.

Mrs. Melnick cried more. The thought of not seeing her children again devastated her. Whom would they call when they needed help? Would Paul finish his culinary training without her emotional and financial support? Would John have the wherewithal to help him? She characterized her husband as a "helpless man" who was so used to being taken care of that he hadn't learned the basics of maintaining himself. "He just found out that there was a filter in the dryer!" she exclaimed. She feared that Mr. Melnick would languish, although she acknowledged Anabel's ability to support him. The parrot was especially attached to her husband and enjoyed not only spending time with him but also imitating Mrs. Melnick's voice.

"Right now I think how much more I should have done through the years," Mrs. Melnick went on. "I will even think about when I was a little girl that I was cruel to somebody. And it flashes back. I will even think of that, and I think, 'I wish I would have been a better person.' Oftentimes I think of that, but without depression. I am not brow-beating myself, because I did do some nice things, too. But I wish I would have done more nice things, even as a child. I think how my God loves me and He is so alive to me, and I know He is going to forgive me for these things, but I just wish . . ."

Nadia

Over the next few weeks, Mrs. Melnick's bowel incontinence became a regular problem. When she got up in the morning, she often defecated on the floor. Although she agreed with Sue that stool hardeners were likely to cause her the even more severe problem of constipation, she hoped there was an alternative solution to her problem. Sue didn't have one, however, and started feeling inadequate as a nurse. Mrs. Melnick seemed to want things Sue couldn't offer, and rejected things she could. When it came to her personal hygiene, for example, she declined Sue's attempts to help her. Only Nadia's help was acceptable to her. Emotionally, Sue found herself disengaging from Mrs. Melnick. She turned her attention to technical problems, such as the need to provide Mrs. Melnick with an electric hospital bed and to find people who would be able to stay with her when she started requiring round-the-clock care.

Nadia still saw Mrs. Melnick five days a week and spent many hours talking with her about her life, her family, television, politics, faith, and a host of other topics. She had gotten to know Mrs. Melnick well, and she liked her. Yet the strength of Mrs. Melnick's attachment to her made her personally and professionally uncomfortable. Personally, she found her patient intrusive. Mrs. Melnick wanted to know everything about her. She even asked to meet Nadia's children, but Nadia gently refused. She explained that it would be emotionally taxing for them to interact with dying patients and exhausting for Nadia herself to keep answering their questions about death. Mrs. Melnick understood Nadia's refusal and apologized for having suggested such a meeting.

Professionally, Nadia felt drained. "My job sucks the life out of me," she said to me. "Then I don't have it to give to my kids, and I don't feel like reading with them, I don't feel like playing with them, because I have given all my guts to Katie or so-and-so all week. It becomes stressful to me going to Katie every day, every day, every day. I need a break from her. I started to feel like the attachment is getting greater, and when she emphasizes how she depends on me and that her comfort level is only there with me as far as personal care, that gets to me. I feel like she is depending on me too much." On her days off Nadia felt tortured by the idea that Mrs. Melnick did not shower. At the same time, she recognized a side of Mrs. Melnick that few others were privy to. It was a vulnerable side, a scared side, that was trying to gain minimal control over a horrifying and uncontrollable situation. "It is like knowing that a Mack truck is going to run over you and watching it come toward you," Nadia said. "Can you imagine the intensity of that?"

The bed

To Sue's surprise, Mrs. Melnick agreed to the delivery of an electric hospital bed, though she made it clear that she wasn't going to use it unless she absolutely had to. She also confirmed that Pat, a childhood friend of hers who lived in Ohio, was going to take care of her during her final days. Pat, she said, would help her smoke when she was no longer able to hold a cigarette. "I am totally addicted," she said laughingly. "I will have withdrawals if I stop smoking, and I have enough troubles. I don't want withdrawal."

The bed was brought to the Melnicks free of charge in the beginning of February. It was placed in Mrs. Melnick's bedroom, next to the queen-size bed. Mrs. Melnick was alone at the time of its delivery. The sight of the bed upset her. "Once I am in the hospital bed," she told me later in tears, "I know for sure it is down, down, down. That is a big turning point." Wendy, the social worker from hospice, spent a visit discussing with Mrs. Melnick what this bed meant to her. Lena joined that conversation, too. Mother and daughter admitted that the hospital bed symbolized the imminence of Mrs. Melnick's death. Lena sobbed the first time she saw it. She sat across from it in shock. Soon after, she was joined by her father who put his arm around her and wept himself for the first time.

"She is just basically a prisoner of the chair"

No one had expected Mrs. Melnick to make it to February. Valentine's Day was just around the corner. In acknowledgment of her mother's second victory, Lena replaced the Christmas tree ornaments with red hearts. Mrs. Melnick was happy and thankful for being alive, but she cried frequently during our meetings. Her bowels continued to move unexpectedly. Accidents took place on a daily basis and required Lena to clean up after her. Her incontinence was degrading to Mrs. Melnick. Together with the arrival of the electric hospital bed, she added it to the milestones of her decline. Still, she said, "I have never questioned 'why me.' I just accept what is happening day by day. Look, the doctors said I would not be here. I just put my faith in God, and I am here. God knows. He wrote the book. He knows the beginning and the end. He knows why I'm here. God has His reason for the bowel movements, too."

Lena was not as accepting of her mother's ailments. She saw Mrs. Melnick's cancer as an "unseen monster" that was robbing her of her dignity. She was overwhelmed not only by Mrs. Melnick's unpredictable bowels but by her overall deterioration. Her stalwart mother had now turned into a fragile woman with a "cabbage patch" face, no hair, a distended belly, flaccid skin, and feet that looked like "balloons." Lena still felt resentment toward her mother, but caring for her had brought her into a new relationship with her after all. Now she started feeling protective toward her and wanted to make sure that she was going to leave this life in peace.

On March 3, Mrs. Melnick received a wheelchair. In the morning she often took morphine to tolerate the short ride from her bedroom to the living room. Without it, she reported unbearable pain. She knew that many patients in her condition chose to stay in bed, but that was the last thing she wanted. If nothing else, Mrs. Melnick was determined to spend her remaining days in her overstuffed chair. Her face had swelled up further, her eyes sunken in dark circles. Her lower legs showed signs of mottling. "There is no other word for it," she said to me, while taking slow and shaky puffs on her cigarette, "I am waiting to die. I am not going to get better, I am getting worse, and there is less and less I can do. I am waiting to die. That is it."

"She is really, really, really scared," Paul told me after one of his visits. "I could just see it in her eyes. Her favorite saying now is, 'Boy, does this suck!' She never talked like that before. Then you have to crack up. She says, 'One of these days I would like to wake up and this is all a nightmare. It has to be a dream.' I just laugh and say, 'Yeah. Unfortunately it is not.' I tell her, 'You always were brain dead, and now it is true,' and she laughs. When I come here it seems like she cries more because I ask her a lot of questions, like 'How do you really feel?' and she will say 'Okay.' I will say, 'Bullshit! Tell me. I want to know.' Then she will cry."

March was an exhausting month for everyone. Each day seemed to drag on longer than the one before. Mrs. Melnick was tired of waiting, and every member of the family hoped that death would come soon. "She is just basically a prisoner of the chair," said Paul. My interviews with Mrs. Melnick became slow and scattered. She told me that she couldn't think, but made every effort to answer my questions. She felt weaker and drowsier every day. She stopped taking showers because she had lost the strength and the motor skills they required. She received sponge baths instead, which she saw as a precious alternative, for she wanted to stay clean until the end. The problem with her loose bowels slowly resolved itself. Now she was constipated and had to cope with abdominal cramps and pressure. Enemas did not always work. She reported that she had hemorrhoids, more pain, scalp itching, thrush, and a possible vaginal infection, but with the treatments she received, she asserted that she was adjusting well. "It is very important to me to adjust," she said softly. "I don't want the disease to control me. I want to control the disease."

"I stay in with my honey"

In the third week of March, Lena took her father's place at the dry-cleaning store. This enabled Mr. Melnick to stay at home. He would lift Mrs. Melnick in and out of chairs and then retreat to a quiet world of his own. He came across to me as a recluse. No one knew how he was feeling. He spent many hours in the living room watching television or interacting sweetly with Anabel. He rarely participated in conversations with visitors and, at times, even failed to acknowledge their presence. I never invited him for an interview because he seemed uncomfortable when I paid attention to him. Mrs. Melnick was concerned. One time, in the middle of our interview, she turned to him and asked, "John, do you want to say something? How are you feeling now with it getting closer to the time? You know, how do you feel about death? It could be only two more weeks and I could be dead, but how do you feel about that?"

Mr. Melnick said he didn't like it at all. That was the end of the discussion.

Although Mr. Melnick hadn't said much in his answer, he had at least indicated that he was aware of his wife's poor prognosis. That in itself was an important development because, until then, he had always denied the severity of Mrs. Melnick's illness and resented her requests for help. Sue, Nadia, and Wendy had all worried that he would not be a compassionate caregiver. But now, to their surprise, they saw him changing. First, he started emptying Mrs. Melnick's commode. A few days later he began lighting her cigarettes, and when I saw him, he was getting ready to rub lotion on her head. "I have not been out in I don't know how many days," he said to me. "I stay in with my honey."

"I am still in shock that John is doing all this," said Mrs. Melnick. "He never did that. I was starting to feel, you know, my kids love me, they are close, and my husband is still cold, and then all of a sudden he is just wonderful. I think he is finally realizing that this is happening, but it is more than that. He just never did those things for me."

On March 20, Mrs. Melnick declared that her time was soon to come. The reason she wasn't dead yet, she explained, was because God had granted her extra time to see her niece, Helen. Helen was raised in a troubled family, and as a teenager had turned to Mrs. Melnick for help. Mrs. Melnick took Helen in and practically raised her for several years. "She is like a daughter to me," she said. Both of the things that Mrs. Melnick had prayed for had now come true: her husband attended to her lovingly, and Helen was on her way for a three-day visit. "God answers prayers," Mrs. Melnick said with a smile.

By the end of March, Helen had come and gone. Mrs. Melnick already missed her, but was too sick to indulge her sadness. With Easter approaching, Lena decorated the Christmas tree with paper eggs and flowers. Lena wanted to be at home with her mother, but had to work at the store instead. She prayed that someone would finally buy their business; it had been for sale for 15 months, and, with the turmoil surrounding Mrs. Melnick's illness, it had not been going well. She was tired and distraught, wishing that her mother would die soon because she couldn't stand to see her suffer. She now felt more love for her than ever before, she said to me. But she also worried. She didn't think her mother would be able to let go without acknowledging the mistakes she had made in her life and making peace with the people she had hurt.

Pat, Mrs. Melnick's friend from Ohio, spent her first evening with Mrs. Melnick reminiscing about the past and assuring her about the future. She told sto-

ries about their youth, their husbands, and children. That same evening Pat
asked Mrs. Melnick to stop fighting. Pat acknowledged that she had done a wonderful job staying alive, but she also noted that she looked exhausted. Pat asked
her to let God take care of her. She talked to her about the happiness she was
going to have in Heaven. And she assured her that she was a good person who
would soon see her beloved Lord. She pleaded with Mrs. Melnick to let go.

"Prescription for K. Melnick—please knock"

On Friday, April 4, Paul and Carl came to see their mother. By this time Mrs.
Melnick was unable to swallow soft foods. Morphine, an anticonvulsant, her
antianxiety medication, and an antiemetic pill were all given to her rectally,
which caused her pain. All of her other medications were discontinued. Sue explained to Mr. Melnick that instead of having to insert four pills into his wife's
rectum, he could have a pharmacist compound the medications into a single
gel-cap suppository. That was costly, however, so Mr. Melnick elected not to
do it.

With a glassy stare, Mrs. Melnick asked Lena to close the store and stay
home. A quiet tension filled the house. Mrs. Melnick's breathing was uneven.
She went through moments of apnea. Her knees were mottled and her urine
output decreased. Nadia spent her visit that day washing Mrs. Melnick's face
and moistening her lips. She took the opportunity to tell Mrs. Melnick goodbye. "I thought about how I would like to say it," she told me later. "Katie," she
said, "the time may be coming soon, and I just want you to know that I feel very
fortunate to have gotten to know you, and I really feel that we have become
special friends. Even though I have to maintain a certain professional level, I
consider you someone that I would have loved to be friends with, even if we
had not met under these circumstances." Then she left.

An uneasy quiet fell upon the Melnicks once again. Suddenly Mrs. Melnick
opened her eyes. "I am going to Hell!" she shouted. Her voice was astoundingly loud. Lena heard it in her bedroom. Mr. Melnick ran to her side and reassured her that she was a good person, she was not going to Hell, she had done
many good things over the years, there was no reason to worry. But Mrs. Melnick insisted she knew better. With the few words she could utter, she asked for
a Catholic priest to absolve her of her sins. The priest arrived a few hours later.
He spent some private time with Mrs. Melnick and left. "I felt fortunate to be
part of everything," said Lena when she described this afternoon to me later.
"My mother apologized for things she said way back when, and how she had
such a problem with alcohol. She knows Jesus Christ is her savior, but I guess
with the brain tumor she got too confused." That evening Lena called hospice
to report that Mrs. Melnick was seeing angels.

April 5 was the first day Mrs. Melnick couldn't get out of bed. She was surrounded by Mr. Melnick, her three children, and Pat, all of whom were carefully watching her every breath. In the afternoon, she started moaning. Assuming that she was in pain, Paul and Lena went to the pharmacy to pick up a prescription for more morphine. When they arrived at the drugstore, they found a note on the door saying, "Prescription for K. Melnick—please knock."

"Boy, is that nice," Lena remembered thinking at the time. "They close the store, but they realize how bad we need the prescription. They are going to let me get it. That is really nice of them." She knocked, feeling happy but also nervous, because she didn't really know what was happening with her mother. The pharmacist came to the door, looking solemn. "Hi," Lena said, showing her checkbook. "I am here for my prescriptions for Katie Melnick."

As she started to write the check the pharmacist shook his head.

"What happened?" Lena asked. "You don't have the morphine, or what is the matter?"

"No, no," the pharmacist replied. "We got a call ten minutes ago that you are not going to be needing it any more."

Lena stood stunned. "She died?"

"I think so," the pharmacist said, his eyes filling up with tears.

Mrs. Melnick had taken her last breath only minutes earlier, lying next to her neatly folded prayer blanket. Pat reported that her death was peaceful. "Paul and I were not meant to be there," Lena said to me later.

The Melnicks were in shock. They cried. They wailed. They held each other. They called Nadia who came to the house immediately. Lena gave Nadia the gift that her mother had bought for her. It was a small porcelain vase. With it came a card from Mrs. Melnick, which Nadia recalled "just moved me because it was almost as if she was talking to me, her words, that she was glad to have had me for a nurse and how she appreciated me."

Mrs. Melnick's body had a look of exhaustion about it. The black bags under her eyes and her dry and wrinkled skin gave the impression she had been struggling. Nadia compared her to a traveler who had just crossed the Sahara Desert and died. When the undertaker arrived, the Melnicks withdrew into a bedroom. They didn't want to see Mrs. Melnick's final exit. But soon they heard Anabel shout, "Bye-bye, Melnick!" as the undertaker carried the body out of the house.

"There were just too many memories"

Mrs. Melnick was cremated. Her funeral went as planned. It was attended by about 25 people, including Sue, Nadia, Wendy, and two other personal care nurses from hospice. Anabel sat in Mr. Melnick's car. Tearful, Mr. Melnick asked Wendy for a follow-up bereavement visit. Then he and his family drove to Maryland with Mrs. Melnick's ashes. They stayed there for a week. At the end of April, Mr. Melnick and Lena were back at work. When they saw Wendy they told her that their trip to Maryland had made them feel better, for it reunited them with old friends. What they found most difficult was returning home. Everything in their apartment reminded them of Mrs. Melnick. The empty, overstuffed living room chair startled them. They wanted to move out. But they also stated that they no longer felt the need for bereavement visits from hospice. They thanked Wendy for all her help and gave her three gifts from Mrs. Melnick. One was for her, another for Sue, and a third one for me.

"It is like she's still alive," said Paul with a chuckle when I spoke to him a few weeks later. "I was going to get a pair of shoes for the funeral and I was thinking, 'Oh, I'd better get a nice pair or she is going to bitch. I don't want to go home and face the music.' And it was like, 'Wait a minute! She isn't there! That is why I'm going to get the shoes.' I was laughing. She was probably laughing too, saying, 'You idiot! I have really got you trained!'"

In May, Mr. Melnick and Lena closed the store. It had been an unprofitable business, full of painful memories, and they were happy to get rid of it. Then they separated. Mr. Melnick went to Georgia to spend the summer with his brother, and Lena stayed with Anabel in Lancaster County. She had just started dating a man with whom she was eager to spend more time. Her father advised her to move to a new apartment, but she couldn't find anything as affordable as their own. Adjusting to a new life was difficult for her. She said:

> Oh, I miss Mom so bad. I do. I know she is in a better place. I understand, it was her time. God took her and I understand that, but it hurts so bad. Everywhere you look I see her glasses, her cream, her shoes, or her clothing or something, and it is just difficult. My dad and I were so used to taking care of her, it is still instilled in me: I have got to get home—I don't know what I am going to do, but I have got to do something. My dad was a real wreck for a while. It was bad. He broke up a lot. I never saw anything like that. He could not stay in the business. There were just too many memories.

In August, five months after Mrs. Melnick's death, Lena still had dreams that her mother was alive and cured. Mrs. Melnick's closet started to smell to her like smoke. Her mother had not gotten around to donating her clothes, so she decided to go through them herself and give many of them away. The only thought that uplifted her was that her mother had made peace with her before she died. She said, "That made me feel so good because I wanted so badly, so desperately, to be close with her, and she just could not become close with any woman. I felt like I was on cloud nine. I was like, 'Thank you so much,' and I am crying and I was saying, 'I love you so much, you have no idea,' and she was like, 'I know, I know.'"

Lena and her boyfriend got engaged in July. A month later, Mr. Melnick called his daughter from Georgia to announce that he had bought a house in his brother's neighborhood. Lena felt abandoned, but she was also relieved that her father had started a new life for himself. His brother had been a good friend to him all their lives, and that closeness between them comforted her. "I hope he is not thinking he can run away from the memories or the emotions, because they are going to come haunting back," she said to me. She wished she could ask her father directly about his feelings, but she had learned that Mr. Melnick was too private to answer such a question. "I cannot imagine my life without my dad now," Lena said to me. "Not at all. One day he had a very rough morning, and we both cried together, and I was holding him, and we were holding each other and just talking, and he said, 'I love you.' He said, 'Thank you.' He said, 'I thank God for you.' He said, 'I don't know what I would do without you,' and it made me feel really good. When you don't hear things and then you do, you are like, 'Wow.'"

18

Susan Mulroney
A Private Matter

Narrated by PATRICIA BOSTON

Susan Mulroney had always considered herself a very private person. She had many friends and a caring family, but all her life she prided herself on being very independent and in control of her own affairs. She never liked to burden family or friends with her problems. When she was diagnosed with advanced cervical cancer at the age of 47, she did not talk much about it to anyone. During the next few months, she remained stoic in the face of her illness and tried to continue with her life normally, as though nothing eventful had taken place. But chemotherapy did not work and she felt increasingly tired, physically weak, and unable to cope on her own. As the cancer progressed she was admitted to the hospital for reassessment of her condition. Her oncologists informed her that the only remaining option was palliative care.

Not wishing to burden family members, Susan chose to be admitted to the Palliative Care Unit, where her condition rapidly became worse. Her physical symptoms were controlled and she seemed comfortable. But no one could tell how she was coping emotionally with the knowledge that she would soon die. Susan preferred to keep her feelings to herself. When people tried to talk with her, she usually found them intrusive. Ten days following her admission to the Palliative Care Unit, she died. Except for one close friend, no one knew much about how she had felt or what the last few months of her life had been like. "If only I had known the truth," Susan's sister said, "I could have done something. I feel let down, cheated. How could I have not known that things were so bad?"

A private life

Susan Mulroney was a school teacher. Born in Montreal, she was raised by parents of Irish descent and lived in an English-speaking area of Montreal. In her early twenties she married Richard Gratton, a wealthy business man. She loved children and it would have given her great joy to have been a mother. But Susan and Richard did not have any children. After some years the couple began to have marital difficulties and Susan filed for a divorce. After a few years, Richard remarried. Susan did not, although she met many potential suitors.

In the years following her divorce Susan threw herself more heavily into her career. She enjoyed teaching in the early grades of high school, and her activities at the school helped to alleviate the sadness of not having children of her own. She became active in school policy and administration. After further study in curriculum development and special education she was able to become an independent education specialist.

With the extra qualifications came an increase in her salary, which enabled her to afford comfort and beautiful things. Following the breakup of her marriage she moved to a large, spacious, penthouse apartment in a green area of the city. She loved her apartment with its panoramic views. On a clear day she could see mountain peaks as far as one hundred miles away.

The apartment was a refuge of peace and solitude. Though Susan had family and many friends, women and men, she liked living alone. Had she met "the right person" she wouldn't have been averse to the idea of remarriage. She met a few men with whom she could go to the theater and concerts, but there had been no single person she wanted to be with for a lifetime. As the years passed, she couldn't imagine not being able to go home to her own place. She always felt peaceful there. Many of the things in her apartment she had collected on her vacations abroad: porcelain china figurines, delicate wood carvings, and many fine pieces of Eastern artwork, tapestries, and crocheted work.

Susan Mulroney did have a few special people in her life—her sister Judy and her friend Jack Peterson. Judy was 18 years Susan's senior and, being the older sister, had always felt protective toward Susan. When the girls were growing up, their mother was ill with multiple sclerosis. More often than not she was unable to care for the two girls as well as she would have liked. Judy had always looked out for Susan, making sure she got to school on time and helping her with homework as well as making meals. "I was more like the mother in the home," Judy recalled to me. Over the years, the two sisters joked about what would happen when they were older and Judy became ill and infirm. With such a great age difference between the two women, they assumed Judy would be the one "to go first." Susan had anticipated looking after Judy in her old age, saying to her laughingly, "I'll take care of you when you get old and you're in a wheelchair."

Despite their age difference, the two sisters had formed a close bond. For a while, when their lives took different paths through marriage and careers, they saw less of each other. Susan had married a business man, Judy, a lawyer. Later, when both sisters were divorced, they renewed their bonds from childhood. They were able to do a lot more together, such as vacations, weekend trips, shopping, and theater. They laughed a lot and had fun together. "It was as if we were like schoolgirls again," Judy later recalled. On their vacations they went mostly to Florida and Barbados in the winter, but also to Africa, India, and Southeast Asia. Once they went on safari.

Despite all the time together and all the trips and outings, there were, Judy said, "limits to how far people could go into Susan's private thoughts. I always knew when I should stop questioning her about something, when what we were talking about was off limits."

The person in whom Susan felt she could confide most of all was Jack Peterson, a colleague at work. The two worked together as teachers for 20 years and saw each other daily. If Susan was facing some dilemma in her teaching or with a colleague, she could talk to Jack, knowing that nothing she told him would be taken any further. It was a "real friendship," Susan told me. Jack later recalled:

> I respected her need for privacy. But it was what you could call a real, honest, good type of relationship. I could say anything to her and she would say anything to me. I would say I knew most details. If she had a man friend and wasn't sure about the relationship, she'd feel okay about talking things through with me. I think in a way, she felt safe with me. We were pals in every sense of the word.

Susan believed she had led a healthy life. She never smoked. She might have had the odd glass of wine at a restaurant for dinner, but she wasn't someone who sat at home and drank alone. When she cooked for herself, she enjoyed healthy food, vegetables in season, and a lot of fruit. She was active in sports and loved bicycling. On a good day in the spring or summer she could cycle up to 20 miles, she told me, without "taking so much as a second breath." Sometimes she would take the bike paths that run along the St. Lawrence River and cycle to Quebec villages such as St. Zotique and Beauparé, as far as 30 or 40 miles on a round trip. When the weather didn't permit bicycling, she took long walks or a jog in the countryside. Even in winter, in temperatures of –15°F, she thought nothing of bundling up in her parka and boots and taking a long, brisk walk. Susan was rarely sick.

"You could have told her it was stage IV and she would have said, 'Stage IV out of what?'"

I was not able to ascertain precisely when Susan first noticed some unusual symptoms. The first anyone else knew of them was when she mentioned to Jack that she was having pains in her lower back. At the time, Susan had simply joked, "I'm just getting old." She also told Judy about the pain, saying it was because she was "getting too close to 50." In just three years' time she would have lived half a century. Judy also wondered if "getting older" might be the correct diagnosis, for Susan worked hard at school and wasn't getting any younger. As Judy later recalled to me, "She always brought home work from school. She would correct the children's books and that. We used to tease her and call her 'the bag lady.' And [when she told us her back hurt] we told her, 'Look, maybe you've got too much stuff in your bags. Too many books. You're getting older.'"

Susan had other symptoms as well, but she didn't tell anyone. She did say once that she didn't feel herself, but did not go into detail. Sometimes when Jack visited her Susan appeared to be preoccupied with medical books, especially gynecological books. He thought that was odd, but then Susan had a curious mind and loved to read, frequently having a book somewhere nearby. Then she began to frequent medical bookstores and health clinics where she could get the latest information on gynecological illnesses. By then Jack felt "something wasn't right" because she seemed so single-minded about this kind of information. But she did not go to see a doctor. Looking back, Jack thought that Susan must have had a clear idea that "something was very wrong."

When, in December 1994, Susan did at last consult Dr. Paul, her gynecologist, he examined her and took a pap smear. One week later, his secretary telephoned and asked if Susan could see Dr. Paul at his office regarding the results. The pap smear was reported as Stage IV, which meant that she had cancer in her cervix. When Dr. Paul told Susan this, she accepted the news calmly. She was not a medical person, so it was not immediately clear to her what that meant. Jack's wife, Rita, however, was a nurse and she knew what a stage IV pap smear meant: something was seriously wrong.

Jack was surprised that his friend was taking such difficult news so calmly. He wondered if Susan was making an overly optimistic assumption that her cancer would be cured. He tried talking to her about her feelings, but Susan did not want to discuss feelings. She would call Jack to go for a cup of coffee or a chat, but if he tried to ask about her illness, it was to no avail. "I just want to get on with my life," she curtly responded.

Rita did not want to interfere in any way, but she thought that stage IV must mean that the cancer was already at a very advanced stage. Jack recalled:

> When Susan got the news from Dr. Paul, it seemed funny that she never went through any crying fits or anything. She seemed to accept everything. It was,

"Okay! It's business as usual." She seemed to accept everything easily, almost too easily. In many ways, I don't think she knew what stage IV meant. You could have told her it was stage IV and she would have said, "Stage IV out of what? Stage X or stage XI?" She'd never been exposed to anything medical in that sense.

Dr. Paul urgently referred Susan to Dr. Lieberman, a surgical oncologist who immediately ordered tests to determine how far the cancer had spread. The cancer was very advanced, Dr. Lieberman explained to Susan, but he would do all he could to arrest its growth. Susan received chemotherapy and, some weeks later, radiotherapy externally and internally to the uterine cavity. She told Judy that she had cancer and was getting it treated. Judy was frightened. Susan had led such a healthy life! Why her? She would have liked to have asked more questions and perhaps have a chat with Dr. Paul. But her only function was to accompany Susan to the chemotherapy clinic for treatments, and there were to be no questions asked. As Judy later recalled,

> I would sit and wait with her while she got to see the doctor and when she went for blood tests. She always seemed to be handling it. Sometimes she'd be irritable when she was getting the blood tests, because we'd sit and wait and wait and wait. But she wouldn't talk about it. Sometimes she'd say, "That's it, I'm not waiting any more," and I'd almost have to sit on her and I'd say, "No, no. We need to wait." Then she'd go in to see the doctor and I'd have to wait outside. She never ever mentioned what he said and I never asked.

Susan had a way of changing the subject very quickly if one asked questions she was not prepared to answer. As Jack said, "She'd tell you right off, 'I don't want to talk about it,' and she'd immediately go on to something else. You could try to bring her back, but then she'd get irritated and clam up altogether."

"I am going to die"

Susan underwent radiotherapy and chemotherapy throughout most of 1995. During this period she tried to continue with her life as though very little of any real consequence were happening. She loved to go shopping and buy clothes. Sometimes she'd go downtown and "spend every cent she had on a new dress." "She was a clothes horse," Jack later recalled. She still wanted the social life she had enjoyed before with her sister. She went to restaurants and movies and acted as if nothing were wrong. She continued to bicycle, walk, and jog. Sometimes she called Jack and Rita to ask if they wanted to go for a few hours of biking. Rita Peterson was not much for biking, so Jack would go. They would bike for miles.

Yet her condition worsened. She developed increasing pain in her back and legs, and sometimes had sharp cramps in her abdomen. She had less and less appetite, even for her favorite foods. Sometimes she would eat a meal and immediately feel full and sick after it. Even a bowl of fresh fruit was difficult to digest. Sometimes it was easier just to vomit what she ate.

In November Dr. Lieberman informed Susan that there was no further treatment for her cancer. It was possible that one of the oncology surgeons at the hospital would be able to suggest another option, but from Dr. Lieberman's standpoint, there was no further treatment, "nothing at all." It was now just 10 months since Dr. Paul had first broken the news that she had cervical cancer.

On November 20, 1995, Susan came into the hospital's surgical ward for further assessment. The surgeon, Dr. Simpson, explained to her that, surgically, there was nothing to be done. The tumors had spread to her bladder and bowel. Dr. Simpson was patient but direct, probably because Susan was that way herself. As Jack later said to me, "she expected you to lay things right on the nose, no messing around."

It was at this time that Susan told Jack about her condition. "I am going to die," she said. Still, after informing both Jack and Judy about the severity of her illness, she did not talk about her feelings to either friends or family. Susan struck them all as stoic and strong. Even now she seemed hopeful and positive. She was matter-of-fact, concerned with the practicalities of what she needed in the way of night clothes and toiletries in the hospital. When she was in the hospital she talked about the activities on the ward, the person in the next bed, or something minor or inconsequential a particular nurse or doctor had said. She did not open herself up for any discussion. Jack said:

> At times, you felt you were walking on eggs. Because she wouldn't feel comfortable if you pushed her on any piece of information she gave you. What she told you, that was her choice to make. And if I ever pushed her on how she felt about something, she'd back off. And then I'd end up feeling uncomfortable that I'd put her in that position.

Cold white walls and white coats

As Susan's symptoms rapidly became more acute, Dr. Lieberman and Dr. Simpson referred her to the Palliative Care Service. Susan would need more specialized management of her pain and discomfort, and she would also need greater emotional support than the surgical team was able to provide. When she was seen and examined by Dr. Webster of the Palliative Care Service, Dr. Webster noted the gravity of her condition. Susan was thin, her abdomen was full and hard on palpation, and she had skin edema. She was experiencing mid-back and epigastric pain, nausea, and vomiting. She was uncomfortable from constipation as an immediate result of pressure of the tumors on her bowel. Her red blood count was low, and she had reportedly been vomiting "coffee grounds" during the previous 24 hours, which was a sign of gastrointestinal bleeding. There was a risk of major gastrointestinal hemorrhage. Dr. Webster set up a medication plan with comfort and pain relief as her ultimate goal, prescribing the following: omeprezole 40 mg orally every four hours for epigastric pain; prochlorperazine 10 mg by mouth or rectum three times daily, and dimenhydrinate as needed for nausea and vomiting; morphine 5–10 mg orally every four hours and nortriptyline 25 mg orally every four hours for pain; and, for constipation, docusate and bisacodyl.

Dr. Webster also explained the nature and goals of the Palliative Care Service, and the various options that were available. Susan could stay on the surgical unit, she could be transferred onto the Palliative Care Unit, or, if someone could take care of her, it was possible she could go home. Susan needed to think about this carefully. There was no denying that she needed full-time care. But she would much rather go home and be alone. Besides, it was Christmas time. She could not imagine what it would be like not to be in her own home at Christmas. Judy offered to move in with her if she wanted to be in her own apartment, but Susan kept saying, "I don't want to be a burden to anyone." Judy told me later, "It wasn't a burden. It would have been a gift to care for her." But she also remembered that during the past year when she had tried to care for Susan at home, she had always felt "a bit in the way."

Susan felt that the surgical unit was "cold" and "sterile." It was generally noisy with the bustle of daily clinical activities. There was no view to speak of from her window, and when she looked around she saw "cold white walls and a lot of people in white coats—all very white!" It was also hard to have to share her room; at times, she felt "closed in." The previous week the woman in the next bed had cried out in pain at night after her surgery; this week she was going home, excited and jubilant that she would leave the hospital and be at home in her own bed. This was hard for Susan to take. During the day the nursing station was noisy and intrusive. The Palliative Care Unit sounded "nice and quiet." She had heard there was carpeting rather than linoleum on the floors. She told Dr. Webster she wanted to go to the Palliative Care Unit.

At this point I received a call from Dr. Webster, who had learned that Susan was interested in being a participant in our study. She was, she had told Dr. Webster, "first and foremost a teacher." If it would help other caregivers and medical staff to learn from her experiences, she would like to be involved.

Our first meeting took place in the surgical unit. The unit was brightly decorated with silver tinsel streamers, balloons, and colorful posters announcing holiday parties. There was an atmosphere of busyness, energy, and healthy noise about the place. Physicians, patients on stretchers being wheeled to or from the operating rooms, nurses, aides delivering meal trays—everything seemed to be in motion. At the nursing station, papers, forms, and charts passed to and fro among nurses, doctors, and clerks. People called out "Merry Christmas!" to one another. As I passed the nursing station to get to Susan

Mulroney's room I wondered how she must be feeling in the midst of all this buoyancy. Would she be thinking about Christmas?

Her room was depressing and cold. On the wall was a polished plaque, stating that the ward acknowledged the memory of a deceased benefactor. Seen vaguely in the midst of massed flowers on the windowsill and the white and blue draperies, the plaque gave me an eerie feeling of being in the antechamber of a funeral home. It would have seemed far cheerier had there been a few pictures over the beds to relieve the stark white walls. I couldn't imagine wanting to stay here knowing I was going to die. Susan smiled as she greeted me. Then she stared straight ahead, hardly making any eye contact. It was as though she were thinking about something other than our conversation. Despite her frailty I noticed how attractive she was and that she looked much younger than her age. She had short, cropped, dark hair, clear, unwrinkled skin, and pale blue eyes that had a soft, innocent, wide-eyed stare.

"I am just waiting around here now," she said. Her words were clipped. I thought she sounded nervous and frightened. "I think it will be a little nicer [on the Palliative Care Unit]. It will be quiet and people will have more time." She was sitting upright in bed, propped up by several pillows. She looked pale and her skin had a slight yellowish tinge to it. She wore a dark green velvet housecoat. Was she cold, I wondered? She said she liked to keep her housecoat on for getting in and out of bed. "I'm sick," she said, "but not so sick I can't do things for myself." She knew her diagnosis and that her cancer had advanced to a point where her doctor could offer no further treatment. But, she said, "I'm not ready to give up yet. I'm not sure how long I've got. There are still questions to be answered. I'm not ready to give up; now I have to work harder to get past the hurdles."

While it was not clear to me exactly what the hurdles were to Susan, it was clear that she still retained some hope that her life would carry on for as long as she could fight her illness. She asked Dr. Webster, who had come with me on this visit, if the oncologists could look into the possibility of more treatments. Later that day, Dr. Lieberman came to see her. Gently, he reiterated that there was nothing more the team could offer surgically or through radiotherapy. Perhaps Susan already knew the answers Dr. Lieberman would have for her. But as she told Jack later, "I had to be sure that everything possible has been done, even if I am dying."

Christmas time

On December 7, 1995, shortly after our first meeting, Susan was transferred to the Palliative Care Unit. It was Christmas time, and yes, she did think of that, she told me when I came to see her on the unit. It was a holiday she loved. She would have liked to have been at home, but not if someone had to be there to take care of her "like a child." "I like to be alone at Christmas," she said, "to enjoy it in my own way." But being at home alone, even though it was Christmas, was not an option.

The Palliative Care Unit was decorated for the holidays, not only for Christmas but also for Hanukkah. At the entrance there was a large menorah with candles on one side and a brightly lit, tinsel-decorated Christmas tree on the other. Notice boards advertised choir services and Christmas and Hanukkah concerts. At the holiday tea that day, carols and Hanukkah songs were sung by the music therapist and her group. This made Susan think of the children at her school and their caroling. She loved to decorate the classroom. Right now the children would be making greeting cards and paper maché toys to give as holiday gifts to their families. "It was magic for them!" Susan said. As Susan and I talked, I couldn't help feeling uncomfortable, perhaps a little guilty, at my own Christmas at home with a caring family. I also loved Christmas and its music. I thought of the concerts I planned to listen to and remembered that on this very same evening I would hear a live performance of Handel's *Messiah* in one of Montreal's most beautiful churches.

Even if she was in the hospital, Susan resolved to do a few small things for the holiday. She had always delighted in giving presents to Judy's two young grandchildren, Sasha and Nick. She loved them both as her own. She asked Judy to buy some of their favorite toys and to put them under the tree at their home. Even if she could not be there to see the children unwrap their gifts, it would give her pleasure just to think about them on Christmas Day. I thought it sad and at the same time admired her courage and selflessness. It was hard for me to imagine why Susan had chosen to be transferred to the Palliative Care Unit instead of being at home at Christmas with her sister who could help care for her. I wasn't sure if I could have made that same choice. But each time I visited her she reiterated that it was the right decision.

Her condition seemed to be deteriorating. After five days on the unit she looked more ill and pale. Now she looked directly at me, wide-eyed, when she spoke. I thought there was honesty and dignity in her gaze. "I know I am going downhill," she said to me. "Maybe I don't have long to go, but I will still fight as long as I have breath in me." She did not elaborate on these feelings, though at times I wished I could press her to do so. But fearing she would find further questions intrusive and recalling her need for privacy, I held back. Over the next few days she talked about the changes that were taking place in her body. It took greater effort to get up alone and go to the bathroom. She was now experiencing some difficult symptoms, including pain, but this was manageable with Dr. Webster's help. She had difficulty keeping down food and would sometimes vomit right after a meal. The dimenhydrinate prescribed by Dr. Webster did help to stave off the feelings of nausea, however. She was now re-

ceiving morphine 5–10 mg every four hours for the pain in her back. Sometimes she dreamed a lot or fell into a half sleep. Dr. Webster had explained that
this could be a side effect of the morphine and suggested that the regular
dosage of morphine be reduced to avoid excessive drowsiness and perhaps the
disturbing dreams. Susan tried this and for a while she felt comfortable and
clearer in her mind.

Only the light, padded footsteps of the palliative care team broke the tranquility of the ward. Susan appreciated her nurses. Barbara, her primary nurse,
seemed kind and had time to help. What was most important to Susan was to
feel comfortable and to have someone there to help her when she needed to
vomit. Barbara did this and had special ways of easing her back and the pain in
her stomach, such as arranging the pillows under her knees as she lay in bed.
She also felt more comfortable if she lay in certain positions. This way she
needed less medication. Susan also liked Barbara because she "didn't pry."

Barbara had cared for patients like Susan Mulroney during her years as a
palliative care nurse. She acknowledged that when one is used to having complete control of one's life and being independent, it's harder to give in and say,
"Now I'm dying." Barbara worried that she did not spend as much time as she
would have liked with Susan, at least to allow an opportunity for Susan to talk if
she needed to. Several people had died within the last five days, and there was
a shortage of staff on the unit, which made it harder to provide one-to-one
care. With this type of work, Barbara said, one needed to have time beyond the
usual nurse–patient ratio in the general health system. People who were dying
needed nursing time.

To Barbara, Susan seemed very stoic and strong on the surface. But there
was something about the way she was coping that made Barbara feel very uncomfortable. "The more I interacted with this patient," Barbara commented to
me, "I had the feeling she was frightened and alone. I felt a lot of tension, and
that she was dealing with a lot of feelings about having come on our unit. She
has some family support and good friends, but there is more there and I feel I
need the time."

But it was hard to talk to Susan. Denise, one of the volunteers on the unit,
resolved to spend time trying. But, Denise told me, "she talks in short sentences and there is a long pause before she will say something. She says that
her sister will have a hard time with her being on this unit. She says she is fine,
but I wonder if she is the one who is having a hard time. She says that coming
on the unit is like 'a slap in the face.' She doesn't want to elaborate." Jack said
that Susan had a way of closing her eyes and pretending sleep or tiredness if
she wanted to end a conversation. Sometimes she would start to retch or cough
and ask the person to return later. Susan often found that easier than "to be so
blunt as to tell the person to leave." Although she did feel tired or nauseous, it
was also a way of avoiding difficult topics.

Susan told me that she wanted to be as helpful as she could with our research project. "It is important for education," she said, and education and learning were important for everyone. But she needed to think about things on her own, too. "I need to feel I'm independent and for that I need my privacy," she said.

For me, as an interviewer, this was a difficult challenge. I had to respect Susan's privacy, and I was committed to conducting an interview that her comfort level would allow. I felt we were learning from Susan, and yet I wondered if there wasn't more to be learned. Sometimes after leaving an interview I felt a sense of helplessness, that perhaps we would never really communicate. I was struck by the detachment that existed between us, particularly in me. I felt very much the intruder, often thinking that I had no place in this very significant piece of this person's life. I tried to think how I could become closer to her, and yet at the same time it seemed that Susan wanted the distance—at least from me, a stranger—because, after all, I was a stranger.

All the key people

As Christmas drew near and Susan's illness seemed to worsen, more and more people came to visit. Richard, her ex-husband, sometimes came and sat on the sofa in her room, but they didn't talk very much. Susan would lie for long periods, apparently awake but with her eyes closed. Richard would sit deep in thought, looking out the window onto the bustle of the city below. His face looked sad. He did not feel like talking to me, either. The whole situation was sad, he said.

Judy brought in stuffed animals, flowers, and orchids, which she knew her sister loved. The flowers' scent filled the room. Their bright blue, pink, and purple colors seemed to give brightness and voice to a place where no one was talking. Judy would sit at the foot of her sister's bed. When Susan appeared to be asleep, Judy would tiptoe outside into the corridor, where she would cry helplessly. I met her there at one of these times. She looked exhausted. "I can't believe it," she said to me. "Everything has happened so fast. She's so young. I always thought I'd be the one to go first." It was especially hard, she continued, because Susan had never really talked about how ill she was. Surely she had known for some time that the cancer was serious. They had not talked, and Judy hadn't really been aware of the seriousness of it all, until now.

When Susan did open her eyes and acknowledge someone, it was usually when Jack was there on his own. A few days earlier, a pastoral care worker had stopped by to visit and suggested that Susan write a journal of her thoughts and experiences. Susan liked that idea and asked Jack to help. He brought in a tape recorder so Susan could dictate her thoughts, which she felt comfortable doing with Jack. But after a few days she felt too tired and weak.

Dr. Webster visited several times a day. Susan lay in bed peacefully and quietly, covered by knitted quilts and soft toy animals. She rarely spoke, and when she did she would often drift in and out of sleep in the middle of a thought, which was clearly distressing to her. Dr. Webster noted that she was slipping fast into a coma. Dr. Webster considered offering her some intravenous hydration, which can sometimes help to reduce a patient's confusion in the last few days of a terminal illness by balancing the electrolytes. Except for ice chips and lemon swabs that the nurses were using to moisten the inside of her mouth, Susan had taken no fluids by mouth. The decision was a difficult one. Susan now looked peaceful and comfortable. A short time later, Barbara reported to Dr. Webster that Susan had passed melena stools, which meant that she was undergoing a gastrointestinal hemorrhage. Dr. Webster concluded now that intravenous hydration would not be helpful.

Dr. Webster tried to spend as much time as she could with Susan's family to answer their questions and comfort them. Now all the key people in Susan's life had assembled in her room or in the small kitchen down the hall. They were having a very difficult time. Edward, her brother, and his wife June, having just arrived from Vancouver, were shocked and angry. Edward felt some information was missing, and asked whether the cancer had been picked up late because his sister ignored some early warning signals and did not seek medical attention in time. Dr. Webster recognized how difficult it was for family members who had not been in touch with the process of their relative's illness. She was not surprised that Edward appeared angry and that he was questioning whether everything had been done. Indeed, all of Susan's family struggled with the idea that she was now dying of an incurable cancer. Only Jack said he was taking things well. "I think it has been easier for me," he later explained. "We were close friends, and even if she didn't tell me everything, I was more prepared. Susan did confide in me a lot."

Susan never came out of her coma. A few days before Christmas she died in the presence of Judy, Jack, and Rita. She had been a patient on the Palliative Care Unit for just 10 days.

"They say it takes time"

People were not sure if Susan would have liked a formal religious ceremony at her funeral service. Throughout her illness she never expressed her religious beliefs to anyone. She had described herself to me as "not an especially religious person." She had been baptized a Catholic, but she disliked overt displays of religiosity. She did talk to the pastoral worker on the Palliative Care Unit, but expressed little interest in talking about God or religion, nor had she expressed interest in receiving the Last Sacraments. "I have not lived my life that way, why now?" she said. While her family wanted to respect her beliefs, they decided that a Catholic service would be the most fitting, since she was a baptized Catholic. A requiem mass was held in the small parish church near her home where she had lived for the past 20 years.

Richard, her former husband, attended with his wife Alison. Judy came with her children and grandchildren. Richard's mother was there, as were Edward and June. Susan's funeral was attended by the many friends, colleagues, and students whom she had taught and who had come to know her over the years.

Jack also attended the funeral, taking a seat with Rita at the back of the church. "I guess I didn't really see myself as legitimate family," he recalled. Jack felt touched and gratified when Judy made a special point of inviting both his wife and him to sit near the front of the church with the family. Still, it didn't feel right. It was an odd feeling, he told me. He felt he had known Susan Mulroney like his own sister. But that was then; it wasn't his place to intrude now. "I'm not family," he said.

At first, in the days immediately after the funeral, Judy felt fear and a sick feeling in her stomach. She didn't feel afraid of anything in particular but rather a pervasive sense of being "nervous," as if something were suddenly going to happen. It was hard to imagine that she couldn't just pick up the phone and talk to Susan, to ask her to go shopping or perhaps to go for a drive on a sunny day.

As the weeks passed, Judy's sense of loss, "the big hole," did not diminish. The funeral was over and everyone had gone home. There were fewer telephone calls. She could still go over to her son's house and babysit her two grandchildren. But everything seemed so empty. As time passed, the emptiness seemed to get worse instead of better. There were days when Judy felt she "just couldn't go on." She tried to keep busy with her young grandchildren. Being with the children gives one a sense of purpose, she said. Although other things kept her busy, as well, sometimes it was hard to concentrate on what anyone said. It was hard, she said, to concentrate on other people's lives when there was so much going on in your own mind.

Sometimes, Judy would try to find solace by taking out a photograph of her sister. But that gave limited comfort, for after Susan learned that there was no cure for her illness, she destroyed whatever personal papers and photographs she could find. Because she was "a private person," Judy explained, "she didn't want anyone intruding on her private life after she was gone." Judy had a few pictures, but it was hard not to have a good recent photograph to remind her of her sister.

Judy became resentful and angry. Sometimes she felt angry toward her sister, sometimes toward her doctors, and sometimes toward her brother. She wondered why Susan had not talked about her illness. Why had she not told her own sister when she knew that she didn't have long to live? When they would get together, "she would behave as though nothing was wrong." Judy didn't feel she could ask questions, and yet as time went on, it was obvious that Susan was seriously ill. What had Susan been thinking? How much had she been informed about her disease? She did not have a husband or children. There was Jack. But surely as a family member, Judy should have been consulted. Once when she approached her sister's doctor, the only thing he would say was "your sister is seriously ill." The only time a physician had discussed anything with Judy was when Susan was dying on the Palliative Care Unit and after she had died. She was grateful to Dr. Webster for her frankness and openness at the end. She felt let down by Edward. He was their only brother. Why had he not taken more of an active role during the course of Susan's illness? "He didn't bother with her for the whole year," Judy said to me. "And rather than hurt her or get her upset, I never said anything. I just told her that I called him and told him she was sick. He had called a couple of times and when finally, at the end, when Dr. Webster had suggested I should call him right away, it took him three days before he got here." Judy paused, then continued, "Anyway, he was here for the funeral and for a few days after that. But he never got involved in her illness."

Still, Judy went on, people couldn't help what happened. It's nobody's fault. "You can't go on blaming people," she said. "I feel angry that she could not have lived longer, but most of the time now I think, what was there that anybody could do? There wasn't anything!" She reached for a tissue and cried. "I'm like this a lot of the time," she said after a moment. "I miss her. I still can't believe it. I just can't believe it."

Judy did not really see the need to seek professional help for her grief. The palliative care bereavement services had called to see how things were. They were very kind, but she did not want to see a bereavement counselor. What could anyone do? "I lost both of my parents and I've been through a divorce. It's something I'll have to get over," she said. "They say it takes time."

I do not know how Susan's brother Edward and his wife have fared. A few days following the funeral they left for home. The last time Edward had seen his sister was a year before her death. They had not had a close relationship.

Jack Peterson also struggled with his relationship to Susan, her illness, and her death. He struggled with the "unfairness" and wondered if there was more he could have done to help. He had suggested a lawyer who could help with Susan's estate. Jack still felt he was in an odd position, for he was a close friend, but not a family member. It was clear that Susan's brother, Edward, wanted the will to be settled in a way that would ensure the best legal arrangement for himself and the family. It was better that the family hired "a good investment counselor."

Still, Susan had been a close, dear friend and it was hard to believe she was really gone. Sometimes Jack went over in his mind those last days on the Palliative Care Unit. The memory was so vivid, he told me. He could still see Susan lying there, dying in the quietness. Sometimes he wondered if Susan could hear anything in those last hours of her life. He thought about what Dr. Webster had said when Susan appeared to be unconscious: "If you talk to her she will be able to hear; if you say something she will hear." But Jack had not talked to her at that moment. As the last days came and people drifted in and out of the room wanting to say goodbye, Jack still wondered if Susan would have heard anything.

Another thing that sometimes puzzled him was why Susan had not received intravenous feeding in those last hours before she died. Perhaps "it wasn't medically correct" to give people intravenous feeding when they were dying, he said to me. But should people still not be treated? He went on, "I would think that someone who is in palliative care who's having difficulty eating should continue to receive intravenous feeding. She was not eating at all, maybe a few sips of water before she went unconscious. I didn't think she'd get more radiation or chemotherapy or anything, but I say to myself, if the disease is going to kill me, okay fine. But say a person who's dying has an infected finger; I still say that the antibiotics should be given, even if the person is dying."

Although Jack understood Susan's need for privacy, as the months passed he was often plagued with thoughts that maybe he should have encouraged more of a dialogue with his friend, especially during those last weeks when it had become clear to everyone that all treatment had failed. He said:

> I still get those nagging doubts about whether I should have talked more about the fact that she was dying. We had known each other for so many years and had been through a lot together. Should I have pushed it? Maybe yes, maybe no. But I console myself by saying, well you know, if she really wanted to talk about it, she would have. She didn't. I think it was more important for her to go out for lunch and have a laugh. But still you have those little doubts.

Six months after Susan's death her family was still trying to cope with their loss. The estate was still in the process of being settled. Judy made a point of contacting Jack and Rita and asked if Rita would like to have Susan's collection of Spode china figurines. She knew that Rita loved to collect china and remembered Susan talking about it. It was right, she said, that "Rita should have the Spode."

Jack told me he was touched by Judy's offer. He also spoke to me about "the bigger picture." Jack believed strongly in an afterlife. He knew that his friend had not been a practicing Catholic, but he held on to his own strong faith, and told me of his "personal assurance that there were spiritual rewards beyond this life." He then said to me, "It's easier when you have a faith and you're very sure of it. I believe Susan has gone to a better place than this. Christian faith tells us, there's something beyond and the person has gone to a reward, a reward of something better."

19

Costas Metrakis
"It Was Not a Peaceful Death"

Narrated by PATRICIA BOSTON

It was unusual for the palliative care team to see someone like Costas Metrakis, a 58-year-old man who had only recently been diagnosed with terminal illness, on the Palliative Care Unit. Usually, the people they cared for, and their families, had time to absorb some of the anguish and turmoil that accompanies the news of a fatal illness. For the Metrakis family there was no time. From the date of his diagnosis of incurable cancer of the stomach to his reluctant admission to palliative care was a period of only two weeks.

The whole family felt numbed. They could not accept palliative care. "It is a place where they send people to die," Elie Metrakis, the patient's wife, said. Reluctantly, recognizing that help for Mr. Metrakis's symptoms would be available on the unit, the couple agreed to be transferred there from the medical ward. After only three days on the unit, despite his burdensome symptoms, Mr. Metrakis asked to go home. The palliative care team mobilized the support they could and Mr. Metrakis went home on a weekend pass. As soon as he came back to the unit he insisted on returning home again. Four days later he was dead.

A healthy life

Mr. Metrakis lived in Canada for many years, though it was not his homeland. Born in Lebanon of Greek parents, he was the oldest of six children in a close-knit family. The family moved to Greece when he was young, and his parents died soon thereafter. Mr. Metrakis married in the 1960s and he and his wife Elie moved to Canada. Most of his family remained in Greece, but one sister, Sophia, moved to Canada at about the same time and was living close by in Montreal. Sophia was especially close to Mr. Metrakis. He had been like a father to her after the death of their parents.

Mr. Metrakis lived with his wife and children in a wealthy, English-speaking suburb of Montreal. Although their small, two-story home was comfortable, it stood out in rather simple contrast to other ornate and stately homes of the neighborhood. Their three children (two sons, aged 21 and 17, and a daughter, aged 15) all lived at home. Mr. Metrakis's first love was his family. His wife and children and his sister Sophia were the most important part of his life. They had built their lives in Montreal. They had made a comfortable home and had become immersed in activities in the local Greek community. While they did not profess to be deeply religious, they regularly attended services at the local chapel.

Mr. Metrakis was a professional artist. He spent much of his life on the road exhibiting his work, but as Mrs. Metrakis recalled, he missed his family when he was on the road. He would call home frequently late at night to see how everyone was doing. His wife and children anticipated his calls and would stay up late waiting for the phone to ring.

A sudden transition

Costas Metrakis loved his life as an artist and enjoyed traveling to various North American cities to exhibit his work. Although he was not a young man, he had energy and stamina and would often return home enthusiastically recounting stories of his travels. Late in September 1995, he started experiencing frequent episodes of heartburn. For a few months he ignored the discomfort, attributing it to eating the wrong kind of food. The symptoms persisted and in May 1996, he consulted his family doctor, Dr. Gorges. The first test, a gastroscopy, was normal, so he was sent for an upper gastrointestinal X-ray. This test was also normal. Mr. Metrakis was instructed to relieve his heartburn with an antacid.

The symptoms continued. He continued to take antacids, but by now had developed frequent episodes of vomiting, which got progressively worse. He was able to eat, but then 10 to 15 minutes later he would vomit. Mr. Metrakis was becoming weak, and he noticed that he had lost 15 pounds. In mid-November 1996, Dr. Gorges sent him for further investigations. A computed tomography (CT) scan of his abdomen was ordered and finally done a few weeks later. He waited for the report for a week. He was now vomiting continuously and was unable to keep down any food. On November 28, weak and dehydrated, he went to the hospital emergency department. During his examination by the emergency physician, the CT scan report was located. It showed metastatic disease to the abdominal cavity with ascites. Although there was no obvious primary tumor seen, a lesion of the stomach was suspected. Lying on his cot in the emergency department, Mr. Metrakis was not yet aware of these results.

The medical ward

Mr. Metrakis was admitted to the hospital with the diagnosis of gastric outlet obstruction. The doctors suspected a gastric tumor but wanted further studies. The resident doctor who had seen Mr. Metrakis in the emergency department wrote in the chart that the medical team, rather than the surgeons, would continue to follow Mr. Metrakis "as the case is mainly palliative." He was not a candidate for surgical treatment of the tumor. Already the medical team was expecting the worst.

Mr. Metrakis's room on the medical ward was not especially comfortable and it was cramped, since Mr. Metrakis shared it with three other patients. Mr. Metrakis occupied a bed near the window and Mrs. Metrakis and her sister-in-law, Sophia, made it as cozy as they could. They brought in flowers and photos from home. The windowsill became congested as more and more bouquets and plants were added to its tiny space.

Mr. Metrakis underwent a second gastroscopy three days after his admission. Two days later, the diagnosis was made. The pathology report confirmed that Mr. Metrakis had advanced gastric cancer.

By the time Dr. Gorges came to visit him in the hospital, Mr. Metrakis had already been informed of his diagnosis by the hospital physicians. The hospital staff felt that Mr. Metrakis understood the gravity of his situation. Dr. Gorges spoke with Mr. Metrakis about what was known and the two men agreed that Mr. Metrakis should get a complete picture of his options, including a surgical consult.

The next few days in the hospital, Mr. Metrakis was seen by many physicians. The medical oncologists were consulted to discuss the role of experimental therapy in treating Mr. Metrakis's disease. Although they could not offer any curative treatment, they were willing to offer experimental chemotherapy for palliation. It was a difficult decision. Mr. Metrakis was still trying to face the fact that he had stomach cancer and he needed time to think. Two days later, he agreed to the experimental treatment. The next decision was how Mr. Metrakis was going to be fed. He needed a way to receive nutrition during his chemotherapy but his stomach was full of tumor. Normally, patients with disease as advanced as this are not offered tube feeding. However, once the physicians embarked on the chemotherapy course they had to find a way to provide nutrition to Mr. Metrakis. It was possible to insert a feeding tube into the small intestine, a procedure known as a jejunostomy. Mr. Metrakis agreed to this, but he was still numb from the sudden course of events.

When Mr. Metrakis went into the operating room to have a jejunostomy tube inserted, things did not go smoothly. The surgeon called the medical oncologist to the operating room. He had found an extensive spread of the cancer involving most of the small bowel and the abdominal cavity. The jejunostomy could not be done and the surgeon now felt that experimental treatment would probably be of no benefit either. The medical oncology team discussed Mr. Metrakis's case, and told Mrs. Metrakis that a palliative approach, emphasizing comfort rather than prolonging life, was the only option. Her husband knew nothing of this, as he was still asleep following the surgery.

When he woke up and heard the news, Costas Metrakis was confronted with the breathtaking transition from thinking of himself as a relatively healthy person with indigestion to being terminally ill with only a few weeks to live. Within a space of two weeks he had learned that he had cancer, had to make a decision about what could be done, had prepared himself for experimental therapy, and then discovered that his condition was too severe to receive it. Now he was hearing that palliative care was the best that could be offered.

Palliative care was not an acceptable option to the Metrakis family. Dr. Thompson, the first palliative care consulting physician to visit Mr. Metrakis, later recalled to me:

> When I arrived, I found a man who looked physically not too bad, except that he had gastric outlet obstruction and he was very, very scared. And we already knew from the scans that there was a lot of intraabdominal disease. His sister and wife were totally denying the situation and were telling me that we hadn't read the tests right, and they would get others because we didn't know what we were talking about, and they would get their own Greek physician involved because we were wrong. His wife asked me, "Can't they just take out his bowel and clean it off and then put it back in?" And I was trying to tell them, "Well, I'm sorry. This is what it is."

Whereas Mr. Metrakis was in shock, his sister Sophia was devastated. She couldn't bring herself even to talk to the palliative care consulting physicians. When Dr. Clermont, the palliative care fellow, came to the medical ward to talk to the Metrakis family about the role of palliative care and what might be offered, Sophia told her to leave the room. She said, "Why does everyone come and tell him he is dying? It is depressing for him. OK, we know he is sick. But people don't have to keep telling him all the time." Sophia angrily demanded to know why no one had discovered Costas's cancer when there was still time to do something about it. "Why didn't the doctors find the tumor before?" she asked. "You know that he had an ultrasound in the summer and they didn't see anything. How could they have not seen anything? The doctors tell us that the tumor is everywhere now, but why didn't they see it when they did the ultrasound? All they did was give him Maalox and send him home!" Now Costas was meeting a team of doctors who weren't going to do anything for him. Sophia wept with anger and grief.

Dr. Clermont tried to explain that sometimes gastric tumors develop very fast. She suggested that perhaps Mr. Metrakis's tumor had been too small to see when he had those tests. She said that Mr. Metrakis's tumor had been very aggressive and perhaps it had spread quickly. She promised to come back to the medical ward each day to see what she could offer to alleviate Mr. Metrakis's symptoms.

Elie Metrakis couldn't understand why the doctors needed to tell her husband the truth about his diagnosis. When I spoke with her about this later she told me:

> It was crazy when we were told that he had only one month to live. I asked the doctors not to tell him. It made me so mad. He was afraid of dying and I didn't want him to know. But the doctors said it was the policy of the hospital. It is a hard thing to know you are dying. It would have been better if he didn't know.

Elie told Dr. Clermont that her husband had always been "scared of dying." He had always disliked flowers and candles because "they reminded him of death." If he had not been told, he would never have suspected he was dying, she said. He might have suspected that things were bad and that he was very sick, but not that he was dying.

"A crazy period"

Mr. Metrakis's difficulty in making decisions was not only due to the speed of events or to his state of shock in the face of terrible news but to the fact that many physicians had become involved in his care and each one had his or her own point of view. The family was continually bombarded with different messages within a short period of time. Some physicians discussed palliative treatments and symptom control, while others talked about chemotherapy and surgery. Dr. Gorges had at first led the family to believe that there wasn't *anything* wrong. When Mr. Metrakis was in the hospital, Dr. Gorges had told them that, even if it was cancer, there was a lot that could be done. So the family kept hoping. Then, another doctor at the hospital told them that Mr. Metrakis had only one month to live. The family called Dr. Gorges, who told them that was impossible; there were *so many* things that could be done, including feeding Mr. Metrakis through a tube. Then, after Mr. Metrakis had the laparotomy, all the doctors, including Dr. Gorges, seemed to be in agreement: the situation was hopeless.

Within a few days of receiving the definitive diagnosis, Mr. Metrakis developed symptoms of total gastric outlet obstruction. He could not keep any food down at all. It was now necessary to hydrate him intravenously. The medical team asked the palliative care consultants to transfer Mr. Metrakis to the Palliative Care Unit. When Dr. Thompson came to the medical ward to make her assessment, she quickly saw how highly charged the situation was. The family was barely ready to consider any kind of palliative care involvement; they were certainly not ready for Mr. Metrakis to move physically to the Palliative Care Unit. Dr. Thompson told Mr. Metrakis that because he wanted to continue his IV hydration and vitamins, he should stay on the medical floor. In the meantime, she added, she would stay involved to help keep him as comfortable as possible.

That weekend, Dr. Langley, another palliative care physician, was on call. A friend of his who also knew the Metrakis family had called Dr. Langley, expressing concern about Costas. The mutual friend knew about the Palliative Care Unit and wanted the palliative care team to be involved in the case. Dr. Langley went to see Mr. Metrakis, but he was asleep, so he spoke with Mrs. Metrakis. He encouraged the family to come to the unit and offered to give Mrs. Metrakis a tour. As Dr. Langley later explained to me, it was routine for the Palliative Care Service to show the unit to prospective patients and their families "as a way of defusing any anxiety about [it] being a 'death house.'"

Dr. Langley thought Mrs. Metrakis's response to the tour seemed "very positive." As far as he could tell she seemed to like the general layout of the unit, the patients' rooms, the kitchen, and the large, home-like lounge. He was wrong. As he later heard, Mrs. Metrakis had been upset "about any number of things" after her tour, though he did not know exactly what had upset her.

Within the palliative care team there was disagreement on what immediate actions to recommend. Dr. Langley was under the impression that the family wanted to move to the Palliative Care Unit and felt it would be helpful to them. "We just have so many more resources to be helpful," he commented to me. "I mean, that's our job. Time after time the ward does make a difference and it happens very quickly over a few days, very few days. I was just hoping that might be a catalyst in some ways for him, and for them." At the same time, Dr. Langley knew that the family was in tremendous turmoil and under pressure to try to come to terms with the rapid progression of Mr. Metrakis's illness. "I'm quick to realize," he continued, "that the relationships and the care in other settings, on other wards, is often exemplary and that you have to be careful in moving somebody to [the Palliative Care Unit] that you're not interrupting the most helpful relationship they have, which is with the nurse who's giving them chemotherapy, or the cleaning woman who always comes in to see them in the morning, or whatever."

For her part, judging from her interactions with the Metrakis family, Dr. Thompson felt that such a move was premature. The family had made it explicit to her that they wanted a cure. Mr. Metrakis had asked for anything that would prolong his life. When he heard about palliative care he had said, "All I can say is that I am a fighter and I will fight this all the way." Mrs. Metrakis was also looking for treatment. She was urging the medical team to add vitamins to her husband's intravenous nutrition.

The nurses and physicians on the medical unit team were also in conflict about whether Mr. Metrakis should go to the Palliative Care Unit at this time. The nursing assessment recorded:

> Transfer to palliative care not appropriate at this time; patient unable to discuss death but is clinging to life which [to him equals] intravenous therapy. [The family] sees the multidisciplinary team as taking away his fluids.

Excerpts from the notes by several different members of the multidisciplinary team further illustrate the conflicts:

> We believe that it is not possible to treat him effectively and that the care plan should be palliative. Too somnolent to discuss with patient at this time. . . . Patient and family reluctant [to agree] to PCU transfer because of hydration issue. . . . Family reluctant to stop IV hydration because it would shorten his life. Gave info re: PCU and possibility of going home. . . . Wife and family not ready to see IV discontinued. Not ready for PCU. . . . I believe the patient would do best in PCU. . . . For psychological reasons the patient should stay on the medical ward. . . . Condition is not improving. Would do best in PCU.

Normally, palliative care physicians have time to allow the family's process of adaptation to take place at a pace that allows the family to absorb the fact that the chance of a cure is remote or impossible. Indeed, one of the reasons patients with advanced cancer have been disproportionately represented in hospice and palliative care programs is the "fit" between the (typically) slow, but progressively deteriorating course of the disease and the philosophy of open communication and psychosocial support while patients and families gradually absorb the bad news. In Mr. Metrakis's case, however, events had been proceeding much faster than the palliative care team was used to.

Finally, after a week of discussions, Mr. Metrakis decided to move to the Palliative Care Unit. On November 29, Dr. Clermont wrote in the chart: "Discussed palliative care goals. Patient agrees to transfer but to discuss with his family." In an attempt to help the family with this transition, Dr. Langley was asked to see the patient once more. After his discussion with Mr. and Mrs. Metrakis, they were willing to accept the transfer. It was December 1.

The Palliative Care Unit

At 6:00 p.m. that evening, Dr. Clermont was rushing to see her last patient of the day before going home. She had just finished her formal admission of Mr. Metrakis to the Palliative Care Unit, including a careful physical examination and a conversation with Mr. Metrakis, and had written her notes in the medical record. As she passed Mr. Metrakis's room on her way to the elevator she was stopped by Mrs. Metrakis and Sophia. With a worried look, Mrs. Metrakis told Dr. Clermont she needed to talk to her. Dr. Clermont asked if it could wait, or was Mr. Metrakis having some trouble settling onto the ward? Mrs. Metrakis said, "It's just a quick question." Dr. Clermont paused and waited. "Everything's OK," Mrs. Metrakis said. "It's just that we heard people come here to die."

Dr. Clermont knew this was not going to be a short conversation. "Well, yes," she said, "I guess some people come to this ward to die. Other people come to this ward for pain control. Some people die here, but some people also go home from here. Who told you that people come here to die?"

Mrs. Metrakis and Sophia answered in unison, "People on the other ward."

"The doctors?" Dr. Clermont asked.

"No, no," Sophia said. "The families of the other patients in our room."

Mrs. Metrakis said, "I thought this is where they send all the patients in the hospital who were going to die."

"Actually," Dr. Clermont said, "patients die on many wards in the hospital. They don't just send all the dying patients to one ward. This ward is a very special ward where people can come and have specialized doctors take care of any symptoms they are having, and make sure that they are comfortable."

"Oh," Mrs. Metrakis responded, without much conviction.

Dr. Clermont was watching her closely now. "Did you think they were sending Mr. Metrakis here to die?" she asked quietly. Mrs. Metrakis nodded tearfully. Dr. Clermont added, "That must have been terrible."

There was a long moment while Dr. Clermont waited for Mrs. Metrakis to regain her composure. Then Dr. Clermont put her arm around Mrs. Metrakis's shoulder, saying, "We want to help Mr. Metrakis to be comfortable and for him to spend as much time with the people he loves as possible."

"We need to get him home," Mrs. Metrakis said. She stood silently for another long moment. "I'd better get back to my husband," she said. "I've been away for quite a long time." She and Sophia then went back into Mr. Metrakis's room.

By the time Mr. Metrakis was transferred to the PCU he had many severe symptoms: intractable vomiting, nausea, persistent hiccoughs, and abdominal pain. Medical management of these symptoms was very difficult. When Mrs. Metrakis described the situation to me she related that her husband was never comfortable. "He continued vomiting and hiccoughing," she told me, "all the time vomiting and hiccoughing. It was so frustrating."

I met the Metrakis family soon after their arrival on the unit. Mr. Metrakis's single room was much larger than the area he had occupied in his four-bed room on the medical ward. There were reclining easy chairs for family members and visitors, and there was enough space to set up a folding cot. But the room wasn't as colorfully decorated as the windowsill Mr. Metrakis had in his corner of the room on the medical ward. In place of the bouquets and plants were a few faded flowers. Despite the get-well cards, mementos, and drawings that Mrs. Metrakis pinned onto a cork bulletin board on the wall, the atmosphere in the room was somber.

When I entered the room for the first time, Mr. Metrakis lay motionless on his side, his face turned toward the door. His bed, with its crisp white sheets, seemed freshly made. Several large, puffy pillows surrounded his body, one comfortably tucked in behind his back, another positioned underneath his right arm. Though the room was quiet, Mr. Metrakis was clearly awake. His dark eyes were wide open; they followed me as I walked toward his bed. Still, I felt the need to whisper. "How are you?" I asked.

"I want to go home now," he responded. "I want to go home to see my children. This is no place for children."

It seemed an effort for him to talk. He took long pauses between each sentence, carefully choosing his words. But he ignored my suggestion that we stop talking for fear of overtiring him. "When they give me something to stop vomiting, I can go home to my children," he went on. "My wife will take care of me there."

Elie Metrakis was sitting in a chair facing the foot of the bed. She seemed able to concentrate only on her husband, staring at him for long periods whether he was asleep or awake. Sophia situated herself at one side of her brother's bed. She was very tender in her interactions with her brother, often stroking his hair or caressing his arm, but to me she looked very angry and distraught. When I introduced myself, she didn't smile. Her dark eyes seemed to look through me, almost accusingly. But along with the rest of the family, she did agree to participate in our project. Mrs. Metrakis didn't seem as openly angry. I thought she was frightened, perhaps still stunned at hearing her husband's diagnosis. Although I could not be certain, I had the sense that the two women rarely talked to each other. There was little eye contact between them and I seldom saw them seek solace from one another. They did not embrace or hug each other. Once, when Elie Metrakis had come out of the room to talk to Dr. Thompson, Sophia followed behind her and abruptly started interrogating Dr. Thompson about her brother's progress as if Mrs. Metrakis were not there.

Despite the severity of Mr. Metrakis's symptoms, the Metrakis family requested that he be discharged home almost from the moment he arrived on the unit. It was not unusual for patients to leave with short-term passes, for a weekend or longer. Sometimes patients would be discharged home for a while and return to the unit when and if they felt the need. However, this particular request on the part of the Metrakis family presented extraordinary nursing and medical challenges. Mr. Metrakis still had a catheter draining from the surgical incision in his abdomen. He was receiving subcutaneous hydration by a process known as hypodermoclysis, which provides hydration without the use of an intravenous line. He was hooked up to a syringe driver to receive subcutaneous steroid medications and octreotide to alleviate his vomiting and abdominal pain. Oxygen would also be required as his condition deteriorated. In addition, he was very weak. As one member of the team recalled to me later, he was "vomiting, sometimes without relief, and when he wasn't vomiting, he was sleeping. I thought he was dying."

Mrs. Metrakis still felt that her husband would be better off at home. He was "sad" on the Palliative Care Unit, and whenever the children came to the hospital to visit, the whole encounter was upsetting. Whenever the children left Mr. Metrakis would get upset and vomit. When Dr. Clermont suggested that the vomiting might be from the blockage in his bowels, Mrs. Metrakis simply repeated that being at home would be better. She would set his bedroom up on the first floor of their home with a commode, she said. She would hire a private nurse for nights. She would learn how to regulate the syringe driver and give injections. She would learn to insert the small needles under his skin that were providing his fluid intake via hypodermoclysis, and would monitor them and reinsert them if necessary to keep them functioning properly.

A nursing discharge planning meeting was arranged to explore in detail what would be required to accomplish the family's goal. The next day, however, Mrs. Metrakis changed her mind. Now it seemed to her that Costas was too sick to come home after all. Over the next three days the intensity of Mr. and Mrs. Metrakis's desire for him to go home fluctuated with the intensity and severity of his symptoms. If they were not controlled, he wanted to stay in the hospital; if he was doing well, he wanted to go home.

Finally, everyone agreed to try to get Mr. Metrakis home for a weekend. It would be a trial, to see if it were possible for him to stay at home for a longer period. In addition to their desire to accommodate Mr. Metrakis if at all possible, the team felt that time at home was important because the family, especially his children, were having a difficult time talking about Mr. Metrakis's illness. It was too painful for Mr. Metrakis to talk to them about his diagnosis, so they did not even know the true seriousness of their father's condition until his admission to the Palliative Care Unit. He did not want the children to see him like this, so ill in bed on the unit. Since it didn't seem likely that the children would visit while Mr. Metrakis was in the hospital, the team thought a weekend at home might help the family as a whole to come to terms with what was happening. When Dr. Clermont told Mrs. Metrakis that they would try to help them get home, Mrs. Metrakis smiled. It was the first time anyone on the team had seen her smile.

Home

On December 4, 1996, three days after being admitted to the Palliative Care Unit, Mr. Metrakis was back home. Dr. Clermont called him two days later, early in the morning, to see how things were going. Mr. Metrakis said he felt well and wanted to stay at home for two more days. Dr. Clermont offered to make a home visit. She wanted to see how the family was managing. When she arrived she was led upstairs to the master bedroom. Mr. Metrakis was lying in bed. Mrs. Metrakis was sitting on the bed next to him. Dr. Clermont sat near Mr. Metrakis on a small stool. Mr. Metrakis said he had had a lot of vomiting, but still, "it is better at home. I've built up this house all of my life. My kids are here and my wife is here all of the time." He had a lot of good memories. He could be more relaxed. When the children were home they would come to his room and they could talk about what they did during the day.

Dr. Clermont could see that Mr. Metrakis was comfortable at home, but Mrs. Metrakis did not seem as comfortable. She seemed a little insecure managing the complicated medical treatments, though she was handling them well. Mr. Metrakis was not being visited by the palliative home care nurses because he was technically still an inpatient, home on a pass. The family could telephone the Palliative Care Unit ward nurses if they had a question. Mrs. Metrakis had some nursing support from the community health center, but relied mainly on her family for support. It was also better for her at home because she did not have to travel to be with her husband. They had a lot of visitors, too, which was good, though her husband did get tired. But on the other hand, it was hard to ask them to leave, for these were friends who had worked together for 30 years. Everyone was "OK," Mrs. Metrakis said of the family. "We all do our things and everyone acts as if nothing is wrong."

Dr. Clermont was worried by this remark. "Something *is* wrong," she said to Mrs. Metrakis. "Mr. Metrakis is sick." From Mrs. Metrakis's point of view, however, that was not the issue. She wanted to maintain hope for a cure at all costs. It had been upsetting for her that in the hospital the doctors kept telling them that he had only a month to live. They kept saying, "There is no hope. There is no hope." But, Mrs. Metrakis said, "I have to hope."

Four days later, once his weekend pass was over, Mr. Metrakis returned to the unit. The doctors tried to control his persistent vomiting and hiccoughs, but the medications often made Mr. Metrakis drowsy, and this was unacceptable to the family. After one day Mr. Metrakis asked if he could return home again. Another four-day pass was arranged, with the understanding that Mr. Metrakis would stay at home permanently if at all possible.

Mr. Metrakis's physical condition was rapidly deteriorating. He had now developed a fever and was increasingly short of breath. Dr. Thompson suspected he had developed pneumonia. He also still had a catheter draining from his laparotomy incision. But Mr. Metrakis still wanted to go home. He would likely die there, and soon. The team believed it was important to prepare Mrs. Metrakis for this. Dr. Clermont spoke with her the next day.

"How are you feeling about going home?" she asked.

"Good," Mrs. Metrakis replied. "I think it will be OK. It's just the vomiting."

Dr. Thompson had consulted a gastroenterologist to see if he could perform a procedure that would involve inserting a tube to drain her husband's stomach through the abdominal wall, thus preventing the vomiting. Dr. Clermont asked Mrs. Metrakis if she had spoken to the gastroenterologist.

"He told us there is nothing he can do," she said. "The cancer is all over the stomach and prevents him from putting the tube in, just like they had said before at the surgery."

"Well, I guess that means that we will have to continue to adjust the medications to see if they will help," Dr. Clermont said. She paused briefly. "I want to talk to you about some difficult things now. Would that be OK?"

Mrs. Metrakis said, "Yes."

"I want to know if you have thought about what to do if Mr. Metrakis dies at home. If you keep him at home, it is possible that he may die there."

"I don't want to think about it," Mrs. Metrakis said.

"Do you think Mr. Metrakis has thought about it?" Dr. Clermont asked.

"Yes, I know he has."

"What has he been thinking about?"

Mrs. Metrakis's voice broke. "If he dies, he wants me to burn him and then scatter his ashes in Greece," she said, looking away and trying to keep her composure.

Dr. Clermont waited several moments before speaking again. Then she said, "It's very difficult to think about losing someone that you love. I can see that you love Mr. Metrakis very much and I know that he loves you, too. It is hard to lose such a good friend."

"Yes," Mrs. Metrakis said in a whisper.

"It was not a peaceful death"

The next morning the Palliative Care Unit nurses gave Mr. Metrakis a bath and washed his hair, and went over his medications one more time with Mrs. Metrakis. The community health agency and the palliative home care service had been informed that the patient would need to be followed at home. Mr. Metrakis went home with his wife and Sophia by ambulance. It was Thursday, December 12.

On Monday, December 16, Dr. Thompson made a home visit. The palliative home care nurse had not had a chance to visit because of the intervening weekend. When Dr. Thompson arrived at the house, Sophia opened the door looking very upset. Sophia led Dr. Thompson to the bedroom where Mr. Metrakis was lying semi-comatose and breathless on the double bed. He was vomiting very frequently. It was obvious that he was dying. Mrs. Metrakis was hovering near the bed, anxious and tearful. She had not slept for days and looked exhausted. At one point she looked up at Dr. Thompson and said, "He has not drained much from his abdominal catheter. Could it be that his cancer has disappeared?"

Dr. Thompson said that the only important thing to do at the moment was to make her husband as comfortable as possible. She suggested morphine for his shortness of breath and for any pain he might be experiencing, and chlorpromazine suppositories to calm him when he became agitated. Then Dr. Thompson took Sophia and Sophia's husband into the kitchen. Sophia had barely looked at Dr. Thompson since she had arrived. But now Dr. Thompson felt compelled to tell her that her brother was dying. "How long will it be?" Sophia wanted to know. Dr. Thompson said it was hard to say for sure, that she had seen things go on like this for several days sometimes. Because Mr. Metrakis was struggling to breathe, looked fearful, and seemed to be in some pain, Dr. Thompson recommended maintaining the dose of morphine. Sophia looked uncertain, but when they came back into the bedroom Mrs. Metrakis agreed that her husband should sleep if that was the only way to control his discomfort. However, she asked Dr. Thompson if Mr. Metrakis could be given his intravenous digoxin (heart medication) since he had not had it yet that day. Dr. Thompson explained gently that the digoxin would not be helpful at this time. She felt that the best intervention would be to maintain the patient's comfort and to allow him to relax and sleep. In fact, the digoxin would not have helped, Dr. Thompson later said, because Mr. Metrakis was dying. As Dr. Thompson was preparing to leave, Mrs. Metrakis was tearful but seemed accepting of Mr. Metrakis's weakened state. Speaking through her extreme fatigue she told Dr. Thompson, "I want to take care of him here throughout the night." Dr. Thompson told her that she was doing a tremendous job.

A few hours later Mr. Metrakis died. Mrs. Metrakis called the funeral home herself and arranged with them to remove her husband's body. Later she told Dr. Thompson she thought he had been in a lot of pain at the end. From Dr. Thompson's point of view Mr. Metrakis had died with a great deal of fear and "angst," though she did not think that he had been in a great deal of physical pain, at least relative to many other deaths she had witnessed. She was upset to think that Mrs. Metrakis would retain this impression. Still, she herself could not be absolutely sure, and in any event, she reflected later, "it was not a peaceful death."

"It feels like he has gone on a trip"

Mr. Metrakis was well known and well loved by many people, and most of them were in shock at the suddenness of his death. There was a very large attendance at the funeral. Then it was Christmas time. The holidays were very difficult for the family—it seemed that they would never end—though Mrs. Metrakis said later that the constant stream of visitors helped the time pass. Friends kept up a steady supply of food and gifts, and kept the family company.

Marion, a bereavement counselor with the Palliative Care Service, made several telephone calls to Mrs. Metrakis over the next several weeks to see how things were going and to ask if she could be of help. Though Mrs. Metrakis was always polite, Marion had the feeling she did not really want to be called. When Dr. Clermont called, however, Mrs. Metrakis seemed glad to have the chance to talk, even though there were also times when messages went unanswered.

In one conversation with Dr. Clermont that took place in February 1997, Mrs. Metrakis told her that the family was going to the cemetery every day to light a candle at Mr. Metrakis's grave. (She made no reference to her husband's request to have his ashes scattered in Greece, and we have no other information that helps resolve this apparent inconsistency.) Mrs. Metrakis said they were still wondering, still trying to piece together the events of the past year. "We continue our routine," she said, "but it is an adjustment for everyone. We keep thinking he is coming back. It is like he is away traveling. I keep thinking he will call at night, like he used to, when he was working and traveling. It feels like he has gone on a trip."

Months after Mr. Metrakis's death, the family still persisted that he should not have been told the truth about his prognosis. Mrs. Metrakis was still upset that the doctors had told him that he was dying. Why did they have to do that? He had always been terrified of everything having to do with death and dying. If they had not told him, he never would have suspected things were that bad. It just didn't seem fair, she told Dr. Clermont. She had thought there was a cure for cancer. Now she knew this was untrue. Later I wondered whether we should not reconsider how we convey information to the patient. Present guidelines state that the patient has the full right to information about his or her diagnosis and treatment, if they express a wish to have this information. Mr. Metrakis may have wanted to know (although we have no details on this). But Mrs. Metrakis would now retain the memory that her husband had died knowing fully that he had a terminal cancer diagnosis, something he had dreaded all of his life.

Later that month the Palliative Care Unit held a memorial service. Both Mrs. Metrakis and Sophia attended. By coincidence the service took place on Mr. Metrakis's birthday. Sophia brought a picture of her brother, taken when he was in his twenties. Sophia sobbed during the ceremony, but Mrs. Metrakis looked detached and distant. The last time Marion called her on the telephone she said she was fine and that "everyone is coping." Marion was not convinced, but simply left the door open in case Mrs. Metrakis should want to talk to her at a later time.

20

Joey Court
Death of a Child

Narrated by YANNA LAMBRINIDOU

The death of a child is a relatively rare event in medicine. Joey Court was born with an unusual and invariably fatal medical disorder (in the interest of his family's privacy we have withheld the name of his condition). His parents anticipated Joey's death from the first year of his life, but tried their best to treat him as they would any other child. Nine years later, and they finally made the difficult decision to withhold further life-prolonging treatment, and they called on the home care services of hospice. To their surprise, Joey lived another five months while relying solely on palliative interventions. This narrative is about a family coming to terms with a child's death. It touches on several themes in pediatric hospice care—the decision to terminate aggressive treatments; the anticipation of death; the grief and bereavement of family members of all ages; and the question, "why?"

"Joey recognizes us and his grandparents"

I remember vividly the first time I drove into the Courts' driveway. It was a hot summer day in August 1996, and I was a bit nervous. All I had heard about Joey, the elder of two sons, was that he was a nine-year-old boy who had the mental capacity and motor skills of a three-month-old baby. Joey was unable to

355

hold his head up. I had difficulty imagining what he looked like or how I would be able to interact with him. My arrival was announced promptly by Coco, a Labrador retriever whose dark brown coat had inspired his name. Behind Coco appeared Amanda Court, a thin woman in her early thirties whose warm smile did nothing to hide the dark circles under her eyes. Mrs. Court welcomed me into the house and introduced me to Mike, her four-year-old son, who leaned against her shyly and smiled. She then led the way to the den, where Joey spent his days. His parents carried him down from his football-themed bedroom in the morning and took him back up at night.

Joey was lying on the sofa with his head propped up with pillows. Mrs. Court spoke to him sweetly. She told him my name and allowed me to stroke him gently on the cheek. Joey's face looked like the face of a nine-year-old boy. He had thick, black hair, brown eyes, sparkling teeth, and a sweet smile that appeared often when he received attention. His atrophic body, however, weighed only 28 pounds. He looked fragile, bony, and pale. He wore diapers under his sweat pants and his feet were kept warm with tiny socks. I greeted him like I would a baby. Staring straight ahead, he waved his arms. "Joey recognizes us and his grandparents," explained Mrs. Court. "He knows voices. He does say about six things." But only she and her husband could understand his utterances.

Mike interpreted his brother's arm movements to mean "Let's play!" Quickly, he placed his miniature hockey figures on Joey's chest and moved them slowly to give him the opportunity to watch. It was hard for me to tell how well Joey could see this.

I was surprised by Mrs. Court's willingness to participate in our study. The demands of her life seemed so rigorous that I didn't understand when she would find the time to talk to me. Joey required round-the-clock physical care that fell almost exclusively on her shoulders. He depended on liquid medications, frequent turning, and constant supervision so as not to sink his face in his pillow and suffocate. His father Brian looked after him in the evenings. Having to work 12–14 hours a day in the maintenance department of a large housing complex, he wasn't able to help more than that. Mike, on the other hand, was starved for attention. As an avid ice-hockey player and fan, he begged his mother to play with his miniature hockey figures and join him in an interactive ice-hockey television game. When Mrs. Court was too busy to tend to his needs, Mike often refused to eat or demanded that he be fed just like his brother. Mrs. Court also had a part-time job as an administrative assistant at a local recreation center, for it was through her employment that she received health insurance.

Although I didn't interview Mrs. Court that day, I could tell that she was happy to have the opportunity to talk. In fact, she showed eagerness to spend time alone with me to speak more openly about her situation. She interacted

lovingly with both of her children and related caringly toward me. But her noticeable thinness, high energy, and preoccupation with the needs of her oldest
son gave me the impression that she was filled with tension. I wondered if she
ever relaxed.

With a shaky voice she told me that in the nine years of his life, Joey had undergone too many hospitalizations. He had suffered more than any child de-
serves. And because of the rareness of his disorder, he had been experimented
on as well. Mrs. Court would never forget the day when she was planning to
give Joey his first haircut. She stepped out of his hospital room for a short break
only to come back to a baby whose head had been shaved and pierced with intravenous needles. Still, she and Brian drew much of their support from a national network of parents and professionals committed to helping children with
Joey's condition. On my way out that day, Mrs. Court exclaimed that our time
together had already helped her. The ability to share some of her experiences
with an interested listener had given her relief.

"He does not walk, he does not sit up, he does not do anything on his own"

Our second meeting lasted nearly two hours. Mrs. Court and I sat on the living
room sofa while Joey napped in the adjacent den. Mike was in day care, Mr.
Court was at work, and Coco sprawled out lazily in front of us. I asked Mrs.
Court to tell me about Joey. She told me that she and her husband had always
wanted a big family. As a sports fan, she said with a laugh, Brian had wanted
enough children for a football team. Early on, however, Amanda had managed
to talk him down to four. When she became pregnant with their first child Mrs.
Court had the "perfect pregnancy." She gained the right amount of weight, ate
well, and exercised. She encountered no complications, and when Joey was
born he looked healthy. But he couldn't keep his food down. On the fourth day
of his life, his physicians discovered that he was missing a kidney and that a significant portion of his small intestine did not function. In recounting Joey's first
surgery, which lasted approximately five hours, Mrs. Court began to cry. "It just
makes me think of the way he was so little, and he really had a hard life," she
said as tears rolled down her cheeks. She told me that after removing the non-
functioning portion of her son's intestine, the surgeon announced that Joey was
likely to die. If, however, he were to survive, he had a good chance of leading a
normal life. Joey did survive, but he spent two of the first twelve months of his
life in the hospital. Until his second year, he was fed intravenously.

By the time Joey was six months old Mr. and Mrs. Court thought that the worst
of their troubles were over, but they were wrong. One day Joey stopped breathing, and when they saw him turn blue they rushed him to the emergency room

where they were told he was having seizures. It was at this time that Joey was diagnosed with a rare congenital disorder that usually limits the life of children to two or three years. The message Mrs. Court took home from the physician was, as she phrased it, "Your child is never going to walk, never going to talk, never do anything. You are going to have this vegetable child for as long as he lives."

Looking back at Joey's diagnosis, Mrs. Court said to me, "We know now that he has done a lot more than they told us he would ever do. I mean, they told us, 'We have to tell you the worst of what could happen,' even though they could not tell us exactly what was going to happen. He reaches out to Daddy when Daddy is there to hold him, and it was kind of neat every time he did a little thing like that. That was a big boost to us, to say, 'This child is not as bad off as they said he was going to be!'" Mrs. Court paused and lowered her voice. "But, he kind of is," she said. "He does not walk, he does not sit up, he does not do anything on his own. He will always be like a baby."

Joey never learned to chew. His diet consisted primarily of pureed foods and thickened liquids. He had difficulty keeping his food down and an inability to expectorate the copious mucus that accumulated in his nose and throat. He had bouts of aspiration pneumonia. He required frequent suctioning and nebulizer treatments, and trips to the hospital were routine. For the first year of his life, his medical bills approached $200,000. Although Amanda's insurance covered a large portion of this expense and the state of Pennsylvania added funds, she and her husband were required to pay what for them was a large amount of money. It took them six years to settle a physical therapy bill that had accumulated over a seven-month period. Moreover, no one had informed them that their son was eligible for medical assistance. Ironically, a few weeks after Joey's fifth birthday, someone notified them about a plan covering children with Joey's condition—but only for the first five years of their lives. The fact that most of Joey's medical expenses could have been covered through public funds fueled the Courts' frustration further. It seemed that unless there was a crisis, Joey's health providers didn't volunteer information about agencies and resources that could help them.

The Courts did find some relief when Joey turned three. The state picked up the cost of his diapers and several agencies paid for expensive equipment to facilitate his care. A wheelchair, a special car seat, a body brace that enabled Joey to sit up, and a special feeding chair were only a few of the supplies they acquired. That same year, Brian and Amanda learned to treat their son's pneumonias at home.

"Oh my gosh! He really does understand this!"

Babysitters were intimidated by Joey's medical needs. Even his grandparents avoided staying alone with him. So, for the first few years of his life, Mr. and

Mrs. Court assumed the sole responsibility for his care. But when Joey reached the age of three, they enrolled him in a school for children with disabilities that offered free physical therapy, sensory stimulation, and recreational activities. Joey loved school. He was mesmerized by different sounds and fulfilled by the individual attention he received. In the evening, he spent time with his father, who adored him. When Mr. Court came home from work, he gave Joey a bath and held him on his lap for hours. The Courts built a swimming pool in their back yard, and bought Joey a floating bodysuit that kept his head firmly above the water. They didn't take vacations, but the Make-A-Wish Foundation offered them a week-long trip to Disney World. "[Joey] loved the rides," recalled Mrs. Court. "The only part he got scared at was when all of a sudden we started shaking, and there was a big fire at the side of us, and you were supposed to feel like you were in an earthquake, and he reached over and grabbed onto my arm. You know, to us that was like, 'Oh my gosh! He really does understand this!'"

Dr. Heather Willis, the Courts' family physician, was always struck by the fact that Brian and Amanda ascribed thoughts and feelings to Joey. She said, "If you heard [Amanda] talk, you almost thought that Joey was a mildly disabled child. I don't know if it was denial, or if it was subtle things that she would respond to because of being with him so much that the rest of us would not see. I don't know. I think Mom was really alert to those subtle ways that he was responding, and the rest of us weren't." When I asked Dr. Willis what she thought about the Courts' approach to Joey's illness, she said:

> My personal feelings are pretty mixed. Because you see the use of resources on someone who does not have a good prognosis—he is really terminal, but you don't know *how* terminal. But we had to admit him to the hospital a few times with high-tech sort of care to get things going again. On the one hand, that makes you feel like, "Why are we doing this?" but on the other hand, you see the parents' involvement with the child and their inability to let go and you think, "No, we can't crush the hope that they have at this point."

Dr. Willis was faced with a common challenge in the care of patients with an incurable illness: how to help a family come to terms with the likelihood that further attempts to prolong life are likely to do more harm than good, without seeming to force unwanted or unacceptable decisions. "I guess there just seems to be a time when they are ready," Dr. Willis continued. "I think you have to say a few things, like 'this is terminal,' and at times you have to point out that your interventions are uncomfortable for the child, and you have to point out that the child is suffering. At some point the family will have to catch on that, yeah, they are suffering and that prolonging things isn't in the best interest of the child."

The Courts worried about Joey every minute of the day. They were in a constant state of readiness to detect unusual sounds and silences and prevent medical crises. Still, they wanted a second child. Although the results of their blood tests remained inconclusive, they didn't seem to suggest that Joey's disorder was genetic. (They have since learned that it was not.) Even if it were, however, they wanted to take the risk. At least, they thought, they knew how to take care of one child with this disorder, so if their second child were born like Joey, they would know how to treat him. Mrs. Court worried constantly during her second pregnancy. Sonograms of the fetus showed no signs of abnormality—which was good news—but no tests were designed to pick up a condition like Joey's. Mike was born in 1991, when Joey was five years old. It took the Courts a year to lose their fear that Mike was sick as well. Only after repeated reassurances from his physicians that he was healthy could they stop interpreting the rapid movements of his eyes as seizures.

"My gosh, I can't help him anymore!"

Like both of his parents, Mike grew up to be protective of Joey. He played with him, talked to him, hugged him and kissed him, and watched carefully when his mother and father tended to Joey's needs. He learned to wipe the sputum off his brother's face, rearrange the pillows under his head, and cover his feet with a small blanket. Mike's attachment to his brother was evident in both good times and bad. When Joey developed aspiration pneumonia, Mike rejected his own food. And when Joey's pneumonia required hospitalization, Mike missed his brother terribly; but he missed his parents, who spent much of their time at Joey's bedside, even more.

During one of Joey's hospitalizations, Mike told his mother that he wanted his brother's disorder. This way, he said, he would be guaranteed his parents' attention. After one of Joey's worst bouts of pneumonia, during which he had such a severe reaction to an antibiotic that he almost died, Mike began to yell. "I think that was his way of coping," Mrs. Court commented to me, "but that is hard on the family, because when he is acting up like that—I mean we are already stressed out—and now, 'Oh my word! We have to handle this child, too!'"

Desperate for support, Mrs. Court asked Joey's case worker if Mike was eligible for psychological help, only to be told that he was too young. The mental health agency involved with the Courts did not offer counseling to children under six, and at this time Mike was only three years old. Amanda tried, with some success, to give Mike more attention. Still, she said to me, "I think Mike's life is really centered around Joey's. It is almost like he does not have a life of his own, because whatever we do as a family is centered around Joey. [If we have a trip planned] and Joey can't go, or Joey is having a bad day, we have to tell Mike, 'Sorry, we can't go today.'"

As the years went by, Joey became harder to handle. Although he was only

28 pounds, his body grew longer, and transferring him from one position to another became physically demanding. Starting in January 1996, Joey's pneumonias began to show signs of resistance to the antibiotics. For a period of four months, from January until April, the Courts made weekly trips to the hospital. Mike, who was almost four at the time, had little tolerance for the intensification of Joey's needs. Then Mrs. Court fell sick. High fever and a severe respiratory infection kept her in bed for a week. She received a letter from her employer stating that, because she had used up both her medical leave and vacation time, her position at the recreation center was in jeopardy. If she were to lose her job, she would also lose her health coverage and the Courts would be driven into bankruptcy. Mrs. Court didn't have the strength to fight. All she could do was hope that her employer would show enough compassion to accept her back when she recovered. In the meantime, she called Dr. Willis to request tranquilizers. "That was a real, real stressful time," she recalled. "That is when my nerves got really bad. I would just lay there for hours and think about all this stuff that could go wrong." Fortunately, her employer did accept her back, and Mrs. Court returned to her part-time job with relief.

At the end of April 1996, the medical team at the hospital told the Courts that they had run out of medications to treat Joey's pneumonias. Instead, they offered to insert a percutaneous endoscopic gastrostomy (PEG) tube into Joey's stomach. Such a device would allow the Courts to feed Joey without requiring him to swallow, and so would prevent him from getting food in his lungs. After serious thought, Brian and Amanda said no. They knew that Joey was terminally ill, and they were aware that he had long outlived his prognosis; at nine years old, he was one of the oldest children living with his disorder. Moreover, he was small, thin, and fragile. Even if he survived the operation, they questioned whether the PEG tube would prolong his life enough to justify additional suffering. A short extension of Joey's life without an improvement in its quality made little sense to them. And even with the PEG tube, Joey was bound to develop more pneumonias from aspirating his own saliva.

To Mr. and Mrs. Court, the battle was over. "You kind of feel helpless," Amanda said. "'My gosh, I can't help him anymore!' You have helped from [when he was little] to nine years old, and now all of a sudden, 'Oh my gosh, I can't do anything!'"

When several of their friends and fellow members of the network that supports children with Joey's condition heard that the Courts had decided to put an end to their son's aggressive treatments, they stopped talking to them.

Hospice

Mr. and Mrs. Court wanted Joey to die at home. Given the high frequency of his pneumonias, they expected to lose him in a matter of weeks. Familiar with the concept of palliative care from earlier discussions with Dr. Willis, they asked her to refer Joey to hospice at the end of April 1996. Although Mrs. Court was mentally prepared for her son's death, she couldn't believe that his time had finally come. Neither she nor her husband was ready to lose Joey. In an effort to protect him from germs, they stopped sending him to school. To keep him limber, they arranged for biweekly home visits from his physical therapist. To the admission nurse, the Courts emphasized that all they wanted from hospice was symptom control for Joey, emotional support for Mike, and hospice volunteers to allow Amanda to work.

For Mike, hospice offered the Illness Support Group within their children's program, "Coping Kids." Twice a month this seven-member group met to explore through play the experience of living with a terminally ill person. Although Mike was only four and a half years old at the time, and the minimum age for participation in Coping Kids was five, Sally Walters, the group's coordinator, agreed to accept him. After a long phone conversation with Mrs. Court, Sally, a serious yet energetic and playful person, felt that Coping Kids had the capacity to help Mike and that Mike had the maturity to work with older children.

For Mrs. Court, hospice provided three volunteers: Amy Rymes, Jessica Austin, and Martha Diamond. Amy, Jessica, and Martha, all women in their fifties with children and grandchildren of their own, agreed to watch Joey on Mondays and Fridays. But Mrs. Court worked three days a week, so she needed one more person to take her place on Wednesdays. Hospice was unable to locate a fourth volunteer. Joey's case worker informed Mrs. Court that she was eligible to apply for a mental health grant that would cover weekly nursing visits, so she submitted an application immediately. In the meantime, Mr. Court secured the permission of his employer to stay at home one day a week. This solution was temporary and conditional. To make up for his lost hours, Brian promised to work on weekends.

"Can I do this?"

"I must say that the first time I went [to the Courts'] I was frightened," said Amy Rymes, in a warm but confessional tone. "You know, I thought, 'Can I do this?'" Amy spent five and a half hours every Monday looking after Joey. She fed him, gave him his medications, turned him over, changed his diaper, and read to him. When he cried, she soothed him by calling out his name. His cooing enthralled her. "When he sat on his chair," Amy noted, "his legs just hung limp, and we put a hassock there so that his feet could prop on that a little bit. But if you ever worked with a ventriloquist or saw a ventriloquist who had a dummy, that is how their legs hang, you know, and I thought how different he is, and yet he is so lovable even though he is not giving you the love back or the hugs. But he needs you. When you dried him, it was like putting a diaper on a little skeleton. There was nothing there. Nothing at all."

Joey threw his head back and forth every time he was given solid foods. He resisted green beans and peanut-butter-and-jelly sandwiches, but he loved applesauce and jello. Often he vomited. Amy's greatest fear was that Joey would choke during her shift and die before his parents were able to get home to him. She knew Joey was fragile and made a point of handling him gently. She would leave his medication cup unrinsed in case she had left a drop that his parents would want to give him later.

Jessica Austin had similar concerns. Unlike Amy, however, Jessica volunteered only in the morning, so she didn't give Joey lunch. She was thankful for that, because she had heard that feedings were a challenge. Jessica was impressed by the care Joey received from his family. Every Friday morning, Jessica watched as Mrs. Court sat on the sofa next to Joey, stroked him, and told him goodbye before she went to work. Jessica was also touched to see Mike carefully cover up the lower part of Joey's body with a blanket before taking off for his grandparents' house. Inspired by the family's expressions of affection, Jessica started talking and singing to Joey herself. She told me that her favorite song was "Jesus loves me, and Jesus loves you, and Jesus loves the little children of the world." She had a feeling that Joey liked that song, for he smiled when he heard it.

Martha Diamond, on the other hand, felt that no matter how much she tried, she could get no reaction out of Joey. The first few times she took care of him, Martha sang songs to calm him down, brought bells to capture his attention, and wore bright clothes to stimulate his vision. But when she didn't see a response from him, she stopped trying. "My feeling was, 'Why are we trying so hard to stimulate him? It is nearly over,'" she said. "That may be a bad attitude, but that is the way I thought: 'Why are we trying to make him progress when he is really regressing?' It is too frustrating to me with no results and so little response."

Martha found lunch time especially exhausting. More often than not, Joey regurgitated, spit, and clenched his teeth. "Maybe the baby activity in a larger body bothered me," she said to me. "I think maybe it did. You know, you look at them and you think, 'Well, it should not be this way,' and, 'They should be eating and swallowing.' I don't know. Maybe it was a mental thing in there about how infant-like his eating was for his looks and his size. I don't know." To pass the time, Martha began watching television and writing letters to her daughter who lived abroad, always keeping one eye on Joey, for she didn't want him to die during her shift. She grew uncomfortable around Mrs. Court. She said that Amanda avoided looking at her in the eyes and resisted her help with household tasks. As time went by, Martha feared that Mrs. Court didn't want her in the house at all.

"All right, start to detach yourself"

Joey never left his mother's thoughts. Mrs. Court wondered constantly if he was thirsty, if his fussiness indicated a sore throat or another aspiration pneumonia, or if he was going to survive his next medical crisis. The idea that Joey's death was imminent terrified her. The day she found the milk in the cupboard and the cereal in the refrigerator she knew for sure that things had caught up with her. She suspected that without her tranquilizers, she would lose her capacity to function. What Mrs. Court appreciated most about hospice was the opportunity they gave her to talk. Because few people in her life understood what it meant to raise a child like Joey, she had often felt alone. The hardship of nurturing a nine-year-old infant was unfathomable to many of her friends. Hospice people were different. Both Maggie Laslett, Joey's nurse, and Claudia James, the hospice social worker, saw what it took to care for Joey. Maggie, a mother of three, showed great respect for Amanda's medical knowledge, nursing skills, and parenting. Claudia, a calm and solicitous young woman, never failed to ask her about her needs and feelings. These women validated Mrs. Court's emotions and assured her of the reasonableness of her decisions. This meant a lot to her.

In the middle of June, after more medical crises, the Courts decided to stop administering more antibiotics. Dr. Willis supported them in this difficult decision. Maggie advised them to prepare for a respiratory crisis and encouraged them to make use of the morphine. She explained that when suctioning and nebulizer treatments didn't resolve Joey's congestion, morphine was a good way to offer him relief. Meanwhile, Joey began looking sleepy. The involuntary twitching of his eyes and the stiffening of his body looked like he was having more seizures. His congestion and dyspnea worsened. He developed fever. During her shift one day, Jessica noticed that Joey was extremely pale, coughed frequently, and had difficulty breathing. "I had a quick prayer," said the hospice volunteer. "'Dear Lord, don't let this child die while I'm here with him.'" She then gave Joey a nebulizer treatment.

On the morning of June 24, Maggie noticed that Joey's skin had turned gray. Three days later, Dr. Willis gave orders for bihourly nebulizer treatments and up to 5 mg of morphine every half hour as needed. Joey looked lifeless. Mike became hyperactive and was aggressive with Coco. But in the midst of his rambunctiousness, he found moments to calm down, talk gently to his brother, and give him a soft kiss on the cheek. Amanda was looking teary, thinner than before, and rarely smiled. She didn't make eye contact with hospice staff. One part of her felt ready to let Joey go, and another part panicked at the thought.

By July 1 the crisis was over. Joey's temperature dropped and his secretions, which were often copious, dissipated with a nasal spray, suctioning, and nebulizer treatments. But Joey still cried often, vomited, rubbed his face against his pillow, and placed his hand in his mouth as if something was bothering him. Mrs.

Court told Claudia that her life felt like a roller coaster. She worried not only about Joey but also about Mike. She was convinced that Joey's ups and downs and the constant level of tension that filled their home was taking a toll on the little boy. He became more hyperactive and disobedient. Especially when he did not attend Coping Kids, Mike yelled, broke rules, and slept poorly at night. One day near the end of July, he stripped himself naked in the presence of a hospice nurse. Another time, after a long day of misbehaving, he looked at his father and said, "I know I was bad, Daddy, and I did not mean to be today, but I have things on my mind that are bothering me."

The month of August unfolded no differently than June and July. Joey had good days and bad days, and so did his family. When September came along and Mike started day care, the Courts were devastated by the fact that Joey wasn't going back to school. Mrs. Court said to me:

> You always expect your children to outlive you. We always knew that this could happen and that he was sick, and he has almost died I don't know how many times. So we have been to this point, but never to the point where now he is not going to school this year. And now hospice is here—it is real final. It is like, now we are there. But it seems like he always keeps pulling out of these bad spells, and I think that is just as hard. It is almost like, if he was going to be sick and get sicker and that was going to be it and this was going to be over with, I think it might almost be easier than the ups and downs.

Mrs. Court seemed to have reduced her interactions with Joey to matters relating to his body. In our conversations I found it almost impossible to get a sense of who Joey was to her—what she loved or what she would miss about him. Her references to him were strictly medical. Amanda herself alluded to the distancing. "As he gets sicker," she said, "I think I withdraw myself more away from him, only because I am preparing myself for what is going to happen. Now that hospice is here you are like, 'All right, start to detach yourself,' only because it is going to be hard in the long run."

Mr. Court seemed to be going in the opposite direction, getting more and more attached to his firstborn son. During Joey's last hospitalization he didn't leave his side. And at night, when he returned home from work, he extended the time he spent with him. Joey showed deep affection for his father. Lovingly, Amanda called him a "daddy's boy." When he heard Brian's voice, he whimpered and begged. "Do you want Daddy to hold you?" Brian would ask sweetly. "Is that what you want?" And when he picked Joey up, father and son seemed to be in bliss.

Mike

In September, Mrs. Court found Mike to be especially "clingy." He had just started preschool, and for the first time in his life he was spending weekdays away from his grandparents. At night he came to his parents' bed for comfort. He started asking them if Joey was going to die. Mr. and Mrs. Court never hid from Mike the seriousness of Joey's condition, but they also didn't know how to talk to him about death. Although Mike used the word himself, they weren't sure what he meant by it. "Does he really understand that once Joey dies he is not going to be laying on the sofa any more?" Mrs. Court wondered. She had told Mike that when people die their spirit goes to Heaven. Then, after watching a burial on television, Mike couldn't understand why the coffin of the deceased was placed in the ground. This contradiction disturbed him.

Brian and Amanda

Mrs. Court always spoke fondly about her husband. When I asked her about the impact of Joey's illness on their relationship she told me that, if anything, Joey's condition had strengthened it. She and Brian stood on a solid foundation, she said, their love and commitment were unshakable. When Joey was born they knew that their struggle was going to bring them closer, and it had. Although she didn't spend much time with her husband, Amanda saw him as her lifelong partner. "When you have kids, your marriage is not yours anymore," she said. "It is almost like you devote your time to your kids until they are old enough to be out and taking care of themselves, and that is when you start to get back together as a couple."

Mrs. Court took care of Joey's medical needs in the day time, and Mr. Court looked after Joey early in the morning and at night. Before going to work, he fed him breakfast, dressed him, carried him from his bedroom to the den, and after work he bathed him and held him on his lap. They had silently agreed on a division of labor in which Brian was responsible for Joey and Amanda was responsible for Mike. "When we plan to go somewhere, just for a picnic or to visit [Brian's] mom or dad or whatever," Mrs. Court said, "Brian will automatically pack Joey's backpack, food, diapers, whatever we need, and I will automatically make sure what Mike needs. I will often say to Brian, 'Do you have Joey's stuff together?' and then I will say, 'I have all of Mike's stuff together. Now we are ready to go.'"

Amy Rymes

Amy, the hospice volunteer, was feeling more and more attached to Joey. She explained that her experience with him had taught her a big lesson about compassion. She had come to see that although Joey was different from other children, he was lovable. He adored his family, liked some foods and disliked others, enjoyed sounds, loved being rubbed on the face, and took pleasure in tossing his arms. Sometimes his physical therapy sessions enabled him to make new movements. Amy laughed one day when she saw him throw one leg over the sofa. She found Joey beautiful. She noticed that when he slept, his black hair shone. He was always clean and every Monday, he was dressed in the T-shirt she had given him. On it was a colorful rainbow and the words, "I am a possibility."

Jessica Austin

Jessica, one of the other volunteers, doubted that Joey was hospice-appropriate. In the middle of September, she told me that aside from his occasional breathing crises, Joey was stable. His condition had not changed since April. Perplexed by his involvement with hospice, she was thinking of alerting her superiors to the situation.

"My name is Mike and my brother Joey is sick"

Sally, the coordinator of Mike's support group, was impressed with the little boy's growth. Mike was the youngest child she had worked with. When he first joined the group he was so "terribly, terribly, terribly shy" that he rarely spoke. But he tried his best to participate in every activity, including the ones that required writing. Mike did not know how to write, but he agreed to draw instead. He looked up to a 13-year-old in the group, and, week after week, made a point of sitting next to him. Sally stressed that in the children's Illness Support Group (in contrast to a separate Loss Group), she didn't dwell on death and dying. Aware that some children maintained hope for their loved ones, she was careful not to shatter their optimism. At the same time, she felt that children like Mike benefited from an environment in which the illness of their relative was acknowledged. "Mike has really come along and, I think, grown and has a better understanding of the fact that his brother is sick," she said. "[He] is now able to say, 'My name is Mike and my brother Joey is sick.'" It was clear to Sally that Mike loved his brother. One of the few times that he spoke was when Sally had invited a nurse to their group. Eagerly, Mike raised his hand and asked questions about human respiration and the function of the stethoscope. Sally had the feeling that Mike would miss Joey because Joey was his most captive audience. She had heard that Mike liked to include his brother in his play, even though Mike did all the talking.

"He just got real ill and just couldn't take it no more"

Friday, September 20, was Joey's 10th birthday. On September 16, Mike declared that he was ready for Joey's party. Brian and Amanda followed Mike in singing "Happy Birthday," but Joey was weak and lethargic, and he struggled to breathe. Mike unwrapped the presents. They included sweat suits from Joey's grandparents, bibs from the volunteers, and shoes from Brian and Amanda.

Three days later, Mike yelled at his mother all the way back from preschool. A note from his teacher explained that his class had just held a funeral for their deceased hermit crab.

When I arrived at the house on September 26, Joey was having another respiratory crisis. After an anxious couple of hours and an emergency visit from Maggie, he began to look better. Amanda seemed to relax, as if a storm had passed. Sweetly, she leaned her forehead on Joey's and looked straight into his eyes. "Joey Court," she said, "you are not to do this to me anymore! You are not to make me afraid anymore and get me so scared!" Later, Maggie told me that she had never seen Mrs. Court so frightened.

When I called to ask about Joey on September 30, I was surprised to hear the voice of Mr. Court. Usually he was at work on weekdays. I introduced myself and asked him about his son. He told me that Joey had died. "It was a little rough yesterday," Brian said calmly. "He just got real ill and just couldn't take it no more. He just fell asleep. So he is gone."

Mrs. Court came to the phone a few moments later. "I can't say we weren't expecting it," she said. "But it's still a shock." She said that Joey never recovered from his last crisis. He developed fever that kept rising, he stopped eating and drinking, and he couldn't breathe. Mrs. Court kept giving him morphine as instructed by Maggie, but on Sunday morning Joey didn't open his eyes. He stopped breathing a few hours later. "It was quick for him though, so we were glad for that," Amanda said. Joey had died with a big smile on his face, she continued. "He did not lay there and struggle or anything," she said, "he just stopped breathing."

Mike didn't quite understand what had happened. He cried at first, because he saw his parents crying, but then he resumed playing. Mrs. Court suspected that Joey's death would become more real to him at the funeral, where he would see Joey's casket placed in the ground. She said that she herself felt "pretty good." Then she added, "I think it will be worse later on."

Hospice nurse Colleen Stone told me that the day of Joey's death was her saddest day with hospice. Colleen knew the Courts, for she had visited them a few times in place of Maggie. On the morning of September 29, she was on weekend duty. Mrs. Court called hospice to say that Joey had died, and Colleen came to pronounce him dead officially. When she arrived, Mike was in the living room running around excitedly. In the den, Amanda, her siblings, Brian's siblings, and all four of Joey's grandparents sat in a circle, crying quietly. Brian picked up Joey and held him in his lap while Colleen listened to his heart. Then Brian handed Joey to the person next to him, stood up, put his arms around Colleen, and sobbed. Everyone took turns holding the deceased boy, and Coco went around the room resting his head on the leg of the person who had him. Brian's mother was startled by the coolness of the corpse. "Get me a blanket, because Joey is cold!" she exclaimed protectively, before she realized what she had said and discreetly laughed it off.

More visitors filed in. At the door, Mike kept announcing that Joey had gone to Heaven. A few times, he said that Joey had died. But every now and then he turned to his mother and asked, "Is Joey going to live with us, Mom?" Until the arrival of the undertaker, almost four hours later, Mike kept himself busy with his toys. But when he saw the hearse he broke into tears. His parents assured him that he would see Joey again at the viewing. The undertaker proceeded to carry the litter into the living room. Everyone watched quietly as Amanda picked up Joey and placed him gently on the small bed. Her lip quivered. The undertaker covered the body with a sheet, and one by one, the 30 visitors kissed Joey goodbye. Brian, Amanda, Mike, and Colleen all stepped out to see the hearse leave. "We waited," Colleen told me, "until we could not see the car anymore."

"Joey is dead, but I am not"

The Courts spent the morning of October 1 at the funeral home. They dressed Joey in one of his new sweat suits and placed his feet in his favorite sneakers. By the time of the viewing they were exhausted. "You almost feel like there are no more tears," Mrs. Court recalled. As friends and relatives were paying their final respects, Mike was busy drawing pictures and laying them at the foot of the white coffin. He had a new teddy bear which he had already named "Joey Bear."

The next day at the cemetery, relatives, friends, church members, co-workers, health providers, school teachers, and hospice staff formed a long line to greet Mr. and Mrs. Court. The two were both cordial but emotionally flat. Mike was excited. Proudly, he ran to his support group leader, Sally, and showed her his bow tie. Sally picked him up and told him that he looked swell. Mike beamed. He then placed his hands on Sally's face and said, "Joey is dead, but I am not." Before she knew it, Sally found herself in front of Joey's casket. Mike wanted to show her the drawings he had made for his brother the previous evening. He told her that Joey was going to take them with him to Heaven. Then he casually lifted Joey's head and rearranged the pillows.

When Mrs. Court saw Amy, the hospice volunteer, in the mourning line, she introduced her to her father and told him that she was indebted to her for her help. Without the support of hospice, she said, she would have not been able to work. Amy saw Joey's death as a miracle. The fact that it had occurred when both Mr. and Mrs. Court were at home was something she had wished for them for months. Looking back at her experience with Joey, she said, "I got more in return than I ever gave." Still, Amy didn't look forward to working with another dying child. She said that her days at the Courts' had exhausted her, not because she worked hard, but because she was constantly on edge.

Maggie, the nurse, was surprised by Joey's death. She hadn't found his last illness to differ significantly from the previous ones and thought that he would overcome it. She felt sad for the Courts and wanted to visit them one more time to say good-bye. In retrospect, Maggie wasn't sure if she had met their needs. Other families, she observed, relied more on hospice than the Courts had. "It must be different to be caring for someone for years and then hospice comes in and is helping out," Maggie reflected. "Probably the intensity of it is not as high as with a family with a very healthy patient who all of a sudden is really sick."

When I spoke with Jessica, she told me she was glad that she hadn't told her superiors that Joey was not hospice-appropriate.

Heather Willis

During Joey's participation in the home care program of hospice, Dr. Willis lost almost all contact with the Courts. In retrospect, she regretted that she hadn't called them herself to hear updates about Joey and give them her support. She also wished that she had stayed in closer contact with Maggie. Aside from signing the medical forms that she sent to her, Dr. Willis didn't communicate with Joey's nurse. "When hospice comes in, they take over, you know," she said. "That is good, and they take over with all the little details of managing the patient's comfort and things like that, and then I will get a message on my desk that hospice would like a change in medicine, or this, or that, and that is fine. But I feel a lot less in touch than when [Amanda and Brian] were coming to me for the management. I wouldn't mind talking to a hospice nurse more. You know, they are sensitive to the doctors and their time and things and try not to bother us during hours, but maybe some of us would like to be bothered."

In addition to attending Joey's viewing, Dr. Willis wrote a letter to Mr. and Mrs. Court complimenting them on the way they had cared for their son. Later, she told me that she attributed Joey's long life to the extraordinary care he had received from his parents. She had supported the Courts in all their decisions, and reflecting on their final choices regarding antibiotics and other life-prolonging care, she said, "If the child is terminal and the family says, 'We don't want to see more suffering,' I am prepared not to actively intervene, and I don't think that is passive euthanasia. That is just letting a disease take its natural course in a person who is going to die of that disease sometime soon anyway."

From the 10 years of work with Mr. and Mrs. Court, Dr. Willis had grown close to them. She remembered all the meetings they had held to discuss Joey's future and all the times she had felt their pain. "I feel like we are going to be friends for life," she said.

"It is so hard that he doesn't need me anymore"

A week after Joey's funeral, I visited Mrs. Court at home. Mike was in preschool and Mr. Court was at work. The living room was filled with flowers. Mrs. Court told me that even though she had expected Joey's death for 10 years, she found it extremely painful. She couldn't imagine not seeing him again. The finality of his death horrified her. Now she knew that her husband had done the right thing when he kept on taking photographs of Joey. Six albums were filled with shots from the first until the tenth year of his life. She relished looking at them.

Because he worked long hours, Mr. Court had not had the opportunity to experience Joey's subtle, day-to-day decline. As a result, his son's death had caught him off guard. Now he walked aimlessly through the house, wondering what to do with himself. He skipped breakfast because he missed feeding Joey. Mrs. Court told me that not having to care for Joey added so much free time to her day that she didn't know what to do with it. "I am just so used to being busy," she said, "that now I go to relax and I get right back up and do something. I think to myself, 'Brian will get home from work,' and I will think, 'Oh my gosh! I had better run to the store quick'—or here or there— 'because tomorrow I can't, because I have Joey!' And then I think, 'No, I don't have to do that now.' If Mike says, 'Mommy, can we play this?' I will look at what time it is, thinking, 'What does Joey need?' or 'Do I have time to do this quick?' I am so used to Joey. It is so hard that he doesn't need me anymore."

Since the day of Joey's death, Mr. and Mrs. Court had dined out twice. They were also planning to take a long-awaited summer trip to Canada. Every day that passed felt easier to Amanda. She told me that what kept her strong was her conviction that Joey was at peace. "We know that he is not suffering," she said, "and I think that has helped us to handle it. This might sound odd, but when the undertaker came to get him and I put him up on the bed, he had a smile on his face and he looked so peaceful, and the undertaker kept that smile on his face for the viewing. Normally they would close the mouth completely.

We said it was a comfort to us, and everybody who was at the viewing said, 'Oh my gosh!' It was an overwhelming feeling of peace."

Joey was buried in a nearby cemetery. The Courts visited him daily. Mike liked talking to his brother. He took flowers to his grave, and on his way to school he stopped with his mother to tell Joey "Good morning." Mrs. Court was surprised to realize how attentive Mike had been to his brother's daily life. She told me that ever since he had received his new teddy bear, Mike acted like Joey was still at home. "By the next day," she said, "he was play-acting that [the teddy bear] was Joey. He was feeding him breakfast the next morning, burping him, and then he laid him on the sofa before he ate. When Mike got up the morning of the funeral and I said, 'What do you want for breakfast?' he said, 'Oh no, Mom, I can't eat breakfast yet. I have to feed Joey.' When we go by the grave he keeps asking me, 'Mom, is his body still there, or did the rest of him go up to Heaven?'"

"My name is Mike and Joey died"

In the middle of November, Mrs. Court looked the most rested I had ever seen her. The dark circles under her eyes had faded and she seemed relaxed. From two tranquilizer pills a day she was now down to a half. The money she and her husband had received from relatives had helped pay off a significant portion of Joey's outstanding medical bills, which had lifted a big burden off their shoulders. But Mrs. Court was still concerned about Mike.

Mike was now five years old. He had been having diarrhea for several days, bit his nails, and acted out in all the ways that he knew irritated his mother. When Amanda refused to feed him like a baby, he didn't eat at all. That was a behavior he used to display when Joey was sick. At dinner the night before, Amanda had resorted to a favorite game to hurry Mike through the meal so they could be on time to church. Mike was dawdling and had eaten almost nothing. Amanda pretended they were in a race to see who could finish eating first.

"Mike, I beat you!" she called out. "All right, Mike, I'm done!"

"Well," Mike replied, "I am going to beat Joey, because Joey is not done yet."

Mike's new Loss Group was a lot bigger than the Illness Group, with an average of 20 children per session. Tracy Torres, a soft-spoken volunteer in her forties, recalled, "You could tell he was frightened to be there. I would sort of coax him a little bit to stay with me, and I would sit beside him, and even then I could tell he was still afraid, and he just did not say much at all." Tracy made a point of staying close to Mike at every meeting, and when it was his turn to introduce himself, she spoke for him. But a few months later, Mike became more open. He giggled and laughed with the other children. He participated eagerly in group activities. And he started to speak for himself. "My name is Mike and Joey died," he said at the beginning of every meeting.

As Christmas approached, Mike began singing songs about Joey's life in Heaven. On the weekends, prior to his ice-hockey practice, he made his father drive by the cemetery to pick up Joey. "We keep reinforcing to him that Joey is always with him, and I think that is just his way of grasping that—to think that he has to drive by to get him," said Mrs. Court. Mike would fasten his brother's seat belt, talk quietly to him in the car, and bring him to hockey practice for luck. But he was worried how Joey was going to celebrate Christmas. His consolation was a little Christmas tree that his aunt had placed on Joey's grave. Mike kept asking questions about Joey's body. Was it all in Heaven? Was some of it in the ground? His parents' answer was always the same: that it was his soul that had gone to Heaven, that Joey had acquired a new body, a healthy one like Mike's. A day or two later, Mike would ask again: What happened to Joey's body?

The Courts received fewer Christmas cards that year, and the families who used to send them photographs of their children, now sent only a card. "They think it is going to hurt our feelings or something like that," Amanda said to me, "because they still have their child and we don't. But I don't look at it that way. I want to see how they are growing." With their own card the Courts sent out a photograph of Mike and one of Joey, taken two weeks before he died. Amanda told me that it meant a lot to her when people talked openly about Joey. She appreciated every sign that her friends remembered her boy. She wanted his memory to live on.

Joey as memory, Joey as spirit

I visited in April 1997, seven months after Joey's death. Since January, Mr. and Mrs. Court had joined the Loss of Child support group at hospice. The monthly meetings of this group, together with bimonthly meetings of the parents group that met in conjunction with Coping Kids, brought the Courts to support group meetings three times a month. Mrs. Court recalled that when she first started attending these meetings she cried on the way there, cried during the meetings, and had a headache all the way back home. Now she looked forward to going. She still cried sometimes, but she also laughed and shared her thoughts freely. In some ways the meetings were drawing her closer to Brian as well, for they were teaching her things about him that she didn't know. Once, the group was talking about personal rituals that people had adopted in their bereavement. When it got to Mr. Court, he said that before he went to bed and when he got up in the morning, he always touched Joey's door. "I didn't know that!" Amanda exclaimed laughingly. "I knew he was close to Joey.

I saw him go by. But I never—when he said that, it was funny, because I did not know he was doing that!"

Mike continued to pick Joey up on his way to hockey practice. When he played well, he attributed it to his brother. When he didn't skate fast enough, he asked Joey to push him harder, and more often than not he sped up. "He is so cute," said Mrs. Court, "because he is so little. [The other kids] are all like 6, up to 12 to 14. He is the littlest guy, and he doesn't even always understand where he is supposed to be. The coaches told Brian that they can tell that his heart and soul is really in there. He goes around and signs autographs for people already. Even for the undertaker! [Mike] says, 'I am going to go to college, probably in Michigan—to Michigan College—and then I am going to play for the Hershey Bears, and then I am going to play for the Colorado Avalanche.' And it is so odd to us, because our kids were so different. We knew Joey would never have a future, and here is one who is planning this huge future. It is so odd. It is almost like we had kids at complete, total, last points on the spectrum."

At the end of April, Coping Kids carried out a memorial service to commemorate the death of the children's loved ones. Amber Dunn, the coordinator of Coping Kids, told me that this service offered children the opportunity to remember, share, and honor their connections to their deceased relatives in ways that funerals often didn't. The service opened with a brief welcoming introduction by a young member of the Loss Group. "Good evening, everyone," said the boy at the center of the stage, "my name is John Balch. Welcome to the Coping Kids memorial service. Tonight is a night to talk about our most special memories and the love we always will have for people who have died." The children then lit candles, sang hymns, played a song that one girl dedicated to her deceased mother, and then one by one they walked toward a large box they called a "treasure chest." Each child announced his or her favorite memory of the departed loved one and deposited an artistic rendering of this memory in the chest. When it was Mike's turn, Tracy asked him if he wanted her to help him describe his memory. Mike declared that he did. "Mike's memory that he treasures is about his brother Joey," Tracy announced into the microphone, and then turned to Mike. "And what do you want to say it was Joey's favorite thing to eat?" she asked. "Applesauce!" said Mike loudly. He then placed his drawing into the treasure chest: a big smiley face, smeared with yellow lines.

After the memorial service, Mike told his parents that he wanted to attend the Coping Kids summer camp, which was scheduled to take place in August. Tracy was amazed by his growth. She told me that she had seen him transform from a child who would not introduce himself in public to "a completely happy-go-lucky boy who will talk at the meeting when we go around the circle." According to Tracy, Mike seemed to have lost his fears of being abandoned. What excited him about the summer camp was that Tracy was going, too.

"Joey pulled the sun up, making it nice"

The last time I saw Mrs. Court was in August 1997. She looked happy, rested, and tanned. The family had recently returned from Canada. The trip was superb, she said. Far away from the physical reminders, she hardly thought about Joey. But when they arrived back home, the house felt empty. The quietness in Joey's room startled her. The next time the Courts attended the Loss of Child Group, Amanda cried all the way through. "Now I am okay again," she said to me. "It was almost like, when we were away, we did not deal with anything, and when you come back, it is like reality hits again—almost like you're starting all over. But it does not take that long to get back to where you were. You just kind of backslide for that short time."

Mrs. Court could hardly believe that it had been a year since Joey's passing. His death was still fresh in her mind. The Courts decorated Joey's grave regularly with flowers, wreaths, wind chimes, and objects that symbolized religious and national holidays. She told me that Mike still talked about Joey, but not nearly as much as before. At Coping Kids he drew a picture, reproduced here, that portrayed his grief as a big, ominous circle hovering over his head. On a windy day, he announced that it was his big brother who was blowing the clouds. When it rained, he claimed that it was Joey who brought the water, and at sunrise he once said, "Joey pulled the sun up, making it nice." Mike had stopped waking up in the middle of the night, and he no longer needed to drive by the cemetery several times a day. Now when he was sad, he talked more

Mike Court's drawing from "Coping Kids."

about his feelings. He told his parents that he played hockey for Joey. One day, he said, he was going to dedicate the Stanley Cup to him.

Mrs. Court continued to browse through her photo albums. She searched in Joey's closet for things she had tucked away years earlier. When she came across Joey's baby book, she opened it to the page where parents record the milestones of their children's growth. She looked to see if there was a space to mark Joey's death. There was no such section.

21

Paula Ferrari
Another Triumph of the Spiritual Over the Practical

Narrated by PATRICIA BOSTON

While on a visit to her parents' birthplace in Italy, Paula Ferrari developed a fever. She also noticed a tendency to fall over and lose her footing without warning. Over the next year these problems progressed. Her doctors told her that her condition was due to amyotrophic lateral sclerosis (ALS), or Lou Gehrig's disease, an incurable degenerative motor neuron disease that leads to progressive weakness of the muscles in the extremities and trunk.

For the next three years, Paula lived with ALS. At first she tried to manage at home and her family rallied and provided all the nursing care they could. But as her disease progressed, she became unable to walk or talk. When she was admitted to the Palliative Care Unit, she was no longer able to eat or swallow on her own and would sometimes choke on her food.

Paula knew that these changes would take place and that her disease would progress until she wouldn't be able to breathe alone. She knew that many others suffering with ALS would have given up and tried to seek physician-assisted suicide if it were legal and available; she had read of such cases. But for Paula Ferrari, to seek help to hasten one's death was an act of total self-deprivation. Death, she insisted to all of those who talked to her about it, is an integral part of our being and existence. To undergo the experience of dying, regardless of the physical suffering it entails, is our ultimate lesson of life. Experiencing suffering offers a unique opportunity to know about ourselves and who we are in our spiritual existence.

Paula did suffer physically. But she stood firmly by her beliefs and never wavered. For her caregivers on the Palliative Care Unit, Paula Ferrari seemed to have mastered the extremes of living with a fatal illness.

Life before illness

Paula Ferrari was born in Philadelphia. She was raised by Italian parents and lived there until she married her husband John, an American citizen. They had four children—two sons, Franco and Greg, and two daughters, Rosa and Rita.

When John got a chemistry teaching job at a Montreal university, the Ferrari family moved there with their young family. After some years of raising the children together, however, things started to fall apart for the Ferraris. The marriage was strained by conflict over financial affairs, and Paula and John each wanted to pursue very different life goals. They decided to separate.

Shortly after arriving from Philadelphia, Paula had enrolled in a masters degree program in philosophy. She began to study seriously many of the spiritual and philosophical questions that had so frequently confronted her over the course of her life. During the years following her marital breakup, she worked as a hospice aide, then as a Roman Catholic chaplain, and finally as a professor and teacher of religious philosophy. She became actively involved in scholars' groups concerned with the relation between religion and spirituality and became known for speaking out publicly on religious political issues. She was a poet, artist, musician, and philosopher, never tiring of speaking about her religious beliefs to anyone who wanted to listen.

In the pursuit of deeper spiritual understanding, Paula traveled to Italy. Although she had been raised in Philadelphia, Italy was the home of her parents and by extension, her heritage. She wanted to renew herself within the context of her Italian roots; to reflect on who she was and to learn her ancestral language.

It was not only her Italian heritage that led her to return to her parents' homeland but also her childhood faith of Catholicism. For a long time she had formally accepted her faith in the teachings of the church. She had embraced her position as a Roman Catholic chaplain. But she constantly wrestled with psychological and spiritual questions, such as the role of beauty and its relation to her own spirituality. She also had many questions about formal teachings of the church, such as the place of women in the church, and some of these were hard for her to reconcile with her own beliefs.

She embraced the monastic life at the Villa Benedictine monastery in the solitude of the Italian mountains; it was a happy life, she later recalled, and a life where she gained much insight. She explored the various dimensions of her experience—her roles as a mother, wife, feminist, and academic—and how she could relate them to her own spirituality. As she practiced the monastic rituals, she began to reconcile her life experience with her spirituality and found a sense of inner spiritual freedom among the nuns and the life they led.

The diagnosis

In my dreams, I travel a lot, walking, talking and guiltily smoking
cigarettes. There's nothing I can do for myself. Like an infant, I
depend on others to survive. I have entered a merciful, if sometimes frustrating, world.

While she was in Italy Paula Ferrari fell. It wasn't a very noticeable or serious fall, but later she told me that she thought it was odd, since she hadn't tripped over anything and this had never happened to her before.

After returning to Montreal, she found that she often stumbled and tripped, seemingly for no reason. Sometimes she needed to hold onto a piece of furniture, just to keep her balance. Her family became increasingly worried. Not only was the unsteadiness persisting but it seemed to be getting worse. Six months after she returned from Italy, Dr. O'Leary, her family doctor, suggested that she undergo a series of tests. When he had the results and informed Paula that she had Lou Gehrig's disease, she couldn't believe it was true.

ALS involves a pervasive and inexorable loss of function. Insidiously, the patient experiences a gradual loss of the use of arms, legs, bladder, and bowel. Swallowing becomes difficult, and ultimately the capacity to breathe diminishes, resulting in death. Dr. O'Leary now reported that Paula Ferrari's tests showed an extensive degeneration of the muscles in three limbs.

As the reality of the disease sank in, Paula's first reaction was hopelessness and despair. "I screamed a lot," she said, recalling this time much later. "The thoughts of losing my children and not living long enough to know my grandchildren were painful," she said. "It was excruciating to me." But it was not only the thought of losing her loved ones that pained her: "I was now forced to mourn the loss of my body," she said. "I was forced to lose control of who I was as I had always known myself."

Coping at home

[John] said, "Don't worry, I won't die—
I'll take care of the kids."
He nearly died this year of cancer,
but I believe him.

We used to be married.
Now he enters my room in the dark
to speak from his heart,
or sit up and watch
'till I fall asleep.°

As she found it harder to walk, Paula decided to move out of her large home and into a small one-bedroom flat in a working-class Italian neighborhood in the west end of the city. The flat was on the ground floor and she wouldn't have to manage stairs. It was also immediately adjacent to the small, traditional Catholic church, Our Lady of Mercy, where she had sometimes attended mass. She could see the street from her front window.

In some ways, she told me, this move continued the spiritual journey she had made the year before, though the simple life of the neighborhood in which she now lived was very different from the solitude of the Italian mountains and the monastery. Paula Ferrari found a comforting innocence in the day-to-day life of the neighborhood. The community was not large, stretching about six blocks to a highway, within a much larger Montreal suburban area. From her window, she could see children playing hockey on the streets and women sweeping their front steps or scrubbing the driveway. On a windy day, she saw rows of men's shirts, socks, and underwear strung on clothes lines between the houses to dry in the tiny backyards. There were a few stores, and a local bakery, which sold large, flat, fresh-baked loaves by the hour, as well as large, ornate, multi-tiered wedding cakes. There were stores where one could purchase milk, beer, cigarettes, shoes, and garden tools, all at the same store. In the daytime, these stores were frequented by black-shawled, elderly women, at night the stores became a quick stop for men to buy cigarettes on the way to the pool hall. Most of the men were craftsmen, skilled laborers, or factory workers. Tomatoes and sunflowers filled the tiny front yards in the late summer months. For a few dollars, some of the men rented small allotment gardens from the city that were close to the railroad tracks or at the edge of the neighborhood and produced plentiful crops of fruit and vegetables.

Her daughter Rita recalled that the apartment had wall-to-wall books, almost up to the ceiling, and her mother had read all of them. She could read in German, Greek, Latin, and Italian. Sometimes she'd have three or four books going at once.

Paula Ferrari had lived alone for many years before her illness, and although she loved people and parties, she was happy being alone. Rita said she thought her mother was quite content with her reading and her cat. She loved to talk and to speak about her work. But it was becoming impossible for her to manage alone, as it became increasingly difficult for her to walk. Each day one of the chil-

°These lines, as well as the lines at the beginnings of subsequent sections, are from poems Paula Ferrari wrote on the Palliative Care Unit.

dren stopped by to visit and to see if they could help—perhaps cook a meal or offer their mother an arm for a walk outside. However, these visits were becoming insufficient, and after a family meeting, John decided that the best thing to do would be to move into her flat and help with her care on a full-time basis.

The move into Paula's flat did not seem unnatural to John, even though they were divorced. The couple had kept up a close friendship since their divorce and in some ways, he still loved his former wife. From John's perspective, the only thing they had ever quarreled about was money. The marital breakup had not been bitter, though in the past years, the couple had pursued different paths. John had met a new woman friend, and Paula had thrust herself into her work on religious philosophy. When he learned about Paula's illness, John thought it best to end his relationship with his friend to devote his time to caring for Paula.

For a while after John moved in, things went well. He did as much as he could: cooking, laundry, driving her to appointments, generally trying to help with whatever Paula needed at the time. But another complication developed: just a few months after he had moved into Paula's flat, John began to feel ill himself, and couldn't do as much for Paula as he would have liked, as he required longer periods of sleep and rest. When he consulted his doctor, he learned he had malignant lymphoma. "It was hard on everybody," he recalled to me. "Our kids then had to take care of the two of us."

Caring for their mother became a major commitment for the four children. A schedule had to be drawn up, and the children committed themselves to daily shifts so that their mother wouldn't be left alone. Franco recalled:

> It was a full-time job, though I'll never regret it. For the longest time I had wanted to travel, but while she was sick, I never felt comfortable leaving the city for more than two weeks. I felt like, what if something happens? or, I'm throwing the workload onto my brother and sisters, because it was a shared workload between us four. So there was that sense of responsibility, and also the sense now that this was precious time with my mother and I shouldn't be taking off, seeing the world or whatever. So all of our plans were put on hold.

"Hey, I'm sick, too, you know!"

Some months following Dr. O'Leary's initial diagnosis, Paula could no longer walk without the aid of a cane or without holding someone's arm. When Dr. O'Leary examined her, he saw that her muscles were rapidly deteriorating; she had increased spasticity of her elbows and knees and a marked change in her overall muscle ability. Rita, Rosa, Greg, and Franco came in daily to share the tasks of Paula's daily toilet care and shopping. Paula needed help to bathe and to dress.

Meanwhile, John's condition stabilized. While in the hospital, he had undergone extensive chemotherapy and was now in remission from his cancer. He felt a bit neglected, even slightly resentful. With all the attention focused on Paula, he felt he had been forced to carry the burden of his own illness alone. He loved his family, but he wanted to say, "Hey, I'm sick, too, you know!" John tried to understand that his children were already heavily involved in Paula's care. They had a strong sense of obligation, in spite of some very difficult days. It was not easy to get outside nursing help. They could get up to 35 hours of home help in a week, but this wasn't really enough for a person who needed care 24 hours a day, seven days a week. Somebody needed to put Paula to bed, take her to the bathroom, help her with every part of daily life. Her children took turns helping her every night. But they felt a lot of stress, and it came out. John recalled:

> The kids would get angry with each other. They just were at their wits' end, you know, because they could come over, there was a schedule, but occasionally someone would mess up. It didn't often happen, but there was stress. You had to be there that night or at a certain time, and that was it.

Paula started to lose her ability to speak, and the community agency nurses said that they couldn't communicate with her. Mrs. Ferrari was "too heavy," they told Rita. She needed to be lifted out of bed, but this task was becoming too hard to manage, they said. They suggested that it was too difficult to care for Mrs. Ferrari at home.

"Well, this is the last step"

The children were also finding it increasingly difficult to cope with the daily physical demands. Sometimes when agency nurses called in sick, by the time a replacement arrived at the house, Mrs. Ferrari had lain in bed until 1:00 in the afternoon. Occasionally Rita or her siblings would call their mother's house and get no answer. When they arrived they would find her in bed, with soiled bedding that had to be changed. They worried about having to leave their mother's door unlocked so people could come in to help her. "So it was a constant worry," Rita explained to me, "and I think it was also a big burden, especially when my sister became pregnant, and we were only three and there was a third night that we had to sleep over and then the next day you get up and go to work. [So we agreed she had to go to palliative care] and it was sad because it was like, well, this is the last step."

Paula could also see how quickly her disease had progressed, and how difficult it was for everyone to manage at home. She saw that everyone was tired.

She thought about death and what it was going to be like to be dying. But these were peaceful thoughts, for she felt an enormous love for God, and felt a security—anticipation almost—and joy in herself that everything would be well. She told a friend, "As we lose control over our lives, we gain the ability to learn a unique lesson of life and perhaps to become closer to God."

She knew it was time and she was ready to go and be cared for at the Palliative Care Unit. It was hard to leave her home. She knew that her disease would progress and that it would not be long before she would completely lose the use of the muscles in her limbs. Not only would her arms and legs be affected but she would lose the use of muscles in her hands and fingers. Eventually, she wouldn't be able to breathe on her own. She thought at the time that she didn't have long to live, perhaps a few months.

In the comfort and peace of her little flat, she had reflected deeply on the kinds of decisions she wanted to make about her care in the last period of her life. Some months before, Mrs. Ferrari had written to Dr. O'Leary, making it clear to him that she did not want to be tube fed or to be kept alive artificially on a respirator. It was not that she wanted to shorten her life—quite the contrary. Dying was "the ultimate experience." It had "something to teach," she said later. But she wanted to be nursed and cared for in as natural a way as could be done. She knew of the care at the Palliative Care Unit, and from her own hospice work of caring for men who were dying from AIDS-related complications, she knew what the philosophy of palliative care entailed. She was not afraid.

In many ways, Mrs. Ferrari remarked to me, this final path on which she was forced to embark had the possibility of becoming "a deep and beautiful time." "Dying had a necessary place," she said. Franco later recalled that his mother "really couldn't understand people who asked for their life to be ended before it was time." There was something to be celebrated in not succumbing to "the practical," as she put it—in other words, to the desire for physician-assisted suicide.

Settling into the routine

Pink sky and two small lavender clouds.
A buttermilk wash floods my window.
Blue sky and green leaves transfigured by light.
Six o'clock: the nurses turn me over.
Adriana empties the trash, Ivo vacuums the hall.
The kitchen courier delivers her menus.

In Dr. O'Leary's letter of referral to palliative care, he noted, "The patient communicates by guttural sounds and by pointing at an alphabet board with a mouth pointer." Dr. O'Leary also stated that he was uncertain how long his patient could be expected to live. He reported: "Her respiratory reserves are minimal and she is choking intermittently which indicates there is a risk of aspiration pneumonia."

Four days later, Paula Ferrari was admitted to the Palliative Care Unit, under the care of Dr. Sylvie Dupuis. She arrived in a beautiful colored skirt with a purple top. Margaret, an experienced palliative care nurse who was assigned to her primary care, recalled that Mrs. Ferrari "looked like she had done her best to be happy when she came." Rita took the week off work because she wanted to help her mother get comfortable and settled. Because it was so hard for her mother to talk and feel understood, Rita was worried that the nurses wouldn't understand her mother. Rita spent every day working with her mother's palliative care nurse to help her learn her mother's routine.

Margaret wondered to herself whether this was such a good idea. She worried that once Rita had to leave and the nurses were on their own, it might be even harder for the patient to adjust again. "She relies on her daughter so much," Margaret commented to me. "She loves her so much, it could be difficult for everyone after Rita leaves." Indeed, because Rita and her family had been the main caretakers for their mother, they knew her routines as well as all the unspoken, daily idiosyncrasies that her care involved. Now there were differences of viewpoint and method as to how to proceed with certain nursing procedures. For example, Rita had specific ideas on how one person could lift Paula back and forth from her bed to the chair. Her own training as a gymnast had oriented her to certain ways of lifting. But the nurses, who had many people to lift and needed to protect their backs, preferred to work in teams, or even to use a mechanical lift, all of which appeared to Rita as intrusive and embarrassing for her mother. As the week passed, Paula's weakening muscles made it very difficult and dangerous for anyone to lift her alone.

Paula was also very clear on how she wanted to be given care. But this was a new place and she didn't know her caregivers yet. Paula wanted to accept these new ward routines, and people tried, but everyone had a different way of approaching her physical care. She knew what she wanted, and although there were many little things she could have said to help the nurses understand her needs, she could not speak clearly enough to make herself understood. As Margaret later recalled:

> She often would break out into uncontrollable crying or laughing, which is part of the disease, but it would be out of her frustration at trying to show us how to put her hands in a certain place; how to move her in bed; how to put her glasses back up on her nose; when just these little things take so long to explain, and she couldn't explain.

The room

A pot of Basil on the windowsill
hides the white chimney,
the suggestion of Ligurian hills
masks the odour of ashes.
The weather is torrid—
if I fail to pay attention
my basil will wilt, wither, and dry.

I first met Paula Ferrari in her room on the unit. She was sitting in a wheel-chair, and attached to her head was an apparatus that held a pointer, which she used with either an alphabet board or a computer to communicate. When she looked up at me she raised her eyebrows, then smiled and made guttural sounds, her way of extending a warm greeting. She had chin-length, slightly graying, dark hair. Although I couldn't be sure how tall she was, I had the impression that she was not tall and perhaps even a little stocky in build. I thought she looked much younger than her 57 years. Using the pointer, she tapped out a message to me on the computer, slowly, almost painfully, it seemed to me. The computer generated a voice. It was hard to know how her real voice sounded, but her welcome was clear: "I am happy to see you," she said. "Thank you."

Paula's room told me much of what I have since learned about her. It was not a large room and was somewhat dark, and it didn't have much of a view. But it was decorated with things from home, all the things which, Paula said, "bring me joy and memories of all the happy things in my life." Her room became a warm and peaceful haven for caregivers and visitors alike to drop in and sit for a while. Even if staff were off duty, it was not unusual for them just to visit. Over and over again, Paula's caregivers' stories described a sense of peace and love that seemed to emanate from her room.

Margaret said, "her room is warm and peaceful. You feel you want to stay in there even when the unit is really busy. It's like when you're in there, sometimes you even forget you're working." This was easy for me to understand. The room was colorful—bright flowers of red and yellow, depending on the season; large green hanging plants; a small herb garden growing on the windowsill. There were paintings of the ocean and woodland scenes, and photographs of Rita, Rosa, Greg, and Franco. A large painting hanging high on the wall, on the righthand side of the bed, displayed forests, with a pathway between the trees. Mrs. Ferrari said, "I want to walk on the road where I can see. The road in the picture leads to the ocean. When I think of the ocean, I think of smells and seaweed." Some time later, Rosa told me that Rita had painted the picture while on a special art scholarship in the Philippines. There were also items from times long past—photographs of Paula with her mother and fa-

ther, old greeting cards with a message of love or encouragement. Pieces of poetry manuscripts lay on a chair or bureau, work from the past and poems that
she was writing now with the aid of the computer and the typing stick.

Relationships and routines

Someone offers me lunch—
I say, "First the neck brace off."
I try to spell it with a chart and a straw between my teeth,
but he mistakes "collar off" for "colour of"
and offers me a spoonful of orange.
It is a very little problem compared with others'.
They've offered to double my "Prozac."

As time went on, the demands of Paula's care became greater and greater. Four
months after her admission, Margaret's nursing record reported:

> Patient needs total care, needs feeding at all meals; oral hygiene needed, drools
> and has dysphagia [difficulty in swallowing]. Patient presents a risk of aspiration
> when eating.

The record went on to report other complications of the disease: she had become constipated and uncomfortable. Other nursing records reported that she
had problems choking when given both fluids and solid foods, and skin rashes
were appearing all over her body. At times she had trouble sleeping at night; it
was sometimes 2:00 a.m. before the night nurse found her asleep, even though
she was taking sedatives. Dr. Dupuis prescribed hyoscine, a medication that
helps to dry out mouth secretions and that can reduce the risk of aspiration,
and docusate to reduce the constipation. She also prescribed chloral hydrate, a
mild sedative that helped her sleep.

Dr. Dupuis's records indicated an increasing flaccidity of Paula's limbs. Now
Mrs. Ferrari routinely needed at least two nurses to help lift her onto the commode beside her bed or into her wheelchair. Rita visited most evenings and
Greg, Franco, and Rosa came two or three times a week. They also tried to
help lift their mother. Everyone tried to use Rita's technique of pivoting her
onto the commode. It could be difficult because sometimes her head and neck
would be in danger of dropping forward if she wasn't positioned carefully. She
was fitted with a large, wide, gauze-covered styrofoam collar to give her neck a
little support. But it was uncomfortable and itchy.

After she had been bathed and dressed and given her usual morning care,
Paula liked to sit in her wheelchair facing the door to the hallway. Here she
would write her thoughts with her straw and alphabet board. She was thrilled
when she got the computer that recorded the typed message through an elec-

tronic voice system. Sometimes she wrote short letters to friends or family, but when she had the energy, she spent much of her time composing poetry—about her day-to-day life, small moments of her hospital routine, memories. Memories were precious and forever binding, she told me.

She loved to watch people and would delight in a small happening on the unit, seeing the color of a volunteer's blouse, or the way the sun would light the colors in a nurse's hair. Although she enjoyed the many visitors who came to see her every day, there were times when she would have liked to have had more solitude, to think and meditate without interruption. The nurses put a sign on her door that read, "Meditating. Please do not disturb." But it was still very difficult for Paula to protect her privacy, for people felt they needed to go in and check on her, and always left the door slightly ajar.

Paula needed to be fed every mouthful of food, which had to be soft in texture and cut up into tiny bits. This procedure required care and delicacy because her choking spasms appeared without warning. The daily record showed that she was choking more despite medication to try to prevent the spasms. The choking usually happened after meals, which meant that there was an increasing risk of aspiration pneumonia.

Communication continued to be very frustrating. Paula had become used to talking by guttural sounds and by expressive facial movements such as raising her eyebrows, closing and opening her eyes, frowning, or smiling. When she couldn't say what she needed, she would become distraught, crying and screaming, and then even more distraught because she could not wipe away her own tears. Sometimes when I went in to sit with her she would look sad and forlorn. I had read that ALS sometimes results in pseudobulbar tearfulness, but I couldn't always be sure what she was thinking. Dr. O'Leary had reported that she had had similar symptoms at home and was receiving fluoxetine which helped to stabilize her emotional state.

These were emotion-filled, difficult days. The volunteer, Jean, first met Paula one evening during suppertime when she was going around the unit to see if anyone needed help with their meal. She noticed that Paula could not feed herself, so she began to feed her the soup that was waiting on the tray. It was not so easy. Jean described the scene to me:

> I was feeding her her soup. She began to pause and looked up at me as though she didn't want the soup. So I stopped feeding it to her. But then she cried out and motioned that, oh yes, she wanted the soup. I saw she was trying to say something else. Then she screamed. Dr. Legare came by at that moment and showed me how to talk to her through the straw and the alphabet board. She pointed to the number 11, and I realized she had been waiting to listen to a special musical concert on the TV on channel 11. Things were fine after that, and she smiled, but I realized what it was like not to be able to communicate. It upset me, and I was kind of drained, exhausted. It was an emotional strain, because I wanted so much to help.

And then she tried to spell out two words for me. Again, I couldn't make the two words out. But I just pretended I understood and went on and smiled. But she's nobody's fool and she saw I didn't understand. So I made her spell it out again. So she spelled it and it said, "Thank you." And I was so touched that it was so important to her to say thank you to people who take care of her. I just left at that point, and I started crying. It touched me to that point. Later I went back into the room and gave her a big hug. John, her former husband, was there, and he just squeezed my wrist. I've been very attached to her since that point.

Passing time

Hilvette feeds me.
She was up last night
celebrating Christmas.
Hilvette says every month has a colour.
The colour of July is brown. Like her.

Despite the many frustrations, Paula Ferrari settled into a daily routine that Rosa later said she had loved, because "it kept meaning and friendships in her life." She would go to mass in the hospital chapel after getting her care in the mornings, take a nap, and then look forward most days for people to come to visit. There were so many who would visit: friends from her neighborhood or the small Italian church where she had attended mass, and from the many charity organizations she belonged to, as well as her family. Paula Ferrari could scarcely talk, but many who came into contact with her, either through an act of caregiving or friendship, felt changed in some way by their encounter with her.

In various ways, she befriended the housekeeping staff, volunteers, nurses, and doctors. Whether it was the person who changed her water pitcher, the volunteer who brought in library books, or the TV repairman, people seemed to know her in some special way. She shared her knowledge and wisdom of poetry writing and became a teacher of poetry to one physician who wrote poetry. One of the volunteers said she had taught him the joy of listening to Bach. She seemed to nurture friendships, old and new, with an energy that far surpassed her doctors' assessment of her medical condition. One of the physicians she had befriended said:

> I feel a deep, personal bond and extreme closeness to her. On the one hand, I think she is the closest person to me. I constantly learn from her about myself and my work. And I never feel I am doing the giving. It is as though she is always the one who gives to me.

The more I came to know her, it seemed as though she had a most extraordinary gift of looking right into your soul.

Often these relationships were built during the process of a routine caregiving task or a special activity or project. Rick, one of the volunteers, said he had come to know Mrs. Ferrari by helping her spell out words with her straw and alphabet board so that she could create her poems. "It was an honor" to help her communicate her poetry, he said. Rick had difficulty explaining his relationship to this patient. He said:

> It's hard to put into words. It goes beyond words, because the relationship is not spoken words. She communicates mostly with her eyes and just certain expressions. But there is obviously a tremendous trust that has developed, a real comfort on her part with me. What has developed is that I'm able to get into her head, to finish her sentences. So I try and save her the energy of finishing her sentences. And I have [come] to know how loving, compassionate and spiritual she is.

Another volunteer, Madeleine, talked about spiritual issues and concerns. Madeleine was used to working with the dying and she had often had the occasion to sit with a patient and listen to some of the fears people expressed. She knew people who had been terrified, who struggled with the question of what would happen to them, who wondered whether there was an afterlife. Paula Ferrari was different. Talking with her, Madeleine said, was "personally and emotionally exciting because spirituality is so much a part of her life. She has thought about her own mortality and who she is has very much to do with how she sees her own relationship to God."

Dr. Dupuis noted that in Mrs. Ferrari's case "her medical problems are of secondary importance to her." "The first level of importance is really her life—what is going on in her life." Dr. Dupuis hadn't experienced this before in a patient with this disease. Most people with ALS had such distressing symptoms that it was all that they could think about. But for Paula Ferrari, it seemed more important to express herself in terms of her own spiritual life.

Mrs. Ferrari did not consider herself religious in a formal sense. Once when I asked about the picture of Jesus that hung at the foot of her hospital bed, she explained that the picture was a "crib picture of the post-resurrection appearances of Jesus." "I painted it," she added. "I painted it in egg tempera. It was fun and I love the theology of it." As if to answer my unasked question, she said, "I do not agree with all of what the church teaches, but I want to be part of its rituals."

Rita, Greg, Franco, Rosa, and John visited the unit regularly. Rita seemed now especially close to her mother and would go every evening to help her write poetry. The poems that Paula wrote now were about love for her children, her life when she was well, memories intermingled with sadness and joy as she approached the end of her life. A particular joy during this period was the birth of her first grandchild. Yet she was worried about Rosa and was sad that she could not be with her for the birth of her child. Her physical problems were less painful to her than this feeling of exclusion.

Looking forward

The first time we met,
your round dark eyes stared
unable to comprehend what I was.
It was mutual.
I fastened upon the craftsmanship of your parts—
the dimple in your elbow,
the transparency of your skin,
and your eyes—entirely iris!
One day you focused,
you smiled, you spoke
serious sounds, happy and sad.
Every day I see you,
you are newer than the day before.

As the time came closer for Rosa's baby to be born, Mrs. Ferrari became more excited. There were periods when she would stare off through the window, worrying whether Rosa and the baby would be healthy and strong. When Rita called and said Rosa was in labor, Mrs. Ferrari spent more and more time in prayer and meditation. She couldn't sleep. Margaret commented that it was as if she were vicariously going through the labor herself.

When the baby was born Paula said, "We think of life, and of the things we know, and the birth of a child is the greatest thing we know as a miracle." Rosa named her baby girl Jenny. Rosa asked Rita and John if there was some way that her mother could visit her on the maternity ward and see her new granddaughter. Dr. Dupuis thought it would be a wonderful experience and the arrangements were made. Paula told Jean, "This is a happy day." Seen through Margaret's eyes, however, it was not the simple visit of a grandmother to see her first grandchild. Paula was not in the role of a grandmother, but more like that of a child herself. As Margaret recalled:

> I came on evening shift and the patient was screaming, crying, and unable to wipe her nose or her drooling mouth. Her husband and son Greg were trying to pull on her heavy coat, but were unable to bend her arm. She was using a straw to point to each letter on her alphabet board, but she constantly dropped the straw in frustration. She wanted her shoes, her glasses, the poinsettia on the table, the beads from the drawer, and the bunny rabbit in her gift bag. Her son Greg tried to put the beads on for his mother, but she cried more. "They're for Rosa!" I was literally seeing her fall apart. Greg said, "Come on, Mom, you're supposed to be happy. The baby is born."

Small kindnesses

Her gentle hands wash me,
her fragrant creams soothe my skin.
His friendly eyes hold me,
his sentences bind my wounds.

The Ferrari family worried that Paula's increasing dependency would mean that she would be treated more and more like a child. Sometimes people who didn't know her "talk in a babying way," Rita said. "My mother understands and accepts that everyone means well," she continued, but she wished that those people would remember that her mother was sharp and alert even if she couldn't talk or do anything for herself. Margaret agreed. The palliative care team had talked about this issue in their patient meetings. She said, "I think we all realize that we sometimes have a tendency to baby people when they are physically helpless."

When caregivers spoke of their own feelings of helplessness and inadequacy it was usually when they couldn't instantly meet a simple request. Often it was a question of incorrectly perceiving Mrs. Ferrari's request for a pillow to be shifted slightly, or to move her hand an inch or two to make it more comfortable. Paula knew they were trying but these moments were still very hard, and the baby talk (almost unconsciously adopted by the staff at times) would make a hard situation feel even worse.

There were also some very rewarding moments, however. She loved the feel of a warm wash cloth on her face, her morning sponge bath, and the smell of the creams that the nurses massaged into her flaccid skin. She would laugh and smile when Margaret combed her hair in the mornings. Once Rita cut her hair and restyled it. When she showed her mother her new haircut in the mirror, Paula chuckled, "If it's okay with you, it's okay with me." Rosa made regular visits to her mother's bedside with Jenny. These were happy times. Paula now had no muscle control and she could not hold Jenny in her arms. Rosa would position the pillow around her so that she could cradle Jenny and feel the baby's body and skin against hers. Sometimes Rosa would hold Jenny's face close to her grandmother's face. Mrs. Ferrari would laugh with loud guttural sounds. One day Rosa said, crying, "She has so much love to give, it's beautiful to watch them together. But I feel sad inside. I know my mother would make a wonderful grandmother." Of Jenny, Mrs. Ferrari said, "She is marvelous. I can't believe it. I need to pinch myself."

Some other changes were taking place in the family's life. Rita was considering leaving Montreal to be with her husband, who had recently been transferred to Atlanta. Paula's condition was weakening day by day. But she had already lived a year after coming to the unit and no one knew how much longer she would live. Rita didn't want to leave, but Paula insisted that Rita go to Atlanta with her husband. It was important to be with him, she told Rita. Greg, Franco, Rosa, and John would all be here to help with her care. So Rita went to Atlanta, resolving to come back for a week each month to help with her mother's care.

Twelve months after Mrs. Ferrari had been admitted to the Palliative Care Unit, the nurses and physicians worried more and more about her choking episodes. There was always a strong risk of aspiration pneumonia. Yet she carried on. Rick, the volunteer, said, "Her lungs are so congested. But it's quite re-markable. Yesterday she called me in to dictate another couple of poems."

The last days

I've been wasting my dying
on frivolous things . . .
I would suffer for others
if I suffered at all . . .
But I'm loved and I know it.
Can I offer God this happiness?

Christine, the music therapist, knew Mrs. Ferrari well. In the beginning, when Mrs. Ferrari was first admitted and could speak a little, she was up in the pallia-tive care lounge more, where there was a grand piano and where volunteer mu-sicians gave afternoon concerts. She had even composed a piece of music with her head pointer. When Mrs. Ferrari could no longer go to the lounge, Chris-tine would bring one of the volunteer musicians into her room, and they would wheel in a smaller piano. But now Mrs. Ferrari was seriously congested with pneumonia and Christine saw that she was dying. Christine hugged her, want-ing to say goodbye. She told me:

> We had a cry and she asked to hear a Beethoven string quartet. The next day I went in and I said, "do you want to hear Beethoven again?" She said yes, and I said, "is it okay if I sit here and listen with you?" And she had some tears and I would dab them. That was our connection.

"Someone like that one compares to one's own life," Christine continued. "You come to work and you are maybe annoyed with children and then you meet with this example of incredible grace in the face of incredible limitations. It was a great learning experience." Christine said that Mrs. Ferrari had somehow connected to what nourished her. "She had humor and faith and she seemed to be living her dying with much more grace and integrity. I am in awe of her."

Margaret also felt that it was close to the end. Over the last weekend Mrs. Ferrari had been short of breath, frightened. Dr. Dupuis increased her mida-zolam a little, to allow her a more peaceful sleep. The hyoscine dosage was in-creased to try and alleviate the profuse secretions that were welling up in her mouth and throat. On Monday Margaret checked the patient list when she came on duty to see if Mrs. Ferrari was there. She was still there.

Now caregivers, friends, and family began to pass by to say goodbye. Some of the staff had gotten to know her very well over the past year. But now the family had begun their vigil at the bedside—Mrs. Ferrari had sent for Rita the day before—and the staff didn't want to intrude on these last hours of family time. Yet it appeared that this was going to be a very personal loss for so many—caregivers, friends, and family alike. Rick, the volunteer, wondered if there would be a chance during these hours to have "just one more connection with her before she passed on." He wasn't sure what he would say. "I could always tell her that I care deeply for her and she means a lot to me," he told me. But he didn't think there would be an opportunity to do that, and there was not. Mrs. Ferrari died a few hours later.

Margaret went into the room to comfort Rita, who had been at the bedside at the moment of death. They hugged and talked with each other, and Rita helped Margaret prepare the body. Rita made her phone calls to Franco, Greg, Rosa, and her father, and to the funeral home. Then she started packing up the room. "There must have been at least 25 bags," Margaret said. She wondered to herself whether Rita should wait for her brothers and sister "just so the room looked natural." Rita did wait, though she felt restless and wanted to go.

When John arrived, the head nurse gently suggested that everyone go into Mrs. Ferrari's room for a prayer, the Universal Prayer that the palliative care staff say together when a patient dies. I was there along with volunteers, primary nurses, nurses from the unit who hadn't directly cared for Mrs. Ferrari, and the physicians. Everyone held hands. John stood at the foot of the bed, crying gently. Rita put her hand inside her mother's hand. The pastoral care worker recited the prayer, ending with the words, "Our love goes with her as we now in silence commend her to Your care." After the prayer, everyone made their way out of the room. The staff went back to the routines of the unit and to caring for the other patients. There was a mood of sadness, a great sense of loss. Some of the nurses were putting their arms around one another. Others squeezed hands, or said a word of comfort.

As everyone filed out, John said, "I really want to thank you on behalf of my family, for all you have done for Paula. We will never forget you." Somebody else (I am not sure who) said quietly, "Ah, but we will never forget her."

II

Working with the Narratives

22

Research Methods

The aims of this chapter are to outline the premises of qualitative research, to show the relevance of qualitative methods to palliative care, and to explain the specific methods underlying this book. The discussion aims to provide an understanding of ethnographic, narrative inquiry, which has been our approach to the experiences of patients, families, and caregivers in palliative care. We outline our rationale for a case narrative study, the ethnographic methods and techniques used to gather and analyze data, the role of the participant-observer, and ethical issues related to qualitative research in palliative care.

Qualitative methodology: an approach to social research

While the physical and natural sciences emphasize quantitative measurement and analysis, the human sciences have a long history in the qualitative research tradition (Denzin and Lincoln, 1994; van Manen, 1988). Late nineteenth-century objections to the creation of generalizable, scientific laws for the purpose of explaining and predicting human behavior prepared the ground for new schools of thought that advocated a focus on "meaning" over "measurement" (Clark, 1997). In the fields of anthropology and sociology, these schools gained popularity by introducing an alternative approach to knowledge making. This approach has come to be called "qualitative research."

Starting in the early twentieth century, anthropologists began to challenge their methodological tradition of theorizing about people in faraway places without getting to know who those people were. Scholars like Franz Boas (1966 [1940]), Bronislaw Malinowski (1922), and their students (e.g., Margaret Mead [1928] and Ruth Benedict [1969]) carved out the beginnings of the "participant-observation" method, whereby intensive fieldwork in nonindustrialized communities produced systematic accounts of native customs and habits. The field of anthropology came to rest on the premise that natural settings should be the primary source of cultural data, and that techniques of participation and observation would lead to a greater understanding of people as researchers learned to think, see, and feel with local people in their own environments (Tedlock, 1991).

During this same period, similar work was undertaken by sociologists. The Chicago School of Sociology, aiming "to avoid moralized or sentimentalized urban reportage in favor of the analysis of urban groups and subcultures, such as immigrants, black migrants, hobos, juvenile delinquents, and others," availed itself of qualitative techniques (Holton, 1996:48). Experience, observation, and participation in real-life events gave rise to such classic studies as William Foote Whyte's *Street Corner Society* (1955), a study of street life among Italian-Americans in Boston, and Erving Goffman's *Asylums* (1961), an analysis of life in a mental hospital and, by extension, in any "total institution," such as a prison or military camp, that denies its occupants their individuality. In the 1970s, qualitative methods of research also emerged in the fields of education, social work, and community development (Patton, 1990; Wolcott, 1973), nursing (Hogstel and Sayner, 1988), and medicine (Mays and Pope, 1995; Pope and Mays, 1995). In all these areas, studies aimed to explore and address social phenomena with important practical implications for individuals, groups, and entire societies.

In spite of these developments, research based on the model of the physical sciences, characterized by the manipulation of variables, experimentation, measurement, and deduction, still has primacy within the medical research community (Clark, 1997; Miller and Crabtree, 1994; Reid, 1996). Health practitioners trained in the medical sciences have been exposed primarily to quantitative, experimental methods, designed to test hypotheses and seek out universal laws. By contrast, qualitative methods, seeking to explore particular settings and experiences, rest on induction and holistic inquiry.

In the social sciences there are clear advantages to both methods. Quantitative experimental methods make it possible to measure the responses of large numbers of people within a limited standardized framework, and thereby facilitate generalizable, statistical aggregations of data (Miller and Crabtree, 1994; Patton, 1990). Qualitative methods explore questions of meaning. The decision as to which approach to employ depends on one's research question and clinical context, as Miller and Crabtree write:

> If the question about one's body, one's life, or power concerns "how many," "how much," "how often," "what size," or numerically measurable associations among phenomena, then a survey research style using the decisions and methods of observational epidemiology is appropriate. If the question asks "if . . . then" or "is . . . more effective than . . ." then an experimental style is reasonable (Miller and Crabtree, 1994:343).

The aim of research, however, is not always to predict relations or test hypotheses. Questions relating to life experience within a dynamic and changing environment, which are usually concerned with multiple meanings, patterns, and complex human relationships, call for a different form of inquiry. Qualitative methods allow us to explore the social world with the assumption that day-to-day realities are both variable and complex. They enable us to understand everyday experience and how people organize and interpret various aspects of their lives. In qualitative approaches, people in their natural settings are the primary source of data, "because human actions are based upon social meanings, intentions, motives, attitudes, and beliefs" (Hammersley and Atkinson, 1983:7). Qualitative researchers focus on what can be explored and described through questions such as "I would like to understand more about . . ." or "I would like to know more about . . ." (Maykut and Morehouse, 1994:53) or "how does it work that way?" They pursue questions of subjective meaning, understanding, and interpretation (Ellis and Flaherty, 1992). Moreover, rather than being separate from the study, qualitative researchers have direct contact with participants. The researchers *are* the instrument of study and their experiences and insights are central to understanding the phenomena under investigation (Patton, 1990).

As M. E. Patton points out, "the advantages of qualitative portrayals of holistic settings is that greater attention can be given to nuance, setting, interdependencies, complexities, idiosyncrasies, and context" (1990:51). To know how caregiving works in the everyday world of palliative care, for example, we need to know firsthand what actually happens in the daily lives of patients, families, and caregivers—to bear witness to their experience. When we ask how we can enhance the quality of palliative care, we first need to know how caregiving works in the present, what caregivers expect to accomplish through their work, and what their institutions and patients expect from them. Our conviction is that these questions are best explored by delving into the depths of subjective experience. In our efforts to do that, we decided to be with patients, their families, and their caregivers through a very trying period in human life. Being with the people one wants to learn something about is the essence of the qualitative, ethnographic approach.

Qualitative research and whole-person palliative care

By themselves, quantitative approaches to research do not address the complexity of the social, psychological, cultural, or spiritual dimensions of illness (Engel, 1977). While the biomedical model of care has provided the means for measuring the patient's biological status, it has done little to foster whole-person palliative care, which emphasizes the intricate and clinically important interactions between body, mind, and spirit. Recognizing that each person is unique and operates within a specific social and cultural context, the philosophy of palliative care assumes a stance of multiple realities. It acknowledges and values not only the caregiver's assessment of the patient but also the patient's and the family's experiences of illness and care. This stance allows the caregivers' understanding of patients, families, and themselves to change and deepen as situations change (Kearney, 1992; Shephard, 1997).

A focus on personal meaning, and on intersubjective knowledge generated through experience, are of primary importance for giving good palliative care. There is a strong emphasis on process as well as on clinical outcome. Care plans are not only based on established scientific models but are also derived from interaction and discussion with the patient and family. Often, preconceived notions of what is optimal care have to be set aside so that the caregiver can hear the patient and meet his or her needs (Baron, 1985). Thus, in both qualitative research and palliative care, the crucial focus is on the perspectives and experiences of individuals, which may not always resonate with conventional medical knowledge. Personal experience is valued as a means of understanding what is important or relevant to patients, either in providing care or conducting research. Stories are given primacy because it is the patient's or family's story that supplies the necessary context for clinical interventions. The first task for both caregivers and researchers is to create an atmosphere of trust and mutual respect, to suspend predetermined beliefs, and to embrace the possibility of conflicting versions of reality.

Participant-observation

In our fieldwork, we drew extensively on participant-observation, a method of inquiry and investigation developed primarily by cultural anthropologists. As participant-observers, we conducted our research by entering into the day-to-day lives of the people with whom we worked. This allowed us to observe each patient's physical condition over time, his or her social interactions with family members and caregivers, and the physical settings in which those interactions occurred. We were allowed to witness both formal and informal moments of illness experiences.

The three of us who carried out this fieldwork directly were Patricia Boston and Anna Towers in Montreal, and Yanna Lambrinidou in Lancaster County. Patricia Boston is a nurse-educator and family therapist affiliated with the Department of Psychiatry and the Palliative Care Service at McGill University, whose doctoral training in education focused on cross-cultural, ethnographic research. Anna Towers was initially trained in family medicine and family therapy, and is now a palliative medicine specialist at the Royal Victoria Hospital. Though she was a day-to-day participant in the work of the Palliative Care Service, she did not function as the researcher in cases in which she had clinical responsibilities. In those cases where she did have a direct clinical role, Patricia Boston was the observer, interviewer, and narrator of the case. Yanna Lambrinidou is a doctoral candidate in the Center for Folklore and Ethnography at the University of Pennsylvania, where she has specialized in ethnographic research methods and cross-cultural studies of health care.

As participant-observers we asked questions such as, "How are you doing today?" "What is happening right now?" "What is important to you at this time?" "How would you describe your life?" Our involvement in the lives of dying patients taught us that the experience of dying was only one part of their life experience. Their identities extended far beyond being a patient. They were working people concerned with their jobs, or about being unemployed; parents concerned about their children; and citizens engaged in the issues of their communities. We could not understand them if we viewed them simply as patients with a terminal illness.

As we participated in patient and family meetings, treatment encounters, and case discussions in patients' homes, in the hospital, and in the inpatient unit of Hospice of Lancaster County, we became part of the social world we were studying, both emotionally and physically. We cried, laughed, helped make beds, and carried groceries. We recorded all these events in detailed field notes. To the best of our abilities, we were able to gain firsthand experience of nuances of communication, nonverbal expressions, and routine caregiving practices. There is no doubt that our perceptions were shaped by our own selective memories and personal interests. Although we could not eliminate the biases of our own standpoint, consistency and repetition of issues and ideas over time within the cases mitigated this effect to some extent.

We must emphasize, however, that we do not consider the narratives in this book to represent either the record of our own subjective states of being during the course of our research or an "objective" depiction of the lives and experiences of the people about whom we wrote. They are, rather, co-constructed versions of the events that took place. To remind the reader of our own part in this construction, we have tried to indicate our involvement in the narratives themselves.

Interviews

Our interviews with patients, families, and caregivers consisted of open-ended, informal, and spontaneous conversations, guided only indirectly by an interview guide that we created at the start of the project. We used this guide as a general and basic checklist of the topic areas we wanted to explore. These areas included the following:

For Patients and Families

- The impact of the patient's illness on the patient's (or family member's) daily life and on the patient's and family's overall quality of life
- The quality of relationship and communication between the patient and family and the members of the palliative care team
- The patient's and family's preferences for receiving care at home or in an institutional setting, and the impact of either setting on the actual experience of care
- The personal meaning and significance the subject attaches to the events of the patient's illness, and the emotional and spiritual resources the participant brings to bear on the situation as it unfolds over time.

For Professional Caregivers

- The personal meaning and significance of caring for the particular patient and family
- The quality of relationship and communication between patient and family and members of the palliative care team
- The functioning of the palliative care team in the course of caring for the patient and family
- Cultural and ethical issues arising in the care of the patient and family.

With the consent of interviewees, we audiotaped each interview, so we could participate fully and without distractions in every conversation. As the participants drew us into their stories, we asked ourselves questions such as: "What is my sense about the narrative content?" "What have I learned that I didn't understand before?" "What are the things I must now try to learn and understand when we meet again?" "How does my present knowledge compare with our thoughts about this particular case?" "How has my knowledge and understanding changed?" Transcribed interviews became part of the ongoing narrative record. Data collection, transcription, description, analysis, and interpretation proceeded simultaneously. In the case of several patients, family members, and caregivers in Montreal who were French speakers, interviews were conducted in their own language by Anna Towers, who is bilingual. For this book, we have translated all French quotations into English.

Journals

In Montreal, both researchers and caregivers kept journals. In Lancaster, caregivers chose not to do that, for they felt that their already demanding schedule didn't leave time for such an involved activity. Journals were variously referred to as a "diary," a "notebook" or "personal record" and contained personal accounts of insights, preliminary understandings, ideas, thoughts, dilemmas, and decisions made during research and caregiving. For the professional caregivers we provided a few questions to prompt their journal keeping. These were:

1. What thoughts or feelings stand our in your mind regarding the interactions you had today with the patient and family? Were there any particularly meaningful or particularly frustrating incidents?
2. Were there any cultural or ethical issues that you want to comment on?
3. Are there any issues that you wish to record regarding the hospital or the health care system in general, as you think it affected the care of this patient today?

In keeping journals the aim was to capture the present moment, while trying to avoid "future recall" as much as possible. We found that personal records facilitated the caregivers' self-reflective process and strengthened their connection to past events during interviews. Our own journals served us in a similar way. They inspired us to reflect, shaped our questions during interviews, and helped us write the narratives in ways that included our own impressions of each event in addition to those of our interviewees.

In summary, the raw data from which our narratives were constructed consist of the hundreds of hours (and pages) of transcribed interviews, and similarly voluminous contemporaneous fieldnotes, as well as the formal documentation of caregiving encounters and patient experiences that we extracted from medical records and nurses' progress notes.

Narrative

A narrative methodology draws on the human tendency to tell stories and to search for meaning in personal experience (Josselson, 1996; Payne, 1997; Polkinghorne, 1988). It assumes that people lead storied lives and tell stories of these lives. (Connelly and Clandinin, 1990). It has been increasingly emphasized in the medical literature that narratives offer a rich resource for both medical education and clinical practice (Barnard, 1992; Brody, 1987; Charon et al., 1995; Hunter, 1991; Kleinman, 1988). Life stories, illness accounts, and personal journals are being used as research data in medicine as a means of understanding feelings, experiences, goals, preferences, and needs in illness and treatment (Barnard, 1986, 1992; Frank, 1992, 1995; Hawkins, 1993; Kleinman, 1988; Manning and Cullam-Swan, 1994). The emergence of the medical narrative has revealed that it is possible to go beyond the traditional clinical case history to understand the course of a patient's illness.

In medical anthropology, the work of Arthur Kleinman, exemplified in *The Illness Narratives* (1988), made a significant departure from the conventional clinical-case genre. This work reported not only symptoms and pathological processes but also patients' subjective experiences. David Barnard's own case narrative work has shown that the illness experience is shaped by the telling and listening to stories over time (Barnard, 1992). As we have already commented in the introduction to this volume, recent books by Ira Byock (1997), Michael Kearney (1996), and Timothy Quill (1996) draw on richly narrated personal experience in caring for the terminally ill. We see our research as providing a complement—and in some respects a further development—to their very important work.

Of course, the narratives in this book are *our* stories, told in *our* voices. In order to transfer the rich, sometimes overwhelming details of many people's experiences into a single narrative, we have had to be selective. We have imposed our sense of theme on experience, which in its pure state has no theme but simply follows the continual flow of life. We have often resorted to devices of narration, scene-setting, and similar features typical of fiction. These narratives are works of fiction in the sense that they are the result of creative, selective, shaping processes that are inherent in all storytelling. We do not present them as the definitive, "objective" story, "the way it was." On the other hand, we have tried to be as faithful as possible to what we witnessed, and we have tried to situate our observations and our identification of themes in the larger context of other empirical and narrative research on palliative care.

To say that there are fictive elements in our narratives is not, of course, to differentiate them in any substantial degree from the many forms of narrative that guide medical practice and medical education (Banks and Hawkins, 1992; Hunter, 1991). For in fact, medical decisions are always rooted in the exchange and creation of stories, which are shaped not only by medical information but also by beliefs, feelings, needs, experiences, impressions, speculations, and perceptions. By acknowledging these fictive elements directly here, and by making frequent reference to our own participation in the cases, we have attempted to provide readers with the information they need to make appropriate critical assessment of the narratives. Our preferred test of the truth value of our narratives is a pragmatic one: do the experiences we have recorded, and the insights they engender, contribute in any significant way to more empathic, competent, and effective palliative care?

Ethics and narrative inquiry

As researchers we encountered three principal ethical issues: (1) adequate informed consent; (2) protecting privacy; and (3) maintaining confidentiality within the team and between the team and patients and families.

All potential participants—patients, families, and caregivers—received a detailed account of our study's purposes and methods prior to making a decision to join the study. No patients were contacted for possible inclusion in the research without a prior inquiry directed to them by a member of their palliative care team. Only after learning from that team member that a patient was willing to meet us and hear more about the project did we visit any patients. In our first meeting with patients, we gave them written materials describing our study in detail and discussed with them what their participation would entail. Only with the permission of patients did we contact other family members and ask for their permission to include them in our interviews and observations. We received very few refusals. Two families withdrew shortly after beginning, one out of concern for the emotional nature of the interviews, and one because of the patient's extreme weakness and fatigue.

We were frank in telling all potential participants that our discussions were likely to touch on painful emotions, sensitive family issues, and private experiences. We assured patients, families, and caregivers, however, that the patient's best interests would always override our research needs. We were prepared to stop interviews, cancel visits, and withdraw from the patient's room at any time. In reality, such requests almost never came. We were also explicit about our plans to publish these narratives, and we explained that we would do everything possible to disguise personal identities. We had the challenge of telling the participants' stories with honesty and integrity while disguising their identity as much as possible. We explained to the participants that, despite the disguises, they would undoubtedly recognize themselves in the narratives, though we believed it to be very unlikely that people not connected with their case would be able to identify them.

We assured all patients that what they told us would remain confidential. But to this assurance we made two precautionary exceptions. The first was that if a patient disclosed to us explicit suicidal intentions, we would be obliged to report this to the palliative care team. The second was that if we learned of patient abuse or of circumstances in which the patient appeared to be in imminent physical danger, we would again feel compelled to break confidentialities and inform their professional caregivers. As it turned out, we encountered neither of these situations.

To professional caregivers we emphasized that we would take note of tensions, disagreements, or resentments among them only if they played a significant role in the patient's care. In some instances they did. But we also assured them that we would take every measure to protect their privacy and that we would not repeat one team member's comments to another without his or her permission.

In the process of collecting data and writing the stories, however, it has become clear that the formal principles underlying informed consent may not account for the uncertainties inherent in the research process. Even though our study was approved by the institutional review boards and ethics committees of the participating institutions, we have become aware that the participant cannot fully appreciate at the outset the implications of being involved in this type of research. We asked the dying and their loved ones to reveal important pieces of themselves, to tell us their experiences of suffering, joy, fear, and pain. We asked them to share moments from the long-forgotten past, presently complicated by life's imminent end. We asked them to reach a level of awareness that, without our questioning, they may well not have reached. As a result, we were always faced with the question or whether or how to proceed when painful memories emerged. After working with us on one case, a caregiver turned down our invitation to participate in interviews concerning a second case. She said that the process of self-reflection had drained her emotionally. Like this caregiver, most participants didn't know what impact our study would have on them when they signed their consent form. Moreover, they didn't know the outcome of their story in advance of its creation. Nor could they know, though they sometimes worried, how their words and actions would be interpreted by the readers of this book.

Despite these risks, many patients, families, and caregivers expressed to us their appreciation for our project. Participants initially volunteered for a variety of reasons. Some felt the project was important for palliative care education and were pleased to have the opportunity to contribute to the improvement of end-of-life care. As one person put it, "It may not be helpful to me personally. I will be long gone. But if my story helps other people to suffer less, then I'd like to help." Another person observed, "I am only a novice in this business of dying but perhaps I can share what I myself am now learning." Some patients joined our study because they liked the idea of taking on an important responsibility and feeling useful at the end of their lives. Other patients craved regular visits by an interested listener. Others saw this study as a unique opportunity to gain posthumous public recognition, or to redeem their misunderstood lives and actions, and some people were actually disappointed that we would not use their real names. We could not do this however, because to do so would have risked exposing the identities of the people who surrounded them.

Several participants told us that they experienced a sense of catharsis in being able to state a personal feeling or opinion. They valued the opportunity to have their perspective heard and, in turn, to learn through their own self-disclosure. Some patients told us that they appreciated the opportunity to re-think their own treatment choices in the process of discussion and reflection. In some cases, they said that the process enabled them to redefine and modify their decisions and desires—an obvious example of the effect of the observer on the observed. As one person put it, "As I talk through the daily events and what is happening, it seems to bring me to think of things I had not thought about before. . . . I believe perhaps I am also learning."

We also quickly discovered that our methodology had an important impact on us. Through our work, we were touched by the people who generously allowed us into their lives, and we were changed by them. We learned from them to value highly the things we take for granted, and to put our lives into perspective. We each experienced profound moments that will remain forever in our memories. We also discovered that in our work there was an element of risk for us as well. We experienced the risk in maintaining relationships with the dying, the risk of loss of closely formed bonds, and the risk that each encounter could challenge our own sense of self and well-being (Boston et al., 1998). In the midst of our own complacency, we had to think through our own perspectives about care at the end of life. As we witnessed different people's courage and resourcefulness, each one of us, at one time or another, wondered, "Will I cope as well?" or "What will happen when I am dying?" We were forced to reflect on the protected and sometimes controlling nature of our roles as clinicians, researchers, and teachers. As we listened to the participants' stories, we were aware that at any time we could seek refuge behind our identities as professionals or scholars. We would never pretend, therefore, that we reached the depths of the other person's experience. We could leave a painful moment behind; the patients and families could not.

References

Banks JT, Hawkins AH (eds). 1992. The art of the case history. *Lit Med* 11(1):1–182.
Barnard D. 1986. A case of amyotrophic lateral sclerosis. *Lit Med* 5:27–42.
Barnard D. 1992. A case of amyotrophic lateral sclerosis: A reprise and a reply. *Lit Med* 11(1):133–146.
Baron R. 1985. An introduction to medical phenomenology: I can't hear you while I'm listening. *Ann Intern Med* 103:606–611.
Benedict R. 1969. Zuni Mythology. New York: AMS Press.
Boas F. 1966 (1940). Race, Language, and Culture. New York: Free Press.

Boston P, Towers A, Barnard D. 1998. Understanding empathy: The caregiver as risk-taker and learner. Unpublished manuscript.

Brody H. 1987. Stories of Sickness. New Haven: Yale University Press.

Byock I. 1997. Dying Well: The Prospect for Growth at the End of Life. New York: Riverhead.

Charon R, Banks JT, Connelly JE, Hawkins AH, Hunter KM, Jones AH, Montello M, Poirier S. 1995. Literature and medicine: Contributions to clinical practice. *Ann Intern Med* 122(8):599–606.

Clark D. 1997. What is qualitative research and what can it contribute to palliative care? *Palliat Med* 11:159–166.

Connelly FM, Clandinin DJ. 1990. Stories of experience and narrative inquiry. *Educational Researcher* 19(5):2–14.

Denzin NK, Lincoln YS (eds). 1994. Handbook of Qualitative Research. Thousand Oaks, CA: Sage.

Ellis G, Flaherty M. 1992. Investigating Subjectivity: Research on Lived Experience. Newbury Park, CA: Sage.

Engel G. 1977. The need for a new medical model: A challenge for biomedicine. *Science* 196:129–136.

Frank AW. 1992. At the Will of the Body: Reflections on Illness. New York: Houghton Mifflin.

Frank AW. 1995. The Wounded Storyteller: Body, Illness, and Ethics. Chicago: University of Chicago Press.

Goffman E. 1961. Asylums: Essays on the Social Situation of Mental Patients and Other Inmates. Chicago: Aldine.

Hammersley M, Atkinson P. 1983. Ethnography Principles in Practice. London: Tavistock Publications.

Hawkins AH. 1993. Reconstructing Illness: Studies in Pathography. West Lafayette, IN: Purdue University Press.

Hogstel MO, Sayner NC. 1988. Nursing Research. New York: McGraw-Hill.

Holton R. 1966. Classical social theory. In: Turner, B (ed). The Blackwell Companion to Social Theory. Oxford: Blackwell.

Hunter KM. 1991. Doctors' Stories: The Narrative Structure of Medical Knowledge. Princeton: Princeton University Press.

Josselson R. 1996. On writing other people's lives: Self-analytic reflections of a narrative researcher. In Josselson R (ed). Ethics and Process in the Narrative Study of Lives. Thousand Oaks, CA: Sage.

Kearney M. 1992. Palliative medicine—just another specialty? *Palliat Med* 6:39–46.

Kearney M. 1996. Mortally Wounded: Stories of Soul Pain, Death, and Healing. New York: Scribner.

Kleinman A. 1988. The Illness Narratives. New York: Basic Books.

Malinowski B. 1922. Argonauts of the Western Pacific: An Account of Native Enterprise and Adventure in the Archipelagoes of Melanesian New Guinea. London: Routledge & Sons.

Manning PK, Cullum-Swan B. 1994. Narrative content and semiotic analysis. In: Denzin NK, Lincoln YS (eds). Handbook of Qualitative Research. Thousand Oaks, CA: Sage.

Maykut P, Morehouse R. 1994. Beginning Qualitative Research: A Philosophic and Practical Guide. London: The Falmer Press.

Mays N, Pope C. 1995. Rigour and qualitative research. *BMJ* 311:109–112.

Mead M. 1928. Coming of Age in Samoa: A Psychological Study in Primitive Youth for Western Civilisation. New York: Blue Ribbon Books.

Miller WL, Crabtree BF. 1994. Clinical research. In: Denzin NK, Lincoln, YS (eds). Handbook of Qualitative Research. Thousand Oaks, CA: Sage.

Patton, ME. 1990. Qualitative Evaluation and Research Methods, 2nd ed. Newbury Park, CA: Sage.

Payne S. 1997. Selecting an approach and design in qualitative research. *Palliat Med* 11:249–252.

Polkinghorne DE. 1988. Narrative Knowing and the Human Sciences. Albany: State University of New York Press.

Pope C, Mays N. 1995. Reaching the parts other methods cannot reach: An introduction to qualitative methods in health and health services research. *BMJ* 311:42–45.

Quill TE. 1996. A Midwife Through the Dying Process: Stories of Healing and Hard Choices at the End of Life. Baltimore: Johns Hopkins University Press.

Reid AJ. 1996. What we want: Qualitative research [editorial]. *Can Family Physician* 42:387–389.

Shephard DAE. 1977. Principles and practice of palliative care. *Can Med Assoc J* 15:-522–526.

Tedlock B. 1991. From participant observation to the observation of participation: The emergence of narrative ethnography. *J Anthropol Res* 47(1):69–94.

van Manen J. 1988. Tales of the Field: On Writing Ethnography. Chicago: University of Chicago Press.

Whyte WF. 1955. Street Corner Society. Chicago: University of Chicago Press.

Wolcott H. 1973. The Man in the Principal's Office. New York: Holt, Rinehart, and Winston.

23

Authors' Comments and Questions for Discussion

Raymond Hynes

Events in terminal illness often progress quickly, and health care professionals must communicate well with the family and with one another. In all cases the palliative care staff needs to assess the degree to which the family want to talk, and whether an intervention is needed to allow for more open communication. The Hynes family asserted that they did not want to discuss emotional issues, and their caregivers did not challenge this.

This case also raises a question regarding research ethics. Mr. Hynes was alone in his hospital room when the medical resident informed him that he had advanced-stage cancer for which there was no cure. Shortly afterwards, while Mr. Hynes was still alone and had not yet spoken with his family, the oncologist approached him regarding the possibility of experimental chemotherapy, which might or might not prolong his life. Decisions need to be made quickly, but whose needs were being served here? Was Mr. Hynes in a good state of mind to make an informed decision about undergoing a treatment that was unlikely to benefit him? Could he have felt comfortable to refuse? It could be argued that the suggestion to Mr. Hynes that he participate in a clinical trial, at what was perhaps the most vulnerable moment of his life, had the decided advantage for the investigators that Mr. Hynes would probably say yes.

It was helpful in this case that the oncologist did not abandon Mr. Hynes when it became clear that he was too ill to receive palliative chemotherapy. There was seamless coordination between oncology and the Palliative Care Service at the Royal Victoria Hospital. In this setting it is routine for oncologists to see patients even though chemotherapy may no longer be an option. In some other settings it may be necessary to transfer the patient to the care of their family physician or to a hospice program. It may be difficult for patients and families to make this transition abruptly. We also imagine that it can be difficult for oncologists to make this transition, especially if they have been looking after the patient for a long time.

Raymond Hynes died at home, which was his wish. He and his family benefited from palliative care services in the home that included visits from a physician. There are several possible models for providing medical services in the home. Often, in the hospice model, a physician will advise on treatment and prescribe medication, but is often not available to see the patient. This can result in less than adequate monitoring and diagnosis of treatable symptoms. In other models, such as the British one, general practitioners will do home visits if required, and they can ask for a home visit by a palliative care consultant in difficult cases. Although models will vary, it is our opinion that one or more well-timed home visits by a physician are invaluable in ensuring good palliative care to patients at home.° To be efficient, such physician care must be regionalized, with clear links between community practitioners and hospital-based palliative care expertise. These are important policy issues that all health care systems need to address.

After her husband's death, Mrs. Hynes would have benefited from a few sessions of bereavement counseling at about six months. The fact that she did not telephone the bereavement service reminds us how difficult it must be for bereaved individuals to ask for the help that they require. In this setting, bereavement counselors only initiate telephone calls for those considered at risk for bereavement complications. All other key persons will receive a letter informing them about the service, and an invitation to attend a memorial event at three months and at one year. More research is needed to explore the potential benefits (or harms) of a more proactive approach, either by the palliative care team or by primary care providers.

Topics for Discussion

1. Mr. Hynes and his family had to deal with bad news—an illness with a relatively quick onset of symptoms, and the diagnosis of an advanced-stage tumor. What are the principles that should be followed in communicating bad news? Were the principles followed in this case?

°Billings J A. 1985. Outpatient Management of Advanced Cancer. Philadelphia: Lippincott.

2. Mr. Hynes had questions about prognosis, and was frustrated with the answers that he received. What do you think about the communication patterns among the physicians, nurse, patient, and family in this case regarding the issue of prognosis? How would you have approached this discussion?

3. At least initially, members of the palliative care team seemed to have expectations that the family communicate differently, that they express their emotions more. What is your view?

4. The family and members of the palliative care team described this as a "successful" death at home. Do you agree? If so, what factors made it successful?

5. Mrs. Hynes went through a typical grief process, given her particular cultural background. What are the elements of such a process? What factors, if present, might have led you to believe that Mrs. Hynes was having an "abnormal" grief reaction?

6. How might cultural differences affect a grief response? What are the implications of this for caregivers?

Albert Hoffer

Why did one of Albert Hoffer's hospice nurses refer to him as "a bird, a corker"? At one level she was referring to Mr. Hoffer's penchant for straight talk, sarcasm, and off-color comments. But Albert Hoffer presented a more basic challenge to the hospice team than a rough-edged personality or mordant wit. To quote the nurse again, he had "his own agenda." The hospice chaplain and several nurses commented that Mr. Hoffer "tested" them. How? By speaking as an educated adult? By insisting on personal privacy? By insisting that his caregivers respect his individuality rather than deliver prepackaged messages of sympathy or reassurance? Put another way, Mr. Hoffer was simply resisting the tendencies toward infantilization and patronization that, no matter how much they are unintended or denied by health care personnel, often infect caregivers' styles of providing care, as Paula Ferrari also discovered.

The team passed their tests. Carl Flynn, in particular, was willing to take risks in his persistent search for a language with which to form a supportive bond with Mr. Hoffer. The language turned out to be a fishing trip, as well as a willingness to engage Mr. Hoffer at a serious existential and theological level. As a result, the chaplain created space for himself to act as a trusted facilitator during several tense family meetings.

This case illustrates well the hospice notion of the family as the unit of care. With considerable resourcefulness, the team responded helpfully to the Hoffers' burdens—not only those arising from Mr. Hoffer's disease but also those from Julia's stroke, and the painful legacies of Mr. Hoffer's past alcoholism. In addition to their skillful symptom control, the team worked very effectively to facilitate emotional communication and brainstorming at the family meetings; and they were both catalysts and witnesses to the acts of reconciliation between father and sons.

The developing relationship between Carl Flynn and Mr. Hoffer illustrates another point. Trainees are sometimes disappointed when they come to a patient's bedside, intending to have a "deep" conversation, only to find that "nothing happens." In fact, patients are often quite selective in the person or persons with whom they will share personal thoughts and feelings. An intimate, confessional moment often requires a period of relationship building before it can occur. Even at that, it won't always happen with everyone who would like to participate in one.°

Topics for Discussion

1. The Hoffer family struggled with the choice between an affordable package of hospice services and the possibility of continuing aggressive treatment of Mr. Hoffer's cancer. What are the policy implications of this system of financing hospice care in the United States? What other systems might avoid these problems?

2. Although addiction is rarely a problem in hospice and palliative care, it emerged as an issue in this case. How should hospice workers respond when they suspect the possible diversion or misuse of narcotics?

3. Comment on the role of the hospice chaplain in this case. What steps did the chaplain take to build rapport with his initially closed and mistrustful patient?

4. Did the hospice team do all they could have done to create trust with this family?

5. One of the hospice nurses said: "The patients who are more vocal, they are more time-consuming, because of their choices. You have to adapt your day to their routine, to uninstitutionalize your thinking." What do you think the nurse means by this? How can we work with patients who disagree with our methods of care, especially when they are not as vocal as Mr. Hoffer?

6. Margaret, the social worker, said that she was "proud of this case." What aspects of the case do you think she was referring to?

7. Frank asked, "Why should a dysfunctional family suddenly function so well"? How did the family help itself to change? How did hospice help the family?

°Barnard D. 1995. The promise of intimacy and the fear of our own undoing. J *Palliat Care* 11(4):22–26.

Klara Bergman

Klara Bergman never really discussed her past experiences of the Holocaust, though from the brief references she made to her experiences of traumatic loss, we know they were ever present. In the final days of her illness, Mrs. Bergman became fearful and suspicious, even in the presence of her most familiar caregivers. There were times when she asked to be freed from her struggles, and times when she wanted relief and for "the end to come quickly." The palliative care team undertook a number of measures to help manage her symptoms. Haloperidol and lorazapam were prescribed in an attempt to alleviate her extreme fearfulness and anxiety, but they were only partly effective. There was an attempt to relieve Mrs. Bergman's pain through music therapy, but "all of her nightmares came flooding back again." She was unable to make the transition from her emotional anguish to spontaneous imagery.

Did the palliative care team fail Mrs. Bergman in assessing that the only way to relieve her suffering was through relief of her symptoms? While palliative care philosophy asserts that the patient's suffering is embedded within the complexities of social, psychological, physical, and spiritual domains, in this case, the team was unable to help Klara Bergman with her spiritual pain.

Topics for Discussion

1. Klara Bergman expressed fear of losing control and being confused while receiving medications to alleviate her pain and discomfort. What problem-solving strategies were used in the process of pharmacological management in this case to minimize the chances of producing confusion?
2. On numerous occasions, Ellen expressed guilt and a feeling of inadequacy in caring for her mother. Was the palliative care team responsive to Ellen's needs? What other kinds of family caregiving strategies could have been employed in this case?
3. As her illness progressed, Klara Bergman made it clear to members of the palliative care team that she was struggling with her religious beliefs. At times, she claimed she "had lost faith in God." What was the approach of the palliative care team? Would any other strategies have helped her deal with these issues?
4. Although she did not discuss details, Klara Bergman did disclose her Holocaust experiences with some of her caregivers. What role, if any, do sociopolitical and cultural factors play in this case?
5. Klara Bergman often said she felt "totally alone" despite the warmth and compassion of life-long friends. What is your appraisal of this situation? Could her family, friends or caregivers have been any more empathic toward Mrs. Bergman?

6. Discuss the problems of evaluating patients for depression in advanced-stage cancer.

7. Regardless of the legal status of euthanasia in Canada at this time, would it have been morally permissible to grant Mrs. Bergman's request for euthanasia? If so, at what point in time would such an action have been appropriate?

Frances Legendre

In contrast to the case of Jenny Doyle, Frances Legendre benefited from receiving both hospice care and active experimental therapy at the same time. Dr. Raymond applied his expertise in symptom control and psychological and spiritual support, while Dr. Singer continued with aggressive experimental therapy. While they were undoubtedly advocates of two contrasting ideologies, it is clear that both physicians managed to submerge their own personal reactions and philosophies in favor of a greater goal, which was to respect the patient's own view of what constituted her quality of life.

Perhaps less visible, and yet vital to this collaborative effort by Dr. Raymond and Dr. Singer, is the implicit successful communication between these two physicians. We do not have details of the many discussions that must have ensued following Mrs. Legendre's change of mind regarding her care. Nevertheless, it is clear that each physician worked through and beyond his personal and professional philosophy and approach to care. However it was done, both physicians managed to eliminate any potential communication problems such as control issues, competition, or power plays in favor of joint problem-solving, mutual understanding, and open communication in the pursuit of common goals.

Topics for Discussion

1. Mr. Legendre described his wife's death as "ideal," yet at several points Mrs. Legendre and her family seemed to have suffered greatly. Was Mrs. Legendre's experience an example of a "good death?"

2. Elisabeth Kübler-Ross and others have proposed that dying people go through a series of stages in their attitudes toward dying. Are these stage-theories helpful in understanding Mrs. Legendre's experience?

3. Some members of the palliative care team questioned the genuineness of Mrs. Legendre's acceptance of death during her first admission to the Palliative Care Unit. Were they justified in their questioning? Are there reliable methods of differentiating between genuine acceptance and denial on the part of patients who seem to be facing imminent death without anxiety or fear?

4. How should members of the palliative care team respond when a patient asks them to join in personal spiritual beliefs that the team members do not share?

5. Mrs. Legendre complained that her oncologists were not always sufficiently aggressive in providing her with experimental treatments for her cancer. What is the physician's responsibility to the patient who demands intensive treatment for advanced disease, when the physician strongly believes that these treatments will do more harm than good?

6. Is the philosophy of palliative care compatible with all-out efforts to prolong life, even at the price of extreme physical suffering? Was it appropriate for Dr. Raymond, as a palliative care physician, to support Mrs. Legendre in her ultimately futile efforts to find a cure?

7. What role did alternative medicine play in this case? What is the physician's responsibility to patients who employ alternative remedies of unproven efficacy, at great personal expense?

8. What aspects of Mrs. Legendre's family's experience are particularly noteworthy in this case? Was the palliative care team appropriately responsive to the family's needs?

9. Are there meaningful differences, clinically and morally, between terminal sedation and euthanasia? Were Mrs. Legendre's physicians justified in refusing her request for medication to hasten her death? How did this aspect of the case affect the overall experiences of the patient, the family, and the palliative care team?

Shamira Cook

This narrative raises three types of issues—technical, sociocultural, and philosophical—that are important in providing excellent, patient-centered hospice and palliative care. Technically, the control of Shamira Cook's symptoms in the last months of her life presented many complicated challenges. The management of her pain was less than optimal. Ms. Cook received very large doses of opioid drugs for pain related to her retroperitoneal tumors and, possibly, her chest tumors. Cancer at these sites usually produces pain of a mixed type, including neuropathic pain, that requires multiple therapeutic approaches, including one or more co-analgesics and, often, anesthetic interventions. Had Ms. Cook received such an approach, she might not have required such large doses of opioids, with their accompanying effects on her cognitive functioning. Anesthetic procedures such as epidural analgesia can be safe and effective in cases such as these. Although the patient is usually hospitalized, it is possible to manage epidural catheters and medication in the home.

An inpatient admission to the Hospice of Lancaster County would have been preferable to assess Ms. Cook's symptoms more carefully and to make necessary adjustments to her symptom management. Apparently, the conflicts between the hospice's expectation that Ms. Cook accept a do-not-resuscitate order and her overall resistance to surrendering aggressive treatment options made this impossible.

It is hard to assess whether the social and racial context of the case contributed to the team's sense of frustration and disappointment after Ms. Cook died. The fact that one of the nurses felt compelled to comment that "not all cases are going to be your white, middle-class, *Leave It To Beaver* or *Ozzie and Harriet* family," suggests that these issues were not far beneath the surface.

Just as significant, however, is a contradiction deep within the hospice ideology of the "good death," a contradiction that appears in other narratives as well. If the stated goal of hospice is to help patients "live well while dying," with the emphasis on living, what if the patient's definition of living is fighting against the disease? Clearly, to Shamira Cook, "living" meant striving to gain as much time as she needed to reclaim and redeem her identity, which she believed had been spoiled by years of substance abuse and parental abuse. Many on the hospice team assumed that Ms. Cook's insistence on more and more treatment showed that she was "in denial," and questioned her appropriateness as a hospice patient. The team's interpretation actually reveals the inadequacy of their dichotomous notions of denial and acceptance. Ms. Cook's fight for more treatment looked indeed like denial to many of her caregivers. Yet as she herself often said, it was precisely her awareness that she was likely to die soon that fueled her urgent struggle for enough time to find out who she really was. We return to the inconsistency in the hospice definition of an appropriate patient in our comments on the case of Stanley Gray.

Topics for Discussion

1. What should our approach be for cancer patients who experience pain and who have a past history of drug abuse?
2. Comment on Yolanda Dixon's involvement with Ms. Cook. Did she demonstrate extreme compassion or was this an example of enmeshment? Do you agree or disagree with Mrs. Dixon that Ms. Cook's doctors had been unclear that her cancer was incurable and that Ms. Cook would have made different choices had they been clearer?
3. How can we help patients maintain hope when cure is no longer possible? Is it possible to redefine hope?
4. Ms. Cook believed that being a hospice patient meant that she would receive only comfort measures until she died—that she would have to give up all hope of extending her life to be accepted by a hospice program.

This is a common assumption. Is this view of hospice requirements accurate? If not, why do many people assume that it is?

5. Ms. Cook demanded that she be resuscitated to the very end of her life. How should physicians approach this issue?

6. For a few months before she died, Ms. Cook was on large doses of opioids and was experiencing somnolence and other side effects. What therapeutic approaches could have been taken to minimize opioid side effects?

7. There are several instances in this narrative where health insurance reimbursement schemes either could not pay for the care Ms. Cook required or limited the care. What other socioeconomic or cultural issues influenced the care Ms. Cook received?

8. What were the possible causes of Ms. Cook's delirium? Discuss strategies to manage delirium at the end of life, including the role of opioid rotation and alternative methods of pain control.

9. Felicia Johnson observed that Shamira Cook died "with elegance." What do you think she meant by that? What is your view?

10. Toward the end of her life Ms. Cook reported a visit from her deceased mother. What is your interpretation of this experience? How might hospice workers respond to patients' reports of contact with the supernatural?

Rose Picard

Mrs. Picard was extraordinarily accepting of her illness and, until the very end, her dying process. Dying can be perceived as being too slow, causing mental anguish to patients and their families. Mrs. Picard had moments when she felt afraid, but was reassured by the presence of her family, or by her faith.

The family asked for sedation in Mrs. Picard's final days. Dr. Morin felt it was appropriate to order sedation, given Mrs. Picard's confusion. It is common in palliative care settings to sedate patients who have confusion from an irreversible cause. Some physicians might wonder whether Mrs. Picard should have received some hydration at the end, with the aim of possibly reducing the confusion.° These are issues that require careful clinical judgment and good communication with the family.

The intense bereavement reaction that Mr. Picard experienced would be categorized as "normal." Linda, however, might have benefited from some counseling, but because of her location, she could not be linked up with the bereavement service of the Palliative Care Unit. There was no record of whether

°Fainsinger R, Bruera E. 1994. The management of dehydration in terminally ill patients. *J Palliat Care* 10(3):55–59.

she had an established relationship with a family physician who might have helped her. This case illuminates the importance of developing coordinated bereavement services.

Topics for Discussion

1. Home care was not an option for Mrs. Picard because of local circumstances. Discuss what types of services, had they been available, might have made it possible for Mrs. Picard to remain at home.
2. Mrs. Picard was admitted to the hospital with bowel obstruction. Discuss the principles and methods for medical management of this condition.
3. Discuss the role of music therapy in this case, and in palliative care more generally.
4. What strategies did different family members employ to cope with the progression of Mrs. Picard's illness? Is it possible to say that some strategies were better than others?
5. Mrs. Picard's oncologist gave her a very specific answer—of "approximately four weeks"—in reply to her direct question as to how long she might live. The prognosis turned out to be very accurate. Discuss the pros and cons of giving patients such precise estimates of the time they have left.
6. What is your view of the family's request to have Mrs. Picard kept sedated, and the nurse's compliance with their request, even though the nurse felt the additional medication might have been unnecessary for Mrs. Picard's comfort?
7. Discuss some of the elements of grieving that family members demonstrated in this case.

Victor Sloski

Shirley Sloski bravely attempted to nurse her husband at home and was determined to continue in spite of his loss of ambulatory functioning, increasing blindness, seizures, and frequent depressive moods. She saw this work as her duty and did it willingly and lovingly.

Palliative care philosophy supports the notion that the patient's loved ones often are the most competent and compassionate caregivers. At the same time, there exists an increasing body of literature in nursing and the broader health field that argues that the family is the unit of care, and that professional caregivers are as much responsible for caring for the family as for the patient.

Mrs. Sloski was tired, distraught, and overburdened, despite Grania's best efforts to provide her with emotional support. In this case, instrumental home care resources were needed on a much larger scale to accommodate Shirley

Sloski's emotional and physical needs, but they were not forthcoming beyond the usual provisions for home care nursing help. Whose needs were being served? Clearly a safe rationale can be provided to the effect that Mrs. Sloski was loyal and dedicated to the full physical and emotional care of her husband. This fits well within the model of the family as caregiver. But it could also be argued that this model serves the health system's needs more than families' needs, acting as a justification for reducing costs by not having to provide highly specialized home care services, while promoting the role of the family as caregiver.[°]

Topics for Discussion

1. Palliative care professionals often state that the family is the unit of care. Their intention is to differentiate palliative care from the narrower focus on the patient alone, which is more characteristic of acute-care medicine. What are the ethical implications of this? Specifically, consider what would have happened if Shirley Sloski had been unable to cope with the increasing burdens of caring for her husband at home, while Victor refused to accept a transfer to the Palliative Care Unit. If the family is the unit of care, where would the palliative care team's ethical obligations lie in this conflict?
2. What is the caregiver's responsibility to the patient who claims that suffering is God's will? Do these responsibilities change if the patient refuses effective pain medication?
3. Describe the nontechnical roles played by the nurses and physicians in the last weeks of Mr. Sloski's life.
4. Comment on the role of cultural and socioeconomic factors in this case.
5. Victor Sloski died one week after his sister's visit, and he died in the brief interval that Mrs. Sloski was away from the bedroom making her telephone call to the hospital. Do you think there is any significance to the timing of Victor's death?

Leonard Patterson

When Hospice of Lancaster County opened its new inpatient facility, shortly before we began our study, visitors and patients alike were overwhelmed by its beauty. It had understated and tasteful color schemes, each room decorated with its own unique wallpaper; elegant hardwood bedframes and night tables; private sun rooms overlooking a garden; and comfortable, roomy common areas and kitchens where families could cook their meals and hang out. Thanks

°Levine C. 1999. The loneliness of the long-term caregiver. N Engl J Med 340(20):1587–1590.

to very generous donations from the community, the Hospice had spared no expense to create what they proudly described as a home-like environment. Still, when Leonard Patterson came there from his ramshackle, filthy apartment, all he could think about was when he would be able to go home. During a four-hour visit (his last) to his apartment, Mr. Patterson leaned back happily amid the dirt, roaches, and reek of cat urine and said, "This is my life. I'm proud of it."

For all its unhome-like feel to Mr. Patterson, the Hospice Center provided him and his wife with essential symptom management and respite care. Yet the startling disjunction between the upper-middle-class aesthetic of the Hospice Center and Mr. Patterson's world is but one of many examples in this case of how all the pieces never quite fit together. Outsiders' views of Mr. Patterson as a loving, almost saintly figure in his neighborhood contrasted with his wife's bitter recollections of his abusiveness and her suspicions about his philandering. The endless strife and secretiveness between Mrs. Patterson and her daughter, particularly when it came to Mrs. Patterson's disability checks, long outlived her husband. Clinical and administrative glitches at the nursing home strained already delicate relations between the nursing home and hospice, and significantly compromised the management of Mr. Patterson's pain.

The sense of disharmony and disconnection persisted in the parallel events that marked Mr. Patterson's last days. While he lay mute and frightened in his nursing home bed, the chaplain encouraging him gently to lift up his fears to God, the police were rushing to Mr. Patterson's apartment in response to a violent screaming match between Mrs. Patterson and her daughter over the dog and cat.

Contemplating all of these jagged edges, we might wonder whether hospice could have done more to smooth things out for Mr. Patterson and his family. A similar question occurs in the case of Richard Johnson. In both of these instances, however, the conflicts that arose during the care of these men, and which were left unresolved after their deaths, were rooted in relationships and personalities with long histories. In Mr. Patterson's case in particular, the difficulties arising from the family history were aggravated by inter-institutional issues within the health and social welfare systems. These cases are therefore excellent examples of the unavoidable interdependence of individual, family, team, and societal factors in the overall effectiveness of hospice and palliative care. To expect the hospice alone to solve all the difficulties associated with dying is unrealistic and unfair.

Topics for Discussion

1. What role did the patient and family's socioeconomic status play in this case? Did their poverty present any special challenges to the hospice team?
2. Comment on the relationships between the hospice team and the staff at

the nursing home. What changes, if any, would you have recommended in these relationships to insure optimal symptom control for Mr. Patterson?

3. To what extent did Mr. Patterson take an active role in the decision making process regarding his enrollment in hospice, his transfer to the nursing home, and his visit back home? Was he able to exercise the maximum appropriate self-determination in light of his physical and mental condition? What should hospice have done if Mr. Patterson had insisted on staying at home throughout his illness rather than returning to die at the nursing home?

4. How did the hospice team define "quality of life" and "the good death" for Mr. Patterson? How did Mr. Patterson define them? Mrs. Patterson?

5. How did the relationships within the Patterson family affect Mr. Patterson's experience of dying? What additional family interventions, if any, would you have recommended to the hospice team?

6. Comment on the role of spirituality and of the hospice chaplain in Mr. Patterson's care.

7. Assuming Mr. Patterson had visceral pain, some of which may have been from his liver and from his rectal tumor, what medication other than opioids might have been helpful? Are there other ways his pain management could have been optimized?

8. Comment on the chaplain's response to Mr. Patterson's request for euthanasia. What alternative responses, if any, would you have recommended?

Miriam Lambert

This narrative may make some readers feel overwhelmed because of the intense suffering that Mrs. Lambert experienced. To put this narrative in perspective, Mrs. Lambert represented a very challenging pain management case. It is rare that the palliative care team fails to control pain and has to resort to sedation. Even with difficult neuropathic pains, combinations of opioids and coanalgesics will control the symptoms in the vast majority of cases. A case of challenging pain like Mrs. Lambert's represents less that 5% of patients experiencing pain in a specialized palliative care center, and even less in a general community health setting. One of the challenges for palliative care is to develop treatment modalities that will reliably control neuropathic pains.

A case such as Mrs. Lambert's will make any palliative care team reflect on their treatment protocols. They will wonder if there was a drug combination that might have worked if tried, and if everything possible from a psychological point of view was done. It is difficult not to experience such cases as failures.

Giving the patient enough time is a built-in principle of good palliative care.

It is routine practice to allow for the necessary time to build a trusting one-on-one relationship with the patient. Mrs. Lambert represented an unusual case because of her intense requirements: she had no close family to support her and required much professional caregiver attention. Within the time constraints of the palliative care team, it may not have been possible to give Mrs. Lambert the time and attention that she needed. In addition, Mrs. Lambert may have been too ill to resolve important issues that need to be worked through over a longer period of time.

Topics for Discussion

1. Persistent uncontrolled pain is rare in palliative care. Often these patients present with a picture that is known as "total pain." What is your understanding of this concept?
2. As you go through the medication record, discuss the various classes of medication that were used and their indications.
3. Discuss the various nonmedical methods that were used to try to control Mrs. Lambert's pain. Can you think of other techniques that might have been tried?
4. Mrs. Lambert had a complex psychological history, and she exhibited acute emotional distress during the course of her terminal illness. Comment on the methods that the various members of the team used to try to help her in this regard. Could they have tried other approaches? Should they have tried fewer?
5. In Mrs. Lambert's case, Dr. Bonin resorted to what may be termed "terminal sedation" in the final days. What is your understanding of this procedure, and the difference between this and euthanasia?

Sadie Fineman

There is now an increasing body of literature that draws attention to the patient's perception of quality of life in terminal illness.[*] This literature emphasizes the physical, psychological, social, and spiritual aspects of the patient's well-being, all of which are to be considered determinants of quality of life and therefore central to the principles underlying end-of-life care. In palliative care it is also stressed that the patient and family have the right to be informed about the disease and about treatment options.

[*] Mount B, Cohen SR. 1997. Quality of life in patients with life-threatening illness. In: Strack S. (ed). Death and the Quest for Meaning: Essays in Honor of Herman Feifel. Northvale, NJ: Jason Aronson, pp 137–152.

Sadie Fineman was never fully informed about her advanced cancer, yet she lived with extraordinary handicaps for a woman of her age. She coped with a malfunctioning biliary tube that drained copiously and soaked the dressings around the tube. Sometimes she experienced extreme pain where the tube was inserted. Mrs. Fineman "knew" she was ill, but at the request of her family, never fully learned the truth about her illness (in contrast to the way the health care team treated the Metrakis family).

What stands out in this case in particular is Sadie Fineman's love of life throughout her illness and up until she died. She never ceased to amaze her family and caregivers by her initiatives to get out to play bridge or Mah-Jong, go for walks, or visit with family. She looked forward to a future of family events and social activities with hope and eager anticipation. She "loved a good wedding." Would it have benefited Mrs. Fineman to have been informed of the full details of her advancing cancer?

Although we frequently employ pejorative terms such as "conspiracy of silence" to describe the way a family and team avoid explicit discussion of diagnostic and prognostic "facts," it appears that in this case these decisions served the patient well. At the same time, there is evidence from the narrative that Sadie Fineman was quite capable of adjusting to the reality of her inevitable death, at her own pace and in her own language.

Topics for Discussion

1. Sadie Fineman and her family made it clear that she wanted to receive nursing care at home. Yet there were times when her need for care exceeded the knowledge and skills of her daughter and the availability of skilled health professionals. Would it have been possible to follow a different approach to accommodate the patient's and family's wishes?

2. Management of Mrs. Fineman's biliary tube posed a nursing challenge for both her caregivers and family. Rachel, Mrs. Fineman's main caregiver at home, was anxious and at times fearful of having to take care of the tube and surrounding skin area. What strategies might have been used to alleviate some of these concerns?

3. Do you agree with the decision of Mrs. Fineman's children to avoid the word "cancer" in their dealings with their mother? What is your appraisal of this situation? Was Mrs. Fineman in denial?

4. In the last days of her illness, Sadie Fineman received a blood transfusion. Despite the severity of her illness, the palliative medical team assessed that a blood transfusion would raise her hemoglobin and permit her to have a few more days of useful life. What is your view of the approach that was taken?

5. What bereavement issues, if any, are raised in this case?

6. What were the most challenging features of caregiving in this case for members of the palliative care team?

Stanley Gray

The question, "When is a patient appropriate for hospice?" is a leitmotif running throughout this book. It is hard to give a definitive answer, and much of it depends on who is asking, and why. Especially in the United States, the answer is complicated by financing schemes for hospice care that require unrealistic, and frequently off-putting, predictions of a patient's imminent death.° Patients and their physicians are understandably reluctant to make these "gloomy prognostications," as Thomas Percival described them in his *Medical Ethics* of 1803. Hospice programs fear the financial and regulatory consequences of carrying too many patients like Stanley Gray, who stunningly outlived his expected end.

Even within our small sample, patients differed greatly in their attitudes toward hospice and palliative care. Some, like Katie Melnick and Martin Roy, seemed to move willingly and gratefully into the programs; others, like Richard Johnson and Jenny Doyle, fought resentfully against them. Some, like Sadie Fineman, never outwardly appeared to acknowledge their impending death, yet gladly availed themselves of every supportive service—including plastic pants—that their caregivers could provide. It seems that patients' and caregivers' agreement that hospice is "appropriate" is frequently the product of a subtle negotiation that is not always explicit—a far more subtle process than is depicted in textbooks of palliative care.

Likewise, hospice programs seem to apply inconsistent standards in judging whether a patient is "appropriate." Again, our sample is small, but if we compare Mr. Gray's case to that of Frances Legendre in Montreal and Jenny Doyle and Shamira Cook in Lancaster, an intriguing hypothesis suggests itself. All three of the other cases raised questions in the minds of the palliative care team as to the appropriateness of the patient's involvement with the program. Mr. Gray's case raised far fewer questions, even though he remained in the program far longer, and his symptoms were by no means any more severe. In fact, Frances Legendre, Jenny Doyle, and Shamira Cook had much more severe pain and other physical and emotional symptoms than Mr. Gray, and they all died after much less time in palliative care. Why, then, did they provoke so much questioning, when Mr. Gray did not?

The answer may be that each of the women actively resisted her disease and sought treatments for it, while Mr. Gray did not. In other words, from the hos-

---

°Fox E et al. 1999. Evaluation of prognostic criteria for determininig hospice eligibility in patients with advanced lung, heart, or liver disease. *JAMA* 282:1638–1645.

pice team's point of view, the mere length of time a patient has to live, or the severity of his or her symptoms, is a less significant criterion for retention in the program than the patient's attitude toward the disease. Hospice professionals are more comfortable with patients who accept death—and are willing to extend those patients' hospice stays indefinitely as long as they maintain that attitude—than they are with patients who resist death, even when those patients actually die sooner and suffer more. We need more data and more case studies like these to test this hypothesis adequately.

Topics for Discussion

1. How did Mr. Gray explain his unexpected medical recovery to himself? What should be the attitudes of health professionals toward patients' explanatory models that do not fit with biomedical understandings? Should they be unconditionally supportive? Is the situation different when the explanatory models are based on religious faith?
2. The hospice chaplain attempted to bring balance to Mr. Gray's theological views, and even suggested an elaborate spiritual exercise to suggest to Mr. Gray that there were other ways he could understand the role of God and Jesus in his life. What is your view of the chaplain's approach?
3. Hospice staff like Naomi Barnes often develop a special attachment to long-term patients like Stanley Gray. How should staff learn to deal with their feelings in such cases?
4. It is accepted practice that in advanced COPD, drugs like bronchodilators and steroids be maximized before opioids are used. Discuss the use of opioids in advanced COPD.
5. Is Mr. Gray terminally ill? Explain your answer.
6. What significant bereavement issues do you believe might arise for Florence Laxton and Cynthia Gray? Do you expect bereavement to be an issue for anyone else in this case?

Martin Roy

It is routine in palliative care to assess level of pain, be it physical, emotional, or spiritual. Patients may present as "good copers," but our assessment antennae are always working! We are trained to label, categorize, and make interpretations—for example, was Martin Roy euphoric or not? There is something that feels "not right" about this case.

The assessment training is embedded in palliative care providers and is almost a reflex. By necessity the process involves objectification, which has implications for the way we view the person. We cannot objectify and empathize in the same moment. We have a duty to go through this process, for example, to screen for depression or to detect masks that may be covering up a lot of emotional pain. Yet psychological assessments are often difficult to make. A case like Martin Roy's shows us how complex these issues are—perhaps more complex than what our literature and concepts can explain. Who knows what Mr. Roy's inner life was really like?

What would the literature on coping say? Patients experiencing life-threatening illness are clearly forced to modify their perceptions and their lives. The coping literature refers to a whole range of "adaptive responses and capacities," as well as ways of managing and reducing stress.°

On the face of it, Mr. Roy fits the definition of a "good coper." He was young but felt that he had led a good and full life. He had a strong, supportive family and, apparently, enough inner resources to manage his life through this period of terminal illness. But something tells us that Mr. Roy fits the criteria too well. Here is a situation of a young man dying at the age of 37. What criteria do we use to assess coping in such a case? We are not the one dying; Mr. Roy is dying—a particular young man with a particular history. Was he exhibiting a pathological reaction? Is there something the palliative care team should have challenged or treated? What theory or language or professional technique will help us understand this?

Topics for Discussion

1. Martin had many of the characteristics of a "good coper." What factors may have led to this?
2. There were occasions during the course of his terminal illness when the members of the palliative care team had concerns about Martin's attitudes and behaviors. Do you think that they were justified in their concerns?
3. Martin developed mental techniques to control his pain. What is the role of such adjuvant techniques in pain control?
4. Comment on the subcutaneous infusion technique that was used to help control Martin's pain both in the hospital and at home. What is the advantage of continuous subcutaneous infusion over other medication delivery systems?
5. Martin had respiratory distress in the last day of his life. Discuss the approach to management of dyspnea in palliative care.
6. Comment on the ways that Martin and Alexandra prepared their children for Martin's death. What did Alexandra do with the children after their father's death that might have helped them adapt? How do grieving

°Lazarus R, Averill JR, Opton EM. 1974. The psychology of coping: Issues in research and assessment. In: Coelho GV, Hamburg DA, Adams JE (eds). Coping and Adaptation. New York: Basic Books.

children respond? How might caregivers help parents deal with their
children's grief?

7. Martin's parents seemed particularly affected by his death. In general,
does the bereavement process of losing an older person differ from that
for the death of a child?

Richard Johnson

This narrative is disturbing because Mr. Johnson was a relatively young man,
dying of a disease that usually affects older men. He had experienced problems
in dealing with previous challenges in his life: his work, the death of his mother,
and the early part of his marriage. In addition, he had the misfortune of experiencing cancer pain that was difficult to control and was prone to developing
side effects from his analgesic medication.

Mr. Johnson needed to be in control. Did he have other needs beyond this?
He pushed hard to get aggressive treatment even when there was a low chance
that this would prolong his life. He did not want palliative care. Was he afraid
to die and unable to discuss it? Dr. Allan tried to get Mr. Johnson to discuss his
fears, but he seemed unable to talk about them, appearing to be an isolated
man. He was unable to share feelings of fear or sadness with his wife, even
though she was constantly at his side. It was as if he had never come to terms
with his mother's death 20 years before.

Mr. Johnson's fear of losing control was with him to the very end. He was not
able to trust his wife to make decisions on his behalf, he trusted no one. He was
apparently a religious, church-going Catholic, and yet this seemed to bring him
no comfort. Mrs. Johnson had similar difficulties. She wanted some control,
but then experienced doubt and guilt. These feelings continued throughout the
bereavement follow-up period.

In palliative care we come across families who present complex medical and
psychosocial scenarios such as this. Sometimes, even with our best efforts, we
do not succeed in making the situation better.

Topics for Discussion

1. When his disease was far advanced, Mr. Johnson pushed for aggressive,
experimental chemotherapy. How do you feel about patients who opt for
experimental protocols that have low chance of prolonging life? How can
hospice or palliative care services help such a patient?

2. How did the issue of autonomy play out in this narrative? Do palliative
care proponents inflict emotional distress by pushing a strict palliative
care philosophy onto undecided individuals?

3. What is your view about how the DNR orders were handled in this case? How should this issue be handled? Should the patient or relatives or both be involved in the decision? Should resuscitation be offered at all if experience tells the physician it is highly unlikely to succeed?

4. Mr. Johnson's pain was not easy to control. Discuss the two different kinds of pain that Mr. Johnson had and what medications or other techniques could have been used to try to control his pain while minimizing side effects.

5. Mr. Johnson developed agitated delirium in the last days of his life. Discuss the approach to management of this condition.

6. Mrs. Johnson could be said to have developed a complicated mourning pattern. What are the risk factors for a complicated bereavement? What are some of the elements of complicated mourning? How can palliative care services help with complicated grief?

7. Comment on the ways children understand death at various stages of their development. What issues do you believe will be important to Simon as he deals with his grief?

Jenny Doyle

Jenny Doyle was caught between two ideologies. One was the ideology of modern North American oncology, which identifies hope with ever-more daring and aggressive curative or life-prolonging efforts, even in the advanced stages of disease.[°] The other was the ideology of hospice, which places the highest value on acceptance of death and on foregoing intensive curative treatments that can prolong physical suffering.[†] Each of these ideologies is well intentioned, each expresses a commitment to nonabandonment of patients, and each serves some patients well. When they clash as they did in this case, they do not serve patients well.

The oncologists' ideology was closer to Jenny Doyle's own goals and values, although the hospice team justifiably wondered if she was getting a clear and realistic picture of her situation, especially in light of Dr. Stein's comment that his "interactions with Jenny have been good because she gets better—so that makes it a lot easier on everybody." Yet, if the oncologists' ability to see Mrs. Doyle's situation accurately was hampered by their own comfort level, what can be said of hospice's vision of her? Sandra Dunn commented that the thought of Jenny dying in Las Vegas was "upsetting" (to whom?). She offered the astonish-

°Good MD, Good BJ, Schaffer C, Lind, SE. 1990. American oncology and the discourse on hope. *Culture, Medicine and Psychiatry* 14:59–79.

†Ackerman F. 1997. Goldilocks and Mrs. Ilych: A critical look at the "philosophy of hospice." *Cambridge Quarterly of Healthcare Ethics* 6:314–324.

ing definition of hospice's mission to be "the voice of reality" (whose?). Somewhere between, and certainly distorted by, these partly self-serving ideological stances is the actual situation of the patient. The true challenge of this and several other cases in this book is providing optimally individualized care to an assertive and highly motivated person, who needs a well-integrated and prolonged combination of active treatment and palliative care.

Despite these conflicts and barriers, the hospice team tried to stay involved to the very end, providing support and companionship that Andrew Doyle, in particular, found helpful. The moment of Jenny's death was ugly, and for both Kim and Andrew, the first year of bereavement was filled with ambivalence and hard feelings. These are factors, however, that are rarely within a hospice team's power to control. The course of bereavement will usually depend as much on a family's prior history as on the interventions of even the most sensitive counselor or volunteer.

Topics for Discussion

1. It is always difficult to discuss prognosis with cancer patients. What were the specific problems regarding prognostication in this case? Could they have been minimized?

2. The hospice social worker commented that at times hospice "must be the voice of reality." What did she mean by this? What is your opinion of this description of the hospice team's role?

3. How does this case illustrate tensions between an interpretation of hospice philosophy that equates hospice with terminal care, and a philosophy of palliative care that is relatively independent of the imminence of death? What strategies might have made it possible for Jenny to have more continuity between comfort-oriented palliative care and her efforts to fight actively against her disease?

4. According to Mrs. Doyle, when Dr. Richards first met her, Dr. Richards said, "When I see someone functioning as well as you are—walking, talking, breathing, telling me that they are caring for their apartment, telling me that they are looking to get back to driving, and things like this—this does not spell 'hospice patient' to me." Comment on Dr. Richards's implied criteria for referral to hospice.

5. Pamidronate, a biphosphanate, assumes a significant role in the clinical management of Jenny's case. Discuss the role of biphosphanates in palliative care.

6. Roberta Smalley called Jenny a "perfect hospice kind of patient." Do you agree? Is there such a thing as a "perfect" hospice patient? If so, what are the characteristics of such a patient?

7. Comment on the phases of the bereavement process for Andrew and Kim.

Jasmine Claude

In a few of the narratives in this book, differences in religious views between the patient and some of the health care givers led to tension, as some staff members question the genuineness or authenticity of the patient's statements of faith. These differences are usually not expressed directly but emerge as significant private thoughts—in this case, from the physicians. These views affected markedly the perceptions the physicians formed of Mrs. Claude, who had developed an unshakable faith in God. The reactions of the palliative care staff ranged from curiosity, fascination, and inspiration to skepticism. According to palliative care philosophy, caregivers have a duty to address and support the patient's religious and spiritual beliefs. Yet some of Mrs. Claude's caregivers seemed to be more comfortable with making "objective" and psychological interpretations regarding her strong belief in God.

Obviously, it is not possible for caregivers not to have particular opinions and beliefs. However, it is fruitful to reflect on how these views may either benefit or harm patients. Has our advancement of knowledge in the psychosocial domains of illness begun to outweigh our ability to accept patients' personal attestations of religious faith?

The palliative care staff marvelled at Mrs. Claude's extraordinary coping abilities. Some of the staff may have actually idealized her. Do we serve patients well when we label them as "strong" and "good copers"? Are we preventing them from displaying their doubts and fears? At the same time, we may do them a disservice if we go digging for doubts and fears.

Topics for Discussion

1. Why do you think that the palliative care staff were fascinated by this "good coper" who demonstrated an extraordinary degree of strength and courage?
2. In the narrative, Mrs. Claude's ward nurse, Rosemary, expressed how difficult it is not to become reactive when faced with some of the emotions that patients often express, especially anger. Has this been an issue in your own work? How can we deal with these kinds of issues?
3. What happens when God enters the picture? Do you think that the palliative care staff might have done Mrs. Claude a disservice with their attitudes concerning her faith?
4. Mrs. Claude posed some interesting dilemmas regarding the role of faith,

spirituality, or religion. How do these become reconciled in the clinical and personal life of palliative care givers? What do we do when we are not clear about personal faith in our own minds?

5. Why do you think that the staff had such a marked reaction to Mrs. Claude's sudden death? How can staff members organize themselves to deal with strong emotions that are evoked by their work?

6. In this case, in several instances the patient thought her prognosis was better than it actually was. Should the palliative care team have challenged this? (It might have allowed her family to come from Haiti sooner.)

Katie Melnick

In his seminal paper, "The Nature of Suffering and the Goals of Medicine," Eric J. Cassell expounds on the individuality of suffering and insists that the only sure way to find out if and how a medical patient is suffering is to ask.° Katie Melnick taught her family, her caregivers, and our interviewer many specific details of her suffering—details we could have easily missed in the face of the extraordinary serenity she derived from her religious faith. Indeed, the progressive levels of her disability and helplessness not only marked her successive experiences of suffering but were also the milestones by which Mrs. Melnick gauged her own closeness to death. The symbolism of the hospital bed, her need for the wheelchair, and, finally and most distressingly, her loss of control over her bowel movements, were crucial to a full understanding of her suffering.

Even her faith led to a moment of guilt and terror as Mrs. Melnick faced her alcoholic past in the last days of her life. Yet her faith was also a powerful resource that enabled her to be open and honest with her family about dying. Though it may well have triggered the fearful moments on her deathbed, her faith also enabled remarkable openness. Because of her certainty that she was living and dying with God, Mrs. Melnick did not have to suppress her anxiety and fears for fear that their expression would trap her in despair.

We also learn a great deal about family members' ambivalence in the face of loss. John and Lena, in particular, expressed widely varying feelings toward Mrs. Melnick over the last months of her life, and into their bereavement. John was initially cold, distant and judgmental, and yet by the end of Katie's life he was able to caress her bald scalp and boast that he was "staying in with my honey." Lena had been severely wounded by her mother, and wanted to nurse Mrs. Melnick in part to bind up her own wounds, and the wounds in their rela-

---

°Cassell EJ. 1982. The nature of suffering and the goals of medicine. *N Eng J Med* 306:639–645.

tionship. Lena's intense swings of feeling during the last weeks of her mother's
life and over the first months of her bereavement suggest that her tasks remain
unfinished.

Topics for Discussion

1. Mrs. Melnick's faith in God was a very prominent aspect of her life and of
   her death. In what ways, specifically, did her faith serve as a support to
   her during her illness? Comment on the moments of fear and despair she
   felt just before she died. Did that experience seem consistent or inconsistent with the life of faith she had lived up to that point?
2. Discuss the impact of the secret history of alcohol abuse on the family's
   experience of Mrs. Melnick's death. Should the hospice team have tried
   to help Lena and her parents come to terms more openly with this history? Why or why not?
3. Comment on the relationship between Nadia and Mrs. Melnick, and on
   Nadia's reactions to the intensity of her work with her patient. How can
   hospice or palliative care programs help their staff avoid emotional exhaustion or burnout?
4. What role did financial concerns play in this case?
5. Mrs. Melnick had some very concrete worries about what the last stages
   of her illness would be like. What approach should hospice workers or
   physicians take when patients express fears about the actual process of
   dying?
6. John Melnick remained quite aloof and distant from his wife until the last
   days of her illness. Could the hospice team have intervened to bring him
   closer to his wife sooner? Should they have done so?

Susan Mulroney

Susan Mulroney considered herself "a very private person" and her illness "a
private matter." As her illness progressed, her caregivers on the Palliative Care
Unit increasingly worried that Ms. Mulroney was "not expressing her feelings."
It made them uncomfortable to think that this patient had fears and feelings
that she was choosing not to share with them.

Ms. Mulroney's silence worried her caregivers. Why? Did her lack of disclo-
sure fail to comply with generally accepted health care teachings regarding patient and family communication? Contemporary communication literature in
the health sciences argues that "functional communication" is characterized by
openness, spontaneity, authenticity, and self-disclosure. Conversely, in "dys-

functional communication" the person's intentions are "covert or hidden."° At what point is the authority of the literature superseded by the patient's right to choose?

Topics for Discussion

1. Contemporary North American psychosocial literature frequently proposes that healthy family functioning depends upon open communication. Susan Mulroney was always a private person and shared few of her thoughts and feelings, even with those close to her. She was uncomfortable when asked about her illness. What is the responsibility or role of palliative care when the patient prefers not to talk?
2. Susan would have liked to have been at home for the final phase of her illness, especially since it was Christmas time. But she was explicit that she did not want anyone to be at home with her, even though she was too ill to be left alone. Could any other strategies have been adopted to help Susan realize her wish?
3. During the last hours of Susan's life some family members expressed the wish that she receive intravenous hydration. Jack Peterson, in particular, wondered if it was ethical not to provide Susan with nutrition and hydration, even though she was dying. What is your view?
4. After Susan's death the family expressed feelings of wishing they could have done more, and had many unanswered questions. Judy Mulroney, in particular, had feelings of anger and resentment toward her brother. Yet the family did not pursue offers of help from the bereavement team. What issues of family grieving are implied in this case, and what is the palliative care team's overall responsibility to a family with unresolved grief?
5. Jack Peterson knew Susan very well. They had a trusting friendship, and in some ways knew each other like sister and brother. Yet as a friend, Jack felt that his role after Susan died was limited. What is the responsibility of the team when the patient's "family" is a friend?
6. Jack felt particularly awkward when he and Rita arrived at the funeral and tried to decide where to sit. In some ways his discomfort calls to mind the concept of disenfranchised grief. What is your understanding of this concept? Are there people who, by virtue of their status or relationship to the deceased, are particularly vulnerable to disenfranchised grief?

°Friedman M. 1998. Family communication patterns and processes. In: Friedman M. Family Nursing: Research, Theory, and Practice, 4th ed. Stamford, CT: Appleton & Lange, pp 231–263.

Costas Metrakis

A short time before he was transferred to the Palliative Care Unit, Costas Metrakis was told the truth about his cancer diagnosis: there was no hope for a cure. Yet it had been his family's explicit wish that Mr. Metrakis not be told the truth, and that hope, and efforts toward a cure, be maintained.

When Mr. Metrakis was transferred to the unit, the Metrakis family perceived it as a place where he was to die. They expressed feelings of anger and betrayal in their interactions with the palliative care team and, in turn, the team found it impossible to build a trusting relationship or any form of therapeutic alliance with their patient or the family. After Mr. Metrakis's death, Mrs. Metrakis continued to ask herself and others, "Why did they have to tell him?"

The family's own rules and beliefs regarding communication of bad news were clearly disregarded, in spite of the fact that there now exists convincing evidence in the communication and palliative care literature that it is necessary to explore and assess how much a patient wants to know about his or her illness or prognosis.

At a broader level, we must also consider our own beliefs in Western society regarding what constitutes healthy patient–physician communication. Not all cultures value the pursuit of truth in the face of a terminal diagnosis.° In some families, the Western concept of open communication as being synonymous with functional communication may prove dysfunctional in practice, if it contradicts the family's belief system and cultural mores.

Topics for Discussion

1. What effects did the sudden transition from diagnosis to palliative treatment have on the palliative care team's relationship with the Metrakis family?
2. Mrs. Metrakis and Sophia expressed dismay when Mr. Metrakis was told the truth about his diagnosis. What is your view? Were the doctors correct that there was no hope? Did the family understand correctly what the physicians tried to communicate?
3. When the medical team consulted the palliative care service physicians for the purposes of transfer to palliative care, there were conflicting points of view on how to proceed. How would you have proceeded in this case?
4. In your opinion, how common is it for patients and families to assume

° Boston P. 1999. Culture and cancer: The relevance of cultural orientation within cancer education programmes. *Eur J Cancer Care* 2:72–76.

that palliative care is "where they send people to die"? Is this an appropriate assumption? If not, what steps might palliative care professionals take to counteract it?

5. What concerns do you have about the bereavement process for the Metrakis family? Could or should the bereavement follow-up service have proceeded any differently in this case?

Joey Court

The hospice team had precious little to do at the bedside in this case. This was due in part to the nature of Joey's illness—he had been terminally ill from birth and his parents had become quite familiar with the demanding routines of his care—and to his inability to interact verbally. But it was primarily due to Amanda Court's extraordinary competence and devotion to Joey's every need. There was simply no room at the bedside for anyone else, as the hospice nurses and volunteers all discovered at one time or another. Amanda was physically and emotionally exhausted; her own health was affected by her non-stop nursing care. The rigors of care were aggravated for most of Joey's life by Amanda's (and to some extent Brian's) fierce determination to treat Joey as a "normal" child while trying to provide a normal upbringing for Mike.

Hospice's real contributions to this case occurred away from the bedside, in the support groups for Amanda and Brian and for Mike. Bereavement support is relatively underemphasized in hospice and palliative care education, despite the fact that it is always mentioned among the primary goals of hospice care and is part of the definition of a Medicare-eligible hospice program. This may result from the fact that bereavement is experienced in the family's private life, and is therefore largely invisible to caregivers who focus mainly on the dying person. According to data provided by Hospice of Lancaster County, approximately 40% of the families who have had a relative die in the hospice program request some form of active bereavement support (regular phone calls, visits at home, or involvement in a support group). The Royal Victoria Hospital Palliative Care Service reports a slightly lower percentage, around 35%–40%. For comparison, St. Christopher's Hospice in London provides active bereavement support to 25% of their bereaved families in a typical year (Cicely Saunders, personal communication).

Amanda and Brian drew extensively from their support groups at Hospice of Lancaster County. Entering the program emotionally devastated, exhausted, and needy, they gradually emerged as providers of support to others, and found this transition to be part of their own healing.

When the griever is a young child, the stakes are particularly high. This narrative sheds a great deal of light on the experiences and needs of the youngest grievers, a group who are often invisible to caregivers, whether the dying patient is old or young.[°][†] Amanda and Brian, in concert with the Hospice of Lancaster County Coping Kids program, were sensitive to Mike's needs. Their sensitivity extended to Mike's cognitive-developmental stage, at which death, while significant to the four- or five year-old, is typically believed to be reversible. They involved Mike as much as possible in Joey's day-to-day care, and provided appropriate rituals to help him communicate feelings, say goodbye, and feel safe and loved. For his part, Mike was very shy when he started with Coping Kids, and ended up social, friendly, and expressive.

Topics for Discussion

1. Are there features of palliative care for children that are significantly different from those of palliative care for adults?
2. Comment on the relationship and communication between Dr. Willis and the hospice team. What are some ways to improve communication between hospice and the treating physician?
3. Comment on Dr. Willis's philosophy in dealing with parents of children with life-threatening illness. How would you approach a family who insists on maintaining intensive, life-prolonging treatment that, in your professional judgment, is of no benefit, or that seems to be doing more harm than good for the child?
4. Why do you think that several friends stopped speaking to the Courts after they decided to withhold further life-prolonging treatments for Joey? Were Brian and Amanda justified in making this decision?
5. To accept Mike into the Illness Support Group, Sally Walters had to make an exception to the hospice rule that requires group members to be at least 5 years old. Discuss the age requirement of bereavement services for children and ways that palliative care programs can support the very young.
6. What were the main benefits the Courts received from their involvement in the various bereavement support groups? How might you describe the potential benefits of such a group to a family who appear reluctant to participate?
7. Comment on the various reactions of the hospice nurses and volunteers to their work with Joey and his family.

[°]Walker C. 1993. Sibling bereavement and grief responses. *J Palliat Nursing* 8:325–334.
[†]Corr C, Corr D. 1998. Key elements in a framework for helping grieving children and adolescents. *Illness, Crisis, and Loss* 6:142–160.

Paula Ferrari

Paula Ferrari exhibited a courage and fortitude in the face of devastating illness that is rarely seen. She taught and believed that dying is the ultimate learning experience. Mrs. Ferrari's presence on the Palliative Care Unit touched everyone who knew her in a special and unique way. As Rosa said, she was loved by everybody.

Without exception, Paula Ferrari's caregivers perceived her as someone who gave to them. She provided spiritual comfort for many of her helpers and some sought solace in her mere presence. But was Paula Ferrari altogether without spiritual pain? Often she would cry out in anguish or in sheer frustration at not being able to use her typewriter to simply chat with people, as she had previously so loved to do. The numerous times she found it hard to tell others what she needed often resulted in long periods of crying and sadness. What of her own anguish in these dark periods of helplessness and frustration? Did the comfort and solace Mrs. Ferrari so frequently bestowed on others in fact obscure the need for her caregivers to attend to her spiritual nourishment? Was the image of Paula Ferrari as a strong, courageous, and spiritually whole woman such that her caregivers may not have always seen the doubts, fears, and dark days of her suffering?

Topics for Discussion

1. Mrs. Ferrari made it clear throughout her illness that she wanted to fully experience her dying. She did not want her consciousness diminished through terminal sedation. Yet there were times when she experienced prolonged and uncontrollable suffering despite all efforts to make her comfortable. What value did she find in the conscious experience of suffering and dying that made it worthwhile to her to endure these difficulties?
2. What measures of quality of life are appropriate for understanding Mrs. Ferrari's experience or for evaluating her care?
3. Mrs. Ferrari's family wanted to care for her at home but were not able to cope. What were the strengths and limitations of the Palliative Care Unit in creating a home-like environment?
4. Some of Mrs. Ferrari's caregivers were influenced by her and attached to her beyond the usual role of caregiving in a palliative care setting. Was this appropriate?
5. At times members of the palliative care team found it impossible to communicate with Mrs. Ferrari, which resulted in unmet needs on the part of the patient and an expressed sense of helplessness and frustration by her

caregivers. What problem-solving strategies might have helped to alleviate this problem?

6. Discuss Mrs. Ferrari's relationship to her religious faith, and the more general role of and meaning of spirituality in her experience of suffering and dying.

7. To what extent were the palliative care staff able to empathize with Mrs. Ferrari?

Bibliography

Principles and practice of palliative care

Berger AM, Portenoy RK, Weissman DE (eds.) 1998. Principles and Practice of Supportive Oncology. Philadelphia: Lippincott-Raven.

Billings JA. 1998. What is palliative care? *J Palliat Med* 1(1):73–81.

Bosanquet N, Salisbury C (eds.) 1999. Providing a Palliative Care Service: Towards an Evidence Base. Oxford: Oxford University Press.

Byock I. 1996. Beyond symptom management. *Euro J Palliat Care* 3(3):125–130.

Byock I. 1997. Dying Well: The Prospect for Growth at the End of Life. New York: Riverhead Books.

Cassell EJ. 1991. The Nature of Suffering and the Goals of Medicine. New York: Oxford University Press.

Cassell EJ. 1982. The nature of suffering and the goals of medicine. *N Eng J Med* 306(11):639–645.

Clark D, Hockley J, Ahmedzai S (eds.) 1997. New Themes in Palliative Care. Buckingham, England: Open University Press.

Council on Ethical and Judicial Affairs, American Medical Association. Council report. 1996. Good care of the dying patient. *JAMA* 275(6):474–478.

Doyle D, Hanks GW, MacDonald N (eds.) 1998. Oxford Textbook of Palliative Medicine, 2nd ed. Oxford: Oxford University Press.

Dush DM. 1993. High-tech, aggressive palliative care: In the service of quality of life. *J Palliat Care* 9(1):37–41.

Field MJ, Cassel CK (eds.) 1997. Approaching Death: Improving Care at the End of Life. Washington, DC: National Academy Press.

Holland J (ed). 1998. Psycho-oncology. Oxford: Oxford University Press.

Magno J. 1992. USA hospice care in the 1990s. *Palliat Med* 6:158–65.

Meier D, Morrison R, Cassel C. 1997. Improving palliative care. *Ann Intern Med* 127(3):225–230.

Mount BM. 1992. Volunteer support services: A key component of palliative care. *J Palliat Care* 8(1):59–64.

Pickett M, Cooley ME, Gordon DB. 1998. Palliative care: Past, present and future perspectives. *Semin Oncol Nurs* 14(2):86–94.

Saunders C, Baines M. 1983. Living with Dying: The Management of Terminal Disease. Oxford: Oxford University Press.

Sheehan DC, Forman WB (eds). 1996. Hospice and Palliative Care: Concepts and Practice. Boston: Jones and Bartlett.

Twycross R. 1997. Introducing Palliative Care, 2nd ed. Oxford: Radcliffe Medical Press.

Weissman DE. 1997. Consultation in palliative medicine. *Arch Intern Med* 157(7): 733–737.

Pain and symptom control

General

Baider L, Uziely B, De-Nour A. 1994. Progressive muscle relaxation and guided imagery in cancer patients. *Gen Hosp Psychiatry* 16:340–347.

Cherny NI, Portenoy RK. 1994. Sedation in the management of refractory symptoms: Guidelines for evaluation and treatment. *J Palliat Care* 10(2):31–38.

Farr WC. 1990. The use of corticosteroids for symptom management in terminally ill patients. *Am J Hospice Care* 7:41–46.

MacDonald N (ed.) 1998. Palliative Medicine: A Case-Based Manual. Oxford: Oxford University Press.

Oliver DJ. 1985. The use of the syringe driver in terminal care. *Br J Clin Pharmacol* 20:515–516.

Twycross R. 1997. Symptom Management in Advanced Cancer. Oxford: Radcliffe Medical Press.

Pain

Bloomfield DJ. 1998. Should bisphosphonates be part of the standard therapy of patients with multiple myeloma or bone metastases from other cancers? An evidence-based review. *J Clin Oncol* 16(3):1218–1225.

Cherny NI, Arbit E, Jain S. 1996. Invasive techniques in the management of cancer pain. *Hematol Oncol Clin North Am* 10(1):121–137.

Ersek M, Ferrell BR. 1994. Providing relief from cancer pain by assisting in the search for meaning. *J Palliat Care* 10(4):15–22.

Fallon MT, Welsh J. 1996. The role of ketamine in pain control. *Eur J Palliat Care* 3:143–146.

Hanks GW, de Conno F, Ripamonti C, Ventafridda V, Hanna M, McQuay HJ, Mercadante S, Meynadier J, Poulain P, Roca i Casas J. 1996. Morphine in cancer pain: Modes of administration. *BMJ* 312:823–826.

Jacox A, Carr DB, Payne R et al. 1994. Management of Cancer Pain. Clinical Practice Guideline No. 9. AHCPR Publication No. 94-0592. Rockville, MD: Agency for Health Care Policy and Research, U.S. Department of Health and Human Services, Public Health Service.

Levy MH. 1996. Pharmacologic treatment of cancer pain. *N Engl J Med* 335(15): 1124–1132.

Luczak J, Dickenson AH, Kotlinksa-Lemieszek A. 1995. The role of ketamine, an NMDA receptor antagonist, in the management of pain. *Prog Palliat Care* 3:127–134.

McQuay HJ, Carroll D, Jadad AR, Wiffen P, Moore A. 1995. Anticonvulsant drugs for management of pain: A systematic review. *BMJ* 311:1047–1052.

McQuay HJ, Tramer M, Nye BA, Carroll D, Wiffen PJ, Moore RA. 1996. A systematic review of antidepressants in neuropathic pain. *Pain* 68:217–227.

Morris DB. 1991. The Culture of Pain. Berkeley: University of California Press.

Pace V. 1995. The use of nonsteroidal anti-inflammatory drugs in cancer. *Palliat Med* 9:273–286.

Robinson RG, Preston DF, Schiefelbein M, Baster KG. 1995. Strontium-89 therapy for the palliation of pain due to osseous metastases. *JAMA* 274(5):420–424.

Spross JA, Wolff Burke M. 1995. Nonpharmacological management of cancer pain. In: McGuire DB, Henke Yarbro C, Ferrell BR (eds). Cancer Pain Management, 2nd ed. London: Jones and Bartlett, pp 159–205.

Twycross R. 1994. Pain Relief in Advanced Cancer. Edinburgh: Churchill Livingstone.

World Health Organization. 1990. Cancer Pain Relief and Palliative Care. Geneva: WHO.

World Health Organization. 1996. Cancer Pain Relief, 2nd ed. Geneva: WHO.

Dyspnea

Davis CL. 1994. The therapeutics of dyspnea. *Cancer Surv* 21:85–98.

Dudgeon DL. 1996. Management of dyspnea and cough in patients with cancer. *Hematol Oncol Clin North Am* 10(1):157–169.

Bowel obstruction

Ripamonti C. 1994. Management of bowel obstruction in advanced cancer patients. *J Pain Symptom Manag* 9(3):193–200.

Fainsinger RL, Spanchynski K, Hanson J, Bruera E. 1994. Symptom control in terminally ill patients with malignant bowel obstruction. *J Pain Symptom Manag* 9:12–18.

Nausea/vomiting

Regnard C, Comiskey M. 1992. Nausea and vomiting in advanced cancer—a flow diagram. *Palliat Med* 6:146–151.

Twycross R, Back I. 1998. Nausea and vomiting in advanced cancer. *Eur J Palliat Care* 5(2):39–45.

Delirium/confusion

Shuster JL. 1998. Delirium, confusion and agitation at the end of life. *J Palliat Med* 1(2):178–186.

Spiritual care

Kearney M. 1996. Mortally Wounded: Stories of Soul Pain, Death and Healing. New York: Scribner.

Kearney M, Mount B. Spiritual care of the dying patient. In Chochinov HM, Breitbart W (eds). Psychiatric Dimensions of Palliative Medicine. New York: Oxford University Press (in press).

Ley DCH, Corless IB. 1988. Spirituality and hospice care. *Death Stud* 12:101–110.

Longaker C. 1997. Facing Death and Finding Hope. New York: Bantam Doubleday.

Lunn L. 1993. Spiritual concerns in palliation. In: Saunders C, Sykes N (eds). The Management of Terminal Malignant Disease, 3rd ed. London: Edward Arnold, pp 213–225.

Rutland-Wallis MA. 1996. When dying is living: Hospice pastoral care and education. *J Pastoral Care* 50(1):41–48.

Spiritual Care Work Group of the International Work Group on Death, Dying, and Bereavement. 1990. Assumptions and principles of spiritual care. *Death Stud* 14:75–81.

Communication

Buckman R. 1992. How to Break Bad News. Baltimore: Johns Hopkins University Press.

Callanan M, Kelley P. 1992. Final Gifts: Understanding the Special Awareness, Needs, and Communications of the Dying. New York: Poseidon Press.

Faulkner A, Maguire P. 1994. Talking to Cancer Patients and Their Relatives. Oxford: Oxford University Press.

Surbone A, Zwitter M (eds). 1997. Communication with the Cancer Patient: Information and Truth. New York: Annals of the New York Academy of Sciences.

Music Therapy

Aldridge D (ed). 1999. Music Therapy in Palliative Care: New Voices. London: Jessica Kingsley.

Lee C (ed). 1995. Lonely Waters: Proceedings of the International Conference on Music Therapy in Palliative Care. Oxford: Sobell Publications.

Munro S, Mount B. 1978. Music therapy in palliative care. *Cana Med Assoc J* 119:1029–1034.

Rytcor M, Salmon D. 1998. Bibliography for music therapy in palliative care, 1963–1997. *Am J Hospice Palliat Care* 15(3):174–180.

Salmon D. 1993. Music and emotion in palliative care. *J Palliat Care* 1993; 9(4):48–52.

Art therapy

Connell C. 1998. Something Understood: Art Therapy in Cancer Care. London: Wrexham Publications.

Pratt A, Wood M (eds). 1998. Art Therapy in Palliative Care. London: Routledge.

Rudloff L. 1985. Michael: An illustrated story of a young man with cancer. *Am J Art Ther* 24:49–62.

Ethical issues in palliative care

Battin MP, Rhodes R, Silvers A (eds). 1998. Physician-Assisted Suicide: Expanding the Debate. New York: Routledge.

Block SD, Billings JA. 1994. Patient requests to hasten death: evaluation and management in terminal care. *Arch Intern Med* 154:2039–2047.

Brenner R. 1997. Issues of access in a diverse society. *Hospice J* 12(2):9–16.

Burt RA. 1997. The Supreme Court speaks—not assisted suicide but a constitutional right to palliative care. *N Engl J Med* 337(17):1234–1236.

Cherny NI, Coyle N, Foley KM. 1994. The treatment of suffering when patients request elective death. *J Palliat Care* 10(2):71–79.

Council on Ethical and Judicial Affairs, American Medical Association. 1992. Decisions near the end of life. *JAMA* 267(16):2229–2233.

Emanuel EJ. 1994. Euthanasia: Historical, ethical and empiric perspectives. *Arch Intern Med* 154:1890–1901.

Foley K. 1997. Competent care of the dying instead of physician-assisted suicide [editorial]. *N Engl J Med* 336(1):54–58.

Haines IE, Zalcberg J, Buchanan D. 1990. Not-for-resuscitation orders in cancer patients—principles of decision-making. *Med J Aust* 153:225–229.

Henderson S, Fins JJ, Moskowitz EH. 1998. Resuscitation in hospice. *Hastings Cent Rep* 28(6):20–22

Kinzbrunner B. 1995. Ethical dilemmas in hospice and palliative care. *Supportive Care Cancer* 3(1):28–36.

MacDonald N. 1994. From the front lines. *J Palliat Care* 10(3):44–47.

Mount B, Hamilton P. 1994. When palliative care fails to control suffering [and commentaries]. *J Palliat Care* 10:24–30.

Of Life and Death: Report of the Special Senate Committee on Euthanasia and Assisted Suicide. Ottawa: Minister of Supply and Services Canada, 1995.

Olweny CLM. 1994. Ethics of palliative care medicine: Palliative care for the rich nations only! *J Palliat Care* 10(3):17–22.

Portenoy RK (ed.) 1991. Special issue on medical ethics: Physician-assisted suicide and euthanasia. *J Pain Symptom Manag* 6:279–339.

Randall F, Downie RS. 1996. Palliative Care Ethics: A Good Companion. Oxford: Oxford University Press.

Roy DJ. 1995. Ethics and complexity in palliative care [editorial]. *J Palliat Care* 11(4):3–4.

Van der Maas PJ, van Delden JJM, Pijnenborg L, Looman CWN. 1991. Euthanasia and other medical decisions concerning the end of life. *Lancet* 338:669–674.

Vanderpool HY. 1978. The ethics of terminal care. *JAMA* 239(9):850–852.

Sociocultural issues

Blackhall LJ, Murphy ST, Frank G, Michel V, Azen S. 1995. Ethnicity and attitudes toward patient autonomy. *JAMA* 274(10):820–825.

Burrs FA. 1995. The African-American experience: Breaking the barriers to hospices. *Hospice J* 10(2):15–18.

Die Trill M, Holland J. 1993. Cross-cultural differences in the care of patients with cancer: A review. *Gen Hosp Psychiatry* 15:21–30.

Field D, Hockey J, Small N (eds). 1997. Death, Gender, and Ethnicity. London: Routledge.

Gamble VN. 1997. Under the shadow of Tuskegee: African-Americans and health care. *Am J Public Health* 87:1773–1778.

Garro C. 1990. Culture, pain and cancer. *J Palliat Care* 6(3):34–44.

Gostin LO. 1995. Informed consent, cultural sensitivity and respect for persons. *JAMA* 274(10):844–845.

Irish DP, Lundquist KF, Nelsen VJ (eds). 1993. Ethnic Variations in Dying, Death, and Grief. Washington, DC: Taylor and Francis.

Krell R. 1997. Confronting despair: The Holocaust survivor's struggle with ordinary life and ordinary death. *Cana Med Assoc J* 157(6):741–744.

National Hospice Organization, Task Force on Access to Hospice Care by Minorities. 1994. Caring For Our Own With Respect, Dignity and Love the Hospice Way. Arlington, VA: National Hospice Organization.

Sankar A. 1991. Ritual and dying: A cultural analysis of social support for caregivers. *Gerontologist* 31(1):43–50.

Secundy MG (ed). 1991. Trials, Tribulation, and Celebrations: African-American Perspectives on Health, Illness, Aging, and Loss. Yarmouth, ME: Intercultural Press.

Grief and bereavement

Bertman S (ed). 1999. Grief and the Healing Arts: Creativity as Therapy. Amityville, NY: Baywood.

Doka KJ (ed). 1989. Disenfranchised Grief: Recognizing Hidden Sorrow. Lexington, MA: Lexington Press.

Klass D, Silverman PR, Nickman SL (eds). 1996. Continuing Bonds: New Understandings of Grief. Washington: Taylor and Francis.

Parkes CM. 1996. Bereavement: Studies of Grief in Adult Life, 3rd ed. London: Routledge.

Rando TA. 1993. Treatment of Complicated Mourning. Champaign, IL: Research Press.

Stroebe MS, Stroebe W, Hansson RO (eds). 1993. Handbook of Bereavement. Cambridge: Cambridge University Press.

Woof WR, Carter YH. 1997. The grieving adult and the general practitioner: A literature review in two parts (part 1). *Br J Gen Pract* 47:443–448.

Woof WR, Carter YH. 1997. The grieving adult and the general practitioner: A literature review in two parts (part 2). *Br J Gen Pract* 47:509–514.

Staff support

Barnard D. 1995. The promise of intimacy and the fear of our own undoing. *J Palliat Care* 11(4):22–26.

Vachon MLS. 1987. Occupational Stress in the Care of the Critically Ill, the Dying and the Bereaved. New York: Hemisphere Press.

Vachon MLS. 1995. Staff stress in hospice/palliative care: A review. *Palliat Med* 9:91–113.

Vachon MLS. 1998. Caring for the caregiver in oncology and palliative care. *Semin Oncol Nurs* 14(2):152–157.

Palliative care education

Barnard D, Quill T, Hafferty FW, Arnold R, Plumb J, Bulger R, Field M. 1999. Preparing the ground: Contributions of the pre-clinical years to medical education for care near the end of life. *Acad Med* 74:499–505.

Billings JA, Block S. 1997. Palliative care in undergraduate medical education: Status report and future directions. *JAMA* 278(9):733–738.

Block S, Bernier GM, Crawley LM, Farber S, Kuhl D, Nelson W, O'Donnell J, Sandy L, Ury W. 1998. Incorporating palliative care into primary care education: Principles, challenges and opportunities. *J Gen Intern Med* 13(11):768–773.

Danis M, Federman D, Fins J, Fox E, Kastenbaum B, Lanken PN, Long K, Lowenstein E, Lynn J, Rouse F, Tulsky J. Incorporating palliative care into critical care education: Principles, challenges, and opportunities. *Crit Care Med* (in press).

Kearney M. 1992. Palliative medicine—just another specialty? *Palliat Med* 6:39–46.

James CR. 1993. The problematic nature of education in palliative care. *J Palliat Care* 9(4):5–10.

Sheldon F, Smith P. 1996. The life so short, the craft so long: A model for post-basic education in palliative care. *Palliat Med* 10:99–104.

Steel K, Ribbe M, Ahronheim J, Hedrick H, Selwyn PA, Forman W, Keay T. 1999. Incorporating education on palliative care into the long-term care setting. *Am Geriatr Soc* 47:904–907.

Weissman DE, Block SD, Blank L, Cain J, Cassem N, Danoff D, Foley K, Meier D, Schyve P, Theige D, Wheeler HB. 1999. Incorporating palliative care education into the acute care hospital setting. *Acad Med* 74:871–877.

Index of Themes